REGNUM STUDIES IN MISSION

Asian and Pentecostal

The Charismatic Face of Christianity in Asia

Second Edition

Series Preface

Regnum Studies in Mission are born from the lived experience of Christians and Christian communities in mission, especially but not solely in the fast growing churches among the poor of the world. These churches have more to tell than stories of growth. They are making significant impacts on their cultures in the cause of Christ. They are producing 'cultural products' which express the reality of Christian faith, hope and love in their societies.

Regnum Studies in Mission are the fruit often of rigorous research to the highest international standards and always of authentic Christian engagement in the transformation of people and societies. And these are for the world. The formation of Christian theology, missiology and practice in the twenty-first century will depend to a great extent on the active participation of growing churches contributing biblical and culturally appropriate expressions of Christian practice to inform World Christianity.

Series Editors

Julie C. Ma — Oxford Centre for Mission Studies, Oxford, UK
Wonsuk Ma — Oxford Centre for Mission Studies, Oxford, UK
Doug Petersen — Vanguard University, Costa Mesa, CA, USA
Terence Ranger — University of Oxford, Oxford, UK
C.B. Samuel — Emmanuel Hospital Association, Delhi, India
Chris Sugden — Anglican Mainstream, Oxford, UK

REGNUM STUDIES IN MISSION

Asian and Pentecostal

The Charismatic Face of Christianity in Asia

Second Edition

Edited by
Allan Anderson
Edmond Tang

Foreword by Cecil M. Robeck, Jr.

WIPF & STOCK · Eugene, Oregon

Wipf and Stock Publishers
199 W 8th Ave, Suite 3
Eugene, OR 97401

Asian and Pentecostal
The Charismatic Face of Christianity in Asia, Second Edition
By Anderson, Allan and Tang, Edmond
Copyright©2011 Regnum Books International
ISBN 13: 978-1-61097-917-7
Publication date 12/1/2011
Previously published by Regnum, 2011

This Edition published by Wipf and Stock Publishers
by arrangement with Regnum Books International

regnum

Contents

Acknowledgements

I want to thank all those who made this publication possible. First and foremost, to the twenty-five authors whose work appears here, and who kept the deadlines given with typical Asian efficiency, in spite of extremely busy lifestyles. Then to all the respondents to papers and participants in the stimulating conference on Asian Pentecostalism convened by the Graduate Institute for Theology and Religion at the University of Birmingham, and held at Fircroft College in Selly Oak, Birmingham in September 2001, who came here from many parts of Asia, Europe and North America. Those who helped with the administration during the conference: Carol Bebawi, Roli dela Cruz and Elijah Kim. This book is a direct result of that conference, and all the plenary and case study papers appear here in a modified form. Thanks also to those who agreed to contribute to the book after the conference was over, to fill in some of the gaps.

A special word of thanks is due to four people in particular: to my co-editor, colleague and friend Edmond Tang, whose idea it was to have the conference in the first place and who made all the administrative arrangements for it. Margaret Allen, long-time secretary at the China Desk of the Churches Together in Britain and Ireland, whose painstaking copy-editing produced the final typescript. Chris Sugden of Regnum who enthusiastically endorsed the publication by Regnum, and Erik Lai in Kuala Lumpur who carried all the printing burdens with remarkable efficiency at short notice.

Above all, I want to thank the great God and Father of the Lord Jesus Christ, who by his Spirit is moving all over the world in this twenty-first century in every country and culture. This book is a testimony to a part of that moving in the most populous continent on earth.

The editors wish to thank all those responsible for the second edition of this book, in particular Wonsuk Ma, who initiated it, his team at Regnum Books who worked on the project including Kate Harris, former Managing Editor of Regnum, and Emily Bowerman who produced the index.

Allan Anderson and Edmond Tang
Birmingham, March 2011

For the New Edition

This revised edition incorporates a completely new copyediting and many corrections with a new cover. However, the editors did not attempt to update data. We are also glad that this edition will become widely available through Regnum's North American partner.

The editors and contributors owe a great debt to the current Regnum team for their careful work, particularly Ms Parrizzad Pound and Mr Tony Gray.

The Editors
Spring 2011

List of Contributors[1]

Allan ANDERSON is Head of the School of philosophy, Theology and Religion and Professor of Global Pentecostal Studies at the University of Birmingham, England

Hyeon Sung BAE was Professor of Theology at Hansei University, Seoul, Korea and now pastors a Korean church in Southern California.

Michael BERGUNDER is Professor of Missiology and the History of Religion at the University of Heidelberg, Germany.

Simon CHAN is Dean of Studies and Lecturer in Systematic Theology at Trinity Theological College, Singapore.

CHIN Khua Khai is an Assemblies of God minister from Myanmar, currently working among Burmese immigrants in Southern California, U.S.A.

DENG Zhaongming is former researcher in the Institute for Sino-Christian Studies and editor of the *Bridge* (now ceased), periodical reporting on the church in China, based in Hong Kong.

Roger E. HEDLUND is the former Director of the Dictionary of South Asian Christianity project at the Mylapore Institute for Indigenous Studies, Chennai, India.

Walter J. HOLLENWEGER is Emeritus Professor of Mission at the University of Birmingham, England and lives in Krattigen, Switzerland.

HWA Yung was the Director of the Centre for the Study of Christianity in Asia at Trinity Theological College, Singapore and is the Methodist Bishop of Malaysia.

Chong Hee JEONG is a minister of the Presbyterian Church in Seoul, South Korea.

Jae Yong JEONG served as an Assemblies of God missionary in the Philippines, and is a pastor in the Assemblies of God, Seoul, South Korea.

Young-Hoon LEE is the senior pastor of the Yoido Full Gospel Church, Seoul, Korea

Julie MA is Missiology Research Tutor, Oxford Centre for Mission Studies, Oxford, England.

Wonsuk MA is David Yonggi Cho Research Tutor of Global Christianity and Executive Director of Oxford Centre for Mission Studies, Oxford, England.

David MARTIN is Emeritus Professor of Sociology at the London School of Economics, England.

Gotthard OBLAU coordinates a theological training programme jointly run by immigrant churches and the United Evangelical Mission in Wuppertal, Germany.

---

[1] Names are alphabetically arranged according to family names, which are printed in the upper cases.

Paulson PULIKOTTIL is Assistant Professor of Biblical Studies at Union Biblical Seminary, Pune, India, and President of the Asian Pentecostal Society.

Mark A. ROBINSON is President of GAP International Projects and doctoral candidate at the University of Queensland, Brisbane, Australia.

Paul Tsuchido SHEW is a doctoral candidate at Fuller Theological Seminary, researcher at Seigakuin University and associate pastor in the Omori Megumi Church, Tokyo, Japan.

Joseph SUICO is General Secretary of the Philippine General Council of the Assemblies of God, Manila, Philippines.

TAN Jin Huat is Academic Dean at the Seminari Theoloji Malaysia, in Seremban, lecturing in New Testament, Homiletics and Malaysian Church History.

Edmond TANG is Director of the Research Unit for East Asian Christian Studies at the University of Birmingham, England.

Gani WIYONO is Lecturer in Church History and Theology at Sekolah Tinggi Teologi (Satyabhakti) Advanced School of Theology, Malang, Indonesia.

Lode L. WOSTYN, CICM, is Dean and Professor of Theology at St Louis University, Baguio City, the Philippines.

Amos YONG is Research Professor of Theology at Regent University, Virginia Beach, Virginia, U.S.A.

Foreword

'Charismatic' religious expression is coming of age. It is much in the news these days as the numbers of adherents in the southern and eastern hemispheres surge past all expectations. Not only is it an experience-friendly movement that has impacted the lives of multiplied millions of people, it is a movement that is finally getting the attention it deserves by the academy.

What is emerging from recent studies is the realization that this is not a single, unified, monolithic movement; it is better understood as a 'movement of movements' that share a core of common beliefs and common experiences. One cannot generalize from continent to continent, from region to region, from denomination to denomination, and in some cases, from congregation to congregation when describing this 'movement'. In a sense, it is a movement very much at home in a 'Post-Modern' setting while holding, in some cases quite strongly, to a variety of 'Pre-Modern' and 'Modern' worldviews.

The editors of this volume have drawn well from a range of scholars, from veterans to newly emerging ones. The majority of them are Asians and insiders, who understand the feel and the diversity of Asian Pentecostalism like few others. This volume stands in the venerable tradition of Professor Walter J. Hollenweger, who pioneered the program that Professor Anderson now oversees at the University of Birmingham.

This volume is a first in the study of Asian Pentecostalism at several levels. It provides us with the first 'big picture' view of the varieties of Charismatic religion in the most populous region of the world while at the same time offering in-depth cameos of specific churches in specific situations there. It is a first coordinated attempt to provide the perspectives of 'Eastern' authors that will go far in disabusing many 'Western' readers of the idea that they have successfully planted mere clones of existing Western Pentecostal/Charismatic congregations in Asia. It is a first in that it provides an argument for the integrity of this Movement in Asia, with a uniquely Asian history in a context unlike anything found in the West. It is a first in so far as it helps us to understand and appreciate the cultural accommodations that the Movement has made to communicate its essence to Asians without violating the spirit of those who first carried the message.

Thus, questions of Pentecostal Historiography, the relationship between the Gospel and culture, the develop of uniquely Asian perspectives on historic theological categories, and the analysis of early and emerging social structures and the routinization of charisma that inevitably follows, all work together to provide the reader with a fresh and nuanced understanding of what is labeled *Asian and Pentecostal.*

This book comes highly recommended for use in courses on Global Pentecostalism, Asian Church History, Modern Church History, as well as a resource for those who want to know what God is saying through the Charismatic face of Christianity in Asia'.

Cecil M. Robeck, Jr.
Professor of Church History and Ecumenics
Director of the David J. du Plessis Center for Christian Spirituality
Fuller Theological Seminary, Pasadena, CA

Introduction
The Charismatic Face of Christianity in Asia

Allan Anderson

Pentecostalism has been described as the fastest growing global religion of the 20th century,[1] aving grown in only one century to over 500 million who would identify with it in one of its many different forms.[2] Its growth rate worldwide is possibly unprecedented in the history of religions. Pentecostalism has become a global phenomenon that has made an impact upon almost every country on earth.[3] The Pentecostal movement began in the early 1900s as a simple, spontaneous and emotional form of Christianity,[4] claiming that the 'gifts of the Spirit', as recorded in the New Testament book of Acts,[5] including such phenomena as glossolalia (speaking in tongues), healings and various 'signs and wonders', were occurring again, and that the church was being restored in an end-time revival that would culminate in the second coming of Christ.

In the 1950s and 1960s the growth of Pentecostalism began to accelerate and it developed into many diverse church forms and varieties, differing according to historical, religious and socio-cultural contexts, but recognisable as having 'Pentecostal' characteristics or distinctives.[6]

---

[1] I am grateful to Mark Robinson for permission to adapt parts of an earlier introduction to his paper and its references for this section of this introduction. J.Z. Smith and W.S. Green (eds.), *The HarperCollins Dictionary of Religion* (San Francisco: HarperCollins, 1995), 835.

[2] David B. Barrett, George T. Kurian and Todd M. Johnson (eds.), *World Christian Encyclopedia*, 2nd ed., vol. (New York: Oxford University Press, 2001). See these statistics discussed further in Allan Anderson, 'Diversity in the Definition of "Pentecostal/Charismatic" and its Ecumenical Implications' (Paper presented at the 31st Annual Meeting of the Society for Pentecostal Studies, Lakeland, Florida, March 2002)..

[3] Karla Poewe, *Charismatic Christianity as a Global Culture* (Los Angeles: University of Southern California Press, 1994).

[4] Harvey Cox, *Fire From Heaven: The Rise of Pentecostal Spirituality and the Reshaping of Religion in the Twenty-first Century* (London: Cassell, 1996), 15.

[5] Walter J. Hollenweger, *Pentecostalism: Origins and Developments Worldwide* (Peabody: Hendrickson, 1997), 2.

[6] S. Hunt, M. Hamilton and T. Walker (eds.), 'Introduction: Tongues, Toronto and the Millenium', in *Charismatic Christianity: Sociological Perspectives* (New York: St. Martins Press, 1997), 2.

Since the 1960s the movement has expanded rapidly through 'classical' Pentecostal denominations born in the U.S.A., indigenous and autochthonous movements especially in Africa and Asia, but Pentecostalism has also pervaded every part of world Christianity (both Protestant and Catholic), through the 'Charismatic movement'.[7] In some countries of the world affected by revival movements, like India, Korea, China and parts of Africa, distinct forms of Pentecostalism have existed for a long time (although not always given this label), and these have affected the character of the classical Pentecostalism and the Charismatic movement that came much later to these areas.

Although the meaning of 'Pentecostal' is debated in this book and will continue to be elude us for a long time, in its simplest sense the term refers to ecstatic forms of Christianity defined in terms of special gifts given by the Holy Spirit.[8] Most Pentecostals, especially in Asia, are also generally regarded as being 'Evangelical' in theology, that is, embracing a literalistic approach to the Bible as the Word of God, and believing in a personal, often individualistic salvation, moral chastity or 'living a holy life', and being active in personal evangelism. Some of the vignettes from different parts of Asia in this book as well as the theological presuppositions of many of its authors will be obvious illustrations of these characteristics.

In recent years, the Pentecostal and Charismatic experience has become a prominent characteristic of many forms of Christianity worldwide, and Asia is certainly no exception. Scholars write of the 'Pentecostalization' of Asian Christianity, while Harvey Cox speaks of 'the rapid spread of the Spirit-oriented forms of Christianity in Asia'.[9] According to the World Christian Encyclopedia, Christianity formed 9.6% of the total population of Asia in 2000, some 313 million people.[10] The 'explosive' growth of Pentecostalism in several Asian countries was described with an estimated 135 million Pentecostals/ Charismatics in Asia, comparing favourably with 80 million in North America, 141 million in Latin America, 126 million in Africa and only 38 million in Europe.[11] According to these statisticians at least, Asia has the second largest number of Pentecostals/Charismatics of any continent of

---

[7] Hollenweger, *Pentecostalism*, 2.

[8] David Stoll, *Is Latin America Turning Protestant?* (Berkeley: University of California Press, 1990), 4. Stoll's definition does not include Catholic Charismatics, as he sees Pentecostalism as a form of Protestantism in Latin America.

[9] Cox, 214.

[10] Barrett et. al., 13. According to another estimate, Christianity formed 8.6% of the Asian population in 2000, some 316 million people: Patrick Johnstone and Jason Mandryk, *Operation World* (Carlisle, UK: Paternoster, 2001), 41.

[11] Barrett et. al., 13-15. Johnstone & Mandryk (21, 32, 34, 41, 52) have significantly lower figures. They estimate 87 million Pentecostals and Charismatics in Asia, compared to 72 million in North America, 85 million in Latin America, 84 million in Africa and 14 million in Europe.

the world, and seems to be fast catching up with the largest, Latin America. Together with Africa, these three continents have some three quarters of all the Pentecostals and Charismatics in the world. Further, at least a third of the Asian Christian population is Charismatic or Pentecostal, a proportion that continues to steadily rise. Much of the growth in Asian Christianity has taken place in particular countries like China, South Korea, South India, the Philippines and Indonesia, and mainly among Pentecostals and Charismatics. After Brazil and the U.S.A., China and India have the third and fifth largest numbers of Pentecostals/ Charismatics of any country in the world.[12]

Clearly, an important religious movement in Asia like this deserves careful study. To focus on this rapidly changing phenomenon, the Research Unit for East Asian Christian Studies and the Research Unit for Pentecostal Studies at the Graduate Institute for Theology and Religion of the University of Birmingham convened a conference in September 2001 with the rather vague title 'The Significance of Asian Pentecostalism'. This was the second conference on Pentecostalism held at Selly Oak, Birmingham, the first held in 1996 in honour of Walter J. Hollenweger, and published in the collection *Pentecostals After a Century*.[13] Much has been written on the growth and development of Pentecostalism in the continents of North America, Latin America and Africa, and even European Pentecostalism has been fairly well researched. But Asia, although the world's largest continent with the greatest religio-cultural diversity (including a significant Christian population), has had comparatively scant attention, especially in the western academic world. Just as Pentecostalism in Latin America and Africa has had profound effects, so Asian Christianity's significant Charismatic character has implications for global Christianity that are far-reaching—but so little has been written about it. That is why we consider this truly a groundbreaking publication, as it appears to be the first time, certainly in the English language, that such a comprehensive attempt has been made to discuss Charismatic Christianity in Asia.

Over twenty scholars from eight Asian nations as well as several from Europe and one from North America converged in Selly Oak for the four-day conference. Some were emerging scholars who were Pentecostals themselves, but the ecumenical character of the conference was reflected by speakers also coming from Roman Catholic, Anglican, Methodist, Lutheran and Reformed perspectives. Walter Hollenweger, Emeritus Professor of Mission at the University of Birmingham and for many the founding father of Pentecostal Studies, gave the opening address in which he discussed questions of religious pluralism from a Barthian perspective. The Conference papers consisted of ten

---

[12] Barrett, et. al., 860.

[13] Allan Anderson and Walter J. Hollenweger (eds.), *Pentecostals After a Century: Global Perspectives on a Movement in Transition* (Sheffield: Sheffield Academic Press, 1999).

plenary papers and six case studies from different Asian countries. The plenaries addressed major themes: Asian Pentecostalism's contribution to ecumenism (Hollenweger), sociological issues in studying the movements (David Martin), Pentecostalism's relevance for a theology of religions in Asia (Amos Yong), historiographical challenges (Allan Anderson) and methodological issues (Michael Bergunder), the latter looking at the South Indian context. Three plenary sessions dealt with the significant contributions of Pentecostalism to Christianity in South Korea (Hyeon Sung Bae and Chong Hee Jeong), China (Gotthard Oblau) and the Catholic Charismatic movement in the Philippines (Lode Wostyn). A further plenary concentrated on theological perspectives on Pentecostalism and the Asian church (Hwa Yung and Wonsuk Ma). The final plenary session was a summation and conference report (Simon Chan and Edmond Tang). Except for those sessions with two plenary speakers, formal responses were given to each paper followed by questions and general discussion. The six case studies were held at two venues simultaneously and were intended to provide contemporary information and reflection on Pentecostalism in particular Asian countries: India (Paulson Pulikottil), Indonesia (Gani Wiyono), the Philippines (Joseph Suico), Malaysia (Tan Jin Huat), China (Deng Zhaoming) and Korea (Young Hoon Lee). These too were followed by times of questions and open discussion.

One speaker remarked that the particular mix of scholars across denominational and national divides might not have been possible if the conference had been held in Asia. It was indeed a unique occasion, and we were aware of its significance. The conference papers have been rearranged in this publication and seven additional studies are included that were written since the conference: one by Julie Ma on Asian Pentecostal women, and six other regional studies to complement the others, on Pentecostal and Charismatic Christianity in India (Roger Hedlund), Myanmar (Chin Khai), Indonesia (Mark Robinson), the Philippines (Jae Yong Jeong), China (Edmond Tang) and Japan (Paul Shew). The result, we believe, is a unique and valuable publication that will make this information and theological reflection available to the wider world.

The first part of the book comprises seven thematic papers where issues are raised relating to the theological, sociological and historical study of Pentecostalism in Asia. In the opening paper, Walter Hollenweger deals with how Asian Pentecostals could contribute to a better understanding of ecumenical dialogue and religious pluralism within their unique context. David Martin, one of the best-known sociologists of religion in the English speaking world, addresses those issues to be faced in the study of Pentecostalism, and compares the Asian context to the very different contexts of the other continents. He provides the reader with very interesting insights into the processes of globalisation, and outlines what he sees as some of the challenges for ongoing research. Hwa Yung, a leading evangelical theologian from Singapore, discusses the Pentecostal nature of the Asian church, and suggests that 'indigenous Christianity' in Asia is more likely to be 'Pentecostal' in its emphases, particularly in regard to its spirituality and encounter with the spirit world. Wonsuk Ma, with his wife Julie, have been Korean Pentecostal missionaries in the Philippines for many years, and operate a network of emerging Asian Pentecostal scholars. Wonsuk Ma, editor of the *Asian Journal of Pentecostal Studies,* deals comprehensively with the impact of classical Pentecostalism on Asian Christianity, looking at a wide range of contemporary issues. Next comes a fascinating study by Chinese American Pentecostal theologian Amos Yong on a comparison of the concept of the 'demonic' in popular Buddhism and in Pentecostalism, and its implications for Christian pneumatology and understanding the religious consciousness of Asia. Julie Ma then considers the plight of Asian women in society and in the church, with examples of Asian Pentecostal women in ministry. My paper on historiography closes this part of the book, with a discussion of the problems involved in the writing of Pentecostal history from a western-centred perspective, and the need to tell the stories of those heroes of Pentecostal history from Asia, Africa and Latin America. The thematic papers set the stage for the regional studies that follow.

The rest of the book deals with the history, development and the current situation of Charismatic Christianity in specific Asian countries, beginning in the west with India and concluding with the 'Far East' in Japan and Korea. We have divided this into three regional sections: Part 2 on South Asia (mainly India, but also Sri Lanka and Nepal), Part 3 on South East Asia (Myanmar, Malaysia, Indonesia and the Philippines) and Part 4 on East Asia (China, South Korea and Japan). Certain countries have been given more attention than others because of greater resources available and the size of Pentecostal and Charismatic Christianity in these countries; but this is not to suggest that it is not equally as significant in such countries as Thailand or Singapore. West and Central Asia, with their large Muslim majorities, are not covered in this publication, and Pentecostalism in these countries is a very small and often heavily persecuted minority. Asian Pentecostalism, like its counterparts in Africa and Latin America, has a distinct character moulded by the particular contexts of its various peoples. These contexts must be taken into account when assessing this vibrant part of world Christianity, and in this book we will not be able to consider all of them. Despite the inevitable gaps, this is a pioneering contribution towards understanding the changing face of Asian Christianity in the 21st Century. But an overview of some of the 'hot spots' in Asian Pentecostalism in this introduction will set the stage for the detailed papers that follow.

The earliest Pentecostal revival in Asia was probably that associated with the Tamil evangelist Aroolappen, in Tamil Nadu, India, as far back as 1860.[14] In the 1905-1907 revival that occurred at Pandita Ramabai's Mukti Mission in Pune, India, young women baptised by the Spirit saw visions, fell into trances and spoke in tongues. Significantly, Ramabai understood this revival to be the means by which the Holy Spirit was creating an indigenous form of Indian Christianity. [15] Although not directly bringing about new Pentecostal denominations, the Mukti revival had far-reaching consequences resulting, inter alia, in Pentecostalism spreading to Chile in South America for the first time. After a penetrating methodological paper on the study of Pentecostal history in India by Michael Bergunder that has important implications for the study of the movement worldwide, two further papers on Indian Pentecostalism concentrate on the forms of the movement that arose from the 1930s onwards. Roger Hedlund presents us with an array of vibrant indigenous Pentecostal churches from all over India, Sri Lanka and Nepal. These movements literally bustle with activity, showing the creativity of these South Asian Pentecostals as they embark not only on church-planting and evangelism, but also a remarkable variety of social upliftment projects. Most indigenous Indian Pentecostal denominations have strict rules for members, including opposition to all forms of jewellery and the ordination of women. One independent Pentecostal church, the Pentecostal Mission, encourages celibacy for the increase of spiritual power, and Paulson Pulikottil's paper discusses this movement and its context among the Dalits. Pentecostalism is clearly the fastest growing form of Christianity in what will soon be the most populous nation on earth. According to the *World Christian Encyclopedia*, over half of India's 62 million Christians in 2000 were Pentecostal/Charismatic.[16]

In South East Asia, the greatest Pentecostal expansion has occurred in Indonesia and the Philippines, but there are also significant Pentecostal and Charismatic minorities in Myanmar, Malaysia and Singapore, the subjects of the first two papers in the third part of the book. The case of Myanmar is extremely interesting, for no western missionary has been allowed to operate there for almost four decades, and Pentecostalism has developed independently into an indigenous movement, particularly among the interior minorities, the Karens and the Chins, the focus of Chin Khai's paper. Tan Jin Huat deals with a very different situation in Malaysia, where western Pentecostal missionaries

---

[14] Ivan M. Satyavrata, 'Contextual Perspectives on Pentecostalism as a Global Culture: A South Asian View', in M.W. Dempster, B.D. Klaus, and D. Petersen (eds.), *The Globalization of Pentecostalism: A Religion made to Travel* (Oxford: Regnum 1999), 205.

[15] Shamsundar M. Adhav, *Pandita Ramabai* (Madras: Christian Literature Society, 1979), 216.

[16] Barrett, et.al., 360.

have operated vigorously and continuously since the 1930s. There, Pentecostalism has expanded mainly among the Chinese and Indian minorities, but the author suggests that 75% of all evangelical Christians in Malaysia are Pentecostal/Charismatic. There are between nine and twelve million Pentecostals in Indonesia, a country with a Muslim majority, which makes the 'Indonesian Revival' (more correctly, Revivals) following the overthrow of Sukarno's government in 1965 unique. One revival was concentrated in West Timor, but over two million Javanese became Christians between 1965 and 1971, the greatest ever turning of Muslims to Christianity.[17] The two complementary papers by Gani Wiyono, an Indonesian Pentecostal theologian, and Mark Robinson, an Australian Pentecostal minister in Indonesia, reflect on this enormous and energetic Pentecostal movement about which so little has been written.

In the Philippines, Pentecostals have grown to such an extent that they are regarded as a serious challenge to the majority Catholic church.[18] David Martin says that sociologically the Philippines may be likened to Latin America, with a Catholic colonising power and rapidly growing Pentecostalism. One estimate put the number of Pentecostals and Charismatics at 20 million, or 26% of the total population, the highest proportion anywhere in Asia, the majority being Catholic Charismatics.[19] Joseph Suico, a Filipino Pentecostal, discusses the growth of classical and independent forms of Pentecostalism, and Lode Wostyn, sympathetic Catholic priest and theologian, in a fascinating study examines the enormous Catholic Charismatic renewal movement in the country and its implications for the future of the Church. There are also distinctly indigenous Filipino movements of a Pentecostal character, some of which have been regarded as 'pseudo-Christian', such as the Santuala movement among the mountain peoples of Luzon. In addition, large new Filipino Charismatic churches have been established, like the Jesus is Lord Fellowship founded by Eddie Villaneuva in 1978 and the Bread of Life Ministries begun by Butch Conde in 1983. Jeong Jae Yong's paper reflects on these developments, taken from his thirteen years experience as a Korean missionary in the Philippines and his doctoral thesis in which he reflects on the relationship between Filipino indigenous religions and Pentecostalism.[20]

---

[17] Avery T. Willis, *Indonesian Revival: Why Two Million Came to Christ* (South Pasadena: William Carey Library, 1977), xv.
[18] Robert C. Salazar (ed), *New Religious Movements in Asia and the Pacific Islands: Implications for Church and Society* (Manila: De La Salle University, 1994), 190.
[19] Barrett, et, al., 594.
[20] Jae Yong Jeong, 'Filipino Pentecostal Spirituality: An Investigation into Filipino Indigenous Spirituality and Pentecostalism in the Philippines' (ThD thesis, University of Birmingham, 2001).

The expansion of Pentecostalism in the 'Far East' is an extraordinary story. We know that classical Pentecostal missionaries were active in China as early as 1907, but there were estimated to be a total of only five million Christians in mainland China at the time of the exodus of western missionaries in 1949. Today, China has probably the largest number of Pentecostal and Charismatic Christians in Asia, and among the largest in the world. It is extremely difficult to assess church membership in China, especially in the case of movements unrecognised by the government. One estimate put the number at around 69 million,[21] but government figures are much lower, admitting to no more than twenty million. Whatever the truth, there has nevertheless been a remarkable growth of Christianity in China recently, much of which has taken place in unregistered indigenous churches. The differences between these indigenous and independent churches and the forms of Pentecostalism found in the West are considerable, and may be likened to the phenomena of African initiated churches, where distinctively African forms of Christianity have consciously rejected western forms.[22] Chinese churches have developed in isolation from the rest of Christianity for at least fifty years, and independent churches grew rapidly when they were faced with severe opposition. Two of the largest of these churches, the True Jesus Church and the Jesus Family, may be considered Pentecostal, and are referred to in China as 'Old Three-Self' churches. All church activities in China were banned in 1966, but recommenced at the end of the 1970s, after which there appears to have been rapid growth.[23] The Chinese churches that re-emerged, in the words of Daniel Bays, 'revealed some striking continuities with the earlier period of revivalism'.[24] The house church movements are widely diverse, but are characterised by being both revivalist and fundamentalist. Our three papers on the Chinese indigenous churches reflect on these developments. Deng Zhaoming, for many years editor of the influential Hong Kong based Christian news magazine *Bridge*, writes from his personal knowledge of the indigenous churches, as does Gotthard Oblau, who both ask whether these churches may be considered 'Pentecostal'. Edmond Tang explains why there has been a dearth of written research on Chinese indigenous churches in his paper.

The growth of Pentecostalism in South Korea has been dramatic and well documented, not only in terms of Pentecostal churches, but also in the

---

[21] Johnstone & Mandryk, 160. *The World Christian Encyclopedia* (Barrett et. al, 191) puts the figure at 54 million.

[22] See Allan Anderson, *African Reformation: African Initiated Christianity in the 20th Century* (Trenton, NJ & Asmara, Eritrea: Africa World Press, 2001).

[23] Salazar, 70.

[24] Daniel H. Bays, 'Christian Revival in China, 1900-1937', in E.L. Blumhofer and R. Balmer (eds.), *Modern Christian Revivals* (Urbana: University of Illinois Press, 1993), 174.

'Pentecostalization' of Korean Protestantism, by which most Protestants are affected by a Pentecostal emphasis.[25] Korean Protestantism has had a history of revivalism, the most notable being the Wonsan revival of 1903 and the 'Korean Pentecost' that commenced at Pyongyang in 1907. Preachers whose ministries were accompanied by miracles and healings (especially Presbyterian pastors Sun Joo Kil and Ik Du Kim and Methodist minister Yong Do Lee continued the revival until the 1930s.[26] This was clearly a 'Charismatic' movement, although classical Pentecostalism only arrived in Korea in 1928. Progress was at first slow, but the most remarkable growth took place under the ministry of David Yonggi Cho and his mother-in-law, who began a small tent church in Seoul in 1958 with five members, which grew until by 1982, classical Pentecostals were the third largest Protestant group in South Korea with over half a million members, half of whom were in Cho's single congregation. These events are described and reflected on in the three Korean contributions, two by scholars from Cho's Yoido Full Gospel Church (Lee and Bae), and one by a Presbyterian scholar (Jeong), a sympathetic outsider who wrote his doctoral thesis at Birmingham on Pentecostalism in Korea.[27] Young Hoon Lee gives us an historical account of the Korean revival movements known as the Holy Spirit movements, beginning in 1907, and culminating in the ecumenical potential of Pentecostalism in Korea today. Hyeon Sung Bae offers a spirited defence of the theology of the pastor of the world's biggest church, Yonggi Cho, as 'Full Gospel' theology, which he argues is an indigenised form of Korean theology. Chong Hee Jeong's discussion of the relationship between 'indigenous Pentecostalism' and the revival movements in 'mainline' Korean Protestantism demonstrates that the categories and paradigms used to discuss Pentecostalism in the West are inappropriate in Asia.

The question of how Korean Pentecostalism interacts with traditional shamanism and Confucianism is a fascinating, if controversial one. Perhaps one explanation that can be ventured is that Pentecostalism is a culturally indigenous form of Korean Christianity interacting with and confronting these older religions and philosophies.[28] Korea also has the phenomenon of mass urbanisation, and the Pentecostal churches have provided places of spiritual security and personal communities for people unsettled by rapid social change.

---

[25] David Martin, *Tongues of Fire: The Explosion of Protestantism in Latin America* (Oxford: Blackwell, 1990), 146.
[26] Jae Bum Lee , 'Pentecostal Type Distinctives and Korean Protestant Church Growth' (PhD thesis, Fuller Theological Seminary, 1986), 181-86.
[27] Chong Hee Jeong , 'The Formation and Development of Korean Pentecostalism from the Perspective of a Dynamic Contextual Theology' (ThD thesis, University of Birmingham, 2001).
[28] Allan Anderson, 'Pentecostalism in East Asia: Indigenous Oriental Christianity?' *Pneuma: The Journal for the Society for Pentecostal Studies* 22:1 (2000), 115-32.

Although these factors might account for the remarkable growth of Pentecostal movements in Korea, Harvey Cox has suggested two more underlying factors: 'for any religion to grow in today's world it must possess two capabilities: it must be able to include and transform at least certain elements of pre-existing religions which still retain a strong grip on the cultural subconscious' and 'it must also equip people to live in rapidly changing societies'. He says that these two 'key ingredients' are found in Korean Pentecostalism.[29]

Behind many of these essays are questions and insights relating to the relationships between all of Asia's ancient religions and Charismatic Christianity. One wonders how many of the new generation of Asian Pentecostal scholars will begin to move away from the North American theological paradigms thrust on their forebears by a western mission education, and engage in an Asian Pentecostal theology that takes *both* the transformation of ancient Asian religions *and* their inclusion seriously. The Pentecostal tendency, inherited from western missionaries, to demonise God's revelation in ancient religions is not helpful and creates unnecessary conflict. These essays are offered in the hope that they will stimulate further research into a neglected but vitally important area of Christian studies. The many and various forms of Asian Pentecostalism certainly represent a truly remarkable expression of Christianity that will be with us for a long time to come, and we ignore this at our peril. This book presents the Charismatic face of Christianity in Asia that is becoming its most prominent expression. I submit that the voices of these (mostly) Asian scholars are an important contribution to our understanding Pentecostalism in Asia, they will open to the academic world new vistas in research and orientation, and they will set parameters for the future study of Christianity in the world's largest and most diverse continent.

---

[29] Cox, 219.

PART ONE

THEMATIC

The Contribution of Asian Pentecostalism to Ecumenical Christianity: Hopes and Questions of a Barthian Theologian

Walter J. Hollenweger

Karl Barth and the Dialogue with Non-Christians

I grew up in the proletarian oral culture of Swiss Pentecostalism, but I was trained in the most rigid methods of biblical exegesis. My teachers were Fritz Blanks (a pioneer in Anabaptist research), Hans Conzelmann, Eduard Schweizer, Gerhard Ebeling and Karl Barth. I knew Rudolf Bultman and Ernst Kasemann personally. These men have influenced my theological biography as much as the practice of Pentecostal prayer and testimony.[1]

As to Karl Barth, I first have to clear up a number of misunderstandings. Just as with biblical texts, the works of Karl Barth have to be interpreted in their cultural and political context. He was a contextual theologian. Because of the serious alcohol problem there, he founded in his first parish in Safenwil a society for teetotallers. He also started a Trade Union because of the miserable work conditions of his parishioners. One should not forget that at this time Switzerland was something of a Third World country with widespread poverty and social problems. Later Karl Barth became a professor in Germany without ever having presented a doctoral dissertation to any university. In fact, if he had submitted his now famous commentary on the Epistle to the Romans he would have failed in any theological faculty. I had this statement confirmed by a number of New Testament scholars.

This is in itself an important observation and it suggests the question: Why is it that probably one of the most influential contemporary theological works, a seminal book for European theology, was not recognized by the then theological establishment? Karl Barth is not alone in this. Bonhoeffer, the other great theologian of the last century, was highly controversial because, so it was said, he mixed up politics and religion, because he 'spoiled' the purity of the

---

[1] Lynne Price, *Theology Out of Place: Walter J. Hollenweger* (Sheffield: Sheffield Academic Press. 2002). Jan A.B. Jongeneel (ed.), *Pentecost. Mission and Ecumenism: Essays in Intercultural Theology* (Frankfurt, New York: Peter Lang, 1992).

gospel (as understood by the Lutheran German bishops).[2] He was even refused a place in the prayer list of the Confessing Church because he was 'only' a political and not a religious martyr.

Karl Barth later collected about twenty honorary degrees from sundry universities around the world. When he was appointed professor in Germany—without, as I said, having written a doctoral dissertation—he again engaged himself with his context, which was the context of the German Catholic, Protestant and Free churches. These churches (including the German Pentecostal churches) saw in Adolf Hitler a kind of a saviour who would protect Germany from decadent western influence and from the Communist onslaught. The devotion to National Socialism and the ideology of the master-race became a kind of *theologia naturalis*, a natural theology, born and raised on German ground. To this Barth said an unequivocal 'no'. According to Barth there is only one source of revelation and this is Christ. All the rest is pure paganism, albeit in Christian disguise. It has to be rejected. This is the *Sitz im Leben* of Karl Barth's 'no' to all religion. According to him, the gospel is the crisis of all religion, including Christian religion.

However, when Barth's son, Christoph, came home from his missionary stay in Indonesia, he said to his father: 'You know, religion is not all bad and it is not totally void of divine revelation'. Barth, the father, listened with great attention to his son's stories and concluded (at this time he was already 80 years old) that if he could start his theological career again, he would write his *Church Dogmatics* not only in dialogue with the Bible, the Church Fathers and the reformers, but also in an exchange with the great religions of our time.[3]

My conclusion: If anybody rejects dialogue with religions on the basis of Barth's *Church Dogmatics* he or she is a Barthian fundamentalist, that is to say he or she is simply repeating now what Barth had to say in the thirties of the last century against the nationalistic neo-paganism in the churches. A real Barthian, however, does what Karl Barth would do in our contemporary situation, namely enter into a critical dialogue with non-Christian religions. I try to be such a Barthian.

From such a perspective one reads the Bible differently. One discovers, for instance, that the biblical authors did not shy away from intense contacts with non-Jewish and non-Christian people and texts. Think of 1 Cor. 13, probably

---

[2] W.J. Hollenweger, 'Dietrich Bonhoeffer and William J. Seymour. A Comparison between Two Ecumenists', *NorskTidssktift for Misjon* (N.E. Bloch-Hoell 1985), 39, 78-83. W.J. Hollenweger, *Bonhoeffer Requiem* (available in English and German from Verlag Metanoia, CH 8963 Kindhausen, Switzerland).

[3] This is based on oral communication from the Barth family. See also the note on Karl Barth in a review of Jacques S.J. Dupuis, *Towards a Christian Theology of Religious Pluralism* (Maryknoll, NY: Orbis Books, 1997) by William J. Nottinghill in *International Review of Mission* 356 (January-April 2001), 156-57, 198..

the most famous text of the New Testament. Any critical commentary shows that in this chapter Paul quotes copiously from popular hellenistic sources. The genius of this chapter is that he puts these texts together in a collage of great beauty. He even manages to write a whole chapter on love without mentioning Christ. 1 Cor. 13 is a Christian text because of the context of the whole first epistle to the Corinthians.

Or one may remember the famous Christmas legend of the magi. These eastern astrologers found the way to the cradle not on the basis of an evangelistic campaign but on the basis of their pagan astrology, while the Bible reading scribes in Jerusalem were involved in a plot to kill the child Jesus. It is remarkable how the commentaries try to soften this clear statement of the missiologist Matthew. They say that this text shows the end of pagan magic. They say that 'myrrh, gold and frankincense' are faith and repentance. None of this is in the text. It is remarkable how so-called 'Bible-believing' expositors disregard the biblical text if it does not suit them. The text shows: The treasures the magi brought to Jesus were the symbols of their culture and religion.

Finally, second Isaiah (45.1) sees in the pagan king Cyrus even an anointed, a messiah, a Christ. That is an extraordinary statement. If it were not in the Bible, its author would be excommunicated straightaway and blamed as an evil syncretizer and falsifier of the biblical message.

Dialogue and Syncretism

Here, it seems to me, Asian Pentecostals can help us a lot. Most of them have family members who are Buddhists, Hindus, Muslims, Taoists or adherents of any other religion. They have a specific down-to-earth knowledge of non-Christian religions. I expect them to show us a way to enter into a genuine dialogue with non-Christians without giving up our loyalty to Christ.[4] Let me explain. At Fuller Theological Seminary I had to tutor a Japanese student. He was a first generation Christian. I asked him about his relationship to his father, who was Buddhist: 'Does your father come to your Christmas celebration?' The student answered positively. 'And you', I continued, 'do you attend Buddhist celebrations with your father, at least now and then?'The student became very uneasy. In the end he said: 'The missionaries are against it'. 'I am sorry, that is not my question', I insisted, 'What do *you* do?'After long reflection he said, 'At first I did not go with him. But now I think it is right to do so. But it is difficult because the missionaries say that this is wrong'.

I would like to comment on this. I think that western missionaries are the least qualified to judge this matter, because they thoughtlessly follow the gods of

---

[4] See on this the chapter in this volume by Amos Yong (93-128) and the literature which he indicates.

their ancestors. They cling religiously to the priorities of capitalism, and this against the clear testimony of Scripture. Listen to this text:

> And the merchants of the earth weep and mourn for the great city, since no one buys their cargo any more, cargo of gold, silver, jewels and pearls, fine linen, purple silk and scarlet, all kinds of scented wood, cinnamon spice, incense, myrrh, frankincense, wine, oil, fine flour and wheat, cattle and sheep, horses and chariots, and slaves, that is human souls. The merchants who became rich in the trade with goods, animals and people weep aloud for in one hour all this wealth has been laid waste. The merchants, the great men of this earth, who deceived all the nations with their *pharmakeia* (Rev. 18.23), who bewitched plants, animals and people with their pharmaceutical industry, they weep and mourn.[5]

In comparison with the witchcraft of modern merchants, of modern *pharmakeia*, of modern *pharmakoi* (Rev. 21.8; 22.15), where *pharmakeia*, etc. is translated by 'sorcery', the religious practices of non-Christian religions are relatively harmless. At any rate, before we condemn others for their religion it would be better to consider our own witchcraft. Indeed, the marriage between Christianity and capitalism is rather a dangerous syncretism.[6] I often ask myself, Why do many Pentecostals only judge the sins in the bedrooms and not those in the *boardrooms*?

In re-reading the papers of the conference I detect some uneasiness among Asian Pentecostals towards the assumption that *all forms* of Christianity—including the evangelical ones—are syncretistic, since the Bible is already a syncretistic document (Leonardo Boff). That does not prevent it from being inspired—on the contrary, it shows us how to distinguish between theologically responsible and theologically irresponsible forms of syncretism.

One such theologically irresponsible form of syncretism is the introduction of the categories of 'supernatural' against the 'natural' into the theological discourse. Supernatural phenomena, so it is argued, are directly caused by God (or the Holy Spirit), natural ones are not. However, 'supernatural' is not a biblical category. *Hyperphysiko* does not exist in the New Testament. The Bible does not distinguish theologically between things we may understand and things which we do not (yet) understand. All creation is God's creation. The fact that we do not understand a phenomenon does not make it more divine. Rather, it says something about our perception, which changes from culture to culture. In fact, the category of the 'supernatural' was an invention of European

---

[5] See the play *Neuer Himmel - neue Erde. Die Visionen der Offenbarung*. A critical interpretation of Apokalypsis, Verlag Metanoia.

[6] More on this in Hollenweger, 'Syncretism and Capitalism', *Asian Journal of Pentecostal Studies* 2:1 (1999), 41-61. See also the chapter 'A Plea for a Theologically Responsible Syncretism', in Hollenweger, *Pentecostalism. Origins and Developments Worldwide* (Peabody, Me: Hendrickson, 1997), 132-141.

scholasticism. These thinkers had taken on board Greek philosophical insights together with remnants of our religious pagan past (insights which argued for an ontological difference between divine and natural phenomena). Catholic popular piety and anti-Enlightenment theologians in Europe have cherished this unbiblical and pagan split of reality up to this day. By way of the evangelical missionary movement, it was passed on to the Third World churches and is now presented as genuine Asian theology. What a joke! Where in Chinese, Indian, Korean or Indonesian thinking is the distinction between 'natural' and 'supernatural' documented? And even if it were, this worldview is in strict contradiction to biblical thinking. This European scholasticism may have had its function in its place and time. Today it confuses the issues and splits the world of phenomena—according to our momentary perception—into divine and less divine things. Furthermore, in contrast to the Corinthians (and also in contrast to Max Weber), Paul includes service (Rom. 12.7; 1 Cor. 12.5), exhortation (Rom. 12.8), acts of mercy (Rom. 12.8), liberality (Rom. 12.8), and even being single or being married (1 Cor. 7.7) among the charismata. It is clear that for Paul, the fact that a gift is not 'understandable' is not a criterion for its divinity. On the other hand, he introduces functional criteria, such as being useful (1 Cor. 12.7), being open to criticism (1 Cor. 14.29), even to criticism from outside (1 Cor. 14.22). He strongly refutes the widespread religious conception of his time that the unusual, the so-called 'supernatural', is divine or spiritual. The spirituality of an action is not shown by its phenomenology but by its function in the body of Christ and in society. There are no phenomena which for him are closer to God because they are spectacular.

Our Relationship with Nature

Many Asians have a special relationship with nature, with animals. This is partly due to their understanding of reincarnation. They have a great respect for animals. Many of them are therefore vegetarians. It is said that some Himalayan people speak with the animals when they encounter them. I tried this out myself in the Swiss Alps when I met an ibex. It stood on the small mountain path and looked straight at me. It did not run away. In amazement it seemed to ask, 'Why do you make so much noise with your feet?' I told him that I could not walk so elegantly up the mountains as he could. Therefore it might be kind to let me pass on the narrow path. The ibex thought for a moment, then he turned around slowly and silently. With great ease he climbed up the rock face.

Similar experiences make Asian Pentecostals less prone to exploiting nature, the air, the water, and all natural resources. Since ecology is becoming a question of life and death for all of us, this is an important issue. If we continue polluting the air and the sea, the next generation will be in great trouble. The sea level will rise and not only Amsterdam, London and Hamburg, but also Los

Angeles and many islands and coastal regions around the Pacific will be flooded. This is not a divine destiny. It is a man-made catastrophe.

Perhaps the ecological awareness of Asian Pentecostals could become not only a theological quality but also an economic necessity. The great insurance companies are already financing ecological projects because in the future they will no longer be able to finance the damage which their colleagues in the chemical, motor and food industries are causing. It only needs a few more tanker accidents, a few more cattle epidemics, and the insurance companies will either have to raise their rates drastically or go bankrupt. This is not a particularly religious topic. One can read about it in the specialized financial periodicals like the *Financial Times*.

I therefore expect Asian Pentecostals to stir up the conscience of their European and North American co-religionists (for instance at the World Pentecostal Conference) and remind them of their responsibility. Many Pentecostals are nowadays in responsible academic, political and industrial positions. They can—if they so wish—have an influence on the future of our planet. They can, for instance, ask their North American colleagues to vote for those politicians who are willing to sign the Kyoto Protocol. That would be a relevant understanding of sanctification and Pentecostal piety.

Let us take a more recent example. Cows are vegetarians. We, especially we Europeans, have made them eat the dead bodies of their fellow cows. This is unnatural and it was done out of sheer greed. The result is known. It is a minor catastrophe for the farmers and the food industry in Europe. Think of the epidemics we would produce if we— instead of burying our dead—processed them into tinned meat and ate them, exactly as we have done with the cows. BSE is not an accident, it is not a punishment from God, it is the result of our own stupidity and greed. It is said that organic farming is too expensive. The contrary is the case. In the long run a sustainable industry and agriculture, a reasonable trade system, will be more economical. These facts are all very well known in the managerial and government offices. They do not have the courage to tell us the truth because for many years they have said the opposite. It is always difficult to avow that we have been wrong. The Bible calls this change of attitude 'repentance'. And Pentecostals know something about repentance and forgiveness. That is why they can admit to having been wrong.

Our Understanding of Mission

If mission is about church growth (which I believe is the case), then the time of European and North American missionaries to the Third World is over. Third World evangelists can do the job better and more efficiently, as the statistics show with overwhelming clarity. There is no longer any need for us white people to evangelize the people of Asia. We should rather concentrate on mission in our own countries. Asian Pentecostals know this quite well.[7] The question is, will they say to their North American and European headquarters, 'Thank you for all you have done. Now, your time is over. We no longer need you. ' That will, of course, create some friction, for western mission is not only about church growth but it is also about exporting and increasing our western forms of Christianity. In other words: It is a new form of colonialism.

Many papers mention pre-Azusa Pentecostal revivals in Asia. If that is a historical notice, it is only of historical significance. As a trained historian I can mention off-hand a dozen Pentecostal outbreaks in Europe which happened before 1907. But if it is a missiological question—which I suspect it is—then of course it means that the Holy Spirit does not only work, nor does she (*Ruach Yahwe* is female) work primarily through western thinkers. By now, that should be clear. However, much of that which is presented as an 'Asian contribution' is just western evangelicalism. That does not disqualify it, but it makes it very difficult to discover in it anything typically Asian. Perhaps this form of evangelicalism is a form of future Christianity. But to my mind, it carries with it far too much rationalism, Aristotelianism and scholasticism to become a universal form of Christian reflection. I have not given up hope. Who knows, Asian Pentecostalism might develop a form of evangelicalism which is not sold on scholastic rationalism and capitalistic egoism but is open to the pressing needs of their countries which I try to describe in this essay. Such a theology would not seek to conform to some abstract theological principle but would be organized around the real spiritual and physical needs of the respective countries. That leads me directly to my next issue.

If mission is about *justice in the world*, in particular about justice in the trade system, then the mission fields are not the Philippines, India or Indonesia, but the places where decisions are taken, namely, Frankfort, Zurich, London and New York. There the instruments are forged to win a few corrupt members of the local elite in Latin America, in Asia and in Africa. They are trained to do their dirty work as mercenaries of an international trade in human souls and goods. It is here that mission societies can invest their financial and human power of liberation to these people. I know that many of them are not happy with their work. As Jesus delivered Zaccheus from his sinful life, so modern missionaries can—together with financial and economic specialists—help modern 'exploiters' to find alternatives.

If mission is about *clear and biblical theology*, then we western theologians have first to do our homework and realize that our kind of theology is heavily influenced by non-biblical factors. When Thomas of Aquinas introduced the logical thought patterns of a pagan philosopher (Aristotle) into theology, that

---

[7] More on this in Hollenweger, 'An Irresponsible Silence', in the forthcoming Mazibuko Festschrift, edited by Roswith Gerloff (Pietermaritzburg, South Africa. Cluster Publications).

was a stroke of genius. But it was also a form of syncretism, for it forced biblical texts into a logical system. However, the Bible is not a logical book. The God of the Bible can contradict himself. He can change his mind. The Bible handles contradictions, tensions and conflicts with great skill. To demand from all Christians, even from those for whom Aristotle is not culturally relevant, that they follow this type of theology is again a form of colonialism.

Of course the biblical message must be presented in a coherent form. But why should logicality be the only form of coherence? The coherence of the Bible is of another nature. It is much more narrative. Biblical coherence expresses itself in doxologies, hymns and testimonies. This is a form of theology which seems to me not only clear and biblical but also more universal. If mission has also to further theological clarity, this has to be done *together with* the Third World Christians and not merely *for* them. That might also be a contribution to *ecumenical cooperation*, another form of mission which is greatly neglected at the present time.

Finally, Pentecostals are interested in the *Holy Spirit.* Asian Pentecostals in particular know that the Holy Spirit is not confined to Christianity. The biblical record makes it clear that all people are endowed with the Spirit, not only Christians (Acts 2.17; the Old Testament, in particular Gen. 2.7). We live because the *Creator Spiritus* is in us. If God takes his spirit back we die. This is not confined to Christians. It is said that the *Creator Spiritus* is different from the *Spiritus Sanctus.* We would then have two spirits. That looks to me like pure speculation with no biblical basis. Of course, there are many different dimensions to the Holy Spirit. Paul, for instance, seems to concentrate the activities of the Holy Spirit on Christians, in particular with the starting point in baptism. Here again, we have to see that the biblical authors are not compelled by the rigidity of logic. Depending on the context in which they theologize, they will present their message differently without being embarrassed by the fact that another author will present things in another way.

If, therefore, the Spirit is in principle in all people—although not all people are obedient to the Spirit—it is no longer strange to expect truth also outside Christianity. How to discover this truth, how it is going to enlighten our Christian theology and praxis, that is something I would very much like to learn from our Asian Pentecostal friends.

For a European theologian, however, it is striking to discover that the great advocates of religious tolerance in the past were not the Christian churches but people who were critical vis-à-vis Christianity. Catholics and Protestants disagreed in all things. Only in one thing did they agree, namely that Anabaptists, Jews, so-called anti-Trinitarians and other nonconformists had to be harassed, persecuted, burned and drowned.

Those who pleaded for tolerance were not the great theologians, neither were they the reformers. All these observations make me suspicious of the belief that the Holy Spirit is at work only within Christianity. Sometimes God speaks to us through non-Christians. If we Christians are stubborn he can even use an ass if he wants to (Num. 22.28).

Issues Affecting the Study of Pentecostalism in Asia

David Martin

I have no expertise with regard to Asia, so I presume my role here is simply to indicate what I would take into account and how I might proceed when studying Pentecostalism in Asia. However, I can begin by underlining an obvious difference between the situation encountered in Asia and the situations encountered elsewhere. In Europe, Pentecostalism mostly encounters secularized societies with established churches. In Protestant regions it has become a recognized presence in the Free Church sector, and its novel manifestations often take the form of faith churches with a health and wealth gospel.[1] In Catholic countries, and even more so in Orthodox ones, it encounters an assumption about the identity of nation and faith, and so the suggestion is made that it is intrusive and alien. Exactly the same is true of Latin America, except that in Latin America the political secularism of radicals and the left is less powerful than in Europe, and the monopoly exercized by the Catholic Church is more ramshackle. (Analytically one needs to treat the Philippines as similar to Latin America.)

North America and sub-Saharan Africa are very different, yet they share a common pluralism and little connection between a given faith and national identity.[2] North America and most English-speaking African countries also share a diffuse Protestantism and the presence of several churches which had state connections in Europe and retain informal links with power in their diaspora. Thus in both North America and Africa, Pentecostalism is a version of what is already familiar and unthreatening except to rival denominations. Yet the USA, where Pentecostalism first took off, already has an established revivalist tradition and massive evangelical emplacements resistant to corrosion from below. In the middle ranges of society the Pentecostal impulse emerges in modified form as the Charismatic movement within historic denominations. The Charismatic movement is also strong in the middling sectors of society in Africa, but established evangelicalism is not all that secure, especially in the younger generation. Where Africa resembles Latin America rather than North America is in the existence of spiritist cults capable of being re-formed under the aegis of the Holy Spirit.

---

[1] Simon Coleman, *The Word and the World: the Globalization of Charismatic Christianity* (Cambridge: Cambridge University Press, 2001).

[2] Paul Gifford, *African Christianity: Its Public Role* (London: Hurst, 1998).

Such varying global conditions help define the special characteristics of Asia, where there are massive emplacements of major world religions closely related to historic culture, to identity and, in many cases, linked to assertive nationalism. Insofar as Pentecostalism can be regarded as western, and indeed North American, it encounters resistance as an alien import, in company with Christianity itself. Moreover, few Asian countries are pluralistic, even where there is more than one form of historic religion and Pentecostalism may find it difficult to secure a base and avoid moves to contain and isolate it.

That points to opportunities in Asia among the excluded or the peripheral, except that such groups have already been receptive to other forms of Christianity, so that Pentecostalism becomes the latest wave of Christianity among certain minorities.[3] This appeal to minorities is not restricted to Asia, of course: Pentecostalism has an appeal to Gypsies in Europe and to some minority peoples in Latin America. Often such groups are stigmatized as inferior and Pentecostalism acts as a revitalization and assertion of moral standing. The most important instance of this revitalization in the Asian context is Korea, where openness to Christianity is associated with hostility to Chinese and Japanese neighbours.[4]

The remaining possibilities in Asia relate to different degrees of pluralism. There are sectors of capitalist penetration in Asia where some mix of Pentecostalism and Charismatic Christianity has an appeal, one which is reinforced by international networks, many of them North American. Thus the network, say in Singapore, may link business people with similar groups in (say) Lagos, Seoul, Los Angeles, or São Paulo. Here the boundaries of Pentecostalism are often blurred because very similar movements are making headway within the historic churches, notably the Roman Catholic Church, forcing these bodies to validate or extrude them.

Another version of pluralism, more restricted in its range, is located in the vast Chinese diaspora. Chinese are found in many parts of South-East Asia, and constitute a forward-looking active group, apt for Pentecostalism. If, as in Malaysia and Indonesia, the majority is Muslim, the Chinese are differentially inclined to Christianity.[5] The religious difference may then be compounded by the ethnic and economic differences to create considerable tension with the state and the majority culture.

Even more important than the Chinese diaspora is China itself, given that the historic religions were attacked by the Communist regime, leaving a partial

---

[3] Susan Billington Harper, *The Shadow of the Mahatma* (Grand Rapids: Eerdmans, 2000).

[4] Richard Fox Young and Mark Mullins (eds.), *Perspectives on Christianity in Korea and Japan*.

[5] Michael Northcott, 'A Survey of the Rise of Charismatic Christianity in Malaysia', *Asian Journal of Theology* 4:1 (1990), 266-78.

vacuum when Communism itself went into decay and became little more than the ideological vesture of power. In China the vacuum was made greater by the disorientations of the exodus to the cities, so that a faith which dealt in personal relations and family stability might have a great deal to offer. What Pentecostalism offers is a portable faith and identity shepherding millions in moral and economic safety to the modern megacity, not just in China but all over the developing world.[6]

So, then, certain characteristic possibilities for the expansion have been identified in the Asian context. There are, first of all, two possibilities of global scope: the trek to the megacity, which involves internal movement, and then the networks of international movement between the plurastic entrepôts of contemporary capitalism from Singapore to Lagos.[7] The third possibility with regard to peripheral or excluded peoples also has its echoes elsewhere, especially in Latin America, but has special characteristics in Asia given that the historic religion holding the centre is non-Christian and maybe militantly so. Moreover, Pentecostalism is a relatively late Christian newcomer and so may find the niche partly occupied, for example by Baptists or Anglicans. What will be of particular interest is whether Pentecostalism is more capable of making an impact on the centre than its Christian predecessors.

It is in this context of the resistant centre that one has to raise the issue of 'functional equivalents' to Pentecostalism emerging within the majority religion either as separate movements or mutations of the majority faith. This is important, since a movement engendered out of the resources of the indigenous culture has the advantage of not being alien and so may restrict the resonance of the Pentecostal appeal. An interesting illustration of how this comes about is found in the contrasting situations of Korea, Japan and Taiwan. In Korea the current of nationalism has been positively related to Christianity, given the threat of powerful Buddhist/Confucian neighbours. That means that Pentecostalism may expand in the wake of previous Christian expansions, drawing both on the indigenous faiths of Buddhism and shamanism and from Methodism and Presbyterianism. In Korea the Buddhist revival comes quite late, though it is quite powerful. However, in Japan and Taiwan nationalism is negatively related to Christianity, and massive new religious movements have emerged which take up some of what would otherwise be Pentecostal social roles.[8]

---

[6] Alan Hunter and Kim-Kwong Chan, *Protestantism in Contemporary China* (Cambridge:Cambridge University Press, 1993).

[7] Tong Chee Kiong, 'The Rationalization of Religion in Singapore', in Tong Chee Kiong et al. (eds.), *Imagining Singapore* (Singapore:Times Academic Press), 276-98.

[8] Robert Weller and Julia Chien-Yu Huang, 'Merit and Mothering: Women and Welfare in Chinese Buddhism', *The Journal of Asian Studies* 57:2 (1998), 379-96.

It may also be that certain modern forms of Hindu religiosity have had a similar effect in India, say among Dalits as the principal Christian target group and an identical question might be asked of the Falungong in China. Of course, the very notion of 'functional equivalent' requires careful handling. It implies that proselytization is often analogous to niche marketing and raises the question of how great is the 'equivalence' with respect to the satisfaction of social and psychological 'needs'. Some forms of Pentecostalism are themselves quite explicit about this as in David Yonggi Cho's maxim 'Find need and meet need'. What perhaps Yonggi Cho failed to note was the way in which 'functional equivalents' in Japan constricted the space available for his mission compared with Korea.[9]

The reference above to Buddhist revival raises certain interesting questions which are always waiting in the wings once penetration achieves a certain degree of success. One question is how far penetration eventually means assimilation of the pre-existent ethos and how far that ethos becomes adjusted to reduce the unique advantages enjoyed by the newcomer. Another and related question relates to whether there is a ceiling to success round about 20-25%, which includes the effects of too much rapidly created plant. That can easily be discussed through a comparison between Korea and Guatemala, and such a comparison will in turn raise issues (a) about the effects of economic booms and busts, and (b) about the effects of major penetration into the middle class and of post-modern conditions as these affect particular advanced sectors. In short, is the success of Pentecostalism tied to a phase of social development, which may eventually curtail or alter it?

Behind all such considerations is the degree to which a new proselytizing movement is experienced and resisted as alien and culturally distant. Being alien and being culturally distant overlap in meaning but are not identical. To be alien is simply to be defined as coming from elsewhere, which in the modern world mostly means the USA, whereas cultural distance includes the proximity of Pentecostal practices, such as exorcism, to indigenous practices. So each has to be taken in turn.

With respect to the alien character of Pentecostalism, the Philippines may provide an interesting example. As already suggested, the Philippines fits at least as much into the Latin American pattern as the Asian. The majority faith is Catholic and was of Spanish provenance and there are a number of groups for which Catholicism itself is either alien or at any rate a thin overlay of an indigenous practice. One has to ask, therefore, not only how far Pentecostalism may be resisted as an alien import by the Catholic majority, but whether Pentecostalism offers minority groups a chance to leap over the local majority by adopting a new identity from elsewhere. The question as to majority resistance to alien import is endemic, and gains particular force in the

---

[9] Richard Fox Young and Mark Mullins *op.cit.*

Philippines on account of its status during the last century as a client state of the USA. That in itself immediately opens a universe of comparisons, for example, with Puerto Rico. Such a comparison facilitates the fundamental question as how far Pentecostalism is related to US influence and how far it may come to be associated with nationalistic resistance to that influence.[10]

It is here that the issue of cultural distance becomes relevant. Pentecostalism, after all, differs somewhat from earlier forms of expansive Protestant Christianity in having crossed the faith of poor whites with the faith of poor blacks and having brought under the aegis of the Holy Spirit innumerable spiritistic cults. It may, therefore, the more easily achieve some consonance with forms of indigenous spirituality than other more rationalized versions of Protestantism, and that in turn could increase identification with indigenous movements of nationalistic protest.

In the Philippines that raises the question as to how far Pentecostalism is faced with other kinds of functional equivalents from within the majority religion of Catholicism, either through the identification of the Catholic Church with movements against corruption or more specifically through Liberation Theology. With respect to Liberation Theology, the same questions have to be asked as in Latin America with respect to certain similarities of form and differences of content, as well such borrowings as may occur in the course of rival expansions.

Nor is this question restricted to the Philippines. In India Pentecostalism competes with Social Gospel Christianity as well as Liberationism, while in Korea a Pentecostalism which has been rather passive and perhaps conformist politically, competes with an active Catholicism willing and able to confront governmental corruption and US influence.[11]

At this point perhaps, one may turn more directly to the problems associated with the dialectic of centre and periphery. At both centre and periphery there may be a desire to achieve identities different from that of the majority tradition, which are facilitated by Pentecostalism as a transnational movement. However, in the case of the periphery, it is clear that Pentecostalism is providing an appeal to a group rather than individuals and may come to have ethnic character not unlike that of Calvinistic Methodism in Wales. The role may be made more complex by the fissiparous character of Pentecostalism in rivalry with pre-existing varieties of Protestantism, and in any case is quite likely to lead to tension at the border with the ethno-religiosity of the

---

[10] Jae Yong Jeong, 'Filipino Pentecostal Spirituality' (Th.D dissertation, Birmingham University, 2001).

[11] Paul Freston, *Evangelicals and Politics in Asia, Africa and Latin America* (Cambridge: Cambridge University Press), 2001.

majority.[12] A state, identified with that ethno-religiosity and perhaps promoting it as a vehicle of national solidarity, can easily perceive an ethno-religiosity at the periphery as a hostile salient. At the very least, this may lead to propaganda defining the adoption of Pentecostalism as treason against the authentic national spirit and its historic roots. It will be interesting to see, for example, how current changes in Nepal, including the revolutionary Maoist movement, affect perceptions of conversion in areas inhabited by ethnic minorities.[13] There is also the issue, frequently raised by anthropologists, as to the divisive effects of missionizing on the social solidarity of minority groups, given that different segments may be differentially associated with particular denominations, or through counter-definition with a revival of the indigenous religion. Any analysis has to concern itself with these complex forms of definition and counter-definition.

With regard to penetration at the centre, that is obviously more difficult than penetration at the periphery; but when it does occur, it is correspondingly significant. An interesting issue here is whether Pentecostalism is associated primarily with an international modernity or with a religiosity which takes seriously the reality and potency of the old spirits. If the former is the case it may well be that Pentecostalism proper shades off into various forms of charismatic religiosity appealing to a mobile metropolitan clientele, particularly in the business community. At any rate, the appropriate universes of comparison might be Kathmandu, Rangoon and Bangkok. For example, in Bangkok, one may ask how far has Pentecostalism broken out of the association of Christianity with minorities to include indigenous Thais and in Kathmandu one may ask how many broadly Charismatic or Evangelical groups of an international provenance are also active in the capital.[14]

The Thai example introduces a further question to do with the partial retention of Thai religious understandings, such as the system of merit, within a Pentecostal framework. Pentecostalism is widely identified with a decisive break. But in some parts of Asia the break includes a retention whereby the old forms and even the old spirits live out a ghostly life within the Pentecostal body. Korea provides an obvious example. Though Koreans are sometimes reluctant to admit a shamanistic stratum within the national culture, it is evident that shamanistic elements are rather easily incorporated in the faith of the Holy Spirit. In a very similar manner Confucian understandings of filial piety and male pre-eminence may reappear within Pentecostalism and that is true not

---

[12] David Martin, *Tongues of Fire* (Oxford: Blackwell, 1990) and *Pentecostalism: Tthe World Their Parish* (Oxford: Blackwell, 2001).

[13] Blandine Ripert, 'Christianisme et Pouvoirs Locaux dans une vallée Tamang du Népal Centrale', *Archives de Sciences Sociales des Religions* 99 (July-Sep. 1997), 69-86.

[14] Edwin Zehner, 'Thai Protestants and Local Supernaturalism: Changing Configurations', *Journal of Southeast Asian Studies* 27:2 (September 1996).

only in Korea itself but in the Korean diaspora, including the large diaspora in the USA.

Diaspora may well provide a concluding theme, because Pentecostalism is a movement well adapted to the mobility of contemporary global society. Koreans go to the Philippines and the USA, bearing their portable faith into new and challenging environments. One has to ask about Pentecostalism in a series of way-stations along global trails. Pastors in particular engage in a global version of the old Methodist circuit. In this way they are a challenge to all established faiths based on local identity and historic continuity and, moreover, deserve special study as religious entrepreneurs and a buried intelligentsia. Pentecostalism lives in interstices, and in the Pacific Islands, as also in Cape Verde in the Atlantic, it undermines the old models relating to place and time.[15] The Pacific Islands, being relatively small, were often converted to forms of Christianity which were able to replace older religions by something approaching the Christendom model, for example, Methodism in Tonga and Fiji. Thus the key to Pentecostalism, in Asia as elsewhere, lies in examining it as a movement, with an international potency not merely reinforced by its North American connections but by combinations of ancient and modern elements assisting rapid indigenization.

Perhaps I might conclude by emphasizing the key themes in the above with respect to a sociological perspective on Pentecostalism in Asia. The first and most characteristic relates to the identification of relevant comparisons, whether these are between major civilizations or between countries as, for example, Korea and Guatemala, or between versions of the same tendency as, for example, 'faith'doctrines in Singapore, Buenos Aires and Lagos. The second relates to the Great Trek to the megacity and with that conditions of economic expansion or contraction. It is all too easy to reach for off-the-peg explanations in terms of whatever happens to be the local situation, because there are some plausible conditions always to hand. The third relates to effects of cultural distance, including North American influence and the response of the culture or religion concerned in terms of revitalization. That is linked to the fourth theme, which is the capacity of a culture to produce functional equivalents. The fifth theme relates to the local possibilities for pluralism, given that Pentecostalism is an instalment of pluralism, as well as internally fissiparous. The sixth theme relates to differential appeals to groups which are excluded or at the periphery. The seventh and last theme is crucial because it is concerned with the possible role of Pentecostalism as expanding and contracting in relation to a particular social phase.

---

[15] Anne Stensfold, 'A Wave of Conversion:Protestantism in Cape Verde', *Religion* 29:4 (1995), 337-46; Manfred Erst (ed.), *Winds of Change: Rapidly Growing Religious Groups in the Pacific* (Suva: Pacific Council of Churches, 1994).

Lastly, let me say something by way of addendum about authenticity, which I realize is contentious. To describe a culture as authentic is simultaneously to identify it, which is problematic, and to approve of it, which is arguably none of our business. In general, people do not know their culture is authentic until an intelligentsia tells them so in the course of constructing national identity. In the case of England, its nation-building occurred so long ago that we cannot know what is authentic. After all, our culture is an amalgam based on borrowings and we cannot locate a pure identity or even think of removing what we believe are accretions. Authenticity, then, is what is imputed to certain elements of folk practice by the entrepreneurs of nationalism, or else it may be the adoption of a culture of the margins of the remote because it offers mental respite from the discontents of modernity. In either case it is a selection in particular of symbols serving to define essential difference in relation to the other or an idealization. In the case of the British Isles, nostalgia for the Celtic, including the Celtic church is precisely a case in point.

We have to be cautious, then, about such nostalgias or, in the case of colonized cultures, feelings of guilt associated with the instinct for retrieval. It is not our role to mark other people's moral scripts in terms of negative or positive. In the long run after all, we have all been colonized or been at a margin. We cannot implicitly seek to constrain peoples within some concept of their time and an original culture. 'Merrie Korea' is about as persuasive as 'Merrie England' or 'Merrie Scotland'.

Authenticity is a discourse of inclusion or exclusion, and in that role peculiarly relevant to Pentecostalism. According to David Lehmann in *Struggle for the Spirit* (1996), the radicalism of Pentecostalism consists in indifference to whether the erudite guardians of the Brazilian ethos choose to regard it as authentic. Whatever we think about that, it remains all too true that we are so sensitive to the approval of western elites or national elites fired by western nationalism that we commend Pentecostalism not on its own account, but because as a faith in the Spirit it accords with the animation and vitality of indigenous culture; or we disapprove of Pentecostalism because we define it as alien and modern and contrary to indigenous practice. Of course, if we choose to deploy a discourse of inclusion or exclusion that is up to us, so long as we are clear that such a discourse is ideological, and so long as we recognize that cultures are always changing and in receipt of new materials which may be enriching as well as corrosive.

Pentecostalism and the Asian Church

Hwa Yung

This paper was originally intended to be a study of how Asian Christianity has responded or is responding to the various forms of Pentecostalism,[1] both indigenous and western. But the facts are such that I am increasingly convinced that another approach would be much more helpful for our understanding of Pentecostalism in the Asian church. Rather than to focus on how Asian Christianity is responding to the Pentecostal/Charismatic renewal, it appears that it would be more useful to ask another question. To what extent is what is call Pentecostalism in the west essentially the same as indigenous Christianity in the non-western world?

This is not an entirely new line of approach. As we shall see, others have already raised the same question. However, before proceeding, we will first look at the impact of the Pentecostal/Charismatic renewal in Asia.

The Impact of Pentecostalism in Asia

There is abundant evidence that Pentecostalism today is widespread in Asian churches today. Various recent writings have already drawn attention to this fact. The statistics for Asia in mid-AD 2000 is as follows:[2]

Total population	3,697 Million
Number of Christians	
▪ Adherents	313 Million
▪ Professing Christians	199 Million
Number of Pentecostals & Charismatics	135 Million

---

[1] I am using the term 'Pentecostalism' here not strictly with reference to classical Pentecostalism alone, but in a broader sense to the whole global Pentecostal/Charismatic renewal in the 20th century.

[2] David B. Barrett and T.M. Johnson, *World Christian Encyclopedia*, 2 vols. (Oxford & New York: Oxford University Press, 2001), I, 13; David B. Barrett, 'The Widespread Holy Spirit Renewal', in Vinson Synan (ed.), *The Century of the Holy Spirit: 100 Years of Pentecostal and Charismatic Renewal, 1901-2001* (Nashville, TN: Thomas Nelson, 2001), 381-414 (388).

Of these, Classical Pentecostals form 5%, Charismatics 16%, and Neocharismatics 79%. These three groups are often classified respectively as 1st, 2nd and 3rd waves renewal members.[3] Further, large numbers of those classified under 2nd wave Charismatics are Roman Catholics, especially in India and Philippines.[4] Also classified under 3rd wave Neocharismatics are the following indigenous groups from different parts of Asia:

Filipino indigenous Pentecostals/Charismatics	6.8 Million
Han Chinese indigenous Pentecostals/Charismatics	49.7 Million
Indian indigenous Pentecostals/Charismatics	16.6 Million
Indonesia indigenous Pentecostals	6.8 Million
Korean indigenous Pentecostals/Charismatics	3.3 Million

The above figures show that about two-thirds of all professing Christians in Asia are Pentecostals, Charismatics or Neocharismatics. And a very high proportion of these are found within churches which arose out of indigenous Christian movements, rather than in traditional denominations brought from the west.

We see the same pattern in the growth of individual congregations. Hong Young-gi[5] has pointed out that of the fifteen mega-churches in Korea which have adult attendance of 12 000 and more, nine are Pentecostal/Charismatic churches. Denominational-wise, there are two Presbyterians (Tong-Hap), two Methodist, three Assemblies of God, one Unification Holiness and one Southern Baptist. And the largest of these, and possibly the largest in the world, is Yoido Full Gospel Church in Seoul under the Pentecostal Yonggi Cho which has a regular adult attendance of 230 000. In Metro Manila, Philippines, a recent study showed that eight out of the ten fastest growing congregations are Pentecostal- Charismatic.[6] Similar observations would also apply to Malaysia and Singapore contexts with which I am personally familiar. A large majority of the fastest growing churches and the largest local congregations are Pentecostal- Charismatic in character.

Finally, whereas much attention has been given to countries like Korea and China, relatively much less has been reported about India. But the above

---

[3] See below for explanation of terms.

[4] See Stanley M Burgess, 'Charismatic Movements', in Scott W. Sunquist, et. al. (ed.) *A Dictionary of Asian Christianity* (Grand Rapids, MI: Eerdmans, 2001), 132-134.

[5] Young-gi Hong, 'The Backgrounds and Characteristics of the Charismatic Mega-Churches in Korea', *Asian Journal of Pentecostal Studies* 3:1 (2000), 99-118.

[6] Jungja Ma, 'Pentecostal Challenges in East and South-East Asia', in Murray W. Dempster, et. al. (eds.), *The Globalization of Pentecostalism: A Religion Made to Travel* (Oxford: Regnum, 1999), 183-202 (196).

figures show clearly that Pentecostalism has also impacted India strongly. Mention should be made, in particular, of one key Pentecostal/Charismatic figure, D.G.S. Dhinakaran. He first came into prominence in the 1970s. One recent study suggests that 'Probably no figure in India at the present time has a more far-reaching influence for the development of Pentecostal/Charismatic Christianity than Bro. Dhinakaran'.[7]

The above evidence demonstrates clearly the widespread impact of Pentecostalism on the Asian church today. But how is this to be understood in relation to the growth of Pentecostalism on the one hand and the Asian church on the other?

The Prevailing Interpretation

Much of the existing literature follows what can be called the prevailing interpretation which speaks of three waves of Pentecostal/Charismatic renewal.[8] The first wave of classical Pentecostalism began on 1 Jan 1901 at Charles F. Parham's Bethel Bible School in the Topeka, Kansas. The subsequent revival of 1906-1907 at Azusa Street, Los Angeles, under William J. Seymour, led to the spread of classical Pentecostalism to many countries through its missionaries. The second wave came in the form of the penetration of Pentecostalism into the historic Protestant and Roman Catholic churches. This is the Charismatic movement which 'also originated primarily in the United States'[9] around 1960, and historically is often linked to Dennis Bennett, the Episcopal rector in Van Nuys, California, as the initiator. From there it spread to other denominations, including Catholics and the Orthodox churches. The third wave of renewal, according to Vinson Synan, began in 1981 with John Wimber's ministry at Fuller Theological Seminary. Further, according to him, 'By 2000 the third wavers, also called 'neo-charismatics', were credited with some 295 million members worldwide'.[10]

Thus the Pentecostal/Charismatic renewal is perceived to have begun essentially in the United States with classical Pentecostalism. It then spread outwards into other parts of the world, first via first-wave Pentecostal missionaries, and then via the second-wave Charismatics and the third-wave

---

[7] Michael Bergunder, '"Ministry of Compassion": D.G.S. Dhinakaran, Christian-Healer Prophet from Tamilnadu', in Roger E. Hedlund (ed.), *Christianity in India: The Emergence of an Indigenous Community* (Chennai: MIIS, and Delhi, ISPCK, 2000), 158-174 (174).

[8] E.g. Burgess, 'Charismatic Movements', 132; Vinson Synan (ed.), *The Century of the Holy Spirit: 100 Years of Pentecostal and Charismatic Renewal, 1901-2001* (Nashville, TN: Thomas Nelson, 2001), 1-13.

[9] Synan, *The Century of the Holy Spirit*, 8.

[10] Synan, *The Century of the Holy Spirit*, 9.

Neocharismatics. Although not everyone sees it this way, it has nonetheless been the interpretation of the Pentecostal/Charismatic phenomenon accepted by most. However, this is now being challenged for various reasons.

To begin with, this interpretation assumes that the primary identity of the global Pentecostal/Charismatic movement is found in its historical linkage to classical Pentecostalism's self-definition of itself, in terms of a post-conversion experience of Spirit baptism as evidenced by speaking of tongues. But this doctrine, which is so central to the classical Pentecostalism derived from the experiences of Charles Parham and William Seymour, is itself being questioned from within by some. The Pentecostal New Testament scholar, Gordon Fee, for example, has raised serious questions about whether the doctrine of an essential post-conversion experience of Spirit baptism can be sustained on biblical grounds.[11]

Fee's critique also finds support from writings outside the classical Pentecostal tradition. Various scholars have further argued that the belief, that speaking in tongues in the necessary sign of being baptized in or filled with the Spirit, cannot be sustained on exegetical grounds. Indeed many within the Pentecostal/Charismatic movement today do not place the same emphasis on tongues as classical Pentecostalism once did. If this is the case, then what is central to classical Pentecostalism's self-definition of itself, namely, the post-conversion experience of Spirit baptism leading to speaking in tongues, cannot be taken as the defining characteristic of the whole Pentecostal/Charismatic movement today.

What then should be the defining characteristic of the whole Pentecostal/Charismatic movement today? It appears that it would be much more appropriate to define Pentecostalism or the Pentecostal/Charismatic movement by what is most distinctive about it, which is the strong emphasis on the work of the Holy Spirit as understood in New Testament. Thus Everett Wilson's statement that 'Pentecostalism, the faith of apostolic signs and wonders, represents itself as a *self-validating expression of primitive Christianity*'[12] is as good a definition as any.

Understood this way, the Three-Wave theory, which sees everything flowing out of American classical Pentecostalism, will be readily seen as a schematized but highly inadequate interpretation of the renewal movement. This is clearly

---

[11] Gordon Fee, *Gospel and Spirit: Issues in New Testament Hermeneutics* (Peabody, MA: Hendrikson, 1991), 105-119. See also Walter J. Hollenweger, 'Rethinking Spirit Baptism: The Natural and the Supernatural', in Allan H. Anderson and Walter J. Hollenweger (eds.), *Pentecostals after a Century: Global Perspectives on a Movement in Transition* (Sheffield: Sheffield Academic Press, 1999), 164-172 (167-169).

[12] Everett A. Wilson, 'They Crossed the Red Sea, Didn't They? Critical History and Pentecostal Beginnings', in Murray W. Dempster, et. al. (eds.), *The Globalization of Pentecostalism: A Religion Made to Travel*, ed. (Oxford: Regnum, 1999), 85-115 (110).

demonstrated by the history of renewal, both in the west and the rest of the world.

In the west, there were clear antecedents of the Pentecostal/Charismatic renewal even before the 20th century. One of the most notable was the Catholic Apostolic Church of Edward Irving, beginning in London in 1831. Again, Pentecostal/Charismatic experiences like being 'slain in the Spirit', 'holy laughter', 'jerking', and the like were known occurrences in Holiness Camp meetings in the 19th century American frontier.[13] Going back further, early Methodism under John Wesley also manifested the phenomena of being 'slain in the Spirit', and cases of healing as well. Jack Deere also unearthed evidence of prophecy exercised by Scottish Presbyterians during the 16th century Reformation.[14] Other examples are also known.[15] To see the movement as beginning with Parham and Seymour at the turn of the 20th century is surely an oversimplification.

Further some scholars have also pointed out that the Pentecostal/Charismatic phenomenon have a multiplicity of beginnings in different cultures. As Everett A. Wilson has noted, Pentecostalism is not just another American phenomenon which then became globalized in the 20th century.

Rather, it 'has broken out or has been rediscovered or been appropriated recurrently since the beginning of this century—if not before'.[16] Therefore, he argues that the study of Pentecostalism,

> ...need not focus exclusively on U.S. precedents, since...non-Western groups have cultivated their own analogous, cognate forms (including their own founders, origins and subcultures), but in a variety of settings, in different ways and with their own spiritual achievements. If they exhibit similar if not identical Pentecostal features, it is notable that they have never had more than the most tenuous ties to the North American institutionsl...Because of their chronological priority and large and rapidly growing memberships, should non-Western movements not be considered in assessing the formative years of the movement?[17]

In other words, non-western beginnings of the Pentecostal/Charismatic phenomenon have to be taken seriously in their own right, and assessed accordingly.

This reinterpretation of Pentecostalism has been suggested by others also. Allan H. Anderson in titling his study of the phenomenon in Asia,

---

[13] Vinson Synan, *The Holiness-Pentecostal Tradition: Charismatic Movements in the Twentieth Century* (Grand Rapids, MI: Eerdmans, 1997), 11-14.

[14] Jack Deere, *Surprised by the Voice of God* (Eastbourne: Kingsway, 1996), 64-78.

[15] For a brief list of 'signs and winders' in the western church history, see John Wimber, *Power Evangelism-Signs and Wonders Today* (London: Hodder, 1985), 151-66.

[16] Wilson, 'They Crossed the Red Sea', 107-108.

[17] Wilson, 'They Crossed the Red Sea', 109-110.

'Pentecostalism in East Asia: Indigenous Oriental Christianity?'[18] is essentially making the same point.

Similarly, although David Barrett uses the 'three waves' language in his analysis, he nevertheless understands it in a substantially different manner from those who take an Americo-centric view of Pentecostal/Charismatic history. Rather than the three successive waves of the prevailing three-wave theory, Barrett speaks instead of the three *simultaneous* waves of renewal impacting global Christianity. Further, he refers to the majority those in the 'third wave' as non-white indigenous neo-Charismatics. These are described as 'Apparent/seemingly/largely pentecostal or semipentecostal members of *this 250–year old movement of churches indigenous to Christians in non-white races across the world, and begun without reference to Western Christianity*'.[19]

It is evident from these considerations that the traditional 'three-waves-flowing-from-one-main-center' approach, is in serious need of modification. As a schematic way of seeing the work of the renewal by the Holy Spirit, it applies reasonably well to the western churches. It also applies to churches in the non-western world which have been or are being strongly influenced by the changing currents in western Christianity. Examples of these would be English-speaking urban churches in many parts of Asia. But when it comes to churches that do not have the same degree of contact with the west, it clearly becomes an arbitrary imposition which often hinders us from understanding the real dynamics at work in many non-western churches. The fact is that much of indigenous Christianity in Asia has often borne the marks of classical Pentecostalism, 'the faith of apostolic signs and wonders', even though in many cases their origins were independent. We will now look at some of the historical evidence in support of this assertion.

Indigenous Christianity in Asia Has Often Been Characterized by Pentecostal/Charismatic Experiences

For the purpose of clarity, the evidence will be divided into pre- and post-Azusa Street categories.

Pre-Azusa Street Pentecostal/Charismatic Manifestations in Asian Christianity

Examples of outbreak of Pentecostalism are clearly found in 19th century Asia. Gary B. McGee in an article on 'Pentecostalism' in the Asian church recounts some of these.

---

[18] Allan H. Anderson, 'Pentecostalism in East Asia: Indigenous Oriental Christianity?' *Pneuma* 22 (Spring 2000), 115-132.

[19] Barrett, 'The Widespread Holy Spirit Renewal', 382, 390 & 404. Italics are mine.

Reports of revival movements in Asia in the 19th ceuntury sometimes contain descriptions of Pentecostal-like phenomena: visions, dreams, prophecies, miracles, persons falling prostrate, and in rare instances speaking in tongues. Participants sought the 'outpouring' of the Holy Spirit for holy living and empowerment to evangelize.... These developments did not always occur as a result of events in the West. In some cases, unusual happenings accompanied the ministries of missionaries and national believers as they evangelized and established churches'.[20]

Among the 'Pentecostal-like' incidents listed by him are the movements in Tirunelveli (1860-65), led in part by John Christian Aroolappen, and Travancore (1873-81) by Justus Joseph, both in India, among the Bataks in Sumatra under Rhenish missionaries, in Central Java under the indigenous leader Sadrach Surapranata, among Karens in Myanmar, and the work of Chinese leaders such as Hsi Shengmo. He goes on to state that, 'Thus, by the time the first Pentecostal missionaries arrived in Asia from the United States in 1907, Pentecostal-like movements and expressions had appeared for almost half a century in various places. These precedents have relevance for understanding contemporary Pentecostal churches and the ongoing charismatic renewal of other Asian churches'.[21]

Special mention must be made of three nationals: Hsi of China, and Aroolappen and Pandita Ramabai of India. Hsi Shengmo (1835-1896) or Pastor Hsi, as in his biography of that name,[22] was a Chinese who ministered in Shanxi Province, China. He came from a scholarly family of above average means. A Confucian scholar, but he became addicted to opium in his thirties. When converted to Christianity in 1879, he took on the name Shengmo, meaning 'demon overcomer'. His ministry was marked by a devotion to the Bible, deep prayer life, and manifestations of spiritual gifts, especially in the area of exorcism and healing. His most notable achievement was probably the establishment of some forty-five drug rehabilitation centers for opium addicts in four provinces. These also served as bases for church-planting. His ministry has been described as 'apostolic' by D. Martyn Lloyd-Jones.[23]

John Christian Arrolappen oversaw a revival which broke out in Tirunelveli in May 1860. G.H. Lang in his biography quotes a first hand account as follows:

---

[20] Gary B. McGee, 'Pentecostalism', in Scott W. Sunquist, et. al. (eds.), *A Dictionary of Asian Christianity* (Grand Rapids, MI: Eerdmans, 2001), 646-650 (647).

[21] McGee, 'Pentecostalism', p. 647.

[22] Mrs. Howard Taylor, *Pastor Hsi: Confucian Scholar and Christian* (London: Overseas Missionary Fellowship, 1900, rev. 1949, 1989).

[23] Taylor, *Pastor Hsi*, vii.

The 'Spirit' was poured out upon many of those assembled, and there was a great shaking, attended with certain 'gifts', viz. Speaking with tongues, seeing of visions, interpretation of tongues and prophecy...the fruits of the Spirit are manifest—there is a hatred of sin of all kinds, casting off of jewels, etc., love and unity, with peace and joy in the Holy Ghost, great love for and searching of God's holy word, with a strong desire for private and social prayer.'[24]

This may well be the first recorded (as opposed to those not recorded!) outbreak of Pentecostalism in India. There was at least one other recorded incident of a similar nature, the outpouring of the Spirit at the Mukti Mission of Pandita Ramabai in Pune, on 30th June, 1905. Ramabai, a Brahmin covert fluent in Sanskrit, was of course the most well-known indigenous Christian woman of India. Accounts of the revival reported simultaneous loud praying with weeping, confession of sins, sensations of burning and speaking of tongues. From there the revival spread to Gujarat where both nationals and Christian Missionary Alliance missionaries went through similar experiences.[25]

Post-Azusa Street Pentecostalism in Asian Christianity

The accounts in the preceding section by themselves are sufficient to debunk the traditional interpretation of the Pentecostal/Charismatic renewal as three waves of revival flowing out of America, beginning in 1906. But further evidence can be found in post-Azusa Street happenings throughout Asia, whose origins owe little or nothing to western Pentecostalism.

We will begin with two of the most well-known Christians of Asia, Sadhu Sundar Singh (1889-1929) of India and John Sung (1901-1944) of China. Sundar Singh was born a Sikh, and brought up in both the Sikh religion and the Hindu *bhakti* tradition. He was converted through a dramatic experience at the age of fifteen, wherein he saw a vision of the living Christ in his room within hours of the time of his planned suicide. Soon he was baptized and at the age of sixteen, in fulfillment of his dead mother's hopes, became a *sadhu*, but as a Christian. He entered an Anglican seminary but left after less than a year because he found the whole atmosphere too foreign. Instead, wearing the ocher robes of an Indian holy man, he began an itinerant ministry all over India,

---

[24] G.H. Lang, *The History and Diaries of an Indian Christian: J. C. Aroolapan* (London: M.F. Robinson & Co., 1939), 198-99; quoted in Ivan M. Satyavrata, 'Contextual Perspectives on Pentecostalism as a Global Culture: A South Asian View', in Murray W. Dempster, et. al. (eds.), *The Globalization of Pentecostalism: A Religion Made to Travel* (Oxford: Regnum, 1999), 203-221 (205).

[25] Satyavrata, 'Contextual Perspective', 204.

Tibet, and, eventually, the world. One writer asserts that 'no Indian Christian has exercised an influence even remotely comparable to Sundar Singh's'.[26]

He adopted the lifestyle of an Indian holy man, walking bare-footed from place to place. His preaching style was not based on some western apologetic approaches, but instead employed parables, pictures and analogies that were familiar to the Indian mind. In an age when the western missionaries had little to say about signs and wonders, he regularly experienced miracles, visions, and spiritual experiences in his own life and ministry—things that both the New Testament and Indian worldviews understood readily and affirmed. Interestingly, although he had a clearly demonstrable gift of healing, he soon refrained from exercising it because he feared that it would divert attention away from faith in Christ to himself as a miracle worker.[27]

John Sung was probably the greatest evangelist and revivalist of 20th century China. Born in the home of a Methodist pastor in Fujian, in south-east China, at a time of intense revolutionary fervor, John Sung went off to America in 1920 for university studies. A brilliant student, he graduated with a Ph.D. in chemistry within six years of his arrival there. After another most eventful year in the U.S., which included a semester at Union, New York, then as it is now a bastion of liberal Christianity, and six months in a mental hospital, he returned home in 1927. In the next fifteen years, he poured out his heart and soul in a most amazing ministry, and in due course became the greatest evangelist that China ever produced. Although not often recognized as such in the existing literature on the period, his ministry brought thousands to Christ, and revival to hundreds of Chinese churches in China and South-East Asia. Leslie T. Lyall, a veteran China Inland Mission member, authored the best biography on John Sung available. Writing some ten years after his death, he states: 'In every province of China and among the overseas Chinese communities in the islands of the South China Sea, in the U.S.A., in the West Indies, in Great Britain, and wherever Chinese Christians are to be found…very many leaders in the Church to-day were either converted or had their lives greatly changed in the campaigns conducted by this extraordinary servant of God'.[28]

Sung ministered in a time when much of the Christianity taught in the west was largely shaped by a rationalistic worldview which could not accommodate signs and wonders easily. But the response of many Chinese Christians even then was often different from that in the west. Leslie Lyall notes that 'Prayer for the sick has always been a natural part of the faith of Chinese Christians.

---

[26] Eric J. Sharpe, 'The Legacy of Sadhu Sundar Singh', *Internat. Bulletin of Missionary Research* 14:4 (1990), 161-167 (166).

[27] A.J. Appasamy, *Sundar Singh: A Biography* (London: Lutterworth Press, 1958), 97-100.

[28] Leslie T. Lyall, *John Sung: Flame for God in the Far East,* 4th ed. (London: Overseas Missionary Fellowship, 1956), xxii.

Many a church has been founded on the basis of prayer heard and answered for the chronically ill, or people raised from critical illnesses. God has answered prayer in so many thousands of cases that Christians in China expect miracles to happen and they undoubtedly do'.[29]

It was no different in the case of John Sung's ministry. Lyall records numerous cases of healing in his ministry including a woman's almost instant recovery from a near fatal heart attack, and the lame, leprous, deaf and dumb being made whole.[30] Such reports have further been substantiated by eye-witnesses of his ministry, some of whom are still alive today. One such is the daughter of a Chinese preacher, a girl of about twelve at the time he visited Penang, in what was then British Malaya, in the late 1930s. She tells of large numbers of people lining-up for prayer for healing. John Sung did not even have time to ask them about their illnesses, but merely prayed for each in tongues as he ministered healing in Christ's name![31]

Other phenomena generally associated with Pentecostalism were also found in Sung's life and ministry. As noted already, he regularly prayed in tongues, a gift he first received on March 25, 1934.[32] He also regularly exercised what many today would call the gift of knowledge or prophecy in the course of his preaching. He would point to specific people in the congregation, rebuking and calling them to repent from specific sins.[33] He also saw clearly that it was western control that was often a crucial hindrance to the growth of the church in China. Repeatedly he stated in his diary his conviction that only after the missionaries leave and western funds stopped from coming would the Chinese church really move forward.[34] His closest and most trusted missionary friend, William E. Schubert, in his brief *I Remember John Sung* draws attention to the same issue. He recounts how towards the end of Sung's life, 'Dr. Sung also told a missionary friend of ours that God had revealed to him that there would be a great revival in China, but that the missionaries would have to leave first'![35]

---

[29] Lyall, *John Sung*, 132.

[30] Lyall, *John Sung*, 10-11, 132-137, 168, 174, 178-179.

[31] Mrs. Khoo Hock Siang, Trinity Methodist Church, Penang, in personal conversation with the author.

[32] John Sung, *The Diaries of John Sung*, trans. Stephen L. Sheng (Brighton, MI: Luke H. Sheng and Stephen L. Sheng, 1995), 29.

[33] Lyall, *John Sung*, 151. Similar stories have been related to the author by eye-witnesses or by those who heard them from such in both Sibu and Sitiawan, Malaysia.

[34] Sung, *Diaries*, 34, 54, 183.

[35] William E. Schubert, *I Remember John Sung* (Singapore: Far Eastern Bible College Press, 1976), 65-66.

This proved to be the most amazing prophecy concerning the Chinese church in the 20[36]th century.[36]

The point that is being made here is that neither Sundar Singh and Sung, two of the most influential Asian Christians in the first half of the 20th century, were classical Pentecostals. Nor were they influenced by them. Both were examples of indigenous Christianity in Asia. Yet they were fully Pentecostal in the New Testament sense of exercising a ministry of 'signs and wonders', and represented Primitive Christianity at its best in the modern world.

Another example is the Indonesian revival of the 1960s and early 70s. Observers reported many examples of 'signs and wonders', some of which bear obvious signs of embellishments. Yet there are enough creditable accounts to showed that 'signs and wonders' were often common occurrences. Kurt Koch's account of the revival, from the point of view of a sympathetic western observer, points to 'signs and wonders' as one of the key reasons for the growth of the church.[37] An indirect confirmation of this also comes from a report in the June 1971 issue of *East Asia Millions*, the official magazine of the Overseas Missionary Fellowship, and recounted by J. Edwin Orr. It tells of an Indonesian team seeking to reach out to Muslims in South Thailand, and demonstrated God's power through prayer by asking the rain to stop. This led to their being invited back to the local mosque where discussions with the imams went on into the wee hours of the morning.[38] Similar happenings are also reported in the autobiography of Petrus Octavianus,[39] one of the key leaders of the Indonesian revival.

The last piece of evidence is drawn from the growth of Christianity in China over the past 50 years or so. Anderson[40] has already drawn attention to two of the indigenous Pentecostal churches, the True Jesus Church and the Jesus Family. A third church, the Local Church or Little Flock of Watchman Nee, is also reported to have manifested Pentecostal-like characteristics. It is well-known that Watchman Nee himself was not a Pentecostal, although the report quoted by Anderson[41] that he might have spoken in tongues may well be right. Certainly the Little Flock churches among S. E. Asian Chinese today are not Pentecostal churches. Yet Nee himself was certainly involved in

---

[36] It is important to note that at the time that Schubert's book was published, the international Christian community was still largely unaware of what was happening in Chinese church during the dark years of the Cultural Revolution in China.

[37] Kurt Koch, *The Revival in Indonesia* (Grand Rapids, MI: Kregel, 1971).

[38] J. Edwin Orr, *Evangelical Awakenings in East Asia* (Minneapolis, MN: Bethany Fellowship, 1975), 146.

[39] Petrus Octavianus, *My Life for the Lord and My Neighbours: A Forty-One Years of Service to the Lord (1957-1998)* (Privately published, 1998), 57-58. A much fuller English version of the Indonesian original is expected in 2002.

[40] Anderson, 'Pentecostalism in East Asia', 118-123.

[41] Anderson, 'Pentecostalism in East Asia', 121.

deliverance ministry against demonic powers. In one account, he recounted a spectacular breakthrough in evangelism on an island off the China coast after the power of *Ta Wang,* the chief deity worshipped on the island, was broken through prayer.[42] This is a clear example of what present-day Pentecostals and Charismatics call 'power encounters'. This only goes to confirm that the line drawn between Pentecostal and non-Pentecostal churches in China is nowhere a clear one. The latest reports on the growth of the various branches of the church in China in the past 25 years or so demonstrate that signs and wonders are widespread, and not confined to only Pentecostal churches at all. Indeed, even some of the Three-Self Patriotic Movement churches and magazines are reporting similar occurrences.[43]

Pentecostalism and the Asian Church—An Alternative Interpretation

The total weight of the above evidence is such that an alternative interpretation is required. What does that entail?

The Three-Wave Americo-Centric Interpretation of Pentecostalism Has Only Partial Validity

The traditional three-wave Americo-centric interpretation which see three waves of renewal coming out of the United States has only partial validity. It applies broadly in the western church, and also to those churches in the non-western world which has been strongly influenced by American Christianity. But that is as far as it goes.

Further, the sharp distinction drawn between Pentecostal/Charismatic churches and non-Pentecostal/Charismatic ones is again a western one. The reason is that indigenous Christianity in Asia and Africa[44] have invariably borne the marks of Pentecostalism. This is not because they were directly or even indirectly influence by western Pentecostalism, although some would have been. Rather it is because these indigenous Christians, like Sundar Singh and John Sung, merely read the Bible from within the context of their own cultures and worldviews, and in simple faith put its teachings into practice. The result was indigenous Christianity which bears great similarity to western Pentecostalism, simply because both bear similarities to New Testament Christianity!

---

[42] Watchman Nee, *Sit, Walk and Stand* (London & Eastbourne: Victory Press, 1957), 57-63.

[43] Tony Lambert, *China's Christian Millions: The Costly Revival* (London: Monarch Books, 1999), 109-120. See also Gothard Oblau's paper in this volume.

[44] Cf. in particular, the African Independent Churches.

The Problem of Worldview

At the heart of the matter is a difference in worldviews. Western Christianity, at least among the more educated, in the 20th century has been largely controlled by a dualistic worldview, with its naturalistic and mechanistic view of the physical world. Within such a worldview, the supernatural tends to be marginalized, whether it is about God or demons. This worldview is partly rooted in the Enlightenment with its narrow empiricism and skeptical rationalism, which paved the way for a rejection of the supernatural and the adoption of a mechanistic worldview. Parallel to this has been the adoption of Greek dualism into the western worldview via Patristic theology which dichotomized the world into two separate realms.[45]

Given this background, we can easily understand Paul Hiebert's description of the modern western mind as having a two-tier view of reality.[46] The dualistic view of reality sees the world in terms of soul and body, spirit and matter, and sacred and secular. Further, this dualism effectively splits the world into two separate, almost iron-clad and unrelated parts, which Hiebert speaks of as the upper and lower realms of high religion and science respectively.[47] The former deals with spiritual and other worldly matters, with beliefs in God and inner religious experience; the latter deals with this-worldly and secular matters which are governed by scientific laws within a mechanistic and closed

---

[45] The early incorporation of the Platonic body-soul distinction into Christian theology had laid the foundation of a pervasive dualism within western thought. Indeed, the Chinese theologian, Carver Yu, in a sustained argument, *Being and Relation: A Theological Critique of Western Dualism and Individualism* (Edinburgh: Scottish Academic Press, 1987), has asserted that the roots of western dualism can be traced even further back to the pre-Socratic Greeks. The adoption of their understanding of reality as 'reality-in-itself', uncontaminated by anything other than itself, led to the view that reality is made up of discrete self-subsistent things, with dynamic interaction and interpenetration of being categorically excluded in principle (64-114). This perception of the unrelatedness of the world gave rise to the dualistic model of reality in the western mind, with all its implications, in contrast to a holistic biblical one (147-235).

[46] Paul G. Hiebert, *Anthropological Reflections on Missiological Issues* (Grand Rapids: Baker, 1994), 189-201.

[47] Hiebert in *Anthropological Reflections* (199) speaks of the two realms of high religion and science. Elsewhere he also speaks of the western worldview as being sharply dichotomized 'between the *supernatural* and the *natural*. The former has to do with other worldly concerns, such as God, Satan, heaven, hell, sin, salvation, prayer and miracles. Nature—the world of matter, space, and time—was increasingly seen as an autonomous realm operating according to natural laws that could be understood by scientists and used to solve human problems on this earth' (219). In Hiebert's conception, the first two realms of the high religion and science correspond to the supernatural and natural realms.

universe. But there is no real interpenetration and interaction between the two tiers!

Within such a worldview there is simply no place in which to fit the miraculous dimension, answers to prayer, the ministration of angels, the work of demonic powers, and related ideas—the very realm where Pentecostalism makes its impact. Hence the modern worldview became increasingly naturalistic in that the world can be understood without recourse to religious ideas. This naturalistic and dualistic worldview contrast sharply with the supernaturalistic and more holistic worldviews that are found in most non-western cultures.

Many in the western church have accepted the western scientific worldview as a sufficient description of reality. These included both liberals and conservatives. Consequently they cannot cope with Pentecostalism. But even in the west, there are those who have not adopt such a worldview entirely. One need only to note the large sections on witchcraft and the occult in many western bookshops as proof of this. It would probably be true to say that the anti-supernaturalistic worldview never really took root amongst the less educated and lower social classes in western society. Consequently, it was here that Pentecostalism flourished in the first half of the 20th century.

The picture in the non-western world was rather different. Most non-westerners possess a supernaturalistic worldview, which even a modern western scientific education could not fully eradicate easily. It is part and parcel of their cultural and religious backgrounds. Consequently, a truly indigenous Christianity in Asia has to be supernaturalistic, and therefore Pentecostal!

The Resultant Mix in Asia Today

The net result of all these is that what we find in Asia, and in other parts of the non-western world, is a most interesting mix. There is a very small minority of Christians who have been influenced by the modern western scientific worldview and liberal theology. They cannot cope with the renewal sweeping across much of Asia today. There is a second group that is far larger. They are theologically conservative or evangelical. But their western education and evangelical theology learnt from the west make it difficult for them to know what to do with signs and wonders. Their theology does not allow them to reject the supernatural because the bible takes the miraculous seriously. Yet many try to rationalize it away. But like the first group, they continue to reject the Pentecostal/Charismatic renewal.

This brings us to the third group. Most come out of the same background as the second group, and in some cases as the first. Their numbers are increasingly growing at the expense of those in the second group, although it is sometimes difficult to demarcate the two. But they can be found in almost every denomination, from the Roman Catholic to the Brethren. They have never been entirely comfortable with the western conservative or liberal theologies they were brought up in, because these are rooted in a worldview which is alien to their own cultures and to biblical Christianity. In moving into some Pentecostal/Charismatic version of Christianity, they are unconsciously laying claim to a recovery of their own indigenous Asian worldviews which take the supernatural seriously. Many have stayed on in their original denominations. Others have left to join the fourth group, which consists of those who became Christians in Pentecostal denominations brought from the west. These include the Assemblies of God, Foursquare Church, and the like, as well the newer Charismatic independent churches.

Finally there is a fifth group consisting of those who belong to the churches who did not originated through direct western influence but through indigenous leadership, and who are usually open to signs and wonders. In China these include groups like the True Jesus Church, the Jesus Family and the house church movement. In places like Indonesia, they would include some of the churches which emerged out the revivals of the 1960s and 70s. In Malaysia and Singapore, probably the most notable would be the New Testament Church started by the Hong Kong actress, Kong Duen Yee, popularly known as Mui Yee, in 1963. Her ministry which stressed the baptism of the Spirit and the speaking of tongues drew many followers, not least from the very conservative Chinese Brethren churches. It should be noted that most of these indigenous churches have remained in the mainstream of the Christian movement, as evidenced by their adherence to the basic tenets of the faith found in the creeds. But some are in danger of extremism and heresy.

To sum up, what is seen as a major evangelical and Pentecostal/Charismatic renewal today is largely a coming together of the third, fourth and fifth groups in the life of the Asian church. It is the result of the Holy Spirit's work which began at different times, cultures and places. They are united together by their commitment to the Lordship of Christ and the authority of the Bible in life and belief, and their adherence to the foundational beliefs of the church as defined by the historic creeds. At the same time they are characterized by a common acceptance of the empowering of the Spirit, and his acts of signs and wonders in the life of the church. These streams of renewal are now coming together and coalescing in an amazing manner, both in Asia and many other parts of the world. It is *this complex, untidy and yet profound mix* that is being referred to when the term Pentecostal/Charismatic movement is used here.

To fail to appreciate the multi-dimensional and multi-cultural manner in which the Holy Spirit has worked, and to straightjacket him by an Americo-centric interpretation of Pentecostalism is to make him less than a God of all nations!

Concluding Comments

I will conclude with three comments. The first is that, if a truly indigenous Christianity in Asia invariably tends to take signs and wonders seriously, then

Pentecostalism is actually a most powerful contextualizing force for churches in the non-western world. The movement takes seriously the supernatural dimension of human existence—something which modernity shaped by the Enlightenment has ignored. By encouraging the church to go back to the New Testament and to reappropriate Primitive Christianity at its best once again today, it is helping non-western Christians to address the whole supernatural dimension in their cultures. Much of supposed ecumenical and evangelical theology written in Asia fails to be truly contextual precisely at this point. They do not and cannot engage the Asian world of demonic spirits, astrology, and the occult, as well as the wholism of Asian worldviews. Consequently they fail to speak to our cultures with power.[48] The plain fact today is that it is those churches and theologies that have taken the supernatural seriously that are in forefront of the growth of Christianity in Asia today.

The second comment is that we need to recognize an inherent danger here. Pentecostalism has highlighted the inadequacy of the modern western scientific worldview. But this does not mean that we should set that aside in favor of some non-western or pre-modern version of a supernaturalistic worldview. The danger of doing so is that we will end up slipping back into an animistic worldview, or adopting that of the New Age or of post-modernity, all of which are equally unchristian. Some of the discussions today on spiritual warfare err precisely at this point. There is an urgent need for the churches in Asia to work out what constitutes a Christian worldview and how that is allowed to speak with Pentecostal power to the prevailing worldviews of our cultures.

Finally, there is a growing vitality in Asian Christianity. Yet, too often the models that we are still adopting are western ones. This is unfortunately also true of the charismatic renewal that is sweeping across many cities in urban Asia. Many of the leaders consciously or unconsciously seek to emulate some western, especially American, Pentecostal preachers with their various versions of the 'health and wealth gospel', without recognizing its inimical influence. It is precisely at this point that we need to look again at some of our own Asian heroes, like Sadhu Sundar Singh and John Sung. These people certainly knew what Pentecostal power mean. At the same time, they combined outstanding demonstrations of signs and wonders in their ministries with a strong biblical stress on holiness and sacrificial living. They serve as far better role models than many of the dispensers of the prosperity gospel today.

---

[48] I have argued this at length in *Mangoes or Bananas: The Quest for an Authentic Asian Christian Theology* (Oxford: Regnum, 1997), esp. 71-76.

Asian (Classical) Pentecostal Theology in Context

Wonsuk Ma

Introduction

The publication of the *New International Dictionary of the Pentecostal and Charismatic Movements*[1] affords, for the first time, an organized effort to pay close attention to the Pentecostal movement in Asia (and perhaps other regions of the world beyond North America and Europe). For this reason, the editors of the *Dictionary* are to be commended. However, coverage remains less than adequate in relation to the phenomenal expansion of this movement as well as the impressive discovery of important old and buried evidence from the early days. The explosive growth of the movement in the non-western world has also encouraged younger Pentecostal scholars to reflect on the work of the Spirit in various contexts.[2] Equally significant is the appearance of the revised edition of the *World Christian Encyclopedia*.[3] This work is particularly meaningful to Pentecostals, just as the first edition has been, because the *Encyclopedia* presents a larger picture of the movement's growth in the past decade. Two items need to be taken note of at this point. Although David Barrett has been updating statistics annually in the International Bulletin of Missionary Research, the future growth pattern can also be predicted. The second item

---

[1] Edited by Stanley M. Burgess and Eduard M. van der Maas (Grand Rapids: Zondervan, 2002). This is a revised and expanded version of . Stanley M. Burgess, Gary B. McGee, and Patrick H. Alexander (eds.), *Dictionary of the Pentecostal and Charismatic Movements* (Grand Rapids: Zondervan, 1987), henceforth *NIDPCM*.

[2] Also to be noted are two modest attempts made by non-western Pentecostals: Theological Symposium for Asian Church Leaders (Seoul, 1998, organized by Young-hoon Lee and Wonsuk Ma), and Theological Symposium of Non-western Pentecostalism (i.e. Asia, Africa and Latin America; Anaheim, 2001, organized by Paulson Pulikottil [Asia, representing Asian Pentecostal Society], Miguel Alvarez [Latin America], and Mathew Clark [Africa] together with Young-hoon Lee and Wonsuk Ma). Both gatherings were deliberately planned a day prior to the opening of the Pentecostal World Conference.

[3] David B. Barrett, George T. Kurian, and Todd M. Johnson (eds.), *World Christian Encyclopedia: A Comparative Survey of Churches and Religions in the Modern World*, 2nd ed., 2 vols. (Oxford: Oxford University Press, 2001), henceforth, indicated as *WCE*. Figures quoted in this study are from the projected numbers for 'mid-2000'.

providing an equally important resource on this subject is found in the *Asian Journal of Pentecostal Studies*. In spite of the short span of this journal's existence, it has published a dozen historical studies on the Pentecostal movement in various Asian countries, fully expecting to continue such documentation in the future.

This paper is an attempt, stemming from my own personal involvement, observation and research, to describe in general terms the common traits of the Asian Pentecostal movement. Discussion is focused on the interaction between the Pentecostal movement and its new-found environment, that is the Asian cultural-religious 'soil' on the one hand, and the contemporary 'weather' (including the politico-economic) on the other. As the process of theologizing primarily purports to bring Christian 'truth' into a specific human context, it is hoped that this probing will contribute to the process of establishing the role, characteristics, and future of Asian Pentecostal theology.[4] This is not a comprehensive study, but a selective one to examine several important theological topics which illustrate the process of Asian Pentecostal theologizing. Presented are some unique struggles of the Pentecostal movement as it engages the Asian context. In the end, I hope, Asian Pentecostals are encouraged to be more intentional in the theologizing process.

The present discussion is primarily centred on classical Pentecostalism,[5] whose roots are traced to the twentieth century outbreak of the Spirit in western countries. There are two major reasons for this limitation. First, the author is most familiar with this Pentecostal tradition as he grew up in this environment. However, 'classical' Pentecostalism in Asia is not identical to its western counterpart. Second, although the number of classical Pentecostal believers worldwide is the smallest among the three major 'Pentecostal/Charismatic' groups,[6] classical Pentecostals have developed more of their own theological institutions, archives and publications than the other two have. Their structured organizations and longer history have allowed them to develop this infrastructure. Undoubtedly, they are able to provide forums for dialogue, theological reflection and suggestions for the future.

As a study of this nature is attempted, the researcher faces two inherent difficulties. First, the research must consider the immense cultural variety in

---

[4] A more detailed discussion of theologization, particularly for Asian Pentecostalism, is found in Wonsuk Ma, 'Toward an Asian Pentecostal Theology', *Asian Journal of Pentecostal Studies* 1:1 (1998), 15-41.

[5] Various categories of Pentecostalism in Asia are not always clear. For instance, Classical Pentecostalism in Asia has as its clear distinction organizational matters, but when it comes to theology and practice it often appears to be more like Charismatic Christianity. This is a subject that deserves a thorough treatment.

[6] See the recent figures published in *World Christian Encyclopedia*, I, 19-23, esp. the charts on 20-21.

Asia. As we look at the socio-cultural context, there is a danger of generalization or wild confusion if an attempt is made to highlight in detail the multitude of differences. Thus, there are times when generalization becomes inevitable. The second situation, the lack of historical documentation of Pentecostalism in various Asian countries, increases the challenge. This lack of preserved records might be blamed on the unique Pentecostal ethos. It was not until the 1990s that serious efforts in historical record keeping began to emerge both in Asian[7] as well as other non-western continents.[8]

Pentecostalism and the Asian Context

When the Pentecostal message was brought to the Asian soil, a lively interaction took place between this 'foreign' element and the native contextual elements. The following are several key factors with which the Pentecostal movement has engaged that have emerged as general characteristics of this Asian movement.

Young Movement

The movement can be described in a number of ways. One factor is that Asia is relatively young. For instance, 37% of the entire population of the Philippines is now below 15 years old,[9] therefore, Pentecostal churches are filled with this younger generation. This may be true of Christianity in general as well. Interestingly, a demographic survey of Pentecostal/Charismatic congregations in comparison with 'mainline' denominations reveals that the greater proportion of these groups is young people. In Asia, this may partly be attributed to the 'modern' worship style, affirmative messages, 'entertaining' singing, and other factors, while the traditional churches, including Roman Catholic ones, appear to be more 'old-fashioned'. For instance, the phenomenal growth of the City Harvest Church (Rev. Kong Hee) or the better-known saga of the Faith Community Baptist Church (Rev. Laurence Kong) in Singapore reveal a showcase of modern Pentecostal demography. It was observed at the

---

[7] Some examples are the development of higher theological education such as the Master of Divinity programmes in Korea, the Philippines, Singapore, Indonesia and others. Also noted is the formation of the Asian Pentecostal Society (1998), Forum for Pentecostal Scholars in India, and the appearance of academic journals such as the *Asian Journal of Pentecostal Studies* (1998), *Australasian Pentecostal Studies* (1998), and *Church & Spirit* (1999) among those published in English.

[8] Perhaps one notable publication is Walter J. Hollenweger, *Pentecostalism: Origin and Developments Worldwide* (Peabody, MA: Hendrickson, 1997) that forcefully argues the 'non-western' nature of the Pentecostal tradition, among other traits.

[9] 'Philippines', *WCE*, I, 594-601 (594).

City Harvest Church's 14th anniversary service in August 2001, attended by more than ten thousand in a national stadium, that the majority of people there were young professionals speaking English as their first language.[10] This stands in stark contrast to the mainline churches where attenders are older, often Chinese-speaking people. Barrett's study reveals that two thirds of Pentecostal converts are the result of evangelistic activities, while one third is demographic growth (through birth).[11] As time passes, this may change, but with the sheer number of young people in Asia, Pentecostal churches will continue to attract this generation.

Another way to describe Pentecostalism is by noting the simple historical fact that the movement is a relatively new one. Although recent research convincingly challenges the old notion that the Pentecostal movement was 'made in the USA' at the beginning of the twentieth century, most agree that Pentecostalism in general is only about one century old. However, in Asia, modern Pentecostalism did not begin to exert its influence with reasonable visibility until the post-colonial period, that is, from the 1950s.[12] In countries such as Vietnam, Nepal or Mongolia,[13] the Pentecostal message was introduced after World War II, although there are also countries where Pentecostal-like revival dates back as early as the nineteenth century.[14]

Apart from indigenous Pentecostal groups, Pentecostal missionaries came primarily from the United States, the United Kingdom and Scandinavian nations. In spite of European involvement in the early history of the Pentecostal message in places like Thailand, Japan, Indonesia, India and Pakistan, North American influence has been significant, especially in the developing stages of the movement. For instance, even the first European Pentecostal missionaries to Indonesia were 'sent' by a church in Seattle, Washington. Because of the late emergence of Asian Pentecostalism, other Protestant groups and Roman Catholics preceded Pentecostal missionaries. Many of the early Pentecostal

---

[10] Chin Do Kham related his participation in this occasion. Their website (www.chc.org.sg/version3/main.htm) contains not only various information such as a brief history and current membership (reported to be more than 13,000), but also various media reports, Most reports feature young professional members of the church, particularly young women (checked Oct 1, 2001).

[11] *WCE*, I, 19.

[12] One example is China. By the time of the Communist take-over in 1949, the total Pentecostal adherents were 500,000, but declined to 150,000 by 1970 after the Cultural Revolution: D. H. Bays and T. M Johnson, 'China', *NIDPCM*, 58-64 (64).

[13] Joshua, 'Pentecostalism in Vietnam: A History of the Assemblies of God', *AJPS* 4:2 (2001), 307-26. Joshua is not a real name. Bal Krishna Sharma, 'A History of the Pentecostal Movement in Nepal', *AJPS* 4:2 (2001), 295-305. Mongolian Pentecostal movement began in the early 1990s.

[14] One example is the Travancore revival in 1860, where healing, prophecy and speaking in tongues were present. See below for detail.

missionaries were directly or indirectly influenced by the Azusa Street revival (1906-1909), as the earliest arrivals began in 1907. For instance, Marie and Cornelis Groesbeek, and Stien and Dirkrichard van Klaveren came to Indonesia around 1920,[15] M.L. Ryan to Japan in 1907,[16] Alfred G. Garr to China in 1907,[17] Mary Rumsey to Korea in 1930,[18] George Berg to India in 1908,[19] and six *balikbayan* (overseas returnees) Filipinos to the Philippines around 1925.[20] Therefore the imported Pentecostal message carried an obvious American flavour.

In many Asian nations, except for the Philippines, US Americans were relatively less involved in colonial rule. More positively, the USA was viewed to have brought long-awaited liberation to many Asian nations during the rather harsh Japanese oppression in the 1930s and 1940s. Even in the Philippines, the USA ceased being the colonizer and became the liberator during the Japanese war as US forces defeated the occupying Japanese Imperial Army. Thus Pentecostalism, often commonly perceived as a North American religious movement, had less colonial connotations than other older Christian denominations. Consequently, without the colonialism of the past, the movement 'walked through' Asia's new independent national life.[21]

---

[15] 'A History of the Pentecostal Movement in Indonesia', *AJPS* 4:1 (2001), 131-48 (134-36). The author is not known.

[16] Masakazu Suzuki, 'A New Look at the Pre-war History of the Japan Assemblies of God', *AJPS* 4:2 (2001), 239-67 (243). Paul Tsuchido Shew, 'A Forgotten History: Correcting the Historical Record of the Roots of Pentecostalism in Japan', *AJPS* 5:1 (2002, forthcoming) makes a similar inquiry independent of Suzuki.

[17] Bays & Johnson, *China*, 59.

[18] Suzuki, 'A New Look at the Pre-war History', 252. Vinson Synan, *The Holiness and Pentecostal Tradition: Charismatic Movement in the Twentieth Century*, 2nd ed. (Grand Rapids: Eerdmans, 1997), 139 believes that Rumsey came to Korea in 1928. A Korean Pentecostal historian, Young-hoon Lee, comp., *A History of the Assemblies of God* [in Korean] (Seoul: Seoul Books, 1998), 196-97 agrees with Synan.

[19] George, *Pentecostal Beginnings in Travancore*, 224. Berg began his missionary work in India from 1901, but after his visit to the Azusa Street mission, he returned to India as a Pentecostal.

[20] Trinidad E. Seleky, 'Six Filipinos and One American: Pioneers of the Assemblies of God in the Philippines', *AJPS* 4:1 (2001), 119-29 (121).

[21] This is not to deny attempts for the 'post-colonial' reinterpretation of the Pentecostal history. See, for instance, Paulson Pulikottil, 'As East and West Met in God's Own Country: Encounter of Western Pentecostalism with Native Pentecostalism in Kerala' (a paper presented at the International Symposium on Non-western Pentecostalism, Anaheim, CA, USA on May 28, 2001) later published in *AJPS*.

Precursors to Pentecostal Mission

It is important to recognize that in addition to the direct influence of the western Pentecostal movement, Asian Pentecostalism is shaped through various revivals and a unique Asian spiritual awareness. At least in two places, powerful revivals unrelated to the North American Pentecostal movement are recorded.

The Indian revival began in the Madras Province in 1860-75, soon followed by the Travancore revival in 1874-75. Scholars report that typical Pentecostal manifestations occurred such as prophesying, tongues, healing, and even glossographia (or 'writing in tongues').[22] These revivals prepared for the advent of the western Pentecostal activities in the early twentieth century in several important ways. One was the emergence of powerful national evangelists who spread the revival to other provinces and developed useful structures for evangelism, church planting and training of workers. Burgess includes a short history of Sarasvati Mary Ramabai who was at the centre of the Mukti revival in 1905-1906, which was characterized by experiences like 'being slain in the spirit' and the baptism in the 'Holy Ghost and fire' with a burning sensation.[23] The first Pentecostal missionaries who arrived in 1907 found an already ploughed land.

The much-celebrated Pyongyang Revival in Korea in 1907[24] was marked by intense prayer and repentance based on concentrated Bible studies. In this revival, where only men were allowed due to the limited space available, both missionaries and nationals began to confess their sins and asked for forgiveness. Clark describes an evening meeting:

> After a short sermon...man after man would rise, confess his sin, break down and weep and then throw himself on the floor and beat the floor with his fists in a perfect agony of conviction.... Sometimes, after a confession, the whole audience would break out into audible prayer, and the effect of that audience of hundreds of men praying together in audible prayer was something indescribable. Again, after another confession, they would break out into uncontrollable weeping and we would all weep together. We couldn't help it. And so the meeting went on until 2

---

[22] Details of this revival have been well documented particularly by Pentecostal scholars: e.g. A. C. George, 'Pentecostal Beginnings of Travancore, South India', *Asian Journal of Pentecostal Studies* 4:2 (2001), 215-237 (220-224); Stanley M. Burgess, 'Pentecostalism in India: An Overview', *AJPS* 4:1 (2001), 85-98 (87-89); Paulson Pulikottil, 'As East and West Met in God's Own Country', *Asian Journal of Pentecostal Studies* 5:1 (Jan, 2002), 5-22.

[23] Burgess, *Pentecostalism in India*, 88-89.

[24] For a brief review, see Young-hoon Lee, 'Korean Pentecostal: The Great Revival of 1907', *Asian Journal of Pentecostal Studies* 4:1 (2001), 73-84.

a.m., with confession and weeping and praying.... We had prayed to God for an outpouring of His Holy Spirit upon the People and it had come.[25]

The stories of this revival were later collected and published by Blair and Hunt under the title, *The Korean Pentecost*. The revival was closely likened to the day of Pentecost:

> Just as on the day of Pentecost, they were altogether in one place, on one accord praying, and suddenly there came from heaven the sound as of rushing of a mighty wind, and it filled all the house where there were sitting.[26]

These precursors to the later Pentecostal movement in India and Korea have several common characteristics, in addition to their 'Pentecostal' manifestations: 1) both took place under colonial rule (British and Japanese); 2) both impacted on the whole nation or at least whole regions of their nations; and more importantly for our discussion, 3) both shaped patterns for spiritual renewal. It is also noted that both countries are significant in the growth of Pentecostal churches and with regard to the wider church and its mission.

Poverty

Most agree that the number one problem of Asia is poverty. One only needs to see the staggering statistics in various reports to realize this fact.[27] Such a chronic state of challenge has been attributed to various factors such as rapid population growth, limited resources, political corruption, limited technological development, poor infrastructure, and the like.

Traditional religions in Asia were not successful in responding to basic human needs. Buddhism, Hinduism, Taoism, Shintoism and Islam have offered moral and spiritual guidance with promises for a good afterlife. In Asia, shamanism in its various forms has provided a response to 'mundane' issues like blessings, good fortune and good health. Because of this and other factors, the traditional Asian religions have incorporated shamanistic elements into their belief systems and this process has resulted in the development of a syncretistic religious form, often referred to as a 'folk' version of the respective religion.

Traditional Christianity, often perceived as a new and/or 'imported' religion, has not necessarily fared any better than the traditional religions. In addition to

---

[25] Allen D. Clark, *A History of the Church in Korea* (Seoul: Christian Literature Society of Korea, 1971), 160-62.

[26] William Blair and Bruce Hunt, *The Korean Pentecostal and the Suffering Which Followed* (Carlisle: Banner of Truth, 1977), 74.

[27] For instance, see Lee C. Wanak, 'Theological Education and the Role of Teachers in the 21st Century: A look at the Asia Pacific Region', *Journal of Asian Mission* 2:1 (March 2000), 3-24 (5-6).

the perception that Christianity is a religion of the colonizers or national elites ('collaborators' with the colonial force), Christianity tended to be excessively spiritual and thus otherworldly. For instance, according to some historians, missionaries carefully spiritualized the explosive 1907 Pyongyang Revival in Korea,[28] motivated by a desire to prevent the church from politically confronting the Japanese who had annexed Korea. Naturally the prevailing message from the pulpit was repentance,[29] deep communion with God, holy living, and future hope. Thus a dualistic mindset was promoted, producing the belief that *this* world is evil and hopeless while true hope is in the *other* world. It is no small wonder that this revival produced a host of deeply committed Christian leaders who later gave their lives to keep their Christian faith, particularly in contradiction to the Japanese insistence on Shinto worship. One such leader was Rev. Ki-chul Joo, a well-known martyr, who served as pastor of the Jangdae-hyun Church, where the Pyongyang revival began. This exemplary pattern of Christian living continued even after Korea obtained independence (but as a divided nation). This was especially so during the tragic Korean War when the North Korean Communistcommunist army was extremely cruel to Christians.

The emergence of a powerful Pentecostal message was felt again in South Korea in the 1970s when Cho Yonggi's message of blessing affected the nation. As South Korea's military regime was waging an all-out economic campaign to eradicate the chronic poverty in society, material blessing was openly preached as part of the message of a 'good God'. Soon, testimonies of God's blessing began to appear in various forms, including Cho's sermons and in various publications. His holistic soteriology includes redemption from poverty which is, according to Cho, a part of God's curse. Whether through a positive attitude toward life and God, a committed work ethic based on a perception of an immanent God, miraculous acts of God, or a combination of some or all of these, Pentecostal Christians began to achieve impressive upward mobility over the decades, a trend that has also been well observed among Latin American Pentecostals.[30] Although this may be criticized as an Asian adaptation of the prosperity gospel popularized by televangelists in the West, the social context for the seemingly similar message is radically different.

---

[28] Young-hoon Lee, 'Korean Pentecost: The Great Revival of 1907', *AJPS* 4:1 (2001), 85-98 (82).

[29] E.g. the sermon of W.N. Blair which began the Pyongyang revival was titled 'We Are All Members of the Body of Christ' and the emphasis was on unity and repentance based on 1 Cor. 12.27. Allen D. Clark, *A History of the Church in Korea* (Seoul: Christian Literature Society, 1971), 160-61.

[30] See the entire book of Richard Shaull and Waldo Cesar, *Pentecostalism and the Future of the Christian Churches: Promises, Limitations, Challenges* (Grand Rapids: Eerdmans, 2000).

Unless one has struggled to provide three meals a day for an entire family, one should not quickly criticize this as an egotistic religion. For many desperate minds, a God who cannot provide the basic needs for survival is not a true God, especially when, before conversion, their ancestor spirits were able to 'bless' them. Of course it is problematic, as the Korean Pentecostal churches have discovered, if Christians fail to move in Christian maturity beyond 'blessing' theology.

Religion of the Powerless Masses

'Powerlessness' can be traced to various socio-economic structures. There are two levels of powerlessness with which Pentecostalism has interacted fruitfully. First of all, on a personal level, Asian masses are prisoners of social caste systems, either explicitly or implicitly. Historically, this century-old social system was further reinforced by colonial powers which facilitated the minority elite groups in acquiring much of the nation's wealth, at the same time remaining loyal to the colonial authorities. That is, the elites are born elite, as much as the deprived ones are born as oppressed individuals who remain oppressed. On the other hand the majority of the nation was deprived of economic, educational and political opportunities. The powerless continue to be powerless generation after generation. Hence, liberation theology was an attempt to empower this voiceless mass in society.

Unlike liberation theology, Minjung theology (the Korean cousin of liberation theology) and Dalit theology (the Indian attempt) whose starting point is in the idea of a change in structure, the Pentecostal movement brought a spiritual dynamic to deprived lives. This Pentecostal revolution is possible because true renewal begins with a change in the innermost core of a human being. Only the power of the Holy Spirit makes this change possible. From this change, other changes follow, be it personal or social transformation. When asked what was the Pentecostal social programme, a Latin American Pentecostal leader answered, 'We are the programme'. It is no wonder that many reports indicate a change in lifestyle among Latin American Pentecostals[31] and this pattern is replicated in Asia.

Understandably, the Pentecostal message further reinforces the concept of positive and dynamic change. It is to the credit of Pentecostalism that this movement introduced a more positive, this-worldly message to the prevailing pessimistic or even escapist world of Christian thought. Yonggi Cho's message, for example, placed strong emphasis on the concept of a 'good God', 'faith', and 'God's blessing'. Although traditional church leaders often criticized this

---

[31] For this reason, Minjung theology has been never considered to be Pentecostal by Korean Christianity including Minjung adherents themselves, except some of our western friends, e.g. Hollenweger, *Pentecostalism*, 99-105.

proactive and positive message, a drastic paradigm shift took place over decades in the minds of Korean Christians. The rapid growth of Cho's church to a staggering 700,000 became a symbol of this positive Christian attitude. Through the effective use of mass media (magazines, tracts, radio, etc.) Cho's message gained an unprecedented popularity, not only among Christian individuals but also among non-believers.

Equally as critical as individual deprivation is the sense of corporate powerlessness, the second level. Most Asian nations are still haunted by their colonial past,[32] coming from a humiliating loss of nationhood, identity and dignity. The recent confrontation over the issue of conflicting history textbooks between Japan and neighbouring countries including Korea and China epitomizes these longstanding and haunting feelings. Japanese history has been recently revised by many of their historians, primarily to glorify and justify the Japanese invasion of and brutality over its annexed nations. For victims during these historical events this activity is viewed as more than a mere internal matter, but is perceived as the unjust whitewashing of Japanese war crimes. Several former 'comfort women', those Koreans (among others) forced to be sex slaves for the Japanese Imperial Army, now mostly in their 70s, are speaking up about their shameful experiences in army camps in the light of this historical whitewashing.

Most Asian nations newly liberated from the colonialism of the past went through a drastic and often painful process of politico-economic change. The major challenge of this post-colonial era was the restoration of national identity and corporate dignity as well as the restoration of individual identify and dignity. Clearly, it will take far more than political independence and diplomatic status to achieve a full restoration. It requires more than economic development and political power. It will take a radical transformation in the people of these nations. This is where the growth of the church becomes important. The church's presence must be felt in these societies. That Asian Pentecostal/Charismatic churches are leading church growth today is seen in various countries like Korea, the Philippines, India, China, and even Vietnam.[33]

---

[32] This is the second of the seven 'critical Asian principles' according to Emerito P. Nacpil, 'The Critical Asian Principles', in *Asian Christian Theology: Emerging Themes*, rev. ed. of *What Asian Christians Are Thinking*, ed. Douglas J. Elwood (Philadelphia: Westminster, 1980), 56-59 (57). Other principles are: 1) plural nature of culture and religion; 2) drive for modernization; 3) desire for self-identity and cultural integrity; 4) home of living religions; 5) in search of a form of social order; and 6) Christianity is a minority.

[33] Young-gi Hong, 'The Backgrounds and Characteristics of the Charismatic Mega-churches in Korea', *AJPS* 3:1 (Jan 2000), 99-118, esp. 104-105 concludes 12 of 15 Korean mega-churches, with more than 10,000 adult Sunday attendants, are Pentecostal/ charismatic in their worship, practice, and message.

Another intriguing link is found between Pentecostalism and nationalism (or patriotism to be more precise), especially among some indigenous Pentecostal groups. Rev. Woon-mong Nah, the founder of the Yongmoon Prayer Mountain, has been a prominent Christian leader particularly from the 1950s to the '70s. Through his peculiar teaching that Korea is a second Israel, he challenged his Bible school students to march toward the heavily fortified Demilitarised Zone between North and South Korea. This action raised high alert on both sides of the border. Equally prominent is the institutionalizing of the national prayer altar, which is solely dedicated to 24-hour per day non-stop prayer for national peace and security. Since the inception of this prayer altar, more prayer mountains have been opened and dedicated primarily to prayer for national welfare. Another example is the Makuya (Tabernacle) group in Japan established by Ikuro Teshima in 1948. In this variation of the 'Non-church Movement' (*mukyokai*) of Kanzo Uchimura, the Makuya Church includes Pentecostal-like worship and belief and propagates that Japan is 'a spiritual temple of Christ'.[34] It is true that Christians tend to be more patriotic than the general public, but some evidence seems to suggest that Pentecostals are even more so. The fact that Christians were the most persecuted group by North Korea's communist army during the Korean War further proves the point. However, patriotism does not necessarily equate to the endorsement of a political system.

Asian Religiosity and Worldviews

Pentecostalism in general, and more specifically non-western Pentecostalism, has been hailed by several writers[35] for recovering and incorporating 'primal spirituality', which traditional Christianity has shied away from. Actually, inherent in the Pentecostal worldview are elements commonly found in shamanistic beliefs. These include an awareness of the spiritual world, an expectation of the supernatural and more importantly, the expectation that God or gods are involved in human activities on a daily basis.[36] This 'black root' of

[34] Makito Nagasawa, 'Makuya Pentecostalism: A Survey', *AJPS* 3:2 (July 2000), 203-218 (208-209).

[35] For example, Harvey Cox, *Fire from Heaven: The Rise of Pentecostal Spirituality and the Reshaping of Religion in the Twenty-First Century* (Reading, MA: Addison-Wesley, 1995), 82-83, also 99-110.

[36] For a comparison between Pentecostal and shamanistic worldview (in this case, Kankana-eys in the northern Philippines), see Julie C. Ma, *When the Spirit Meets the Spirits: Pentecostal Ministry among the Kankana-ey Tribe in the Philippines* (Frankfurt am Main: Peter Lang, 2000), 187-231. Also Bays & Johnson, 'China', 62 contends that this similarity in the worldviews is the mark of native Pentecostal movements. Rodney L. Henry, *Filipino Spirit World: A Challenge to the Church* (Manila: OMF Literature, 1986) observes how western missionaries are incapable of handling this worldview.

Pentecostalism, according to Hollenweger's designation,[37] can find its true home not in the western church, but in the non-western thought world. No matter how modern a society may look, basically Asian minds are shamanistic in orientation.[38] This is where Asian Pentecostals have challenges as well as promises in their future.

Now, how shamanism influences Asian Pentecostalism is a much-debated subject. Interestingly, it appears that western scholars insist that Asian Pentecostals are shamanistic while Asian Pentecostals themselves persistently deny this charge. This ongoing disagreement stems from at least two differing perspectives between western writers and Asian Pentecostals.

It is important to remember that Christianity in general and Pentecostalism in particular are young in Asia, with the exception of India. Basically, western 'conversion' develops within the context of a 'Christianized' social culture—even if that culture is only nominally Christianized—or people may move from nominalism in their faith to become committed Christians. In contrast, Asians come to Christianity (or Pentecostalism) from a radically 'pagan' cultural-religious past. Even today, considering only 7% of Asia is Christian, the majority of conversions in Asia are first generational. That is, the new believer is often the very first one in a given family to become a Christian. Today many Asians become Christians at risk of their lives. This is not a simple matter of changing one's religion. It is denouncing the old lifestyle, religion, and often the rituals a family performs for all deceased ancestors. This responsibility falls especially hard upon the eldest son. For instance, my wife's entire family disowned her when she became Christian, more specifically Pentecostal. She was literally thrown out of her home at the age of sixteen. In the end, all her siblings followed her path, and even their mother confessed her faith in Christ before her death. Had my wife participated in shamanistic rituals with the family (that is borrowing from the form of the old, and yet privately and secretly filling it with a new Christian meaning), her Christian witness would not have shone as it has until now. In fact, any such 'compromise' would have been viewed as a lack of serious commitment, and it would have undermined the value of her newfound faith.

If one makes such a radical decision, this often requires a radical severance in Asia. This is never an easy choice, but it is a clean one. If the new believer shows any hint of 'compromise', more often than not their Christian witness is lost. Of course this is not the only valid way for a Christian to relate his or her family and 'old' environment. Nevertheless, Clark argues that such a radical anti-cultural lifestyle or martyr-like commitment, is the main contributing factor in the growth of Korean churches. If the uniqueness of Pentecostalism is

---

[37] Hollenweger, *Pentecostalism*, 17-24.
[38] E.g. Simon Chan, 'An Asian Review', *Journal of Pentecostal Theology* 4 (1994), 35-40.

found in the radical anti-cultural nature of the movement, this should be preserved. Modern-day martyrs have increased and most of these come from the non-western world. This is because their clear stands are against the old religion. I would stress that the greatest number of modern-day martyrs are among Pentecostal believers. It is reported that the highest number of Indonesian churches that were burned by Muslim radicals are Pentecostal. The general superintendent of the Assemblies of God in Iran was martyred just a few years ago.[39] A Vietnamese Pentecostal group has an unwritten rule for ordination that the candidate must have been imprisoned at least once before submitting for ordination. Young Chinese Christians (predominantly young women) are regularly introduced as being imprisoned for the cause of their faith in Christ.

In such a 'hostile' situation Pentecostals seldom 'borrow' old cultural or religious forms or practices. For instance Korean Pentecostalism developed several unique practices such as unison prayer, however these did not come from shamanistic traditions but from the prayer mountain movement. Some worship forms came from the West. Even some syncretistic Pentecostal groups show their reluctance in adapting traditional Christian religious forms. For instance, the Santuala group of the northern Philippines, practising what appears to be a syncretistic form of Pentecostalism, has developed several peculiar 'Christian forms' but they are by no means close to shamanistic ones.[40] Julie Ma's research also proves that the successful Pentecostal mission among a tribal group in the northern Philippines shows no trace of 'adaptation' of any 'old' forms.[41] When the Makuya group of Japan added folk elements such as walking on live charcoal in their Pentecostal-like worship they were immediately considered to be outside orthodox Christianity.

In truth, Pentecostals have consciously maintained an absolute distance from the native cultural and religious practices. I said, 'consciously', because I am aware that there may be shamanistic religious features that could have been incorporated without consciousness. In Korea, the first 'litmus paper' test of the relationship between Christianity and traditional religions (in Korea's case,

---

[39] A news report on the murder of an Iranian Pentecostal leader, *The Pentecost Evangel* (March 27, 1994), 24.

[40] Julie C. Ma, 'Santuala: A Case of Pentecostal Syncretism', *AJPS* 3:1 (Jan 2000), 61-82 (64-67).

[41] Julie C. Ma, *When the Spirit Meets the Spirits*. Mathew Clark, 'Asian Pentecostal Theology: A Perspective from Africa', *AJPS* 4:2 (2001), 181-99 (190) rightly points out that a western scholar missed Ma's point: 'It is unfortunate that a...clearly upheld commitment to Christian absolutes by J. Ma is dismissed by Hollenweger in his preface to the work, e.g. 'All in all, this is the report of a not yet recognized but de facto marriage between pre-Christian and Christian elements'.

shamanism) is the issue of ancestor veneration.[42] In the early 1980s, when Yonggi Cho made a slight suggestion for a young Christian to 'greet' the deceased ancestors before a portrait (he compared it with bringing flowers to the grave in the West), he promptly received charges that he was a 'heretic'. The only native religious element legitimately taken from traditional shamanism is the so-called 'primal spirituality'.[43]

It is also critical to note that there are abundant notions of universal spirits in shamanistic expressions. Unlike the West, which has a basically Christian philosophical background (although this is questionable in some details), the shamanistic mind has no mechanism to interchange the shamanistic spirits, especially universal ones, with the Holy Spirit.[44] Without this 'exchange mechanism', a Christian notion of the Holy Spirit can easily be subsumed into the traditional idea of universal spirits, such as *chi*.

Korean Pentecostalism, especially the religion that Yonggi Cho has preached, has been labelled 'shamanistic' by Evangelical Christians in Korea. However, the charge is not because Cho borrows shamanistic forms or practices in his Pentecostal ministry. Cox missed this entirely, and even when he visited Korea and dialogued with Pentecostal and Evangelical theologians, he continued this claim.[45] Traditional Korean Christianity had been a 'high' religion with much emphasis on puritanical and ethical teachings. Because of the oppressive circumstances of the Japanese occupation, the Christian outlook was totally eschatological. Because of the radical departure from old practices among most Korean Christians, they did not fall into the trap of split-level Christianity, resorting to traditional religions for daily 'low'-level issues.[46]

---

[42] This is also true of African Pentecostals. See Clark, 'Asian Pentecostal Theology', 184.

[43] Perhaps more serious attempts, intentionally or otherwise, may be found among the Third Wavers as accused by some missiologists as Christian shamanism. See, for example, Robert J. Priest, Thomas Campbell, and Bradford A. Mullen, 'Missiological Syncretism: The New Animistic Paradigm', in *Spiritual Power and Mission: Raising the Issues*, Evangelical Missiological Society Series 3, ed. Edward Rommen (Pasadena, CA: William Carey Library, 1995), 9-87. The response of Kraft is found in the same volume: Charles H. Kraft, *Christian Animism' or God-Given Authority?* 88-136. Also see a reflection on some of the Third wave's assumptions and practices in Wonsuk Ma, 'A 'First Waver's Looks at the "Third Wave": A Pentecostal Reflection on Charles Kraft's Power Encounter Terminology', *Pneuma* 19 (1997), 189-206.

[44] Chan, 'An Asian Review', 40.

[45] See the record of dialogue in *Sungnyung-kwa Kyohoi Gaengshin* [The Holy Spirit and Church Renewal] (Seoul: International Theological Institute, 1997), 99-134. Cox preached in a Sunday service with thousands of worshippers as his audience.

[46] David S. Lim, 'A Critique of Modernity in Protestant Missions in the Philippines', *Journal of Asian Mission* 2:2 (2000), 149-177 (156 n. 29).

Pentecostal preachers brought daily issues into the religious dimension. Messages began to include not only the traditional topics such as sin, salvation, heaven, etc. but also provision for daily needs, healing, God's favour in business and others. Cho's message, for example, was quickly characterized as the message of God's blessing, not only spiritual but also physical and material. Asking for 'blessing' was traditionally reserved for lower religions like shamanism or syncretistic Buddhism, this alleged *gibok sinang* (literally meaning 'belief in prayer-for-blessing') is considered 'shamanistic'. And this is the Korean 'shamanism' controversy that has surrounded Cho for decades, which is radically different from why Cox or Hollenweger characterized Korean Pentecostalism as 'shamanistic'.[47]

Our short discussion brings us to the conclusion that Asian Pentecostalism has conspicuously distanced itself from the traditional religious forms and concepts, while actively engaging with contemporary socio-economic settings. My contacts with underground Chinese believers seem to confirm the thesis.

In the light of the foregoing discussion, a word from an Asian Pentecostal to our concerned friends in the West may be in order. This word is especially for those who seem to have developed a romanticism concerning shamanism. It is important to be properly informed before pronouncing a diagnosis and prognosis. Neither Cox nor Hollenweger seem to have had first-hand experience or information on Korean Pentecostalism, heavily relying upon second-hand knowledge, most likely from their students. It is important to verify that this information is not only accurate but is also a fair representation. Most probably, their major sources (students) were not Pentecostals as Koreans would see it, and this I would emphasize!

Now when it comes to contextualization (or syncretization in Hollenweger's term),[48] one requires extreme care. However noble contextualization may appear, this is an extremely complex and delicate task. Contextualization has to employ forms that are part of the receptor culture and assign a new (that is, Christian) meaning to it, so that receptors will not view the Christian message as 'foreign'. One has to remember that non-western culture pays great attention to the form as much as to the contents. Hastening without serious

---

[47] It is interesting that Hollenweger, *Pentecostalism*, 99-105 fails to refer to Cho in his discussion of Korean Pentecostalism, while Minjung theology receives much attention. Cho, the pastor of the largest Pentecostal congregation, receives just one footnote treatment (100 n. 2), and this seems to imply either partial knowledge, or a bias against, Korean Pentecostalism as Koreans would commonly understand what it is to be. The revised version of Barrett's 'South Korea', *WCE*, I, 682-87 (686) not only wrongly categorizes Cho's large congregation of (Korean) Assemblies of God under 'Jesus Assembly of God Korea', but also sees him (who has served the Chair of the World Assemblies of God Fellowship, perhaps the largest 'classical' Pentecostal denomination worldwide) as 'neocharismatic'.

[48] E.g. Walter J. Hollenweger, 'Syncretism and Capitalism', *AJPS* 2:1 (1999), 47-61.

contemplation is the enemy of proper contextualization. Sometimes common sense may work: 'No medicine' is better than 'wrong medicine'. Outside help in this process is rather limited and can be likened to an attempt to help a chick struggling to break away the shell of its egg. Once you try to help (by cracking the shell), it will die. (Of course, we will watch very carefully whether this 'help' comes from a place where Pentecostalism is flourishing or dying.) Let us Asians do this task, carefully interacting with our surroundings, although this sometimes means giving up our own lives for the sake of God's kingdom and the future generations. Let time work for us, too. In my estimation, at least a generation will need to pass before a cultural symbol (often with a religious connotation) becomes 'neutral' in the minds of people. The West had the benefit of two thousand years of diluting, redefining, and refining old 'pagan' symbols, rituals, and concepts. The West can assist us by sharing their experiences but Asians have to undertake this important task.

Issues for Asian Pentecostals

There are a number of important issues that Asian Pentecostals will face in the new century. Some of them have already appeared on the horizon. Due to the phenomenal growth in the past and future growth expected (a Christian in Asia has to evangelize thirteen fellow Asians for Christ), the role of Asian Pentecostalism is expected to be significant. Some of the issues ahead are as follows, although not every one of them is uniquely Asian.

What/Who Is Pentecostal?

In the past decade or so the question, 'What is Pentecostal?' has occupied the centre stage of discussions and will continue to do so. Part of the ambiguity comes from the rapid expansion and complex characteristics this question acquires as it interacts with various socio-cultural and religious settings, partly because of the movement's (or the Spirit's) creative adaptability. Hence, it is simply impossible to come up with a satisfactory definition. Maybe a question should be raised as to whether the term 'Pentecostal' should be abandoned. Alternative terms are possible, as Korean Christianity popularly has called such a movement 'the movement of the Holy Spirit' or the 'Holy Spirit movement'. The problem with these terms or any other possible term is that their definition may be used too broadly to encompass any revival and renewal of the church. A good maxim in missiological circles may be instructive: 'If everything is mission, nothing is mission'. On the other hand, extremely narrow definitions will no longer serve adequately the diverse and complex nature of the movement. For instance, the foundational doctrine of Spirit baptism among Classical Pentecostals will no longer apply to the Charismatics, the Third Wave, nor the vast array of indigenous groups.

This leads to a modest proposal: first, work on the 'generic' use of the term 'Pentecostal' and then let the various streams (e.g. 'classical Pentecostalism') add their distinct elements. One working definition, as employed in this paper, could be 'A Christian movement where vitality of the Spirit in the life of believers and the church receives a special emphasis resulting in the manifest operation of spiritual gifts, the presence of miracles, lively worship, renewal in the body of Christ, and committed zeal for winning souls through the empowerment of the Spirit'. (One may recognize that there is no one group that is 'perfectly Pentecostal' but all identifying groups are 'partially Pentecostal'.)

Whether or not such a proposed definition of Pentecostalism is acceptable, the important task of opening discussion on this issue has now been brought before the global academic community. As scholars, we constantly need to refine 'our' identity through continuous dialogue. I repeat, 'our' identity because it is critical that in this process 'insiders' , that is Asian Pentecostals, not only take part but also take the lead. Often in the past the 'polite' nature of Asians has robbed us of our own critical roles. This is *first of all* a warning to my fellow Asian Pentecostals.

Groups that are More Pentecostal but Less Christian[49]

This issue is directly related to the matter of definition. Pentecostalism, due to its rich spiritual and experiential dimension, has the potential to circulate among less 'Christian' religious groups while practising some 'Pentecostal' elements. At present Asia has a constant rise of 'heretic' or questionable groups with Pentecostal-like spiritual practices such as prophecy, visions, healings, miracles, and even speaking-in-tongues. These provide attractive elements for other religions which adapt certain Pentecostal elements, especially sensational ones, into their movements.

Tae-sun Park was a gifted follower of Woon-mong Nah. During his crusade in Seoul there was significant manifestation of God's power. Soon Park left the Yongmoon Prayer Mountain and began the *Singang-chon* (Village of Faith) movement. Its communal living, questionable doctrinal teaching (including a claim that he was the 'olive' branch prophesied in the Old Testament), ethical problems and reported forced labour cases led to a general condemnation by the Korean church. And yet Park continued to claim the power of the Holy Spirit. I wonder if African Initiated Churches are such a group, where their commitment to traditional Christian beliefs is in question while Pentecostal-like practices are evident.

Because of these types of events, it is sensible to place the true definition of Pentecostalism within the context of traditional Christianity. Thus, any group

---

[49] This expression was suggested by Stanley M. Burgess in a conversation with the author in August 2001 in Baguio, Philippines.

that is less than Christian, in spite of its 'full' Pentecostal characteristics, should not necessarily be called Pentecostal, and Asian Christians should continue to discern groups of this kind.

The Issue of Suffering

The triumphalist attitude of the modern Pentecostal/Charismatic theology and ethos has left very little room for human suffering.[50] Perhaps this was not part of the original Pentecostal spirituality which had immediate eschatological expectations and a strong sense of missionary calling. The majority of adherents came from low social strata and practiced such things as 'praying through' and 'tarrying', not to mention their commitment to holiness. Even with these elements, healing was often claimed to be a matter of 'receiving' what was already paid for on the cross.[51] As this eschatological or *other-worldly* orientation was slowly changed to a more *this-worldly* look (especially after the advent of the Charismatic movement in the 1960s) the theological outlook of Pentecostal/Charismatic churches began to be influenced by super televangelists who brought ready-made solutions for every problem. Healing, blessing and miracles are claimed, but often with a self-centred orientation rather than from a mission-oriented motivation that was characteristic of early Pentecostal believers.

The positive attitude of Pentecostalism has made many wonderful contributions to the church, as exemplified above in the case of Korean Christianity. In spite of this the overly simplistic and triumphalist theology of 'kingdom now' (or its variety) has betrayed the true reality of human life where suffering is an integral component. It has also been destructive of the eschatological tension that New Testament believers had been taught to live with for so long. These problems have almost created a sense that Pentecostalism is a cheap version of Christianity, or as Tom Smail puts it, 'post-cross' Christianity.[52] This not only distorted the concept of commitment in Christianity but also fostered unscriptural expectations of God's power on

---

[50] Interestingly, this was one of the two the major reasons why early Pentecostal missionaries in China were not accepted by fellow missionaries. Garr claimed to be able to speak native languages supernaturally and instantly angered many missionaries, while denouncing the methods of other mission agencies in China. Bays & Johnson, *China*, 60-61.

[51] Such an attitude made taking medicine a sinful act or lack of faith. See Vinson Synan, 'A Healer in the House?: A Historical Perspective on Healing in the Pentecostal/ Charismatic Tradition', *AJPS* 3:2 (July 2000), 189-201 (193-94) for Alexander Dewie's position.

[52] Tom Smail, 'The Cross and the Spirit', in *Charismatic Renewal: The Search for a Theology*, eds. Tom Smail, Andrew Walker, and Nigel Wright (London: SPCK, 1995), 49-70 (56-58).

our behalf. Although this is not preached explicitly it is conceivable that Christians with long-term illness may likely lose their place in a local Pentecostal church when the message of unconditional healing which actually only requires faith is implicitly proclaimed from the pulpit. In reality the old fallacy is recycled: if one is not healed, it is either because of hidden sin or lack of faith, since Jesus paid for all healing. For this reason, it is encouraging to see more appearances of Pentecostal reflection on the reality of suffering in human life.[53] The Asian masses suffer on a daily basis from structural oppression and poverty.

Another important aspect is 'voluntary suffering' among Asian Christians and Pentecostals. As briefly discussed above, becoming a Christian is at times a life-and-death decision and has resulted in many cases of persecution. In Barrett's analysis, there are three major sources of persecution against Christians: secular governments, atheists, and Muslims.[54] Courageous reports coming from China, North Korea, Vietnam, Laos, Cambodia, Myanmar, Nepal, Bhutan and Tibet attest to the first two sources of Christian suffering. The recent trial of several western humanitarian workers by the Afghanistan authorities illustrates the harsh reality that some Asian Christians have chosen to live with as they have chosen to follow Jesus. The case becomes worse when Asian Christians, already vulnerable to various forms of suffering, have strong and aggressive evangelistic zeal. Pentecostals fall in this category and thus they are more susceptible to suffering and persecution.[55] As both involuntary and voluntary suffering continues among Asian Christians, I encourage Asian Pentecostal scholarship to pursue this topic in order to bring a healthy balance to wider Pentecostal theology.

The Social Responsibility of Pentecostal Christianity

Pentecostalism was originally identified with the Fundamentalist wing of Christianity, even though Fundamentalists mounted the greatest attack against the new movement. It was because of the Pentecostals' unilateral identification with this conservative wing, their deep commitment to the word of God, and their literalist view of the Bible that this uncomfortable alliance seemed

---

[53] For instance, two articles in the upcoming *Spirit and Spirituality: Essays in Honor of Russell P. Spittler*, eds. Wonsuk Ma and Robert P. Menzies (forthcoming) includes William W. Menzies, 'Reflections on Suffering: A Pentecostal Perspective' and Veli-Matti Kärkkäinen, 'Theology of the Cross: A Stumbling Block to Pentecostal/ Charismatic Spirituality?'

[54] Barrett, *WCE*, I, 11.

[55] Barrett, *WCE*, I, 20 shows that Pentecostals provide 38% of the evangelistic 'harvesters', even if Pentecostal/Charismatic Christianity is only 26% of world Christianity.

justified.[56] It may be helpful to remember that the Pentecostal movement was born and grew during the turbulent period of tension between liberal and conservative Christianity.[57] This changed as Pentecostals were politically identified with evangelicals in the second part of the last century. This political alliance of the Pentecostals with conservative wings of the church naturally moved them away from social issues, which was generally considered part of a liberal agenda.

However, this does not imply that Pentecostalism does not make social contributions. Witnesses in Latin America reflect the most impressive indication that the Pentecostal movement has a powerful and unique potential for social transformation. Several approaches to social issues have been tried by Pentecostals (often in mission settings), and many were proven to be effective. For example, Latin American ChildCare Ministry has provided thousands of children from low-income families with quality education. This successful ministry has drawn much attention.[58] People like Lilian Trasher among Egyptian orphans and Mark Buntain among the Calcutta poor, represent the best of the Pentecostal contribution to social transformation.[59] And yet Pentecostals, like their evangelical cousins, 'minister' to the victims as a

---

[56] See Russell P. Spittler, 'Are Pentecostals and Charismatics Fundamentalists? A Review of American Uses of These Categories', in Karla Poewe (ed.), *Charismatic Christianity as a Global Culture*, Studies in Comparative Religion (Columbia: University of South Carolina Press), 103–116; H.V. Synan, 'Fundamentalism', *Dictionary of the Pentecostal and Charismatic Movements*, 324-27 (326-27); Hollenweger, *Pentecostalism*, 192.

[57] This does not mean that Pentecostals did not have any dealings with the liberal wing of the church. See, for example, Cecil M. Robeck, Jr., 'Assemblies of God and Ecumenical Corporation' in *Pentecostalism in Context: Essays in Honor of William W. Menzies*, eds. Wonsuk Ma and Robert P. Menzies (Sheffield: Sheffield Academic Press, 1997), 107-105.

[58] Douglas Petersen wrote a PhD dissertation investigating this ministry and later published: *Not by Might, Nor by Power: A Pentecostal Theology of Social Concern in Latin America* (Oxford & Irvine, CA: Regnum, 1996). Also see the entire issue of *Transformation* 16:2 (1999) dedicated to the theme of 'A Pentecostal Approach to Evangelization and Social Action'.

[59] For Buntain, see Douglas Wead, *The Compassionate Touch* (Carol Stream, IL: Creation Books, 1977) and S. Shemeth, 'Buntain, Daniel, Mark (1923-)', in *Dictionary of Pentecostal and Charismatic Movements*, eds. Stanley M. Burgess and Gary B. McGee (Grand Rapids: Zondervan, 1988), 101-102. For Trasher, see S. Shemeth, 'Trasher, Lillian Hunt (1887-1961)', in *Dictionary of Pentecostal and Charismatic Movements*, 852-53; J. Beatty, 'Nile Mother', *AG Heritage* 4 (Winter, 1984-85), 1, 3-6, 8; D. Crouch, 'Why They Called Her the Greatest Woman in Egypt', *AG Heritage* 4, 7-8.

priority rather than actively trying to reform the social and political structures which are perceived to have caused the evil in the first place.[60]

Perhaps one significant case of a social contribution may be found among Malaysian Pentecostal churches. In this Muslim nation, evangelism of Muslim Malays is extremely limited and is a severe violation of the law. This may have encouraged Pentecostal churches to explore creative avenues to demonstrate God's love in action. A small Tamil Pentecostal church in Kuala Lumpur began an orphanage and home for the elderly. Another small Pentecostal congregation in Malacca (or Melaka) began a drug rehabilitation centre. One mid-size Pentecostal church in Kuala Lumpur began a dialysis centre for poor kidney patients. While financial assistance from the government for drug rehabilitation programmes should be considered a factor, another encouraging case of a social contribution is seen in Pentecostal drug rehabilitation programmes. The fact cannot be ignored that there are high success rates in these church-based programmes. Now more churches in Malaysia are opening various social service facilities and programmes. We should learn more about this significant work, which warrants serious research in the future.

The strong emphasis of Pentecostal churches in northern India on social services also proves that such approaches tend to be more common where direct evangelistic opportunities are limited. Unlike South India, early Pentecostal missionaries in northern India established institutions including orphanages, industrial schools, elementary schools, and medical services such as leper asylums and dispensaries.[61]

Perhaps a fundamental question relevant to our discussion is: Why does social corruption increase in some Asian countries where the Pentecostal/Charismatic movement has exploded?[62] This is an urgent question which Pentecostal communities have to ponder seriously. Such a question encompasses not only individual responsibility but also structural reform.

Beyond Blessing

Because of the dire context in Asia where daily survival is at stake, Pentecostalism has rightly addressed several immediate issues by introducing

---

[60] For a Korean Pentecostal case, see Wonsuk Ma, 'The Work of the Holy Spirit in the Social Dimension: A Study of Korean Pentecostal Churches' [in Korean], in *Sanctification of a Christian in the Work of the Holy Spirit* (Seoul: International Theological Institute, 1997), 141-75.

[61] G.B. McGee and S.M. Burgess , 'India', *NIDPCM*, 123.

[62] A Singaporean 'Charismatic' theologian, Yeo Choo Lak, 'New President, Fresh Hopes: Doing Theology in the Philippines', *Journal of Asian Mission* 1:1 (March 1999), 81-92 raises this poignant question after he had moved to the Philippines.

God, who responds to the needs of his people. However this theological orientation needs to be supplemented with an ultimate theological goal.

Asian classical Pentecostalism is not so 'classical', that is, it does not always reflect the early Pentecostal beliefs and practices faithfully. This discrepancy is often found among the non-English speaking Asian nations. Early Pentecostals in the West made a clear theological connection between the fullness of the Spirit (or more popularly called 'baptism in the Spirit') and mission. This is based on how early Pentecostals understood the ultimate purpose of the Spirit's coming: empowerment for witness (Acts 1.8). Charles Parham even argued that the tongues are ultimately a missionary gift bypassing the painful language learning process in the mission field.[63] Although this was soon discovered not to be the case, early Pentecostals continued their conviction that Spirit baptism is for evangelism and mission. This missionary-oriented belief in the work of the Spirit is not always found among Asian Pentecostals. Perhaps with the influence of Charismatic theology (often less, or even non-missionary, but with a renewal emphasis on individuals and churches) in the later part of the previous century, Asian Pentecostals have a more self-centred, blessing-oriented theological outlook than the true classical Pentecostals. Of course the new Asian context contributed to this theological orientation. However the trend obviously betrays the very purpose of the Spirit's work among God's people: to make a self-giving missionary people.

It is rather unfortunate that Pentecostal churches have had phenomenal church growth but have failed to provide the next clear theological goal beyond blessing and beyond 'me'. A good case is the Yoido Full Gospel Church, the largest single congregation in the world. Its emphasis on prayer, a positive attitude, the cell system, the mobilization of the laity and various programmes made the Yoido Full Gospel Church the locomotive of Korean church growth. Yoido's Church Growth International has attracted thousands of church leaders from all over the world to learn its secrets of church growth. The message of blessing was the driving force in mobilizing people for evangelism and commitment. However since the 1990s this church has lost its leading role in church growth as the church stopped growing. Various factors have been suggested, but one convincing argument is the changing society and human needs. People began to question whether blessing is the ultimate goal of Christian faith. When Christians were looking for a theological goal beyond blessing, the Yoido Church was not able to articulate the noble Pentecostal theology of mission as the ultimate goal of Christian living, blessing and Spirit

---

[63] James R. Goff, Jr., *Fields White unto Harvest: Chares F. Parham and the Missionary Origin of Pentecostalism* (Fayetteville, Arkansas: University of Arkansas Press, 1988), 164-65; also idem, 'Initial Tongues in the Theology of Charles Fox Parham', in Gary B. McGee (ed.), *Initial Evidence: Historical and Biblical Perspectives on the Pentecostal Doctrine of Spirit Baptism* (Peabody, MA: Hendrickson, 1991), 57-71 (64-65).

baptism. In fact, the 'blessing' could have been theologically interpreted as part
of the empowerment for witnessing (Acts 1.8). Certainly classical Pentecostal
scholarship has an important responsibility to articulate this central theological
goal of Pentecostal experiences.

Ecumenical Potential

This less articulated[64] but equally important and widely practised contribution
of the movement will continue to challenge Asian Pentecostals. Robeck draws
his argument for the ecumenical potential of Pentecostalism from the
inter-confessional composition of the Azusa Street revival. Although there was
no theological articulation on this revolutionary phenomenon, the unifying
work of the Spirit was powerfully demonstrated, although the human work of
segregation was equally evident. This spontaneous ecumenism is particularly
significant in the light of the concerted and organized efforts of the World
Council of Churches to achieve visible (although certainly short of organic)
unity. Pentecostal ecumenism takes place 'spontaneously' and 'intuitively'.[65]

In a sense Asian Pentecostals, like many other evangelical denominations,
are the product of western missionary (and often denominational) efforts. One
problem with evangelical missionary work is the strong denominational
orientation which almost ignores commitment to ecumenism. This argument
can be further substantiated by a general observation of the difference between
English-speaking and non-English speaking countries. For instance in Korea (a
non-English speaking country) one can hardly find an independent Charismatic
church, while all churches are widely open to Pentecostal influences.[66] On the
other hand in the Philippines (an English-speaking nation) Charismatic groups
have to be independent, except Roman Catholic Charismatic groups, while
denominational churches have strictly kept the 'foreign' (that is, Pentecostal)

---

[64] The first articulation of the ecumenical potential of the Pentecostal movement is by
Cecil M. Robeck, Jr., 'Taking Stock of Pentecostalism: The Personal Reflections of a
Retiring Editor', *Pneuma* 15:1 (1993), 35-60. However, from the earliest days, this
potential was well noted: e.g., Frank Bartleman, *Azusa Street: The Roots of Modern-day
Pentecost* (South Plainfield, NJ: Logos, 1980 reprint), 167-73 as early as in 1925;
Donald Gee, *Toward Pentecostal Unity* (Springfield, MO: Gospel Publishing House,
1961) has a subtitle: An Earnest Plea for Spirit-filled Believers to Unite for World
Evangelization.

[65] Koichi Kitano, 'Spontaneous Ecumenicity between Catholics and Protestants in
Charismatic Movement: A Case Study' (PhD dissertation, Centro Escolar University,
Manila, 1981).

[66] For instance, Chang-sup Shin, 'Assessing the Impact of Pentecostalism on the Korean
Presbyterian Church in Light of Calvin's Theology', *Chongshin Theological Journal* 3:1
(1998), 115-131 discusses pros and cons of the 'Pentecostalization' of the Presbyterian
churches in Korea.

influences away. In the case of Korea missionaries have had limited access to influence the Christian masses because of the language barrier and thus it is the national leaders who have had more freedom to shape their theology. In the Philippines on the other hand, missionaries from their western 'headquarters' are promptly dispatched to clean up any perceived theological 'impurity'. Only recently have non-Pentecostal denominations begun to adopt Pentecostal/Charismatic types of music.

Likewise it seems that the role of Asian Pentecostal leaders is to pursue this visionary ecumenical goal, first among various Pentecostal and Charismatic groups and then move to the larger church world. With the maturity and growth of Asian Pentecostal churches, national churches can now set their own agenda and allow missionaries to be partners in these pursuits instead of missionaries setting the agenda for national churches. Some churches were even divided, not due to doctrinal differences, but due to more than one mission agency's involvement in the establishment of national churches. For instance there are three Assemblies of God groups in Thailand, primarily because early missionaries from Canada, the USA, and Finland failed to form one national Assemblies of God body. Although nationals are as guilty as missionaries for church divisions, genuine efforts to bring churches together will always produce positive effects even if structural unity may not be achieved immediately. After all, the Spirit makes us one.

The Spirit outside of the Church

Traditionally, perhaps due to the lack of articulation, Pentecostal understanding of the Spirit has been limited to the Christian life, more specifically to the empowering aspect of the Spirit's work. This narrowly defined pneumatology has in turn produced highly dynamic effects as well as producing phenomenal church growth and missions promotion among Pentecostals. However as more interaction is taking place with other Christian traditions Pentecostals have been challenged to expand their narrow pneumatology.[67] Asian Pentecostals are further challenged to rethink the scope of their pneumatology in light of their pluralistic religious context.

Although an average Asian Pentecostal is not ready to accept the argument that the Spirit is given to 'all' including male and female, young and old, slaves and free (Joel 2.28-29),[68] one can easily admit that the Spirit of God is involved in creation and its sustenance. For instance, when the Lord takes 'his spirit',

---

[67] My personal involvement in an ecumenical dialogue has compelled me to expand the scope of my understanding of the work of the Spirit. Also see Veli-Matti Kärkkäinen, '"Truth on Fire": Pentecostal Theology of Mission and the Challenge of a New Millennium', *Asian Journal of Pentecostal Studies* 3:1 (Jan. 2000), 33-60 (54-56).

[68] E.g. Jurgen Moltmann and Hollenweger.

away we cease to exist (Job 34:14). Then it is not difficult to admit that the Spirit works outside of the church. Now applying this thesis will not be easy and Asian Pentecostals have to struggle with some hard questions in their contexts, such as: 'Is the Spirit in cultures?', or 'Is the Spirit working in other religions?' Complexity and plurality in racial make-up and religious orientations throughout the many Asian societies no longer allows the old simplistic crusading mentality of days gone by. Asian Pentecostals must prayerfully and academically think through these issues now and in the years to come.

Racial Concerns

Racial conflict has become the foremost political issue since the end of the cold war era. As seen in recent conflicts (such as Bosnia) racial issues often involve religious struggles. At the end of World War II, many Asian countries became independent, at times resulting in arbitrary demarcation of borders. For instance, West Pakistan and East Pakistan existed as one nation in spite of differences in history, religion and particularly the geographical division between the two parts. The latter became Bangladesh only after many racial and religious war casualties. The case of East Timor's independence from Indonesia is a recent example. Racial tension is like a time bomb in many Asian nations. Some of them are Malaysia, Indonesia, China (with Tibet and the western Muslim provinces), the Philippines, Sri Lanka and others.

How Pentecostalism can bring a positive contribution to this issue is not an easy question. However, a harmonious inter-racial Christian life can be a powerful sign of the Spirit's work. Although in some countries such racial harmony is simply impossible, places like Singapore have shown good interracial Christian potential. If the Azusa Street revival was characterized by spontaneous interracial fellowship, the Spirit can also help us to be agents of reconciliation. After all, as early Pentecostals claimed, 'the colour line was washed away in the blood [of Jesus]'.[69]

Concluding Words

While promises are bright for the future of Asian Pentecostalism, the challenges are ample. Emerging new issues in the Asian context will make the challenge more acute. This will certainly require more than a regurgitation of western Pentecostal theology. Asian theologians will need to create new theological categories to respond meaningfully to what Asia uniquely faces. For instance the recent issue of intergenerational curse/blessing found its cognitive

---

[69] As testified by Frank Bartleman of the Azusa Street interracial miracle, *Azusa Street: The Roots of Modern-day Pentecost* (South Plainfield, NJ: Logos, 1980 reprint), 54.

home right among Asian Pentecostals. Another example is the popular Chi-gong practices in Hong Kong, China and Korea. Chi is an old Chinese concept referring to a universal energy of life. Street-side 'institutes' claim to be able to charge this cosmic energy of life into individuals. How Pentecostal churches should discern and judge this practice is a uniquely Asian Pentecostal theological issue and challenge. Every sector of the Asian Pentecostal church in general needs to work hard to maximize Pentecostalism's potential. My concluding thought is specifically directed to the academic community.

Over the century of Pentecostal history this spiritual dynamic of Pentecostalism has produced excellent practitioners including pastors, evangelists and missionaries, but not many reflective scholars. Perhaps this is still better than the reverse scenario: few practitioners but many thinkers. Only since the second half of the last century has the movement begun to see the emergence of serious scholarship, first in historical studies and then biblical studies.[70] Pentecostal seminaries began to appear only in the 1960s.[71] When this seemingly anti-intellectual spiritual dynamic is planted in the Asian soil where learning is highly prized a new form of Pentecostal intellectuals can be expected. We may have seen a small sign of this expectation. For instance among the Foursquare Pentecostals the Gospel Theological Seminary in Korea has opened the first graduate level courses, which includes a Master of Theology programme. Hansei University (of the Korean Assemblies of God) recently began to offer doctoral programmes. Asia Pacific Theological Seminary (Assemblies of God) now offers post-graduate programmes including a Master of Theology in Pentecostal Studies, a projected Doctor of Ministry in Pentecostal Ministries and a joint PhD programme with a British university. There are at least a dozen Pentecostal schools in Asia offering graduate programmes.

Two Pentecostal journals in English are produced in Asia[72] in addition to numerous academic periodicals produced in national languages, particularly in Japan and Korea. *Australasian Pentecostal Studies* is also published in this part of the globe. The Asian Pentecostal Society in its short history has provided not only an annual forum among Asian Pentecostal thinkers but also leadership to

---

[70] For a survey of the emergence of biblical scholarship among Pentecostals, see Wonsuk Ma, 'Pentecostal Biblical Studies: Yesterday, Today and Tomorrow', in Murray W. Dempster, Byron D. Klaus, and Douglas Petersen (eds.), *The Globalization of Pentecostalism: A Religion Made to Travel* (Oxford: Regnum, 1999), 52-69.

[71] For a comprehensive survey of Pentecostal education, see L.F. Wilson, 'Bible Institutes, Colleges, Universities', *Dictionary of the Pentecostal and Charismatic Movements*, 57-65.

[72] *The Spirit and Church* by Gospel Theological Seminary, Daejon, Korea, and *Asian Journal of Pentecostal Studies* by Asia Pacific Theological Seminary, Baguio, Philippines.

bring Pentecostal scholars from other non-western continents for theological reflection. All these seem to indicate a bright future for Asian Pentecostals.

However, the challenges are equally great, some of which I have discussed above. For the academic community two words of caution may be proper. First, Asian Pentecostalism can be meaningfully explored and developed only in the global Pentecostal context. In spite of its explosive growth, knowing that this success has not been of human design or achievement but of the Spirit, Asian Pentecostal thinkers must actively and humbly seek to learn from and work with western colleagues and other non-western friends. The future of the movement is something all of us need to work toward intentionally. Thus, global networking will be critical, and for this, as an Asian Pentecostal, the organizers of the Asian Pentecostal Conference (Birmingham, 2001) deserve warm commendation. The earnest request that this conference be an on-going effort should be seriously considered.

Today, I renew my two pleas: 1) the creation of a global Pentecostal scholarly forum; and 2) the launch of a Pentecostal abstract for the purpose of a comprehensive compilation of all the scholarly writings on Pentecostal subjects, whatever languages they are written in. These writings need to be abstracted as a service of and to the Pentecostal academic community. The networking among Pentecostal scholars may take place as early as in 2004 during the 20th Pentecostal World Conference in Johannesburg, South Africa.[73]

Second, the Asian Pentecostals, especially those of the academic community, need to carefully guard themselves from extreme Pentecostal scholasticism. Obsession with academic pursuit can easily suffocate spiritual dynamics if not carefully guarded. This is exactly why traditional Pentecostalism has been anti-intellectual. While trying to correct this historical suspicion, Asian Pentecostals cannot afford to make a bigger mistake: a spiritual movement without spiritual dynamics. Asian theological reflection can be a strength to the Pentecostal movement worldwide or it can be a curse. We must be conscientious and careful in our scholastic endeavours.

Asian Pentecostals have reason to celebrate. This movement has made a unique contribution to global Pentecostalism, and by God's grace will continue to do so in the future. May God help us to listen to him, and obey his bidding through the power of his Holy Spirit.

---

[73] See Mathew Clark, 'International Symposium on Non-Western Pentecostalism', *Asian Journal of Pentecostal Studies* 5:1 (2002), 1-4.

The Demonic in Pentecostal/Charismatic Christianity and in the Religious Consciousness of Asia

Amos Yong

Introduction

In this paper, I want to continue to explore what I call a pneumatological approach to the phenomenon of human religiosity that I have begun to develop elsewhere.[1] I remain convinced that such an approach, which emphasizes the spiritual dimensions of human life and experience, holds promise for further understanding the interrelatedness of God and creation. This is because pneumatology itself opens up different horizons and perspectives and draws into the interreligious encounter other comparative categories by which human religiousness is further illuminated. Here I hope to develop this thesis through engaging in dialogue with the Buddhist tradition, specifically on the topic of demonology.

Demonology is itself a central feature both of the spiritual aspect of reality and of human religiosity.[2] It connects issues of ultimate (other-worldly) concern to issues of immediate (this-worldly) concern. I believe its consideration is a crucial component of any pneumatological approach to the religions, not only because any discussion of the spiritual aspect of human

---

[1] See Yong, *Discerning the Spirit(s): A Pentecostal-Charismatic Contribution to Christian Theology of Religions* (JPTSup 20; Sheffield, UK: Sheffield Academic Press, 2000), and *The Holy Spirit and the Non-Christian Faiths: Toward a Pneumatological Theology of Religions* (Grand Rapids: Baker Academic, 2003). It needs to be clearly stated that the following discussion reflects the ruminations of an Asian born but American raised and educated Pentecostal. Some of my Asian colleagues contributing to this volume are suspicious about the viability of this project for a variety of reasons. I must admit that my own interests are not motivated by issues pertaining directly to theological inculturation in the regions of Asia. However, insofar as the following proceeds as part of a serious attempt to rethink pneumatology from a globally informed Pentecostal perspective, towards that end I request that what follows be taken seriously as an attempt to do Pentecostal theology within both an Asian-American and a global Pentecostal context.

[2] See Bruce Long, 'Demons: An Overview', in Mircea Eliade (ed.), *The Encyclopedia of Religion*, 16 vols. (New York: Macmillan, 1987), IV, 282-88.

experience exclusive of the demonic remains impoverished, but also because of the importance of being able to discern divine from non-divine and demonic spirits which are at work in the religious experiences of humankind.

Along these lines, I submit that a potentially fruitful line of inquiry is available to us through a comparative study of the demonic in Pentecostal Christianity and what Melvin Spiro calls the 'little traditions' of Buddhism in Asia. Within the Burmese context, Spiro argues for the distinction between the 'great tradition' of elite Buddhism with its sacred texts and doctrines and the 'little tradition' of popularly practised Buddhism with its rituals and festivals drawn from the assimilation of textual Buddhism with indigenous traditions.[3] However one might wish to take issue with this categorization, for purposes of beginning the Buddhist-Christian dialogue proposed in this paper I wish to exploit Spiro's distinction heuristically as a means of distinguishing between 'high-church' and 'low-church' Christianity, with the latter including Pentecostal Christianity in Asia. As the discussion proceeds, I believe that the artificiality of these distinctions—both for the Buddhist and the Christian traditions—will be evident. For the moment, however, I want to inquire not only into what a comparative analysis of Pentecostal and popular Buddhist demonologies tell us about the religious consciousness of Asia, but also about what this might mean for both the Christian theological and the buddhological traditions.

Because of my conviction that theology emerges out of the human experience on the ground rather than solely from an abstract rationalistic encounter with alleged deposits of revelation from above, the following methodological parameters will guide our inquiry. First, Christian theology needs to correlate biblical scholarship and practical ministry with the various social and scientific disciplines. Each needs to illuminate the other. In the context of the twenty-first century, theology fails unless it is multidisciplinary. Only an interdisciplinary method can be genuinely comparative, and that would include, of course, both cross-cultural and cross-religious comparativism. Second, an interdisciplinary, social-scientific approach is empirical through and through. This means that theology not only pays descriptive attention to the actual histories, phenomenologies and experiences of religious persons and traditions, but also attempts to understand how these inform the normative beliefs and expressions of Christian life in particular and religious life in general. This emphasis on the concrete manifestations of religiousness arises in part out of my own (Pentecostal) conviction that however else Christians

---

[3] Cf. Melford E. Spiro, *Buddhism and Society: A Great Tradition and Its Burmese Vicissitudes*, 2nd ed. (Berkeley, Los Angeles, London: University of California Press, 1982). In connection with this two-traditions theory, see Richard S. Cohen, 'Nâga, Yaksinâ, Buddha: Local Deities and Local Buddhism at Ajanta', *History of Religions* 37:4 (1998), 360-400.

encounter God through the Holy Spirit, such encounters are inevitably kinesthetic, material and embodied (i.e. through healings, tongues, the shout, the dance, being 'slain in the Spirit', and so on). Finally, even if I do not embrace postmodernism as a whole uncritically, I take the postmodern turns 'to the subject' and 'to the community' seriously. These turns require that heretofore marginalized voices be admitted back into all conversations. With regard to religious inquiry and theological reflection specifically, this means that not only do Pentecostal voices and experiences count in general but, more importantly, Asian Pentecostal voices and experiences need to be heard in all their particularities. Further, any theology worth its salt in a religiously plural world will also need to attend not only to voices from the 'great tradition of Buddhism', but also to Sinhalese and Tantric (in the case of this paper), and other 'local' Buddhist voices and experiences as well. Each needs to be heard in all of its distinctiveness not because the postmodern turns land one finally in relativism, but because all truth is God's truth wherever it might be found and needs to be accounted for in any theology that makes claims which aspire to universal truthfulness.[4]

With these methodological convictions in hand, I propose to proceed as follows. The first section provides a brief overview of demonology in the Christian tradition in general and in Pentecostal Christianity (in Asia) in particular. The middle section, the most extensive of this paper, will focus on the demonic in Buddhist traditions and practices. The concluding section will return to the task of reflecting on the possibilities and problems confronting a cross-cultural and interreligious theology that nevertheless is distinctively Christian.

Pentecostal Demonologies and the Asian Context[5]

As a whole, Pentecostal demonological beliefs are traditioned much less formally through theological treatises but rather through the testimony, the sermon and other popularly produced and marketed materials. This characteristic of Pentecostal demonology means that the demonic in the Pentecostal imagination retains a connection with pre-modern Christian views in many respects. Our approach to Pentecostal demonologies will be through

---

[4] The details of the theological method operative here can be found in my *Spirit-Word-Community: Theological Hermeneutics in Trinitarian Perspective, New Critical Thinking in Biblical Studies and Theology* (Burlington, VT: Ashgate, 2002).

[5] The papers published in this volume evoked extensive discussion about the definition of 'Pentecostal' at the conference in Birmingham where they were originally presented. I would argue that the problem of defining 'Pentecostal' also bedevils attempts to define 'demonology' or 'Asian'. My response is to take a polythetic, pluralistic, non-essentialistic and *a posteriori* strategy to all definitions.

the hermeneutic by which Pentecostals read and understand the biblical materials.

Christian traditions and the demonic

For our purposes, three aspects of the biblical data concerning the demonic are pertinent to Pentecostal demonologies.[6] First, the devil and his demons are understood as personal, spiritual and malevolent beings who are responsible for the human experience of temptation, suffering and evil. In this regard, there is a holistic understanding of the interrelatedness of the material and spiritual realms of creation. Humans can interact with demons even while demonic activity can influence affairs in the material world. Second, the life, death and resurrection of Jesus Christ has triumphed over the devil and his demons. Redemption has been accomplished, and death, the last weapon of the devil, has been vanquished. Victory over temptation is provided through life in the Spirit. Finally, this overcoming the suffering and evil wrought by the devil and his demons can be experienced in part now in anticipation of the eschatological once-for-all triumph over these aspects of embodied experience. The devil and his demons can and should be resisted and rebuked in the name of Jesus and they will have to flee. For their engagement with the powers of darkness, Christians have been given divinely appointed weapons—especially a suit of spiritual armour along with the power of fasting and prayer and the sword of the Word of God—which are more than adequate for the task of standing against and exorcising their enemy.

This brief overview of Pentecostal demonologies leaves out much that is relevant to understanding the religious situation in Asia. As a specifically Pentecostal reading of the Christian Testament data regarding the demonic, the preceding sketch provides no hint about the evolution of ideas in contrast to the understanding of the ancient Hebrews as recorded in the First Testament. In the latter, *ha Satan* ('the Satan') in the book of Job represents more an office or a function in the divine council rather than a personal spiritual being. The divine council is itself ambiguously described within the pages of the Hebrew Bible, its members perhaps being appointed to oversee human affairs.[7] Yet while they serve as 'gods' on the one hand, they are also depicted as not much more then

---

[6] My own work seeks to ask theological questions about the demonic that builds on the biblical exegesis of others. See, e.g. Stephen F. Noll, *Angels of Light, Powers of Darkness: Thinking Biblically about Angels, Satan and Principalities* (Downers Grove: InterVarsity Press, 1998), and Keith Ferdinando, *The Triumph of Christ in African Perspective: A Study of Demonology and Redemption in the African Context* (Carlisle, UK: Paternoster Press, 1999), esp. section two.

[7] Job 1.6; 2.1. cf. E. Theodore Mullen, Jr, *The Divine Council in Canaanite and Early Hebrew Literature*, Harvard Semitic Monographs 24 (Chico, CA: Scholars Press, 1980).

mere mortals on the other.[8] Further, the departed dead, another category of immaterial beings, 'exist' in limbo in the underworld of Shades, occasionally re-appearing and having intercourse with the living.[9]

In the Second Testament, the distinction is now clearly made between good angels who are ministering servants of God and humankind and fallen angels who are demons ruled by Satan.[10] The divine council appears to have been disbanded since cosmic authority is now dualistically conceived—perhaps due to the influence of Zoroastrianism on post-exilic Jewish theology—between the one God and his angels on the one side and the demons of paganism on the other.[11] The departed dead, *daimones*, appear to have been released from the confines of Sheol and, insofar as they now roam or wander the earth at all, they do so as demons on the one hand and yet subject to the triumphant ministry, life, death and resurrection of Christ on the other.[12] The righteous dead now seem to have a new resting place in Abraham's bosom and no longer play an important role except perhaps as witnesses to the race run by the Christian.[13]

The vagueness of the biblical data on points of detail, however, served as a catalyst for a variety of patristic and medieval speculations regarding the realms of the dead and the demonic.[14] The witness and examples of early Christian martyrs and the memories they etched on the Christian imagination combined with the convergence of Christian and pagan cultures in the post-Constantinian era to bring about the cult of the saints in which the Christian dead were venerated and to whom supplications were offered. It would be a mistake, however, to think of this as applicable solely at the level of the masses since ample evidence exists that the bishops were central players in developing both the devotional and liturgical aspects of this tradition. The result could therefore only be distorted if seen as a bifurcation of 'authentic' Christianity on the one hand and 'corrupted' Christianity on the other. In reality, things were much more complex. Lay and hierarchical Christianity were intrinsically connected with the generations (the spirits of the dead) who preceded them, and all 'three'

---

[8] Cf. Ps. 82.1, 6.

[9] Cf. 1 Sam. 28.

[10] Heb. 1.14; Rev. 12.9-10.

[11] 1 Cor. 8.4-6; 10.20.

[12] See Peter Bolt, 'Jesus, the Daimons and the Dead', in Anthony N.S. Lane (ed.), *The Unseen World: Christian Reflections on Angels, Demons, and the Heavenly Realm* (Grand Rapids: Baker Book House, and Carlisle, UK: Paternoster Press, 1996), 75-102.

[13] Luke 16.22; Heb. 12.1.

[14] For historical surveys of the demonic in western Christianity, see Christopher Nugent, *Masks of Satan: The Demonic in History* (Westminster, MD: Christian Classics, 1983), and Jeffrey Burton Russell, *The Prince of Darkness: Radical Evil and the Power of Good in History* (Ithaca and London: Cornell University Press, 1988).

groups were understood as being at the same time participants in an unseen world of benevolent and malevolent beings.[15]

Modern Christians have, by and large, rejected most of these medieval notions regarding the cult of the saints and the demonic as superstitions. While the latent power of evil in the human condition is acknowledged, it has also been largely depersonalized.[16] Psychological analysis, demythologization, and secularization, among other developments, have combined to produce naturalistic and mechanistic worldviews devoid of spiritual beings, whether they be saints, angels or demons. Even with the arrival of the new age movement, spiritual forces are psychologized and understood as latent within the human soul, generally speaking, rather than being external, invasive, and threatening personal agents in their own right. It is against this background that conservative Christian and Pentecostal views of the demonic can and should be understood to be both biblicistic and premodern in various respects.

Pentecostal demonologies

Contemporary Pentecostal demonologies are concerned with two basic questions: 1) Can Christians be demon-possessed? 2) How can Christians effectively deal with the attacks of the devil and his demons in the various arenas of life? Both sets of questions, it is clear, are deeply practical, existential and soteriological. Let us look briefly at the former.

Pentecostals disagree among themselves about whether or not Christians can be demon-possessed. For the purposes at hand, I do not wish to go into the details of this debate or even to clearly define its terms (such as the possible distinctions proffered between being demonized and being demon-possessed). Whatever one believes about these questions, two observations are pertinent to our inquiry. First, the question of demon possession itself reflects fundamental intuitions in the Pentecostal worldview. Thus Pentecostals testify to having been protected or delivered from demonic attacks and from triumphing over extenuating circumstances that reflect demonic activity and Pentecostal literature is replete with dualistic imagery and metaphors which undergird their division of the forces of the cosmos into hostile and friendly spiritual beings. The conviction throughout is that there is more to reality than what is engaged with the physical senses.

---

[15] For a historical perspective, see Peter Brown, *The Cult of the Saints: Its Rise and Function in Latin Christianity* (Chicago: The University of Chicago Press, 1981).

[16] See e.g. Alan M. Olson (ed.), *Disguises of the Demonic: Contemporary Perspectives on the Power of Evil* (New York: Association Press, 1975), and Howard Vann Pendley III, 'Views of the Demonic in Recent Religious Thought' (Ph.D. diss., Southern Baptist Theological Seminary 1976).

The second observation relates to the sociological, soteriological and theological backgrounds that impinge on the issues at stake. Sociologically, for example, does the distinction between elitist and popular Christianity made above further our understanding about why this is a question of significance for Pentecostals? Is it significant, for example, that western Pentecostal demonologies lay much less emphasis than African or Asian Pentecostal ones on this issue? Even when Asian Pentecostals deny that Christians can be demon-possessed, might it be the case that the concern itself is driven by the social location of Pentecostal experiences that parallel that of the indigenous traditions from which they have (perhaps recently) been converted? Does the widespread indigenous belief in ancestors—both benevolent and malevolent—throughout Asia have anything to do with how Pentecostals interpret Scripture on the one hand and, on the other, how they understand their own conversion experiences to have relocated them cosmologically?[17]

Yet regardless of how one understands the sociological issue, it cannot be denied that deep soteriological anxieties are manifest in Pentecostal demonologies. Pentecostals, like other human beings, are concerned about succeeding rather than failing physically, economically, socio-politically and interpersonally. They are interested in living in health and peaceably and in experiencing well-being. They, like everybody else, want to avoid suffering, tragedy and the taint of evil. And, insofar as one's life is not what it should be due to inexplicable circumstances beyond one's personal control, relief is sought in the supernatural realm. Here, the power of God through the Holy Spirit is invoked against the powers of darkness since it is the latter with which the Christian ultimately wrestles behind the manifestations of the phenomenal world.[18]

But what about the Enlightenment critique and (it would be claimed) exposure of the demonic as nothing more than a figment of the human imagination? This raises the theological question in a pointed way: do demons exist or not? Of course, this assumes that one can (and either should or should not) have a realist theology of demons; but things might not be so simple. In the

---

[17] Thus it is interesting to note that a recent article in an Asian Pentecostal journal does not appear to reflect Asian Pentecostal concerns. All the sources referred to are western. The author argues against apriorism in biblical exegesis that has results opposed to his own findings, but does not entertain the possibility that such apriorism may be operative in his own work which does not offer countering empirical evidence. See Steven S. Carter, 'Demon Possession and the Christian', *Asian Journal of Pentecostal Studies* 3:1 (2000), 19-31.

[18] An ethnographic study of Pentecostals in the Northern Luzon of the Philippines documents these attitudes and practices; see Julie C. Ma, *When the Spirit Meets the Spirits: Pentecostal Ministry among the Kankana-ey Tribe in the Philippines*, Studies in the Intercultural History of Christianity 118 (Frankfurt, Bern, New York and Wein: Peter Lang, 2000).

secular West, Pentecostal Christians are slowly beginning to grapple with this set of questions as well. Thus Pentecostal systematic theologies written in the West confront the question and defend it, beginning with biblical exposition.[19] This raises, however, the prior metaphysical, cosmological, socio-structural and hermeneutical frameworks within which such exegesis is to be understood. Until Pentecostals wrestle seriously with these meta-questions in conjunction with their exegesis, it can hardly be said that their interpretations of the Bible will be taken seriously by those in the modern West.

Can the same critique be applied to Asian Pentecostal demonologies? Perhaps and perhaps not. While some regions of Asia are clearly modern in their technologies and development, others are not. Singaporeans and Japanese might be more inclined to agree that demons are psychological projections thanmight be, for example, Dalit Indians and Kankana-ey villagers in northern Luzon. The sociological question reappears at just this juncture, thus returning us to the hermeneutical circle. For the moment, however, I wish to expand on the sociological issues in an attempt to understand how Asian Pentecostals deal with the second question mentioned above: that of responding to the demonic in the various arenas of human life.

Exorcising the Demonic

Pentecostals the world over have two interrelated strategies in dealing with demonic: exorcism and spiritual warfare. Both can be and are usually applied together either at the individual or the corporate level, even if it is generally the case that exorcisms are focused on the deliverance of individuals (even if conducted through communal rituals) while spiritual warfare is targeted toward transforming socio-political, ideological and religious situations. The literature on both is immense, even if the praxis of spiritual warfare is a much more recent development in Pentecostal and Third-Wave circles more specifically. Since the remainder of this paper will attempt to compare and contrast Pentecostal and Asian Buddhist rites of exorcism focused on individuals, I will say little about spiritual warfare except that it is currently in vogue, especially among the more missionary minded Pentecostal practitioners.[20]

---

[19] Cf. Guy P. Duffield and Nathaniel M. Van Cleave, *Foundations of Pentecostal Theology* (Los Angeles: LIFE Bible College, 1983), 479-96, and Frank Macchia, 'Created Spirit Beings: Satan and Demons', in Stanley Horton (ed.), *Systematic Theology* (rev. ed.; Springfield, MO: Logion Press, 1995), 194-213. Yeow Choo Lak, an Asian Charismatic evangelical educated in the West, takes a similar approach by beginning with Scripture: *To God Be the Glory! Doctrines on God and Creation* (Singapore: Trinity Theological College Publication, 1981), 175-81.

[20] E.g. Julie Ma, *When the Spirit Meets the Spirits*, passim; and Wonsuk Ma, 'A "First Waver"' Looks at the "Third Wave": A Pentecostal Reflection on Charles Kraft's Power

Central to the practice of both spiritual warfare and exorcism, however, is the power encounter.[21] Whereas spiritual warfare attempts to deal with the powers as spiritual realities presiding over religious, cultural, ideological, social, institutional and geo-political structures, exorcism deals with personal demonic beings oppressing families and, especially, individual lives. In the Asian Pentecostal context, the power of the Holy Spirit is understood to oppose, destroy, and put to flight the powers of darkness. Thus Christian conversion facilitates the movement of persons and families from out of the domain of demonic (previously ancestral, and other super-human) spirits and into that of the Holy Spirit. The following provides a skeletal outline of Christian exorcism set more specifically within the context of Asian Pentecostalism.

Exorcism has been integral to Christian practice following the paradigmatic life of Jesus.[22] Central components of Christian exorcism include preparatory prayer and fasting, especially on the part of those who serve in the ministry of exorcism; confession of Jesus' lordship; identification of the offending spirits, usually by name, through the spiritual gift of discernment of spirits; laying on of hands and anointing with oil; rebuking, binding and/or casting out of the evil spirits, usually through invocation of the name of Jesus and the quotation of Scripture as the Word of God; followed up with baptism in water (at least historically) and then discipleship aimed at a purified environment and lifestyle. At various times and places in the history of Christianity, some of these elements have been emphasized while others have been neglected. The format outlined here is simply a loose structure which guides, but does not predetermine, exorcist rituals.

While we are currently lacking in reliable ethnographic studies of exorcism among Pentecostals, it is safe to say that many of these techniques are brought into play at some point or other in the ritual process.[23] However, distinctively

---

Encounter Terminology', *Pneuma: The Journal of the Society for Pentecostal Studies* 19 (1997), 189-206.

[21] See Opal L. Reddin (ed.), *Power Encounter: A Pentecostal Perspective*, rev. ed. (Springfield, MO: Central Bible College Press Publishers, 1999); Kevin Springer (ed.), *Power Encounters among Christians in the Western World* (San Francisco: Harper & Row, 1988); and C. Peter Wagner, *Confronting the Powers* (Ventura, CA: Regal Books, 1996).

[22] Cf. Graham Twelftree, *Jesus the Exorcist: A Contribution to the Study of the Historical Jesus* (Peabody, MA: Hendrickson Publishers, 1993); Elmo Nauman, Jr., *Exorcism through the Ages* (New York: Philosophical Library, 1974); and Matthew Linn and Dennis Linn (eds.), *Deliverance Prayer* (New York: Paulist Press, 1981).

[23] For a brief anthropological account of exorcism in Mexican (Yucatan) Pentecostalism set within a theory of religion, see Felicitas D. Goodman, *How About Demons? Possession and Exorcism in the Modern World* (Bloomington and Indianapolis: Indiana University Press, 1988), ch. 4.

Pentecostal elements can also be clearly identified. These include reliance on the charism of discernment of spirits which is understood to be available especially to those ritual exorcists—whether laypersons or ministers—who have been filled with or have received the Holy Spirit; the presence of the Bible as a sacred and numinous object signifying the power of the divine word to which the demonic is subject; the occasional glossolalic utterance symbolizing the presence and activity of the divine Spirit; the application of anointing oil upon the forehead of the afflicted; and the casting forth of the evil spirit(s) into the abyss, their destined abode. Finally, even during but especially upon successful exorcism, fervent prayer for Spirit-baptism is offered up on behalf of the afflicted one which correlates with the belief that a body inhabited by the Holy Spirit provides no 'room' for habitation by evil spirits.[24]

Asian Pentecostal exorcisms deviate little from these basic forms with the exception that one gets the impression the ritual practices exude peculiarly local flavours. The rites of exorcism in Pentecostalism in India and in Korea, for example, include additional components which synthesize the biblical materials and the indigenous Hindu and shamanistic traditions. Thus congregational worship including features such as rounds of mantra-like incantations of biblical phrases, the visualisation of healing through the spiritual gift of faith, animated hand gestures and resounding handclaps symbolizing the reversal of fright which chases away demons[25] and the repetitious pronouncement of formulaic blessings on the individual are all important aspects of the deliverance ministry.[26] Of course, both Indian and Korean Pentecostals emphatically deny charges of syncretism and insist on the biblical bases of their practices via a concordistic hermeneutic.

Ultimately, the goal in Asian Pentecostal exorcisms is deliverance from oppression by the powers of darkness in all of its forms. Symptoms of demonic presence and activity include physical illnesses, emotional imbalance, mental disturbances, financial troubles, sleeplessness accompanied by nightmares, and other such debilitating phenomena. Successful exorcisms usually mean

---

[24] See, e.g. Francis McNutt, *Deliverance from Evil Spirits: A Practical Manual* (Grand Rapids: Chosen Books, 1995), and L.G. McClung, Jr, 'Exorcism', in Stanley M. Burgess, Gary B. McGee and Patrick H. Alexander (eds.), *Dictionary of Pentecostal and Charismatic Movements* (Grand Rapids: Zondervan Publishing House/Regency Reference Library, 1988), 290-94.

[25] Cf. Job 27.23.

[26] See e.g. Lionel Caplan, 'The Popular Culture of Evil in Urban South India', in David Parkin (ed.), *The Anthropology of Evil* (Oxford, UK, and New York, NY: Basil Blackwell, 1985), 110-27, esp. 122-23; Michael Bergunder, 'Miracle Healing and Exorcism: The South Indian Pentecostal Movement in the Context of Popular Hinduism', *International Review of Mission* 90 (2001), 103-12; and Harvey Cox, *Fire from Heaven: The Rise of Pentecostal Spirituality and the Reshaping of Religion in the Twenty-First Century* (Reading, MA: Addison-Wesley, 1995), 218-28.

wholeness of mind, body, soul and spirit The healed individual gives testimony to the life-transforming power of the Holy Spirit and is reintegrated into the social and ecclesial communities at large.

Asian Buddhism and the Demonic

Christians as a whole and Pentecostal Christians in particular, of course, are not the only ones who have wrestled with the reality of the demonic. In what follows I want to examine the Asian religious consciousness through the lens of Buddhist demonologies. I begin with textual Buddhism and proceed to an examination of how this has been assimilated into popular beliefs and practices specifically as revealed in indigenous rites of exorcism. The conclusion of this section asks about the articulation and explication of the demonic in the Buddhist worldview.

Textual/Doctrinal Issues in Buddhist Demonology

To begin with, an important distinction needs to be made. It is noteworthy that the Asian mind distinguishes between the demonic and the category of evil.[27] Demons are not inherently evil in and of themselves, especially since, according to the Buddhist notion of dependent origination, nothing possesses essential selfhood. Rather, demons, like all other supernatural and natural beings, are caught in the samsaric process and therefore may be either benign or malevolent depending on the relationship at issue. Alternatively, the case can also be made that the demonic in Buddhism signifies nothing more than the capacity of the human psyche to reify its fears. While I will return to take up this question later, the roots of this notion of the demonic are easily traceable to

---

[27] As Martin Southwold, says, 'There is no concept of radical evil in Buddhism'. If, that is, we distinguish between evil as 'bad', and evil as 'radically horrific'. Is it then the case that 'Radical evil is associated with demonology, which is itself associated with theism… [and, specifically] with monotheism?'; See Southwold, 'Buddhism and Evil', in David Parkin (ed.), *The Anthropology of Evil* (Oxford and New York: Basil Blackwell, 1985), 128-41 (138 and 139). For further discussions of the problem of evil in the Asian context, see Medagama Vajiragnana, 'ATheoretical Explanation of Evil in Theravada Buddhism', in William Cenkner (ed.), *Evil and the Response of World Religions* (St. Paul: Paragon House, 1997), 99-108; T.O. Ling, *Buddhism and the Mythology of Evil: A Study in Theravâda Buddhism* (London: George Allen & Unwin, 1962); Arthur L. Herman, *The Problem of Evil and Indian Thought* (Delhi, Varanasi, and Patna: Motilal Banarsidass, 1976); Wendy Doniger O'Flaherty, *The Origins of Evil in Hindu Mythology*, 2nd ed. (Berkeley, Los Angeles, London: University of California Press, 1980); and James W. Boyd, *Satan and Marâ: Christian and Buddhist Symbols of Evil*, Studies in the History of Religions Supplements to Numen 27 (Leiden: E. J. Brill, 1975).

the Indian religious background from which Buddhism emerged. There, the illusoriness of phenomenal experience is posited against the eternal reality of Brahman.

Yet it was this same Hindu background which provided the fertile soil for the emergence of the demonic in Buddhism. The gods of Vedic religion were transmuted over time, and emerged as a pantheon of Buddhist supernatural beings.[28] Early on, the figures Kâma (lit. 'desire'), originally a Vedic deity of sensual love and worldly enjoyment and Yama (lit. 'restraint' or 'death'), originally a Brahmanic deity, were absorbed by Buddhism. What emerged was the notion of a supernatural being, first as a sympathetic onlooker to the laws of karma (especially in the *Anguttara Nikaya*), evolving then into the chief of departed souls (the god of death), and finally, in the post-Nikaya canon, to the 'king of the law' who judges and dispenses punishment.[29] Thus the development of the premier Buddhist symbol of the demonic—Mâra—as that of tempter who arouses desires which lead to death.

It is in this context that the richness and complexity of Mâra in the Buddhist scriptures is to be understood.[30] To begin with, Mâra and his daughters, the devas, oppose the Buddha and the spread of enlightenment (*Digha Nikaya* 2.103-12). He obstructs the practising of meditation, attempts to divert the living out of the eightfold path and hinders the proclamation of the Dharma by appearing in variously attractive (especially the devas) or repulsive guises, often accompanied by disturbing noises and terrifying phenomena (such as landslides or earthquakes). The result is a fourfold characterization of Mâra as *skadhamâra*, *klesarâma*, *devaputramâra*, and *mrtyumâra*. The first is Mâra who epitomizes the conditions of *dukkha*—i.e. the cycles of death and rebirth—and is thereby equated with the wheel of samsara.[31] *Klesarâma* and *devaputramâra* point, respectively, to the internal and external causal aspects of karma-producing acts of defilement. The former is the confusion and perplexity that arises from ignorance and perverse and false views.[32] The latter derives

---

[28] M.M.J. Marasinghe, *Gods in Early Buddhism: A Study in Their Social and Mythological Milieu as Depicted in the Nikâyas of the Pâli Canon* (Sri Lanka: University of Sri Lanka, Vidyalankara Campus, 1974); and Alice Getty, *The Gods of Northern Buddhism: Their History and Iconography*, 2nd ed. (Oxford: Oxford University Press, 1928; reprint, New York: Dover Publications, 1988).

[29] For more on Yama in Vedic and early Buddhist texts, see Alex Wayman, 'Studies in Yama and Mâra', *Indo-Iranian Journal* 3 (1959), 44-73, and 112-31.

[30] On Mara, see, besides Ling and Boyd (cited above), Ernst Windisch, *Mâra und Buddha* (Leipzig: S. Hirzel, 1895); Lowell W. Bloss, 'The Taming of Mâra: Witnessing to the Buddha's Virtues', *History of Religions* 18:2 (1978), 156-76; and Chandra Wikramagamage, 'Mâra as Evil in Buddhism', in William Cenkner (ed.), *Evil and the Response of World Religions* (St. Paul: Paragon House, 1997), 109-15.

[31] Itivuttaka 40, 50, 58.

[32] Udana 3, 33, 38; Anguttara Nikaya 2.17, 52.

from Mâra who obstructs and interrupts by being a deceiver and by inspiring factions.[33] As such, he stands as the enemy of human beings, holding them in bondage. *Mrtyumâra*, finally, synthesizes the various meanings of Mâra as death itself: Death' is both the essential meaning of the concept Mâra and the essential character of all conditions and defilements of samsara. The whole of samsara is characterized by *mrtyumâra'*.[34]

However the Buddha, as the completely awakened one, sees through Mâra and the devas, and is therefore able to counteract all of Mâra's efforts to destroy enlightenment.[35] The path of the Buddha enables others to overcome Mâra.[36] Enlightenment dispels ignorance and chases the darkness away precisely by illuminating the nature of the opposition as Mâra.[37] Thus those who would also wish to subdue Mâra should follow the example of the Buddha and invoke the Dharma. Triumph over Mâra is ensured through the cultivation of wisdom and the practice of mindfulness at the heart of the Eightfold Path.[38] So on the one hand whether or not one conquers Mâra depends on one's practice. On the other hand, however, the Buddha is the ultimately awakened one and it is therefore only through the power of the Buddha and his Dharma that Mâra can be vanquished.

In keeping with Spiro's distinction between the great and little traditions of Buddhism mentioned above, the argument could certainly be made that there exist two types of Mâra references. At the monastic level, Mâra signifies the totality of that which is *dukkha* as well as the entire range of defilements. It therefore serves more highly abstract and catechetical purposes connected with training of novice monks in the practice of meditation. At the level of popular belief and practice, Mâra is a mythological figure in the sense of being pictured in highly imaginative ways. Yet his (and that of the devas') presence and activity amidst the felt *dukkha* of the world of the living is certainly not doubted, nor to be taken lightly. But to begin qualifying Spiro's distinction would be to recognize that the everyday intercourse between the sangha and the laity means a highly fluid notion of Mâra operates, such that both sides understand each other. Further, learned Buddhist intellectuals reaching back to Asanga and Nâgârjuna also referred to Mâra and the deva-figures.[39]

---

[33] Samyutta Nikaya 1.65ff; Vinaya Pitaka 3.69.

[34] Boyd, *Satan and Marâ*, 109.

[35] Digha Nikaya 1:87, 111, 150, 224; 2:127; 3:7, 84, 146.

[36] Sutta Nipata, 733, 1095.

[37] Ling, *Buddhism and the Mythology of Evil*, 53.

[38] Dhammapada 40-46; Majjhima Nikaya 3.88ff.; 3.109ff.; Dhammapada 34-37.

[39] Boyd, *Satan and Marâ*, 131.

At this point it is important to emphasize the cosmological backdrop pertinent to the worldview of both monk and layperson.[40] It is here that what is distinctively Buddhist or Hindu versus that which is rooted in local and indigenous traditions becomes very difficult to sort out.

Depending on the region, one encounters varying numbers of cosmic levels inclusive of heavens, hells, and the earthly abode in between, each replete with their ever-shifting population of natural, spiritual and supernatural beings. Deities in the latter category number over five hundred and include Buddhas, bodhisattvas, goddesses, defenders or protectors, arhats, and a variety of devas.[41] The categories of protectors and devas, however, contain morally ambiguous beings, at times designated gods, at other times demigods, demons, devils, or monsters, sometimes each of these pertaining to the same being albeit not at the same time. And this dynamic cosmology is easily correlated with canonical Pali Buddhism insofar as the latter distinguishes twelve classifications of Mâra according to the threefold division of *skandha* (the human sense aggregates), *dhatu* (the elements of nature), and *ayatana* (the various spheres of the cosmos). Minimally, Mâra and the devas as symbols of the demonic are understood as personal beings on the human plane, even while retaining supernatural deity-like features possessed by heavenly beings at the cosmic level as well as demonic features possessed by creatures of the hellish underworld.

Yet in the Buddhist cosmology, each of these worlds interpenetrates with the others. Because of the complexities involved in identifying 'who's who' in the Buddhist cosmos, it will be more helpful for us to understand the symbolic function of Mâra within the Buddhist conceptualization of the unseen spiritual world. Here the *Petavatthu* is of some assistance.[42] While most scholars agree that the *Petavatthu* is a relatively late compilation, perhaps c.100-200 CE, it nevertheless reflects the popular Buddhist concern with karmic retribution in the afterlife. *Petas*—Pali, or *pretas* in Sanskrit, literally meaning 'he who has gone forth', or 'he is completely gone herefrom' or 'the departed one'[43]—are

---

[40] Two helpful works in this regard are W. Randolph Kloetzli, *Buddhist Cosmology: Science and Theology in the Images of Motion and Light* (Delhi: Motilal Banarsidass, 1989); and Akira Sadakata, *Buddhist Cosmology: Philosophy and Origins*, trans. Gaynor Sekimori (Tokyo: Kôsei Publishing, 1997).

[41] The number 500 plus comes from J. Deniker, 'Introduction' to Getty, *The Gods of Northern Buddhism*, xlix; cf. L.A. Waddell, 'Demons and Spirits (Buddhist)', in James Hastings (ed.), *The Encyclopedia of Religion and Ethics*, 13 vols. (New York: Scribner's, 1910-), 571-72.

[42] See the 'Introduction' to the *Petavatthu* in I.B. Horner (ed.), *The Minor Anthologies of the Pali Canon*, part IV, *Petavatthu: Stories of the Departed*, trans. H.S. Gehman (London and Boston: Pali Text Society/Routledge & Kegan Paul, 1974).

[43] Bimala Churn Law, *The Buddhist Conception of Spirits*, 2nd ed. (Sonarpur Varanasi, India: Bhartiya Publishing House, 1974 reprint), 1.

distinguishable between those who are higher (devas) as opposed to lower (*petas*) and those who are happy (*vimanavatthu*) versus unhappy (*petavatthu*). Those in the latter categories compare well with the demonic as popularly conceived. The form of these *petas* is frequently repulsive, e.g. as in the physiognomy of a pig representing those who were gluttons in their previous life;[44] a foul-smelling, cancerous mouth representing habitual liars;[45] or a woman described as having a smelly, ugly, filthy body swarming with flies, inexorably thirsty but without anything to drink and subsisting only on the flesh of her dead son mixed with pus and blood—all of which combine as retribution for her causing the miscarriage of her husband's other wife through taking a false oath.[46] Yet in each case, the *petas* are more suffering spirits burdened in the afterlife with the effects of their own karma than they are malevolent beings.

The purpose of the *Petavatthu*, however, is more important than the gory details. Its goal is to establish the ritual of gifts to the Sangha as an efficacious means of releasing *petas* from their unhappy state. The various *vatthus* (stories) therefore contrast the merit earned by those who have been generous in a correct manner to the holy men or the unfortunate, with the demerit of those who have not been. The contrast is supposed to shape the response of the readers toward right action and right karma. In this way, social reciprocity between layperson and monk is advocated since the feeding of monks results in an accumulation of merit and a more desirable afterlife.[47] The primary thrust of the *Petavatthu* is therefore not to show the way to Nirvana, but to motivate the masses toward the sowing of good seeds so as to avoid the woeful existence of condemnation as wandering and tormented ghosts in the next life.

And yet, as Morris Opler points out, such motivational techniques betray the fact that even at the popular level most Asians do not believe in karma as an iron law. Rather misfortune, sickness, and other stresses and anxieties are caused just as much by supernatural beings such as petas, devas, or ghosts—understood primarily to be unhappy departed ancestors—as they are by the unrighteous deeds of one's previous life. It is only because this is the case that it is possible for one to improve one's situation not only through good deeds but also through spirit-possession, exorcisms, placating one's ancestors,

---

[44] Sukarapeta 1:2.

[45] Putimukhapeta 1:3.

[46] Pancaputtakhadakapeta 1:5.

[47] Note that the object of the gifts are always bhikkhus, the Sangha, or other lay devotees of the Buddha, not just any person. As Law points out: 'even gifts without measure of untold wealth to ordinary denizens of the earth can never produce the same effect as the gift of a small thing to a venerable follower of the Buddhist persuasion' (*The Buddhist Conception of Spirits*, 107). This is, then, what legitimizes and even encourages the mendicant lifestyle of the renunciant.

etc.[48] This sets the stage for our consideration of Asian religious rituals of exorcism whereby the demonic is confronted, engaged, and vanquished—Buddhist style!

The Praxis of Buddhist Exorcisms

The foregoing has shown how Mâra (along with the devas and the *petas*) symbolizes all that opposes human well-being and wholeness in this life and in the hereafter, as well as how it functions soteriologically and structurally in Buddhist societies. In both cases, the way forward for Buddhists is through the Buddha and his Dharma. Mâra and the Buddha are therefore intimately linked as opposing forces played out in the human realm.[49] Insofar as the religious consciousness of Asia has imbibed the spirit of Buddhism, it is thereby coloured by the dynamics of the confrontation between the forces of Mâra leading to bondage on the one hand and that of the Buddha leading to liberation on the other. I propose to examine this cosmic struggle as particularized in two Buddhist traditions of exorcism: the Theravadin in Sri Lanka, and the Mahâyâna in Tibet. The following will present highly condensed summaries of the available ethnographic literature.

THERAVADA BUDDHISM IN SRI LANKA

Theravada Buddhism is itself a complex tradition with various faces spread out throughout South and Southeast Asia. Any attempt to understand Theravadin notions of the demonic would necessarily have to take into account data stretching from Sri Lanka to Myanmar (formerly Burma) and Thailand.[50] The following discussion focuses on exorcism in Sinhalese Buddhism, which is itself dynamic and complex.

---

[48] See Morris E. Opler, 'Spirit Possession in a Rural Area of Northern India', in William A. Lessa and Evon Z. Vogt (eds.), *Reader in Comparative Religion: An Anthropological Approach* (Evanston, IL, and White Plains, NY: Row, Peterson and Company, 1958), 553-66.

[49] This interconnectedness is seen in Kamitsuka Yoshiko, 'The Concept of Mâra and the Idea of Expelling Demons', trans. Amy Lynn Miller and Thomas H. Peterson, *Taoist Resources* 6:2 (1996), 30-50.

[50] Burmese Buddhism has been discussed in detail by Spiro in *Buddhism and Society*, and *Burmese Supernaturalism*, expanded ed. (Philadelphia: Institute for the Study of Human Issues, 1978). Thai Buddhism is treated extensively by Stanley Jeyaraja Tambiah, *Buddhism and the Spirit Cults in North-East Thailand* (Cambridge: Cambridge University Press, 1970), and *The Buddhist Saints of the Forest and the Cult of Amulets: A Study in Charisma, Hagiography, Sectarianism, and Millennial Buddhism*, Cambridge Studies in Social Anthropology 49 (Cambridge: Cambridge University Press, 1984). See also Donald K. Swearer, *The Buddhist World of Southeast Asia* (Albany, NY: SUNY Press, 1995).

The centrality of the Pali scriptures to Sinhalese Buddhism accounts in part for the basic features of its demonology and its rites of exorcism.[51] In a complex, multitiered cosmos, human health and prosperity is most immediately implicated by the activity of various deities, devas, and *petas* (*yakkas*). When afflicted, the Sinhalese seek out various healers including holy men, Buddhist monks, astrologers, oracles, priests, traditional medicine men, and exorcists (*edura*). If the problem is diagnosed as originating from demonic sources, rituals of exorcism are performed.

Exorcism rituals are elaborate events among the Sinhalese. These ceremonies follow a conventional order that includes the following elements: acknowledgement of the supreme deities (Vishnu, Shiva, Brahma) via the mystical *om*; greeting of the Buddha; addressing the deity or *peta/yakka* concerned; chanting the proper mantra, usually in the incomprehensible formulae of Sanskrit, Elu or other (e.g. Tamil) languages, identified to deal with the issue at hand and the particular deity or demon responsible for it; various propitiatory or exorcism actions, as appropriate; affirmation of *âsvahâ* or its cognates, indicating approval of the recitation, e.g. 'this will be good' (a parallel to the Christian 'amen'); the application of *yantras* which function as protective amulets; and closing by reverencing the Buddha. The mantras and chants are especially crucial, being understood to work variously—e.g. because the Buddha answers the chant exercised in faith; because of the powers inherent in the Buddha's name, teachings, and words; because the chanter abides by or promises to abide 'in' the Buddha's precepts; or even because the chanters/utterers are empowered through the ritual process to transform themselves and their situations.[52]

Yet this skeletal outline is itself misleading as it does not tell half the story of what transpires during the exorcism. As extended events, they include dramatic,

---

[51] For full accounts, see Paul Wirz, *Exorcism and the Art of Healing in Ceylon* (Leiden: E. J. Brill, 1954), and Bruce Kapferer, *A Celebration of Demons: Exorcism and the Aesthetics of Healing in Sri Lanka* (Bloomington: Indiana University Press, 1983). For shorter accounts, consult Michael M. Ames, 'Magical-animism and Buddhism: A Structural Analysis of the Sinhalese Religious System', *Journal of Asian Studies* 23 (1964), 21-52, and 'Tovil: Exorcism by White Magic', *Natural History* 87:1 (1978), 42-48; John Halverson, 'Dynamics of Exorcism: The Sinhalese Sanniyakuma', *History of Religions* 10:4 (1971), 334-59; Lorna Rhodes Amarasingham, 'The Misery of the Embodied: Representations of Women in Sinhalese Myth', in Judith Hoch-Smith and Anita Spring (eds.), *Women in Ritual and Symbolic Roles* (New York and London: Plenum Press, 1978), 101-26; and Tissa Kariyawasam, 'The Deities and Demons in the Folklore of the Sinhala Buddhists', *Dialogue*, New Series 17:1-3 (1990), 82-90.

[52] Cf. Spiro, *Buddhism and Society*, 147-53. As Swearer notes, 'Even in the Pali texts themselves the Buddha is said to have approved chanting the Karaniya Metta Sutta to ward off evil spirits...' (*The Buddhist World of Southeast Asia*, 27). Contemporary speech-act theory helps us understand how the Buddhist scriptures are used as well as how they are authorized and expected to be used by the faithful Buddhist.

musical, dance and comic components alongside traditional spirit possession activity. The exorcists appear in terrifying demonic masks and outfits that symbolize the offending party. They are confronted, scolded, and tamed by both the exorcist and the congregation, as it were, before being restored to their rightful place in the cosmic order. Thus the demons are reminded of their subservient role, especially to the Buddha, and are rejected as illegitimate intruders into the realm of human affairs.[53]

Sinhalese exorcisms are therefore designed to unveil the true, benign nature of the demons. Through the ceremony, death is itself ritualized, deceived (as it has deceived), banished (with regard to the fear of death), and reassimilated (in recognition of human finitude and frailty). The goal is the healing of the individual and his or her restoration back toward normal participation in the community.

MAHÂYÂNA BUDDHISM IN TIBET

Similar doctrinal and ritual structures can be detected in the complexities of Tantric or Tibetan Buddhism.[54] A ritualistic and magical tradition focused primarily on this-worldly benefits, Tantric Buddhism is the convergence of indigenous Tibetan elements and almost all of the Brahmanical and Hindu deities into the stream of Mahâyâna beliefs and practices as the latter spread eastward during the first few centuries of the common era.[55] The pantheon of deities, demons and other supernatural beings is even more bewildering in this context. Demonic figures are especially wrathful and terrifying, including vampires, witches, zombies, goblins, and other malignant spiritual beings. Tibetans turn to lamas, Buddhist monks and priests and other specialists for help with their afflictions, misfortunes and other tragedies.

Religious ceremonies either appease or exorcise the responsible demons. Yet the Tibetan background also serves to put a specific spin both on the ceremonial features themselves and on what is assumed to occur during the ritual process. Generally, Tibetan exorcisms include sacrificial objects and

---

[53] See Kapferer, *A Celebration of Demons*, esp. ch. 6, 'The Demonic Illusion: Demons and the Cosmic Hierarchy', 111-28.

[54] On demonology and exorcisms in Tibetan Buddhism, see Réne de Nebesky-Wojkowitz, *Oracles and Demons of Tibet: The Cult and Iconography of the Tibetan Protective Deities* (S-Gravenhage and The Hague: Mouton & Co., 1956); Sherry B. Ortner, 'The White-Black Ones: The Sherpa View of Human Nature', in James F. Fisher (ed.), *Himalayan Anthropology: The Indo-Tibetan Interface* (The Hague and Paris: Mouton Publishers, 1978), 263-85; and Edwin Bernbaum, 'Wrathful Deities', *Parabola* 6:4 (1981), 56-61.

[55] On the eastward movement of the Mahayana tradition, see Matsunaga Yâkei, 'From Indian Tantric Buddhism to Japanese Buddhism', in Minoru Kiyota (ed.), *Japanese Buddhism: Its Tradition, New Religions and Interaction with Christianity* (Tokyo and Los Angeles: Buddhist Books International, 1987), 47-54.

offerings, oracular possession, prophetic trances (a type of shamanism), various methods of divination, destructive magic as well as protection against black magic, and the rite of 'weathermaking'. Further, because demons (*geg*, lit. 'hindrances') are considered to symbolize resistant and oppositional realities both external and internal to the afflicted, the practice of *chod*—'cutting off'—is designed to assist the yogi to understand the illusory and deceptive capacity of the mind. Visualisation of the slicing up of the body represents the letting go and detachment from the illusory self, including that which is symptomatic— whether in the form of illness, death, or other phenomena—of the presence and activity of the demonic. The goal in these cases is liberation not only of the self but also of the demonic 'others', considered as they are along with all sentient beings to be in the samsaric process and therefore deceived but capable also of eventual awakening.

The interrelatedness between the realm of the demonic and that of the Buddha is clearly observable in way in which the *Heart Sutra* is used by Tibetan exorcists.[56] Redacted at some point during the first few centuries CE, the central point of the sutra is that the awakened sage recognizes the emptiness of all things, including all discriminations of the mind and perceptions of the senses. Awakened ones are therefore those whose 'minds are without obstruction' and, as such, without fear.[57]

It is not difficult to see, then, how in the Tibetan setting the *Sutra* functions as an extended mantra against the demonic. It is chanted up to 252 times during each fully completed ritual within all four major schools of Tibetan Buddhism. The officiant begins by setting in place a painting or statue of the Buddha, whose authority he assumes, surrounded by multiple images, icons, and representations of the otherwise invisible Mâras or the afflicting demon(s). Throughout the ritual, offerings, gifts and absolutions, including an effigy of the patron seeking relief, are offered the demon(s) which serve in part as the ransom whereby they are appealed to to release the oppressed party. Handclaps are strategically located along with the physical turning around of the Mâra images and accumulating offerings and gifts outward, facing away from the Buddha, after every nine repetitions of the *Sutra*. This signifies the gradual expelling of the demonic Mâras from the patron who has come under the

---

[56] For introductory material to the *Heart Sutra*, see Donald S. Lopez, Jr, *The Heart Sutra Explained: Indian and Tibetan Commentaries* (Albany, NY: State University of New York Press, 1988), 3-8. The following draws from Lopez's *Elaborations on Emptiness: Uses of the eart Sutra* (Princeton: Princeton University Press, 1996), 216-38, and 'Exorcising Demons with a Sutra', in Donald Lopez, Jr. (ed.), *Religions of Tibet in Practice* (Princeton: Princeton University Press, 1997), 511-26.

[57] The text of the *Heart Sutra* is most easily accessible in Edward Conze, *Buddhist Scriptures* (London: Penguin Books, 1959), 162-64; the translation I quote here is from Lopez's *Elaborations on Emptiness*, vii.

protection of the Buddha. At various moments throughout the ritual, the demons are identified by name, rebuked, and exorcized. At the end of this exhausting ritual, a benediction is pronounced as well as a dedication: 'By coming under the power of the four [Mâras] in this existence, one is bereft of happiness and tormented by millions of suffering. Until one attains the vajra-like samâdhi, this rite is an amazing method of exorcism'.[58]

In each case—whether it be through techniques of visualisation, or through the ritual use of a sutra—the Buddhist soteriological structures are fairly clear. The realm of the demonic is the source of human disease, but yet remains subservient to the power of the Buddha and his Dharma. The latter serve as a means of righting the disorder rampant in the cosmos, and of restoring the desired physical, psychological, mental, social and spiritual order. And central to the ritual process is the combination of exorcism as well as the illumination or awakening of the mind to reality and to the truth of the Dharma.

Buddhist Traditions and the Hermeneutics of Demonology

In limiting our inquiry to the Sinhalese and Tibetan cases, we have not even begun to wrestle with the varieties of East Asian Buddhism and the complexities that attend understandings of the demonic that are inextricably woven into millennia-old traditions of ancestor veneration and worship. What are we to make of this array of data? In this section, I want to pose the hermeneutical question to Buddhism. This is also at the same time necessarily ontological and at least demonological (if not even theological) insofar as questions of meaning cannot be divorced from questions of reality and questions of truthfulness. In what follows, then, I will attempt to correlate interpretations of the demonic suggested by Buddhist practitioners themselves with those suggested by students of Buddhism in Asia.

In my own survey of the literature I believe I have uncovered five broad categories of responses to the question: How do Asian Buddhists understand the demonic and what do they really believe about it? I will describe these briefly in no particular order. The overlap that is discernible at various places, however, means that the following should be considered as a heuristic sketch that anticipates the cross-cultural and interreligious theology of the demonic which I will develop in section three.

First, at the popular level, demons are real beings who cause sickness, misfortune and tragedy in the world of the living. More often than not, demonic entities are understood as unfulfilled spirits of deceased ancestors who, because of untimely death or unfortunate circumstances surrounding death, have not been adequately laid to rest and therefore return to haunt their descendants. In this view, intercourse between the demonic and human realms is a given. If the

---

[58] Quoted in Lopez, 'Exorcising Demons with a Sutra', 515.

offending spirit is identified as an ancestor of the family, appropriate measures are taken to appease and placate the disturbed spirit in order to alleviate the situation; if the offending spirit is identified as either a complete or relative stranger to the family lineage, then exorcism is in order.

The next three views are interrelated and pertain more to the Buddhist intelligentsia, although reflective lay Buddhists are aware of some of them to a greater or lesser degree and may even espouse varying versions of each view at some level. I call them the non-dualist, the psychological, and the skilful means views. The *non-dualist* view is a logical extension of the dynamic cosmologies of Buddhism with their interdependent gods, demons and other sentient beings. Especially in the Mahâyâna tradition, the fluid movement between the various realms of heavens, earth and hells correlated with the emerging conviction that heaven is in some sense equivalent to hell and that samsara is nirvana, and vice-versa. The result is that ultimately there is no ontological divide between the divine and the demonic. As such, demons, along with all other things, are codependently originated phenomena. This means that demons are not essentially morally wicked, malevolent, or evil. Rather each demonic manifestation is an aspect of consciousness that is finally non-dual.

The *psychological* view sees the demonic as projections of the mind. This was clearly realized by the twelfth century Tibetan Buddhist monk, Milarepa, who sought to understand why traditional exorcism techniques did not work against the threatening demons. Milarepa eventually dispelled his 'tormentors' by way of recognizing them for what they were: projections of his own mind, ultimately of the same nature of luminosity and emptiness.[59] This connects well with Sinhalese understandings of the trickery and illusions represented by the demonic. Buddhists, however, do not then see the demonic as simply illusory. Given the non-dualism between mind and reality, elements of consciousness are just as real as is being confronted by a tiger or a samurai warrior. This means that how one responds to each reality one confronts at the level of consciousness is just as important, and in fact intrinsic to, how one responds ritually (through exorcisms or otherwise), existentially and practically, since each response is not only to the demonic but also to oneself and one's total situation.

The *skilful means* view builds on the Buddhist doctrine of *upaya*, the notion that different persons at different times and places are aided by different techniques in their quest for enlightenment. In this scheme, the Buddha's Dharma depicts Mâra as one of the ways of getting disciples to move forward in their cultivation of enlightenment. In fact, the Buddha himself can be manifest in both divinely glorious and demonically hideous forms, although perhaps at different moments. The Sinhalese ritual clearly demonstrates the

---

[59] On Milarepa, see Judith Simmer-Brown, 'Inviting the Demon', *Parabola* 22:2 (1997), 12-19.

trickery involved in exposing the false identity of the demonic even while unveiling the true reality of the Buddha. The benediction following the Tibetan ritual of exorcism reflects the conviction that chanting the *Heart Sutra* is the best one can do not only to deal with demonic intrusions into one's life now, but also to move one along toward the ultimate goal of enlightenment. Demons are therefore manifestations of the wheel of samsara and serve to inspire living human beings to attain better rebirths and ultimately to escape rebirth altogether. Both groups of sentient beings need to treat each other appropriately in order to further their own soteriological goals.

Inevitably, then, Buddhists who believe Mâra to be *upaya* have perennially exercized what might be called a hermeneutic of demythologization regarding their understanding of the demonic.[60] Thus Mâra is considered to be a bridge to move one from Hindu or other popular demonological beliefs toward a Buddhist metaphysical view of reality. Or Mâra represents the realm of samsara that hinders the realisation of nirvana. Or Mâra captures the experience of evil as emergent from both within and yet, mysteriously, also confronts one from without. Or Mâra serves as a focal symbol that reinforces the personal and social responsibility to participate in the cosmic battle against the unholy. In all of these, Mâra provides an entire conceptual explanatory framework by which one not only understands the experience of *dukkha*, but also is shown how such can be overcome. Fundamentally, then, the Tathagata takes on different, oftentimes demonic, forms in order to save the diversity of persons in the Asian continent. In this as well as the other two 'elitist' demonologies, the demonic serves primarily as a soteriological category, both with regard to this life and the one to come.

The fifth and last category of responses approaches the question of what the demonic means from a socio-structural and socio-political perspective. Here, the suggestions of cultural anthropologists like Spiro regarding the demonic in Burmese society may also be pertinent elsewhere, including beyond the confines of the world of Buddhism. Spiro proposes that

> nats [the Burmese *petas* or departed dead] are associated with, literally, every structural level of traditional Burmese society, beginning with the individual, and proceeding through the ascending levels of household, kinsmen, village, district,

---

[60] In my view, 'demythologization' adequately describes, in essence, the following summary of Buddhist responses drawn from Ling, *Buddhism and the Mythology of Evil*, 162-64. Previously, Ling writes, 'Satan and Mâra are symbols; this means that their function is principally to facilitate a transition of viewpoint for those accustomed to thinking in demonic terms, rather than to embody absolute truth. The mythological figures are means to an end, rather than ends in themselves' (90). Interestingly, it is also arguable that Buddhists were much more adept at demythologizing their symbols for evil early on than Christians, perhaps due to the analytical bent of Buddhist intellectuals and to the historical bent of Christians.

region and nation. According to this analysis there is a perfect fit between the nat structure and the social structure.... Taken, then, as a political relationship, the relationship between nat and people is one between lord and subjects, which, for traditional Burma...is a despotic relationship.... Being despotic they evoke the same sentiments evoked by government. These sentiments can be easily expressed. Since they cause trouble, avoid them; if they cannot be avoided, placate them; if their assistance is desired, bribe (propitiate) them.[61]

The reality of the demonic is here correlated with the oppressive socio-economic and political conditions under which Buddhists all over Asia exist. Again, however, that does not mean that the demonic are purely symbolic or imaginary realities. Considered in this framework, rituals of exorcism do reorder the Buddhist social life and relationships. Therefore, to my mind, to say that this is a reductionist interpretation of Buddhist demonology misses the point. The issue in the light of non-dual Buddhism is not whether or not demons exist, but how they exist, what are their functions, and how they can and should be dealt with.

Toward a Pentecostal/Christian and Cross-Cultural Demonology

I want to emphasize that the comparative theological project I am exploring here is motivated by the quest for understanding and the possibility of experiencing transformation that comes from such understanding. In fact, in agreement with the Dutch Pentecostal theologian, Jean Jacques Suurmond, I would say that the outpouring of the Spirit is precisely what enables humans to encounter and engage others, including religious others, in deep and authentic ways.[62] Having said that, I also need to acknowledge both the difficulty of doing comparative theology and comparative religion in the postmodern world and Jonathan Z. Smith's contention that, historically, comparative projects have always been driven by apologetic purposes, even if these are unannounced.[63] Any apologetic motivations on my part, however, are consciously secondary to my stated intentions. Whether or not other Pentecostals can agree with me on this issue is an important matter, but one which I cannot address here.

My concluding reflections have necessarily to be brief in this already overly lengthy paper. Here, I want to draw some phenomenological comparisons, probe the contrasts within the larger soteriological framework of both traditions

---

[61] Spiro, *Burmese Supernaturalism*, 131, 138.

[62] Suurmond, *Word and Spirit at Play: Towards a Charismatic Theology*, trans. John Bowden (Grand Rapids: Eerdmans, 1994), 201.

[63] See esp. Smith, *Imagining Religion: From Jonestown to Babylon* (Chicago: University of Chicago Press, 1983), and *Drudgery Divine: On the Comparison of Early Christianities and the Religions of Late Antiquity* (Chicago: University of Chicago Press, 1990).

and then pose the hermeneutical question regarding the demonic from a Christian perspective. Again, the latter is also at the same time necessarily ontological and certainly theological. Since I am first and foremost a Christian theologian rather than a buddhologist or even orientalist, the following shifts from asking or answering questions for Buddhists to doing so for Christians. The overarching question taken up in this final section is what a cross-cultural and more specifically Buddhist-Christian theology of the demonic looks like from a Pentecostal and pneumatological perspective.

Comparisons and Contrasts:
From Phenomenology toward a Soteriology of the Demonic

Phenomenologically, there are many similarities, at least on the surface, which are observable between Christian and Buddhist views of the demonic. Members in both traditions believe there is more to reality than meets the eye and engages the senses. In fact, this supernatural realm is intrinsically interrelated with the material world, and this with regard to both this-worldly and other-worldly matters of concern. The demonic is often, if not always, the source of the experience of evil, suffering and *dukkha* in general. It is therefore to be resisted and, in dire cases, to be exorcized.

Exorcisms also display phenomenological similarities. In both traditions, a supreme power is recognized: that of Jesus by the Holy Spirit and that of the Buddha through the Dharma and the sangha; the invocation of their respective names are central; the identification of the offending spirits is standard fare; mantra-like repetitions of various phrases of worship and exorcism formulas are commonplace; visualization is frequently employed; and the clap and other physical gestures are manifest. Christians emphasize baptism (in water for non-Pentecostals and in the Spirit for Pentecostals) and a life of discipleship in the way of Jesus as an ongoing antidote, while Buddhists emphasize the importance of living according to Buddhist precepts and walking the Eightfold Path.

On the other side, the differences between both traditions should not be overlooked and may in fact be more important for carving out a cross-cultural and interreligious theology of the demonic. These differences can be best sketched as cosmological/theological and soteriological. According to the former, the tensions in both traditions between dualism and monism are clearly evident. For Pentecostals, the demonic is conceived realistically, even if demonic power is itself finally subservient to the divine. In the Christian tradition, there is a clearer penultimate dualism between, for example, good and fallen (or demonic) angels and an emergent distinction between the latter category of spiritual beings and the spirits of the dead. Ultimately, however, God is supreme over both the living and the dead as well as over the devil and his minions. Yet even in this case one wonders whether or not there is a point of contact between penultimate dualism-ultimate monism in Christianity and reality as conventional or reality as it is in Buddhism?

At the level of popular mythology—conventional reality, as Buddhists acknowledge it—deities can degenerate into demons and demons can ascend up the spiritual path toward divinisation. Translated into popular practice, deceased human beings may return to haunt the living as demonic spirits or may return to bless the living as benevolent ancestors. At the elitist or enlightened level, gods and demons along with all sentient beings are understood in non-dualistic terms. And, given the centrality of the doctrines of karma and rebirth—both highly complex notions with a variety of Buddhist interpretations, it should be noted—to the overall cosmology, the spirits of the dead, whether that be ancestors, nats, or *petas* etc., become important players in the world of the living (considered, of course, as holistically interconnected with the world of the dead).

Soteriologically, the Christian belief in a personal devil requires a more literal understanding of exorcism. Buddhists, on the other hand, range across the spectrum of seeing exorcism literally as the expelling of demonic beings on the one side to seeing exorcism as a psychological purging of the mind and the dispelling of ignorance and illusion on the other side, with various forms of propitiation and placation of the demonic as well as of spirits of the dead in the middle. Another difference concerns the soteriological function of the demonic in both traditions. Christians do not believe the devil or the powers of darkness can in any way counteract ultimate salvation which rests on the gratuitous providence of God, even while the devil and his minions can, by bringing temptation, trials, tribulation, suffering, and pain, be divine tools to test and strengthen the faith of the believer. Buddhists, on the other hand, see Mâra as supremely concerned with hindering awakening and the attainment of nirvana, and as such an active reality in the samsaric process. This is because, generally speaking, Christians are tempted, as if by external forces, while Buddhists are inclined, as if internally, toward 'evil'; Christians are deceived by external lies while Buddhists are confused and perplexed by obfuscations about reality. In short, Christians take the suffering of life either as provisionally intended by God or as the result of evil forces acting in the world which is basically created good, albeit one that is now fallen due to sin, while Buddhists take life as intrinsically *dukkha*. As James Boyd puts it, 'whereas a dominant characteristic of the Christian mythology could be referred to as a sense of *horrendum* [Satan as darkness], the Buddhist experience may more accurately be characterized by *fascinans* [Mâra as luminousness]'.[64]

---

[64] Cf. James Boyd, *Satan and Marâ*, 144-54 and 166-67 (154).

Interpreting the Demonic:
Toward a Cross-cultural and Interreligious Theology of Evil

A number of hermeneutical strategies can be adopted in moving from phenomenology and soteriology to theology. In what follows, I want to briefly explore an exegetical and an ethical approach to a cross-cultural and interreligious—specifically Buddhist-Christian—theology of the demonic.

One exegetical approach in the context of the Buddhist-Christian dialogue would be to focus on engaging the various scriptural texts from the perspective of the other tradition. Thus John Keenan's Mahâyâna reading of Mark's gospel unveils an extremely suggestive demonology. On Keenan's reading, Jesus' way is the 'middle way', a dialectical but synthetic trek between the emptiness of no-self and dependent co-arising, toward engagement with 'suchness' (reality such as it is). His 'enlightenment' is the realization of the truth both of emptiness at the heart of reality and of dependent co-arising as reality itself. The appropriate response is *not* immersion into either apart from the other which would lead to nihilism (emphasizing emptiness) on the one hand or hedonism (emphasizing dependent co-origination) on the other. Rather enlightenment requires re-engaging the conventionality of dependent co-origination in light of the truth of emptiness. The demonic in Mark, then, symbolizes the reality of emptiness without the realization of dependent co-origination, leading to nihilism portrayed specifically in and through the demoniacs at the synagogue in Capernaum and at the Gerasene tombs, the deaf and dumb boy and even Peter who was rebuked by Jesus.[65] On the other side, of course, is the demonic as exemplified in the hedonistic overindulgence on the sensory pleasures of what arises in this world.

I would ask, in light of Keenan's interpretation, whether it is appropriate to consider the tradition of esoteric (Tantric) Buddhism, which—in reaction to the renunciation tradition of Theravada Buddhism—affirms worldly desires as emancipation itself, even as it insists all things are a manifestation of the Dharmakaya, to be a ready-made conduit for the emergence of the demonic? Thus, its deities (and demons) are 'possessed of anger, desire, passion, and other intense feelings'.[66] Can it be said then that these are those who have

---

[65] John P. Keenan, *The Gospel of Mark: A Mahâyâna Reading* (Maryknoll: Orbis Books, 1995), 67-73, 138-43, 200-04, and 219-22; cf. also Keenan's exegesis on other Markan passages that mention the demons and Satan, 101-13, 179-80.

[66] Sadakata, *Buddhist Cosmology*, 139-40. As Radmila Moacanin puts it, 'In the Tantric system, any worldly pleasure [and, I would add, any worldly displeasure as well], any experience of the senses, any occasion in this world can become an opportunity for enlightenment when wisdom is applied'; 'Tantric Buddhism and Jung: Connections, Similarities and Differences', in Daniel J. Meckel and Robert L. Moore (eds.), *Self and Liberation: The Jung/Buddhism Dialogue* (New York and Mahwah, NJ: Paulist Press, 1992), 275-301 (284).

disregarded the truth of emptiness and immersed themselves fully into the world of dependent co-arising, only to allow the emergence of a pure (demonic) hedonism? Is there, in other words, a hedonistic form of Buddhist manifestation which would be demonic in character? On the other side, is there a nihilistic type of Buddhist renunciation, for example, which might exhibit equally demonic features?

Put in Pentecostal terms, is the oppression of the demonic experienced in Sinhalese and Tantric Buddhism, etc. perhaps an expression of spiritual forces which seek to destroy human life precisely by throwing it out of balance and by inculcating a spirit of fear rather than one of love, power and a sound mind?[67] Alternatively, is the demonic in Buddhism a manifestation of powers of darkness that seek to hinder awakening to the divine gift of life?[68] In this case, the awakening which is to be embraced is not that of the Buddha but that of the prodigal son, whose eyes were opened to the love of the Father. More explicitly, it is the awakening that comes about through the reception of the gospel proclaimed by the power of the Spirit whereby blind eyes are opened, the prisoners are set free and the oppressed are delivered.[69]

For our purposes, it is important to recognize Keenan's main point, which is to emphasize Jesus as a paradigmatic exemplar of how to engage the world (of dependent coorigination) and the demonic. This connects well with Pentecostal exegetical intuitions about the demonic, especially in their focus on the extended ending of the Markan text.[70] Here, the emphasis is on the heralding of the new age, not only in terms of the availability of the good news of salvation to all, but also in the fact that this new age is not solely a spiritual one but a radically material and embodied existence in this world as well. Thus the passing away of the old order and the arrival of the new Kingdom of God is characterized by the signs which accompany believers: casting out of demons in Jesus' name, speaking in new tongues, picking up serpents and drinking deadly poisons without being harmed and healing of the sick.[71]

The results, ultimately, may be characterized either as soteriological or as ethical, depending on the dominant categorical framework that is adopted. For our purposes, however, the fundamental questions become: how does being a follower of Jesus influence the life that one lives and what kind of life is that? This ethical component has been at the forefront of a number of attempts at a comparative Buddhist-Christian demonology.[72] The goal of exorcism is, after

---

[67] Cf. 2 Tim. 1.7.

[68] Cf. Eph. 6.12ff.

[69] Cf. Lk. 4.18.

[70] Mk. 16.9-20.

[71] Mk 16.17-18.

[72] See e.g. Aloysius Pieris, S.J., 'Prophetic Humour and the Exposure of Demons: Christian Hope in the Light of a Buddhist Exorcism', *East Asian Pastoral Review* 32:3/

all, Christian discipleship in the broadest sense, including life empowered by the Holy Spirit. And, from the Buddhist perspective, 'the way to overcome Mâra is the same way that leads to liberation in the Buddhist sense'—i.e. through the Eightfold Path with its three basic criteria for distinguishing between good and evil that include respect for self, respect for others, and the Dharma.[73] In both traditions, this leads logically to an ever-expanding ethical vision, moving out from the preoccupation with oneself toward one's relationships with others, towards a consideration of others on their own terms apart from their relationship with oneself and therefore, potentially, toward an environmental or cosmic ethic. At this level of theological ethics, is it too much to agree with Trevor Ling that, 'Here is to be seen an example of how two major religious traditions may learn from each other; the symbols may illuminate each other: for what they symbolize is better understood in the light of both symbols than in the light of either one of them alone'?[74]

Continuing Questions for the Buddhist-Christian Dialogue

Both the Buddhist and Christian mythologies disclose that there are 'light' as well as 'dark' features to various experiences of evil. Satan is sometimes called Lucifer, disguised as an angel of light, and Mâra is sometimes called the Dark One and associated with 'smokiness' and 'murkiness'. The Christian can speak of bondage to this world just as the Buddhist does of samsara, and the Buddhist mythologically portrays the cause or source of evil as external to oneself just as the Christian does. But whereas the Christian maximizes externality and the sense of *horrendum*, minimizing *fascinans* and humanity's contribution to the power of evil (as viewed within the limited context of the Satan mythology), the Buddhist maximizes the inherent bondage to samsara and the *fascinans* character of it, while minimizing the externality and *horrendum* features of such experiences. Perhaps each tradition, by illuminating different aspects of the existentially known character of evil, when brought together will help us to a fuller understanding on the generic level of the human experience of evil.[75]

I want to close this essay by making one disclaimer and raising a few theological questions from a Pentecostal perspective in the light of the foregoing discussion. The disclaimer is to insist that this paper is only a preliminary attempt to compare and contrast one area of belief and practice across two drastically different traditions which rarely have been considered

---

4 (1995), 178-91, and Brian Tognotti, 'Christian Demonology in the Light of Buddhist Mindfulness', *Dialogue*, New Series 17:1-3 (1990), 91-103.

[73] See Medagama Vajiragnana, 'A Theoretical Explanation of Evil in Theravada Buddhism', 103.

[74] Ling, *Buddhism and the Mythology of Evil*, 93.

[75] Boyd, *Satan and Marâ*, 166-67.

together. Much more work needs to be done on all fronts—empirical, socio-psychological, historical, exegetical, and theological—before we can begin to make confident comparisons and contrasts. The present comparative categories, while helpful in certain respects, remain highly western in origin and with regard to the interests brought to the table (as evidenced in the quotation opening this subsection). Asian voices, both those recently converted and those who are second generation converts (since first generation converts tend to reject all associations with the traditions which they have left) to Christianity from Buddhism (and vice versa) need to be engaged in this discussion.

Three clusters of theological questions in closing. The first concerns the missiological thrust of Christianity in general and of Pentecostalism in particular. The questions here are legion. To what extent is Christian mission to include interreligious dialogue alongside kerygmatic proclamation? What does it mean to contextualize the gospel in any local area—i.e. to be specific to the case studies in this paper, to what degree should the worldview of popular Sinhalese or Tantric Buddhism be considered as a *praeparatio evangelica* or to what degree should those worldviews be demythologized? More generally, in light of the preceding discussion, what exactly is the relationship between Buddhism and Christianity in Asia and elsewhere? And, in all of these questions, what, from the Christian perspective, is the role of the Holy Spirit in the missionizing process and what does it mean for Christians to follow the leading of the Spirit in their living out the gospel?

The second set of questions is the practical one that arises out of the concern of this essay. How should Christians understand and engage the demonic in the Asian context? Should Christian praxis take into account Buddhist approaches to the demonic in Asia? What light does psychological, socio-anthropological and other perspectives on exorcism shed on the nature of the demonic and its presence and activity in the human realm? What exactly is the human condition, both in terms of its material and spiritual dimensions and of their relationship? How are the trials and sufferings of human beings best addressed, such that the human situation is engaged holistically? What does salvation mean, in this life and in the life to come? What does spiritual warfare and warfare prayer mean in a cultural-religious situation where the demonic takes many shapes, forms and guises? How is the once-for-all victory of Jesus Christ over the demonic to be understood and played out in the religious situation of Asia?

This leads, finally, to the theological question underneath this entire discussion. The missiological and pragmatist orientations, however soteriological they may be, in and of themselves lead to reductionist understandings and are finally inadequate to deal with the ontological and theological questions concerning the reality of the demonic. This is because missionary contexts are dynamic and the questions which one generation confronts are not going to be the same as that of succeeding generations.[76] The fact that the two-traditions theory is currently being challenged by those who see Buddhism as a holistic life-and-world view is a case in point about how modern and postmodern perspectives are highlighting the fluidity and interconnectedness of both the questions and the contexts within which questions are being posed. So even to ask whether or not demons are real in our time is not the same question as the same string of words in the premodern context.

Yet a still different question necessarily deals with the reality of the experiences of Christians and Buddhists in Asia and elsewhere. These experiences raise, in turn, the following kinds of strictly theological questions for a cross-cultural, interreligious, and Buddhist-Christian demonology: In light of the ambiguous nature of the demonic in Buddhism and the possibility of even Mâra's ultimate salvation, should Christians perhaps look again at the question of the final end of the demonic in light of Origen's doctrine of *apokatastasis* which has been marginal, at best, in the theological tradition? Does the non-dual emphasis in Buddhism open up new lines of consideration of the demonic as the 'hidden' side of God, perhaps in dialogue with Augustinian, Lutheran, mystical and Neo-Platonic traditions in Christianity? What does the Buddhist doctrine of *upaya* have to tell Christians about their experience of the demonic and what does that mean theologically with regard to the ontological reality of evil? Finally, among other questions (recognizing the difficulty of applying these categories outside of the western context), does the fact that both premodern and postmodern ideas about the demonic have coexisted for two millennia in the world of Buddhist Asia tell us anything about the viability of their coexistence in the western world and what might that mean theologically about *homo religiosus*? On these issues, then, perhaps the religious consciousness of Asia remains a fertile arena for investigation, not only for insight into the human condition in general, but also to further both Buddhist and Christian understandings of the world in both its empirical and spiritual dimensions, and of the relationship of both to that reality which is ultimate.[77]

---

[76] I make this argument in part two of my 'Going Where the Spirit Goes...: Engaging the Spirit(s) in Julie Ma's Pneumatological Missiology', *Journal of Pentecostal Theology*, forthcoming.

[77] My thanks to Robert Beckford (University of Birmingham), Paul Reasoner (Bethel College, St. Paul, MN), Patrick Uhlmann (University of California at Los Angeles), and Bockja Kim (Hong Kong University) for their critical comments on previous drafts of this paper. It is much the better because of their input. Needless to say, remaining errors of fact and interpretation are my own responsibility.

Asian Women and Pentecostal Ministry

Julie C. Ma

According to Jewish custom, the Feast of Pentecost was celebrated only by men. However, both men and women experienced the outpouring of the Holy Spirit on that day.[1] Peter's preaching from the prophet Joel was that 'sons and daughters' would prophesy,[2] and this has since been a key encouragement for women to enter Christian ministry. This was particularly true for those with roots in the nineteenth century Holiness movement.[3] Pentecostals have believed strongly in the notion of the call of God. Both unmarried and married women have worked in various ministry settings primarily to fulfil their sense of calling. They are church planters, preachers, counsellors, teachers and doctors in far-off corners of the world. Their God-given gifts and empowerment are used for particular purposes and tasks, and this sense of divine call was more significant than limitations set by institutions and mission organizations.

In local ministry settings, women are also used effectively. Some women have enormously influenced churches, schools and, in Korea, prayer mountains. Women work hard with their distinctive spiritual gifts and strong commitment. However, often Asian women in general have been deprived of their calling and their potential because their culture has commonly failed to recognize women's leadership qualities and capabilities, both in society and in the church. Although there are some improvements in women's roles in various ways, due to the influence of globalization, full recognition is still minimal.

In this paper I would like to discuss several critical women's issues arising in Asia, such as women's involvement in the mission field, and their ministry in the local setting.

A Reflection on Personal Experience

Becoming a working partner with my husband, I had to experience a rather uncomfortable change. Korean culture expected a pastor's wife to be active at home but not in ministry. However, once we were in the mission field, both

---

[1] Acts 1.14-15; 2.1

[2] Joel 2.28-29.

[3] Barbara Cavaness, 'God Calling: Women in Assemblies of God Mission', *Pneuma: The Journal of the Society for Pentecostal Studies* 16:1 (1994), 49-62.

husband and wife were expected to be equally active in this work. I had to push myself hard so that I would not just remain as an 'indoor mama', just doing house chores. Although I had to push myself, I did not know how far I could go. If I went too far, people might have criticized me. On the other hand, if I remained as a typical Asian woman, keeping myself quiet, I would not have been more than a housewife. The decision was made to stretch myself as much as I could within the opportunity afforded me.

In particular, our ministry among the Kankana-ey tribe in the Philippines has assisted me in obtaining new horizons on women's roles in God's Kingdom. A historical study of the Assemblies of God mission among the tribal group in the mountains in northern Luzon reports the interesting fact that the initial ministry among the Kankana-ey people was started by a single widow missionary from North America, Elva Vanderbout, together with a few local leaders.[4] Until she began her mission in the mountains, no missionaries or local ministers of the denomination had attempted mountain ministry. Vanderbout reached this tribal people with the distinctive Christian message of God's power. Through the gospel of divine power and its manifestation, churches were built and the work was effectively carried out. Her commitment to spread the gospel was remarkable and resulted in bringing many people to Christ.

I want to urge Asian women to find their unique self-identity as Christian women. Many Asian women tend to restrict themselves within their home or to a limited number of areas. I would like to encourage them to liberate themselves from this unjustifiably limited perspective.

Women of the Bible in Ministry

Deborah is an outstanding woman leader in the Old Testament. Judges 4.1-15 notes a story of conquest through her leadership. This narrative is about Israel combating with Canaan, which is understood as a sturdy nation with a strong military force.[5] The Israelites were, for a long period of time, brutally exploited by the Canaanites. The unbearable persecutions of the Canaanites finally caused the Israelites to implore help from God.[6] The brave judge Deborah, the woman who led Israel at this time, determined to do something by leading the battle against Canaan. She commanded Barak, son of Abinoam, to get ten thousand men of Naphtali and Zebulun and direct them to Mount Tabor. The fascinating fact in this description is the human plot incorporated in God's strategy as Deborah said what she heard from God, 'I will lure Sisera, the commander of Jabin's army, with his chariots and his troops to the Kishon

---

[4] Julie Ma, 'Elva Vanderbout: A Woman Pioneer of Pentecostal Mission among Igorots', *Journal of Asian Mission* 3:1 (2001), 121-140.

[5] Arthur E. Cundall, *Judges and Ruth* (Downers Grove, IL: InterVarsity Press, 1968), 88.

[6] Judges 4.

River and give him into your hands'. Deborah revealed her tremendous faith, bravery and skill, all of which enabled her to succeed. She assured herself and Barak of God's victory for her nation.[7] Deborah ordered Barak, 'Go! this is the day the Lord has given Sisera into your hands. Has not the Lord gone ahead of you'. As Deborah prophesied, God routed Sisera, the commander of Jabin's army of Canaan, and all his chariots and army. Sisera deserted his chariot and darted away on foot. Deborah's leadership was recognized in the battle against the Canaanites. Her wisdom was used in the battle to bring the victory. Israel was assured that God was with his people and fought for them.

In the New Testament, although women did not necessarily occupy major positions, they were significantly used by God to complete his purpose. Women who followed the Lord during his ministry witnessed the final moment of his death.[8] Matthew records the account of women who followed Jesus from Galilee to care for his needs, including Mary Magdalene, Mary the mother of James and Joses, and the mother of Zebedee's sons.[9] These women never left the tomb where the body of Jesus was placed, which shows their heart and love for the Lord as against any fear arising from cultural expectations, and in spite of the guards. Matthew notes, 'The angel said to the women, "Do not be afraid, for I know that you are looking for Jesus, who was crucified. He is not here; he has risen, as he said"'. Then the angel commissioned the women to move promptly to Galilee and report to the fearful disciples that the Lord had risen from the dead. On the way there, to their great joy, the women encountered Jesus. He repeated the order to go to Galilee and tell his disciples that he would appear to them. The women received the commission twice, from the angel and from Jesus himself.[10] These women became the messengers who brought the good news of the resurrection of Jesus to the disciples. Although the women never spent much time with Christ, they proved their faith in him to be much stronger than that of the disciples and they were used significantly during Christ's final moments on earth.

Women's Social Issues in Asia

Here, I will highlight just a few issues out of many.

---

[7] Julie Ma, When the Spirit Meets the Spirits: Pentecostal Ministry among the *Kankana-ey* Tribe in the Philippines (Frankfurt-am-Main: Peter Lang, 2000), 166.

[8] Julie Ma, 'A Missionary Challenge to Asian Pentecostals: Power Mission and Its Effect' (Paper Presented in Asian Pentecostal Society Annual Meeting, Manila Philippines, 2000).

[9] Matthew 27.55-56.

[10] Matthew 28.5-7, 10.

The Abuse of Women

In some countries in Asia, women are dehumanized. Although women are faced with more opportunities in society and better treatment in this new century, traditional attitudes towards women persist. Women are not given proper consideration and recognition of their role in society and in the church. Just a few years ago, women were victims of government, military and social oppression. One particular women's organization, the Christian Conference of Asian Women's Concerns Consultation held a conference in Ginowan Seminar House (also known as The Ecumenical Peach Centre), Okinawa, Japan, from 19-25 June, 1992, under the catchwords, 'Called to be Peacemakers'. Participants came from Korea, Japan, Taiwan, Philippines, Hong Kong, Sri Lanka, Australia and Papua New Guinea.[11] Out of the many striking facts reported from this conference, I want to note the issue of the 'dehumanization of women'[12] and give an overview of the abuse of Asian women in the past.

> Through such cruel confinement in refugee camps that their humanity is destroyed (70% of the world's 13 million refugees are women), women killed their babies in Okinawa in World War II, and Korean 'comfort women' committed suicide in Japan. Through abject poverty, women and children in the Philippines, Taiwan, Thailand and other Asian countries have been sold and stolen, and women are being prostituted, especially around military bases and for the entertainment of tourists. These circumstances lead to the perversion of children in military training, and women taking up arms in Sri Lanka where they are encouraged to commit suicide if they are caught.

This gives the impression that women were indeed the victims of war and were heart-broken. What about the current era? Are women less victims and better treated better than in the past? My immediate response is a qualified 'yes'. Being better treated does not necessarily mean being equal with males. I am not talking from a feministic activist's viewpoint but from that of one who believes in justice for all humanity.

In Vietnam, girls have fewer opportunities for the benefits of education than boys. There are basic differences in the opportunities for boys and girls who finish primary schooling to proceed to government secondary school. Places are normally determined by an examination and frequently the girls have lower chances due to their poor performance in the exam. The primary reason for this is that girls spend far more time than boys working at household chores.[13]

---

[11] *Sowing the Grains of Peace: A Resource Handbook for Building Peace* (Okinawa, Japan: Northeast Asia Subregional Women's Consultation Ginowan Seminar, June 1992), 1.
[12] *Sowing the Grains of Peace*, 33.
[13] Margaret McDonald, *Women in Development: Viet Nam* (Manila: Asian Development Bank, 1995), 43.

In 1955, Malaysia formulated the Employment Act for the benefit of workers.[14] This is core legislation regulating all labour relations[15] and some provisions apply in an equal manner to men and women, such as contracts of service, salary, break time, amount of working time, holidays, annual leave, sick leave and so on. Certain aspects of employment, however, are unfavourable to female workers. Against stipulations in the Act, female employees in the private sector are paid lower wages compared to male workers for doing an equal amount of labour.[16] In the public sector, however, women are given equal pay, and a trend has developed that Malaysian women are given increasing opportunities to participate in the national growth of the country in areas of the economy and the work market, as well as better access to education and health.[17]

In China, women encounter unfair treatment when seeking employment. A 1997 investigation approved by an official newspaper for students discovered that female graduates from colleges and universities face greater rejection rates than male graduates in the labour market. Women counted for 34% of total graduates in 1996, but in that year 27 out of 42 government organizations in Beijing declined to interview female candidates for vacancies. According to the Beijing Graduate Employment Consulting Centre, discrimination against women is a social difficulty which can only be resolved when social and economic standards have risen.[18]

Women have gradually progressed into better places and have become better treated than back in the 1940s. However there needs to be greater improvements in women's positions and opportunities, and better recognition in society and even in the church.

Violence Against Women and Girls[19]

The Universal Declaration of Human Rights[20] provides liberty for each individual, male or female, fundamental to human life. For women, these rights have been violated in the following ways: sexual assault, sexual harassment, and verbal mistreatment intended to disgrace them. The employment of

---

[14] Aminah Ahmad, *Women in Malaysia* (Manila: Asian Development Bank, 1998), 12

[15] *Women in Malaysia*, 12

[16] *Women in Malaysia*, 12

[17] *Women in Malaysia*, 4

[18] *Women in the People's Republic of China* (Manila: Asian Development Bank, 1998), 35.

[19] Jeanne Frances I. Illo, *Women in the Philippines* (Manila: Asian Development Bank, 1997), 16.

[20] Rina David and Penny Azarcon de la Cruz, 'Towards Our Own Image: An Alternative Philippines Report on Women and Media', Pamphlet Series 1 (Quezon City: Philippines Women's Research Collective, 1985), 16.

women's bodies to sell cars and other goods objectifies women. Moreover, scenes of rape or other forms of violation against women are needlessly shown in films, soap operas, and comic books.[21]

Men in Korea enter military service at around age 19 or 20. Certain characters of Korean men are reshaped during their military training. The influence of Confucianism on the minds of Korean men is another factor, particularly in the valuing of women. *Sowing the Grains of Peace* well depicts Korea men:

> From an early age, men receive military training and in adulthood they join the army and continue to live in militarized society. From there they acquire militaristic values and ways of thinking. This becomes tied to the Confucious value systems which emphasize the predominance of man over woman. They regard women as objects, with a low position, as assistants or the subdued ones. Assault and battery of wives, discriminatory treatment and low wages at work, human trafficking (kidnapping women for prostitution) sexual torturing, physical violence are committed by men who are deeply influence by militarization.[22]

Some years ago, a policeman in Korea detained a girl student and tormented her sexually and another group of policemen raped a woman. In 1980, a new military policy was introduced called the '35 Policy'. This is to 'subdue people's consciousness through sex, sport and the screen'.[23] Information concerning the use of women in the entertainment industry in South Korea demonstrates that 5-7.5% (or 120,000-150,000) of the female populace is drawn in. This statistic also includes the women who followed the locations of the US Army in Korea.[24]

A Philippine government survey noted that on average, one of every ten women had been forced, and a much smaller percentage had been pressurized to engage in sex with someone. Some of the victims searched for help from places like the Women's Crisis Center,[25] *Lihok Pilipina*, in Cebu City and in Metro Manila, and hospitals like the Philippine General Hospital. It should be noted that physical and sexual exploitation is not only a problem of human rights in a society but also part of an economic issue. Women who work at night report experiences of broken limbs or severe bruising. They often hide the signs of their pain from follow workers.[26]

---

[21] Rina David and Penny Azarcon-de la Cruz, 'Towards Our Own Image: An Alternative Philippines Report on Women and Media', 16.

[22] Jeanne Hayes, *Sowing the Grains of Peace*, 13.

[23] Jeanne Hayes, *Sowing the Grains of Peace*, 13.

[24] Jeanne Hayes, *Sowing the Grains of Peace*. p. 13.

[25] Jeanne Frances I. Illo, *Women in the Philippines*, 17.

[26] Jeanne Frances I. Illo, *Women in the Philippines*, 16-17

Children also are subject to local violence. A survey shows that from 1991-96 as many as 8,355 maltreatment of children cases were reported to the Department of Social Welfare and Development in the Philippines.[27] All victims of child abuse were girls between the ages of 11 and 17, and more than half of the girls had been sexually abused. The victims indicated or showed symptoms of sexually transmitted diseases.[28] Most incidents of child abuse occurred at home while the victims were alone, with the parents being away for work. The majority of the perpetrators were discovered to be male relatives.[29]

A distinctive violent act towards women has been sexual abuse. They became prey to the sexual exploitation of men. I would like to speculate on this issue, concerning how long it will last, and if there are any possible ways to minimize it.

Less Opportunity for Education

Philippine women are fortunate to have the benefit of education. At the national level there are virtually no gender gaps in literacy and school attendance rates, although there are regional variations. For example, about 50% of children drop out before they reach the sixth grade. Among adults, female illiteracy dramatically exceeds male illiteracy. The illiteracy problem in Mindanao can be traced to two factors, with divergent gender effects: the peace and order problem, which has affected school attendance of boys and cultural prescriptions that inhibit the education of girls.[30]

Briefly mentioned earlier, women in Vietnam have little opportunity for education. Poverty is one of the main reasons for not attending school. There is a considerable burden on needy families in sending their children to school. Furthermore, girls in poor families experience severe disadvantages because if parents are forced to take children out of school through financial difficulty they will take out girls before boys.[31]

---

[27] Jeanne Frances I. Illo, *Women in the Philippines*, 17.

[28] University of the Philippines Center for Women's Studies and the United Nations Children's Fund (UCWS/UNICEF), 'Breaking the Silence: The Realities of Family Violence in the Philippines and Recommendations for Change' (A report undertaken by the UCWS foundation, Inc. for Women in Development Interagency Committee Fourth Country Programme for Children, with funding assistance from the United Nations Children's Fund, 1996).

[29] University of the Philippines Center for Women's Studies, the Department of Social Welfare and Development, and the United Nations Children's Fund, 'Today's Girl-Children: Tomorrow's Women' (Info Kit for the launching of the Week of the Girl-Child, 1997).

[30] Jeanne Frances I. Illo, *Women in the Philippines*, 58.

[31] ADUKI Pty, *Poverty in Viet Nam*, April 19, 1995.

In China, according to a survey in 1998, female school enrolments at primary, secondary and higher education levels as a proportion of entire enrolments from 1982-96 show a general improvement in female enrolment over this period. However there is still a gap between male and female enrolment, with the gap broadening as the education level increases.[32]

In some Asian countries such as Japan, Korea, Singapore, Malaysia and Hong Kong, women may have a better opportunity for higher education than women in Muslim countries like Indonesia, who unfortunately have very little opportunity or exposure to higher education.

Selected Asian Women in Pentecostal Ministry

There are many Asian women who sincerely respond to the call of God. I have selected and described four outstanding women (two Koreans and two Filipinas), who had an enormous impact on the Pentecostal church and beyond. Other women's ministries will be noted later in this paper more briefly.

Jashil Choi

Jashil Choi served as associate pastor at the Yoido Full Gospel Church in Seoul, Korea, pastored by Yonggi Cho, her son-in-law. She was born in 1915 in Haeju City in Whang-Hae Province of North Korea during the Japanese occupation. At the age of twelve she and her mother happened to attend a tent revival meeting held by Rev Sung-Bong Lee, a well-known revival preacher in early Korean church history. At this meeting they accepted Christ as their personal Saviour. After moving to Seoul she opened a new business and became successful. However she encountered a tragic incident when her mother and her oldest daughter died with ten days of each other. This incident affected Choi so badly that she had manifold illnesses. She entered the Full Gospel Bible College for theological training for her future ministr[33] and it was here that she met Yonggi Cho and later became his mother-in-law. She was particularly prominent in several ministries.

CHILD EVANGELISM

Since the early days of Bible college, Choi was extensively involved in child evangelism. A motivation for this ministry came from Matthew 5.16, 'Let your light shine before men, that they may see your good deeds and praise your Father in heaven'. Choi had a distinctive gift in approaching children for

---

[32] Asian Development Bank: *Women in the People's Republic of China* (Manila: ADB, 1998), 30.

[33] Jashil Choi, *I Was a Hallelujah Woman* [in Korean] (Seoul, Korea: Seoul Press, 1978), 1-125.

evangelism and her natural ability caused her to draw many children to Christ. Her ministry was normally characterized by intense and earnest prayer. She spent more time in prayer and fasting for effective evangelism than for other forms of ministry. It is well known that her prayer with fasting was a significant support to Yonggi Choi's successful pastoral work leading to the largest congregation in the world.

The church she pioneered with Yonggi Cho in the rural outskirts of Seoul moved to the city centre to accommodate the increasing members. Soon after the move the membership grew to 18,000 and the growth continued in the next seven years. Yonggi Cho did not hesitate to attribute this unprecedented growth primarily to Choi's spiritual insights and gifts. At that time the church became particularly known for its healing ministry.[34]

ESTABLISHING A PRAYER MOUNTAIN:

Choi felt strongly moved to start a prayer mountain. Such an urgent feeling directed her every night to a public cemetery in Osan-ri, close to the border with North Korea, to spend time in prayer. Establishing a prayer mountain in that particular location was not favoured by church leaders, in addition to the financial challenges involved. At the end, however, she prevailed and the prayer mountain was established. This ministry rapidly began to attract people, not only from all over the country, but also from Japan and other parts of the world. Visitors experienced a new and powerful spiritual dimension through prayer with fasting. The Osan-ri prayer mountain became the first international facility for prayer and fasting. Many experienced healing of incurable sicknesses through dedicated and passionate prayer accompanied with fasting. Such news quickly spread throughout the countries and more people visited the prayer mountain.

Certainly fasting is a long Christian spiritual tradition. It is often an ultimate form of earnest and extended supplication. In the Osan-ri Prayer Mountain, some people fasted even for forty days. It is a spiritual wrestling between supplicant and the divine Being.[35]

INTERNATIONAL MINISTRY

Choi's ministry slowly moved beyond Korea and expanded to other nations. The country that she ministered in with great passion was Japan. Choi's anointed message accompanied by the work of the Spirit influenced many Japanese churches and leaders. She also ministered in Thailand, Hong Kong, the United States and Germany. Her ministry was characterized by her passion and openness to a great work of the Holy Spirit. She was particularly motivated

---

[34] Choi., *I Was a Hallelujah Woman*, 355-356.

[35] Julie Ma, 'Korean Pentecostal Spirituality: A Case Study of Jashil Choi', in *Spirit and Spirituality: Essays in Honor of Russell P. Spittler* (London: T & T Clark, forthcoming).

by Acts 1,8, 'But you will receive power when the Holy Spirit comes on you; and you will be my witnesses in Jerusalem and in all Judea and Samaria and to the ends of the earth'.[36]

Seen-Ok Ahn

Seen-Ok Ahn (Kim before her marriage) was born in Pyongyang, now the capital city of North Korea, in 1924. She started attending church as a child, although her parents were not Christians. Her first ministry experience was in an orphanage where she met her husband who took care of the orphans. As the Korean War broke out in 1950, they fled North Korea and moved to the south.[37] *Educational Ministry*: In 1953 Ahn and her husband began to teach war refugee students. This soon grew into a formal Christian school in Daejon City. Today, the ministry comprises six different schools in the city with approximately 8,000 students and 400 teachers.[38] While working in this ministry, God opened a door for her to receive theological training in the United States. Such an experience helped her broaden her perspective on educating young people.[39] The schools hold chapel services on a regular basis, which provides the students with an opportunity to hear the Word of God and to accept Christ into their hearts. Besides this, the schools incorporated a Bible subject in their curriculum, which became an indirect means of evangelism among the students. In fact, many students who graduated from the school committed their lives to full time ministry and mission work.

PRISON MINISTRY

Ahn did not just limit herself to education, but she expanded into other work. She was involved in evangelism among prisoners for more than twenty years. She preached the gospel to diverse criminals and subsequently won many souls to Christ. Her boldness for Christ led her to an auspicious place like a prison where men were dominant and there she presented the good news. Together with the Holy Spirit, the result of her ministry was overwhelming.

---

[36] Choi, *I Was a Hallelujah Woman*, 437-460.

[37] Yeol-soo Eim, 'Pentecostalism and Public School: The Case Study of Rev Dr Seen-ok Ahn (Paper presented in the first Asian Pentecostal Society in Four Square Seminary in DaeJun, Korea, May 21, 1999), 2.

[38] Eim, 'Pentecostalism and Public School', 3 reports specific names of the school. The names of the school are Daesung Junior High School (only boys), Daesung Girls' Junior High School, Daesung High School, Daesung Commercial Girls' High School, Sungnam Junior High School, and Sungnam Junior School (boys and girls).

[39] Department of Planning, *The Statistics of the School in 1999* (Taejon: Daesung Christian School, 1999).

Besides the above distinctive ministries, Ahn pioneered a church that grew rapidly in number, to the point where it is the largest church among the Foursquare churches in Korea. Her spiritual life was remarkable and when she was sixty years old she committed herself to forty days of fasting. People around her were so concerned about her health but she went through it well.[40] Ahn continues to exercise her spirituality in prayer and fasting even today.

Trinidad Seleky

Trinidad Seleky (Esperanza before marriage) was born in 1922 in Pangasinan, Philippines. She was one of a few prominent women in Pentecostal churches. Seleky graduated from Bethel Bible College in 1948, Northwest College in Kirkland, Washington in 1962 and she completed a Master's degree at Fuller Theological Seminary. In fact, she was the first Filipino graduate from this seminary. The most significant contribution she made was educating and training future Asian church leaders at Asia Pacific Theological Seminary. In 1967 she joined the teaching staff and served many years in its administration. Besides teaching courses in education in the seminary, she conducted seminars, was involved in various ministries such as vacation Bible school, youth camps, children's crusade, Sunday school curriculum development and training Christian education workers. She travelled all over the Philippines teaching and sharing the burden of the Christian education ministry.

From 1980-87, Seleky served the Philippine General Council of the Assemblies of God as Treasurer as well as National Director of the Sunday School Department of the Assemblies of God. She was the liaison person between the seminary and other evangelical organizations in the Philippines. She also provided leadership for the Philippine Association of Christian Education, which developed a Doctor of Education programme. In May 1987, Seleky had conferred on her a Doctor of Divinity degree by the Southern California Theological Seminary. Her dedication to teaching and God's ministry was remarkable.[41]

Virgie Cruz

Virgie Cruz was a Filipina born in 1930 in Paete, Laguna, Philippines. Cruz ministered as an international evangelist and was founding pastor of a large church in Manila. She conducted many evangelistic crusades in cities within the country and internationally. The result was so immense that hundreds of souls gave their lives to Christ and further committed themselves to his service.

---

[40] Seen-ok Ahn, *Fasting Prayer* (Cassette tapes, January 15, 1988).
[41] Lue Gomez, the Secretary to President of Asia Pacific Theological Seminary, October 5, 2001, provided the Information.

Her dynamic message, together with the work of the Holy Spirit, penetrated the hearts of people and made them repent. Her vibrant leadership encouraged church members to be involved in active evangelism. While the church was growing, it expanded its ministry into diverse realms caring for the community, helping the poor, reaching young people, and so on. Cruz influenced and challenged numerous young people during her pastoral work to engage in the ministry of the gospel.

Other Women

God has used countless Asian women. In Malaysia, Susan Tang has for more than twenty years been planting and pastoring churches in Sabah. Her dedication to God's Kingdom has resulted in not only many converts and churches, but countless pastors and evangelists, dedicating their lives to the Lord. Another woman, Teo Kwee Keng has pastored a thriving church in Batu Pahat, Malaysia for fourteen years, pioneering at least four other churches in the area during that time, and serving at a number of preaching points.[42] Norma Lam from the same country has served as a woman missionary in the Philippines, teaching at an international seminary for twelve years. While teaching there, she extended herself into local mission work together with the Filipino missionaries, Anita Swartz and Adeline Ladera, who have worked together in the Ministry Development Programme of the seminary. The regular mission work consists of evangelism, medical service, preaching and teaching in mountain village churches. Her ministry extends to the Philippines, Cambodia, Indonesia, China, Malaysia (her home country), Singapore, and many other Asian countries.

Numerous Asian women have served as cross-cultural missionaries. Nora Catipon, a Filipino single missionary, went to Cambodia to teach in the Bible School. Another woman, Erlynda Reyes has joined an international training ministry working with a missionary staff from many other countries. In the 1960s Maria Gomez in East Timor was called to service on a particular island where a prison stands and various criminals were confined. She and her husband spent many years planting the seed of the gospel through the means of building churches and training young people. One night when they had an evening service the Holy Spirit fell upon the congregation, people confessed their sins and great healing took place. Now the whole island is called an 'Assemblies of God island'. Gomez is the current General Superintendent in East Timor.[43] In Singapore, Lula Baird, Lau To Chan, Sarah Johnson and Jean

---

[42] Cavaness, 'God Calling', 49-62.

[43] Bill Snider, speaking at the Mission Emphasis Week in Asia Pacific Theological Seminary, October 10, 2001.

Wagner were instrumental in the establishing of Grace Assembly from 1950-60, now a thriving church of nearly 1,700 parishioners.[44]

There are several devoted women in the mountains of northern Luzon. Pynie Pacasen is one good example. Being a Kankana-ey woman, she crossed her ethnic boundaries and has preached the gospel to the Kalango-ya tribal people. In more than ten years she has established five congregations among the Kalango-ya tribe. Her ministry has involved hiking on mountain trails for more than ten hours every week, often in heavy rain or under treacherous heat. The mountain trails were heavily infested with Communist guerrillas for many year. Through her ministry, many young mountain people have been trained as Christian workers.

A broader perspective of Asian Pentecostal women's involvement in ministry is well summarized by Cavaness in the Assemblies of God context:

> Women made up 26% of the list of the Assemblies of God ordained and licensed ministers in Indonesia, 36% of the list in Malaysia and 34% of the list in Singapore (totalling over 250 women). The Assemblies of God in the Philippines has a lot of women pastors and workers, and women make up about one-half (100) of the number of foreign missionaries being sent out from Singapore AG churches. The more than 130 AG Bible schools and one seminary in Asia Pacific have large contingents of female students preparing for ministry.[45]

Asian women may have received their encouragement from women missionaries, as seen in the case of Vanderbout. Ruth Breusch was a missionary to India and made a great impact on local churches,[46] while Naomi Dowdey in Singapore founded and pastored the largest Assemblies of God church there. Lilian Trasher, who went to Egypt in 1910, broke her engagement to answer God's call and served Egyptian children for twenty-five years with no furlough. When she died in 1961 she was greatly honoured by the Egyptian government for her social service, taking care of 1,400 children and widows at the orphanage in Assiout, Egypt. In fifty years she ministered to more than 20,000 children and widows.[47]

Challenges and Conclusion

God does not call people on the basis of gender, race, abilities, education, or economic status, but calls both men and women to fulfil his work. Pentecostals assert that God bestows power on his people on the basis of faith and

---

[44] Fred Abeysekera, *The History of the Assemblies of God of Singapore* (Singapore: Abundant Press, 1992), 206-13.
[45] Cavaness, 'God Calling', p. 59.
[46] Cavaness, 'God Calling', p. 58.
[47] Caveness, 'God Calling', p. 59.

obedience, nothing more. David Roebuck remarks about the early stage of Pentecostal women ministers:

> In almost every case, a female minister significantly influenced these women's understanding of their call to ministry. Without denigrating the role of the Holy Spirit or of significant males in their lives, the presence of a powerful female role model was remarkable.[48]

If we acknowledge that the call and empowerment of God applies to females as well as males, women's role in various ministries like teaching, preaching, leadership, mission and administration should be recognized and even encouraged without limitations. However, in churches almost all leadership positions are taken by men and they have the powerful voice in decision-making. It is interesting that in most congregations there are more female than male members. This gender discrimination in leadership is also common in institutions and mission organizations. It is particularly true among Asian churches because of their patriarchal culture. Thus, Christian women in Asia have great challenges to overcome.

Women should be given a greater opportunity for higher education, through which they can develop their academic skills. In August 2001, Ruth Peever, an English professor at Asia Pacific Theological Seminary and a former missionary to China for sixteen years, delivered a lecture on the advantage of higher education to young people from Korea. She stated that her experience in China was that her doctoral degree suddenly opened many doors, especially into places that were exclusive and of high profile for ministry. The president of one university in China honoured her for her high academic degree. Asian women should be encouraged to strive for higher education and academic challenge for better involvement in ministry.

The ordination of women is not permitted in many denominations in Asia. A simple answer to this problem from a denominational leader in Korea was, 'You'd better get married'. I personally do not have a strong desire to be ordained. However, ordination may open doors for ministry that otherwise would not be available. Pentecostal denominations have stood out in this socio-ecclesial culture of Asia. Although not uniformly, the majority of Pentecostal denominations in Asia have ordained women for ministry. For instance, the general councils of the Assemblies of God in countries like the Philippines, Malaysia and Singapore have an impressive proportion of women ministers. In Korea, the number is rapidly rising. Their achievements are

---

[48] David G. Roebuck, 'Go and Tell My Brother?: The Waning of Women's Voices in American Pentecostalism' (a paper presented at the Twentieth Annual Meeting of the society for Pentecostal Studies, Dallas, TX, November 8-10, 1990), F-18.

especially noticeable in mission. However, when we look at leadership, it is still a male-dominated world.

If Christ liberated all humanity, including women, on the cross, Pentecostals should endeavour to liberate women in every area of ministry, not just a few selected areas like Christian education. Historically, the Pentecostal movement liberated social outcasts like the native Americans, women, and laity. Since we know that God called and empowered both women and men,[49] they have to have the same opportunity to fulfil their calling. I also believe that women themselves have to make an effort to improve themselves. Thus, women must encourage themselves. The bottom line is that everyone, men or women, should have a chance to fulfil their God-given calling.

---

[49] E.g., Cheryl Bridges Johns, 'Pentecostals and the Praxis of Liberation: A Proposal for Subversive Theological Education', *Transformation* 11:1 (January/March, 1994), 11 notes that 'the active presence of the Holy Spirit…calls for a radical balance in ministry of males and females, black and whites, rich and poor'.

Revising Pentecostal History in Global Perspective

Allan Anderson

The Context of Pentecostal Historiography

This paper outlines what is seen to be a fundamental misconception in the writing of Pentecostal history that needs correcting.[1] The writing of the global history of Pentecostalism, at least in the English language, has mostly reflected a bias interpreting that history from western, and predominantly North American, perspectives. The vital and often more significant work of Asian, African and South American Pentecostal pioneers has been neglected, if not completely ignored. This is true of most of the histories, whether written by outsiders or insiders, by historians, sociologists or theologians. Some of these histories add the biases of denomination and race, and most of the earlier ones were not written by professional historians and tended to be hagiographies. All literature is influenced by the presuppositions of its authors, and history is no exception. Furthermore, history is usually written with a particular goal in mind; to achieve this, the author is constantly selecting, sifting and interpreting sources and events. In order to understand the importance of and need for rewriting Pentecostal history, it is first necessary to critically examine the presuppositions of existing histories.

Some of the first academic histories were written by outsiders: Lutheran theologian Nils Bloch-Hoell (whose work first appeared in Norwegian in 1956);[2] British sociologist Malcolm Calley on African Caribbean Pentecostals in Britain;[3] Swiss sociologist Christian Lalive d'Epinay on Chilean movements;[4] a global study by Swiss ecumenist and Professor of Mission at the University of Birmingham, Walter Hollenweger;[5] and several North Americans,

---

[1] I am grateful to Gary McGee for his helpful comments made on an earlier draft of this paper.

[2] Nils Bloch-Hoell, *The Pentecostal Movement* (London: Allen & Unwin, 1964).

[3] Malcolm J. Calley, *God's People: West Indian Pentecostal Sects in England* (London & New York: Oxford University Press, 1965).

[4] Christian Lalive d'Epinay, *Haven of the Masses: A Study of the Pentecostal Movement in Chile* (London: Lutterworth Press, 1969).

[5] Walter J. Hollenweger, *The Pentecostals* (London: SCM Press, 1972).

including the seminal study by social historian Robert Mapes Anderson;[6] a widely acclaimed study of theological roots by historian Donald Dayton;[7] and more recently a study by Episcopalian William Faupel,[8] a study by Harvard theologian and one-time secularisation theorist Harvey Cox,[9] and one by Grant Wacker, historian of religion.[10] Hollenweger, Faupel and Wacker, all former Pentecostals, have written sympathetic studies, and Dayton and Cox have a largely positive appraisal, even if the latter's phenomenological conclusions are looked at somewhat warily by 'classical' Pentecostals themselves. From within North American Pentecostalism has come a string of noteworthy histories, from the earliest ones by Frank Bartleman, chronicler of the Asuza Street Revival[11] and Stanley Frodsham,[12] an early Assemblies of God historian, to include the more recent works by Edith Blumhofer,[13] Charles Conn[14] and Vinson Synan,[15] among many others. The earlier histories tended to see Pentecostalism as emerging in the USA 'suddenly from heaven', and they took what has been described as a 'providential' view of history, tending to discount or ignore 'natural' causes of the rise of the movement.[16] Joe Creech suggests that

---

[6] Robert Mapes Anderson, *Vision of the Disinherited: The Making of American Pentecostalism* (New York: Oxford University Press, 1979).

[7] Donald Dayton, *The Theological Roots of Pentecostalism* (Metuchen, NJ & London: Scarecrow Press, 1987).

[8] D. William Faupel, *The Everlasting Gospel: The Significance of Eschatology in the Development of Pentecostal Thought* (Sheffield: Sheffield Academic Press, 1996).

[9] Harvey Cox, *Fire from Heaven: The Rise of Pentecostal Spirituality and the Reshaping of Religion in the Twenty-first Century* (London: Cassell, 1996).

[10] Grant Wacker, *Heaven Below: Early Pentecostals and American Culture* (Cambridge, MA & London: Harvard University Press, 2001).

[11] Frank Bartleman, *Azusa Street* (South Plainfield, NJ: Bridge Publishing, 1980).

[12] Stanley Frodsham, *With Signs Following: The Story of the Pentecostal Revival in the Twentieth Century* (Springfield, MO: Gospel Publishing House, 1946).

[13] Edith L. Blumhofer, *The Assemblies of God: A Chapter in the Story of American Pentecostalism*, 2 vols. (Springfield, MO: Gospel Publishing House, 1989); Blumhofer, *Restoring the Faith: The Assemblies of God, Pentecostalism, and American Culture* (Urbana & Chicago: University of Illinois Press, 1993).

[14] Charles W. Conn, *Like a Mighty Army: A History of the Church of God 1886-1976* (Cleveland, TN: Pathway Press, 1977).

[15] Vinson Synan, *The Holiness-Pentecostal Movement in the United States* (Grand Rapids: Eerdmans, 1971); item, *The Holiness-Pentecostal Tradition: Charismatic Movements in the Twentieth Century* (Grand Rapids & Cambridge: Eerdmans, 1997).

[16] Grant Wacker, 'Are the Golden Oldies Still Worth Playing? Reflections on History Writing Among Early Pentecostals', *Pneuma* 8:2 (Fall 1986), 81-100 (84); Augustus Cerillo, 'The Beginnings of American Pentecostalism: A Historiographical Overview', in E.L. Blumhofer, R.P. Spittler & G.A. Wacker (eds), *Pentecostal Currents in American Protestantism* (Urbana & Chicago: University of Illinois Press, 1999), 229-259 (229).

Bartleman's account in particular created the 'central myth of origin' that has persisted to the present, and that this 'myth' was based on theological and historical paradigms that overlooked other points of origin.[17] The first (1988) edition of the *Dictionary of Pentecostal and Charismatic Movements*, edited by Stanley Burgess and Gary McGee,[18] provides further historical material on (mostly) western Pentecostalism. It is predominantly North American in focus, with some attention given to Europe, but the world of the great majority of Pentecostals is almost entirely absent. The editors are aware of this in their Preface, but betray their presuppositions there: 'It is necessary first to concentrate on North America and Europe, where classical Pentecostalism and the charismatic movement originate'.[19] This list of Pentecostal historians is by no means an exhaustive one. Bearing in mind that some studies are intentionally North American in focus, and at the risk of oversimplification, it may not be inaccurate to state that most histories declare or imply that Pentecostalism, fanning out from the western world and in particular from the USA, grew and expanded in Asia, Africa, the Pacific and Latin America because of the work of a number of western 'missionaries' who carried the 'full gospel' to the ends of the earth.

In these histories, the various presuppositions of the writers are often transparent, some of which are now easily dismissed. Bloch-Hoell's study abounds with innuendos showing that he probably thought that many Pentecostals were psychologically unstable and neurotic.[20] This deprivation theory is repeated in a more subtle form by Lalive d'Epinay and Robert Anderson, who saw Pentecostalism as a refuge for the socially marginalized and underprivileged poor, the 'vision of the disinherited', as Anderson put it, where 'ecstatic religious experience' was 'a surrogate for success in the social struggle'.[21] Wacker's most recent contribution, in contrast, sees early North American Pentecostals as representative of the entire spectrum of society, including the wealthy middle class.[22] At least as far as the origins of Pentecostalism are concerned, the heroes and heroines or *dramatis personae,* are Westerners, who are regarded as the main role players responsible for the global expansion of Pentecostalism. The commencement of the movement is

---

[17] Joe Creech, 'Visions of Glory: The Place of the Azusa Street Revival in Pentecostal History', *Church History* 65 (September 1996), 405-424 (406, 408).

[18] S.M. Burgess & G.M. McGee (eds.), *Dictionary of Pentecostal and Charismatic Movements* (Grand Rapids: Zondervan, 1988).

[19] Burgess & McGee, *Dictionary*, vii. I understand that the second edition of this work (2001) contains more 'non-western' material, but was not yet published at the time of writing.

[20] Bloch-Hoell, *Pentecostal Movement*, 21, 32.

[21] Anderson, *Vision*, 152.

[22] Wacker, *Heaven Below*, 216.

always situated in the USA, whether in Cherokee County, North Carolina in the 1890s (according to some Church of God historians), Charles Parham's movement in Topeka, Kansas in 1901 (where many historians start) or the Azusa Street revival led by William Seymour in Los Angeles, 1906 (which most agree was the driving force behind the rapid spread of the movement).

Although the exact place of origin is disputed, the primacy of Azusa Street as the heart or 'cradle' of Pentecostalism was reaffirmed in the 1970s, largely through the influence of Walter Hollenweger. Writers began to assert the important role of this predominantly African-American church as the generator of Pentecostal churches all over the world.[23] Grant Wacker pointed out that the early histories of the movement suffered from what he called a 'ritualization of Pentecostal history' that included a 'white racial bias' that ignored the central influence of black culture on Pentecostal worship and theology, and in his view, the 'more serious distortion' of a 'persistent gender bias' in which the leading role of women was overlooked.[24] These race and gender distortions are indeed serious problems that must be overcome, but there may be even graver issues that face Pentecostal historiography. In all these historical interpretations, some of which indeed attempted to correct errors of the past, the vital role of thousands of indigenous workers in the early Pentecostal movement, particularly in Asia and Africa, was ignored, overlooked or minimized. In early Pentecostal periodicals carrying reports of missionaries, if the indigenous workers are mentioned at all it is usually as anonymous 'native workers' or at best, they are mentioned by a single name, often misspelled.

This serious omission arises from the environment in which Pentecostal missions were carried out and this environment is often not given due consideration in the writing of history. The experiences of Pentecostals throughout the world cannot be separated from the wider context of political and social power.[25] The beginning of the twentieth century was the heyday of colonialism, when western European nations governed and exploited the majority of people on earth. This rampant colonialization was often transferred into the ecclesiastical realm and was reflected in the attitudes of missionaries who so often moved in the shadows of colonizers. In the late nineteenth century in North America and Europe there was an almost universal belief, from conservatives to Marxists, in the superiority of western culture and civilization. This was the ideology that fired colonialists and missionaries alike and the

---

[23] Douglas J. Nelson, 'For Such a Time as This: The Story of William J Seymour and the Azusa Street Revival' (PhD thesis, University of Birmingham, 1981); Iain MacRobert, *The Black Roots and White Racism of Early Pentecostalism in the USA* (Basingstoke: Macmillan, 1988).

[24] Wacker, 'Golden Oldies', 95.

[25] Jim Sharpe, 'History from Below', in Peter Burke (ed.), *New Perspectives on Historical Writing* (Cambridge: Polity Press, 1991), 24-41 (33).

belief lingered long into the twentieth century.[26] It undoubtedly affected Pentecostal missionaries too, even if subconsciously. Early Pentecostals in western Europe and North America were impassioned with ideas of 'global spiritual conquest',[27] an expansionist conviction influenced by premillennial eschatological expectations that the nations of the world had to be 'possessed' for Christ before his imminent coming to rule the earth. This was a long tradition rooted in the nineteenth century evangelical awakenings. Undoubtedly, the 'manifest destiny' of the United States influenced Pentecostal missions used to thinking in expansionist terms. Brouwer, Gifford and Rose in their book *Exporting the American Gospel,* say that US Americans have a belief in 'America's special place among nations' and 'a conviction that other peoples ought to be guided and ruled by American principles, both civil and religious'. They point out that Pentecostals have joined other US Christians whom they term 'fundamentalists' in accepting 'this global-political mission as part of their own program of intense religious evangelization'.[28] Coupled with a belief in the superiority of forms of Christianity 'made in America' is a conviction in the superiority of the political and social system found in the USA. This neo-imperialism has been that which has often alienated North American missionaries from local national leaders, and certainly the perceived hegemony bolstered by US economic and military muscle has not helped the negative image.

In recent years, the 'southward swing of the Christian centre of gravity',[29] which has made Pentecostalism more African and Asian than western, heightens the urgency of this debate. Most Pentecostals now live in Asia, Africa and Latin America. The leading Protestant missionary-sending nations are no longer the United States, Britain, Sweden or Germany, but India, South Korea, Brazil and Nigeria.[30] At the beginning of the twenty-first century, the largest Pentecostal congregations in London, England and in Kiev, Ukraine, each with several thousands of members, are led by African pastors. In Africa itself, the history of very large numbers of Christians can only be understood within that context. In Asia, where the largest number of evangelical Christians in any continent of the world live, most are of a Pentecostal and Charismatic

---

[26] Henk Wesseling, 'Overseas History', in Peter Burke (ed.), *New Perspectives on Historical Writing* (Cambridge: Polity Press, 1991), 67-92 (75).

[27] Wacker, *Heaven Below,* 263.

[28] Steve Brouwer, Paul Gifford & Susan D. Rose, *Exporting the American Gospel: Global Christian Fundamentalism* (New York: Routledge, 1996), 14, 17.

[29] Andrew F Walls, 'Of Ivory Towers and Ashrams: Some Reflections on Theological Scholarship in Africa', *Journal of African Christian Thought* 3:1 (June 2000), 1.

[30] Larry D Pate, 'The Dramatic Growth of Two-Thirds World Missions', in William D Taylor (ed.), *Internationalising Missionary Training* (Exeter: Paternoster Press, 1991), 35

type; and Latin America has the largest number of Pentecostals in any continent. Barrett and Johnson's annual statistics give dramatic evidence of how rapidly the western share of world Christianity has decreased. In 1900, 77% of the world's Christian population was in Europe and North America. By 2000, only 37% of the two billion Christians in the world were from these two northern continents and their projection for 2025 is 29%. Furthermore, 26% of the world's Christians are now 'Pentecostal/ Charismatics', expected to rise to 31% by 2025.[31] The 'southward swing' is more evident in Pentecostalism than in most other forms of Christianity. Much of the dramatic church growth in Asia, Africa and Latin America has taken place in Pentecostal and indigenous and independent Pentecostal-like churches, and I would guess that at least three-quarters of Pentecostalism today is found in these continents. Classical Pentecostal churches with roots in North America like the Assemblies of God, have probably only some 8% of their world associate membership in North America, with at least 80% in the 'Third World' continents.[32]

We obviously need to know who and what is responsible for this explosion of Charismatic Christianity. There are glaring gaps in our knowledge. We would be forgiven for asking where all the indigenous heroines and heroes of Pentecostal history have gone. Like the soldiers of the protest folksong of the sixties, they have 'gone to graveyards every one', and we might parody the refrain: 'When will we ever learn'? The historians and chroniclers of the past have sent thousands of Pentecostal labourers to their unnamed graves. The historical processes leading to the fundamental changes in global Pentecostal demographics must be charted accurately. Hopefully, however, it is not too late to correct past distortions. In much of the writing of Pentecostal history until the present day, the 'objects' of western missionary efforts, now the great majority of Pentecostals in the world, remain marginalized.

This situation has begun to improve with the welcome appearance in the past two decades of academic theses and books that relate to the history of Pentecostalism outside the western world, including studies on movements in Argentina,[33] Chile,[34] Ghana,[35] South Africa,[36] South India,[37] the Philippines,[38]

---

[31] David B. Barrett & Todd M. Johnson, 'Annual Statistical Table on Global Mission: 2001', *International Bulletin of Missionary Research* 25:1 (January 2001), 25.

[32] One estimate puts the total number of adherents of the World Assemblies of God Fellowship in 1997 at some 30 million, of which about 2½ million are in North America. Everett AWilson, *Strategy of the Spirit: J Philip Hogan and the Growth of the Assemblies of God Worldwide 1960-1990* (Carlisle: Regnum, 1997), 3, 107, 183.

[33] José Norberto Saracco, 'Argentine Pentecostalism: Its History and Theology' (PhD thesis, University of Birmingham, 1990).

[34] Juan Sepúlveda, 'Gospel and Culture in Latin American Protestantism: Toward a New Theological Appreciation of Syncretism' (PhD thesis, University of Birmingham, 1996).

[35] Kingsley Larbi, *Pentecostalism*; Johnson Asamoah-Gyadu, 'Renewal within African Christianity: A Study of Some Current Historical and Theological Developments within

Korea,[39] a translation of Willis Hoover's personal reflections on the history of Chilean Pentecostalism [40] and several others. But the great gaps in our information remain. Pentecostal anthropologist Ronald Bueno reminds us that we need to 'rehistoricize' Pentecostal experiences and identities by considering the contribution of the 'local', the 'Pentecostalisms', if we are really to understand the 'global', Pentecostalism.[41] 'Pentecostalism' that is made in the USA is only one part of the total picture of many forms of 'Pentecostalisms', and the hidden treasures of these local histories need to be discovered.

An Azusa Street 'Jerusalem'?

Frank Bartleman spoke of Azusa Street as the 'American Jerusalem'.[42] But the 'made in the USA' assumption is one of the great disservices done to worldwide Pentecostalism and is reflected in the ongoing debate about Pentecostal origins. Augustus Cerillo suggests that there are at least four approaches to this subject and that one theory of the complex origins of

---

Independent Indigenous Pentecostalism in Ghana' (PhD thesis, University of Birmingham, 2000).

[36] Allan Anderson, *Moya: The Holy Spirit in an African Context*. (Pretoria: University of South Africa Press, 1991); idem, *Bazalwane: African Pentecostals in South Africa* (Pretoria: University of South Africa Press, 1992); idem, *Zion and Pentecost: The Spirituality and Experience of Pentecostal and Zionist/Apostolic Churches in South Africa* (Pretoria: University of South Africa Press, 2000); and Allan Anderson and Samuel Otwang, *Tumelo: The Faith of African Pentecostals in South Africa* (Pretoria: University of South Africa Press, 1993).

[37] Michael Bergunder, *Die Südindische Pfingstbewegung im 20. Jahrhundert* (Frankfurt am Main: Peter Lang, 1999).

[38] Jae Yong Jeong , 'Filipino Pentecostal Spirituality: An Investigation into Filipino Indigenous Spirituality and Pentecostalism in the Philippines' (ThD thesis, University of Birmingham, 2001).

[39] Jae Bum Lee, 'Pentecostal Type Distinctives and Korean Protestant Church Growth' (PhD thesis, Fuller Theological Seminary, 1986); Boo Woong Yoo, *Korean Pentecostalism: Its History and Theology* (New York: Peter Lang, 1988); Young Hoon Lee, 'The Holy Spirit Movement in Korea: Its Historical and Doctrinal Development' (PhD thesis, Temple University, 1996); Chong Hee Jeong, 'The Formation and Development of Korean Pentecostalism from the Perspective of a Dynamic Contextual Theology' (ThD thesis, University of Birmingham, 2001).

[40] Willis C. Hoover, *History of the Pentecostal Revival in Chile*, trans. Mario G. Hoover (Santiago, Chile: Imprenta Eben-Ezer, 2000).

[41] Ronald N. Bueno, 'Listening to the Margins: Re-historicizing Pentecostal Experiences and Identities', in M.W. Dempster, B.D. Klaus, & D. Petersen (eds), *The Globalization of Pentecostalism: A Religion made to Travel* (Oxford: Regnum, 1999), 269.

[42] Bartleman, *Azusa Street*, 63.

Pentecostalism cannot be emphasized to the exclusion of others.[43] The most popular theory in the more recent written histories seems to be one that places the Azusa Street revival in Los Angeles at the centre of Pentecostalism, the 'Jerusalem' out of which the Pentecostal gospel reached out to the 'ends of the earth'. The first two decades of the Pentecostal movement were marked by feverish and often sacrificial mission activities. By 1910, only four years after the commencement of the Azusa Street revival, it was reported that Pentecostal missionaries from Europe and North America were in over fifty nations of the world.[44] From its beginning, Pentecostalism in the western world was characterized by an emphasis on evangelistic outreach, and all Pentecostal missionary strategy placed evangelism at the top of its priorities, linked as it was to a particular premillenial eschatology. The Pentecostal revival resulted in a category of ordinary but 'called' people called 'missionaries' spreading out to every corner of the globe within a remarkably short space of time. Harvey Cox suggests that the rapid spread of the movement was because of its heady and spontaneous spirituality, 'like the spread of a salubrious contagion'.[45] It touched people emotionally and its emphasis on experience was spread through testimony and personal contact. Faupel chronicles the sending out of workers from Azusa Street's Apostolic Faith Mission, the role of this congregation as a magnet to which Christian leaders were drawn, the creation of new Pentecostal centres and the spread to the nations of the world. In these various early expanding activities, a lack of central organization resulted in what Faupel describes as 'creative chaos'.[46]

Despite the significance of the Azusa Street revival as a centre of African-American (and oral) Pentecostalism that profoundly affected its nature, when this is assumed to be the 'Jerusalem' from which the 'full gospel' reaches out to the nations of earth, the truth is distorted and smacks of cultural imperialism.[47] There were several centres of Pentecostalism from which great

---

[43] Augustus Cerillo, Jr, 'Interpretative Approaches to the History of American Pentecostal Origins', *Pneuma* 19:1 (1997), 29-49; Cecil M. Robeck, 'Pentecostal Origins in Global Perspective', in H.D. Hunter and P.D. Hocken (eds.), *All Together in One Place: Theological Papers from the Brighton Conference on World Evangelization* (Sheffield: Sheffield Academic Press, 1993), 166.

[44] Faupel, *Everlasting Gospel*, 212-6; Robeck, 'Pentecostal Origins', 176-7; Wacker, *Heaven Below*, 264.

[45] Cox, *Fire from Heaven*, 71.

[46] Faupel, 213-222; Gary B. McGee, 'Pentecostals and their Various Strategies for Global Mission: A Historical Assessment', in M.W. Dempster, B.D. Klaus & D. Petersen (eds.), *Called and Empowered: Global Mission in Pentecostal Perspective* (Peabody: Hendrickson, 1991), 208.

[47] This theme is repeated in a footnote to a recent article by L. Grant McClung, Jr., 'Try to Get People Saved': Revisiting the Paradigm of an Urgent Pentecostal Missiology', in *Globalization of Pentecostalism*, 49, n. 11.

expansion took place, even in North America. There were many 'Jerusalems': Pyongyang, Korea; Beijing, China; Pune, India; Wakkerstroom, South Africa; Lagos, Nigeria; Valparaiso, Chile; Belem, Brazil; Oslo, Norway; and Sunderland, England—among other centres. Pentecostalism has many varieties, and not just the North American 'classical Pentecostal' kind. My understanding of 'Pentecostalism' includes 'Charismatic' Christianity and those movements where the practice of gifts of the Spirit is encouraged, which may include or exclude speaking in tongues. As Everett Wilson has observed, Pentecostalism has had many beginnings, and there are many 'Pentecostalisms'.[48] Azusa Street was certainly significant in reminding North American Pentecostals of their non-racial and ecumenical origins and ethos. The Azusa Street revival was an interracial fellowship that was unique and has given inspiration to many. It has motivated Black South African Pentecostals, for many decades denied basic human dignities by their white counterparts in the same Pentecostal denominations, some of which were founded by Azusa Street missionaries.[49] The stimulus of the movement from a predominantly black church led by Seymour, undoubtedly rooted in the African-American culture of the nineteenth century, is certainly significant. Many of the early manifestations of Pentecostalism were found in the religious expressions of the slaves in North America and were themselves a reflection of the African religious culture from which they had been forcefully abducted. Seymour was deeply affected by this slave spirituality. It was this holistic spirituality that made the Pentecostal message so suitable to cultures all over the world where experience of divine intervention was more important than creeds, controversies and doctrinal arguments that soon racked the North American movement.

Although Pentecostal missiologist Paul Pomerville continued the earlier 'providential' view of Pentecostal history, he declared that Pentecostalism had originated in a series of roughly spontaneous and universal beginnings in different parts of the world, and that no attempt should be made to restrict its commencement to one geographical location such as Los Angeles.[50] This represented a new approach to the problem of origins, but Pomerville's

---

[48] Everett A Wilson, 'They Crossed the Red Sea, Didn't They? Critical History and Pentecostal Beginnings', in *Globalization of Pentecostalism*, 107.

[49] Allan Anderson, 'Dangerous Memories for South African Pentecostals', in Allan Anderson and Walter J. Hollenweger (eds.), *Pentecostals after a Century: Global Perspectives on a Movement in Transition* (Sheffield: Sheffield Academic Press, 1999), 105; Anderson, *Bazalwane*, 23; Anderson, *Zion and Pentecost*, 58, 85. Emissaries from Azusa Street and Zion City, Tom Hezmalhalch and John G. Lake, who reported back to Seymour, founded the first Pentecostal church in South Africa, the Apostolic Faith Mission, in 1908. Henry M. Turney, who went to South Africa in 1909 and was associated with the formation of the Assemblies of God there, was an Azusa Street product.

[50] Paul Pomerville, *The Third Force in Missions* (Peabody, MA: Hendrickson, 1985), 52.

insistence on spontaneity meant that he tended to ignore the complexity of historical and social factors that linked the different 'outpourings' to each other. Without minimizing the importance of Azusa Street, due recognition must be given to places in the world where Pentecostal revival broke out independently of this event and in some cases even predated it. One example is the 'Korean Pentecost', which began among missionaries in Pyongyang in 1903 and soon spread to thousands of Korean people. This revival seemed to have been unaffected by nineteenth century 'Evangelical awakenings'; it predated the 1904 Welsh Revival, and it quickly took on an indigenous character all of its own.[51] The Korean revival affected revivals in China like the Manchurian Revival of 1908[52] and irrevocably changed the face of East Asian Christianity. In this context, it is important to note which movement preceded which. Korean Pentecostals are unanimous in acknowledging the contribution of the earlier revival to their own movement. The revival greatly influenced the present dominance of the Charismatic movement in the Presbyterian and Methodist churches there, many of whose characteristic practices have been absorbed by the 'classical' Pentecostal churches (like Yonggi Cho's Yoido Full Gospel Church) that came over two decades later. Furthermore, although strictly speaking this is not a 'classical Pentecostal' revival and in spite of North American Protestant missionary participation in its beginning, early Korean revival leaders in the Presbyterian and Methodist churches were much more 'Pentecostal' than the missionaries would have wanted them to be and their characteristic revival practices persist in Protestant and Pentecostal churches in Korea today.[53]

In the case of China, Daniel Bays has shown that the influence of Pentecostalism has 'accelerated the development of indigenous churches', particularly because Pentecostals were closer to the 'traditional folk religiosity' with its 'lively sense of the supernatural' than other churches were. Most of the Chinese indigenous churches today are Pentecostal 'in explicit identity or in orientation'. Bays says that Pentecostalism in China, 'especially its egalitarian style and its provision of direct revelation to all', also facilitated the development of churches independent of foreign missions.[54] This was equally

---

[51] Chong Hee Jeong , 'Formation and Development'.

[52] Daniel H. Bays, 'Christian Revival in China, 1900-1937', in E.L. Blumhofer & R. Balmer (eds.), *Modern Christian Revivals* (Urbana & Chicago: University of Illinois Press, 1993), 163.

[53] Jae Bum Lee, 'Pentecostal Type Distinctives'; Young Hoon Lee, 'The Holy Spirit Movement in Korea'; Chong Hee Jeong, 'Formation and Development'.

[54] Daniel Bays, 'The Protestant Missionary Establishment and the Pentecostal Movement', in E.L. Blumhofer, R.P. Spittler & G.A. Wacker (eds.), *Pentecostal Currents in American Protestantism* (Urbana & Chicago: University of Illinois Press, 1999), 63.

true of Pentecostalism in Africa and Latin America—something the early Pentecostal missionaries from the West could not have anticipated and probably would not have encouraged.

Similarly in India, the 1905-1907 revival at Pandita Ramabai's Mukti Mission in Poona, in which young women baptized by the Spirit had seen visions, fallen into trances and spoken in tongues, began before the Azusa Street revival, although tongues first occurred there in December 1906.[55] This revival was understood by Ramabai herself to be the means by which the Holy Spirit was creating an indigenous form of Indian Christianity.[56] She penned these prophetically significant words at the time:

> Let the revival come to Indians so as to suit their nature and feelings. God has made them. He knows their nature, and He will work out His purpose in them in a way which may not conform to the ways of Western people and their lifelong training. Let the English and other Western Missionaries begin to study the Indian nature, I mean the religious inclinations, the emotional side of the Indian mind. Let them not try to conduct revival meetings and devotional exercises altogether in Western ways and conform to Western etiquette. If our Western teachers and foreignised Indian leaders want the work of God to be carried on among us in their own way, they are sure to stop or spoil it.[57]

The Apostolic Faith, the periodical from Azusa Street, greeted news of this revival in its November 1906 issue with 'Hallelujah! God is sending the Pentecost to India. He is no respecter of persons'. There is no mention of missionaries or of Ramabai's mission, but it suggests that there, 'natives... simply taught of God' were responsible for the outpouring of the Spirit, and that the gifts of the Spirit were given to 'simple, unlearned members of the body of Christ'.[58] Of course, the Indian people are not named, not even the internationally famous Pandita Ramabai. Nevertheless, Pentecostal missionaries worked with the Mukti Mission for many years and Ramabai

---

[55] Gary McGee, '"Latter Rain" Falling in the East: Early-Twentieth-Century Pentecostalism in India and the Debate over Speaking in Tongues', *Church History* 68 (September 1999), 648-665. Tongues first occurred in India in July 1906, after the Azusa Street revival had begun; but this developed independently of Azusa (personal communication from Gary McGee).

[56] Shamsundar M. Adhav, *Pandita Ramabai* (Madras: Christian Literature Society, 1979), 216.

[57] Pandita Ramabai, 'Stray Thoughts on the Revival', *The Bombay Guardian,* November 4th, 1905, 9.

[58] *Apostolic Faith* 3, 1. Another report on the revival in India is printed in *The Apostolic Faith* the following month: *Apostolic Faith* 4, 4. A report in *The Apostolic Faith* in September 1907 (10, 4) suggests that the Mukti revival did not experience tongues until December 1906, after receiving reports from Los Angeles, but tongues appeared elsewhere in the Indian revival earlier (McGee, 'Latter Rain', 654-56).

received support from the fledgling Pentecostal movement in Britain, where she was mentioned in the Pentecostal periodical *Confidence*.[59] However, the original Pentecostal outpouring in India took place much earlier than Mukti, in Tamil Nadu in 1860-65 under the Tamil evangelist Aroolappen, and in Travancore in 1873-81.[60] As McGee points out, Pentecostalism had already established itself in India 'before word of Azusa reached the subcontinent'.[61] Although the Tamil Nadu and Mukti revivals themselves may not have resulted directly in the formation of Pentecostal denominations, the Mukti revival in particular had other far-reaching consequences that penetrated parts of the world untouched by Azusa Street.

Perhaps the most important of these consequences crossed two oceans to South America. In 1907, North American revivalist Willis Hoover, Methodist Episcopal minister in Valparaiso, Chile, heard of the Mukti revival through a pamphlet by his wife's former classmate Minnie Abrams. Later, he enquired about the Pentecostal revivals in other places, especially those in Venezuela, Norway and India among his fellow Methodists.[62] The revival in Hoover's church in 1909 resulted in his expulsion from the Methodist Church in 1910 and the formation of the Methodist Pentecostal Church, to become an indigenous church and the largest non-Catholic denomination in Chile.[63] The vast majority of Chilean Pentecostals, who now form some 20% of the total population of their country, are quite different from 'classical' Pentecostals in North America and trace their origins to the Valparaiso events.[64] In 1909 Luis Francescon took the Pentecostal message to Italian communities in Brazil; and in 1911 two Swedish immigrants to the United States, Gunnar Vingren and Daniel Berg, began what became the Assemblies of God in Brazil three years before it was constituted in the USA. This is now the largest Protestant denomination in Latin America and the largest Assemblies of God in any nation, quite independent of its North American counterpart.[65] The first missionaries to Brazil were connected to William Durham's church in Chicago, but were separate from the North American movement and looked to Sweden

---

[59] *Confidence* 1:6 (September 1908), 10. I am indebted to the Donald Gee Research Centre, Mattersey, England, and their director David Gerard, for permission to read their early Pentecostal periodicals *Confidence*, *Flames of Fire*, and *Things New and Old*.

[60] McGee, 'Latter Rain', 649; Ivan M. Satyavrata, 'Contextual Perspectives on Pentecostalism as a Global Culture: A South Asian View', in *Globalization of Pentecostalism*, 205.

[61] McGee, 'Latter Rain', 650.

[62] Hoover, *History*, 9, 164.

[63] Peter Wagner, *Look Out! The Pentecostals are Coming* (Carol Stream: Creation House, 1973), 17; Juan Sepúlveda, 'Indigenous Pentecostalism and the Chilean Experience', Anderson & Hollenweger, *Pentecostals after a Century*, 111-2.

[64] Sepúlveda, 'Indigenous Pentecostalism', 113-15.

[65] Wagner, 23-25.

for their main support.[66] However, although western missionaries are usually given the credit for the foundation of these large denominations, their rapid growth was mainly due to the efforts of the unknown indigenous workers. Douglas Petersen has shown that in Central America strong Pentecostal churches emerged 'with little external assistance or foreign control'.[67] All over the world there were untold thousands of indigenous revivalists without western connections responsible for the spread of the Pentecostal gospel. In the Ivory Coast and the Gold Coast (now Ghana), the Liberian Kru, William Wade Harris spearheaded a revival in 1914 quite distinct from the western Pentecostal movement, but with many Pentecostal phenomena including healing and speaking in tongues. This revival resulted in 120,000 conversions in a year, the largest influx of Africans to Christianity the continent had ever seen. Whether Harris had any encounter with African-American missionaries from Azusa Street working in Liberia we may never know, but there were certainly no connections thereafter. Chinese evangelists crisscrossed that vast nation with a Pentecostal message similar to but distinct from its western counterpart, resulting in many thousands of conversions to Christianity. A Chinese preacher, Mok Lai Chi, was responsible for the early spread of Pentecostalism in Hong Kong and started a Pentecostal newspaper there in 1908.[68] These various Pentecostal revivals were not primarily a movement from the western world to 'foreign lands', but more significantly movements within these continents themselves.

An obscure history of Pentecostalism has been taken for granted for so long that the multitudes of nameless ones responsible for its grassroots expansion have passed into history unremembered and their memory is now very difficult to retrieve. Everett Wilson's essay on Pentecostal historiography warns us of the futility of expecting either 'to find a homogeneous Pentecostal type at the beginning' or 'to assume that the experience of the first set of Pentecostals provides a model for the future'. He says that it is the ordinary people, those 'who were not at all certain where they were going' who carried the movement through its various stages to make an impact. He points out that the future of Pentecostalism lies not with the North Americans but with the autonomous churches in Africa, Asia and Latin America, whose origins often predate those of the 'classical Pentecostals' in the West.[69] Klaus and Triplett remind us that Pentecostals in the West 'have a tendency toward triumphalist affirmation of

---

[66] I am indebted to David Bundy for this insight after a personal conversation.

[67] Douglas Petersen, 'The Formation of Popular, National, Autonomous Pentecostal churches in Central America', *Pneuma* 16:1 (1994), 23.

[68] Bays, 'Protestant Missionary Establishment', 54.

[69] Wilson, 103-104, 106, 109.

missionary effectiveness'.[70] This is often bolstered by statistics proclaiming that 'Pentecostals/ Charismatics' are now second only to Catholics as the world's largest Christian grouping.[71] When this is assumed implicitly to be largely the work of 'white' missions, the scenario becomes even more incredulous. Despite the undeniably courageous work of the early Pentecostal missionaries from the West, the more important contribution of indigenous evangelists and pastors must be properly recognized. A hankering after a 'conquest of the heathen' that has tended to dominate Pentecostal missions from the West creates more problems than it attempts to solve, particularly in those parts of the world where Christianity has been linked with colonial expansionism.[72] Most of Pentecostalism's rapid expansion in the twentieth century was not mainly the result of the labours of missionaries from North America and western Europe to Africa, Asia and Latin America. It was rather the result of the spontaneous indigenization of the Pentecostal message by thousands of preachers who traversed these continents with a new message of the power of the Spirit, healing the sick, and casting out demons. This may be one of the most important reconstructions necessary in Pentecostal historiography.

Reading Between the Lines

One of the reasons for the distorted picture we have of Pentecostal history is the problem of documentary sources. Our writing of early Pentecostal history outside the western world almost entirely depends on letters, reports and periodicals of western Pentecostals and their missionaries. These documents were loaded for western consumption in order to bolster financial and prayer support in North America and Europe; and so the reports mostly talked about the activities of the missionaries themselves and not their so-called 'native workers'. History cannot be understood from written sources alone, especially when these sources are the only written documents from this period and almost exclusively reflect the 'official' positions of power and privilege of their authors. We have to 'read in between the lines' of the documents, minutes and newsletters to discover the hints of a wider world than that being described. This is certainly a hazardous exercise, for the possibilities of misinterpretation become greater with incomplete information, especially in the case of those who have already died and whose voices have been 'lost'. The importance of retrieving oral traditions is underlined here, for the stories of those still living who remember the past must be recorded for posterity. In several parts of the

---

[70] Byron D. Klaus and Loren O. Triplett, 'National Leadership in Pentecostal Missions', in Dempster, Klaus & Petersen (eds.), *Called and Empowered*, 232.

[71] Gary B. McGee, 'Pentecostal Missiology: Moving beyond Triumphalism to Face the Issues', *Pneuma* 16:2 (1994), 276.

[72] Satyavrata, 212.

world, the early histories of Pentecostalism are still within living memories, and these must be recounted before it is too late. Of course, the further back in time we go, the more difficult it is to recover the histories 'from below', as the sources become scarcer.[73]

Some of the 'reading between the lines' that is done might cast early Pentecostal missionaries in less favourable light. There can be little doubt that many of the secessions that took place early on in western Pentecostal mission efforts in Africa and elsewhere were at least partly the result of cultural and social insensitivities on the part of the missionaries.[74] Early Pentecostal missionaries frequently referred in their newsletters to the 'objects' of mission as 'the heathen',[75] and were slow to recognize indigenous leadership when it arose with creative alternatives to western forms of Pentecostalism. Missionary paternalism, even if it was 'benevolent' paternalism, was widely practised. In country after country, white Pentecostals followed the example of other expatriate missionaries and kept control of churches and their indigenous founders, and especially of the finances they raised in western Europe and North America. Most wrote home as if they were mainly (if not solely) responsible for the progress of the Pentecostal work there. The truth was often that the churches grew in spite of (and not because of) these missionaries. As Gary McGee has remarked,

> Historically, most Pentecostal missionaries paternally guided their converts and mission churches until after World War II (for some to the present). Ironically, in their zeal to encourage converts to seek spiritual gifts... they actually denied them the gifts of administration and leadership.[76]

To give an example from South Africa, in the formation of the Apostolic Faith Mission, African pastors were denied executive leadership, were given only nominal and local leadership opportunities, the races were almost immediately separated in baptisms and church gatherings, and apartheid had became the accepted practice of the church. Although African pastors and evangelists were largely responsible for the growth of the Pentecostal movement in South Africa, they were written out of history—with the exception of Nicholas Bhengu, whose enormous contribution to the development of the South African Assemblies of God was impossible to ignore.[77] It cannot be wondered that the schisms that occurred within the Apostolic Faith movement from 1910 onwards

---

[73] Sharpe, 'History from Below', 26.

[74] Allan Anderson, 'Signs and Blunders: Pentecostal Mission Issues at "Home and Abroad" in the Twentieth Century', *Journal of Asian Mission* 2:2 (2000), 193-210.

[75] *Confidence*, 1:2 (May 1908), 19; Kathleen Miller, 'Orissa, India', *Confidence* 2:5 (May 1909), 110.

[76] McGee, 'Pentecostal Missiology', 279.

[77] Anderson, *Zion and Pentecost*, 89-93.

resulted in hundreds of other denominations, including the creation of the largest church in South Africa today, the Zion Christian Church. The founder of this church, Engenas Lekganyane, was a preacher in the Apostolic Faith Mission and a fellow worker with John G. Lake.[78] Because these early African Pentecostals were seen as the 'opposition' to the work of white Pentecostals, they were often accused of 'misconduct' and thought of as unable to lead churches. One could argue that their work was more effective and relevant to their context, and they developed in quite different directions from that of the churches from which they seceded. These African Pentecostal churches, although perhaps not 'classical Pentecostals' in the usual sense of the word, practice characteristic Pentecostal spiritual gifts (especially healing, prophecy and speaking in tongues), and now represent almost half of the African population of South Africa.[79]

There are also examples from later Pentecostal history. In Africa's most populous nation Nigeria, the Christ Apostolic Church was founded in 1941 by Pentecostal evangelist Joseph Babalola, after British Pentecostal missionaries from the Apostolic Church objected to Africans sprinkling the 'water of life' (water that had been prayed over) in healing rituals. African Pentecostal churches in Nigeria today far outnumber those founded by European missionaries. The African leaders in turn found the missionaries' use of quinine to prevent malaria inconsistent with their proclamation of divine healing. We can only wonder whether water or quinine had the upper hand in the exercise of faith in this instance! At about the same time in Ghana, British Apostolic missionaries found a large African church wanting to work with them, but the Europeans insisted that they substitute their calabash rattles used in worship (part of a well established African Christian tradition) for tambourines. The missionaries reported that the Africans had thought that the missionaries wanted to deprive them of their power to ward off evil spirits. The same missionaries later fell out with the Africans over the use of quinine. Many of these and similar struggles were evidence of cultural misunderstandings and insensitivity that could have been avoided.

Sometimes western Pentecostal missionaries were patronizing and impolite about the people they were 'serving', and their racism was blatant. One missionary woman writing from Mbabane, Swaziland in 1911, spoke of the work among 'the native boys', quickly explaining that 'all [African males] are called 'boys'—from infancy to grey hairs'. Another Pentecostal missionary in Johannesburg writes of the 'Holy Spirit coming down on these black boys [mine workers] in such power'.[80] The use of 'boys' to refer to grown African

---

[78] Anderson, *Zion and Pentecost*, 60-70.

[79] Anderson, *Zion and Pentecost*, 13, 41.

[80] Frances Taylor, Mbabane, Swaziland, *Confidence* 4:1 (January 1911), 16; Eleazar & Lizzie Ann Jenkins, Johannesburg, *Confidence* 4:1 (January 1911), 18.

men was a common practice among Pentecostal missionaries.[81] Another
Pentecostal missionary in the Congo used a whip to 'discipline' his African
luggage bearers and boasted of the effectiveness of this 'thrashing'.[82] A British
Pentecostal Missionary Union (PMU) missionary in Tibet, Frank Trevitt,
reported that they had 'only wild Tibetans about us continually',[83] and spoke of
Tibet as 'this dark, priest-ridden country'.[84] McGee quotes an Assemblies of
God missionary in Burkina Faso who said that although the Mossi people were
'mentally inferior to other tribes', they could 'be trained to a very satisfactory
degree'.[85]

Nevertheless, the exploits of western missionaries were certainly impressive,
and we cannot assume that all were racist bigots. We can only greatly admire
their sacrificial efforts and in most cases their selfless dedication, as many even
laid down their lives through the ravages of tropical disease. They were often
very successful in adapting to extremely difficult circumstances; and many
showed a servant heart and genuinely loved the people they worked with. They
achieved much against what sometimes seemed overwhelming odds. But many
of these missionaries supposedly responsible for the spread of the Pentecostal
gospel throughout the world were by no means exemplary. For them, 'mission'
was understood as 'foreign mission' (mostly cross-cultural, from 'white' to
'other' peoples), and they were mostly untrained and inexperienced. Their only
qualification was the baptism in the Spirit and a divine call, their motivation
was to evangelize the world before the imminent coming of Christ, and so
evangelism was more important than education or 'civilization'.[86] Pentecostal
workers from the white Anglo-Saxon Protestant world usually saw their
mission in terms of from a civilized, Christian 'home' to a Satanic and pagan
'foreign land', where sometimes their own personal difficulties, prejudices (and
possible failures) in adapting to a radically different culture, living conditions
and religion were projected in their newsletters home. In 1911, one English
missionary expressed this fear as she wrote home from western China:

> Please pray for us and the people here, who are living and dying in Satan's
> kingdom. His reign here is no uncertain one, but a terrible, fearful, crushing rule,

---

[81] e.g. A.W. Richardson, 'Kalembe Lembe, Congo', *Confidence* (October-December
1921), 61; James Salter, 'Mwanza, Congo;, *Things New and Old* 3:1 (April 1923), 7.
[82] Fred Johnstone, 'Kalamba Mukenya, Kasai', *Confidence* 8:5 (May 1915), 98.
[83] Frank Trevitt, 'Taocheo', *Flames of Fire* 9 (January 1913), 5.
[84] Frank Trevitt, 'Taocheo', *Confidence* 6:3 (March 1913), 62.
[85] McGee, 'Pentecostals and their Various Strategies', 211.
[86] Walter J. Hollenweger, 'The Black Roots of Pentecostalism', in Allan Anderson &
Walter J. Hollenweger (eds), *Pentecostals after a Century: Global Perspectives on a
Movement in Transition* (Sheffield: Sheffield Academic Press, 1999), 34.

driving the people to wickedness and sin such as is not dreamt of in England. It is a force which can be felt everywhere, an awful living presence.[87]

They went out, like many other Christian missionaries before them, with a fundamental conviction that the North Atlantic was a 'Christian' realm, that they were sent as 'light' to 'darkness' and that the ancient cultures and religions of the nations to which they were sent were 'heathen', 'pagan' and 'demonic', to be 'conquered' for Christ.[88] Western culture was 'Christian' culture and all other cultures were dark problems to be solved by the light of the gospel, replacing the old 'paganism' with the new 'Christianity'.[89] Missionaries went out with the conviction that their 'future labours' would be among 'the poor heathen in darkness'.[90]

Religious intolerance and bigoted ignorance was a common feature of some of their reports, illustrated by their attitude to other religions. British PMU missionary in India in 1914, Grace Elkington, lamented: 'Oh, what a dark, sad land this seems to be, and the longer one lives in it, the more one feels the darkness all around'.[91] Almost four years later, she wrote of Hindu temples as 'the works of the devil', and that 'a favourite god of the Hindus', was 'supposed to be an incarnation of the second person of the Hindu Trinity'.[92] Another missionary discussed Hinduism, quoting Paul: 'they sacrifice to devils, and not to God' and said that 'The Devil' was 'at the bottom of all their worship'.[93] At a missionary convention in London in 1924, Walter Clifford, on furlough from India, described Hinduism as 'a religion of fear, not a religion of love' and that many of the Indian holy men were 'demon possessed', because 'you can see the devil shining out of their eyes. They have given themselves over to him'.[94] In north-west India, A.L. Slocum complained about the opposition of Muslims, using pejorative terms: 'Satan seems so entrenched in these Mussulmans that my efforts seem only a drop in the bucket'.[95] Young PMU worker Frank Trevitt (who died in China in 1916) sent back this report from 'dark China', obviously identifying a treasured Chinese national symbol with the devil:

---

[87] Constance Skarratt, 'PMU, India', *Confidence* 4:9 (September 1911), 214.

[88] A. Kok in *Flames of Fire* 35 (February 1916), 4.

[89] Wilbert R. Shenk, 'Recasting Theology of Mission: Impulses from the Non-Western World', *International Bulletin of Missionary Research* 25:3 (July 2001), 100.

[90] Jessie Biggs, 'SS Fushimi Maru', *Flames of Fire* 49 (May 1917), 40.

[91] Grace Elkington, 'Partabgarth', *Confidence* 7:12 (December 1914), 238.

[92] Grace Elkington, 'India', *Confidence* 11:3 (July-September 1918), 57.

[93] 1 Corinthians 10.20; H. Boyce in *Confidence* 10:1 (January-February 1917), 11.

[94] *Redemption Tidings* 1:2 (October 1924), 17.

[95] *The Pentecostal Witness* 1 (July 1924), 4.

This is heathendom truly, without light or love, not even as much as a dumb beast would have. Well, we have seen much of this spirit, which truly is the 'Dragon's' spirit, which is as you know, China's ensign... Oh, how one's heart longs and sighs for the coming of Christ's glorious Ensign, to be placed where the Dragon holds such sway.[96]

Later on, Trevitt referred to Tibetan Lama priests as Satan's 'wicked messengers', and that 'Satan through them hates Christ in us'.[97] John Beruldsen reported on a visit to a Mongolian 'Lama Temple' in Beijing and describes a priest worshipping 'a large idol from 90 to 100 English feet high'. He comments, 'One could almost smell and feel the atmosphere of hell in these places. Poor benighted people! The power of God could save them from it all, if only they knew it'.[98] Fanny Jenner, observing religious rituals in Yunnan, China wrote, 'the heathen spent one whole day in worshipping the graves of relatives—burning incense and weeping and wailing. Oh the mockery of it all. How Satan blinds their minds!'[99] Elizabeth Biggs reports from Likiang on a visit to a Tibetan Buddhist lamasery that 'the seat of Satan might be a good name for such a place', because 'the demonic power was keenly felt, and the wicked faces of these lamas haunted us for many days after'.[100] Miss Agar tells of the 'tortures of the Buddhist Purgatory' and how she was 'anew impressed with the strong resemblance between Roman Catholicism and Buddhism'.[101] One can surmise that their converts and the 'native workers', who had spent their lives in these ancient religions, would have had a more nuanced and better informed view of their old beliefs, and thus would have been more able to communicate effectively in this religious worldview.

Racism was too frequent in missionary reports. The conference address published in *Confidence* by a missionary from Africa, Miss Doeking, 'Leopard's Spots or God's masterpiece, which?', who referred to African people as follows:

The savage is God's opportunity, the masterpiece of our common creator, who delights in tackling impossibilities...unless the superior races are ready to humble themselves, we may yet witness such an awakening of the despised races as will put to shame the pride of their superiors.[102]

[96] Frank Trevitt in *Confidence* 4:8 (August 1911), 191.
[97] Frank Trevitt in *Confidence* 5:9 (May 1912), 215; 5:12 (December 1912), 286.
[98] John C. Beruldsen, 'North China', *Confidence* 6:4 (April 1913), 84.
[99] Fanny Jenner, 'Yunnanfu', *Confidence* 8:6 (June 1915), 118.
[100] Elizabeth M. Biggs, 'Likiang', *Flames of Fire* 48 (April 1917), 29.
[101] Miss Agar in *Confidence* 8: 6 (June 1915), 119.
[102] A.E. Doeking in *Confidence* 8:8 (August 1915), 154.

The so-called 'superior races' of Europe were at that very time engaged in such a horrible and dehumanizing war that the rest of the world could be forgiven for wondering who were actually the 'savages'. The incriminations went on. In South Africa, the Apostolic Faith Mission had by 1917 separated the 'white' churches from the others, and declared, 'we do not teach or encourage social equality between Whites and Natives'.[103] An English worker in India described her visit to a 'low caste village' with a 'little organ' singing hymns, and commented, 'They are so dull and ignorant and have to be taught like children in the K.G. classes', but added patronizingly, 'They followed intelligently, as was shown by their remarks'.[104] Her companion missionary obviously felt the same way, speaking of 'these village women of India', and 'how dull they are, and how slow to grasp anything new'.[105]

In the light of these and many other reports, it is no wonder that missionaries saw themselves as the prime movers in the Pentecostal revival. The people they were working with were too 'far gone' to be able to exercise really effective leadership in the churches that were springing up. There were exceptions to this bigotry, however. PMU chairman Cecil Polhill urged his missionaries to pursue indigenization, in an interesting article published in the organization's periodical, *Flames of Fire* in 1917. With remarkable insight for this period, nurtured by his many years of association with the China Inland Mission, he asserted:

> Is not that day far nearer in not a few of our fields of work in Asia and Africa than we as yet commonly recognize? The Christians are reckoned by their thousands and tens of thousands. In nature and temperament they are far better qualified than we to present the message to their fellow countrymen. Intellectually they are often fully our equals. Spiritually the power that works in us is also the power that works in them….These are things of high mission policy. Meanwhile the biggest service that the individual missionary can offer will over and over again be known and trusted as a true friend, quietly to live down antipathy and suspicion where it exists, watchfully and generously to seek for opportunities of surrendering to the native brother or sister a task which the foreigner could more easily fulfil himself.[106]

There are signs that PMU missionaries took his advice seriously, but that not all Pentecostal missionaries were convinced of the virtues of indigenous leadership. A PMU woman worker in India, Minnie Thomas, replied to Polhill's urging that 'for India at least, it is quite a new thought that the churches should be in the hands of Indian Pastors and Elders', and added

---

[103] Anderson, *Zion and Pentecost*, 86.
[104] Grace Elkington in *Flames of Fire* 27 (May 1915), 3.
[105] B. Jones in *Flames of Fire* 33 (November-December 1915), 9.
[106] Cecil Polhill, *Flames of Fire* 49 (May 1917), 38.

wistfully, 'but I am sure it is the *Lord's* plan'.[107] In spite of these and other hesitations, indigenous leadership was to become one of the strongest features of Pentecostalism throughout the world.[108] Four years earlier in 1913, Dutch Pentecostal missionary Arie Kok of the PMU from the western Yunnan province in China had begun to rely more on indigenous helpers for the progress of the work, and writes:

> I feel that if the natives themselves do not carry the good news to their own people, the task will be impossible for us foreigners.... The Lord is teaching us more and more that the natives are the best evangelists to their own people. So we are praying and believing for a band of native witnesses, filled with the love and the Spirit of God, who are to carry the glad tidings to their own villages.[109]

By this time missionaries in China were turning their attention to learning to be more sensitive to the cultures and languages of the people and the churches were quickly turning indigenous. The missionaries may not have foreseen or planned this result, but it was one that was to be of vital importance for the future. The evacuation of most western missionaries from China in 1949 meant that a strong, indigenous church could continue to gain strength without them. Missions like Burton's Congo Evangelistic Mission rejected the use of interpreters and thus forced their workers to learn languages, for as James Salter rightly observed, 'To learn the language is the way to the hearts of the people'.[110] But the paternalism of Burton's policy was clearly stated in 1925, and was characteristic of most western Pentecostal missions at the time: 'The great needs are Spirit-filled native evangelists, and a few white workers to superintend and help them'.[111] Forty-five years after Burton had begun this mission in 1915 it was still directed by an all white Field Executive Council and had sixty-five missionaries working in fourteen mission compounds. When all the missionaries were forced to leave the Congo during the civil war of 1960, the churches they left behind began to multiply much more rapidly than before. The result of this seeming setback was that ten years later these churches had more than doubled in number.[112] In all these cases we know the names of the missionaries, but those of the indigenous leaders of the churches are harder to come by.

---

[107] Minnie A. Thomas, 'Arungabad District, India', *Flames of Fire* 48 (April 1917), 31.
[108] James Salter in *Things New and Old* 1:6 (January 1922), 45; 2:4 (October 1922), 7.
[109] A. & E. Kok, 'Likiang-fu', *Confidence* 6:10 (October 1913), 206-207.
[110] James Salter, 'Address, Derby Hall, London', *Things New and Old* 3:3 (August 1923), 1.
[111] W.F.P. Burton in *Redemption Tidings* 1:4 (January 1925), 12.
[112] Two missionaries were killed in the Congolese war, and Burton and his missionaries were evacuated in 1960. Harold Womersley, *Wm. F.P. Burton: Congo Pioneer* (Eastbourne: Victory Press, 1973), 77, 113.

Towards a New Pentecostal Historiography

Historians speak of a 'new history' written in deliberate reaction against traditional history and its paradigms. The 'new history' is concerned with the whole of human activity, 'history from below' rather than 'history from above', history taken from the perspective of the poor and powerless rather than the rich and powerful.[113] In the writing of Pentecostal history there needs to be a sort of 'affirmative action' to redress the balance, where the contribution of indigenous workers, pastors and evangelists is emphasized. We need to plumb the depths of our oral histories and bring to light that which has been concealed for so long. Consequently, the work of the western missionaries, who came from countries of power and wrote newsletters for their own specific purposes, is put into correct perspective. We cannot continue to ignore the failings of these missionaries and give an exaggerated importance to people whose role was usually catalytic and not central. Asia, Africa and Latin America have their own Christian heroes who are not just western missionaries there! The voices of these Pentecostal and Charismatic pioneers should be heard in the writing of our histories. African writers have pointed out that in the western world information on western missionaries to Africa 'is many times disproportionate to their role and contribution', mainly because of the scarcity of written information on African Christians.[114] The same is true of Asia, the Pacific and Latin America. A serious and extensive rewriting of global Pentecostal history needs to be done, in which the enormous contributions of the indigenous pioneers is properly recognized, so that US American classical Pentecostals in particular shed their often-heard assumption that Pentecostalism is a 'made in the USA' product that has been exported to the world.

The Pentecostal experience of the power of the Spirit was the reason for the unprecedented flexibility on the part of its emissaries to the various cultures into which the Pentecostal message was taken. But the historiographical imperialism and ethnocentrism of the past must be rectified. The revising of the history of Pentecostalism in the twenty-first century must be undertaken, not by emphasizing the missionary 'heroes' of the powerful and wealthy nations of the world, but by giving a voice to the people living in the world's most marginalized parts. We must 'listen to the margins',[115] by allowing the hitherto voiceless and often nameless ones to speak, and by recognizing the contribution of those unsung Pentecostal labourers of the past who have been overlooked in

---

[113] Peter Burke, 'Overture: The New History, its Past and its Future', in Peter Burke (ed), *New Perspectives on Historical Writing* (Cambridge: Polity Press, 1991), 2-4.

[114] Watson A.O. Omulokoli, 'Researching and Writing Christian Biography in Africa: A Challenge to Evangelical Studies in Global Context', *Journal of African Christian Thought* 3:1 (June 2000), 41.

[115] Ronald N. Bueno, 'Listening to the Margins: Re-historicizing Pentecostal Experiences and Identities', in *Globalization of Pentecostalism*, 268.

our histories and hagiographies. Then together we will come to a honest appraisal of our histories and be better able to suggest solutions to the problems of division, parochialism, racism and ethnocentrism that plague Pentecostalism today, seeking to do all this in the power of the Spirit, but especially in the humility of the Cross.

PART TWO

SOUTH ASIA

Constructing Indian Pentecostalism:
On Issues of Methodology and Representation

Michael Bergunder

What is Pentecostalism?[1] The academic study of and the discussion within the Pentecostal movement up to now shows that this is a very complex question. A wide range of answers has been given, reaching from extremely narrow definitions to very broad ones. Certain circles of White Pentecostalism in the United States, for instance, sometimes try to narrow down Pentecostalism to a sub-category of American evangelicalism.[2] In sharp contrast to that stands the approach of David Barrett, who considers a very broad variety of churches, organizations and networks as representative of Pentecostalism.[3] Current Pentecostal and non-Pentecostal academic study tends to use such a broad understanding of Pentecostalism; and when it comes to statistics even Pentecostals (who otherwise count themselves as evangelicals) refer to Barrett's findings that c. 25% of World Christianity is Pentecostal.[4]

Admittedly, a narrow understanding has some real advantages. It would enable a comprehensive definition of Pentecostalism, because a clear-cut dogmatic basis could be formulated (e.g. evangelicalism plus tongues speaking

---

[1] Here, Pentecostalism is understood as a very general term that includes Charismatics, Neo-Pentecostals, Faith movement, and so on.

[2] Cf. e.g. C.M. Robeck, 'Art. National Association of Evangelicals', in S.M. Burgess, et al. (eds.), *Dictionary of Pentecostal and Charismatic Movments* (Grand Rapids: Zondervan, 1990), 634-636. It is noteworthy that also in recent sociological literature Pentecostals will often be lumped together with evangelicals, cf. e.g. P. Freston, *Evangelicals and Politics in Asia, Africa and Latin America* (Cambridge: Cambridge University Press, 2001).

[3] Cf. D.B. Barrett, 'Art. Statistics, Global', in S.M. Burgess et al. (eds.), *Dictionary of Pentecostal and Charismatic Movements* (Grand Rapids: Zondervan, 1990), 810-830.

[4] The recent statistics are found in D. Barrett et al. (eds.), *World Christian Encyclopedia* (Oxford: Oxford University Press, 2001), 4 (table 1-1). For a broad understanding of Pentecostalism in modern Pentecostal scholarship cf. e.g. W.J. Hollenweger, *Charismatisch-pfingstliches Christentum* (Göttingen: Vandenhoeck & Ruprecht, 1997 [Engl. as *Pentecostalism*, 1998]); A.H. Anderson & W.J. Hollenweger (eds.), *Pentecostals after a Century* (Sheffield: Sheffield Academic Press, 1999); A.H. Anderson, 'Stretching the Definitions?', *Journal of Pentecostal Theology* 10:1 (2001), 98-119, but cf. also the critique of G.B. McGee, 'Pentecostal Missiology', *Pneuma* 16 (1994), 275-281 (277).

as initial evidence of Spirit baptism) and an institutional framework assigned (e.g. Pentecostal member-churches of the National Association of Evangelicals). Nevertheless, its heuristic value would be very limited as it is absolutely counterintuitive and arbitrarily separates phenomena that belong together. As the acceptance of Barrett's figures already indicates, even the most evangelical oriented Pentecostals refer in certain contexts to more inclusive identities of Pentecostalism.

From an academic point of view there is no alternative to a broad understanding of Pentecostalism, but so far not much has been done to substantiate this approach in a methodologically satisfying manner. The most serious problem lies in the fact that a broad understanding of Pentecostalism neither refers to a common dogmatic basis nor to a common institutional framework (international umbrella organizations like the Pentecostal World Conference only cover very tiny fragments of the Pentecostal movement). Nevertheless academic research of the last decades has proved the usefulness of a broad understanding of Pentecostalism as a single global phenomenon. But its unity can't be described in the way traditional church history deals with Orthodoxy, Catholicism, Lutheranism and so on. New ways should be found to trace an international discursive network called Pentecostalism.

Looking at the current discussion, three complexes of questions seem to be most hotly debated in the context of constructing Pentecostalism. First: did Pentecostalism originate in the United States and spread out to the rest of the world from there? Second: how is it possible to define Pentecostalism as a global religious movement in a meaningful manner without resorting to specific theological tenets as a basis for definition? Third: how is Pentecostalism to be described within regional contexts (the question of 'indigenous' Pentecostalism)? This article searches for models to answer these three questions more appropriately and it will test their heuristic value on Indian cases. If it proves possible to make some progress in this complexity of problems, a better theoretical understanding of Pentecostalism could be the result.

The first two sections of this article are written from a strictly historical point of view with no immediate theological agenda in mind, though I am fully aware that 'historiographical perspectives are not just history' but that they may 'express and articulate theological visions'.[5] Therefore I will explicitly refer to theological implications where I am aware of my own theological concerns.

---

[5] D.W. Dayton, 'Yet Another Layer of the Onion', *The Ecumenical Review* 40 (1988), 87-110 (102). Cf. also Robeck who says: 'Whoever determines the identity for the Pentecostal movement is placed in a unique and privileged role. In this definitional act, there is power'. C.M. Robeck, 'Pentecostal Origins from a Global Perspective', in H.D. Hunter & P.D. Hocken (eds.), *All Together in One Place* (Sheffield: Sheffield Academic Press, 1993), 166-180. (169).

Compared with the other two, the third section is explicitly theological though I am trying to avoid getting too much into normative issues.

Beginnings of Pentecostalism

In the last few decades vigorous historical research into the beginnings of the Pentecostal movement has started. This has been done to a great extent by Pentecostal scholars themselves who tried to overcome an uncritical, more or less hagiographical tradition of telling about the beginnings as was common within their churches. This tradition, often called the 'providential approach',[6] was based on the belief that Pentecostalism was 'a spontaneous, providentially generated, [world wide] end-time religious revival, a movement fundamentally discontinuous with 1,900 years of Christian history';[7] but such a notion is hardly compatible with academic history. Therefore the '"new' Pentecostal historiography'[8] is trying to relate the emergence of Pentecostalism to nineteenth century theological roots and to its contemporary social and cultural context. It was Donald Dayton's *Theological Roots of Pentecostalism* (1987) that set the standard for that new endeavour.[9] Dayton argued in a richly textured historical analysis that the theological patterns of Pentecostalism could be traced back to nineteenth century Wesleyan, Reformed, and Higher Life holiness circles in the United States. At the turn of the twentieth century, this vast network of holiness institutions and movements constituted 'a sort of pre-Pentecostal tinderbox awaiting the spark that would set it off'.[10] Numerous important studies have come out more recently that further prove the continuity between Pentecostalism and nineteenth century popular American evangelicalism, though there are discussions about the details (e.g. Wesleyan versus Reformed roots).[11] Pentecostal and non-Pentecostal historians now

---

[6] S.M. Burgess, 'Interpretative Approaches to the History of American Pentecostal Origins', *Pneuma* 19 (1997), 29-52 (31-36); Grant Wacker, 'Art. Bibliography and Historiography of Pentecostalism (US)', in S.M. Burgess et al. (eds.), *Dictionary of Pentecostal and Charismatic Movements* (Grand Rapids: Zondervan, 1990), 65-76 (69-76)

[7] Cerillo, 'Interpretative Approaches to the History of American Pentecostal Origins', 32.

[8] A. Cerillo, 'The Beginnings of American Pentecostalism', in: E.L. Blumhofer et al. (eds.), *Pentecostal Currents in American Protestantism* (Urbana: University of Illinois Press, 1999), 229-259 (229).

[9] Cf. D.W. Dayton, *Theological Roots of Pentecostalism* (Metuchen: Scarecrow, 1987).

[10] Dayton, *Theological Roots of Pentecostalism*, 174.

[11] Cf. e.g. I. MacRobert, *The Black Roots and White Racism of early Pentecostalism in the USA* (Basingstoke: Macmillan, 1988); D.W. Faupel, *The Everlasting Gospel* (Sheffield: Sheffield Academic Press, 1996); G. Wacker, *Heaven Below* (Cambridge: Harvard University Press, 2001).

consider Topeka and Azusa Street as the outcome of a specific American (and to some extent British) religious history.

As a side effect, this strict historical approach rejects the notion that Pentecostalism was a worldwide revival from its very beginnings. This thesis of multiple, worldwide origins of Pentecostalism was the popular self-understanding of early Pentecostals and became an integral part of the providential historical self-understanding in Pentecostal circles (e.g. it is part of the famous popular histories of Donald Gee and Stanley H. Frodsham).[12] Nevertheless, from an academic point of view, this kind of Americanization of Pentecostal historiography seemed to be inevitable, as Robeck rightly states: '...without wishing to be triumphalistic, the evidence gathered in all serious quests for origins of the modern Pentecostal movement appears inevitably to point to North America'.[13] However it is not without problems that historiography now runs counter to the early Pentecostal self-understanding as a global movement and that worldwide Pentecostalism becomes necessarily the result of Pentecostal missionary work from North America. Especially among scholars who focus their research on the non-western Pentecostal movement, there is a certain uneasiness with such an American-centred history as this doesn't seem to do justice to the multifaceted and global nature of the Pentecostal phenomenon.

In the following, I would like to offer a way out of the dilemma when I argue that there is an additional historical root of Pentecostalism that has been somewhat neglected as a distinctive category so far: the *missionary movement*. The nineteenth century, up to the beginning of World War I in 1914, was the heyday of colonialism. Under the brutal rule of colonial powers nearly the whole world was brought into the reach of the West. In that situation, parts of western Christianity reacted with missionary initiatives to spread the Christian faith in Africa and Asia and a huge number of missionary societies were founded for that purpose.[14] The specific conditions on the 'mission fields'

---

[12] S.H. Frodsham, *With Signs Following* (Springfield: Gospel Publishing House, 1946), 53, 'One remarkable feature of the Latter-Rain outpouring in the early days was the way the Spirit of God fell upon one and another in different parts of the world who had never come in contact with anyone who had received the Pentecostal experience'; D. Gee, *Wind and Flame* (Croyden: Assemblies of God Publishing House, 1967), 29-30, '... yet there was also occurring a truly spontaneous and simultaneous Revival on Pentecostal lines in widely separated places. The only agency was a deep hunger for such a Revival produced in the hearts of Christians by the Holy Spirit Himself'.

[13] Robeck, 'Pentecostal Origins from a Global Perspective', 170. Cf. already Nichol who called the United States the 'Birthplace of Twentieth-Century Pentecostalism': J.T. Nichol, *Pentecostalism* (New York: Harper and Row, 1966), 25.

[14] Cf. S. Neill, *A History of Christian Missions* (Harmondsworth: Penguin, 1964); W.R. Hutchison, *Errand to the world* (Chicago: Univ. of Chicago Press, 1987). For the

brought many Protestant missionary societies into close contact with each other and in the course of time a global missionary network beyond denominational boundaries developed. This emerging global network led to the famous World Missionary Conference at Edinburgh in 1910 that is arguably the beginning of the ecumenical movement.[15]

Religious revivals always played a crucial role in the missionary movement as they influenced many of the missionary recruits. However, in the second half of the nineteenth century a development took place that is of special interest with regard to Pentecostalism. It was during that time that premillennialism permeated evangelical circles in Britain (first in the Brethren movement) and in the United States (in the prophecy conferences, starting in New York 1878). This was accompanied by a new missionary awareness: 'On the great missionary movement hangs the appointed hour of the millennial dawn, of the marriage of the Lamb, of the glory of the resurrection, of the time of the restitution of all things'.[16] As a result several so-called 'faith missions' were founded.[17] The idea of faith missions (strictly interdenominational, no fixed salary, missionaries are members not employees of the mission, and so on) was first formulated in Hudson Taylor's China Inland Mission (London 1865), but became widely popular through the work of Fanny and Grattan Guinness, who founded the East London Training Institute in 1873. The Guinnesses influenced A.B. Simpson and the Christian and Missionary Alliance (1887) and, during a journey through the United States in 1889, Fanny Guinness was instrumental in starting the Boston Missionary Training Institute (A.J. Gordon) and the Chicago Evangelization Society (later Moody Bible Institute). Another very enthusiastic promoter of faith missions was Arthur Tappan Pierson, a Christian journalist, who edited the *Missionary Review of the World* from 1886 (in 1891 joined by A.J. Gordon as co-editor). The Student Volunteer Missionary Union (1886) was also part of this premillennial-oriented evangelical missionary network and was inspired by Dwight L. Moody and led by John R. Mott. The latter chose the motto 'the evangelization of the world in this generation' (originally coined by Pierson) for this organization.[18] Through this vast network, American holiness circles became part of the global missionary movement and this in turn affirmed a strong missionary awareness among

---

connection between western missionary activities and colonialism, see, cf. H. Gründer, *Welteroberung und Christentum* (Gütersloh: Gütersloher Verl.-Haus Mohn, 1992).

[15] Cf. R. Rouse & S. Neill, *A History of the Ecumenical Movement, 1517-1968* (Geneva: World Council of Churches, 1994).

[16] Annual Report of the International Missionary Alliance 1892, 62, quoted in K. Fiedler, *Ganz auf Vertrauen* (Giessen, Basel: Brunnen, 1992 [Engl. transl. Oxford: Regnum Books 1994]), 364, n. 77.

[17] Cf. Fiedler, *Ganz auf Vertrauen*, 65-102; 359-370.

[18] Cf. G. Rosenkranz, *Die christliche Mission* (München: Chr. Kaiser, 1977), 218, 219.

them. It was this missionary awareness that became a decisive theological root for Pentecostalism, because it gives some clues why tongues speaking became so important for the movement.[19]

Charles Parham created the threefold theological formula that was used at Azusa Street: '1) Tongue speech as the initial evidence of Holy Spirit Baptism, 2) Spirit-filled believers as the 'sealed' Bride of Christ, and 3) Xenoglossic tongues as the tool for dramatic endtime revival'.[20] It is arguable that the idea of xenoglossic tongues ('missionary tongues') was the most important aspect among these three points. In the early days, Pentecostals thought that their glossolalia was actually foreign tongues for missionary purposes. This was hitherto rather overlooked, as the Pentecostal movement quietly gave up the idea of xenoglossia later. Nevertheless a number of sources point to the fact that Parham got his emphasis on tongues speaking from the missionary movement.

William Faupel shows convincingly the deep influence of the missionary movement on Parham.[21] The premillennialist missionary strategy was not aiming at converting the whole world to Christianity, but to be a witness to all nations and to give the chance to as many people as possible to accept the Christian message before Christ's Second Coming. Within such a perspective, time was running out and it became an urgent question as to how possible successful missionary work could be with such a limited timeframe. For one thing, the extremely time-consuming learning of foreign languages was felt to be a major obstacle. In this connection, isolated reports about the occurrence of the gift of xenoglossia spread in missionary circles.[22] Very prominent was the tale of a young woman called Jennie Glassey who had received African languages through the Holy Spirit in 1895.[23] The Glassey case became known to Charles Parham and impressed him very much, as it seemed to prove that God could enable missionaries by giving them the necessary foreign

---

[19] Dayton, *Theological Roots of Pentecostalism*, 167 did not identify a theological root for tongues speaking: 'Nearly every wing of late nineteenth-century revivalism was teaching in one form or another all the basic themes of Pentecostalism except for the experience of glossolalia, or speaking in tongues'. The following reflections are mainly based on the findings of J.R. Goff, *Fields White Unto Harvest* (Fayetteville: University of Arkansas Press, 1988); Faupel, *The Everlasting Gospel*, and G.B. McGee, 'Shortcut to Language Preparations?', *International Bulletin of Missionary Research* 25 (2001), 118-123.

[20] Goff, *Fields White Unto Harvest*, 173.

[21] Cf. Faupel, *The Everlasting Gospel*, 115-186.

[22] Cf. McGee, 'Shortcut to Language Preparations?'.

[23] Cf. Goff, *Fields White Unto Harvest*, 72-73; H.D. Hunter, 'Beniah at the Apostolic Crossroads', *Cyberjournal for Pentecostal-Charismatic Research* 1 (1997); McGee, 'Short-cut to Language Preparations?'.

languages.[24] Furthermore, in premillennial circles the idea was widespread that the Second Coming of Christ would be preceded by a worldwide revival that would greatly enlarge missionary work. Through the influence of Frank Sandford, Charles Parham accepted this notion and then brought it all together into the new Pentecostal 'Latter Rain' concept.[25]

These two points which Parham developed under the influence of the missionary movement (missionary tongues and worldwide revival) became part of the core self-understanding of the Azusa Street Revival in 1906, as can be seen from its periodical *The Apostolic Faith*.[26] For the participants of Azusa Street it was very clear that tongues speaking meant missionary tongues for a worldwide end-time revival that now had started in Los Angeles. To prove this claim it was of utmost importance that the revival would develop into a global phenomenon within a very short time. This pressure gave Azusa Street an extremely global outlook from its very start.

As already mentioned, many evangelicals at home and in the 'mission fields' shared the idea of a worldwide end-time revival. Moreover, Azusa Street falls in a time when many thought that such a revival had already started. The revival chronicler Edwin Orr speaks of a global 'Fifth General Awakening' between 1900-1910 (including Keswick, the Torrey and Alexander evangelistic ministry, the Welsh revival, the Khasi Hills revival, the Mukti Mission, and the Korean Revival).[27] During that time the global missionary movement that was connected through a very dense network of extensive correspondence and personal contacts was very much focussed on revival matters: 'What was remarkable was that missionaries and national believers in obscure places in India, the Far East, Africa and Latin America seemed to move at the same time to pray for phenomenal revival in their fields and world wide'.[28] Contemporary outsiders, like Frederick Henke, saw Azusa Street simply as small part of this

---

[24] Cf. Faupel, *The Everlasting Gospel*, 174.

[25] Cf. Faupel, *The Everlasting Gospel*, 167.

[26] 'This is a world-wide revival, the last Pentecostal revival to bring our Jesus' (*Apostolic Faith* 1:1 [Sept. 1906], 4). 'God is solving the missionary problem, sending out new-tongued missionaries on the apostolic faith line, without purse or scrip, and the Lord is going before them preparing the way' (*Apostolic Faith* 1:3 [Nov. 1906], 2).

[27] J.E. Orr, *Evangelical Awakenings in Southern Asia*, 2nd ed. (Minneapolis: Bethany Fellowship, 1976), 99: 'It was the most extensive Evangelical Awakening of all time, reviving Anglican, Baptist, Congregational, Disciples, Lutheran, Methodist, Presbyterian and Reformed churches and other evangelical bodies throughout Europe and North America, Australasia and South Africa, and their daughter churches and missionary causes throughout Asia, Africa and Latin America, winning more than five million folk to an evangelical faith in the two years of greatest impact in each country'. Cf. also J.E. Orr, *The Flaming Tongue* (Chicago: Moody Press, 1973); Orr, *Evangelical Awakenings in Southern Asia*, 99-106.

[28] Orr, *Evangelical Awakenings in Southern Asia*, 100.

revival: 'This speaking in tongues is but one of a series of such phenomena as 'tongues of fire', 'rushing of a mighty wind', 'interpretation of tongues', jerking, writhing, and falling to the ground, which are occurring in connection with a world-wide religious revival'.[29] Moreover, Orr is of the opinion that during this 'Fifth General Awakening' Pentecostalism was not a crucial factor but only an indirect by-product.[30]

It is important to keep in mind the relatively small impact of the Azusa Street revival at that time, because it contradicts the self-understanding of the Pentecostal movement. Azusa Street claimed to be the definitive formula for and sure beginning of the end-time revival, fulfilling all revival hopes that were transmitted through the missionary movement. So they claimed the whole ongoing revival movement for themselves: 'The present world-wide revival was rocked in the cradle of little Wales. It was 'brought up' in India, following; becoming full grown in Los Angeles later'.[31] In this situation, it became crucial to get their views accepted within the international evangelical circles. Azusa Street went global from the very start and began to channel their message through the vast international evangelical and missionary network that was receptive to revivals. As the Azusa Street participants were themselves part of this network and as the Pentecostal formula contained mainly elements that were familiar to those circles (fivefold gospel and end-time revival), they found easy access.

It is amazing to see how quickly the Azusa Street revival received positive responses in different parts of the world. However, as Joe Creech has rightly emphasized,[32] to join the Azusa Street revival was not necessarily connected with formal changes in institutional structure and ethos or theological traditions; nor did this establish formal institutional ties with Azusa Street. It spread because individuals and organizations generally accepted that a second Pentecost with the experience of tongues speaking and other spiritual gifts like healing and prophecy had happened and they declared themselves to be part of it. In that way, very different and divergent streams could join the Pentecostal movement, as nearly everybody who desired it could become part of it. Because of that, internal tensions and splits were a fundamental part of the movement right from its beginnings. The spread of the Azusa Street revival was essentially a kind of networking within evangelical and missionary circles. It

---

[29] F.G. Henke, 'The Gift of Tongues and Related Phenomena at the Present Day', *American Journal of Theology* 13 (1909), 193-206 (193).
[30] 'Indirectly it [the Fifth General Awakening] produced Pentecostalism' (Orr, *Evangelical Awakenings in Southern Asia*, 99). Cf. also Faupel, *The Everlasting Gospel*, 190.
[31] F. Bartleman, *Azusa Street* (S. Plainfield: Bridge Publishing, 1980 [first published 1925]), 19.
[32] Cf. J. Creech, 'Visions of Glory', *Church History* 65 (1996), 405-424.

took place at least in three different ways: correspondence and magazines; evangelistic journeys and other personal contacts; and missionary work. Some examples to emphasize this threefold global outreach might illustrate this.[33]

In September 1906 Azusa Street started its first journal, *The Apostolic Faith*, with 5,000 copies; half a year later it was already printing 40,000. Numerous new Pentecostal periodicals started and existing ones became Pentecostal all over North America and far beyond. It is said that within the first year of the Azusa Street revival vernacular Pentecostal newspapers were printed in Norway, Germany, China, Japan, Palestine, and Brazil.[34] This publication network was accompanied by immense and intensive correspondence. In January 1907, it was reported that up to fifty letters reached Azusa Street alone every day.[35] Nearly all Pentecostal groups in the early years maintained extensive international mail networks. One gets the impression that each corresponded with every one. Through these written channels an imagined global Pentecostal community was created that assured the individual believer of the international success of the revival and made it attractive to join in.

But it was also through personal contacts that the message was spread. Right from the beginning the specific worship practice—heavily shaped by Black spirituality[36]—of Azusa Street was passed on through common worship when people flocked from all over the country and even abroad to Los Angeles to 'get their Pentecost'. Besides, quite a number of Pentecostal leaders undertook global evangelistic tours, so that 'Pentecostals' geographic restlessness seemed so pronounced that the movement eventually became synonymous with itinerancy'.[37] For instance Anseln Howard Post was an early member of Azusa Street and in 1907 started his travels abroad that took him as far as South Africa, England, Wales and Ceylon.[38] Thomas Ball Barratt had come from Norway to the USA and became Pentecostal after he had visited Azusa Street in 1906; and in 1908-1909 he travelled through much of Europe and undertook a

---

[33] For a good concise overview cf. Faupel, *The Everlasting Gospel*, 212-227.

[34] Wacker, *Heaven Below*, 263.

[35] Cf. *Apostolic Faith* 1:5 (Jan. 1907), 4.

[36] On the question of Black spirituality at Azusa Street and its difference from Parham's teachings, cf. MacRobert, *The Black Roots*; Hollenweger, *Charismatisch-pfingstliches Christentum*, 31-56; D.D. Daniels, 'Everybody Bids You Welcome', in M.W. Dempster et al. (eds.), *The Globalization of Pentecostalism* (Oxford: Regnum Books, 1999), 222-52. But cf. also A. Taves, *Fits, Trances, and Visions* (Princeton: Princeton University Press, 1999), 328-337, who opens up new perspectives to explain the different spiritualities between Parham and Azusa Street.

[37] Wacker, *Heaven Below*, 215.

[38] Cf. G.B. McGee, 'Art. Post, Anseln Howard', in S.M. Burgess et al. (eds.), *Dictionary of Pentecostal and Charismatic Movements* (Grand Rapids: Zondervan, 1990), 720.

journey to India.[39] Daniel Awrey circled the globe in 1909, in 1910-11 he was in India and China and he died in Liberia in 1913.[40] Frank Bartleman, after he had already travelled extensively in the USA, started in 1910 on a round-the-world trip via Europe, Palestine, Egypt, India, Ceylon, China, Japan, and Hawaii.[41] These evangelists and several others travelled along established evangelical networks, and in the 'mission fields' they tried to impress their beliefs on missionaries open to the evangelical revival teachings.

However, the most spectacular global outreach of early Azusa Street were the missionaries who went out being confident that they were equipped with foreign tongues to preach the Pentecostal message in the vernacular. Quite a few former faith missionaries participated in Azusa Street (e.g. Samuel J. Mead and George E. Berg) and even helped to identify specific African or Asian languages allegedly being spoken by some in worship services as is amply reported in *The Apostolic Faith*. Boosted by the impression that he had spoken Bengali at Azusa Street,

A.G. Garr and his wife (who supposedly spoke Tibetan and Chinese) started for India where they arrived at the beginning of 1907.[42] S.J. Mead, former missionary with William Taylor in Africa for twenty years, organized a missionary party that allegedly had received African languages to go to Africa and the group embarked in December 1906.[43] In September 1907, M.L. Ryan collected a dozen men and women to go to Japan, clearly confident that they would be equipped with the necessary languages through missionary tongues.[44] When these missionaries arrived at their 'mission fields', they naturally became disillusioned because missionary tongues were not available,[45] but it seems that only a very few abandoned their Pentecostal objectives. Some returned early, some concentrated on revival preaching among western missionaries, like the

---

[39] T.B. Barratt, *When the Fire Fell and an Outline of My Life* (Oslo, 1927); N. Bloch-Hoell, *The Pentecostal Movement* (Oslo: Universistetsforlaget, 1964), 68.

[40] *Apostolic Faith* 1:2 (Oct. 1906), 4; H.D. Hunter, *International Pentecostal Holiness Church* (http://www.pctii.org/arc/iphc.html, 13.03.2002); Bartleman, *Azusa Street*, 83.

[41] Bartleman, *Azusa Street*, 146.

[42] *Apostolic Faith* 1:1 (Sept. 1906), 4; *Apostolic Faith* 1:2 (Oct. 1906), 2.

[43] Cf. Faupel, *The Everlasting Gospel*, 220-21.

[44] Cf. Wacker, *Heaven Below*, 86.

[45] As Pentecostal theologian Gary B. McGee, *This Gospel...Shall Be Preached* (Springfield: Gospel Publishing House, 1986), 45 clearly stated: 'Evidence of any early Pentecostal missionary ever receiving a new language in this manner does not exist'. Cf. also Henke, 'The Gift of Tongues and Related Phenomena at the Present Day', 205-206. A theological reflection on the failing of missionary tongues is now going on within Pentecostal theology, cf. J.E. Powers, 'Missionary Tongues?', *Journal of Pentecostal Theology* 17 (2000), 39-55.

Garrs, and others stayed and turned to traditional methods;[46] in that way they played an essential role in establishing an international Pentecostal network.

This threefold global outreach of early Pentecostalism was not without success. Many faith missionaries (especially from the Christian and Missionary Alliance) joined the new Pentecostal network, as did also quite a few indigenous workers of faith missions.[47] At the end of 1908 the Pentecostal movement had taken root in around fifty countries all over the world[48] and it could be stated that it had virtually 'circled the globe'.[49] So a real worldwide network was established. Only then was it seen that Azusa Street had proved to be the start of a worldwide revival, because without an immediate global establishment the revival would have fallen short of all expectations according to its self-image.

Putting the Pentecostal beginnings into such a global context means that only this worldwide network could be named Pentecostalism in the true sense. Azusa Street was the prelude, but the beginning of Pentecostalism was attained when a global Pentecostal network was established. Neither a creed, an institution nor a place was the beginning of Pentecostalism but a vast and vague international network; and in that specific sense Pentecostalism was a global movement right from its beginnings. India is a good example of this.

Beginnings of Pentecostalism in India

India played an important role in the worldwide revival that took place in the first decade of the twentieth century, especially through the events in the Khasi

---

[46] It is seems to be not entirely clear whether all early Pentecostal missionaries initially believed they were equipped with missionary tongues. Further research should bring clarification, because already at Azusa Street we find the clear notion that tongues were not necessarily for use in a foreign field 'but as a sign to you of Penteocost' as G.A. Cook wrote to T.B. Barratt in October 1906. See D. Bundy, 'Spiritual Advice to a Seeker', *Pneuma* 14 (1992), 159-170 (164). Robeck gives further examples from the early times where speaking in tongues was not connected to foreign languages. See W.F. Carother, Nov. 1906; 'Report of Chicago Revival' (Summer 1907); C.H. Mason, Feb./March 1907), cf. C.M. Robeck, *Making Sense of Pentecostalism in a Global Context: Papers from the 28th Annual Meeting of the Society for Pentecostal Studies* (Springfield, MO, 1999), 8.

[47] From China we know that in addition to that indigenous workers from established missions joined the Pentecostal fold, cf. D. Bays, 'The Protestant Missionary Establishment and the Pentecostal Movement', in E.L. Blumhofer et al. (eds.), *Pentecostal Currents in American Protestantism* (Urbana: University of Illinois Press, 1999), 50-67 (61); for India cf. below.

[48] Cf. Faupel, *The Everlasting Gospel*, 15 n. 6.

[49] *Apostolic Faith* (Ore.), July-August 1908, 1; *Latter Rain Evangel*, March 1909, 5; quoted in Wacker, *Heaven Below*, 263.

Hills and at Mukti Mission. At the end of the nineteenth century expectations for a new revival were high in India too.[50] In 1898, Pandita Ramabai attended the Keswick convention and requested the people there to pray for a missionary awakening among the Indians.[51] Ramabai, a Marathi Brahman convert, led a missionary and charity organization called Mukti Mission that was backed by foreign help and many western missionaries took part in its work.[52] In the year 1903, she sent her daughter Manoramabai to Australia along with her very close collaborator, the American Minnie F. Abrams, to monitor the evangelistic efforts of the Torrey and Alexander team.[53] Influenced by the revival in Wales 1904-1906, the Welsh Presbyterian mission in northeast India experienced a great awakening in the Khasi Hills which introduced Christianity to the whole region.[54] The news of these events soon spread throughout India and abroad and it also caught the keen attention of Ramabai. Under the influence of events in Australia and Wales, she started a special prayer circle in 1905 that led to a great revival at Mukti Mission in Kedgaon.[55] In the years 1906-1907, it was accompanied by various manifestations such as speaking in tongues. Different Americans who worked for the mission and had heard from Azusa Street started similarly speaking in tongues and interpreted the Mukti Mission as proof of the worldwide Pentecostal end-time revival.[56] However, as McGee and Blumhofer have emphasized,[57] Mukti Mission also shows that even among its very Pentecostal protagonists, the role of tongues speaking as initial evidence and a missionary tool was considered less important in India than at Azusa Street. Moreover Ramabai and the Mukti Mission as an institution later definitely backed out of the Pentecostal movement and interpreted the revival there as part of the larger evangelical awakening in the first decade of the twentieth century. This fact is often overlooked in popular Pentecostal hagiographical appropriation of the Mukti Mission.

---

[50] Cf. Orr, *Evangelical Awakenings in Southern Asia*, 107-111; G.B. McGee, '"Latter Rain" Falling in the East', *Church History* 68 (1999), 648-65 (651-53).

[51] Cf. Orr, *Evangelical Awakenings in Southern Asia*, 144; McGee, '"Latter Rain' Falling in the East", 651.

[52] For Pandita Ramabai and Mukti Mission, cf. N. Macnicol, *Pandita Ramabai* (Calcutta: Association Press, 1926); R.K. Dongre and J.F. Patterson, *Pandita Ramabai*, 2nd ed. (Madras: Christian Literature Society, 1969); M. Kosambi (ed.), *Pandita Ramabai Through Her Own Words* (Delhi: Oxford University Press, 2000); E.L. Blumhofer, 'Consuming Fire' (unpublished manuscript, 2001).

[53] Cf. Orr, *Evangelical Awakenings in Southern Asia*, 144.

[54] Cf. F.S. Downs, *North East India in the Nineteenth and Twentieth Centuries* (Bangalore: Church History Association, 1992), 95-96.

[55] Cf. N. MacNicol, *Pandita Ramabai* (Stuttgart: Evang. Missionsverlag, 1930), 161-62; Orr, *Evangelical Awakenings in Southern Asia*, 143-48.

[56] Cf. McGee, '"Latter Rain" Falling in the East'.

[57] Cf. McGee, '"Latter Rain' Falling in the East"; Blumhofer, *Consuming Fire*.

The Mukti Mission became a vital link for the global Pentecostal network that was to be established and it helped create Pentecostalism; but it was not the Pentecostal beginning in India. Other events were similarly important. Pentecostal revival ideas got an important boost in India when the first active participants from Azusa Street landed there. In the beginning of 1907 the Garr couple arrived and held meetings in English for 'missionaries and Christian workers' in Calcutta and as a result regular Pentecostal gatherings at the Carey Baptist Chapel (Bow Bazaar) are reported.[58] Of course they also visited the Mukti Mission. Although their stay was quite controversial among missionaries it certainly further established the Pentecostal network. In 1908, George E. Berg, another active participant at Azusa Street, landed in India and settled at Bangalore, a British civil and military centre at that time. He had already been a missionary in India before and he immediately used his contacts in the Brethren mission in Kerala.[59] In the same year, T.B. Barratt was invited to India by sympathizing missionaries to tell them more about the Pentecostal experience.[60] Most of the time Barratt stayed at Coonoor, a so-called hill station, where most of the western missionaries had gathered to take refuge from the hottest months of the year. During his stay some missionaries and Indians received the new baptism of the Spirit, though there were also seemingly outspoken negative reactions. During his stay in India, Barratt also held meetings at Bombay (today officially Mumbai) and Calcutta (Kolkata), and he visited the Mukti Mission.

Within a very short time a widespread and diffuse Pentecostal network was established in India that could be called the beginning of Pentecostalism in India. It was from this Indian network that a Pentecostal movement was established on the subcontinent through different initiatives. The most far-reaching was the work of George E. Berg, who won quite a few Indian adherents in Kerala through his contacts in the Brethren mission there, including some indigenous leaders mainly from Brethren background but also from Mar Thoma Church and the Anderson Church of God. In the year 1912, Berg returned to the USA for furlough and took part in the 'First World Wide Pentecostal Camp' organized by the Apostolic Faith Mission at Azusa Street. There he met with Robert F. Cook and advised him to follow him as a missionary to India. Cook was to become the key person for the establishment of the first Pentecostal church organizations in Kerala (Indian Pentecostal

---

[58] M.W. Moorhead, 'The Latter Rain in Calcutta, India', *The Pentecostal Evangel*, 17th April, 1920.

[59] To avoid unnecessary confusion for those who are not experts on India geographical names are generally given according to their modern usage accepting some grave anachronisms (e.g. Kerala, Tamilnadu, Karnataka, Andhra Pradesh).

[60] Barratt, *When the Fire Fell*, 157-67. T.B. Barratt stayed in India from 3 April till August 1908. The invitation came from A.N. Groves, together with Maud Orlebar and Max Wood Moorhead.

Church of God, Church of God,[61] Assemblies of God)[62] that have survived to the present day and were the starting point for many more Pentecostal denominations in South India. However, there are many other connections. One example is the founding of the Madras Pentecostal Assembly that can be attributed to two Swedish missionaries, Karin Andersson and Ida Nilson, who in North India had probably been staying in close contact with Mukti Mission. It is said that, as they waited for their ship in Chennai (formerly Madras) on their way back to their country in 1913, they did evangelistic work in Guindy (part of Chennai today) and as a result a Pentecostal congregation started there led by the Tamil Benjamin Jacob.[63] The American missionaries Christian Schoonmaker and Herbert Coxe, to give another example, had originally come to India with the Christian and Missionary Alliance and then became Pentecostals under the decisive influence of the Mukti Mission, eventually working for the Assemblies of God in North India.[64] Moreover, it must also be pointed out that at least two American missionaries who became Pentecostals in India influenced the Pentecostal movement in other parts of the world: Minnie Abrams in Chile, and Alice E. Luce in Mexico and among Hispanic Americans.[65]

Outlining a Definition of Pentecostalism

Pentecostalism could not keep its initial promises. As Faupel has emphasized, by the end of 1908 it had become clear that Pentecostal expectations were not

---

[61] In this article 'Church of God' refers to churches and missionary organizations that are affiliated to Church of God (Cleveland, TN).

[62] In this article 'Assemblies of God' refers to churches and missionary organizations that are affiliated to Assemblies of God (Springfield, MO).

[63] They are quite conflicting reports about the details. Cf. *Balm of Gilead* 50:9 (Dec. 1988), 5; N.G.J. Vasu, *My Mites to My Master* (Madras: Madras Pentecostal Assembly, c. 1950), 15; B. Andreasson and E. Andreasson, *Pingst i Indien* (Stockholm: MissionsInstitutet-PMU, 1989), 33. Cf. also M. Bergunder, *Die südindische Pfingstbewegung im 20. Jahrhundert* (Frankfurt: Peter Lang, 1999), 13, 27.

[64] Cf. M.L. Ketcham, 'History of Pentecost' (unpublished manuscript, 1973); C.H. Schoonmaker, 'My Baptism in the Holy Spirit', in *Cloud of Witnesses To Pentecost in India* (Pamphlet no. 6, Bombay: November 1908); Frodsham, *With Signs Following*, 111-13; E.B. Robinson, 'Art. Schoonmaker, Christian H.', in S.M. Burgess et al. (eds.), *Dictionary of Pentecostal and Charismatic Movements* (Grand Rapids: Zondervan, 1990), 770-71; E.A. Wilson, 'Art. Norton, Albert', in S.M. Burgess et al. (eds.), *Dictionary of Pentecostal and Charismatic Movements* (Grand Rapids: Zondervan, 1990), 641.

[65] Cf. Gee, *Wind and Flame*, 57; W.J. Hollenweger, *Handbuch der Pfingstbewegung*, 10 vols. (Genf, 1965/67), 03.07.013, 1136; McGee, '"Latter Rain" Falling in the East', 664-65.

realized.[66] 'The delay of the parousia and inability to speak in known tongues forced most Pentecostals to reassess their mission'.[67] Unlike many others the Pentecostal revival did not vanish after the initial promises had to be revised. The global network that was established within few years marked the beginning of a movement that would vigorously shape world Christianity in years to come. This divergent, multi-voiced and fragmented movement kept the idea of a common Pentecostal identity, but it appears that it is very difficult for scholars to define this phenomenon appropriately. As Everett Wilson has pointed out, there is no institutional setting of Pentecostalism: 'At no time, within the ranks, did adherents make up a discrete, readily identifiable group'.[68] Moreover Wilson also disputes the existence of an essential theological agenda: 'By almost any standard, Pentecostalism presently is not what Charles Fox Parham or any of his successors has pronounced it to be, but rather what contemporary Brazilians, Koreans and Africans demonstrate that it actually is'.[69] Nevertheless, there are certainly things that form a distinctive Pentecostal identity however vague it might be. One might guess that it has something to do with a certain spiritual praxis (intuitive, experiential Spirit-centred devotion; oral liturgy; firm biblical orientation; narrative theology and testimonies; strong lay participation; healing and so on), but even then it is rather something that is subject to constant change and dependent on mutual affirmation because 'every generation is the first generation'[70] in Pentecostalism. The vigorous debates about Pentecostal identity that are going on within Pentecostal theology will therefore rather help to shape, create and reaffirm this identity than to discover essential categories that could be used as a starting point for a scholarly definition.[71]

If there are no institutional or theological avenues for definition then it might be a good idea to look for a non-essential way of mapping a Pentecostal network as global discursive formation. I would suggest applying two criteria

---

[66] Cf. Faupel, *The Everlasting Gospel*, 228.

[67] Faupel, *The Everlasting Gospel*, 308.

[68] E.A. Wilson, 'They Crossed the Red Sea, Didn't They?', in M.W. Dempster et al. (eds.), *The Globalization of Pentecostalism* (Oxford: Regnum Books, 1999), 85-115 (108).

[69] Wilson, 'They Crossed the Red Sea, Didn't They?', 109.

[70] Wilson, 'They Crossed the Red Sea, Didn't They?', 106.

[71] For that debate cf. e.g. C.B. Johns, 'The Adolescence of Pentecostalism', *Pneuma* 17 (1995), 3-17; J.K.A. Smith, 'The Closing of the Book', *Journal of Pentecostal Theology* 11 (1997), 49-71; S. Chan, *Pentecosal Theology and the Christian Spiritual Tradition* (Sheffield: Sheffield Academic Press, 2000); A. Yong, *Discerning the Spirit(s)* (Sheffield: Sheffield Academic Press, 2000); D.M. Coulter, 'What Meaneth This?', *Journal of Pentecostal Theology* 10:1 (2001), 38-64.; V.-M. Kärkkäinen, 'Toward a Pneumatological Theology of Religions', *International Review of Mission* 91 (2002), 187-98.

for Pentecostalism: the existence of historical connections and synchronous interrelations. Both these criteria have to be applied within a global context, as Pentecostalism is a global movement right from its very beginning. The first criterion demands that all that we count as Pentecostal must be connected within a vast diachronous network that goes back to the beginning of Pentecostalism. That means that the question of direct historical influences becomes a crucial one and that all parallel phenomena that are without historical connections (e.g. Irvingites, cargo movements) must not be called Pentecostal. In addition to historical connections, the second criterion demands that only that which is linked up by some sort of synchronous network can be called Pentecostalism. This purely descriptive definition corresponds, as far as I see, to the way most Pentecostal and non-Pentecostal scholars who prefer a broad definition of Pentecostalism are using the term, though they seldom make their use explicit. Moreover, this definitory proposal does not seem to be counterintuitive to common Pentecostal self-understanding. Although the definition is very much based on common sense, it has some rather harsh consequences for actual research because without establishing a diachronous and synchronous network one must no longer speak of Pentecostalism.

For the establishment of the diachronous network a critical, strictly historical perspective has to be applied. Tracing historical connections usually means to focus on churches that have split and on pastors who changed their affiliation from one Pentecostal denomination to another, often taking with them whole congregations or even a set-up of churches. It is precisely these frictions that are most important for the historian who tries to sketch a diachronous network. The problem is that this approach is usually not in line with the common stereotyped pattern of testimonies and hagiographies that church leaders like to tell. Especially in many popular accounts of denominational histories, the illusion is fostered that the respective church started under direct godly providence and splits or makes contact with other churches or leaders and so on are not thoroughly analysed. But then such accounts do not contribute much to Pentecostal history because they are not about Pentecostalism as such. If we want to write a history of Pentecostalism we have to trace historical connections and this information is often hard to get. They are usually not found in oral testimonies or written documents and are in danger of getting lost when the respective generation has died. It will never be possible to reconstruct the full diachronous interconnections; but it is necessary to have the gaps carefully in mind because without a diachronous network there is no Pentecostalism. In this context it is of utmost importance that the bias of western archival sources and indigenous hagiographical traditions is not reproduced by the historian but is critically broken up and put under hermeneutical suspicion.

Similarly, establishing a synchronous network is very demanding. The description of a major denomination that calls itself Pentecostal does not contribute much to the research of Pentecostalism. Instead it is necessary to map a communicative network between different churches, organizations, and individuals that share the same diachronous network at the specific time period the research is focussing on. Through this synchronous network, theological styles and oral tradition will be made or kept compatible with each other. Theologoumena can be subjected to comparative control and be mutually assimilated so that some sort of common Pentecostal identity will be created. This synchronous network is very fluid and is in no way a closed structure. It always remains open to discussion because it is subject to rapid historical change and its construction will usually depend on certain biases of the scholar who undertakes it. But that does not mean that the power of representation is equally distributed within the synchronous network. On the contrary, representational power depends very much on the control of material and intellectual resources, so that dominant discourses are shaping the synchronous network and need to be thoroughly analysed.

Moreover within the one ideal global synchronous network there are many partial networks (e.g. regional networks, charismatic movements, White American evangelical Pentecostal churches) and if some church or organization is part of the historical but not of the contemporarily existing synchronous network then this is purely a descriptive statement. It could be the case that it was part of the synchronous network in the past and/or became (again) part of the network afterwards. The synchronous network has always tested boundaries, as the case of the African Instituted Churches shows, which share in many aspects common historical roots with the Pentecostal movement and were at a time, at least to some extent, a loose part of a synchronous network;[72] there are many signs that some of them will reclaim a Pentecostal identity and re-enter the synchronous network.[73]

To sum up: Pentecostalism is a constructed category that can be meaningfully applied when it refers to both a diachronous and synchronous network of global dimensions.

Writing the History of the South Indian Pentecostal Movement

The case of the South Indian Pentecostal movement can help illustrate the consequences of these ideas.[74] First of all, as shown above, India was part of the establishment of global Pentecostalism and that means that it is not possible to write its history as the result of a western (or even North American) missionary

---

[72] Cf. D. Maxwell, 'Historicizing Christian Independency', *Journal of African History* 40 (1999), 243-64.

[73] Cf. A.H. Anderson, *African Reformation* (Trenton: Africa World Press, 2001).

[74] The following data of the South Indian Pentecostal movement are based on the material collected in M. Bergunder, *Die südindische Pfingstbewegung im 20. Jahrhundert* (Frankfurt: Peter Lang, 1999 [engl. translation in preparation]).

enterprise because it was already there before western Pentecostal denominations started organized missionary efforts in India. When Pentecostalism became established in India after around 1910, its growth in South India started as a joint enterprise between George E. Berg and a number of Indian co-workers. When Berg visited Kerala in 1911, Robert Cumine, a Tamil-speaking Anglo-Indian from the Kolar Gold Fields near Bangalore who was converted to the Pentecostal faith under his influence, accompanied him. While they were staying in the region of Kottarakara and Adur, Berg approached his Brethren contacts and a small prayer-group under the leadership of Paruttupara Ummachan invited him to their place at Thuyavur (near Adur) and, as a result, they became Pentecostals, being probably the first Pentecostal congregation in South India. During the Kerala tour of 1911, Berg got acquainted with a few young people who followed him to Bangalore where he held Bible studies and instructed them in the Pentecostal faith. Among them were Umman Mammen and Pandalam Mattai who began to work as Pentecostal evangelists after they returned to Kerala. After a serious conflict with Robert F. Cook who had joined him in 1913, Berg left India for good in 1914. During World War I Cook, who wanted to continue the work alone, mainly stayed at the safe garrison of Bangalore, but in winter 1916-17 he undertook, along with Robert Cumine, an evangelistic tour of Kerala with the aim of renewing the contacts made by Berg. During that tour it became manifest that the congregation at Thuvayur had in the meantime developed a lively mission activity under the leadership of Paruttapara Ummachen. Umman Mamman and Pandalam Mattai also had been very active as Pentecostal missionaries in Kerala. In the 1920s more Indian evangelists and leaders, mainly from Brethren or holiness background, joined the Pentecostal faith (e.g. K.E. Abraham and A.J. John in 1923 and K.C. Cherian and P.V. John in 1924). Nevertheless Cook, who permanently moved to Kerala in 1922, exercised quite significant control of the emerging movement as he gave financial support to Indian evangelists and bought church land to build churches (first at Thuyavur in 1919).[75] In the 1920s funds became more easily available because Cook had joined the Assemblies of God and other missionaries of that organization came as missionaries to Kerala (Mary Chapman in 1921, John H. Burgess in 1927, and Martha Kucera in 1928). Nevertheless the Indians with their speaker K.E. Abraham were very critical of attempts to combine financial support with organizational control, especially after the regional Council of Assemblies of God for South India and Ceylon was formed in 1929. The late 1920s and early 1930s was a time when Indian Pentecostal leaders got into serious conflict with Robert F. Cook and among themselves about questions of leadership positions,

---

[75] Saju, *Kerala Pentekosthu Charithram* <*malay*> (Kottayam, Kerala: Good News Publication, 1994), 42.

financial matters, affiliation to western missionary societies and so on.[76] At the end of these quite turbulent conflicts, four larger Pentecostal churches came into being in Kerala in the 1930s, two with direct links to western missions (Assemblies of God, Church of God) and two quite different independent organizations, though not completely without western partners (Ceylon Pentecostal Mission, Indian Pentecostal Church of God). This historical genesis shows that the emerging Pentecostal movement in India could hardly be rendered as the missionary history of western Pentecostal denominations.[77]

Another point concerns the way that a diachronous network is made visible. Diachronous relationships can be described best by biographies which are established through critical reading and thorough investigation. The example of M.O. John, one of the old Pentecostal stalwarts among the Tamils in South India might illustrate that fact. M.O. John (born 1926) came from a Maravar Hindu family in Ammapatti, near Madurai. In 1942 he converted to Christianity and was baptized. He came into contact with Robert F. Cook and his son George who both worked as missionaries of the Church of God at this time. They invited him to Kerala since he faced hostility in his village because of his conversion. He remained an evangelist in the Church of God in Kerala until 1945. Then he went to Madurai where he worked as a casual labourer and there became a member of the Pentecostal congregation led by the Indian M. Benjamin who also belonged to the Church of God at that time. In 1947, M.O. John went back to Kerala and came into contact with the missionary couple Edwards, who worked for the Assemblies of God and sent him to the Bethel Bible School in Kerala. During this period, in 1948, he was married in Punalur and accompanied the Edwards family on a journey to Tamilnadu. After he had finished Bible school, he joined the Edwards in Tamilnadu until 1951. Apparently it was only then that he experienced baptism in the Spirit. Then under the influence of M. Benjamin, who for some time had moved his congregation to the Assemblies of God but after a deep quarrel with one young American missionary had gone back to the Church of God, M.O. John also left the Assemblies of God and joined the Church of God again. In the second half of the 1950s he left the Church of God and lived for a little while with Victor P.D. Kay, one of the important independent Pentecostal leaders of Tamilnadu in Thanjavur who worked together with P.M. Samuel from the Indian

---

[76] The details of this remarkable and complex conflict which cannot be given here, but cf. Bergunder, *Die südindische Pfingstbewegung im 20. Jahrhundert*, 14-26.

[77] Histories that focus on the work of western Pentecostal missionaries are still in vogue (cf. e.g. S.M. Burgess, 'Pentecostalism in India', *Asian Journal of Pentecostal Studies* 4 [2001], 85-98.), but, when the Indians themselves write about their history, the picture changes completely. Cf. Saju, *Kerala Pentekosthu Charithram*; A.C. George, 'Pentecostal Beginnings in Travancore, South India', *Asian Journal of Pentecostal Studies* 4 (2001), 215-37.

Pentecostal Church of God. Through Victor P.D. Kay, M.O. John also came into contact with P.M. Samuel. P.M. Samuel hailed from Kerala and was the leader of the Indian Pentecostal Church of God in Andhra Pradesh. He also controlled the Indian Pentecostal Church of God in Tamilnadu, mainly through the money that he got from foreign partners. In 1959 M.O. John went to Kalupatti, which was near his birthplace. There with the assistance of P.M. Samuel he founded a congregation in the name of the Indian Pentecostal Church of God. P.M. Samuel enabled him to open an orphanage in Kalupatti with the support of the German-based Christian Mission Service. In 1969, M.O. John had finished a church building; however he did not register it in the name of the Indian Pentecostal Church of God but in his own name. In the sequel he was P.M. Samuel's most important co-worker in Tamilnadu. In 1981, as he was not in agreement with a new leadership in the Indian Pentecostal Church of God in Tamilnadu, he left this denomination and made his congregation independent, which was very easy as the property never belonged to the Indian Pentecostal Church of God. In 1994 he joined the Indian Pentecostal Assemblies, another independent Pentecostal denomination in Tamilnadu. His eldest son Ebenezer (born 1953) studied in 1976-77 at Elim Bible Institute, New York. In 1979 in Tirumangalam near Madurai, he founded his own organization the Elim Church of God, which has an American Neocharismatic church as its main sponsor.

In writing a history of the Indian Pentecostal Movement it is exactly this kind of historical interaction that one has to focus on. Nevertheless in a study on Indian Pentecostalism it is also very important to include all the churches and organizations that show historical connections to Pentecostalism, even if they are currently not within the synchronous network.[78] Maybe they were part of the synchronous network at one time and maybe they will (re)claim a Pentecostal identity and re-enter the network. But often there are also groups which are in and out at the same time and which show that the borders are absolutely fluid and impossible to draw clearly. A good example is the Ceylon Pentecostal Mission (since 1984 in India officially under the name The Pentecostal Mission), which currently refuses contact with all other Pentecostal churches and has a whole range of extremely radical and church-dividing exclusive doctrines. Nevertheless numerous Pentecostal pastors were formerly members or even pastors in the Ceylon Pentecostal Mission. Amazingly the

---

[78] E.g. in South India the Bible Mission, Beginning Pentecostal Truth Church, Manujothi Ashram, Yesunamam Churches (cf. Bergunder, *Die südindische Pfingstbewegung im 20. Jahrhundert*, 143-58). Even more important would be the Catholic Charismatic movement which is of considerable strength in South India but has currently no or minimal relationship to the Indian Pentecostal movement. Since the sensational conversion of one of the leaders of the Tamil Catholic charismatics, S.J. Berchmans, to the Pentecostal movement in 1991, the situation has even become worse.

very distinctive doctrines of the Ceylon Pentecostal Mission are scarcely a matter of concern, but on the contrary many pastors, evangelists and lay people of the other Pentecostal churches greatly value the teaching of Ceylon Pentecostal Mission. This is connected with the fact that the Ceylon Pentecostal Mission is the only Indian Pentecostal church to have published on all important theological loci in detailed but easily understood publications. Moreover many members of other Pentecostal churches take part in the conventions of the Ceylon Mission and, conversely, their members (and even some of their pastors) attend these churches' conventions. So it is that the Ceylon Pentecostal Mission, in spite of its strong separatism, has not entirely lost its links with the mainstream of the Indian Pentecostal movement and it is very difficult to tell whether it is in or out of the synchronous network.

Furthermore, writing about the South Indian Pentecostal movement means putting the histories of single denominations or churches into the context of a larger framework that brings them together into one network. This is a very difficult task, but the following sketch of the history of the South Indian Pentecostal movement might give some idea of what is meant.

South Indian Pentecostal History

As already mentioned, the clashes in the late 1930s led to the foundation of four Pentecostal churches in Kerala. These churches maintained a leading position in Kerala, but with their increasing establishment they had to contend time and again with internal quarrels and stagnating tendencies. Hence they were not in a position to offer an adequate framework for integrating younger leading personalities with new ideas. That led to the founding of new churches. As a result Sharon Fellowship (P.J. Thomas, 1953) was born as a direct reaction to the quarrels within the Indian Pentecostal Church of God. Also the New India Church of God (V.A. Thamby, c. 1973) developed itself in the course of its history as a reservoir for many who were dissatisfied with the Pentecostal church to which they once belonged. The leaders of the New India Bible Church (Thomas Philip, Abraham Philip, 1972) did not want their church to be identified outside distinctly as a Pentecostal church and therefore established an independent organization. Gospel for Asia (K.P. Yohannan, 1978) was first founded only as a mission work and began later (1993) to establish its own church structures as a result of its dissatisfaction with the missing missionary dynamic of the existing Pentecostal churches. A common characteristic of all churches mentioned above is that their leadership is in the hands of Syrian Christians.[79] But since the 1940s, new Pentecostal churches were founded in

---

[79] For the problem of Syrian Christian domination within South Indian Pentecostalism see below. Syrian Christians claim to come originally from Hindu Brahman families that were converted by the apostle Thomas. All Syrian Christians were originally members

Kerala which were not led by Syrian Christians but by people groups that were considered much lower on the religio-social ladder: so-called Dalits (and in some cases by Nadars and Ezhavas who normally would not come under the term 'Dalit').[80] The main reason for this was the inability of the churches led by Syrian Christians to integrate Dalit or Nadar leaders. The foundation of the World Missionary Evangelism in Kerala (C.S. Mathew, 1962) is a good example. An extremely special case of the caste-compartmentalization within the Pentecostal movement in Kerala was the establishment of the 'Kerala Division' of the Church of God (K.J. Chacko, 1972), which demonstrates the exclusion of Dalit participation in a Church of God dominated by Syrian Christians. While the churches dominated by Syrian Christians have fostered comparatively closer contact among themselves, they seldom have a close relationship with churches led by Dalits or Nadars.

The South Indian Pentecostal movement established itself outside Kerala only in the second half of the 1940s. However a few remarkable mission activities had already taken place in the period before (in Tamilnadu: Madras Pentecostal Assembly since 1913, Ceylon Pentecostal Mission since 1930s, British Assemblies of God since 1920s; in Andhra Pradesh: Eastern Full Gospel Mission since 1926, Indian Pentecostal Church of God since 1932). Unfortunately very little is known about this.

Despite an earlier series of missionary activities, the Pentecostal movement was able to put down roots in Tamilnadu only after World War II. Two phases could be seen in that process. First of all in the 1940s until the 1960s, there were increased attempts by foreign missions and at the same time important indigenous ecclesiastical formations. After the end of World War II indigenous Pentecostal churches proliferated in Tamilnadu. The Indian Pentecostal Church of God achieved a few missionary successes coming from their stations in Andhra Pradesh. The Ceylon Pentecostal Mission, which attained new missionary strength under the chief pastor Alwin, also played an important role. At the same time, however, several experienced Tamil pastors left the Ceylon Pentecostal Mission and founded their own independent churches (John Rose,

---

of the Syrian Orthodox Church. Now, many of them are also Catholics or Protestants. A speciality of the Syrian Christian community is that, in spite of their confessional divisions, they maintain a common identity, analogous to the Hindu system. They practise an extraordinarily consistent endogamy and they keep very much to themselves in churches dominated by them. Regarding the Syrian Christian identity cf. e.g. G. Menachery (ed.), *The St. Thomas Christian Encyclopedia of India* (Trichur, 1973); S. Visvanathan, *The Christians of Kerala* (Madras: Oxford University Press, 1993); A. Kariyil, *Church and Society in Kerala* (New Delhi: Intercultural Publications, 1995).

[80] Dalit is a modern term that designates people who are considered untouchable in Brahmanical Hinduism, but discrimination didn't end after conversion to Christianity. Cf. e.g. J.C.B. Webster, *The Dalit Christians* (Delhi: I.S.P.C.K., 1992); S. Clarke, *Dalits and Christianity* (Delhi: Oxford University Press, 1998).

Full Gospel Pentecostal Church; S.B. Daniel/S. Ponraj, Pentecostal Church of India; G. Sunderam, Apostolic Christian Assembly). Since most of these pastors had lived together for some time in Malaysia they had close contact with each other and a strong feeling of togetherness, though each of them led independent churches. Several other independent churches began, like in the southernmost part of Tamilnadu where Sadhu Yesudhason became highly respected as the leader of a very influential indigenous church called Kirubasanam.

The second phase began in the 1960s when the foreign mission organizations went over one after the other to indigenous leadership and when it became increasingly possible for the indigenous churches to gain international partners. The result of that convergent development led to the formation of many new indigenous churches, which showed enormous increases since the 1980s and were strongly anchored in the global Pentecostal movement through their foreign partners. Since the 1960s, the Pentecostal movement also began to be deeply rooted in the big cities like Madurai, Coimbatore and Chennai. Chennai in particular experienced big growth and became the most important centre of the movement in southern India. Apart from the especially strong representation of the Assemblies of God, the scene was increasingly marked by many independent regional churches in this city. At the beginning of the twenty-first century, the Tamil-speaking south is arguably the most vibrant centre of Indian Pentecostalism.

The Pentecostal movement in Karnataka remained numerically weak right into the second half of the twentieth century. It was limited almost exclusively to migrants from Tamilnadu, Kerala and Andhra Pradesh, and it scarcely touched the native Kannada speaking population. Until the mid 1990s there were no really large centres of the Pentecostal movement except in Bangalore and in the neighbouring Kolar Gold Fields.

For a long time the Indian Pentecostal Church of God, started mainly by missionaries from Kerala, was the only distinct force of Pentecostalism in Andhra Pradesh. However in the second half of the 1940s, Pentecostalism in Andhra Pradesh entered a new phase. The missionaries from Kerala (who all belonged to the Syrian Christian community) and the new Pentecostal recruits from Andhra Pradesh who were practically all with the Indian Pentecostal Church of God, gave up moving around and became settled. Financial assistance from overseas made it possible for them to build their own churches and to set up local centres which acted very independently (e.g. P.M. Samuel, Vijayawada; P.T. Chacko, Secunderabad; P.L. Paramjothi, Antarvedipalam; K.R. David, Rajamundry; K.S. Joseph, Narasapur). In this way, the Indian Pentecostal Church of God in Andhra Pradesh developed a rather decentralized structure. It proved to be of special significance that the missionaries from Kerala (especially P.M. Samuel and P.T. Chacko) had far more overseas contacts than their colleagues from Andhra Pradesh. So unfair distribution went along with the establishment of local centres and this prepared the ground for recruitment campaigns by the Dallas based World Missionary Evangelism (John E. Douglas Sr.) in the 1960s. This had the result that, with the exception of P.L. Paramjothi, almost all the important Telugu leaders in the Indian Pentecostal Church of God went over to World Missionary Evangelism, which suddenly became the biggest Pentecostal church in Andhra Pradesh. Through World Missionary Evangelism the Indian Pentecostal Church of God suffered a severe setback, but it consolidated its position relatively soon and remained one of the bigger Pentecostal churches in Andhra Pradesh. In the following period it emerged from further secessions comparatively unharmed. Quite different was the situation of World Missionary Evangelism, which was shaken by repeated internal crises and never came to a settled condition. By the end of the 1960s, many more Pentecostal churches were established in Andhra Pradesh. Among these new churches there were significant differences. The missionary success of the classical Pentecostal churches proved to be comparatively modest. In contrast to the rest of South India the Assemblies of God, while successful elsewhere, had scarcely gained a footing in Andhra Pradesh. Indians who had stayed a long time in the USA were returning to Andhra Pradesh to begin their own missions with the backing of foreign sponsors they had found while staying overseas (e.g. Ernest Komanapalli, Manna Rock Church; P.J. Titus, New Testament Church). The fact that they were well acquainted with the Indian as well as the American scene was quite an advantage for numerical success. In addition to that churches in the big cities with a regional emphasis proved their potential for growth and developed their own style. In Vizag, for instance, there were two big churches, independent of one another, whose leaders had never belonged to a Pentecostal congregation and each went his own way in shaping their pastoral work (Krupa Rao's Jesus Christ Prayer and Evangelistic Ministries; and M.A. Paul's Christ's Church). Other independent churches were the result of splitting, where financial help from overseas played a part (e.g. Y.S. John Babu's Sion Fellowship).

'Indigenous' Pentecostalism?

Pentecostalism has been a global endeavour right from its beginning. No country or place can claim the origin of Pentecostalism. Nevertheless many Pentecostal and Charismatic churches in Africa, Asia and Latin America (and also in Europe!) display quite a strong White North American evangelical flavour that has its source in the huge missionary activities undertaken by Pentecostals from the United States. Theological statements of faith are copied from American Pentecostal originals, vernacular theological literature is translated from American sources and in many cases, even worship service and style are shaped by American cultural patterns. This easily gives the impression that being Pentecostal— wherever it might be—means practising an American Pentecostal way of spiritual life; this opinion would even be backed up by the popular self-understanding in quite a lot of Pentecostal circles all over the globe. It is this observation that called to the scene many critics who designated Pentecostalism as an American religion that was exported from the United States to the Third World as a means of ideological control.[81]

It was Walter Hollenweger who first forcefully disputed this one-sided-point of view and showed that there are many other variants of Pentecostalism with theological teachings not directly dependent on American models that can claim the same representational right to be Pentecostal.[82] Hollenweger's insights have shaped a whole generation of new and critical Pentecostal theologians who are now in the lead of Pentecostal scholarship;[83] among them it goes without saying that Pentecostalism must not be defined by North American evangelical standards only.

Next came the anthropologists and sociologists who became interested in non-western Pentecostal communities and started to do field work among them. Especially in the last two decades, a vast amount of research has been done that has deepened the academic knowledge of the Pentecostal movement tremendously.[84] As the most amazing finding, anthropological research showed the Pentecostal movement as a very contextual phenomenon and hardly as something destructive to existing society. Interestingly, this factual contextualization was found in both independent churches and churches with established organizational links to North American denominations. However what anthropologists observed was not the result of a conscious contextual Pentecostal theological agenda which was, as a rule, absent or even categorically rejected by the respective leaders and theological spokespersons.

Slowly, Pentecostal theologians are starting to cope with that situation and—coming from the Hollenwegerian approach but also influenced by a recent study of Harvey Cox[85]—they are trying to make theological sense out of the anthropological data. At present, Pentecostal theologians based in North America and Europe are in the forefront of this discussion[86] and, as a result, the White North American evangelical type is regarded as just one variety of the Pentecostal movement, as can best be seen from the fact that there are now

---

[81] Cf. S. Brouwer et al., *Exporting the American Gospel* (London: Routledge, 1996).

[82] Cf. W.J. Hollenweger, *The Pentecostals* (London: SCM Press, 1972).

[83] Cf. J.A.B. Jongeneel (ed.), *Pentecost, Mission and Ecumenism* (Frankfurt: Peter Lang, 1992).

[84] For an overview on anthropological literature on Latin America cf. M. Bergunder, 'The Pentecostal Movement and Basic Ecclesial Communities in Latin America', *International Review of Mission* 91 (2002), 163-86; for Africa cf. A.H. Anderson, *Zion and Pentecost* (Pretoria: University of South Africa Press, 2000); for India M. Bergunder, 'Miracle Healing and Exorcism', *International Review of Mission* 90 (2001), 103.

[85] Cf. H. Cox, *Fire From Heaven* (London: Cassell, 1996).

[86] Cf. e.g. D. Petersen, *Not By Might Nor By Power* (Oxford: Regnum Books, 1996); Yong, *Discerning the Spirit(s)*; Anderson, *Zion and Pentecost*.

several acknowledged Pentecostal perspectives in the West, like Hispanic-American and African American ('Black') Pentecostalism. [87] Gradually Pentecostal theologians from Asia, Africa and Latin America are joining in this venture[88] and certainly it is vital that they should take the lead in future.

The theological challenge which contemporary Pentecostal theology faces is curiously very similar to that in the mainline churches, where over the last decades concepts of inculturation and contextualization have been hotly discussed.[89] So it is not surprising that Pentecostal theologians sometimes use words like 'contextualization' or 'inculturation' when they go into the issue, but they rarely deal with the philosophical and theological concepts behind it.[90] At present one can observe some uncertainty among Pentecostals as to how to deal hermeneutically with the question of contextualization. That has certainly something to do with widespread reservations against ecumenical theology in general but probably more with the intrinsic difficulties: how to relate contextualization to a meaningful Pentecostal theology of mission (which is also still missing); or how to relate actual contextual performance to often explicit anti-contextual attitudes among the persons involved and so on. However, Pentecostal theology can not avoid these fundamental questions, but if it does tackle these issues it will probably become a heated debate. Moreover as the so-called ecumenical theology is still struggling for meaningful concepts of inculturation and contextualization a distinctive Pentecostal voice would be more than welcome to global academic theology in general.

Nevertheless there is some tendency to avoid this delicate debate by using a much older concept that still has some credit within evangelical circles: indigenization.[91] The concept of indigenization stems from Rufus Anderson and Henry Venn in the nineteenth century who propagated as the aim of mission the 'three selfs': self-government, self-support, and self-propagation. [92] This

---

[87] Cf. e.g. R.I. Gerloff, *A Plea for British Black Theologies* (Frankfurt: Peter Lang, 1992); S. Solivan, *The Spirit, Pathos and Liberation* (Sheffield: Sheffield Academic Press, 1998); Daniels, 'Everybody Bids You Welcome'.

[88] But cf. D. Kim, 'The Healing of Han in Korean Pentecostalism', *Journal of Pentecostal Theology* 15 (1999), 123-39.; J. Sepúlveda, 'Indigenous Pentecostalism and the Chilean Experience', in: A.H. Anderson and W.J. Hollenweger (ed.), *Pentecostals after a Century* (Sheffield: Sheffield Academic Press, 1999), 111-34.

[89] Cf. e.g. G. Collet (ed.), *Theologien der Dritten Welt* (Immensee, 1990); D.J. Bosch, *Transforming Mission* (Maryknoll: Orbis Books, 1991), 420-57; S.B. Bevans, *Models of Contextual Theology* (Maryknoll: Orbis Books, 1992).

[90] But cf. Yong, *Discerning the Spirit(s)*, 206-19.

[91] For a critique cf. Bosch, *Transforming Mission*, 448-50.

[92] Through Melvin Hodges (*The Indigenous Church* [Springfield, MO: Gospel Publishing House, 1953]) this concept became quite well known in Pentecostal circles too.

concept avoids a clear attitude towards inculturation or contextualization. It only emphasizes organizational independence from 'western' Pentecostalism but implies that this would also mean independence from western dominance. Nevertheless one should be careful not to fall prey to a wrong postcolonial reading of 'indigenous' as free from western domination. The ongoing academic discussion on postcolonial theory has shown that the simple binary code western/indigenous does not help to decipher dominant colonial and postcolonial discourses because the colonial encounter was quite complex and produced diverse, hybrid and fluid configurations.[93]

It is too simple to suggest that western denominations like the Assemblies of God try to dominate their non-western sister churches whereas Pentecostal churches in Africa, Asia and Latin America that are without established institutional ties to any western organisation or church would be more free, even if both have indigenous leadership. Oppression must not be narrowed down to the western/non-western antithesis. This would be misleading and would underestimate the effect of dominant discursive practices that work beyond established institutional links. Many independent Pentecostal churches get quite a lot of money from western partners; their leaders have studied at western Bible schools and they regularly entertain westerners as guests or missionaries at Gospel campaigns, and so on.

Moreover beliefs and rituals in indigenous churches are not necessarily more contextualized than in the churches that have official ties to western denominations. Even if one would add a fourth, 'theological' dimension to the above-mentioned three aspects of indigenization one would not get satisfactory results, because according to this logic churches would be most indigenized when they hold the most non-western set of doctrines and practices. But without discussing criteria for relating that to the universal claim of the Christian message and for determining an authentic Christian witness, this theological dimension remains meaningless.

Furthermore the growth rate of independent churches is not inevitably better than that of western denominations. In many regions of Africa, Asia and Latin America, the Assemblies of God are the fastest growing Pentecostal church. Indigenous churches are also not a benefit in themselves because independence does not necessarily mean good governance. If one analyses leadership, corruption, nepotism and similar phenomena, then the line is not at all between western and 'indigenous' Pentecostalism, but in between.

So for the hermeneutical task that lies ahead of Pentecostal theology the concept of indigenization would not be suitable because it falls short of expectations.

---

[93] Cf. e.g. B.J. Moore-Gilbert, *Postcolonial Theory* (London: Verso, 1997); R.J.C. Young, *Postcolonialism* (London: Blackwell, 2001).

Indian Pentecostalism as 'Indigenous' Christianity

At present there is no such thing as contextual theology within Indian Pentecostalism, though there have been some rare examples that somewhat headed in that direction, but rather motivated by the search for immediately effective missionary tools than by the search for new ways of theologizing.[94] Nevertheless things are changing fast and there are quite a few young Pentecostal Indian scholars who seem to be taking up the challenge.[95]

However there is also a tendency to look at Indian Pentecostalism within the straightforward antithesis of 'indigenous' versus 'western', which causes the above-mentioned problems. Roger Hedlund initiated a project on Indian 'Churches of Indigenous Origin', identifying independent Pentecostal churches as the most important representatives.[96] Hedlund, a long-time missionary to India who has a decidedly American evangelical background, shows a genuine openness and appreciation for the disparate Indian church landscape. His intentions are certainly laudable, especially in the context of rising Hindu nationalism that despises Islam and Christianity as foreign western, non-indigenous religions. Nevertheless, if 'indigenous' only means 'under the control of Indians, guided by Indian leaders'[97] then it is not clear why mainline denominations like the Church of South India and the Church of North India

---

[94] Already in 1975, John Thannickal wrote a dissertation in which he researched Hindu and Christian ashrams to find some stimulation for a contextual proclamation of the Christian message, cf. J. Thannickal, 'Ashram: A Communicating Community' (D. Miss. Thesis, School of World Mission, Fuller Theological Seminary, Pasadena, 1975); for information on John Thannickal cf. Bergunder, *Die südindische Pfingstbewegung im 20. Jahrhundert*, 103-104. In the 1980s Sadhu Chellappa started to go to the Hindu scriptures to prove Christ (cf. Bergunder, *Die südindische Pfingstbewegung im 20. Jahrhundert*, 138-39). Moses Choudhary - strongly influenced by Donald McGavran's church growth movement - promotes an accommodation strategy for Christian mission among high caste Hindus so that they can stay with their own people even after going over to Christianity, cf. G. Moses (Gullapalli Vinayak) Choudary, 'Reaching and Discipling Caste Hindus in Andhra Pradesh, India' (A Class Term Paper, Church of God School of Theology, Cleveland, 1980), and Bergunder, *Die südindische Pfingstbewegung im 20. Jahrhundert*, 131-33.

[95] For instance, V.V. Thomas (United Biblical Seminary, Poona) works on a PhD theses on 'Pentecostalism among Dalits in Kerala', and he explicitly relates this research to the concept of 'Dalit theology' which is the Indian variant of liberation theology. Others, like M. Stephen (Faith Theological Seminary, Manakala) or Isaac V. Mathew (Bethel Bible College, Punalur) are trying to make theological sense out of the encounter between Indian Pentecostalism and popular Hindu religiosity.

[96] Cf. R.E. Hedlund, 'Indian Instituted Churches', *Mission Studies* 16:1 (1999), 26-42; R. E. Hedlund (ed.), *Christianity is Indian* (New Delhi: ISPCK, 2000); R.E. Hedlund, *Quest for Identity* (Delhi: ISPCK, 2000).

[97] Hedlund, *Quest for Identity*, 81-82.

are not covered by that term. Accordingly, the assignments of the respective churches remain vague and inconsistent[98] and 'indigenous' remains nothing else but a synonym for 'non-western' or 'native'. A similar example is Indian Pentecostal theologian Paulson Pulikottil who refers to the independent Indian Pentecostal Church of God as an example of 'indigenous Pentecostalism' as against what he calls 'western Pentecostalism'.[99] He is certainly right when he claims an emancipatory, anti-colonial stance among the leaders of the Indian Pentecostal Church of God who successfully resisted any domination by western Pentecostal missionaries. Nevertheless, the postcolonial debate, which Pulikottil is explicitly referring to, goes much further. The subaltern studies project has shown that the anti-colonial national movement was mainly in the interest of the largely Hindu high-caste elites whereas the subalterns (untouchables, tribals, and so on) did not benefit to the same extent.[100]

In the same way, as the leadership of the Indian Pentecostal Church of God was dominated by Syrian Christians—who, as already mentioned, consider themselves as an ethnically defined caste group of very high social status comparable to Brahmans—the perpetuation of an oppressive structure by the exclusion of subaltern groups from leadership positions took place despite indigenous leadership. And it was not only the Indian Pentecostal Church of God at fault. All major Pentecostal (and most of the mainline) denominations in Kerala have Syrian leadership. This Syrian domination goes back quite early. At the beginning of the 1920s the majority of Pentecostals in Kerala were rather from 'low caste' or 'untouchable' background, people who would call themselves Dalits today. Robert F. Cook, the leading western Pentecostal missionary in that area, received positive reactions from different independent Dalit groups and their leaders at that time. For instance Poykayil Yohannan invited him to a central convention of his church in 1923 in which more than a

---

[98] The Syrian Orthodox church though it uses a 'foreign' (Syrian) liturgy can at the same time serve as the 'Original Indigenous Paradigm' (Hedlund, *Quest for Identity*, 23). Likewise, for instance, it is not clear why Pentecostal churches like the Tamil branch of the Church of God (Cleveland) or World Missionary Evangelism (Dallas, Texas) should be good examples for indigenous Pentecostalism (cf. Roger E. Hedlund, *Quest for Identity*, 82, 198). Similarly, Stanley Burgess knows of 'Indian Neocharismatics' which he explicitly considers as part of Hedlund's indigenous Christian movements, but as the most important example, he refers to the New Apostolic Church which is actually a Swiss-based centrally organized church of German-speaking origin with no Pentecostal ties so far (cf. Burgess, 'Pentecostalism in India', 95-96).

[99] Cf. P. Pulikottil, 'As East and West Met in God's Own Country', *Cyberjournal for Pentecostal-Charismatic Research* 10 (2001).

[100] Cf. V. Chaturvedi (ed.), *Mapping Subaltern Studies and the Postcolonial* (London: Verso, 2000).

thousand people gathered.[101] Cook found keen listeners and as a result further invitations followed. In spite of this those intensive contacts did not bring about the entry of Dalit leaders into the Pentecostal movement, whereas at the same time the Syrian Christians established themselves as bearers of the first line of leadership in the Pentecostal churches in Kerala. About the middle of the 1920s many Syrian Christians who had worked as congregational leaders with the Brethren, went over to the Pentecostal movement taking with them their congregations and thus became automatically the leading Pentecostal figures. It seems that the Syrian Christians particularly utilized a two-year absence of Cook (who had gone on furlough to the United States during 1924-26), to establish themselves in the leading church positions. It was arguably the dominance of Syrian Christians that prevented Dalit leaders such as Poykayil Yohannan from joining the Pentecostal movement. In any case, at that time it would have been hardly possible for Pentecostal Dalit pastors to rise up to leadership positions in a major Pentecostal denomination within the Kerala region, although there are remarkable exceptions like P.D. Johnson, who was for ten years (1980-90) District Superintendent of the Assemblies of God in Kerala. As a reaction to that situation Pentecostal churches arose that are based on homogeneous Dalit congregations with Dalit leadership (e.g. World Missionary Evangelism, Kerala Division of the Church of God) but still they are all at a disadvantage against the other Syrian dominated denominations (whether financially, or regarding foreign contacts and so on). These internal oppressive structures of Indian Pentecostalism cannot be named within a hermeneutical framework that is limited to the antithesis of 'indigenous' versus 'western', but one important context for contextual Pentecostal theology lies just here.

Conclusion

In conclusion one could say that constructing Indian Pentecostalism is a very difficult task that encounters quite a few methodological problems. On the one hand there is a historical problem that must be radically freed from theological premises. Moreover Indian Pentecostal historiography has to make sure that it really traces a diachronous and synchronous network of a Pentecostal movement. Otherwise it becomes doubtful whether it makes sense to apply the

---

[101] After his membership in the Church Missionary Society, in the Mar-Thoma Church and lastly with the Brethren, Poykayil Yohannan (who belonged to the Pulaiya community which is considered untouchable by caste Hindus) had founded his own independent church in 1907. See cf. W.S. Hunt, *The Anglican Church in Travancore and Cochin 1816-1916* (Kottayam: Church Missionary Society Press, 1920/1933), II, 235; S. Fuchs, *Godmen on the Warpath* (New Delhi: Munshiram Manoharlal, 1992), 236-38; Saju, *Kerala Pentekosthu Charithram*, 51.

term Pentecostal at all. On the other hand it is very difficult to make theological sense of the peculiarities of Pentecostalism within an Indian context. Anthropologists' observation of factual contextualization could be taken as the starting point of reflective concepts of contextual Pentecostal theology. Constructing Indian Pentecostalism is a task that refers to the very fundamental issues of the academic study of Pentecostalism. So the arguments presented in this paper will hopefully be helpful in the ongoing discussion of how Pentecostalism in general can best be studied.

Indigenous Pentecostalism in India

Roger E. Hedlund

Pentecostal Origins in India

Pentecostalism in India has its roots in Maharashtra at the Ramabai Mukti Mission, Kedgaon, according to various authorities.[1] In 1897 Pandita Ramabai invited Minnie Abrams, one of the earliest Pentecostal missionaries from America, to minister at Kedgaon.[2] In 1905 a spiritual revival at Mukti was to reverberate far beyond Kedgaon.[3] A first-hand account by Minnie Abrams describes the weeping and praying of the repentant Mukti girls as well as the dramatic manifestations which accompanied the new 'baptism of the Holy Ghost and fire'.[4] Preaching bands from Mukti volunteered to spread the gospel in the surrounding villages. The message of Pentecost made its way to other parts of India. Healings, speaking in tongues, prophecy and other 'gifts of the Spirit' were in vogue.[5]

J. Edwin Orr documents the spread of the revival as the Mukti bands carried the message throughout the Maratha country. Characterized by emotional phenomena, the impact of the awakening was long-lasting in terms of conversions and changed lives.[6] The spiritual movement spread across various

---

[1] Ivan M. Saatyavrata, 'Contextual Perspectives on Pentecostalism as a Global Culture: A South Asian View' in Murray W. Dempster, Byron D. Klaus, and Douglas Petersen (eds.), *The Globalization of Pentecostalism: A Religion Made to Travel* (Carlisle, UK, Paternoster, Regnum Books, 1999), 204. See also Gary B. McGee, *This Gospel Shall Be Preached: A History and Theology of Assemblies of God Foreign Missions to 1959* (Springfield, MO: Gospel Publishing House, 1986), 54.

[2] Basil Miller, *Pandita Ramabai: India's Christian Pilgrim* (Pasadena, World-Wide Missions, n.d.), 64.

[3] Ibid., 86-87.

[4] Minnie F.Abrams, *The Baptism of the Holy Ghost & Fire* (Kedgaon, Pandita Ramabai Mukti Mission, second edition,1906, reprinted in1999), 1-3. Walter J. Hollenweger states that in 1963 the Mukti Mission leadership claimed they were totally ignorant of the Pentecostal revival, *Pentecostalism: Origins and Developments Worldwide* (Peabody, Mass., Hendrickson Publishers, 1997), 120.

[5] Ibid., 36.

[6] J. Edwin Orr, *Evangelical Awakenings in India* (New Delhi, Masihi Sahitya Sanstha, 1970), 111-114.

denominations, e.g. Alliance, Anglican, Baptist, Friends, Methodist and Presbyterian.... At Mukti Ramabai channelled the enthusiasm of the believing community into famine relief work as well as social rehabilitation.[7] In this way the spiritual awakening had an enduring influence in Maharashtrian society.

There were also, however, earlier precedents in South India, both in Tamil Nadu and in Kerala. Historian Gary McGee states that 'the most prominent revivals of the nineteenth century characterized by the charismatic gifts of the Holy Spirit occurred in India'.[8] Pentecostalism in South Asia, then, is significantly indigenous in origin. 'The Pentecostal movement that created ripples in South India began as an indigenous movement. It was not until later that revival movements in the West impacted on this indigenous movement'.[9] In 1860 in Tirunelveli, under CMS catechist John Christian Aroolappen, a revival took place with Pentecostal signs including prophecy, tongues, interpretation of tongues, dreams, visions, and intense conviction of sin.[10] A decade later a similar revival was brought to Kerala (Travancore) by Aroolappen.[11]

These and other antecedents prepared the ground for the twentieth century Pentecostal movement in India. As A.C. George observes, Pentecostalism in South India 'was not born in a vacuum. On the contrary, it came out of a church that could boast of almost two thousand years of Christianity'.[12]

Among early Pentecostal missionaries were several from the 1908 Azusa Street Mission revival. These included George Berg and Robert F. Cook, pioneer missionaries whose evangelistic work laid the foundations for the beginnings of the Assemblies of God and the Church of God in Southern India. Cook, who began as an independent missionary, for a while joined the Assemblies of God then separated and, affiliated to the Church of God (Cleveland), attracted a group of committed local preachers who were to become significant Pentecostal leaders. One of them, K.E. Abraham, became founder of the Indian Pentecostal Church of God, a major indigenous Pentecostal denomination from which have sprung numbers of other independent movements. IPC is the largest indigenous Pentecostal movement in India and continues to grow at the rate of one new church per week. In 1997

---

[7] Jessie H. Mair, *Bungalows in Heaven: The Story of Pandita Ramaba* (Kedgaon, Pandita Ramabai Mukti Mission, revised, 1993 reprint), 79.

[8] Gary B. McGee, 'India: Pentecostal and Pentecostal-like Movements (1860-1910)' (an unpublished article, c.1999), cited by A.C. George, 'Pentecostal Beginnings in Travancore, South India', *Asian Journal of Pentecostal Studies* 4:2 (2001), 220.

[9] A.C. George, 'Pentecostal Beginnings in Travancore, South India',*Asian Journal of Pentecostal Studies* 4:2 (July 2001), 220.

[10] Ibid., 222.

[11] Ibid., 223.

[12] Ibid., 216.

there were more than 3,000 local churches in India including 1,700 in Kerala, 700 in Andhra, 210 in Tamil Nadu, 70 in Karnataka, and smaller numbers in other states in North India and the North East.[13]

The IPC is an important expression of Christian nationalism in India prior to India's independence. K.E. Abraham believed that ministry could progress better without foreign missionary domination. Self-supporting churches should be led by self-sacrificing national ministers. Leadership should be in the hands of local Christians. Local churches should manage their own affairs and hold their own property as independent Christian Churches in an independent India. The IPC thus challenged the Assemblies of God and the Church of God which were of missionary origins in India.

From these origins have emerged numerous Pentecostal movements. One example is the Sharon Fellowship Church and its institutions based at Thiruvalla begun by P.J. Thomas after he separated from the IPC in 1953. Today SFC has more than 90,000 members and 450 congregations in Kerala and 350 outside Kerala.[14]

These are but a few of the many Pentecostal denominations in India. The first major scholarly study of South Indian Pentecostalism[15] touches the history of all known Pentecostal bodies in South India, including those of indigenous

---

[13] Information is compiled from a number of sources including an interview with the son of the founder and present head of the IPC, Pastor T.S. Abraham, at Hebron, Kumbanad, on 18 December, 1997. Important sources consulted include the following: Sara Abraham, 'A Critical Evaluation of the Indian Pentecostal Church of God - Its Origin and Development in Kerala' (MTh thesis, Serampore University, 1990); IPC, 'A Handbook of the Indian Pentecostal Church of God' (Kumbanad, Kerala: IPC General Secretary, Hebronpuram, 1994); Samuel Mathew, 'Biblical Leadership: A Theology of Servanthood for the Church in India' (MTh in Missiology thesis, Fuller Theological Seminary, 1989); Abraham Thottumkal Pothen, 'The Indian Pentecostal Church of God and Its Contribution to Church Growth' (MA Missiology thesis, Fuller Theological Seminary, 1988); Saju, *Kerala Penthecosthu Charithram* (Kottayam: Good News Publications,1994); P.J. Titus, 'IPC Movement in Andhra Pradesh' (unpublished paper, 1997); Habel G. Verghese, *K.E. Abraham: An Apostle From Modern India* (Kadambanad, Kerala: Christian Literature Service of India), 1974.

[14] Information is from T.P. Abraham, 'Sharon Fellowship Church' (an unpublished paper, n.d.). Dr Abraham is a theologically-trained leader and educator in the Fellowship to whom I am indebted for much of the information about SFC. Sources for Dr Abraham's paper include *CEM Silver Jubilee Souvenir* (1983); *Burning Flames* edited by Elanthoor Achankunju (1994); 'Sharon Fellowship Church' (an unpublished research paper, Fuller Theological Seminary, 1986). Additional information is from an unpublished paper, 'Sharon Fellowship Church' (n.d.,) by K.V. Daniel of the Voice of the Gospel Ministries, Trichur.

[15] This is a definitive work by a German scholar at Halle University, Michael Bergunder, *Die Südindische Pfingstbewegung im 20.Jahrhundert* (Frankfurt, Peter Lang, 1999), not yet available in English.

origins as well as those of international (foreign missionary) extraction. Bergunder lists a total of 71 Pentecostal bodies in the four southern states. Andhra Pradesh has 14 Pentecostal denominations of which 12 appear to be indigenous in origin. These include the Bible Mission, Christ's Church, Church of God, Indian Pentecostal Church, Jesus Christ Prayer and Evangelistic Ministries, Manna/Rock Church, New Testament Church, Sion Fellowship, and various small churches at Hyderabad and Vizag and throughout Andhra with a total Andhra constituency of 37,500 members.

In Karnataka, out of seven Pentecostal groups, six might be classed as indigenous in origin. These are the Ceylon Pentecostal Mission, Gospel Prayer Hall, Philadelphia Church, Shekinah Gospel Prayer Fellowship, and other small churches of Bangalore and Karnataka with a total of 9,200 members in Karnataka.

In Kerala, 11 out of 15 Pentecostal bodies listed appear to be CIOs, namely: Apostolic Church of Pentecost, Ceylon Pentecostal Mission, Church of God (M.E. Jacob), Church of God (Kerala Division), Church of God (Kerala State), Indian Pentecostal Assembly, Indian Pentecostal Church, International Zion Assembly, New India Bible Church, New India Church of God, Sharon Fellowship, and various small churches of Kerala together comprising some 96,500 believers in Kerala.

But Tamil Nadu has the greatest number with 33 Pentecostal bodies of which 27 appear to be groups of indigenous origin, comprising a total of 124,900 members. Groups listed include the Apostolic Christian Assembly, Apostolic Fellowship Tabernacle, Athumanesar, Beginning Pentecostal Truth Church, Body of Christ, Ceylon Pentecostal Mission, Church of God, Full Gospel Pentecostal Church, Good News Mission, Good Samaritan Fellowship, Good Shepherd Evangelical Church, Indian Pentecostal Assemblies, Indian Pentecostal Church, Jehova Salvation Church, Kirubasanam, Living Word Church, Madras Pentecostal Assembly, Maranatha, Prayer Garden Fellowship, Prince of Peace, Trinity Full Gospel Church, Zion Assemblies of God, and various small churches of the cities and districts of Tamil Nadu.[16]

The above is not an exhaustive listing of South Indian Pentecostals. New groups frequently appear, and other groups are overlooked inadvertently by researchers and compilers. A similar investigation in North India would reveal parallel developments of new indigenous Pentecostal and Charismatic movements in Mumbai, in Punjab, and in Delhi. A common thread running through each of these Pentecostal churches is a conscious expression of their Indian identity and character. Their Pentecostal faith binds them to fellow-believers world-wide. Yet their life and witness at home and in the diaspora are indelibly marked by an Indian identity and character.

---

[16] Ibid., 306-307.

The origins of Pentecostalism in Sri Lanka are closely related to developments in India. The earliest Pentecostal missionaries were not related to any denomination and served as independent Christian workers. The most prominent among them was a woman, Anna Lewini, from Denmark who first arrived in Colombo in 1919, returned to Denmark in 1920, then came again to Sri Lanka where she remained for more than three decades. In 1922 she rented a hall at Borella which became the first assembly of Pentecostal Christians in Sri Lanka, known as Glad Tidings Hall. In 1927 the name was changed to Colombo Gospel Tabernacle.[17]

Anna Lewini was the 'real founder of Pentecostalism in Sri Lanka'.[18] Another figure, however, was to be more prominent, because Anna Lewini deliberately chose a secondary position. 'She labored and founded the mission. Then she prayed for a man to arrive to take over the leadership. When the person arrived she willingly handed over the ministry to that person'.[19] Walter H. Clifford was that person who arrived from India to serve from 1924 to 1948 as an Assemblies of God missionary in Sri Lanka.[20] Clifford's ministry and influence were extensive. He not only laid a solid foundations for the Assemblies of God, but also influenced other denominations.

According to historian Somaratna, 'The Ceylon Pentecostal Mission owes its origin to the ministry of Walter Clifford'.[21] The CPM began as a breakaway group in 1923 led by Alwin R. de Alwis and Pastor Paul. The CPM espoused an ascetic approach to spirituality. Ministers were not to marry and they should wear white. They disdained the use of medicine and gave central importance to the doctrine of the second coming of Christ. Somaratna observes that testimonies of miraculous healing attracted Buddhists and Hindus, and the wearing of white was appropriate culturally in Sri Lanka where Buddhist devotees wore white to visit the temples. The CPM also instituted indigenous forms of worship.[22]

The CPM, despite its name, did not remain confined to Sri Lanka but spread to other countries including South India, the birthplace of Pastor Paul, then known as Ramankutty, born in 1881 to Hindu parents in the village of Engadiyur in Trichur District, Kerala.[23] In 1895, at the age of fourteen,

---

[17] G.P.V. Somaratna, *Origins of the Pentecostal Mission in Sri Lanka* (Nugegoda, Margaya Fellowship, 1996), 12, 16, 18.

[18] G.P.V. Somaratna, *Walter H. Clifford: Apostle of Pentecostalism in Sri Lanka* (Nugegoda, Margaya Fellowship, 1997), 23.

[19] Loc.cit.

[20] Ibid., 25.

[21] Loc.cit.

[22] Somaratna, *Origins...*, 34-35, 40-41.

[23] This information is provided by one a stalwart member, Bro. Paul C. Martin, 'A Brief History of the Ceylon Pentecostal Mission' (Paper presented at the Hyderabad Conference on Indigenous Christian Movements in India, 27-31 October, 1998).

Ramankutty went to Sri Lanka, where he was employed in Colombo by a wealthy Christian, Dr Asarappa, who was himself a Hindu convert to Christianity. This apparently was Ramankutty's first contact with Christianity and the Christian Church. But he had no desire to be a Christian and even refused to accept a Bible. Then in 1899, at the age of eighteen, he had a vision of the Lord Jesus Christ which caused him to begin secretly to pray and meditate on Jesus.[24] This, however, was not the first such vision, nor was it to be the last. His vision in 1899 caused him to recall this childhood experience. Then, in 1902, at the age of twenty two, came a third vision following which Ramankutty could no longer remain a hidden follower of Jesus. This may be viewed as a decisive encounter and call. Ramankutty openly confessed Jesus as Lord, was baptized and given the Christian name 'Paul'.

His ministry developed gradually. It was reported that a leper over whom Paul prayed was cured and a person declared dead was brought to life. People were attracted to his new fellowship, called the Ceylon Pentecostal Mission. Among those who joined was a college lecturer, Alwin R.de Alwis. Under the leadership of Pastor Paul and Bro. Alwin the CPM ministry spread beyond Colombo to Tamil Nadu and Kerala, then to other countries.[25]

The CPM laid the foundation for other Pentecostal ministries, not only in Sri Lanka and India but beyond. Today, says Paul C. Martin, the CPM under various names, is one of the largest Pentecostal movements in the world with branches in several countries. While exact membership figures are not yet available, there are 848 branches world-wide (including 708 in India) and about 3,984 full-time ministers presided over by the current chief pastor C.K. Lazarus.[26] In addition there are numbers of independent assemblies and movements which have severed connections with the CPM. Some of these are prominent, such as the Apostolic Christian Assembly in Tamil Nadu, founded by Pastor G. Sundram, led today by Pastor Sam Sundaram, and many more.

To the north of India, in Nepal, where Christianity has been growing rapidly during the last three decades, the Christian movement from its inception is said to have a Pentecostal character. Even before Nepal opened its doors in 1951, Pentecostal missionaries in India were active on the Nepal border. Some of the converts were trained at the North India Bible Institute of the Assemblies of God at Hardoi. In Nepal converts were exposed to Pentecostal teaching. Besides the Assemblies of God, the Agape Fellowship and many independent churches are Pentecostal or Charismatic.[27] Christianity in Nepal could be described as a 'first century church'.

---

[24] Ibid.

[25] Ibid., 8.

[26] Martin, *op.cit.*, 5, 12.

[27] Bal Krishna Sharma, 'A History of the Pentecostal Movement in Nepal', *Asian Journal of Pentecostal Studies* 4:2 (July 2001), 295-305.

From these scanty glimpses of Pentecostal origins in South India, Sri Lanka and Nepal, we turn for a closer look at Andhra Pradesh, then give some examples from North India and the North East. First a disclaimer. This paper is not exhaustive. It does not claim to cover all the Pentecostals in South Asia. Nor does it explore all the regions of India. At best this may serve as an introduction to a large subject by offering a few examples. These vignettes indicate something of the diversity among Indian Pentecostals. The examples included are some of those which have emerged through indigenous initiative rather than from foreign missionary initiative. The latter are extremely important. They simply are not the focus of the present study. Although Indian Pentecostalism is strongest in Tamil Nadu and Kerala, we begin in South India with Andhra Pradesh, where Pentecostalism has its own identity quite apart from its significant links with Kerala. We then move to parts of North India: Madhya Pradesh, Bihar, Myumbai, Bengal—then finally to the North East with its own distinct history.

Andhra Pradesh: Kerala Outreach & Local Indigeneity

Indigenous Christianity is prominent in Andhra Pradesh, especially in the coastal districts. An interesting feature is that the Christian community is drawn from all sections of society, including a wide spectrum of Hindu castes. According to a 1983 survey, about a quarter of the Christians in East Godavari District were from the forward community, the so-called higher castes.[28] In West Godavari about 16% were from such backgrounds. In Guntur District 10% of the Christians identified themselves as from high caste parentage, and in Krishna District about 12%. In western Krishna District the Church of South India was predominant while in eastern Krishna the independent churches dominated including WME, IPC, and other Pentecostal groups as well as the non-Pentecostal LEF and Bakht Singh assemblies. The independent groups were said to be active in Bible study and outreach, self-supporting, meeting for worship in homes, ministering to members' needs.[29] It seems evident that indigenous Christianity is much more vigorous in Andhra than governmental and other statistics would indicate.

It will be helpful to take a closer look at the numerous independent churches in the city of Visakapatnam, also known as Vizag, many of which are Pentecostal or Charismatic in character. Vizag appears to be a city of indigenous movements and churches with more than 1,000 house churches

---

[28] Santosh Kumar, Yesupadam, and Jonathan, *East Andhra Survey* (Kilpauk, Madras, Church Growth Research Centre, 1983).
[29] Ibid.

reported.[30] I have personally visited and preached in several well-established CIO[31] congregations in the city including Christ's Church, Upper Room, and the New Testament Church. Christ's Church is a prominent CIO which began as a single worship service started sometime after 1972 by Pastor M.A. Paul and his colleagues. This church has experienced rapid growth. Christ's Church today has 50 branches with more than 5,000 members. Pastor M.A. Paul is assisted by associates and elders. Services are conducted in Telugu, English and Oriya. The fellowship operates a children's home, a widows' home and welfare projects and conducts regular conventions and leadership training courses.[32]

Upper Room Prayer Fellowship is the outcome of a revival which began in 1969 in an 'upper room' prayer meeting—hence the name of this church. The prayer group gradually developed into a Sunday worship. Today this Fellowship is a registered society which has spread into three districts of Andhra with fourteen branches having a total membership of about 5,000 members of which 70% are urban. There is no foreign support involved. Emphasis is on church planting through team ministry and prayer cells under the direction of Bro. Sukumar Patnaik who is the present leader.[33]

Bethesda Church, located in Sanjeeviah Colony, Vizag 4, is another CIO registered body which receives no foreign funds. The church was started in 1968 by Pastor J.D. Moses, a retired forest officer, who continued as pastor until his death in 1987 after which Pastor S. Paramanandam, who is a product of Pastor J.D. Moses' ministry, became the leader. This is a Charismatic church with one additional branch and 600 followers from the urban area.[34]

Logos Prayer Fellowship Centre, Reading Room and Development Society, was founded in 1974 by Pastor S. Abraham while he was an employee in the Port Trust. What began as a worship service with one member today has four branches and a local church of 250 members. Ministry is concentrated on slum areas with team and film evangelism. This Pentecostal ministry is a registered society with seven board members. They have published a Telugu hymn book. Within the next five years they plan to begin 100 churches.[35]

Sanjeevaiah Colony, Vizag, also is the headquarter of Rhema Blessing Ministries. Mr N. Anand, an assistant scientist in the Meteorological

---

[30] This figure was mentioned by several local persons during the Initial Meeting of the Indigenous Christian Movements Project on 19 August, 1997, at COTR Seminary, Vizag.

[31] Churches of Indigenous Origin. The CIO abbreviation is derived from the project by that name carried out during 1997-2000 as part of a Pew-funded, OMSC-administered research enablement book-writing grant.

[32] Information provided for the CIO Project by Dr P.J. Titus in a letter to Roger E. Hedlund, 13 January, 1999.

[33] Ibid.

[34] Ibid.

[35] Ibid.

Department of the Government of India, was a product of Pastor M.R. James' ministry in 1975. In 1993 he left his job in order to continue full-time ministry as a pastor of the Logos Prayer Fellowhip. In January 1998 he started a new Charismatic ministry which he registered as Rhema Blessing Ministries. This is an independent ministry without any foreign support. There are ten branches and 800 followers, 80% from the urban area, drawn from Gavara, Velam and Kapu backgrounds. A Telugu magazine, *Rhema Blessings*, is published as well as tracts and a Telugu-English hymn book. The goal is to increase the number of prayer cells and to establish ministries in four coastal districts of Andhra Pradesh.[36]

Faith Home Ministries began in 1980 at Vizag with four members. Pastor Y. Isaac, the founder, came from Guntur and earlier was associated with the Ceylon Pentecostal Mission. This ministry has expanded to incorporate 1,100 believers and five branches (including one in Connecticut, USA). In Vizag they have two Telugu worship services as well as an English service every Sunday. Membership is about 90% urban. Every October and November this fellowship conducts a 40-day Bible training programme. They have produced a Telugu hymn book, audio cassettes, and tracts. *The Voice of the Last Trumpet* is a monthly Telugu publication. Pastor Isaac also conducts healing crusades in different parts of the country. Faith Home Ministries is a registered society with seven board members. This Full Gospel Pentecostal ministry receives no foreign support and has a goal to plant ten churches within a year.[37]

Love-N-Care Ministries, established in 1991 under the leadership of Pastor P. Yesupadam, is reported to be one of the fastest growing Christian movements of Vizag. In 1998 the founder received a vision in which he saw two hands holding a globe with the words 'JESUS CARES'. This vision resulted in the present Love-N-Care Ministries which has 10,000 followers in 103 branches. Membership is 80% rural from Kamma, Kapu, Reddy, Brahmin and tribal backgrounds. Students are given practical training in a one-year outreach course at two discipleship training centres. This Charismatic Movement is active in service to society through three schools, one junior college, three children's homes, one old age home, and other welfare programmes.

Books, tracts, hymnals, newsletters, and a magazine titled *Eternal Life* are printed by Bethany Printers. These ministries are registered under the Societies Registration Act. Pastor Yesupadam plans to begin a 100 bed hospital and a Jesus Cares University by year 2001. Branches have started in USA, Canada and South Korea, and Pastor Yesupadam also plans to extend the ministries to South Africa.[38]

---

[36] Ibid.
[37] Ibid.
[38] Ibid.

New Life Pentecostal Church was established in 1985 by Pastor K.C. Mathew at Sanjay Gandhi Colony, Vizag-40, with a vision to plant churches in unreached villages. Under the joint leadership of K.I. Jameson Mathews and Dr K. Sam Mathews, they now have 64 churches and 3,700 believers in Andhra and Orissa, 75% from the rural area. Members are from Brahmin, Vysya, Kamma, Kapu and tribal backgrounds. The church has a film ministry and outreach team as well as an evening Bible College to train the laity. As a charitable society the church provides assistance to widows and marriage assistance to the poor as well as help to the needy in times of floods and other natural calamities. It also operates a school, a children's home and a tailoring centre and publishes an English magazine. Leadership have goals to plant 2,000 churches by the year 2010, to start children's homes in different places in Andhra and Orissa, and to launch a missionary training centre to train 50 persons per year. They plan to become members of the Evangelical Fellowship of India and of the Pentecostal Fellowship of India.[39]

Christian Faith Ministries Association, founded by Rev. Ch. Daniel in 1976, has 63 branches in five coastal districts of Andhra Pradesh with some 4,000 followers, 90% from the rural area. In association with Campus Crusade for Christ they conduct a film ministry. This Full Gospel Pentecostal Association operates a one-year Bible Institute course, Victory Public School, a dairy farm, and a tailoring centre for women. They publish a Telugu magazine, *Go, or Send*, and have produced a Telugu hymn book.. Rev. Ch. Daniel has plans to begin a hospital and aims to start one church per month in the rural areas.[40]

Jesus Heals Ministries was started in 1984 by Dr G. Luke as a response to the call and vision of God. At present there are 23 branches with 1,300 members, 70% from rural areas. Dr G. Luke is a medical practitioner with a heart for evangelism. As part of a community development plan he has established health centres in the villages. Medical aid, food, clothing, and rescue operations are extended to widows, orphans and others in times of natural calamities. Every month evangelism activities are extended to ten villages. An occasional newsletter is published. An audio and video cassette on health education has been produced. This organization cooperates with government and foreign agencies in a rural health programme. Jesus Heals Ministries is a Pentecostal ministry registered under the Societies Act. Within the next five years they plan to plant 1,000 churches and train 1,000 native missionaries.[41]

Viswas Prarthana Mandiram was begun in 1991 by Pastor G.V. Rao, who resigned from the Telecom Department for this purpose. VPM has three branches with 650 members. Worship is in English and Telugu. This is a

---

[39] Ibid.
[40] Ibid.
[41] Ibid.

Pentecostal ministry registered under the Societies Act. It is a completely urban ministry with church planting as a future goal.[42]

Christian Life Centre Ministries was established in 1985 as a holistic ministry to care for the total needs of humans. The founder, Sudheer K. Mohanty, following a profound spiritual experience of the Lord Jesus Christ, resigned his bank job and entered into full-time Christian ministry in obedience to the call of God. Today CLC has 3,100 followers in 13 churches in Andhra and Orissa, half of them from a rural background. Local people are trained and equipped by the ministry which operates a free education school, children's home, old age home, health centres and other welfare programmes such as constructing water tanks and sponsoring the poor and needy for higher education. CLC publishes books, tracts, hymnals, and audio and video cassettes. A goal is to plant more churches.[43]

The Rt Rev. Dr K.R. Singh is founder-president of the United Christian Interior Ministries. The founder began preaching at an early age, then completed theological education studies in India and in Germany. Singh, who has suffered much for the cause of Christ, started this ministry among Naxelites and other radical groups in the tribal village of Seloor. Some 200 tribal churches have been established.[44]

Near Vizag at Bheemunipatnam is located the COTR Theological Seminary founded by Rev. Dr P.J. Titus in 1983 which today enrols more than 200 students.[45] Some 350 students from various parts of India have earned BTh and MDiv degrees and 300 have done certificate and diploma courses in the Seminary. Other entities in the COTR cluster of ministries include the Nava Jeevan Public School of 625 children, New Life Children's Home catering to the poor and destitute, COTR Hospital providing medical care to the surrounding villages, a free Legal Aid Association, and the COTR Vocational College offering a two-year training course for needy women. The campus serves as headquarters of the New Testament Church of India which claims 200 affiliated local churches and includes a Hindi regional training centre at Delhi. Originally from Kerala, Dr P.J. Titus is a nephew of the late Apostle P.M. Samuel who was the pioneer and founder of the Indian Pentecostal Church of God in Andhra Pradesh. The IPC was registered in 1935 at Eluru and today has hundreds of churches and pastors in the major centres of Andhra Pradesh such as Vajayawada, Warangal, Narasapur, Antervedipalem, Hyderabad-Secunderabad, Rajahmundry, Tadepalligudem, Kakinada, Vizag,

---

[42] Ibid.

[43] Ibid.

[44] Ibid.

[45] COTR and NTCI information is drawn from several visits and from the COTR publication, *The Answer* 15:1 (February 1997).

Amalapuram, Mandapeta, and Khammam District.[46] The Zion Bible College at Vijayawada, started in 1940, now is directed by P.M. Samuel's grandson. Several former IPC pastors have begun independent churches or joined other fellowships such as the WME mission.[47]

Numerous other churches, organizations, and indigenous institutions are found throughout the coastal region. At Chintapally in Vizag District the tribal Christians comprise an indigenous movement known as 'Adinivasi Pragathi Padam'.[48]

Another primary centre of indigenous Christian movements and institutions is Guntur which has numbers of independent assemblies, Pentecostal and other churches. The most notable is the Bible Mission founded by M. Devadas. This indigenous movement is one of the few to have been described in an academic dissertation and publication.[49] The Bible Mission can be classed as a healing movement but appears to shun a distinctly Pentecostal identity. Writings of the founder have been translated and are available in three small books from the headquarters at Guntur. From the first book, *Mithra, The Friend*, we learn something of the theology of Devadas. The second, *Maxims to Rebuke Satan*, in today's parlance might be called a manual for spiritual warfare. The third book, *Praising God for His Divine Qualities*, is a devotional guide or worship manual. In the Preface to this book Rev.John Selvaraj relates, 'One day St Devadas praised God from 8 am to 4 pm remembering his divine quality of Holiness. Praise only, not prayer! There are instances of this kind in his life'.[50] The incident is reminiscent of a Christian Indian *bhakta*. The book is a recital of eleven attributes of God together with prayers and praises to be used in thanksgiving meetings. The second book, dealing with Satan, also is suited to a Christian version of the *bhakti* movement and begins with a chapter 'Praising the Lord for His Divine Qualities'.[51] Then follow chapters intended as guides to believers in times of temptation: Satan's head to be cut off; Prayers to the Lord and reprimands to Satan; Reprimands and rebukes to Satan; Maxims to rebuke Satan; Prayers to God to drive away Devils; Letters of divorce and challenge to Satan; Know your adversary the Satan; and Steps to subdue Satan. This book reveals an apparently straightforward biblical Christology, demonology, and eschatology. A more elaborate theological statement is provided by Devadas's

---

[46] P.J. Titus, 'IPC Movement in Andhra Pradesh' (unpublished paper enclosed with the author's letter of November 15, 1997, to Roger E. Hedlund).

[47] Ibid.

[48] Letter from Revd D.J. Jeremiah of Andhra Christian Theological College, Hyderabad, to Roger E. Hedlund, 11 August, 1997.

[49] P. Solomon Raj, *A Christian Folk-Religion in India* (Frankfurt, Peter Lang, 1986).

[50] 'Preface' in M. Devadas *Praising God for His Divine Qualities* (Guntur, Bible Mission, 1997).

[51] M. Devadas, *Maxims to Rebuke Satan* (Guntur, Bible Mission, 1996), 1-3.

first book, *Mithra*, which is subtitled *God's 'Great Plan of Salvation' for all Mankind Revealed*.[52] The book begins with an invitation to salvation then follows with summary statements on various doctrines and topics together with Bible references. Much of Devadas's teaching was done orally, and this book is a summary of what he taught.

These three books give an impression of Devadas as an Indian *bhakta* with a fairly orthodox Christian doctrine. His teachings are considered normative by the followers. The Bible Mission continues to attract a wide following from Andhra and from bordering Orissa. The Indian identity of the Bible Mission is clearly evident in the career of the founder and in the week-long annual convention near Guntur attended by more than 20,000 devotees.

Guntur also is the home of several lesser-known indigenous Christian expressions. For example, the New Jerusalem Gospel Society at Nagram in Guntur District, founded in 1961 by Dr K. John, reports 75 branch churches with 75 pastors and 4,000 believers working among the neglected section of society 'whose life is very miserable'.[53]

Hyderabad in recent years has become a major centre of indigenous activity. Pastors and other Christian leaders of all denominations in the Twin Cities join regularly in a prayer fellowship: Assemblies of God, Baptist, Brethren, CSI, Lutheran, Mennonite, Pentecostal and Independent churches as well as other Christian organizations. Independent churches in Hyderabad are predominantly Baptist, but Pentecostals also are prominent. In a survey conducted as part of the 'Churches of Indigenous Origins in India' project found 28 independent congregations identifying themselves as Baptist, 24 as Charismatic, 14 as Pentecostal, nine as Fundamentalist, five as Brethren in orientation, four as Mennonite, and six by other descriptions.[54] Several of the Baptist group also identified themselves as Charismatic, others as Fundamentalist which means that   the   Baptist-Brethren-Fundamentalist   grouping   and   the Charismatic-Pentecostal group are about equal in number.

In the Pentecostal/Charismatic category El-Shaddai Church was the smallest with ten members, and the largest was Dr Ernest P. Komanapalli's Rock Church Ministries reporting more than 10,000 members in more than 1,000 churches throughout India. Other large local churches include Vadhuvu Sangam (Bride of Christ Church) with 2,000 members in 10 branches and the Jesus Love Mission reporting 1,000 adult members in four churches. There are many more, Pentecostal as well as non-Pentecostal, in Hyderabad, in the coastal region and in other areas of Andhra.

---

[52] M. Devadas, *Mithra, The Friend* (Guntur, Bible Mission, 1995).

[53] Churches of Indigenous Origins Project data collected by Revd P.S. Shalem Raju, 20 Nov., 1997.

[54] Information compiled by the researcher, Mr Immanuel Paspula, who visited each church during several months in 1997 and 1998.

North India: Missionary Outreach from South and Centre

North India, especially the Hindi-speaking region, has a meagre Christian population. Indifference to the Christian message—and a general unawareness about Christianity—seem characteristic. The Arya Samaj, the Hindu Mahasabha, Rashtriya Swayamsevak Sangh, Vishwa Hindu Parishad and other Hindu organizations—many of a fundamentalist ideology—are prominent in the Hindi region. Linked with political forces, they aim 'to implant the notion that Hindu and India are virtually interchangeable categories and that India should be identified as the nation of Hindus'.[55] These reactionary forces combine to resist change, including a presumptive threat of Christian conversion. Hindu fundamentalism thrives 'as a distinctively extreme reaction to threats to communal identity'.[56]

In this context of hostility, it is not surprising if Christianity has few adherents. Christians comprise but 0.15% of the population of Uttar Pradesh, India's most populous state. India's largest state in terms of territory, Madhya Pradesh is primarily rural with some 71,000 villages. The Christian population is comparatively low, about 400,000. India's largest tribal population is in M.P. Ostensibly a Hindi-speaking state, in actuality scores of languages and local dialects are in use. The entire Bible is available only in Hindi. Bible translation is in progress in a few of the tribal languages. Translation projects are carried out primarily by indigenous missionary agencies together with the Bible Society of India. Literacy and developmental projects also are primarily in the hands of the Christians.

Missionary activity takes several forms. The Pentecostal Church at Itarsi sponsors the Central India Bible College, founded in 1962 by Pastor Kurien Thomas, president, directed by Pastor Matthew Thomas, vice president and principal, which trains Christian workers for the region.[57] The related Fellowship of the Pentecostal Churches of God in India, established in 1966, reports more than 500 workers in 13 fields of service throughout North and South India.[58] This Fellowship is an example of one of the many ministries to

---

[55] Deepak Lal, 'The Economic Impact of Hindu Revivalism' in Martin E. Marrty and R. Scott Appleby (eds.), *Fundamentalisms and the State: Remaking Polities, Economies, and Militance* (Chicago: University of Chicago Press, 1993), 410-426, 418.

[56] Robert Eric Frykenberg, 'Hindu Fundamentalism and the Structural Stability of India' in *Fundamentalisms and the State: Remaking Polities, Economies, and Militance*, 233-255, 236.

[57] Information received in a letter of Dr Matthew K. Thomas to Roger E. Hedlund, 9 March 1998.

[58] Statistics are from Larry D. Pate, *From Every People* (Monrovia, MARC, 1989), 155.

have emerged from the IPC.[59] The Indian Pentecostal Church of God, headquartered in Kumbanand, Kerala, has 44 local churches in M.P.[60]

Indigenous Pentecostal/Charismatic mission agencies serving in Madhya Pradesh include Blessing Youth Mission, Indian Evangelical Team, Native Missionary Movement, along with others.[61] These organizations together with several non-Pentecostal agencies are engaged in a number of translation, literacy, medical, evangelistic and community development projects as part of their ministry of social and spiritual service in this state.

Bihar has a dubious distinction as one of the more backward states of India, despite its considerable natural resources. The Christian community is about 1% of the population of Bihar,[62] historically concentrated mainly in Chotanagpur which was recently bifurcated to create the new state of Jharkhand. Churches are mainly traditional Protestant and Catholic denominations started by foreign missionary initiatives, although a few churches of indigenous origin may be discerned.

Pentecostal groups include the Church of God, Ceylon Pentecostal Mission, Full Gospel Church, Full Gospel New Testament Church, Indian Pentecostal Church, Maranatha Church, Pentecostal Assembly Church, Pentecostal Bethel Church Association, Pentecostal Church of God, Salem Christian Church, Salem Pentecostal Church, and others.[63]

Several indigenous mission agencies also work in Bihar-Jarkhand. Particularly notable, and of Pentecostal type, is the Gospel Echoing Missionary Society. GEMS is a remarkable achievement of one local church in South India, the GEMS House of Prayer at Chrompet, Chennai, whose concentrated missionary outreach has brought an entire new denomination into existence in an area where previously there were no churches. Today the GEMS Church is growing rapidly with 438 workers at 142 centres in 217 locations in the different parts of Bihar as well as in bordering Uttar Pradesh and Madhya Pradesh.

Some 6,000 believers attended the GEMS convention in Bihar during October 1998. Many projects are carried out including three children's homes plus a home for 100 children of stonecutters and a home for 60 children

---

[59] *The Trumpet*, IPC Platinum Jubilee Edition, January-February 1999, 69.

[60] Information is from *A Hand Book of the Indian Pentecostal Church of God 1994'* published by the Office of the General Secretary, Hebron Puram, Kumbanad, Kerala, 1994.

[61] Information from several sources including L. Joshi Jayaprakash, *Evaluation of Indigenous Missions of India* (Kilpauk, Madras, Church Growth Research Centre, 1987), and the *Indian Missions* quarterly magazine, January-March 1998, published by the India Missions Association, Chennai.

[62] S.Vasantharaj Albert, ed., *Bihar: Church and People Groups* (Madras, Church Growth Association of India, 1992).

[63] Ibid., 39.

suffering from polio. GEMS also operates 77 middle schools and 4 English schools including a high school. Out of 69 linguistic dialects in Bihar, GEMS concentrates mainly on three major Hindi dialects of Bhojpuri, Maitali and Magai.[64] Based in Rohdas District, the Mission works mainly in neglected areas of North Bihar, Central and West Bihar. With 7,000 baptized and 8,000 known believers, the total GEMS Christian community in Bihar may be estimated at more than 13,000. In addition, some 15,000 children are cared for in schools. The GEMS approach includes a balanced programme of medical ministry involving a hospital and clinics, free medical camps, education and social services including emancipation of children from bonded labour. Because of this benevolent social dimension the Mission is well-accepted in Bihar, despite some opposition and persecution.[65]

In Mumbai (Bombay) the charismatic New Life Fellowship is a remarkable example of a dynamic urban house church movement which began in 1968 and by 1994 had grown to 1,450 house churches in Mumbai and more than 2,000 throughout India.[66] It is an unusual story. With roots in the 1960s and a small church started in 1968, a foundation of biblical teaching was laid during the 1970s. Then, in 1980, came a dramatic turn-around. Pastor S. Joseph's dream of a mega-church in Bombay was to metamorphose into a plan for 'hundreds of churches' in the city. Each house church would consist of 10-15 members. Thousands came to faith. By 1989 there were more than 1,500 house churches in Bombay with an overall congregation of over 12,000.[67] Pastor Joseph intends that every member should be a disciple and the church should be a church with a mission. To reach people everywhere it is necessary for them to have a church within shouting distance, within walking distance, or within cycling distance.[68] To achieve this objective, house groups were started which have now progressed into house churches. The house group gatherings are the venue for family-centred ministry and evangelism. The focus of the house churches is on corporate life, worship and nurture. Through this means the body is activated and leadership developed. During a May 1992 'Love Bombay' outreach, some 1,200 workers went door to door, bringing a positive response from 13,000 persons of whom 6,000 were added to the church within 26 days. Stemming from a 1993 conference in Goa, there is a greater 'harvest' thrust. Emphasis is

---

[64] Information provided by Mr. Goforth, son of the GEMS mission director in Bihar, Pastor Augustine Jebakumar, by telephone at Chennai-Chrompeth, on 11 January 1999.

[65] Pastor Augustine Jebakumar, telephone interview, Chrompet-Chennai, on 13 January 1999.

[66] S. Subramaniam, 'Strategy to Reach Greater Madras', *DAWN*, 1996, 65.

[67] 'New Life Fellowship' brochure, Mahim, Mumbai, 1997.

[68] Information from an interview with Pastor S. Joseph and the NLF leadership team (Pastors Jerry D'Souza, Shekhar Kallianpur, Shelton Davidson, and Willie Soans) conducted by Roger E. Hedlund at Mahim, Mumbai, on 26 January, 1998.

on prayer and preaching points which become house groups for teaching, healing, and outreach. Then house churches are formed.

NLF owns no property. Large celebration centres consisting of numbers of house churches meet in rented facilities. All 11 major languages of Mumbai are found in the house churches which cross into many different ethnic and sociological groups. The celebration centres are bilingual. The city has been divided into 10 MPUs (million people units) for prayer, research, and outreach. The house church concept is a key strategy, but it is more. The house church is an efficient medium for exercise of spiritual gifts and to develop leaders. Pastor Willie Soans points out that the house church enhances the home, which is where values are shared. 'Value systems are ingrained through living together in a household'.[69] NLF is animated by the example of the New Testament church which moved from house to house in cell groups. Today NLF is present in all the states of India and in each district of one state (Andhra Pradesh). During 1997 the Reach India Project targeted 12 cities with more than 1,500 workers. An estimated 2.6 million homes were visited, 13 million heard the Gospel, and 1,600 believed. In 1998 the aim was to adopt 1,000 villages and see a house church established in each village. NLF methodology taps the human resources of India particularly through the lay leaders.

A closer look at NLF, Mumbai, reveals 140 prayer cells, 511 house groups, 305 house churches, and 122 celebration centres.[70] Various projects are conducted in collaboration with other agencies. The New Life Medical and Educational Trust provides medical care and operates free schools for the poor. In Dharavi, Asia's largest slum, NLF missionaries provide medicines, food and soap. Problems of alcoholism, starvation and other ills are confronted in the slum. House churches have been formed with a cumulative congregation of 350, and free education is provided to many of the poor and exploited children. Without education many are reduced to scavenging. NLF is committed to social action along with proclamation of the good news.[71]

NLF reaches beyond Mumbai. In 1995 the Chembur (Bombay) NLF church began an outreach beyond Mumbai in Sholapur District. Miracles of healing, signs and wonders were recorded. Within a year more than 2,500 people turned to Christ. NLF has begun churches in 24 Sholapur villages where previously there were no churches.[72] During five months in 1997 NLF sent 719 missionaries into 12 important cities where they reported 35,317 people added to the Body of Christ. NLF networks with other churches and agencies in this

---

[69] Willie Soans, 'In Thunder He Spoke', *Vision*, November 1997, 8.

[70] Information from 'NLF Statistics of Mumbai as on 5 January, 1998', Mumbai, New Life Fellowship, 17 February, 1998, 1.

[71] Information from NLF literature including a *Move!* May-June 1997 magazine article, 'Bringing Hope to a Hell called "Dharavi"'.

[72] 'The Book of Acts - Alive & Kicking!' *Move*, May-June, 1997, 18-23.

outreach.[73] Sometimes the outreach effort brings a different kind of response. Five NLF missionaries in another city were beaten with iron rods and tortured by religious fundamentalists opposed to the preaching of the gospel. But this suffering for Christ is viewed as part of the gospel. 'The tortured missionaries want to reach out to their assailant[sic] in love'.[74] And thus the message spreads and the witness grows.

Bengal. Pentecostalism came to Kolkata (Calcutta) early in the twentieth century with the arrival of American missionaries in 1904. From this beginning developed the work of the Assemblies of God and other Pentecostal ministries in Eastern India.[75] Pentecostal churches in Kolkata include eight Assemblies of God, the Ceylon Pentecostal Mission and several independent congregations.

The 1930s appear to have been a time of spiritual awakening in the Himalayas. During this period Sadhu Sundar Singh made visits to Darjeeling. Other visitors of note were evangelist Kamal Prasad Tewari of Allahabad, Sadhu Dhanbahadur Tamang of Nepal, and Sadhu Masih from Gorakhpur.[76] The years 1940-44 became years of revival. The Kalimpong Pentecostal movement began during this time. The Full Gospel Pentecostal Church was founded in 1942. From Kalimpong the Pentecostal message spread to other places in the Himalayas including Sikkim, Bhutan and Nepal.[77] Kalimpong is the headquarters of the Himalaya Crusade founded by Dr S. Sodemba in 1956. S. Sodemba, born in 1926 at Kalimpong, converted during the 1940-41 revival, became active in the spreading Pentecostal movement. New churches were being started wherever the revival spread.[78] In 1962 a group of 20 pastors formed the Full Gospel Pentecostal Church Fellowship which conducts an annual convention.[79] In 1968 Sodemba created the Children's Faith Home which caters to the needs of orphans and the destitute. In 1972 the Himalaya Crusade became a denomination.[80] By 1998 the Crusade reported 125 branches with more than 10,000 members and is engaged in a wide range of activities including schools, conventions, children's homes, relief, welfare, development, leadership training, Bible colleges, literature production, arts and crafts

---

[73] Shekhar Kallianpur, 'The Belligerent Trailblazers!' *Move*, May-June 1997, 14-17, 25.

[74] 'A Night that Froze in Horror', *Move*, May-June, 1997, 12-13, 33-34.

[75] Maynard Ketcham and Wayne Warner, 'When the Pentecostal Fire Fell in Calcutta', in L. Grant McClung (ed.), *Azusa Street and Beyond* (New Jersey, Bridge Publishing, 1986), 27-31.

[76] 'Souvenir', Golden Jubilee Kalimpong Penticostal Movement 1942-92, Himalaya Crusade, Kalimpong, 1992.

[77] Ibid., 7,9.

[78] S. Sodemba, He Danced with the Angels: Fire out of the Himalayan Mountains (Kalimpong,1990), 1-6.

[79] Ibid., 7.

[80] Ibid., 17-28.

industries, and ministries to women and youth.[81] As an outcome, not only have many come to faith, but hundreds are blessed materially and financially, living conditions improved, education has come to the poor—many of whom are receiving rehabilitation and doing advanced degrees, improving their social standing.[82] Apart from the currently affiliated HC branch churches, others have broken away, perhaps a total of 250-300 churches in all combined. Recently Rev. Sodemba has started a theological seminary.[83]

North East India: Revival Movements

North East India has its own distinctive identity and ecclesiastical history. Predominantly Baptist and Presbyterian with pockets of Roman Catholic strength, North East India has felt the impact of several revival movements during the twentieth century.

Meghalaya

The earliest recorded instance was among the Presbyterians in the Khasi-Jaintia Hills in 1897 and resulted in thousands of conversions, then spread to the Presbyterian and Baptist churches of Mizoram.[84] The first major wave of revival among the Khasi Presbyterians followed in 1905-1906 and was characterized by formation of prayer groups, unison singing and dancing.[85] The second wave of revival in 195658 resulted in candidates for theological training and strengthened the ministry of the church.[86] The third wave of the Holy Spirit during the 1990s, in what is now the state of Meghalaya, is regarded as problematic in that many separated from the mainstream Presbyterian, Church of God and Roman Catholic churches and formed new denominations.[87] This revival featured speaking in tongues, healing, prophecy and other spiritual gifts. Indigenous 'breakaway' movements however have an earlier history.

---

[81] Information provided by Dr S. Sodemba for the Churches of Indigenous Origins in India Project, 29 October 1998.

[82] Ibid.

[83] Interview with Revd S. Sodemba at Christian Aid Mission, Charlottesville, 5 June, 1998.

[84] T. Nongsiej, 'Revival Movement in Khasi-Jaintia Hills' in O.L. Snaitang (ed.), *Churches of Indigenous Origins in North East India* (Delhi, ISPCK, 2000), 24-25.

[85] Ibid., 32-33

[86] Ibid., 34-35.

[87] Ibid., 35.

The Assembly Church of Jesus Christ (Full Gospel) came into being in 1930 as the result of a conflict within the Presbyterian Church.[88] The new church initially spread rapidly, then stagnated from 1935 to 1950. In 1956 a revival began which spread to all the Assembly churches. The revival brought change and new congregational life, but was followed by division and separation. Renewal began in 1964 with a new vision for missionary outreach resulting in new churches in Meghalaya and outreach into six other states as well as outside India.[89] In 1965, during the annual Assembly meeting in Shillong, an outbreak of revival brought manifestations of tongues, visions and prophecy. 'The power of God was fully manifested when six hundred believers spoke in other tongues. Pentecost was rehearsed once again. From this time onward, this power did not cease but keep (sic.) working in the church'.[90] During the next five years new churches sprang up and a harvest of progress continued. The historian records significant events during this period into the '90s including the establishing of Doulos Bible Institute in 1978. Leadership development and outreach continued and was extended among the Garos and into Haryana, Punjab and Mumbai. In the early '90s the Assembly hosted a conference of the Pentecostal Fellowship of India, which brought a greater awareness of Charismatic Christianity in North East India.[91]

Quite a different history is that of the Church of the Full Gospel Fellowship, which began as a parachurch organization in Shillong in 1974 but evolved into a church.[92] Initially a fellowship among believers who remained members of various Christian denominations, in 1977 regular Bible studies began at several centres. By 1985 there were seven Bible study centres in and around Shillong. Meanwhile in 1983 the Fellowship was registered as a religious society. The subsequent administrative structure provided for oversight of a full span of church functions and ministries. The Full Gospel Fellowship was declared a church in 1995.[93] The transition was necessitated because of converts who had no church background but were 'from traditional Khasi religion, Hinduism, and former alcoholics, drug addicts and social outcasts'.[94] As a church, the Full Gospel Fellowship has developed rapidly with 60 local churches and Bible study centres in 97 towns and villages of Meghalaya.[95] The Fellowship is a

---

[88] Prosper Ryntathiang and D.Kitbok Ryntathiang, 'The Assembly Church of Jesus Christ (Full Gospel), India' in O.L. Snaitang (ed.), *Churches of Indigenous Origins in North East India* (Delhi, ISPCK, 2000), 67ff.

[89] Ibid., 98-101.

[90] Ibid., 101.

[91] Ibid., 105-118.

[92] Barnold Wankhar, 'The Church of the Full Gospel Fellowship' in O.L. Snaitang (ed.), *Churches of Indigenous Origins in North East India* (Delhi, ISPCK, 2000), 139-149.

[93] Ibid., 143.

[94] Ibid., 143.

[95] Ibid., 143.

fully self-supporting indigenous church. The Statement of Faith is distinctly Pentecostal.

Mizoram

In Mizoram revival movements had a great impact on the development of leaders and the formation of mission societies in the Great Tradition Christianity of the Baptist and Presbyterian churches, states Snaitang, but also led to the emergence of a large number of indigenous Christian movements.[96] Mizoram today is the main centre for the rise of independent Pentecostal/Charismatic groups in North East India. The most prominent among them is Isua Krista Kohhran (the Church of Jesus Christ) which began in 1971 as a break-away from the Baptist Church of Mizoram. 'It is an indigenous church made up of members of the Lai dialect group without any outside connections. It represented a protest against the dominance of the Luseis within the BCM'.[97] By 1975 IKK claimed to have 80 local congregations, 15,000 members and a community of 40,000. Theologically they accept the Bible as their rule of faith and practice baptism and the Lord's Supper much as in the traditional churches.[98] Members are mainly from Baptist and Presbyterian background, but elements of Mizo traditional culture are incorporated along with Pentecostal revivalist practices. Collective participation in decision-making, emphasis on personal experience of God, public testimonies, and active evangelization are features of this growing missionary-minded church.[99]

Tensions between revivalists and their opponents frequently led to separation and formation of new groups. Among the hundred or so Mizo revivalist church movements, Snaitang identifies Tlira Pawl as the earliest, founded in 1913, but now in decline. In 1932 Zakaia Pawl was organized by a disgruntled Presbyterian who for a while associated with the United Pentecostal Church before founding Zakaia Pawl as a spiritual institution on clan-based religious lines. Hminga notes that Zakaia Pawl revived certain pre-Christian festivals and practices such as rice beer drinking bouts and *Puma Zai* (ribald community dance song).[100] Khuangtuaha Pawl was founded in 1942 by a former Presbyterian as a communitarian fellowship modelled after the early church.

---

[96] O.L. Snaitang, *Churches of Indigenous Origins in Northeast India* (Delhi, ISPCK, 2000), 178-179.

[97] Khup Za Go, *A Critical Historical Study of Bible Translations among the Zo People in North East India* (Churachandpur, Manipur, Chin Baptist Literature Board, 1996), 63.

[98] C.L. Hminga, *The Life and Witness of the Churches in Mizoram* (Serkawn, Lunglei, Baptist Church of Mizoram, 1987), 259.

[99] Snaitang, *op.cit.*, 179-180.

[100] Hminga, *op.cit.*, 200.

This group seems to have much in common with the Thiang Zau Pawl (All Free Group) which discarded the Bible in favour of direct guidance from the Spirit of God mediated through the group's leaders.[101] Zathangvunga Pawl is another independent, revivalist, charismatic splinter group founded in 1965 and focusing on community worship and enhancement of spirituality. Zoram Maicham, also started in 1965, combines high spiritual concern with service for the uplift of the poor and needy, the latter being an expression of a traditional Mizo ethic. The Thiangzau Church, begun in 1947, is an expression of Mizo spirituality featuring revival crusades, open-air evangelistic meetings, and attractive praise and worship. The Mizo Israel Pawl is an interesting variation believing itself one of the lost tribes of Israel.[102] After an initial spurt of growth, many of the new movements began to decline, but simultaneously other new groups began.

Apart from these indigenous Christian groups, major Pentecostal denominations include the Assemblies of God and the United Pentecostal Church, both of which are said to be increasing due to revival movements in Nagaland, Manipur and Mizoram.[103] Pentecostal influence became prominent after World War II.[104]

The United Pentecostal Church was inaugurated in 1950. Five pastors were appointed and the UPC soon claimed to have 5,000 members, mainly through transfer. Hminga makes the comment that the UPC was 'most polemic and unscrupulous' in its membership drive.[105] Hminga also points out that the fourth Mizo revival, in 1935, seems to have prepared the way for the UPC 'which soon absorbed many of the extreme revivalists'.[106] The 1935 revival accelerated the conversion movement among the Mizos, but was also accompanied by extraordinary phenomena. 'At the beginning it manifested in dancing and shaking, but it soon developed into speaking with tongues and singing with tongues. Many people claimed to have direct revelations from God and were foretelling things to come'.[107] The so-called 'High Revival' became divisive. 'Church leaders who pleaded for self-control were branded as anti-Holy Spirit and those who did not dance or speak in tongues were regarded as those who had not received the Holy Spirit'.[108] It is not surprising that the United Pentecostal Church has not had a cordial relationship with other churches.

---

[101] Hminga, *Ibid.*, 199.

[102] Snaitang, *op.cit*, 181-83.

[103] Frederick S. Downs, *Christianity in North East India* (Delhi, ISPCK, 1983), 151.

[104] Ibid., 125.

[105] Hminga, *loc.cit.*

[106] Ibid., 198.

[107] Ibid., 161.

[108] Ibid., 162.

Downs makes the interesting observation that the revivals became instruments of indigenization. Practices which had been banned by the missionaries were brought back by the revivalists. 'However much the missionaries might disapprove of some of the traditional practices like dancing, chanting and drum-playing, they could hardly resist what was believed to be the leading of the Holy Spirit in the revivals!'[109]

Manipur

The United Pentecostal Church was introduced into Manipur in 1953, and the headquarters established at Churachandpur in 1957, one among many indigenous Christian movements, Pentecostal and non-Pentecostal, found in the hill areas of Manipur.[110] Snaitang points out that many of these groups contain significant ethnic elements. The Revival Church of God is one such, full gospel in faith, largely Vaiphei in membership with a minority of Thadou-Kukis and Gangtes. This church appears to have incorporated some indigenous practices borrowed from pre-Christian tribal religion.[111] The Christian Revival Church is a highly evangelistic independent revivalist church found mainly among the Thadou-Kukis. 'Its conspicuous concentration among the particular group of people is a common model of the kind of indigenous expression of Christianity in Manipur'.[112] Muanthanga observes, 'Multiplicity of small ethnic groups has produced a myriad of small denominations and churches in Manipur'.[113]

Nagaland.

Nagaland has seen comparatively few independent church movements. Unlike Manipur, in Nagaland the major Baptist denomination has diversified along ethnic lines producing numerous tribal Baptist church associations and theological institutions in keeping with Naga cultural ethos.114 The main independent model, growing out of the revival movement, is the Nagaland Christian Revival Church founded in 1962. Snaitang enumerates seven reasons for its attraction. First and foremost is its biblical principles combined with emphasis on a holy life and the expression of free worship in singing, dancing, tongues, and orchestral prayer. Second, it attracted Naga leaders. Third, emphasis on a personal encounter with Christ. Fourth, the missionary outreach

---

[109] Downs, loc.cit.

[110] Snaitang, op.cit., 184.

[111] Ibid., 185-186.

[112] Ibid., 186.

[113] P.C. Muanthanga, Directory of Churches and Missions in N.E. India (Carey Research & Communication Centre, 1997), 16.

[114] Snaitang, op.cit., 190.

of the church appealed to the mission-minded Naga Baptists. Fifth, trained leadership catered to the spiritual needs of the people through a representative Tribal Church Council and several theological training institutes. Sixth, signs and wonders and healing attract. Seven, persecution and opposition kindled sympathy leading to attraction and growth.[115] The United Pentecostal Church and the Assemblies of God are also active in Nagaland as well as other groups growing out of the revival movements of the past. 'Catholic and Charismatic groups are steadily growing in Nagaland and they may continue to grow at the expense of other groups'.[116]

Both Assam and Arunachal Pradesh report recently-started independent churches, but further information is not available at present. These are but some of the shapers of the Christianity of North East India today.

Conclusion

The Pentecostal movement is alive and well in India. This paper has highlighted several examples drawn from areas of Pentecostal strength. Pentecostalism appears to thrive mainly in regions of pre-existing Christian communities. This reflects its heritage as a revival movement. It seems to have had less impact as an agent of evangelization among non-Christian Buddhist, Hindu, Muslim and tribal populations. Exceptions are anticipated and should be noted. Further research is required.

---

[115] Snaitang, ibid., 188-190.
[116] Muanthanga, *op.cit.*, 26.

Ramankutty Paul:
A Dalit Contribution to Pentecostalism

Paulson Pulikottil

The Dalit Contribution to Pentecostalism

Quite a lot has been written about the contribution of western missionaries to Pentecostalism in India. Narratives about the work of Syrian Christians in Pentecostalism in the Indian subcontinent are plenty. However, the contribution of Dalit[1] Christians to Pentecostalism in the subcontinent is something that has not yet been properly researched. This article examines the contribution of a Dalit Christian by the name of Pastor Ramankutty Paul and his denomination, The Pentecostal Mission, is set against its socio-religious background.

Pastor Paul was a Dalit convert of the Ezhava caste from central Kerala who became a Christian through his employer, another Hindu convert to Christianity. He was born in 1881, and changed his original name, Ramankutty, to Paul and later worked as a catechist of the Church Missionary Society. After his experience of baptism in the Holy Spirit, in 1924 he founded what is now known as The Pentecostal Mission (formerly the Ceylon Pentecostal Mission), a 'full gospel' Pentecostal denomination. Pastor Paul's contribution to establishing The Pentecostal Mission (TPM) is unique in many ways. First of all, it is the first Dalitled Pentecostal denomination in India and the one which integrated Dalits and non-Dalits in its membership and leadership. It has existed without any major divisions for nearly 80 years. Secondly, TPM is the only denomination that defied the limitations that were imposed on the church in the Third World during colonial rule. TPM is the only Indian denomination that has established churches among the populations of other countries, with branches in 19 countries administered from Chennai (Madras), India: Australia, Canada, Costa Rica, Dominican Republic, El Salvador, Fiji, France, Kenya,

---

[1] The fourth caste, *Sudras* and all other lower castes are officially called the Scheduled Castes in the Indian Constitution; Mahatma Gandhi called them *Harijans* meaning 'God's people'. However, in modern writings and theological discussions the word 'Dalit' has replaced 'Harijans' and 'Scheduled Castes'. In this article the word 'Dalit' is used to describe what otherwise would be described as 'Harijans', 'Scheduled Castes', 'lower castes' or 'backward classes'.

Malaysia, Mexico, Nepal, Papua New Guinea, Puerto Rico, Singapore, Sierra Leone, Switzerland, Trinidad and Tobago, UK and USA.[2]

The Dalits and their Plight in Indian Society

The importance of Pastor Paul's contribution can be appreciated only against the background of the social reality of the Dalits. So, in the following pages I sketch briefly the Dalit background from which Pastor Paul emerged. Caste is a uniquely Indian institution. Hutton remarks:

> For although social institutions that resemble caste in one respect or another are not difficult to find elsewhere, and some of them undoubtedly have some association with caste in their ultimate origin, yet caste in its fullest sense, caste, that is, as we know it in India, is an exclusively Indian phenomenon. No comparable institution to be seen anywhere else has anything like the complexity, elaboration and rigidity of caste in India.[3]

Caste is an endogamous reality from which there is no escape except through death. In the Hindu worldview of the unending loop of birth and death, death brings a possibility of being born into a higher caste in the next incarnation, depending on one's merits. However, no amount of hard work, economic achievements or reputation would help one person to change caste in the present life. The lower castes have a very low social and economic status and their caste identity means that no progress is possible. Caste means segregation, since it has the idea that the lower caste pollutes the upper caste by contact or proximity. They are not allowed to use public roads and other public facilities. It also guarantees those who belong to the higher castes a berth in the upper stratum of society. Until 1855, when slavery was abolished in Kerala, many of the lower castes were considered slaves to those of the upper castes. Having been relegated a lower place in society and denied the privileges of education, the lower caste is economically disadvantaged as well. Indian society has been structured along caste lines for centuries, and caste has controlled the economic, social and political life of India's people.

Pastor Paul thus belonged to a community that was considered lower than others, without any rights, and when he was born he was considered to be in a slave caste. In fact, although in south Kerala slave castes were emancipated in 1855, Paul's region, which belonged to central Kerala, only made an official proclamation of emancipation in 1947. He thus belonged to a community which had no freedom of association, expression, or right to own property, and this

---

[2] The Pentecostal Mission: Rules and Regulations of the Church (Madras: Pentecostal Press Trust), n.d., 1-2.

[3] J.H. Hutton, *Caste in India*, 46, cited in Ninan Koshy, *Caste in Kerala Churches* (Bangalore: The Christian Institute for the Study of Religion and Society, 1968), 7.

applied to most of the low caste communities. This throws into greater relief the uniqueness of Raman Paul's important achievement. His background may appear to be similar to that of African Americans in the USA or Blacks in South Africa during apartheid. But caste was more rigorous and oppressive than colour or race. Moreover, when Pentecostalism emerged under Black leadership (or at least partial leadership) in the USA, there were already Black churches under Black leadership. When Pentecostalism appeared under indigenous leadership in India, there were no Dalit-led churches in his part of the world. Raman Paul is thus a solitary figure who stands in stark contrast to his background.

We thus need to look at the plight of the Dalits within the Christian church in Kerala. In Indian society, which is structured along the four major castes and numerous sub-castes, caste identity is carried over to the new religion to which a person is converted since it is endogamous. In India, caste identity and discrimination based on caste prevails even in Christianity and Islam.

Dalits within Kerala Churches

Though born in a Dalit Hindu family, Pastor Paul (then Ramankutty) was employed by a Christian. It was in this family that he received his basic lessons in Christianity. He joined the Church Missionary Society as a catechist, but neither his conversion nor his job as a catechist promised any social or economic mobility to him and the thousands he represented. We need an overall picture of the Christian landscape of Kerala in order to understand this.

Christianity in Kerala was more or less homogenous as far as caste status was concerned until the 1850s, when Dalits changed the scenario by their entrance into Christianity. Christians in Kerala trace their origins back to CE 52, when the Apostle Thomas preached in the south-western coast of India. Christianity was further strengthened by the emigration of Christians from Syria in the third and eighth centuriesCE. Regular contact with the mother church in the Middle East by visits of metropolitans kept Christianity in Kerala thriving until the Islamic conquest of most of the Christian lands after 600. However, Christianity in Kerala continued, but suffered a setback with the arrival of the Portuguese who forcibly converted the Syrian Christians to Roman Catholicism. However the Syrian Christians revolted against Roman domination after fifty years and established their independence, and Roman Catholicism continued to exist side by side with the Oriental Orthodox Christianity in Kerala. In the caste-based society of India, the rulers of Kerala had accorded special privileges to the Syrian Christians. They were considered as a caste second to the Brahmins, though they themselves claimed to be equal to Brahmins. The Syrian Christians of Kerala kept their racial purity and maintained their social status by not admitting to the church any from outside their community. Evangelism and mission were unknown among the Syrian Christian churches in Kerala. Until conversions from Dalits began to take place,

Christianity was considered by the local rulers and population as the religion of the high caste and wealthy traders.

During the nineteenth century, Protestant missionaries were converting people from all castes in the rest of India, but in Kerala, they spent their efforts on reforming the Syrian Christian church. The Protestant missionaries from the West (mainly English) initially worked among the Syrian Christian community with the consent of the bishops until 1836, when the Mavelikara Synod decided to dissolve any partnership with the Protestants. The pastoral letter that Mar Chepat Dionysius sent out to all his parishes in 1836 asserted:

> We being the Jacobite Syrian subjects to the Patriarch of Antioch and observing the Church rites and rules established by the prelates sent by his command cannot therefore deviate from them and as no one possesses authority to preach and teach the doctrine of one religion in the Church of another without the sanction of their respective Patriarch, we cannot permit the same.[4]

Gibbs, the Anglican historian, considers this as a watershed in the history of Christianity in Kerala. He comments that, 'The first phase of the mission in Travancore had come to an end, and the missionaries now turned to direct missionary work among non-Christians'.[5]

The missionary energy thus diverted was aimed at mainly the lower caste communities in Hinduism and it began to bear fruit by 1854. According to Gladstone, in the following years Kerala witnessed great mass conversions from non-Christian communities, especially the Dalits. This redrew the entire Christian landscape of this South Indian state.[6] Gladstone also notes that the reason for mass movements among the Dalits of Kerala was mainly motivated by their aspiration for a better social status, which was actually denied them. The history of the mass movements among the depressed castes in Kerala tells us that it is not money or effort that matters, but being accepted into the community of the people of God. The conversion of the Pulayas and Parayas, as in the case of any other caste, was motivated by the hope of their socio-economic and religious emancipation, and it was part of their struggle for their own progress. They had suffered all humiliations as non-Christians, as slaves.

---

[4] Translated by C.M. Agur, *Church History of Travancore* (Madras: Masillamani, 1903, AES Edition 1990), 122. Travancore is the southern part of the present Kerala state which was formed in 1957 by combining three princely states namely Travancore, Cochin and Malabar, when the states were redrawn on the basis of language. The language of Kerala (and its three constituent parts) is Malayalam.

[5] M.E. Gibbs, *The Anglican Church in India 1600-1970* (Delhi: ISPCK, 1972), 113.

[6] J.W. Gladstone, *Protestant Christianity and People's Movements in Kerala 1850-1936* (Trivandrum: Seminary Publications, 1984), 93-151.

But the discovery of the existence of caste inside the mission shattered their hopes and was too much to bear.[7]

Dalits in the Missionary Churches

Even the western missionaries who condemned caste and for whom it was a strange system did not have an open attitude towards Christians from a Dalit background. They still wanted to keep the caste labels intact and considered themselves racially superior to Christian Dalits. The following incident adequately illustrates the point.

When Charles Mead, a missionary with the London Missionary Society, married an educated Christian woman from the *Paraya* caste (one of the lowest castes) in 1850, it was met with vehement opposition from the other missionaries. This was a remarriage, since his wife had died in 1848, but the issue was not remarriage but that the marriage was with a person of low caste. One of his friends wrote to him in July 1850, 'We deem it our duty most emphatically and most firmly to protest against your taking such a step which in our opinion, would be most injurious to the best interests of the cause of Christ in Travancore'.Another missionary wrote to the authorities of his mission, 'The marriage of Mr Mead to a young native woman, of the Pariah caste, has filled us with surprise, disappointment and sorrow'. Mead's letter to the Foreign Secretary of the LMS is the best commentary on the missionaries' attitude towards caste. He said, 'I am surprised that there is so much of caste sprit amongst missionaries of our own and other societies'.[8] However, Charles Mead and John Cox, who married an Ishava woman ten years after this incident, were forced to leave the service of the LMS. Mead joined the government service while John Cox moved into the plantation business; both continued to live in Kerala until their death.

Not only did the missionaries maintain racial prejudice against the Dalits whom they invited to church but they were unwilling to share leadership with native Christians, whether of Dalit background or not. Gladstone's observation, supported by a number of letters written by the missionaries, is significant here:

> The missionaries were also extremely reluctant to share their administrative authority with their Indian assistants. They wished to maintain the relationship in terms of the ruler and the ruled. It is a deplorable fact that from the time of making plans for the training of Indians for mission work during the 1820s down to the end of the 19th century, there was no concept of building up a body of Christian ministers and workers in India, who would have an equal share in all

---

[7] Gladstone, 138.
[8] Letters quoted by Gladstone, 192-3.

matters related to the Church. The missionaries thought only of creating a team of workers who would work loyally under the missionaries.[9]

Pastor Paul's work under the Church Missionary Society as a Dalit and a catechist was inferior to that of the missionary, with no leadership role and no status in the church or in society. It is from this subaltern status that Ramankutty Paul founded and gave leadership to his international Pentecostal denomination.

Dalits in Kerala Churches

The situation did not improve when the missionaries left and the leadership came into the hands of native people. Koshy's notable study concludes that, even in 1968, people not in the caste system were ignored in church leadership.[10] He notes three aspects of leadership denied to the Dalits: (1) the upper classes dominate church administration; (2) in some churches there is a separate type of parish organization for the Dalits, and this does not get representation in the general councils of the church (only a few persons are nominated); and (3) generally, Dalits do not have representation in church councils, boards, etc. commensurate with their numerical strength.[11]

Iyer's statement on the Christian attitude to caste is remarkable here:

> The average Indian Christian is a staunch observer of castes. It is a moot point whether he is not stricter in his observance of castes than the average Hindu. There is a large number of Christians in the southern Districts of the Madras Presidency who even boast of their being firmer and truer adherents of the caste system than the Hindus.[12]

The native Christians in missionary churches and Dalit Christians in all churches suffered many disadvantages. They were given subservient roles and their freedom of self-expression was curtailed or even denied. This explains why in Kerala there was no Dalit Christian movement or denomination until Pastor Paul came on the scene and why a study of Pastor Paul becomes very significant for understanding Dalit Christianity in general and Dalit Pentecostalism in particular.

---

[9] Gladstone, 184.

[10] Koshy's study focuses on caste in the Syrian Christian churches and other Protestant denominations in Kerala. A study that deals with caste in Catholic tradition in Kerala is George Koilparampil, *Caste in the Catholic Community in Kerala, A Study of Caste Elements in the Inter Rite Relationships of Syrians and Latin* (Cochin: Department of Sociology, St. Teresa's College, 1982), which has more or less similar conclusions.

[11] Koshy, 58.

[12] L.K.A. Iyer, *Anthropology of the Syrian Christians*, cited in Koshy, 9.

William Seymour, the leader of Azusa Street revival is a similar figure, for he was a black pastor, a son of emancipated slaves and physically disabled. However, in several aspects Pastor Paul and Seymour stand poles apart. Seymour had the support and legacy of a large vibrant black Christian movement which was already decades old when the Azusa Street revival began. African American spirituality was well formed, with clear social and theological goals. In contrast, Pastor Paul is a lonely figure: there was no Dalit Christian church, Dalit theology, nor leadership. He emerges with his movement from the shadows of the dominant western missionary and caste-conscious Syrian Christian Church and in an environment outside the church that kept this stigma intact.

TPM as an International Mission

The second aspect of Pastor Paul's contribution to Pentecostalism is that he founded the only Indian church that has branches in foreign countries that are governed from India. In fact, he reversed the direction of cross-cultural world mission. Foreign control of Indian missions and India becoming the target of mission have been topics for heated debate for years. D.T. Niles, one of the leading missiologists of the past century, was concerned about Asia becoming the target of western missions. Verkuyl has summarised his position thus:

> In Niles' judgement, the base of mission has been in the West for too long. It must also come Eeast—ecclesiastically, politically, and geographically. By ecclesiastical 'easternity' he means as sending of missionaries from East to West as well as West to East.[13]

Another important voice in this regard is that of K.T. Paul, the noted Indian Christian statesman. He wanted a moratorium on foreign missions to India because he felt that foreign missions did not help in developing self-governing, self-propagating, self-supporting native churches.

Though not primarily for missiological reasons, but perhaps out of a nationalistic spirit, the early Pentecostals in India also shared similar positions. Pastor K.E. Abraham one of the founders of the Indian Pentecostal Church and a close colleague of Pastor Paul, seems to have held such an aspiration; but it was Pastor Paul who could first establish a 'three self' native church.[14]

---

[13] J. Verkuyl, *Contemporary Missiology, An Introduction* (Grand Rapids: William B. Eerdmans, 1978), 81.

[14] K.E. Abraham, *Humble Servant of Jesus Christ (Yesukristhuvinte Eliya Dasan)* (Kumbanad: Pentecostal Young Peoples Association, 1965), 454. Pastor K.E. Abraham was ordained by Pastor Paul and they worked very closely, though leading two separate denominations until 1933. They parted ways with each other and in Pastor Abraham's

The Indian churches along with other churches in the Third World were also subject to what Verkuyl calls 'Ecclesiastical Colonialism'. He describes this as 'the urge of the missionaries to impose the model of the mother church on the native churches among whom they are working rather than give the people the freedom to shape their own churches in response to the gospel'.[15] Although Verkuyl limits this concept to theological expressions, Ecclesiatical Colonialism also resulted in producing churches dependent upon the foreign mission bodies or denominations. A number of voices have protested against this. I have pointed out how the early Pentecostals of India refused to be mimics of the foreign partners.[16]

I want to suggest in the following pages that the background from which Pastor Paul originates provides some explanation for the emergence of his movement, which stands out in Indian Pentecostal history. It seems that Pastor Paul comes from a community of Dalits greatly influenced by the Dalit social and religious revivals in Kerala during his time. The Ezhava awakening in Kerala led by Sri Narayana Guru,[17] seems to have influenced him at least indirectly, in addition to the influence of Pentecostal lay theology.

Sri Narayana Guru

Sri Narayana Guru was born in 1854 in the southern part of Kerala, then known as Travancore.[18] He did not receive any formal education but educated himself in Ayurvedic medicine, Sanskrit and religious philosophies. He also learned Yoga. All these are denied to the lower castes. Before becoming a religious reformer he used to earn his living working as a cowherd, a farmer and then as a teacher as he taught himself. At the age of thirty he became a wandering mystic. Though married at an early age, he did not lead a married life, we know nothing about his wife and he did not raise a family. His meeting with Chattampi Swamikal, another Hindu reformer who worked for the uplift of the Nayar community, changed the course of his life. He took upon himself the call to work for the revival and the uplift of his own community (the Ezhavas) by establishing a religious centre in 1884.[19] Pastor Paul was then three years old.

---

words, 'we love them as children of God, but stopped having cooperation and spiritual fellowship'. See Abraham, 235.

[15] Verkuyl, 173.

[16] Paulson Pulikottil, 'As East and West Met in God's Own Country: Encounter of Western Pentecostalism with Native Pentecostalism in Kerala', *Asian Journal of Pentecostal Studies* 5:1 (2002), 5-22.

[17] Also spelt 'Sree Narayana Guru'.

[18] His original name was Narayanan. 'Sree' is the honorific equivalent to English 'Mr' and Guru means 'teacher'.

[19] S.N. Rao, 'Sri Narayana Guru's Ecumenical Vision for the Ezhava Community', *Indian Church History Review* 38:2 (1994), 126-134.; a more detailed work on the life of

Writing in 1933, after describing the plight of the Ezhavas (Iluvas) and sketching the reform set in motion by Sri Narayana Guru and his movement, Padmanabha Menon prophesied 'a bright future' for them.[20] Within the short span of fifty years the movement started by Guru had caught the attention of the whole nation, so that Rabindranath Tagore and Mahatma Gandhi visited him. Thousands of Ezhavas were attracted to this movement by the teaching of Sri Narayana Guru, so that no one could ignore it. Guru also visited many parts of Tamil Nadu and made two visits to Sri Lanka (in 1918 and 1923) to propagate his movement.[21]

Guru's main contribution is that he created alternate public spheres for the Ezhavas. The Ezhavas, like other lower caste communities, were denied education, opportunity for employment and suffered restrictions in other realms. Guru not only taught that Ezhavas should receive education, but he established educational centres adjacent to the temples he consecrated. He encouraged the Ezhavas to acquire skills to enable self-employment. He encouraged them to enter various occupations. He thus broke into public spheres that were denied them. But his contribution that is of greatest importance for this study is his entry into religious spheres that were denied the lower castes. When it came to religion, Ezhavas as well as other non-Brahman communities were not allowed to learn Sanskrit, the language of the Hindu scriptures and liturgy. This effectively prevented them from becoming religious teachers and priests. However, Guru had taught himself Sanskrit and he then taught others, thus invading the stronghold of Brahminical Hinduism.

In the time of Guru, the lower castes were not allowed to worship in the Hindu temples. It was only in 1936 that lower castes were allowed to enter Hindu temples through the famous Temple Entry Proclamation of the Travancore Maharaja. In the rest of Kerala, a similar proclamation had to wait until 1947! The lower caste Hindus had created their own religious spaces, which were inhabited by demons and spirits. They were not allowed to worship the gods of the Hindu scriptures. Samuel Mateer divides the Hinduism of this period into two categories: Hinduism and 'devil worship'. In the temples, the gods of the scriptures, Siva, Ganesh, Vishnu, etc. were worshipped; but in the local shrines and private cultic groves the demonic worship of lesser spirits and local deities like Madan and Chattan took place. The religion of the Dalits in

---

Sri Narayan Guru is M.K. Sanoo, *Narayana Guru* (Bombay: Bhartiya Vidya Bhavan, 1978).

[20] K.P. Padmanabha Menon, *A History of Kerala: Written in the form of Notes: Visscher's Letters from Malabar*, vol. 3 (Ernakulam: Cochin Government Press, 1933), 446.

[21] Rao, 129.

this period was considered, even by western writers like Mateer, as different and of less significance than that of Brahminical Hinduism.[22]

The Dalits were thus prevented from having access to the religious spheres of the higher castes by being denied access to both the scriptures and the temples. Furthermore, the Dalits kept themselves away from such spheres by creating their own religious spheres of spirit worship. This segregation is what Guru opposed and brought down. He broke the stronghold of Brahminical Hinduism and destroyed their monopoly in 1888 by installing a Siva idol in Aruvipuram where he was residing at the time. He was opposed by the higher castes because, while no Dalit was allowed to worship Siva or even enter the temples, Guru had installed a Siva idol—something a Brahman alone is permitted to do. Rao points out that Guru had built about sixty temples all over Kerala for Ezhavas to worship, installing various idols and consecrating priests from the Ezhava caste.[23]

Raman Paul and the Ezhava Awakening

It has been pointed out earlier that the Dalits in the Kerala churches were going through a situation similar to that of the non-priestly castes of Hinduism, without the freedom of expression and association within their ecclesiastical traditions. There are a number of reasons why we should consider that the Ezhava awakening in nineteenth century Kerala might have influenced the Pentecostal movement of Ramankutty Paul. First of all, they shared the same racial, geographical and religious space. Both leaders, Guru and Paul, were Hindus of the Ezhava caste and worked in what is now known as Kerala, Tamil Nadu and Sri Lanka. Under the British Raj, South India and Ceylon (Sri Lanka) formed one political identity, even though they were geographically separated by the Pampan Pass. Secondly, Ramankutty Paul came on the scene at a time when the Ezhava awakening was at the height of its impact. No one in Kerala, particularly an Ezhava, could ignore it or be insulated from its influence.

This explains the many similarities between the two movements. The possibility of a Dalit, who was suppressed religiously and socially, leading a movement is the example of Guru—and this is what Ramankutty Paul also achieved. Guru showed by his example that Ezhavas could also create their own alternative public and religious spheres. Ramankutty Paul did this in Pentecostalism.

In Pentecostal historical narratives there is usually an overemphasis on the guidance of the Holy Spirit, but seldom do these narratives examine how the Holy Spirit leads people. Such historical narratives many times overemphasize

---

[22] Samuel Mateer, *The Land of Charity, a Descriptive Account of Travancore and Its People* (London: John Snow , 1870), 158-226.
[23] Rao, 127.

the spiritual and 'supernatural' dimensions at the cost of the natural. Does this 'supernatural' leading have nothing to do with the social and historical contexts? What emerges from this study is that Pentecostal movements do owe a lot to their own social contexts and their histories are rooted in and shaped by such contexts.

PART THREE

SOUTH EAST ASIA

The Assemblies of God
and Pentecostalism in Myanmar

Chin Khua Khai

Introduction

Myanmar, known as Burma before 1989, is a country in mainland South East Asia that shares its borders with China, Laos, Thailand, Bangladesh and India.[1] The estimated population by the year 2000 was 51,539,000 comprised of 135 ethnic groups in which 89.8% are Buddhist, 4.9% Christian, 3.9% Islam, 0.5% Hindu, and 1.2% tribal religions.[2] Catholic Christianity was introduced to the people in Myanmar around 1554, Protestant Christianity in 1807,[3] and Pentecostalism in the 1920s.

Modern Pentecostalism asserted that it had rediscovered the New Testament phenomenon of baptism in the Holy Spirit evidenced with speaking in tongues (glossolalia) at Topeka, Kansas in 1901. Ever since, the Pentecostal witness has spread and reached nations all over the world and is becoming one of the largest Christian families on earth. It also reached Myanmar nationals early in the twentieth century. As in many parts of the world, it is the most dynamic Christian movement in Myanmar today. Three church organizations: the Assemblies of God, the United Pentecostal Church (Oneness),[4] and the Foursquare Church,[5] as well as a number of individual Charismatic[6] churches

---

[1] The editors are grateful to Wonsuk Ma for permission to produce this reworked article that first appeared in the *Asian Journal for Pentecostal Studies* (2002).

[2] Sein Tin, *The Statistical Year Book of Myanmar 1995* (Yangon, Myanmar: Myanmar Statistical Organization), 19-26.

[3] Chin Khua Khai, 'Myanmar Mission Board and Agencies', in A. Scott Moreau (ed.), *Evangelical Dictionary of World Missions* (Grand Rapids: Baker, 2000), 667-68.

[4] J. Ral Buai organized the United Pentecostal Church in 1973. Their belief in modalism (Oneness), speaking in tongue as evidence of salvation, practices such as baptism in the name of Jesus and dancing and rolling and excessive drum beating during the worship are not accepted in the rest of the Pentecostal groups, however.

[5] Philip Ahone founded the Full Gospel Foursquare Church in 1989. Formerly he was a minister in the Assemblies of God and a well-known evangelistic preacher in the early renewal movement. With a few daughter churches, he organized the Foursquare Church.

represent a vital Christianity that encounters both nominal Christian practices and the non-Christian world. Both missionaries and national leaders and believers share a role in contributing towards the emergence and growth of Pentecostalism in Myanmar.

Hector and Sigrid McClean may have been the first resident Pentecostal missionaries to Myanmar, working there during the 1920s. They wrote about their work among the Melee people in upper Myanmar that resulted in the whole tribe becoming Christians.[7] Their work among the Loheh tribe at Ming-tz-shan resulted in a revival where approximately sixty were reported to have received the baptism of the Spirit and many others being converted to Christianity.[8] Nothing further is known about their work.

The Arrival of Assemblies of God Missionaries

The third largest denomination in the country, the Assemblies of God of Myanmar (AG) is the oldest and largest Pentecostal organization that dates its establishment to 1931 and reported a membership of 84,158 in the year 2000.[9] The history of the AG began among the Lisu and Rawang people in the north of the country, where half the members belong today. Initially, the AG began through the extension ministry of missionaries in southwest China, in the Salwin and Mekong river valleys. Ada Buchwater was an English missionary who arrived at Wheisi in the Mekong valley in 1919. In 1921, she made contact and shared the gospel with Lisus from Myanmar, which event was believed to be the first Pentecostal witness to Myanmar nationals. Leonard and Olive Bolton from England arrived in 1924. Their work on the China side of the border had a great impact on the people in Myanmar too. Also, G. Clifford and Lavada Morrison from the USA came to Wheisi for language study in 1926, but fled to Putao, Myanmar when a communist insurrection began in 1927. They went back to Shang Pah in the Salwin river valley in southwest China and opened mission work there in 1931. Morrison described their hazardous trip as the means God had used to bring them to ministry among the tribes of Myanmar:

---

[6] The charismatic movement in Myanmar is a practice of individual believers rather than the church as a whole. It is seen among a few local churches and para-church movements.

[7] Hector McLean, 'A Thousand Family Turn to the Lord', *The Pentecostal Evangel* (March 20, 1926), 6.

[8] H. McLean, 'Pentecostal Revival In Burma', *The Pentecostal Evangel* (September 11, 1926), 11.

[9] Sual Za Go, 'Statistics of the Assemblies of God of Myanmar' (A letter to the author, Jan. 25, 2001).

Then one day God spoke to our hearts and revealed His purpose in it all, saying, 'where there is no vision, the people perish!' I had to lead you out this way by this route to give you an eye vision of a people sitting in darkness and the shadow of death. A people so isolated from the rest of the world, and so secluded in the depth of these mountains that they are in a particularly unknown region, and none had ever taken to them the gospel light. I have chosen you to be my messenger to this people. Will you obey my call?[10]

The actual ministry to the Myanmar interior started in 1931,[11] when two Rawang tribesmen from Myanmar asked Morrisons to visit them. The account was as follows:

Two Rawang tribesmen from Burma traveled over high mountain passes into Salwin Valley carrying packs of Burmese goat wool to trade for Chinese rock salt. They came to Shang Pah, where the Clifford Morrisons were living, and 'happened' on a Pentecostal convention. There they heard for the first time of Jesus who could wash away their sins. One of the men, tears streaming down his face, waved his hand toward the west and exclaimed, 'My people live beyond those mountains.... They have never heard the story you tell of the one True God, and know not the 'Way of Life'... Won't you send someone to my people to tell them about Jesus?'[12]

The Morrisons responded by sending Lisu evangelists, who after three months of hard work, reported that thirty-seven Lisu and Rawang families had become Christians.[13] Bolton also sent indigenous preachers to Lisus in Myanmar. Thus, the work of the AG in southwest China was extended to Myanmar. The work of the Pentecostal mission became more concrete when believers were gathered into a church of a worshipping community. The first AG churches in Myanmar were planted in the Lisu land of Kachin State in 1933.[14] Morrison visited the churches and helped set them in order by electing deacons to oversee the local services. He taught them to tithe, to develop spiritual and physical responsibilities and to be self-reliant. The believers erected church buildings by their own efforts, using local materials such as bamboo. Lay ministries extended the work throughout the pioneering period of the mission. Many notable events were reported to have taken place through the prayers and simple faith of Lisu believers. They gathered in the homes of sick people, prayed all night long—sometimes even two to three days at a time—until it was believed that the sick person was healed. For these

---

[10] Gleen D. Stafford, 2.

[11] This date probably is taken as the beginning of Assemblies of God ministry in Myanmar.

[12] Leonard Bolton, 213.

[13] Bolton, 213-14.

[14] David, *The Assemblies of God in Burma* (unpublished manuscript, no date), 4.

Pentecostals, signs and miracles proved the preaching of gospel and drew people to the Christian faith. Morrison noted a case of healing as follows:

> One of our preachers was telling me how a Baptist family in Burma was led into a deeper experience with the Lord through a case of healing in the family. This man was the headman of the village and his daughter was very sick. They had tried every kind of medicine from the hospital, but to no avail. One of our Lisu workers was present, and under the power of the Spirit he began to sing a hymn in their own tongue, a language he did not know. The people were amazed. The song was so worded that they listened with awe, and so moved that they asked him to prayer for the girl. He did, and the girl was instantly healed.[15]

The work spread quickly through a people movement. The Lisu brought the gospel to the Rawang, and the Rawang in turn brought it to the Lhao-vo. Entire villages converted to Christianity and ceased their traditional religious practices. Their social and religious lives in their bamboo churches were Christ-centred. Herman Tegenfeldt, a Baptist missionary to Kachin land, noted that large numbers of people became Christians in an area in which the AG participated in outreach with other missions.[16]

The Morrisons revisited the work in Myanmar in 1940 and convened a two-week revival meeting. They wrote about the revival:

> Words will never be able to express our joy.... During the first or second service in their midst, the Holy Spirit fell over the whole vast assembly, and over half of the congregation was praising God and singing in an unknown tongue while many were dancing in the Spirit.[17]

The church kept progressing through indigenous workers whose policy was to plant self-propagating, self-supporting, and self-governing churches. The Japanese war subjected the people to persecution and torture and they lost their institutions. Despite this, the church gained more members, so that by the time they convened for a Silver Jubilee in 1956, the AG numbered 7,000 members.

In spite of the developing Pentecostal work in Myanmar, there was no permanent resident missionary until the end of World War II. Pentecostal missionaries from Sweden, Finland, and the Go Ye Fellowship and the Open Bible Standard Church from the USA laboured for a short time prior to World War II, but none of these groups returned to Myanmar after the war and thus

---

[15] Clifford Morrison, 'Speaking in Known Tongues', *The Pentecostal Evangel* (April 3, 1948), 7.

[16] Herman Tegenfeldt, *The Kachin Baptist Church of Burma* (Pasadena: William Carey Library, 1974), 94.

[17] Lavada Morrison, 'Missionary Challenge' (April, 1949), 13.

there was no continuing work.[18] Nevertheless, the years following World War II were great years of advancement for the AG in various areas of Myanmar as resident missionaries came to work there. The Morrisons came to the Lisu land in Myanmar in 1947. They started two schools in 1954 in order to prepare workers. Walter and Lucille Erola from the USA came in 1951. Walter Erola had worked under the Finnish Salem Mission in 1937 but returned as a liaison officer with the conquering British and American forces during the closing days of the war in 1945. He came back with his wife Lucille as an AG missionary and developed a church at Mogok in central Myanmar, with an outreach to other villages nearby. Lucille Erola spoke of a result of their labour: 'Tun Gaun and Ma Tin were a Burmese Buddhist couple who turned to Christ by seeing in their dream the cross of Christ higher than pagodas. They accepted Jesus and were both filled with the Holy Spirit'.[19]

Mr and Mrs Leonard Bolton came to Yangon, the capital city of Myanmar from Chittagong in East Pakistan (now Bangladesh) as missionary transfers in 1956. They noted that since they had landed there thirty years ago, everything had changed, except the 'spiritual darkness'. The city was full of Buddhist monasteries, temples and shrines. They began a meeting at an Indian family home, a rented house on Windamere Road, with a few people who were interested in the Pentecostal message. Bolton noted, 'Church planting here meant rock-bottom pioneering'.[20] The Boltons worked there for a short period but were unable to renew their residence permit, and left the country in 1957.

Glenn and Kathleen Stafford came to Yangon to oversee the urban mission work there in 1957. Their special meetings with visiting evangelists from abroad always attracted crowds. A noteworthy occasion was the evangelistic meetings of Harvey McAlister, which attracted people from all corners of the city; the sick were reported healed and believers experienced the baptism of the Spirit. Another remarkable revival was the ministry of evangelist Mabel Willetts in 1961, when people confessed sins and were converted to Christianity. It was said that the Holy Spirit had fallen on a group of people in the congregation, which was then reported to have developed into a 'veritable deluge'.[21] This event was a hallmark for the church as a future leader received the baptism of the Holy Spirit.

Myo Chit, the present General Superintendent of the AG, had commented on the result of this revival, saying, 'Several of us former anti-Pentecostals

---

[18] Stafford, 3
[19] Walter Erola, 'The Cross Above the Pagoda', *The Pentecostal Evangel* (December 4, 1955), 8, 9.
[20] Bolton, 199.
[21] Stafford, 7.

received the Holy Spirit as a result of their ministry'.[22] Coming from a Plymouth Brethren background, he was strongly anti-Pentecostal, criticizing the Pentecostal mission in Yangon as a 'crazy church'. He also commented that his pride was broken as God baptized him in the Holy Spirit in 1961. He then became affiliated with the Staffords and the Pentecostal church. In 1965, the Staffords invited him into full-time ministry, which he was sure was the call of God and he left his job to assist the Staffords. In March 1966 he succeeded the missionaries as the pastor of Yangon Evangel Church, when the government sent all missionaries home.

Ray and Bethany Trask were the last missionaries to arrive in 1961, continuing the urban ministry at Yangon as the Staffords went on furlough. Ray Trask made several preaching tours to nearby villages and some Buddhists and Hindus became Christians. The Trasks moved to Mogok until the government forced them to leave the country in 1965.

Stafford commented on the revival at a large biennial convention in 1961 attended by more than 3,000 national believers from all parts of the country. Each meeting ended with a call for people to come for prayer at about 11:00 pm, which lasted until midnight. He said,

> These were Pentecostal Christians and we had a 'real' Pentecostal convention... Some repented and confessed sins of long standing; some were convicted of carrying firewood on Sunday, or may be it was killing a chicken on the Lord's day. You might smile at this, but to these sincere Christians they had transgressed their standard and wanted to repent. Others were guilty of greater things and we knew God was working.[23]

The missionaries had always struggled for entrance and resident visas since independence in 1948. The Morrisons returned to the USA to retire in 1959. The Walters left the country for the last time in 1962, not able to renew their visas. No new visas or re-entry visas had been issued to missionaries since 1962,[24] when the military coup took place, and in 1964 Myanmar became a closed country. In March 1966, the Socialist government declared that all foreign missionaries had to leave the country within a month. Maynard Ketchem cited a phrase from the *Guardian*, a local newspaper, about the government order, saying, 'By 30 April 1966, all Christian missionaries must leave Burma'.[25] Ever since that time, no missionary has worked in Myanmar.

---

[22] Myo Chit, 'Even the Buddhist Monks are Listening', *Pentecostal Evangel* (February 10, 1980), 18.
[23] Glenn Stafford, 'Convention Time in Burma', *The Pentecostal Evangel* (July 23, 1961), 11.
[24] Stafford, 10.
[25] Maynard Ketchem, 'A New Day Dawns in Missions', *The Pentecostal Evangel* (July 17, 1966), 12.

However, God did not leave with the missionaries. By 1970, Pentecostals everywhere in the country had steadily grown. In Yangon, the capital city, Myo Chit was left in charge of the Evangel Church since 1966. Attendance dropped so that ten to fifteen people in the Sunday worship services were considered to be a crowd. But the church soon overcame its difficulties. A woman unknown to the pastor was touched by the preaching. As she learned that the church was in debt, she wrote out a cheque to completely cancel the debt. Another family donated land that was their family inheritance, which at first became a centre for short-term Bible training for young people from all over Myanmar, and later became the Evangel Bible College. The Pentecostal message and free worship drew people from all corners of the city and foreign visitors during the 1970s. It had grown to four to five hundred regular attendants by 1980. Healing and miracles were often reported as Myo Chit continued this ministry.

The Renewal Movement and Pentecostalism

The Pentecostal movement has become more visible since a great renewal affected churches among the Chins from the 1970s. The renewal started in local Baptist churches and spread across the country, but later resulted in many Pentecostal churches being planted. The AG has increased its membership by a half since the renewal. The United Pentecostal Church and the Foursquare Church have also sprung up as a result. The renewal movement has brought nominal Christians and non-Christians to conversion. The Chins have been converted to Christianity from tribal religion in a great 'people movement' since the 1900s. Christianity has helped greatly transform Chin society and culture. By 1970, many educated Chins were working in government offices all over the country and many Chin soldiers serving in the army. Unfortunately, second and third generation Christians (not only among the Chins but also everywhere in the country) were nominal in faith and practice.

Early in the 1970s, a burden for renewal came to the Tedim Baptist Church. In January 1973, the pastor Hau Lian Kham with a small group started praying for renewal, and after intense prayer, they conducted week-long open-air evangelistic meetings, which had never been a feature of Christianity in this region. It was reported that the work of the Spirit was so strong that many people repented of sin and became Christians. Eventually, the evangelistic meetings became a launching pad for the renewal movement. Renewal and conversion spread every day through the witness of 'born again' believers. Being 'born again' was an topic of discussion in offices, schools, market places and on the streets. Over several years the renewal continued to spread to many Chin individuals on the periphery of the ecclesiastical structures and lay believers spread the renewal throughout the country. Since this renewal, the AG has become the third largest denomination in the country.[26] Hau Lian Kham, key leader of the renewal movement, gradually shifted his belief and practice from fundamentalism-evangelicalism to Pentecostalism and in 1977 became a member of the AG. He influenced many believers and local churches to turn to Pentecostalism, which has greatly increased the growth of the AG.

It was claimed that miracles often followed this Pentecostal witness. Many people testified of healing from cancer, high blood pressure, tonsillitis, skin disease, and other maladies, and that their vision and hearing had been restored. They spoke of deliverance from the bondage of evil spirits occurring from time to time. I select and describe a few miraculous events that were reported at the time to help better understand this revival among the Chin.[27] Although these events may seem incredible to some readers, they are based on interviews conducted during field research, especially those held with the evangelists mentioned below.

One report concerned an answer to believers' intense prayer. The Tedim AG section celebrated an annual convention at Tungzang. Situated on a mountain, the villagers always had problems with not having enough water. Not knowing how they would cope with a gathering of 3,000 people, the believers prayed for rain and a water supply. Miraculously, a spring broke out in the middle of the village on the day the convention began. This spring supplied enough water for the crowds and still exists today.

Miracles were often reported in the ministry of evangelist Tamki, a convert from Mindat in southern Chin State. Dominated mainly by tribal religion and Buddhism, the people here are greatly attracted by supernatural manifestations, which have often been the means of converting people to Christianity. Tamki often challenged his people with the name of Jesus. It was reported that a group of people plotted to shoot and kill him while he was witnessing, but that to their astonishment, the guns would not fire the bullets. Because of this event demonstrating divine protection, many came to believe his witness and sought to receive Christian faith. He testified to many more miracles in his ministry.

Another report concerned an angel protecting evangelist Khai Khan Suan from being killed. One night, while preaching in a village near Kale, some men from the village tried to kill him. But they were afraid to, for they saw an angel hovering over and protecting the preacher and his evangelistic meetings. Finally, they all became Christians.

The ministry of evangelist Kam Cin Hau was accompanied by many miraculous accounts. He started the 'Back to the Bible' ministry in 1987 as a

---

[26] Chin K. Khai, 'Myanmar Mission Board and Agencies', in A. Scott Moreau (ed.), *Evangelical Dictionary of World Missions* (Grand Rapids: Baker, 2000), 667-68.

[27] I interviewed these people personally about their experiences. For detail see Chin K. Khai, 'Dynamics of Renewal: A Historical Movement Among the Zomi (Chin) in Myanmar' (PhD Dissertation, Fuller Theological Seminary, 1999), 269-75.

response to an ecstatic experience, in which in a vision he was taken to the heavenly abode of Christ and his angels. He reported on some of his most memorable evangelistic meetings. One report in Khuasak during April 1988 spoke of many converts, people being filled with Spirit, 'slain in the Spirit' (falling in a trance to the floor), and receiving healing from sicknesses. While people were 'slain', crying and laughing occurred. At another evangelistic event in Suangzang during May 1988, the audience was 'slain in the Spirit', they confessed their sins and were converted to Christianity. A six-year old boy cried aloud while 'slain', saying that he had a vision of his parents in hell asking for water. The traditional village priest was sick to the point of death, but he was reported healed and converted through prayer during these meetings. At the evangelistic meetings in Heilei village during the same month, people fell 'slain' before the Lord, crying and laughing, being filled with Holy Spirit. They put away their tobacco, *tuibuk* drug, and drinking *zu* (beer), and the workers broke two hundred beer pots in one day. Five to seven thousand attended every evangelistic meeting in Tedim town during July and August 1988. Again it was reported that the work of the Spirit was so powerful that many people were converted, received healing through being 'slain in the Spirit', and were speaking in tongues. These evangelistic meetings were celebrated with singing and dancing 'in the Spirit'. Many children became Christians during these meetings and more than thirty of them went out for evangelism to nearby villages.

The ministry of Lang Do Khup is a Charismatic movement in the Baptist church. He had a turning point in his ministry when a village priest told him how healing the sick comes by worshipping *dawis* (evil spirits), while Christians are powerless to bring such healing. This challenge compelled Khup to pray for the power of healing. He reported one day praying for a lame girl. Nothing happened, so he and his Christian companions returned home. But the Holy Spirit spoke to him to go back and pray for the girl. As he did that, the girl stood up and walked with no help. On another occasion, he said that God spoke to him to raise a dead man, and that doubts and fear came as he prayed. But the Holy Spirit encouraged him to persist in prayer, and finally the dead man came alive. It was reported that during youth meetings at Suangpi village, a women by the name Khup Dim who had been paralysed for twenty years was healed and was jumping and praising God with great joy, and many received the baptism of Holy Spirit with the manifestation of speaking in tongues.

Another example of these reports of miracles is Lian Za Dal, who ministers among Buddhists in Yangon. He was formerly pastor of the Siyin Baptist church, but in 1991 he started a new church to evangelize the neighbouring Buddhists. To his great surprise, during the worship time on the day of Pentecost in 1996, the members started speaking in tongues, prophesying, and seeing visions, manifestations they had not known before. Dal said that the Spirit equipped the members with spiritual gifts. Some boys and girls of about ten years old saw visions of the spiritual realm. Dal himself believed he had been given authority to heal and to command angels in the name of Jesus. Being an educated man trained in the Baptist Theological Seminary, Dal had a hard time accepting all these phenomena. He said that by searching for the will of God and examining everything through the word of God, he became a charismatic preacher in a local Baptist church.

Beliefs and Practices of Pentecostalism in Myanmar

The emphasis on speaking in tongues as a sign of the baptism of the Holy Spirit was a dynamic factor of the Pentecostal renewal. As Pentecostalism developed into a movement in the late 1970s, believers were urged to seek the baptism of the Holy Spirit, also known as being filled with the Holy Spirit, as subsequent to the experience of conversion. As Robert Menzies articulated, the baptism was taught as subsequent to regeneration and was the gateway to receive other spiritual gifts.[28] Therefore, Pentecostals hungrily sought for this special gift, which when they received it, they were renewed with joy, and had an increased desire for the Lord and boldness for witnessing.

The Pentecostals were evangelical in their basic tenants of faith and practice emphasizing the authority of Scripture, salvation in Christ by faith through grace, the urgency of Christ's coming, and the need for an immediate response to the invitation for salvation. Doctrinally, they were distinct from the mainline evangelical bodies only in terms of their emphasis on the charismatic gifts and functions. What Gordon Fee has stated accords with Pentecostals among the Chins. He says:

> Traditionally, they have put their overall theological emphasis precisely where other evangelicals do on the person and work of Christ. Nonetheless, the public expression of tongues, which has so often characterized Pentecostal worship, has also served as much as anything else to distinguish Pentecostals, and very often therefore to separate them, from their other bothers and sisters in Christ.[29]

Moreover, Pentecostals preach and teach the 'full gospel', living a holy life, and the imminent return of Christ—messages that have helped many to deeper commitment. Their message of liberation from poverty and low self-esteem, and their positive attitude has helped lift many from their low self-image. The subject of holy living emphasizes that believers are temples of the Holy Spirit, urging them to keep themselves holy, being separated from 'worldly' habits. As

---

[28] Robert P. Menzies, 'Spirit-Baptism and Spiritual Gifts', in Wonsuk Ma and Robert P. Menzies (eds.), *Pentecostalism in Context, Essay in Honor of William W. Menzies* (Sheffield, England: Sheffield Academic Press, 1997), 48-59.

[29] Gordon D. Fee, 'Toward a Pauline Theology of Glossolalia', in Wonsukma and Robert P. Menzies 9eds.), *Pentecostalism in Context:Essays in Honor of William Menzies* (Sheffiedl, England: Sheffield Academic Press, 1997), 24-27.

a result, Pentecostal believers abstained from their old habits of drinking, smoking, singing secular songs, reading novels, watching movies and anything that would affect their spiritual growth.[30] Also, believers always look forward to the 'rapture' of believers to heaven in their lifetime.

Pentecostal worship is a great transforming event. They have learned that worship is an essential part of being a Christian, and corporate worship a compelling need among believers. Pentecostal worship services are very different from those of the traditional style of worship. The enthusiasm with modern praise and worship choruses and musical instruments and their style of corporate prayer all make the worship services exciting and joyful. Praise and worship with choruses and a few hymns, led with musical accompaniment, and clapping hands are seen in all 'born again' churches. Solos, duets, trios, group singers, and action singers attractively and persuasively support the worship. Choruses composed within their own contexts convey their deep relationship with the Lord, developing theological insights that help people focus on deeper worship and praise.

The Pentecostals do not despise study and knowledge but emphasize the ministry of the Holy Spirit. The *Khanlawhna Hun* (The Revival Hours) is a newsletter that alludes to a scriptural theme taken from Zechariah 4.6, 'Not by might nor by power, but by my Spirit, says the Lord Almighty' (NIV). They acknowledge the Holy Spirit as the only power source, helper, and teacher of the things of God. As a result, the glory of God shown in miracles have always been witnessed and reported.

Prophetic Movements among Chin Pentecostals

In spite of the above phenomena that help build the churches, Pentecostals in Myanmar do face excesses as well. There have often been prophecies that have led believers into error. These prophecies are called *thusuak* or *sawlna*—that is 'forth-telling', commanding someone to do something. It began with certain people who claimed to receive the audible voice of God that demanded certain things be accomplished. If people failed to do these things, then calamity would follow. This, which I call the 'prophetic movement',[31] can be put into two periods: the early prophetic movement (1977-1989) and the later prophetic movement (1990 onwards).

A movement that appeared in 1977 had the phenomena of dancing, crying, rolling on the floor, carrying tables and chairs, and running around the church as a mode of repentance. The followers put on sackcloth, stood in the middle of the village and called for repentance. Furthermore, they claimed to have

---

[30] Forthcoming Chin K. Khai, *The Cross Amid Pagodas* (Baguio, Philippines, APTS Press).

[31] Khai, 'Dynamics of Renewal', 280-88; 350-53

received prophecies, saying that the Holy Spirit spoke to them audibly. They said the Bible was insufficient, and prophecies today were far more important. As these teachings and practices spread, a group tried to raise a dead body at Phaiza village, claiming that God told them to do so, but the body was not raised. They went around the Tedim town believing that God would give them all the people in the town. Their meetings commonly used excessive drum beating, dancing and repeating one song over ten times. They planted crosses in the open ground, waited for the 'rapture' and abstained from certain food and meats. Miracles sometimes followed as participants acted on prophecies. A group of them prepared a metre square piece of ground for the landing of a plane, which was reinterpreted as a spiritual plane that would 'rapture' them. Any prophecy that did not come true was reinterpreted as a testing of faith. The group considered themselves holier than any other believers, for they prayed and committed themselves seriously to their practices. They asserted that the name 'Jesus' was that of an ancient Greek god and stressed *Yashua* as the true name. Therefore, they taught that water baptism in the name of *Yashua* alone gives salvation. They even declared themselves descendants of the Israelites and kept the Sabbath and observed rites of circumcision. Finally, the group split into smaller sects, *Khami Pawl* (Spiritual Group), *Nazareth Khuami Yashua pawl* (Church of Yashua of Nazareth), and some joined the United Pentecostal Church.

John Thang Hum, a pastor at Kalemyo, reported a particular event when a prophetess went to the Tahan AG church and prophesied in a prayer of healing for a sick person in the church. The pastor, Lian Zam, with two of his deacons followed the prophetess with no hesitation. They prayed for the sick but nothing happened. The prophetess then suggested the need to kill a chicken and apply the blood to the body of the sick person. The pastor instantly objected to the prophecy as false, saying that the death of Jesus was sufficient for cleansing sins and healing sickness. Such prophecies were similarly denied as false elsewhere.

Another kind of prophetic movement is called the 'cleansing movement',[32] that came through prophecy appearing in the mid 1990s. Although there are excesses in this movement, generally it has been a positive force in the church. One of the cleansing movements was called the 'cleansing village', mainly an expression of unity among the village churches, with youth and adults together. The evil spirits were cast out of the villages, spiritually unclean things were destroyed or burned down and united worship was celebrated. It has similarities to the traditional *Khuado* feast,[33] a time when villagers chase spirits out of the village.

---

[32] Cleansing here means an act of spiritual deliverance.

[33] *Khuado* feast is a harvest (New Year) festival. It is similar to the water (New Year) festival of ethnic Bama. The Chins celebrate it every year after the harvest. The

Similar to this movement are the 'cleansing houses'. According to prophecy, certain houses would need to be cleansed for good health, prosperity, and the success of the household members. The prophets in visions saw unclean things in the house—things dedicated to evil spirits, materials used for worshipping spirits, and things in which spirits dwelt. These things hindered the household from prosperity and health, and caused sickness and loss among the family members. The prophet and the believers would take the objects and throw them away or burn them in a fire. After that, they would rededicate the house to God with prayer.

Tual Khaw Mang, a retired civil officer, testified to the cleansing of his house at Saizang in 1995. His parents and grandparents were chiefs of the Saizang village and were tribal religionists until they became Christians in 1995. They celebrated a ceremony of dedication and house cleansing as they committed themselves to Christ. To their surprise, problems and sickness came on family members in the following days. As they prayed, a prophet saw in a vision that there were unclean things left in the house, things that were used for demonic worship which needed to be destroyed immediately. Accordingly, they found a sword, a javelin, pots, and things dedicated to their household spirits they had not used for years. As they burned them their problems were resolved and sicknesses healed.

The prophetic movements gave the church a bad name in Chin society, for two main reasons: First, prophecy was misused for personal gain; and second, the prophecy did not always come true. Sometimes the gifts were not practised with consistent discipline. Many of the unfounded prophecies were delivered outside the church, where the prophet or prophetess functioned independently. Such a person did not allow himself or herself to be disciplined by the church leaders.

The Chin churches, particularly the Assemblies of God, rejected these teachings and practices. In 1978, Hau Lian Kham, Myo Chit, Dam Suan Mung, Suak Za Go and other leaders taught biblical criteria by which true prophets and prophecies could be distinguished from the false. First, a true prophecy must be in accord with, not contradicting, the teachings of Scripture. Second, it must edify believers. Third, it must be fulfilled. Fourth, it must glorify the name of Christ. Again in 1997, churches at Kale organized a prophetic conference in 1997 in order to bring the prophetic movement in line with biblical teachings. Dam S. Mung, pastor of the Full Gospel Church at Yangon, taught about the nature and characteristics of prophecy in the Bible and how to handle a prophetic movement. It was reported to be very helpful for local churches.

---

traditional concept of *Khuado* is two kinds: hospitalizing the spirits of forefathers and fighting against evil spirits, chasing them out of the village as well as cleansing the village in order to welcome the new year after harvest. For detail see, Khai, 'Dynamics of Renewal', 75.

Pentecostal Education and Mission

In Myanmar, critics often speak of Pentecostals as emotionalists who are not oriented toward intellectual matters. In reality, however, Pentecostals have emphasized Christian education from the very beginning and have educated many workers. All local churches encourage not only children but also adults to attend their Sunday schools. As early as the mission began, the missionaries conducted short-term schools in various villages that educated the indigenous people. By 1954 there were two schools[34] among the Lisus and Rawangs. They taught Bible lessons as well as reading, writing, and arithmetic. The school at Putao was moved to Myitkyina in 1964 and was named Burma Bible School.[35] The school offered a three-year diploma course in Bible and theological studies. Evangel Bible College was opened in Yangon on 2 August, 1979 with a resident teacher and twenty students. The college followed the curriculum and materials from the International Correspondence Institute (ICI) of Brussels, Belgium.[36] Maranatha Bible College opened at Kale in the northwestern area of the country in 1988 under the supervision and sponsorship of the District Council. Bethel Bible College opened at Tedim in 1991, and is also known as the 'Decade of Harvest Center'. The Apostolic Christian Bible College at Yangon was opened in 1986 and offers a bachelor degree for the United Pentecostal Church. The Full Gospel Bible Training Center at Yangon opened in 1995 and offers a diploma course. The School of Gospel Ministry at Yangon also offers a diploma course. Beside these, there are short-term Bible training schools in different towns and cities. Also, the respective districts and general councils conduct conventions and Bible seminars to mobilize and equip their people for service.

Pentecostals in Myanmar are committed to evangelism and mission work.[37] Churches send home missionaries both to completely unevangelized people and to places where Pentecostal ministry has not yet been started. They believe in church planting as a strategy for growth. They gather the converts to be worshipping communities and then viable churches. Missions have been carried out through a self-supporting programme, as all Pentecostal churches have developed the means to support their missionaries. Kyiyudaw Shubu (Lawm Bawm), meaning 'thanks offering box', is a box in which believers put coins in addition to their tithes and offerings on Sundays with praise to God for the blessings they have received, to support the mission work. Let tashoh sa (khut pham) is a handful of rice which the mother of the household keeps aside whenever she prepares a meal. In the same way, a girl keeps aside a stick of firewood (an sing) out of that which she collects in the forest. After a time, they

---

[34] Tegenfeldt, 287.

[35] Stafford, 8.

[36] Forthcoming Khai, *The Cross Amid Pagodas* (Baguio, Philippines: APTS Press).

[37] Khai, 'Dynamics of Renewal', 310-12, 340-42.

gather all the things they have put aside, sell them, and then hand over the money to the mission department. With these methods the Women's Mission provides support for missionaries.

Conclusion

Pentecostals in Myanmar are growing quickly compared to other denominations. Maynard Ketchem, the field director of Far East Asia for the AG in the USA, at one time stated that the AG in Myanmar was a model church with its self-propagating, self-supporting and self-governing methods.[38] I would like to comment on few theological and mission issues.

Preaching salvation should emphasize a collective approach to the salvation of God. Renewal preachers often addressed individual sin, individual repentance, and individual salvation—a pattern copied from western individualism. This had less impact in Myanmar society because social sin was not addressed, people with group identity were not acknowledged and social change was less concentrated. The image of 'group above self' slowly disappears as the individual emphasis takes over the people movement. Many would-be converts might have been denied acceptance in the church as a result of their inability to restructure their socially determined selves.

Although encountering spirits and power was not a new phenomenon among the Pentecostals, the 'cleansing-prophetic movement' was a breakthrough theoretically as well as practically in the life of the churches. The main distinction from other 'spiritual warfare' practices was that it operated through prophecy. This has to do with the culture in which indigenous religion was practised before. The prophet or prophetess could see in a vision the spirits and their abiding place in the house, the village, or even in the person and animal. These spirits brought calamities to people, and the prophet or prophetess with their followers cast out those spirits in the name of Jesus. The 'cleansing prophetic movement' is a deliverance ministry performed in a collective way. Many Christians, including some Pentecostals, regard prophetic ministry as having no grounds for corroboration or validity and unscriptural. It is the position of this paper that the participants were not telling lies, but rather were recounting real experiences. The prophetic ministry is an act of encountering unseen spirits and supernatural powers in what Paul Hiebert terms the 'excluded middle'.[39] Such events were rampant among people of folk religions, not only in Myanmar but also throughout the world. These are realities that science does not explain, but which merit spiritual recognition, observation, discernment and intervention. To the people in Myanmar, the existence of spirit

---

[38] Maynard L. Ketchem, 'Burma Revisited', *The Pentecostal Evangel* (June 16, 1968), 8.
[39] Paul G. Hiebert, 'The Flaw of the Excluded Middle', *Missiology: An International Review* 10 (1982), 35-47.

beings, demons and souls is not just a myth but a life encounter. Thus, the prophetic movement has offered a necessary and powerful spiritual dimension, but it calls for credibility-and reliability-testing in terms of Scriptural as well as empirical interpretation.

Beside the theological issues, the church in Myanmar always struggles to overcome some mission obstacles. The Buddhist world still remains unshaken by the witness of the gospel of Christ and is a major challenge to Christians in Myanmar, who feel uneasy when nationalism and Buddhism are coined together with the saying, 'A good Bama is a good Buddhist'. Consequently, restriction and discrimination from the government follow many Christian activities. Worship in house churches has been prohibited, crosses on top of mountains and churches were pulled down and burned and Christian publications and literature distribution are restricted. Even promotion to higher positions both in civil and military offices has been stopped for Christians. Christians as a minority group have no voice in this social landscape.

Poverty is another obstacle to growth. The country's economy has fallen to rock bottom, a shortage of major products has occurred for years, and inflation has rocketed up daily. Many small churches could not promote their activities due to a lack of resources. New churches could not raise their own buildings. Ministers do not get enough support, so they struggle for survival. They need both spiritual and moral support.

But in spite of these obstacles, Pentecostal witness always has a great prospect of success. Serving in the power of the Spirit followed by miracles, healing, signs and wonders is a great challenge to Buddhist and traditional practices. In addition, lay believers have been effectively instrumental in spreading the gospel since the beginning of the mission. Therefore, mobilizing and equipping them with deeper theological knowledge and then commissioning them to carry out the task will bring great advancement for the church in its mission.

Pentecostals and Charismatics in Malaysia and Singapore

Tan Jin Huat

The Pentecostal movement arrived in Malaysia in the 1930s, its initial growth was slow for the first three decades, but from the 1970s it grew rapidly in tandem with the Charismatic movement. In the 1960s, the Pentecostals constituted about 25% of evangelical Christians, but by 1985 they were 75%. Moreover, some mainline denominational churches have become Charismatic, and the influence of the Pentecostal/Charismatic movement has become pervasive among Malaysian churches.[1]

This paper seeks to explore the origin and development of the various strands of the Pentecostal/Charismatic movement in Malaysia, which has generally developed along four separate linguistic lines. The first Pentecostal group to arrive in Malaysia was the Ceylon Pentecostal Mission (CPM), later joined by the Assemblies of God, and these worked mainly, though not solely, among migrant Indians and Sri Lankans in Peninsular Malaysia. The second group, the Assemblies of God (AOG), first started with Chinese-speaking work and shortly afterwards with English-speaking work, which later outstripped its Chinese work. An impetus to the Chinese work of the AOG came through the influence of Kong Duen Yee, a Hong Kong actress. The ministry of Dr John Sung among the Chinese-speaking churches in the 1930s could be considered Charismatic, as he held revival meetings in Malaysia (both Peninsular and Sarawak) with great effect, where healing and gifts of the Spirit were manifested. Among the third group, the English speaking churches, the Pentecostal and Charismatic movement has been significantly influential so that new independent churches were started and some mainline churches have since become Charismatic. Fourthly, there was a separate development of Pentecostal expression through revivals among the indigenous people belonging to the Sidang Injil Borneo (SIB) churches in Sarawak, beginning in the 1970s.

---

[1] 'Pentecostalism' has been used to include all movements that emphasize the work of the Holy Spirit (esp. baptism/filling of the Spirit) and the use of his gifts (e.g. tongues, healing and prophecy) in the life and ministry of the church.

Indian and Ceylonese Ministry:
The Ceylon Pentecostal Mission and the Assemblies of God

The earliest stream of Pentecostal influence came through the Ceylon Pentecostal Mission[2] which worked mainly among the migrant workers from India and Ceylon (now Sri Lanka).[3] The first Malaysian work was begun in Ipoh in 1930 by Pastor A.K. Titus and then in Kuala Lumpur by Mr & Mrs V.V. Samuel.[4] During the visit of Chief Pastor Paul, the founder of CPM, with a team of workers to Kuala Lumpur, the first Ceylon Pentecostal Mission Convention was held in December 1931. Though there were few believers, there were conversions, Spirit baptisms and unusual blessings of gifts in kind from various unknown people, which served as an encouragement to them.[5] By 1933, the work had spread to Teluk Anson. From January 1934 till December 1935, Pastor Paul, Pastor Alwin and others came from Ceylon to hold conventions in Singapore, Kuala Lumpur and Ipoh. Their work was disrupted during the Japanese occupation of Malaya (1940-45) and by 1943 there was only one Pentecostal worker left. After 1947, workers from Ceylon and India came to re-establish the work. Due to doctrinal strife, the CPM decided to register itself as the Pentecostal Church of Malaya (PCM) in 1952. But work prior to 1950 among the Indians and Ceylonese fluctuated greatly due to the transitory nature of these migrants.[6] The work in Penang, which began during the 1950s, attracted a number of believers from the Chinese community, where nearly 90% of its congregation was Chinese, but its Chinese members have since declined to about 50% of the present congregation. By 2000, it had a total membership of some 1,000-1,500 with 13 centres. The CPM is predominantly an Indian Church with about 10-15% of Chinese members, only in Kuala Lumpur, Penang and Miri. Out of their fifty full-time workers in the year 2000, six were Chinese.[7]

The basic thrust of its ministry has been to hold regular conventions and to establish Faith Homes which became centres for their ministry. The work grew as a result of notable miracles being performed during the conventions. The

---

[2] Interview with Pastor Matthews, the Superintending Pastor of CPM, Malaysia on 23 April, 2001.

[3] CPM was founded by Pastor Paul in Ceylon (now Sri Lanka) in 1924. See *The Biography of Pastor Paul*. Publication 15 (Chennai: Pentecost Press Trust, 1998), 36.

[4] 'The Origin of the CPM work in Malaysia and Singapore', in *The Pentecostal Messenger,* April 2001, 8, 20-21.

[5] The Biography of Pastor Paul, 106.

[6] By 1957, more than 4 million Indians had come to Malaya and 2.5 million had returned. Of these, two thirds were labourers. The other one third were clerical workers mainly living in the towns.

[7] The CPM does not maintain any written record of membership. Only the pastor knows who the members are.

Chief Pastor and other pastors/full-time workers of the CPM from India made constant (usually annual) visits to hold the conventions at the CPM churches in Singapore, Kuala Lumpur, Penang and Ipoh. During these conventions and divine healing services, there was the preaching of the gospel, ministry time (e.g. prayer for the sick), Bible study on the deeper life, children's programme and 'tarrying' meetings. People were drawn into the church through healing and miracles reported at these conventions. In the CPM, there has also been a strong emphasis on the need to prepare for the Second Coming of Christ and the perfecting of the soul for Christ's coming. Prior to 1945, their emphasis had been on healing which led to conversions. Since 1945, the preaching of the gospel came to be included in the healing services.[8] During its services, everyone speaks in tongues simultaneously and aloud, and sometimes there has been singing and dancing in the Spirit and any other manifestation of the gifts of the Spirit.

The regular ministry of the CPM comprises the Sunday service, Wednesday Bible study and the Saturday 'tarrying' meetings. The tarrying meetings, usually of two hours duration, are meant for members to wait for the anointing of the Spirit and the purification of the soul. The Bible study stresses the deeper life of the Christian. Like any holiness movement, it stresses consecration (the giving up of all that is dear to us) and the victorious overcoming life. At times, after the visit of the Chief Pastor, those accompanying him might stay on to assist in the work of the local churches for a while before returning to India, or they might even stay on permanently. One such person was Pastor Jacob in 1949 who stayed on as Pastor of the Ipoh church. Their work naturally attracted the Indians and Sri Lankans by virtue of that fact that the CPM's workers were mainly from these countries. Sometimes, pastors of the CPM seceded to form independent churches, three of which began working mainly among the poor labouring class Indians in the Tamil settlements and plantations in Ipoh, Kuala Lumpur and Port Dickson from 1935.[9] By 1978, their combined membership only totalled 150, as their even more sectarian outlook and stringent practices kept them very small.

The CPM is generally conservative and trinitarian in its theology, and in practice seeks to obey the Scriptures literally. Full-time workers have been expected to be celibate, living in the Faith Homes where all things are held in common and belong to the Mission, with no individual ownership of property. It is strict in its code in terms of dress and behaviour, and full-time workers are dressed in white without jewellery or cosmetics. But the Chinese full-time workers, though dressed in white, do not wear the traditional Indian dress

---

[8] Interview with Pastor Matthews.

[9] In 1935, Pastor P.C. John began the Ipoh church. In Kuala Lumpur, Pastor J.C. Rose started his church. But in the 1960s, it experienced a split and some twenty of its members joined the English speaking services of the Assemblies of God (AOG).

(white shirt and dhotti). By its doctrine and practice, it encourages a generally sectarian outlook.

The CPM churches have stagnated in numbers since 1970, at around 1,000-1,500.[10] There are a few reasons for this. First, additions into the CPM have been offset by deaths of its older members and by its members (especially women) marrying Christians from other denominations, resulting sometimes in whole families moving into these denominations. Another reason is that some members have found its teaching rather strict and extreme in regard to the deeper life and healing. In particular, its strict stand on healing (that a sick person is not to take any medicine but to depend solely on God for healing) may have been difficult for some to accept. Also, the rise of the Pentecostal (AOG) and Charismatic churches since the 1970s with their emphasis on a 'blessings theology' have made it more attractive and appealing for members to change churches. Also, a limiting factor for those of other races to join the CPM is its practice of an Indianised form of Pentecostalism, which is probably a cause for the decline in the numbers of its Chinese members in Penang. For the present Chinese pastor in the CPM to wear a westernised white shirt and trousers instead of the usual Indian traditional dress may be a way of making its Indianised form of Pentecostalism more palatable to those of different ethnic origin. But the CPM has continued to be perceived as an extreme Indian Christian sect by the other Christian churches.

The Tamil ministry of the Assemblies of God (AOG) did not formally begin until 1968, when Dr Chris Thomas, the first Dean of the Bible Institute of Malaya was asked to initiate the work. A three stage programme was formulated to reach the Tamils: 1) Begin a Tamil Bible Correspondence Course (TBCC), 2) Follow-up through evangelistic campaigns, and 3) Have a short term Tamil Bible School to train workers to plant churches. The TBCC met with an encouraging initial response of 4,000 students with 1,000 finishing the whole (13 lessons) course within the year. Next, evangelistic campaigns were conducted in areas where at least 50 or more students had completed the TBCC.[11] This resulted in 14 Tamil services being started along the major towns in the west coast of Peninsular Malaysia. A Tamil Bible Camp was initiated and later the Malayan Tamil Bible Institute (MTBI) was established in 1972 with its first three students who were all Hindu converts. In 1975, the AOG Tamil ministry had eight churches and 10 preaching points with 450 adult baptized members. By 1985, the work had grown to 20 churches and 34 congregations and a total of 2,115 members. A factor for growth has been due to the work of MBTI graduates. The reduction of Indians in the plantations

---

[10] Chris Thomas, *Diaspora Indians: Church Growth among Indians in West Malaysia* (Penang: MIEC, 1978), 128. In 1978, there were 8 churches with a total of 1,000 members.

[11] These areas included Perlis, Kedah, Penang, Selangor, Pahang and Negri Sembilan.

since the 1980s, which was partly due to government policies, led to a rural-urban drift of Indians, particularly of the second and third generation. Better discipleship programmes and a marriage bureau for match-making single Indian converts consolidated their gains. The result was that the urban Indian congregations became larger than other Indian churches.[12] This trend has continued to the present day.

There are a couple of notable differences between the work of the CPM and AOG. Only since 1974 did the AOG hold special healing services with special speakers from America and India, which attracted many people from other religious backgrounds. Prior to that, there was none. Also, the AOG had better planning and outreach strategy for the work. The CPM and its splinter groups, which were the earliest Pentecostal groups, worked primarily among the migrant Indians and Ceylonese and remained very much on the fringe of Christianity in Malaysia. In contrast, the Tamil ministry of the AOG has been more successful and has grown steadily, especially since the 1980s.

Chinese Ministry: The Assemblies of God and the New Testament Church[13]

Ministry among the Chinese churches from the 1930s to the 1950s should be understood in the light of the influence of Dr John Sung's ministry, which could be considered Charismatic. From 1935-40, he was instrumental in bringing revival to the Chinese churches (mainly Methodist and Presbyterian) in the major towns in Malaysia and Singapore. His revival meetings saw evidences of weeping, conviction of sins, many conversions and changed lives from various sins and addictions, reconciliation of relationships, healing and deliverance of people from the power of the evil spirits and also the word of knowledge.[14] His ministry of 'signs and wonders' brought renewal to the Chinese church, with many committing themselves to full-time Christian ministry. The practice of conservative Chinese Christians praying aloud simultaneously seems to have its origin in John Sung's ministry since the meeting in Baldwin School chapel in March 1931, where John Sung spoke and the Holy Spirit fell on those present and they prayed simultaneously.[15] Also

---

[12] An Indian church is one that conducts its meetings solely in Tamil. An Indian congregation is usually bilingual in its services. By 1985, the Indian church had 995 members and the Indian congregations had 1,120 members.

[13] Interview with Rev Ng Kok Kee, President of Bible College of Malaysia (BCM) on 9 April 2001.

[14] Sheng. *Diaries of John Sung*, 106.

[15] Those present were urged by him to stop praying aloud simultaneously but it happened three times in that meeting so that finally John Sung allowed them to do so. See Schubert, *I Remember John Sung*. 34.

another characteristic of the John Sung revival was the singing of short gospel choruses.[16] Except for speaking in tongues (though it was not absent),[17] John Sung's ministry had all the marks of a modern day Charismatic movement, and became the unconscious benchmark for the mainline Chinese churches to gauge any move of the Spirit or revival.

Against this backdrop, the work of the Assemblies of God (AOG) with its claim of the baptism of the Holy Spirit would have been regarded favourably among Chinese churches. The AOG began its Chinese work in Peninsular Malaysia in 1934, first at Ampang and then moved to the Pudu area in 1935. From 1936-50, the work began slowly among the Chinese-speaking people. Rev Sandhal, with a couple of women missionaries, two local pastors and two local Bible women helped to spread the work through house to house visitation, house gatherings with Bible story time for children, Sunday schools, tuition classes, and youth fellowship activities. By 1940, it became officially affiliated with the Assemblies of God (AOG) in the USA. In 1953, the AOG was registered as an official body with the authorities and erected its first building at Jalan Sayor in 1955,[18] by which time, there were three centres in Singapore and one in Penang. The Malaysian work was initially Chinese speaking. It was from these centres that other AOG churches (both Chinese and English speaking) throughout the country were started.

From 1950-60, with the closure of missionary work in China, there was an influx of American AOG missionaries and the work began to spread to other towns. Work in Penang began in 1953 under Iris Hatchett, (who had been a missionary to China) with four Chinese workers from Hong Kong. The work was bilingual, but with a rapid turnover of missionaries during the mid-1950s there was slow growth. The work rekindled in 1960 and it grew into two separate churches; the Chinese speaking church under Luke Koo and the English speaking church at MacAlister Road under David Baker. From Penang, work spread to Ipoh in 1959 through the efforts of Lula Ashmore Baird and then to Taiping, Aulong village in 1960. The Ipoh church grew rapidly and led to the formation of two churches: Emmanuel AOG, an English-speaking church and First AOG, a Chinese speaking church. In 1959, the Bairds started the Raub AG work. In Kuala Lumpur, First AOG started the Sungei Besi Mission under the leadership of Ms Leong.[19]

---

[16] See *Diaries of John Sung,* for some of these choruses that he composed.

[17] See *Diaries of John Sung,* 29, 32 about John Sung having the experience of speaking in tongues and being asked about it by Pastor Wang Ming Tao. For John Sung, 'the most important thing is the power from the Holy Spirit to witness for the Lord'.

[18] Derek Tan, 'The Assemblies of God' in Hunt, Lee & Roxborogh (ed), *Christianity in Malaysia* (Kuala Lumpur: Seminari Theoloji Malaysia, 1992), 230-33.

[19] Alvin Cheah, 'History of the Assemblies of God Church in Malaysia' (BTh thesis, Bible College of Malaysia, 1987).

The ministry of the Hong Kong actress, Kong Duen Yee, popularly known as Mui Yee, (with her stress on the baptism of the Spirit and speaking in tongues), created quite a stir among the Chinese people. Her visit to Singapore and Malaysia (Kuala Lumpur, Ipoh and Penang) in 1963 was initially sponsored by the AOG which later withdrew its support when she started to make extreme claims and began to organize her own churches, the New Testament Church (NTC).[20] In Singapore, a Brethren elder, Elder Goh Ewe Kheng, who experienced the baptism in the Spirit during one of Mui Yee's meetings, resigned from the Brethren Assembly and started his home fellowship of about a hundred people, which formed the nucleus of what became the Church of Singapore. From the perspective of those who came into the experience of the Holy Spirit, they were forced by circumstances to begin their own church as their former church would not accept them.[21] By the mid-1990s, they had become one of the largest independent Charismatic churches in Singapore.[22] Some factors for its growth included 1) the attitude of Elder Goh Ewe Kheng and the Church of Singapore in maintaining contact with other church leaders in Singapore; 2) the rise of the Charismatic movement in Singapore in 1972 provided them with the avenue of emerging leaders to initiate the Spiritual Renewal Fellowship in 1973 by bringing together not only Pentecostal pastors but pastors and lay-leaders involved in the Charismatic renewal. It is significant that in the mid-1990s Elder Goh Ewe Kheng was chairm of the Evangelical Fellowship of Singapore, indicating the respectability and acceptability that the Church of Singapore has among the Singaporean churches.

In Kuala Lumpur, Mui Yee's act of condemning the Chinese gods and goddesses angered the Chinese community. The mediums and gangsters who went quietly into her gospel and healing meetings with the aim of challenging her had protective charms (needles) on them, which reportedly fell off during the meeting, leaving them powerless. At one stage, mediums and gangsters stood outside the church premises challenging her to come out for a spiritual

---

[20] The New Testament Churches in Malaysia and Singapore have their origin in the ministry of the Hong Kong actress popularly known as Mui Yee (her real name being Kong Duen Yee). After her baptism in the Holy Spirit at a Pentecostal meeting in Hong Kong in 1961, she set herself as an apostle of the church to set up churches that would resemble the early church of the New Testament, both in name (hence the Church of Singapore, the Church of Kuala Lumpur, the Church of Ipoh and the Church of Penang) and in practice, hence their call to purify the evils of denominationalism, that is, to establish nondenominational churches and to encourage the dynamic working of the Holy Spirit and his gifts.

[21] E.K. Sng, *In God's Good Time*, 2nd edn. (Singapore: GCF, 1993), 291.

[22] James Wong, 'The Church in Singapore', in Athyal, Saphir (ed.), *Church in Asia Today: Opportunities and Challenges* (Singapore: Asia Lausanne Committee for World Evangelization, 1996), 299-323.

duel. Wisely she did not oblige, riot police cordoned off the area during the encounter and nothing untoward happened. News of this event spread to the nearby Chinese community provoking both a reaction of hostility as well as a reaction of curiosity and interest about the superior Spirit of the Christians against whom the Chinese mediums were helpless. This power-encounter raised the question among unbelievers in that area of the Christian God being seen as far more powerful than any of the spirits that the Chinese worshipped. With healing of some physical ailments and the conversion of a medium it had some impact on the non-Christian Chinese community.

In Penang, another Brethren Elder from the Burmah Road Gospel Hall, Teh Phai Lian started the Church of Penang (later renamed the Charismatic Church of Penang, CCOP) in 1963 at his house.[23] Four years later, it moved to a bungalow in Jalan Utama. It finally built and dedicated its own building at Bayan Baru in 1998. [24] In a sense there was a stagnation in the Chinese-speaking work, probably due to the children of its members becoming English-speaking and so an English service was started. Also, since the rise of the AOG and the Charismatic movement, the CCOP does not seem to be any more distinctive than the others. In fact, there are more dynamic Pentecostal and Charismatic churches in Penang that have drawn away some of its members. In their meetings there was speaking in tongues, singing in the Spirit, healing and exorcism. Doctrinally, they subscribed to the idea that the NTC is the only true Church of God with a strong emphasis on dying to self, complete submission to the Holy Spirit and willingness to suffer for Christ's sake, sometimes taken to the extreme.

The reactions among the mainline Chinese speaking churches in Malaysia to Mui Yee's ministry had been largely negative. They viewed her teaching as extreme, in particular that of speaking in tongues, and her action of calling her followers to come out of their denominational churches to form their own church as divisive. Moreover, she had been castigated as an instrument of the devil, when news spread that she died of tongue cancer in 1966. The result was great reservation, prejudice and suspicion among the mainline Chinese-speaking churches towards the NTC in particular and the Pentecostal/Charismatic movement in general. This prejudice was to last for some three decades into the early 1990s among the Chinese speaking churches. Over the years, the leaders of the NTC became more sectarian in doctrine, practice and fellowship, hence marginalizing themselves from mainstream Christianity. They experienced a much slower growth in Malaysia compared to their Singapore counterpart. Neither did they gain any substantial following on

---

[23] Andrew Loh, *Treasures of Darkness. Charismatic Renewal. The Malaysian Connection* (Melaka: Percetakan Yinfay Litho, 1991), 7.

[24] Souvenir programme of Charismatic Church of Penang for the dedication of their new building at Bayan Baru on 10 October 1998.

the rise of the Charismatic movement in Malaysia since 1973. Today, they stay on the fringes and continue their activities quietly, including the operation of a church retreat centre near Tapah, which was raided recently (January 2001) by the Malaysian police, not due to any activities of its own but through pressures from Islamic groups.

In short, the Pentecostal movement among the mainline Chinese speaking churches was prejudiced in two ways. First, its claim to power ministry was consciously or unconsciously compared with the powerful ministry of John Sung and found to be only a pale shadow. The second was the prejudice created by the ministry of Mui Yee, which was to have a long-lasting negative effect on the Chinese speaking churches. This inevitably led to the marginalization of the NTC from mainline Christianity. In contrast, the beginning of an openness to the Pentecostal/Charismatic influence among the Chinese churches since the mid-1990s has been slowly felt among students and young adults. An impetus for Charismatic expression among the Chinese Methodist churches has been provided recently by its present president, who has found much support from the younger pastors, youths and young adults.

English-speaking Ministry:
The Assemblies of God and the Charismatic Movement

The AOG first concentrated its work among the Chinese in the Pudu area of Kuala Lumpur in 1934. Its special efforts, like large tent evangelistic meetings for a whole week with an American evangelist and an open air meeting in a neighbouring field in 1936-37, (in addition house to house visitation, house gatherings with Bible story time for children, Sunday schools, tuition classes, and youth fellowship activities) met with the response of a number of converts. With more missionaries since the 1950s, the work grew slowly but steadily, attracting mainly children and youths. The beginnings of a breakthrough came in 1957 at the Youth Camp at Port Dickson, where 20 youths (out of the 80 youths there) became baptized in the Spirit. Since then until the 1970s, youth camps became the focus of spiritual renewal (with emphasis on the baptism of the Holy Spirit and speaking in tongues) and growth with a challenge for full-time Christian ministry. Many responded to the call and went to Bible school.[25]

The founding of the Bible Institute of Malaya (later changed to Bible College of Malaysia, BCM) in 1960 was instrumental in furthering the growth

---

[25] Derek Tan, 'The Assemblies of God', in Hunt, Lee & Roxborogh (ed), *Christianity in Malaysia: A Denominational History*, 237.

of the Pentecostal movement considerably.[26] The BCM graduates from 1960-80 were basically pioneers, evangelists and church planters, since there were very few AOG churches then. By the 1970s, every major town in West Malaysia had an AOG church.[27] Within a span of 25 years from 1962 to 1987, the number of AOG ministers rose sharply from seven to 318 with a total of 200 churches. So the rate of growth among AOG churches, which steadily increased from 1964 to 1974, began to experience a significantly sharp increase in the number of churches and membership from 1974 to 1990. Since the 1990s, there has been a slower pace of growth, but by 2000 there were 291 churches.[28]

The early emphases of the AOG were planting new churches by BCM graduates and evangelism, baptism of the Holy Spirit and speaking in tongues as its initial physical evidence. These BCM graduates started school groups in the major towns, organised youth rallies, open air meetings for children, and giving out tracts in the neighbourhood of the outreach-point. Where it fitted into their agenda, they networked with para-church groups like Navigators and Malaysian Campus Crusade for Christ, to help them in their evangelism and discipleship programmes. In 1976, they cooperated with the Malaysian Campus Crusade for Christ in the 'I found it!' campaign using the four spiritual laws as a means of evangelism. One of its early BCM pioneers started the audio-visual literature ministry which found great support and acceptability among the denominations in the 1960s and 1970s. The AOG stayed focussed on outreach and evangelism and as a result grew steadily.

The 1970s was the heyday of student work among the AOG. In 1971, the AOG churches consisted largely of Chinese Christians, with 80% of them being students in their mid-teens. Student work had the necessary boost through the energetic work of BCM graduates and also the formation of the Inter School Christ's Ambassador in 1971 by Ray Quah, who used Navigators material to disciple new converts. They emphasized Bible reading and study, scripture memorization, discipleship and knowing Christ, normally meeting outside the school compound in community halls. The growth of youth ministry was also fuelled by the AOG Selangor Youth Department, which organized a number of youth rallies at the Kuala Lumpur Town Hall and the Dewan Bahasa dan Pustaka, with attendance in the hundreds. The largest AOG church in Kuala Lumpur, Calvary Church (under Prince Guneratnam since 1972) which began

---

[26] BCM started as a regional centre for training AOG pastors for the South East Asia region. It started with the English speaking programme. The Chinese speaking progamme was only started in 1967.

[27] New AOG churches were started in Butterworth, Taiping and Malacca in 1963, Seremban, Klang, Kajang and Port Klang in 1964, Kuala Lumpur, Ulu Klang, Jinjang (KL) in 1965, and Penang, Alor Star, Batu Pahat, Klang, Kuala Lipis, and Cochrane Rd, KL in the 1970s. See Alvin Cheah, *History of AOG Church*, 19-20.

[28] Interview with Rev. Ng Kok Kee, President of BCM.

in 1960, moved from the parent church, First AOG to its present premises at Damansara in 1968. From 1973-80, it grew rapidly in tandem with the Charismatic renewal occurring in the mainline denominations, to 725 members by 1980,[29] and it planted three churches in the 1970s.

The rise of the Charismatic movement in the early 1970s provided the necessary impetus for the Pentecostal movement to increase significantly. From the mid-1970s to the early 1980s, the influx of young people into the AOG churches was further fuelled by the expulsion of youths involved in the Charismatic movement in the mainline churches in the Klang Valley.[30] In the late 1970s, defection from the new Charismatic churches added to the AOG not only numbers but also leaders who later became pastors in various AOG churches.[31] When the Charismatic renewal had begun to affect the mainline churches, Calvary Church began its outreach, Calvary Charismatic Centre and started with Sunday afternoon meetings in the Merlin Hotel in 1978 for those who were from the other denominations but felt uncomfortable worshipping at an AOG church. This ministry began to attract professionals and businessmen. It was attended by a number of Christians from other denominations who were interested in the baptism of the Holy Spirit or had come into this experience, including Roman Catholic nuns and a couple of Brethren leaders and their members. These later in 1981 formed the Full Gospel Assembly (FGA), Kuala Lumpur which has since become one of the largest Charismatic churches in Malaysia. The reasons for the attendance by Christians from other denominations were varied, ranging from curiosity, genuine seeking for the Pentecostal experience and to learning from the Pentecostals their way of worship and their management of the spiritual gifts in church life and worship.

Since the late 1980s, the AOG churches matured and saw a decline in the numbers of their youth. Instead, the young people were attracted to newer Charismatic churches like Renewal Lutheran Church and FGA and currently Damansara Utama Methodist Church and Sidang Injil Borneo. However, one or two AOG churches were creative in their outlook in using music and the performing arts and so were able to retain their youth. But these more successful pastors were initially AOG youth pastors and had continued to

---

[29] Derek Tan, 'The Assemblies of God', in Hunt, Lee & Roxborogh (ed) *Christianity in Malaysia* (Kuala Lumpur: Seminari Theoloji Malaysia, 1992), 239.

[30] Some 300 youths left both the churches and the AOG churches gained some 200 of them.

[31] TOG under Raymond Row, formerly from St. Paul's PJ, was started in 1974 when he was a student at BIM from 1974-76. It was affiliated with the AOG for a short time before it went independent. It was the fastest growing church around 1975-80. Out of this work came a number of AOG leaders like Ronald Ooi who went on to pastor Penang Christian Centre (PCC) in Penang and Dominic Chan who went on to pastor Glad Tidings, Klang and others who have moved on to serve the Lord in both church and para-church groups like Malaysian Care.

remain in touch with youth work. The AOG churches recognized this weakness in its young people's work and sought to rekindle it with the 'Jam with the Lamb' musical sessions. But this was not approved by the AOG Council and instead was held through the sponsorship of a local church or body like BCM. Ironically, the creative methods of outreach, which were acceptable in the 1960s and 1970s and bore good results, seemed to have become unacceptable to the AOG leadership in the late 1990s and 2000.

During the 1960s till the mid-1970s, the motivation of the AOG ministers was to sacrifice willingly their life for the work of God. This helped them to persevere in the work in small towns like Raub where their numbers were very small. But a change began to take place in 1977, when Pastor Paul Cho Yonggi of Korea came to Singapore to conduct a church growth seminar. In Malaysia, Duane Vierow, a Lutheran pastor had been promoting church growth ideas among the churches. This stress on church growth resulted in a changed outlook among the AOG pastors. Prior to that, the AOG, which had come out of the Holiness movement, valued highly the practice of holiness, which led to a world-negating attitude. Moreover, it valued poverty, sacrifice and suffering for Christ's sake, which resulted in persevering for Christ in difficult situations. But with the church growth movement, the thinking shifted to the concept that if there is church growth, then there is God's blessing; if the church is not growing (interpreted as *numerical* growth), then God is not blessing that church. Once, those who persevered in small towns with small numbers were held as models of faithfulness, but by the late 1970s, their faithfulness to God was in question. The changed outlook caused some hard soul-searching among these pastors. It also meant that BCM graduates since the 1980s did not think of planting churches in the difficult rural areas but sought to serve in the larger urban churches. Since the 1980s, the concept of mega-churches caught the imagination of the pastors who sought to establish large congregation in excess of a thousand members, resulting in a few large AOG churches (like Calvary, Glad Tidings and Grace Assembly) in the Klang Valley.

With this change of thinking, the next step was an easy accommodation to the Prosperity Gospel in the 1980s. The Prosperity Gospel came with the influence of the American Charismatics who came in great numbers in the mid-1980s till the early 1990s; among these was Morris Cerrullo, whose visit was initially sponsored by Grace Assembly (AOG). Among the Charismatics, Abundant Life Centre was the main local centre promoting the Prosperity Gospel, which in turn initially derived its teachings from the American faith-healer T.L. Osborn, especially the concept of seed-faith. The Prosperity theology came in the context of an economic boom in Malaysia in the 1980s and 1990s, which made it more easily accepted among Pentecostals and Charismatics.

In the early to mid-80s, the emphasis was on faith healing and deliverance ministry in addition to praying for the baptism of the Holy Spirit and speaking in tongues as regular features of the revival meetings. The later 1980s saw the rise of the prophetic movement, where personal prophecies were a regular feature during ministry time. The AOG as a whole was generally cautious about this prophetic movement. Churches that had these meetings were very well attended with people seeking personal guidance through prophecies. This practice declined after criticism that it was becoming like a form of Christian fortune-telling. Initially a couple of Charismatic churches encouraged the prophetic movement, but it was Renewal Lutheran Church (RLC) that strongly promoted it. Up to the mid 1980s, the AOG churches saw great increases in their numbers. But with the rise of many newer independent Charismatic churches like Full Gospel Assembly, The Word Centre, Full Gospel Tabernacle, Renewal Lutheran Church, and New Life Restoration Centre, there was a drift of some AOG members to these Charismatic churches, resulting in slower growth in the AOG churches. Moreover, a number of leadership crises among the larger AOG churches in the cities have also dampened its growth in the later 1980s and 1990s.

The Charismatic movement made its presence felt in the mainline churches initially through the ministry of Rev Peter Young in 1972. He was then pastor of St Gabriel's (Anglican) Church and also the general secretary of Scripture Union (SU), the then leading evangelical para-church organization. In 1972, Peter Young had come into the Charismatic experience and in the following year several leaders and members of St Gabriel's Church followed. The movement spread rapidly to members of the nearby Baptist, Methodist and Anglican churches. At this stage, those who became Charismatics were mainly interested individuals from a number of the churches. As a whole, the church leadership of the mainline denominations was cautious and suspicious. News of Peter Young becoming Charismatic spread throughout the evangelical (especially SU) circle of supporters. A mixture of reactions followed. There was strong opposition from a couple of the leading Brethren churches in the Klang Valley, who withdrew support for SU. There was also a cautious wait-and-see attitude with regard to the genuineness of his Charismatic experience. But Peter Young's influence continued to spread among key individual Christian leaders in the various towns in Peninsular Malaysia during the course of his SU work. His stature as an evangelical leader did much to erode the strong prejudice which the evangelical community had for the Pentecostal movement at that time. The main opposition came from the Brethren churches who were the predominant evangelical churches then.[32] They subscribed to a dispensational theology, understood the spiritual gifts to have ceased with the apostles and attributed tongues-speaking to the devil. But Peter

---

[32] See Tan Jin-Huat, 'David Boler: The Man, His Life and Influence', in Ooi Chin Aik and Tan Jin Huat (ed), *Pursuit of God's Cause. A Collection of Essays on the Life and Impact of the Evangelical Church in Malaysia* (Petaling Jaya: National Evangelical Christian Fellowship, 1998), 24.

Young's sound biblical teaching on the Holy Spirit and gentlemanly manners did much to enhance the credibility of the Charismatic movement.

The emerging Charismatic movement spread its influence through organized meetings to promote Charismatic renewal. In the initial years St Gabriel's Church held meetings where Christians were encouraged to seek the baptism of the Holy Spirit. A couple of healing services were also held but not emphasized. Later, a series of seminars on the Holy Spirit was held, which attracted some 150-200 young people from various churches. There were special speakers including Edgar Webb and Rev. Harold Parks. The main emphasis was on the baptism of the Holy Spirit and speaking in tongues, with a few cases of exorcism and deliverance. The success of these meetings led to the formation of the Renewal Fellowship (RF), which was aimed at promoting spiritual renewal among the churches. As an inter-denominational organization it was modelled after the Fountain Trust in England. Those who were initially involved in the pro-tem committee of Renewal fellowship included a few Anglican laypeople including the writer as chair, a Lutheran pastor (Rev Bob Neff), two Pentecostal pastors (Rev Joseph Yong and Ronnie Kon) and a Roman Catholic layperson (Willie Massang). It was important that the RF did not insist on speaking in tongues as the initial physical evidence of the baptism of the Holy Spirit, but only as a possible accompaniment. In certain theological and practical matters, it took a different position from that of the AOG. Under the sponsorship of RF, a couple of seminars were organized. A team from World MAP under Brian Bailey held a series of meetings at St Gabriel's Church, All Saints' Church and Christ Lutheran Church, Setapak. In 1975, a significant seminar was held in which a Baptist minister (Douglas McBain) and a Roman Catholic priest (Ian Petit, a Benedictine monk) ministered together. The evening public meetings at Trinity Methodist Church, Petaling Jaya were packed with some 350-400 people from Anglican, Baptist, Brethren, Evangelical Free, Lutheran (LCMS), Methodist, Pentecostal and Roman Catholic churches. The credentials of the speakers, their theological soundness and their moderate ministry style gave much credence to the emerging Charismatic movement.

Many young people from the various denominations, who had become Charismatics and had felt somewhat alienated from their churches, found the SU music ministry practices and performances of the musical presentations of 'Come Together' and 'If My People', a rallying point for them. These musicals were held at various local churches around the country from 1975-79 and through this group the Charismatic influence spread mainly to young people of other denominations, including the Presbyterians in the south.

In the initial years of the Charismatic movement, there was the perception that those who joined the Charismatic movement were either having psychological problems or were over-emotional young people. It was true that from 1972-76 it consisted mainly of young people ranging from late teens to later twenties. But this situation changed when a slow stream of older adults including Dr Caterall of St. Paul's Church and P.V. Jacobs, Headmaster of St David's High School, Melaka became involved, coupled with the news that the Anglican Bishop of Singapore, Bishop Chiu Ban It and Professor Khoo Oon Teik, Chair of SU Singapore had become Charismatic. Unfortunately, these young enthusiastic Charismatics felt compelled or were forced to leave their denominational churches, thereby swelling greatly the numbers in many AOG churches in the Klang Valley from 1973-81.

The exodus of young people from the mainline churches also gave rise to the formation of new independent Charismatic churches, such as the Tabernacle of God in 1974 under Raymond Row and Latter Rain Church in 1975 under Dexter Low. Both the Tabernacle of God (TOG) and the Latter Rain Church (LRC) were effective in their early years in reaching out to the young people, especially in the universities and colleges. The Latter Rain Church was initially successful in planting a total of 25 churches throughout the country. The LRC, which began in Melaka, moved to Kuala Lumpur in 1978 to work among the university students and began to shed its *kampong* outlook.[33] But their decline began in 1982 and 1991 respectively due to the highly authoritarian style of leadership and internal leadership differences. From TOG, many left for the AOG churches. From LRC, eight churches (of which Gateway Christian Fellowship, Melaka was one of the largest) with a total of 600 members seceded and became unaffiliated independent Charismatic churches,[34] thereby reducing LRC's membership by almost half. But LRC recouped its numbers within a year, having university students as a new group of leaders and reaching its peak in 1989-91.[35] The Latter Rain Church has continued to experience a couple of splits even into the late 1990s. With these breakaways both these churches have been reduced considerably in size.[36]

The next wave of Charismatic renewal from 1979 onwards began to affect older professionals and businessmen. Initially, the main influence came through Dr Peter Tong, a former Brethren member who had joined Calvary Charismatic Centre for a short while before starting the Abundant Life Centre with a couple of other like-minded people from other denominations. At the same time, the Full Gospel Businessmen's Fellowship (FGBMF) was initiated involving almost the same group of people. This network together with the newly formed Full Gospel Assembly (FGA) attracted hundreds of people each month. In the 1980s, there were many conversions among established professionals and some

---

[33] *Kampong* in Malay means 'village'.

[34] The LRC churches that seceded were from Melaka, Muar, Kuala Lumpur, Klang, Ipoh, Taiping, Penang and Alor Star.

[35] In the Petaling Jaya Church alone, there were some 800 members. Personal communication with a former pastor of the LRC, Malcolm Dennis.

[36] Klang Baptist Church, which had turned Charismatic in 1976, left to form its own church but remained within the Baptist denomination.

highly placed business people. Due to a misunderstanding with regard to the functioning of the FGBMF, the AOG churches withdrew their support for the Charismatic movement from the early 1980s. Also, some AOG members were beginning to leave their churches for the fastest growing church, FGA in the 1980s. By 1980, the Roman Catholic (RC) Charismatics, who once joined the Charismatic meetings, were longer present. There are a couple of reasons. During some of the Charismatic meetings and seminars, some speakers spoke out publicly against some RC practices (e.g. veneration of Mary). Also, the RC Church, being aware of their members leaving for Charismatic churches, decided to have their own services for RC Charismatics. One outcome has been the rise of RC churches conducting regular healing services.

During this time, one of the currently largest independent Charismatic churches, Full Gospel Assembly (FGA) was formed. It began in 1979 when two Brethren Church Elders, Dr Koh Eng Kiat and Mr Ang Chui Lai were compelled to leave their Brethren churches. They started a fellowship group at Dr Koh's house for those who had recently left their Brethren churches. By 1980 they had moved into a shop-lot and their numbers rose from 60 to 400. They moved again in May 1981 to the Majestic Hotel. However a group of young people stayed in Petaling Jaya and formed the Full Gospel Tabernacle (FGT). Still FGA continued to grow to 600 people. Towards the end of 1983, FGA moved to its present premises of a cinema hall. By 1990 it had grown to 5,000 and now to some 12,000 people with four congregations, (English speaking, Chinese speaking, Tamil speaking and Bahasa Malaysia speaking).

In the 1980s a number of independent Charismatic churches, particularly from former Brethren churches in Taiping and Ipoh sought affiliation with FGA. Soon they were joined by others in Penang, Seremban and Batu Pahat. In the 1990s, FGA became involved in church planting. Since then there are centres of work in Kuala Selangor, Sungei Buloh, Raub, Puchong and Cheras. An offshoot of FGA was the Tabernacle of Glory (TOG) in the early 1980s. It emphasized power ministries, revelation knowledge and personal prophecies. It invited Benny Hinn and a series of American preachers to speak at its rallies, resulting in very rapid growth. Its decline set in after the pastor exhibited some heretical tendencies and moral impropriety. After his departure in 1995, the church experienced a split with a large number of its members going to other Charismatic churches. There was also a proliferation of other new independent Charismatic churches during the 1980s. Some were formed by leaders or individuals from the mainline churches; among these included The Word Centre under Timothy Phua and Renewal Lutheran Church (RLC) under Pastor Joshua Yee. Returnees from Melbourne who were formerly students at Monash University and were connected with the Waverley Christian Church under Kevin Conner started the New Life Restoration Centre (NLRC) under the leadership of Jeremiah Yap.

In the 1980s FGBMF and FGA were the main centres of Charismatic happenings. They had a continuous stream of invited speakers from overseas as well as organizing seminars for the churches to promote Charismatic renewal. During this time, the AOG view of speaking in tongues became the accepted norm. Deliverance ministry and exorcisms were widely practised in the initial period. But at one stage many individual members went to extremes with the obsession of finding demons in every nook and corner and also excesses in relation to the Prosperity Gospel and the *Name It and Claim It* theology and practices. But these were later greatly reduced. It then gave way to the prophetic movement, which was promoted by TOG. Into the later 1980s and 1990s, RLC also began promoting its Deeper Life Seminars and with it majored on personal prophecies. In 1994, a prophecy was given that the Anglican Bishop of West Malaysia would be healed of his heart problem and would have many years of effective ministry, but he died not long afterwards. Issues and questions in relation to personal prophesies began to surface. This prophetic movement which was in vogue from the later 1980s took a nose-dive since the mid 1990s, as there were many criticisms regarding the practice of personal prophesies. Not only were new independent Charismatic churches being established, but some established churches were also becoming Charismatic. The Full Gospel Businessmen Fellowship meetings (FGBFM) were largely instrumental in encouraging the leaders of these churches (who were professionals and businessmen) into the Charismatic experience. The transition into the Charismatic movement for these churches was relatively smooth since its key leaders were involved in the renewal.

By the mid-1990s the Charismatic renewal had waned and when the Toronto Blessing was in vogue in the mid-1990s, a couple of churches were involved including DUMC and NLRC. It benefited these churches as they saw some growth, but generally, the AOG and Charismatic churches have become extremely cautious regarding this new happening, resulting in a very mixed reaction. Interestingly, those involved in earlier renewal movements have tended to be cautious with the later ones, to the extent of being critical of them. Those who had encouraged the Toronto Blessing were also involved in promoting the Cell Church movement, which has been popularized by Pastor Paul Yonggi Cho of Korea and Lawrence Khong of Faith Community Baptist Church (FCBC), Singapore. DUMC under Daniel Ho had been actively conducting Cell Church seminars for a few years and had seen some rapid growth. Their emphasis has been that each cell group should function like a church with the operation of the gifts of the Spirit.

Indigenous Ministry, Revival and the Sidang Injil Borneo

The Charismatic manifestations in the revivals in East Malaysia began as a separate development from those occurring in Peninsular Malaysia in the 1970s. Revival broke out in the interior of Sarawak among the Kelabits in 1973. The ministry of Indonesian evangelist, Petrus Octavanius who preached at the Easter Convention of the SIB in April 1973 and also at Bario started the process of the revival. Many were converted and renewed. In October that year, a group of young secondary school students were praying when the Holy Spirit fell upon them. The meeting lasted all night, then a few days, and soon involved the whole village. At the meeting for all the churches at Central Bario on 21 October, where the church leaders were also present, the awesome presence of God was felt. There was weeping, confession of sins, worship that lasted for hours into the next day, changed lives, reconciliation of relationships, difficult court cases amicably resolved, deep desire to pray and renewed vigour and zeal for the Lord. During this period, there were manifestation of the gifts of the Spirit like words of knowledge, wisdom, prophecy, discernment and speaking in tongues, which occurred spontaneously. This revival spread through the work of six mission teams comprising schoolteachers, young people, church elders, district and village chiefs.

They went to the nearby surrounding areas and experienced a tremendous work of the Spirit, where many experienced repentance, reconciliation, healing of the sick, deliverance from demonic powers and burning of charms and fetishes, and a renewed love and joy for the Lord.

A second wave of revival came in August 1975 through the ministry of two Indonesian evangelists who came to Bario. In this second wave, there was a sense of exuberance, worship and praise resulting in many short new songs being composed. Again, teams were sent to the same destinations as in the previous wave of revival in 1973. By 1979 the revival had waned and many became spiritually indifferent, particularly those who migrated to the coastal towns for education and job opportunities. Out of this concern and helplessness, people began to gather in groups for prayer in 1979. This resulted in the 'prayer mountain movement' (e.g. Mount Murud ministry) where people gathered at a specific mountain for prayer and intercession at specific times.

In the next wave of revival in 1984-85, Ba Kelalan became the centre where there was a series of spectacular signs and wonders, which received national coverage in the national daily, *The Straits Times* in December 1985. A key figure at this revival was Pa Agong Bangau, a Sidang Injil Borneo (SIB) pastor, who spent long hours in prayer, received visions and operated in the area of gifts of knowledge, wisdom, working of miracles and prophecy. His ministry had a positive impact on the Sidang Injil Borneo (SIB) Church as a whole, even though some expressed a measure of scepticism and reservation. These Charismatic renewals and revivals brought reawakening to the SIB Church and boosted their enthusiasm for God in a way that contributed to the growth of the indigenous church.

Concluding Comments

Prior to the 1950s, the major races (Malays, Chinese and Indians) were generally living separate from each other: Malays in the *kampongs* (villages), Chinese in the tin mines and rubber estates and the Indians in the plantations.

Only in the major towns was there any mixing of these races with the Chinese forming the majority. In the post-independence period, there was a greater urbanization process, which meant that the towns became more cosmopolitan. Also, the geographical segregation of the races in the towns, where the races lived in Malay *kampongs*, Chinese villages and Indian settlements, began to be blurred from the 1970s. When the Pentecostal movement came to Malaysia, it began, grew and developed along racial and linguistic lines according to the geographical segregation of the different races, resulting in English-speaking, Chinese-speaking and Tamil-speaking churches. Only in the major towns were there mixed congregations of both Chinese and Indians in the churches.

The growth of the CPM and the NTC among the Indians-Ceylonese and Chinese respectively has been generally slow as they have been considered as extreme sects, operating on the fringe of mainstream Christianity and also sidelined by the mainline churches. The CPM with its image of having an Indianised form of Pentecostalism has largely confined itself to Indian members. It would need to shed its sectarian image and its Indian cultural dress, which it has been trying to do in recent years, to make it more acceptable and attractive to the other races. Further, the internal splits that they (CPM and NTC) experienced, have been major set-backs for them.

The AOG work, which began in the 1930s among the Chinese, lived under the shadow of the powerful ministry of Dr John Sung in the 1930s. He exercised such a tremendous influence over the Chinese speaking churches even into the 1960s so that the work of the AOG among them looked pale in comparison. Moreover, the ministry of Mui Yee, though it attracted many non-Christians, gave the Pentecostal movement a very negative image (that it is the work of the devil) among the Chinese speaking churches, which was to last into the 1990s. Despite this prejudice, growth of the AOG work among the Chinese community continued although at a much slower pace.

It was in the English-speaking churches that the Pentecostal movement grew, first rather slowly in the 1950s as a result of push-pull factors. On the one hand, there was the influx of American missionaries from China and Asian workers from Hong Kong that gave the work the necessary impetus. But the quick turnover of these workers caused stagnation in the work, particularly in the case of the work in Penang. Its number of missionaries in comparison to the missionaries in the other mainline churches was small and so its impact was smaller in comparison. Nevertheless there was a slight growth. Then in the 1960s there was noticeable growth. The establishment of the Bible College of Malaysia and the pioneering spirit of these young BCM graduates both in planting new churches and establishing youth groups in every major town in Malaysia by the 1970s were major contributing factors. Also during this period, the Pentecostal movement was very much a lay-led movement.

The rapid growth of the AOG also coincided with the rise of the Charismatic movement since the mid-1970s, where large numbers of Charismatics joined AOG churches as they were not accepted in their mainline denominational churches. This Pentecostal/Charismatic movement, which had mainly English-speaking youths in the 1970s, saw the inclusion of professionals and businessmen in the 1980s and early 1990s. With the rise of the Charismatic movement, new independent Charismatic churches proliferated in every major town of Peninsular Malaysia. Of these, FGA Kuala Lumpur has become the largest. These new independent Charismatic churches were lay-led and gave lay participation a wider scope. In the mid 1980s and into the 1990s there was a noticeable movement of some lay people from some of the AOG churches, as the AOG churches had become much more 'clergy' led. The large number of BCM graduates each year resulted in them taking over existing lay ministries with the result that lay participation was given a more limited role.

The issue of whether the Pentecostal movement will be an ageing movement is beyond the scope of this paper. But there seem to be indications of this trend as is evidenced in the leadership of this movement. In the 1970s the leaders were in the late teens and twenties. Today they are in their late thirties to fifties. Moreover the youth population of the AOG, which once constituted 90% of its members, has been reduced to only some 10-15%.

The Pentecostal/Charismatic movement experienced a shift of emphasis and activity in its development since the 1970s. First, the emphasis was on the baptism of the Holy Spirit and speaking in tongues; then it stressed deliverance ministry and faith healing. By the 1980s and 1990s, there was the Health and Wealth Gospel, signs and wonders and personal prophecies movement followed by Spiritual Warfare, Toronto Blessing and then the Cell Church movement. It seems that these movement are fashionable for a while only to be discarded for the next fashion. There is no doubt that the movements have brought in large numbers of people. But the question is, 'After Cell Church, what next?' In all these movements, the hidden danger has been the neglect of proper discipling of the converts and members to Christian maturity.

In a separate development, the Charismatic movement in East Malaysia, which began as a revival in the interior highlands of Bario, Sarawak in 1973, was sparked through the ministry of an Indonesian evangelist, Dr Petrus Octavanius and continued through a series of revivals in 1975, 1979 and 1984-85. From the interior this Charismatic renewal spread to all the SIB churches both in the interior and along the coastal towns of Sarawak. Since 1990 the SIB has begun work in Peninsular Malaysia and has grown significantly.

While the Pentecostal influences among the various linguistic groups were rather independent of each other in the years from the 1930s to the 1970s, the Pentecostal/Charismatic movement of the mid-1980s and 1990s among the English speaking churches provided a contact or meeting point for the various strands of the Pentecostal/Charismatic movement, especially when the new independent Charismatic churches organized seminars that have been open to other churches and also encouraged mission teams that visited the East Malaysian SIB churches. This interchange has the effect of mutual influence so that since the late 1980s Pentecostal and Charismatic churches have become rather indistinguishable.

However the mainline denominational churches (Anglican, Methodist, Lutheran, Presbyterian) have continued to remain cautious about the Pentecostal/Charismatic movement. Some mainline churches have become Charismatic with a modified form of their traditional worship style. Perhaps an indication of the extent of the Pentecostal/Charismatic influence among the evangelicals may be seen in the composition of the leadership in the National Evangelical Christian Fellowship (NECF), where 80% of its leaders in the Executive Council may be considered as Pentecostal or Charismatic.

Pentecostalism in Indonesia

Gani Wiyono

Introduction

From its humble beginning in the first decade of the twentieth century, the Pentecostal movement in Indonesia has grown rapidly. The most recent statistic given by Barrett, Kurian and Johnson reveals that there are approximately 9,450,000 adherents of Pentecostalism in that predominantly Muslim country.[1] It is not the purpose of this essay to provide a comprehensive historical analysis of Indonesian Pentecostalism. Rather it will present a historical overview of the origin, growth and recent development of Pentecostalism in Indonesia. Several case studies will also be presented to illustrate some particular statements.

The Origins of Pentecostalism in Indonesia.

It is difficult to spell out an exact date when Pentecostalism entered Indonesia for very little data (especially written material) is available. However, it seems that Pentecostalism has been present in this archipelago since as early as 1910. Gerrit R. Polman, the early leader of Dutch Pentecostalism had been mailing *Spade Regen* to the Dutch Indies (the former name of Indonesia) since 1909.[2] This bulletin seems to have greatly influenced Dutch descendants who settled at Temanggung, Central Java. As a result, an ecumenical prayer meeting that had Pentecostal nuances was established in 1911. Among those who actively got involved in that prayer meeting were H.E. Horstman of the *Gereformeerd Kerk*,

---

[1] David B. Barrett, George T. Kurian, and Todd M. Johnson (eds.), *World Christian Encyclopedia: A Comparative Survey of Churches and Religion in the Modern World*, 2nd ed. 2 vols. (Oxford, UK: Oxford University Press, 2001), I, 375.

[2] Cornelis van der Laan, *Sectarian Against His Will: Gerrit Roelof Polman and the Birth of Pentecostalism in the Netherland* (Metuchen, N.J. and London: Scarecrow Press, 1991), 186; Cf. M. Tapilatu, 'Gereja-gereja Pentakosta di Indonesia: Suatu Tinjauan tentang Sejarah, Organisasi. Ibadah, Kegiatan, Ajaran dan Sikap Terhadap Gereja-gereja Lain' (ThM Thesis. Jakarta Advanced School of Theology, Jakarta, 1982), 18.

Weirs of the *Hervormd Kerk*, and Van Abkoude, who later became key figures in the early years of Pentecostalism in Indonesia.[3]

In September 1920, in *Spade Regen,* Polman published a request from believers there to send Pentecostal missionaries to Java.[4] Among those who responded to this call were Johann Thiessen, Willem Bernard and his wife, Marie Blekkink, a sister of Mrs Polman, and Mina Hansen.[5] Thiessen returned to Java in 1921,[6] while Bernard, Blekking, and Hansen left for Java in August 1922. Thiessen chose Bandung as his domicile while Bernard, Blekkink, and Hansen settled in Temanggung where they worked with H.E. Horstman.

Almost at the same time, two missionaries of Dutch descent, Richard van Klaveren and Cornelis Groesbeek[7] of Bethel Temple in Seattle, Washington,

---

[3] 'Api Tuhan di Indonesia: Sejarah Masuk dan Berkembangnya Gerakan Pentakosta di Indonesia', *Tiberias* 2:6 (n.d.), 32-33.

[4] Van der Laan, 186

[5] Van der Laan, 186, 198.

[6] Johann Thiessen was born on 22 November 1869 in Odessa, Russia and raised in a Russian Mennonite community. When he was 25, he enrolled in St Chrischonna seminary in Switzerland and studied there for three years. After finishing his seminary, he went to Tapanuli, North Sumatra as a Mennonite missionary and ministered there for 12 years (1901-12). While taking his first furlough, he encountered Pentecostal experience (receiving baptism in the Holy Spirit) in Basel, Switzerland. He then got in touch with and was influenced by some key figures of early European Pentecostalism such as Jonathan Paul of Germany and Gerrit R. Polman of Netherlands.
In 1920 Thiessen participated in the founding of the Dutch Missionary Society and became its vice-president. A year later, he returned to Dutch East-Indies, not as a Mennonite missionary any more but a Pentecostal missionary. On 29 March, 1923 he founded De Pinksterbeweging or Gereja Gerakan Pentakosta (Indonesia Pentecostal Movement Church) in Bandung, and started the publication of *Dit is het.* See Van der Laan, 186-87, 197-98; 'Api Tuhan di Indonesia II: Lawatan Roh Kudus Semakin Meluas', *Tiberias* 2:7 (n.d.), 51-52, for details

[7] Richard van Klaveren and Cornelis E. Groesbeek were former officers in the Salvation Army. In 1919 they attended a tent revival meeting conducted by Bethel Temple, an independent Pentecostal church in Seattle. In that meeting they received Pentecostal experiences. A year later, God called them to do a pioneering work in Java through a vision. They shared this vision with W.H. Offiler, a pastor of Bethel Temple, who then agreed to provide financial support for them.
After months of raising funds, they were still short by US $500.00 of the needed US $2,200.00. Fortunately, there was unexpected financial help from Emily Malquist, a young woman who experienced a divine healing. She was scheduled to undergo a major surgery to remove a cancerous tumour, but the schedule was cancelled due to the falling off of her 8.25 pounds tumour onto the floor. After being examined again by her physician, there was a confirmation that she was totally healed. Prior to this amazing experience, she attended a service in Bethel Temple where W.H. Offiler prayed for her healing. Thus US $500.00 that she previously planned to spend on the surgery was given to Offiler as an offering for sending the missionaries to Java. See Nicky J. Sumual,

arrived in Jakarta to begin pioneering work in the Dutch Indies. Bali was their first targeted place. Unfortunately, before van Klaveren and Groesbeek were able to establish a Pentecostal congregation, the Dutch Indies government ordered them to leave Bali.[8] They then relocated in Surabaya. After being together for a while in Surabaya, van Klaveren and Groesbeek parted. Van Klaveren moved to Lawang, and then ended up doing pioneering work in Jakarta, while the Groesbeeks moved to Cepu where they put much effort into communicating the Pentecostal message to those who attended a weekly meeting in the house of van Gessels, an employee of a Dutch oil company.[9] After a short time, Groesbeek was able to disciple van Gessels, S.I.P. Luimondong, Hornung and A.E. Siwi, who later became prominent leaders in the early years of Pentecostalism in Indonesia. Towards the end of 1923 Groesbeek handed over the leadership of the Cepu congregation to van Gessel. He himself moved to East Java and began a pioneering work in Tunjungan, Surabaya.[10] The fruit of Groesbeek's tireless work is what is now known as *Gereja Pentakosta di Indonesia* or the Pentecostal Church in Indonesia, the largest Pentecostal denomination.[11]

Early Success

Bandung, Temanggung, Cepu and then Surabaya stand high in the brief history of the Pentecostal movement in Indonesia, for from these places Pentecostalism was disseminated throughout the islands that had previously been influenced by Christianity. From Temanggung, the Pentecostal message was propagated primarily in the island of Java;[12] from Bandung, it was carried to different parts of West Java (Cimahi, Jakarta, Bogor, Sukabumi, Cirebon, and Depok) and Central Java (Semarang, Cilacap, Purworejo and Yogyakarta);[13] from Cepu and

---

Pantekosta Indonesia Suatu Sejarah (n.p.: n.d.), 44-46, Theopilus Karunia Djaja, *Sejarah Gereja Pantekosta di Indonesia* (n.p,: n.d.), 14, for details.

[8] Following the murder of a Dutch missionary, J. de Vroom, the Dutch East Indies Government banned Christian mission in Bali. The door was open again on 21 August, 1930 when Tsang Kam Foek was granted permission to work as a missionary among the Chinese population in Bali. For details see Chris Sugden, *Seeking the Asian Face of Jesus: The Practice and Theology of Christian Social Witness in Indonesia and India 1974-96* (Oxford, UK: Regnum Books International, 1997), 44-47.

[9] Sumual, 44-53; Theopilus Karunia Djaja, *Sejarah Gereja Pantekosta di Indonesia* (n.p.: n.d.), 13-15.

[10] Sumual, 57.

[11] Before 1942, Gereja Pentakosta di Indonesia was well-known as Pinkster Gemeente in Nederlandsch Indie.

[12] Th. Van den End and J. Weitjens, *Ragi Carita 2: Sejarah Gereja di Indonesia 1860-an-Sekarang* (Jakarta: BPK Gunung Mulia, 1999), 272.

[13] *Sejarah Gereja-Gereja Pantekosta di Indonesia*, 9

Surabaya, Pentecostal evangelists planted churches in East Java, Sangir Talaud, South, North, Central, and South East Sulawesi, Lampung, North and South Sumatra, Nias, Riau, West Timor, East, West, and South Kalimantan, the Mollucas and Irian Jaya.[14]

Those places, however, were not alone in propagating the Pentecostal message. After World War II other Pentecostal evangelists, who were not directly tied to Pentecostal congregations in Temanggung, Bandung, Cepu, and Surabaya, began to participate in the founding of Pentecostal congregations. Ralph Devin, Kenneth Short, Raymond Busby and other American Assemblies of God missionaries established *Gereja-gereja Sidang Jemaat Allah* (Assemblies of God in Indonesia) in the Mollucas, North Sumatra, Jakarta and Bogor, Minahasa, Kalimantan and some other parts of Indonesia. William Arnold Parson and Eugene Loving of the Pentecostal Church of God in America started Pentecostal congregations which later became *Gereja Pentekosta Missi di Indonesia* (Pentecostal Mission Church in Indonesia) in Ternate, Halmahera, Bacan, and some other islands in the Moluccas.[15]

With such a quick geographical spread, Pentecostalism grew significantly in numbers. It is no wonder that van den End, a church historian of the Indonesian churches, considers that the most fruitful evangelistic activities in Indonesia in the twentieth century were carried out by Pentecostals.[16] Several factors, presented as follows, most likely account for the early success of the Pentecostal movement.

'The Field Was Ready'

When evangelists spread the Pentecostal message throughout Indonesia, all the infrastructure for the effective communication of the gospel (such as: railway, road, telephone and telegraph facilities) were available.[17] The Bible had already been translated into several major dialects. Many people, especially those in the cities, had been freed from illiteracy, resulting in an increasing degree of receptivity to new ideas. The most important factor, however, was the fact that

---

[14] Sumual, 76-77; Karuniajaya, 38-44.

[15] See Josemus Manyira, 'Sejarah dan Perkembangan Gereja Kalvari Pentakosta Misi Betlehem Ternate' (Thesis., STT Satyabhakti, Malang, 2001).

[16] Van den End and Weitjens, 278.

[17] See Sartono Kartodirdjo, 'Latar Belakang Sosio-kultural Dunia Kanak-kanak and Masa Muda Bung Karno' (http://www.kompas.com/kompas-cetak/0106/01/Soekarno/lata50.htm) (Search: July 20, 2001). Kartodirjo explains that in the beginning of the twentieth century, Indonesia, especially Java, underwent a massive political, social, and economical transformation as a result of modernization, promoted by the Dutch East Indies Government. This positive change could not have happened if the Dutch Government had not been compelled to improve the life-quality of people whom they had colonized for more than 200 years.

Bahasa Melayu had become the lingua franca in the cities. Thus Pentecostal evangelists, who mostly worked in the cities, did not need to spend time and energy in learning the local dialects.[18]

Aggressive in Mission

Even today, Pentecostals are well known for their zeal to 'convert' people, both from Christian and non-Christian backgrounds. Consequently they generally disregarded the traditional boundaries of comity long established by mission agencies of Europe. This meant that they were not reluctant to start a Pentecostal congregation even in the places where other Protestant denominations had already established churches.[19]

The Strong Influence of Pietism

As Leonard Halle has shown, Pietism has had a significant influence on the formation of Indonesian Christianity.[20] Since several aspects of Pietistic spirituality, such as an emphasis on otherworldliness, individual experience, and biblical authority had much affinity with Pentecostal spirituality,[21] the presentation of Pentecostalism to Indonesian Christians did not face any very serious problem. Thus, the extensive receptivity to Pentecostalism among Indonesian Christians was only a matter of time.

The Cultural Worldview of Indonesians

Culturally, Indonesians can relate to a supernatural worldview in which spirits exercise significant influence over humans, causing illness, misfortune and even demonic bondage. Therefore the Pentecostal message and practices that boldly declared the victory of God over the power of darkness became attractive to many Indonesians, both believers (non-Pentecostal Christians) and unbelievers (Muslims, Hindus, Buddhists, or tribal religionists). A good example for this can be found in the following case study.

---

[18] Van den End and Weitjens, 276.

[19] Van den End and Weitjens, 275; 'A History of Pentecostal Movement in Indonesia', *AJPS* 4:1 (January 2001), 148.

[20] See Leonard Halle, *Jujur Terhadap Pietisme: Menilai Kembali Reputasi Pietisme pada Gereja-gereja di Indonesia* (Jakarta: BPK Gunung Mulia, 1993), especially chapter 3.

[21] See, *Dictionary of Pentecostal and Charismatic Movement*, 1988 ed. s.v. 'Spirituality, Pentecostal and Charismatic', by Russell P. Spittler.

CASE STUDY 1: THE MINISTRY OF TIMMY SOLISSA IN WAIBOHIT, ISLAND OF BURU.

Timmy Solissa was the chief of the Solissa tribe on the island of Buru. He became a Pentecostal under the ministry of Johan Hukom, an Assemblies of God minister. He was reported to be a man of prayer, bestowed with the gifts of healing and casting out of demons. While doing pioneering work in the southern part of Buru, thirty people who did not like him approached and tried to kill him. In front of them was a very huge tree. Pastor Timmy said, 'Be cautious! That huge tree in front of you is about to fall down'. But the people ignored the warning, since they had already used demonic power to sustain the tree. Seemingly a miracle occurred, when suddenly the tree fell down. The victory of the power of God over the power of darkness finally led not only those thirty people but also many other people to accept Jesus Christ as their Lord.[22]

Churches for the Laity

A wider opportunity given to laypeople to get involved in ministry (inside and outside the church) attracted many to join the Pentecostal movement. According to Johannes Verkuyl, such a democratization of ministry that was rarely available in non-Pentecostal churches was one of the key factors for early Pentecostal success.[23]

The Proliferation of Pentecostal Groups

Besides being full of the bright story of success, the history of the Pentecostal movement in Indonesia is pervaded by the tragic tale of repeated schisms. Starting primarily with one organization, *De Pinkstergemeente in Nederlandsch-Indie* (The Pentecostal Assemblies in the Dutch Indies), which embraced almost all Pentecostal groups in 1924, Indonesian Pentecostalism has been divided into over fifty denominations. The motivations behind these repeated divisions are various. Among them are 1) doctrinal differences regarding the Trinity; 2) disputes over specific issues, such as eating blood, the role of women in ministry and tithing; 3) personal conflicts; and 4) insubordination to leadership.[24] The 'blame' for these schisms can be partially placed in the hands of foreigners. W.H. Offiler of Bethel Temple, as the sender

[22] Amos Mauleki, 'Sejarah Perkembangan Gereja Sidang-sidang Jemaat Allah di Maluku' (BTh thesis, Satyabakti Advance School of Theology, Malang, Indonesia, 2000), 49-52.
[23] Johannes Verkuyl, *Geredja dan Bidat-bidat* (Jakarta: BPK Gunung Mulia, 1962), 61.
[24] See Van den End and Weitjens, 272-73; Fridolin Ukur, dan Frank L. Cooley, *Jerih dan Juang: Laporan Nasional Survai Menyeluruh Gereja di Ind onesia* (Jakarta: Lembaga Penelitian dan Studi-DGI, 1979), 69; Sumual, 78-81.

of missionaries to the Dutch East Indies, for example, introduced the so-called Oneness teaching and forbade women leadership in the church. His move caused Margareth van Alt and van Abkoude to resign from *De Pinkster Gemeente* and to start their own Pentecostal denominations. Van Alt organized *Pinkster Zending* or *Gereja Utusan Pentakosta* (Indonesian Pentecostal Mission Church), while van Abkoude established *De Gemeente van God*, which later joined the Assemblies of God in Indonesia.[25] Despite this tragic tale of schisms, most Pentecostal churches generated by the schisms still have continued to grow at a phenomenal rate. The following case study describes vividly what has been stated above.

The Pentecostal Church in Indonesia or *Gereja Pentekosta di Indonesia* (GPDI) is the oldest Pentecostal denomination,[26] from which most Pentecostal denominations in Indonesia origininate. Between 1931 and 1966, GPDI suffered repeated schisms resulting in the proliferation of Pentecostal groups. These schisms, however, were not able to retard the progress of GPDI, for as Karuniajaya has shown, GPDI grew from a few congregations in the 1920s to 6,277 congregations (with 1.5–2 million members) in 1993.[27]

Other Pentecostal denominations that derived their existence from GPDI also experienced a phenomenal growth. Full Gospel Bethel Church or *Gereja Bethel Injil Sepenuh* (GBIS), after being independent for 12 years, increased its membership to 65,000 in 1969. GPDI *Siburian*, two decades after dissociating itself from GPDI, had 351 congregations with 185,000 members in 1970.[28] *Gereja Isa Almasih* (Church of Jesus Christ, the Messiah) grew from 16 congregations (with 14,986 members) in 1974 to 68 congregations, with 54,200 members) in 1994.[29] Indonesian Bethel Church or *Gereja Bethel Indonesia* (GBI) that separated from GBIS in 1969, grew significantly from 372 congregations, with 51,279 members in 1970 to 2,386 congregations, with 420,133 members in 1991.[30]

---

[25] Frank L. Cooley, *The Growing Seed: The Christian Church in Indonesia* (Jakarta, Indonesia: Christian Publishing House BPK Gunung Mulia, 1982), 68.

[26] The former name of *GPDI* is 'De Pinkster Gemeente in Nederlandsch Indie'. When the Japanese military force ruled over Indonesia, the Dutch name was Indonesianized to become *GPDI*.

[27] Karuniajaya, 3.

[28] Ukur, dan Cooley, 108.

[29] Hiendarto Supatra, ed., *50 Tahun Gereja Isa Almasih* (Semarang: Sinode Gereja Isa Almasih, 1996), 41.

[30] H.L. Senduk, *Sejarah GBI: Suatu Gereja Nasional Yang Termuda* (n.p.: n.d.), 89.

Indigenous Quasi-Pentecostals In Indonesia[31]

There is clear evidence of Pentecostal-like outpourings among indigenous, non-Pentecostal/Charismatic Protestant groups in Indonesia during the twentieth century. Two of these Pentecostal-like outpourings, the Nias and Timor revival, are worth mentioning here since they are quite well documented and widely known in the West.[32]

The Nias Revival

During 1916-22, people of the island of Nias, off the north-west of Sumatra, experienced the so-called *Fangesa Dodo* or the 'Great Repentance' revival. Starting from a place called Humene (about 10 miles from Gunung Sitoli, the main city in the island), a wave of repentance swept over the whole island resulting in remarkable church growth.[33] Peters notes that between 1915 and 1925 there were over 45,000 people added to the Nias churches.[34] Several years later (1940), a new wave of revival came over a number of Nias churches. The more recent movement indeed was not as extensive geographically as the one in 1916-1922, yet still caused remarkable growth. In both cases, Pentecostal-like phenomena such as speaking with tongues, prayer with ecstasy, falling into trances, casting out demons, revelation through visions and dreams, miracles, as well as the restoration of the offices of prophet/prophetesses were reported to be present.[35]

Due to the geographical location of the island of Nias in the midst of the Indian Ocean, this revival seemingly did not have a significant influence on churches in the mainland of Indonesia (Java, Sumatra, Sulawesi, Kalimantan, etc.).

---

[31] Cf. Vinson Synan, *The Holiness-Pentecostal Tradition: Charismatic Movements in the Twentieth Century* (Grand Rapids, MI: Eerdmans, 1997), 283.

[32] Lee Ira Bruckner, 'The History and Character of the Niasan People Movement in Indonesia, 1865-1940' (DMiss dissertation, Fuller Theological Seminary, 1979); David R. Brougham., 'The Work of the Holy Spirit in Church Growth as Seen in Selected Indonesian Case Studies' (DMiss dissertation, Fuller Theological Seminary, 1988); Th. Muller Krueger, *Die Grosse Reue* (Barmen/Wuppertal: Verlag der Rheinischen Mission, 1931); Th. Muller Krueger, *Sedjarah Gereja di Indonesia* (Jakarta: BPK Gunung Mulia, 1959); George W. Peters, *Indonesia Revival: Focus on Timor* (Grand Rapids, MI: Zondervan, 1973); Kurt Koch, *The Revival in Indonesia* (Grand Rapids, MI: Kregel Publications, 1970); G.F. Brookes, 'Spirit Movements in Timor – A Survey' (ThM theses, Melbourne College of Divinity, 1977).

[33] Muller-Krueger, *Sedjarah Geredja di Indonesia*, 237.

[34] Peters, 47.

[35] Peters, 48-49; Brougham, 119, 144, 130, 136; Muller-Krueger, *Sedjarah Geredja di Indonesia*, 238-43; Van den End, 206.

The Timor Revival.

The Timor Revival is one of the major events in the history of Christianity in Timor. It started from a GMIT (*Gereja Masehi Injili Timor* or the Evangelical Christian Church of Timor) congregation in Soe, a cool mountain town situated 68 miles from Kupang (the capital of the province) on 25 September, 1965. From that place the revival swept over the whole island, even to some islands nearby. This revival became one of the significant factors contributing to the amazing growth of GMIT, from 375,000 in 1964 to 517,000 in 1971[36] and the presence of many Charismatic occurrences in the whole area of West Timor.

As in the case of the Nias Revival, the Timor Revival was also accompanied with Pentecostal-like phenomena. Gifts of discernment, knowledge, and revelation through visions and dreams, speaking in tongues, divine healing, and numerous miracles, including water turning into wine, translation from a certain place to another place in the twinkling of an eye, the resurrection of the dead and visible 'tongues of fire' are reported to have been present during the revival.[37]

Whether there was a significant influence of the Timor Revival on Indonesian churches outside the island of Timor is difficult to determine since very little data is available. It seems, however, that the Timor Revival had more influence on the people in the West than in Indonesia, due to the publication of some popular books like Mel Tari's *Like a Mighty Wind*, Kurt Koch's *The Revival in Indonesia* and *New Wine of God,* and Don Crawford's *Miracles in Indonesia.*

The Indonesian Charismatic Movement

The Charismatic movement entered Indonesia in the second half of the 1960s,[38] but was not so influential until the next decade. Sociological reasons have been applied to explain the explosion of the Charismatic movement in Indonesia. Zakharia Ngelow, an Indonesian church historian, for example explains how the National Development Programs, heavy political restrictions programmed by Soeharto's semi-military government and the 'latent' tension between Christians and Muslims caused confusion and spiritual emptiness within the hearts of many people, especially those who were living in the big cities. Unfortunately, in times when people looked for certainty and security, the

---

[36] Peters, 93.

[37] For a detailed description and complete bibliography, consult my article, 'Timor Revival: A Historical Study of the Great Twentieth Century Revival in Indonesia', *Asia Journal of Pentecostal Studies* 4:2 (forthcoming).

[38] Cf. Iman Santoso, 'The Church in Indonesia', in Saphir Atyal (ed.), *Church in Asia Today: Challenges and Opportunities* (Singapore: Asia Lausanne Committee for World Evangelization, 1996), 338.

existing churches failed to meet such needs.[39] Thus when Charismatic conventions offered 'casual' and 'therapeutic' services, warm fellowship, plus a comfortable environment (held mostly in ballrooms of expensive hotels), many churchgoers, primarily those who came from the middle class and intellectual society and mainline churches, came and joined them.

Another thing that may account for the explosion of the Charismatic movement in Indonesia is its ecumenical (interdenominational) character. By refusing to identify themselves with a particular denomination[40] they were able to successfully recruit churchgoers who were unwilling to give up their formal membership yet were not really satisfied by the ministries of their own churches. When attending charismatic gatherings, churchgoers did not consider themselves to have moved out of their formal church, but aimed to deepen their spiritual experience in such ecumenical gatherings.

Today, some charismatic gatherings are still retaining their status as informal-ecclesiastical bodies. The Full Gospel Business Men's Fellowship International (FGBMFI) Indonesia, Charisma Campus Ministry Jakarta and many other unnamed charismatic groups that hold their meetings in hotels and business offices are among those that can be classified into this group. Other groups changed their status to become more institutionalized. The Charismatic Worship Service (CWS), for example, while retaining its inter-denominational character, already considers itself as a church. This can be clearly seen in the CWS mission statement[41] and in the way they minister. Though not ordaining their ministers, CWS has an ecclesiastical structure with associate pastors and deacons, conducts wedding and funeral ceremonies, and performs water baptism for their members.

CASE STUDY 3: THE CHARISMATIC WORSHIP SERVICE (CWS) – JL, SENEN RAYA 46 JAKARTA

In June 1974 Carl Chrisner, a staff member of the US Embassy in Indonesia, arrived in Jakarta. Together with Willy Lasut, an Indonesian army officer and two Assemblies of God missionaries, James Anderson and Tom Hines, he started the Charismatic Worship Service in Reog Room, Hotel Indonesia, Jakarta on 17 November 1974 with 20-30 people (mostly expatriates). Due to their significant growth they had to move to larger facilities a year later. In the following years CWS has continued to grow. Today, under the leadership of

---

[39] See Zakharia J. Ngelow, 'Gerakan Kharismatik di Indonesia', *Berita Oikoumene* (June 1994), 24.

[40] Such attitude is reflected in the way they consider themselves. Instead of using the term 'church' they prefer to use 'service' or 'fellowship' for their gatherings. In fact, when talking about membership they would rather use *peserta* (participants) than *anggota*, a common word for a member of an established ecclesiastical institution.

[41] See Charismatic Worship Service's mission statement in Dibaharuhi Menuju Kepenuhan Kristus: Buku Kenangan 20 Tahun CWS (1974-94), 45.

Soewandoko Roeslim, CWS has over 8,000 members with over 10 daughter churches in different parts of Jakarta, Surabaya, Denpasar, Medan, Manado, Kendari, Bandung and Semarang. In addition to four services in Bahasa Indonesia every Sunday, CWS also has English, Mandarin and Indian services and special services for homeless people and inmates. CWS also develops media ministries. Today, they have their own publisher, Charismata, that publishes *Charismata*, a popular magazine, *Charis*, a journal for pastors and some books.

Catholic Charismatic Renewal

Two factors account for the emergence of the Catholic Charismatic renewal in Indonesia.[42] First was the return of Indonesian lay Catholics who encountered such a Catholic renewal abroad and were willing to share such experiences with their fellow-Catholics in Indonesia. Second was the explosion of Charismatic conventions in the big cities that attracted many lay Catholics. To accommodate and give a proper direction to such a lay movement, the late Mgr Leo Sukoto, Bishop of Jakarta, invited two charismatic speakers, Pastor O'Brien SJ of Bangkok and Pastor H. Schneider of Manila to conduct a seminar for both priests and lay Catholics in May 1976. The topic of the seminar was 'New Life in the Spirit' and the seminar was held in English.[43] This event marked the welcoming of the Charismatic renewal within the body of the Roman Catholic Church in Indonesia.

On 3 March 1977, Pastor L. Sugiri, SJ invited some of those who 'graduated' from O'Brien and Schneider's seminar to conduct a seminar on Charismatic renewal in his parish, in *Mangga Besar* Jakarta. Three hundred people were present and baptized by the Holy Spirit in that seminar. Afterwards, there was a tremendous renewal within the parish, with vibrant spiritual life and the fruit and amazing gifts of the Spirit could be easily seen in the lives of the believers. This encouraged other dioceses, both in Jakarta and some other parts of Indonesia, to conduct similar seminars. As a result the Catholic Charismatic Renewal spread throughout Indonesia.[44] Today it is difficult to count the exact number of Catholic Charismatic groups in Indonesia. A website of Indonesian Catholic Charismatics estimates that there are approximately 1,000,000 Charismatic Catholics in Indonesia.[45] Through the

---

[42] One of the earliest Catholic Charismatic Renewal service was started by Pastor Johanes Indrakusuma, O Carm in Batu, Malang (1975).

[43] 'Sejarah Karismatik di Indonesia', in http://www.katolik.net/karismatik/th-indonesia.htm (22 June, 2001).

[44] Ibid. See also, 'Kembali Kepada Semangat Awal' *Karakter* (November 2000), 51.

[45] http://www. katolik.net/karismatik/evangelisasi.htm (10 July, 2001).

lay movement within these groups, Catholicism in Indonesia has been revitalized.

CASE STUDY 4: THE PROFILE OF THE CATHOLIC CHARISMATIC RENEWAL IN INDONESIA.

The following are several characteristics of the Catholic Charismatic Renewal in Indonesia which has renewed the faith and commitment of many lukewarm Roman Catholics.[46]

- It is basically a lay movement. The role of Catholic priests is as moderators and sometimes facilitators who provide training for laypeople who are willing to serve in the area of teaching, preaching and counselling.
- The locus of their activities is primarily in the prayer groups. There are two kinds of prayer groups in the body of the Catholic Charismatic Renewal in Indonesia. First is the so-called *dekanat*, which is tied directly to a local parish. Second is the so-called *categorical*, whose members are homogeneous (i.e. medical doctors, businessman, women, children, spouses, etc).
- The characteristics of their religious gatherings are: (a) focusing on Jesus, with the ultimate goal of having a deep, personal relationship with Jesus; (b) using a contemporary worship style, which is often found in the Pentecostal/Charismatic services; (c) emphasizing Bible study. All members of Catholic Charismatic Renewal groups bring the Bible with them and read and trust in it; (d) speaking in tongues and other manifestations of the Spirit are allowed.
- They pray for the sick.
- They encourage their members to get involved in evangelism, based on the reading of Acts 2.42 and Mat. 28.18-20.

The Most Recent Development

The Success of Indonesian Bethel Church (Gereja Bethel Indonesia)

In the last few years, there has been a tremendous quantitative growth among Pentecostal churches which are parts of Indonesian Bethel Church (*Gereja Bethel Indonesia -GBI*). Today, especially in the big cities, it is not very difficult to find an Indonesian Bethel Church (*GBI*) whose members number

---

[46] See 'Awam, Pimpin Karismatik Katolik', *Karakter* (Agustus 2000), 14-15; 'Tidak Perlu Saling Menghakimi', *Karakter* (Agustus 2000), 18-22.; 'Pola Persekutuan', in http://www.katolik.net/karismatik/th-indonesia.htm (22 June, 2001); 'Karismatik dan Evangelisasi' (http://www.katolik.net/karismatik/evangelisasi.htm, 23 June, 2001).

over 500 people. Some churches even are reported to have more than 2,000 members, such as:

GBI 'Bethany' Surabaya	+70,000 members[47]
GBI 'Bethany' Jakarta	+40,000 members[48]
GBI 'Bethany' Bandung	+12,000 members[49]
GBI 'Mawar Sharon' Jakarta	+10,000 members[50]
GBI 'Api KemuliaanNya' Jakarta	+3,000 members[51]

Several of the most common characteristics of *GBI* churches, presented as follows, may account for their success.

THE DECENTRALIZATION OF STRUCTURAL ORGANIZATION

All *GBI* are autonomous. Both the national and district leadership cannot force their subordinate (local churches) to follow what they want.[52] Such a structural organization has given more space for creativity and created a policy that meets the contextual need.

ENTERTAINING WORSHIP STYLE.

If other classical Pentecostal churches generally consider worship as secondary, *GBI* churches place worship as a spearhead of their campaigns to recruit members.[53] They develop a contemporary worship style, equipped with excellent musicians, good singers, tambourine dancing groups and perfect sound systems. Often Christian celebrities are invited to please the worshippers, offering distraction from routine and demanding that the hour be engaging in the way the flood of 'entertainment' is.

---

[47] Billy Bruce, 'Indonesian Believers Multiply Under Leadership of Bethel Church of God', *Charisma* 24:11 (June 1999), 27.

[48] Ibid., 27.

[49] Ibid., 27.

[50] 'Gereja Yang Bertumbuh', *Media Komunikasi* (Mei 2000), 36.

[51] 'Gembala Sidang GBI Api KemuliaaNya, Pendeta Alexander Iranata: 'Harus Bertanya, Mengapa Jemaat Lari' *Narwastu* (September 1999), 33.

[52] Senduk, 139-40.

[53] Biworo G. Adinata, 'Mission Strategy of *Gereja* Bethel Indonesia in the Context of Islam and Christian encounter in Indonesia' (a ThM thesis, Fuller Theological Seminary, 1993), 93 wrote, ' The church hymn and music, equally carry the power of sermon. *Gereja Bethel Indonesia* therefore believes that there is tremendous power in Christian praise'.

Most sermons delivered in the *GBI* churches are pragmatic-oriented and 'theologically thin' but communicated to people in a clear and interesting way (pervaded by testimonies, stories and jokes). Perhaps this happens because many pastors have not had formal theological training. Most of them are former businessmen, professionals and even celebrities. Only a few are Bible School or Seminary graduates.

AN AGGRESSIVE 'CHURCH-MARKETING'.

Towards the weekend, not a few *GBI* churches put advertisements in newspapers and Christian broadcasts to recruit more members. Such advertisements generally give an invitation, a description of the place (mostly in hotels or restaurants), the speaker (usually a well-known, popular preacher), 'guest star' (usually a celebrity who will perform a special number or give a testimony) and a prospectively therapeutic service (promising divine healing and other kind of miracles).

EMPHASIS ON THE MIRACULOUS.

Undoubtedly, the miraculous, especially divine healing, has been the central message of typical *GBI* churches. One particular *GBI* church, 'Tiberias' has grown significantly due to the healing ministry performed by the senior pastor, Dr Jesayas Pariadji.[54]

Growing Interest in Higher Theological Education

In the last few years Pentecostals have realized that a decent theological training is very important for having a successful ministry in the present context of Indonesia. Therefore in addition to continuing a practical, short-term approach to ministerial training they also have begun to develop Bible colleges and seminaries. Some Pentecostal denominations, such as the Indonesian Bethel Church (*GBI* or *Gereja Bethel Indonesia*)[55] and the Assemblies of God in Indonesia (*GSJA* or *Gereja Sidang Jemaat Allah*)[56] offer a graduate

---

[54] *GBI* Tiberias regularly publishes a magazine, *Tiberias* which always narrates the healing ministries of J. Pariadji.

[55] With the assistance of the Church of God School of Theology, *Institut Theologia dan Keguruan Indonesia*, well-known as Bethel Seminary Jakarta, offers Master of Arts in Church Ministries and Master of Divinity Programme.

[56] 'Ekklesia' Advanced School of Theology, formerly being known as Jakarta Bible School offers Master of Arts in Pastoral Studies.

programme. The Indonesian Full Gospel Church (*GISI* or *Gereja Injil Seutuh Indonesia*) has even started a Doctor of Ministry programme.[57]

In spite of this growing interest in higher theological education Pentecostals have not produced any significant scholarly works. Most publications are sermonic or devotional since such kinds of literature are relatively easier to write and can be sold in the market. Moreover most academically trained Indonesian Pentecostals are busy ministers who often find it difficult to do research and theological reflection. Besides teaching, they often have to assume pastoral ministries or leadership positions either at a district or national level.

The Persecution of Pentecostal Churches

During the period of 1965–98 there were 514 churches which were closed, vandalized, destroyed, or burnt down. Out of that number, 275 cases took place between 1996 and 30 November, 1998. Included in this total (275) are approximately 121 (44.0%) Pentecostal churches; 18 Catholic churches (6.5%); 12 Indonesian Christian churches or *GKI* (4.4%); 11 Java and East Java Christian churches or *GKJ* and *GKJW* (4.0%); 9 Batak Protestant Christian churches (3.3 %); 8 Western Indonesia Protestant churches or *GPIB* (2.9%); 7 Pasundan Christian churches or *GKP* (2.5%); 89 other denominations (32.4%).[58] Thus, Pentecostal churches rank first for total numbers in the persecution. The question is: How can it be explained? First of all, as aforementioned, among other Christian groups in Indonesia the Pentecostals are the most aggressive in mission.[59] Therefore they are more vulnerable to the attacks of hardline Islamic groups such as the *Front of the Defence of Islam* (Front Pembela Islam) and *Lasykar Jihad*. Furthermore, the presence of Pentecostal churches rarely makes a positive and visible impact in the surrounding community. In some cases, they are even considered as 'the disturber' of the community because of their noisy worship style.[60]

---

[57] With the assistance of Regent University, Virginia, US, Harvest International Theological Seminary Jakarta offers Doctor of Ministry in Leadership.

[58] See the complete list in Paul Tahalele, *The Church and Human Rights in Indonesia* (Surabaya, Indonesia: Indonesia Christian Communication Forum, 1998), 7-20.

[59] See also Martin Lukito Sinaga, 'After the Burning Churches: Civil Society as the Future Form of Christianity in Indonesia', *Asia Journal of Theology* 12:2 (October 1998), 370 who writes, '…the issue of 'christianization' seemed to be one of the factors responsible for the ignition of the religious unrest. This was obvious, since most of the victims were members of the fundamentalist churches who explicitly professed that christianization was their primary goal'. Undoubtedly, 'the fundamentalist churches' referred by Sinaga here includes Pentecostal/Charismatic groups.

[60] A good example for this can be seen in the burning of *GPDI Songong, Rogo Jampi, Banyuwangi, East Java* on Tuesday, 23 December, 1997. For the details, see Paul Tahalele, Frans Parera, Thomas Santoso (eds), *Indonesia di Persimpangan Kekuasaan*

The Explosion of Cell-group Ministry

In recent years, most Indonesian Pentecostal and Charismatic leaders, especially those who minister to people in the cities, have been paying increasing attention to small groups or cell-group ministry. The success of *Gereja Yesus Kristus Tuhan* in Speed Plaza, Jakarta[61] in developing a cell-group ministry, which is resulting in a remarkable church growth may inspire those leaders to develop their own cell groups. But there are more important reasons behind this increasing attention to cell-group ministries. Among these are:

- In Indonesia, where open religious activities may easily provoke Muslims to harm Christians as before, a cell group ministry offers the better choice for it does not gather many people who seemingly bring a sense of threat to the existing Muslim community.
- A cell group ministry offers a friendly atmosphere to non-Christians to participate in Christian worship. Many are afraid of being isolated from their relatives and friends when they go to established churches.
- A cell group ministry provides such a setting where believers may be optimally ministered by and minister to one another.

The Restoration of a Spirit of Togetherness and Unity

Initially, the leadership of the established churches, which later cooperated and formed the Indonesian Council of Churches (ICC)[62] on 28 May, 1950, seemed to close their doors to the renewal movements such as Pentecostalism. The reason behind that rejection was that first, Pentecostalism, as other renewal movements, seemed to be concerned only for personal conversion and salvation, leaving the world with its problems. Second, Pentecostalism, which undoubtedly put much emphasis on emotion but was weak in theology had been considered to have an unbalanced understanding of Christianity. To them such lack of balance could have harmed their members if the door of relationship continued to be open. Third, Pentecostals often betrayed the common ministerial code of ethics, namely 'do not steal each other's sheep'.

Dominasi Kekerasan atas Dialog Publik (Jakarta: Go-East Institute and FKKI, 2001), 216; Alexander Nunuhitu, 'Pandangan Para Pendeta di Jawa Timur Terhadap Penganiayaan Gereja: Suatu Penelitian Deskriptif' (BTh thesis, SatyaBhakti Advanced School of Theology, Malang, 1997), 79-80, found that the improper usage of music and sound-system became one of the factors that initiated the persecution of churches in the East Java.

[61] This church, which is pastored by three ex-engineers, Eddy Leo, Sofyan Sutedja, and Samilton Pangella, has grown remarkably in membership from 70 (in 1979) to 8000 (by 2001).

[62] ICC is related to WCC (World Council of Churches). For this reason this particular Christian fellowship is often designated 'ecumenical'.

However such atmosphere began to change when Dr Mk. Tjakraatmadja, as a representative of ICC, was willing to be present and delivered his speech to 150 Pentecostal pastors from 17 different Pentecostal denominations who had attended the third Congress of Pentecostal Pastors in Indonesia in Bandung on 4-7 October, 1960.[63] In the same year, one particular Pentecostal denomination, the Church of Jesus Christ the Messiah (*Gereja Isa Almasih -GIA*) was accepted as a member of ICC. Later several Pentecostal denominations, such as Indonesia Pentecostal Movement Church (*Gereja Gerakan Pentakosta – GGP*), Surabaya Based Pentecostal Church (*Gereja Pentakosta Pusat Surabaya – GPPS*) and Indonesian Bethel Church (*Gereja Bethel Indonesia – GBI*) followed in the footsteps of GIA, leaving some other Pentecostal denominations to join the Indonesian Evangelical Fellowship (IEC)[64] or Indonesian Pentecostal Council (IPC) later.[65]

Towards the end of the 1980s, signs of the spirit of togetherness and mutual understanding became stronger. In October 1989 a church growth seminar was held in Jakarta. Both presenters and participants for this conference came from all the different Christian groups in Indonesia (the ecumenicals, evangelicals, and Pentecostals) with Yonggi Cho of Yoido Full Gospel Church, Seoul, South Korea as the keynote speaker. This particular seminar demonstrated a profound picture of unity in the diversity of Christianity in Indonesia.

The concrete evidence of the spirit of togetherness between Pentecostals and non-Pentecostals today may be in the National Prayer Network or *Jaringan Doa Nasional* and the Indonesian Christian Communication Forum (ICCF). The former is more 'passive', since it focuses its ministry on praying and fasting for the welfare of the country in general and Christians in particular. The latter however is more 'aggressive'. ICCF puts much effort into making the Christian right to worship in freedom possible all over Indonesia, to renovating churches which were destroyed and burnt, to collecting food and clothing from churches and concerned persons to be distributed to people who live in poverty and to doing human resource empowerment through education, training and networking. These two forums have gained support from many denominations, both from Pentecostal/Charismatics and those which are not.

---

[63] Verkuyl, 32, 36-37.

[64] IEC is related to World Evangelical Fellowship. For this reason, churches that belong to this particular fellowship are often designated 'evangelicals'. IEC was formed in August 1971. One of the major Pentecostal denomination in Indonesia that belongs to IEC is Assemblies of God in Indonesia.

[65] Two major Pentecostal fellowships in Indonesia, Council for Cooperation of Pentecostal Churches in Indonesia or *Dewan Kerjasama Gereja-Gereja Kristen Pantakosta Seluruh Indonesia* and The Pentecostal Fellowship in Indonesia or *Persekutuan Pantekosta Indonesia* merged into one Pentecostal Fellowship, namely Indonesian Pentecostal Council (IPC) or *Dewan Pantekosta Indonesia* on 14 September, 1979. At its inception this particular Pentecostal fellowship had 40 member churches.

Present Opportunities and Challenges

Today, the Pentecostal movement in Indonesia is set in the context of economic turmoil which has gone from bad to worse. Jeff Hammond, a veteran Australian missionary to Indonesia reports that the crisis has caused '... 20 million unemployed and 70 million under-employed, earning on average US $0.50 a day. Half the country's 203 million inhabitants live below an already low poverty line. Some 80 million are starving, half of whom are in danger of imminent death'.[66]

In such a context, the Pentecostal movement in Indonesia is being challenged to develop a keener vision for social concern and service both inside and outside its own community. A more holistic approach which has often been neglected is needed to maintain a balance between preaching the gospel and meeting human needs. By taking part in the struggles and problems of the people, Pentecostals may develop a better relationship with other groups, especially Muslims, which in turn may break the chain of violence and persecution of Christians.

Furthermore, the Indonesian Pentecostal movement today is also existing amid the mushrooming of tribalism, disunity and disintegration. In the last few months, Dayak have fought against Madurese in Central and West Kalimantan; Torajanese against Buginese and Makasarese in South and Central Sulawesi. In such a context, the Pentecostals must show the power of Pentecost in reconciling and uniting all different groups of people by living in unity and love for each other.

A historical overview of the Pentecostal movement in Indonesia has just been presented. Certainly it is far from complete. Much work of collecting, preserving and interpreting the historical data still needs to be done. Indeed, they might 'steal' our time, money and efforts in doing evangelism, feeding the hungry and so on. But it is worth doing, as pronounced by Frykenberg: "Remembering' by enhancing and preserving its own history is one of the crucial means by which a community empowers itself'.[67]

---

[66] Quoted by Wolfgang Fernandez, 'Indonesian Church Leaders Getting Ready for "Niniveh"', *Dawn Report* 36 (November 1998), 2.
[67] Quoted in Stanley M. Burgess, 'Pentecostalism in India: An Overview', *Asia Journal of Pentecostal Theology* 4:1 (2001), 98.

The Growth of Indonesian Pentecostalism

Mark Robinson

Pentecostalism Comes to Indonesia

The Pentecostal revival in the early 1900s in the USA led to many missionaries being sent around the world. By 1910 over 185 Pentecostals from the USA alone had gone overseas as missionaries.[1] Pentecostal missionaries arrived in Asian countries such as China (1907),[2] India (1907),[3] Indonesia (1921),[4] Philippines (1926),[5] Korea (1928),[6] and Thailand (1946).[7]

From its beginnings in 1921 the Pentecostal movement in Indonesia has grown to approximately ten to twelve million people and spread to the main islands and major cities and towns. To understand how, where, when and why Pentecostalism has grown from then to now, I will track the development of the movement through the twentieth century, considering the various stages it has passed through. To assist this tracking process I will sub-divide Indonesian Pentecostal church history into the periods that also relate to the political history of Indonesia. While the major events relating to the expansion of

---

[1] G.B. McGee, 'Missions, Overseas (North America)' in Stanley M. Burgess and Gary B. McGee (eds.), *Dictionary of Pentecostal and Charismatic Movements* (Grand Rapids: Zondervan, 1988), 610-625 (612)

[2] D. Bays, 'The Protestant Missionary Establishment and the Pentecostal Movement' in Edith. L. Blumhofer, Russell.P. Spittler and Grant. A. Wacker (eds.), *Pentecostal Currents in American Protestantism* (Urbana: University of Illinois Press, 1999), 50-67 (52).

[3] S. Burgess, 'Pentecostalism in India: An Overview', *Asian Journal of Pentecostal Studies* 4:1 (January 2001), 85-98 (89).

[4] T. van den End, *Ragi Carita: Sejarah Gereja Di Indonesia 2 - 1860-an – sekarang* [A History of the Church in Indonesia, vol 2 – 1860 – present] (Jakarta: Pt BPKGunung Mulia, 1989), 256.

[5] S. Trinidad, 'Six Filipinos and One American: pioneers of the Assemblies of God in the Philippines', *Asian Journal of Pentecostal Studies* 4:1 (January 2001), 119-121 (121).

[6] Y.H. Lee, 'Korean Pentecost: The Great Revival of 1907' in *Asian Journal of Pentecostal Studies* 4:1 (January 2001), 73-83. (73).

[7] J. Hosack, 'The Arrival of Pentecostals and Charismatics in Thailand', *Asian Journal of Pentecostal Studies* 4:1 (January 2001), 109-117 (110).

Pentecostalism in Indonesia do not perfectly mirror these political divisions, the political eras and events associated with them do have some bearing on the church's growth and development. I will describe the twentieth century history of the Pentecostal movement in Indonesia according to five periods: 1) pioneer missionaries in the Dutch Colonial period (1921-42); 2) church indigenization in the Japanese occupation and struggle for independence (1942-49); 3) steady success in Sukarno's Old Order (1949-68); 4) accelerated growth in Suharto's New Order (1968-98); and 5) new opportunities in the new millennium (1998-present).

Pioneer Missionaries in the Dutch Colonial Period 1921-42

The 'Dutch East Indies', as Indonesia was known in 1900, was a Dutch colony consisting of various islands, peoples, cultures and religions. Indonesian society was religiously pluralist, consisting of various syncretistic mixes of ethnic religions, Hinduism, Buddhism, Islam and Christianity. It is estimated that the majority of Indonesians were Muslims, about 90%,[8] who mainly lived in villages and could be categorized according to varying levels of intensity of their profession of Islam. Differences in their Islamic faith existed for various regional, historic, political, theological and ethnic reasons.

When Pentecostalism came to Indonesia, Roman Catholicism and Protestant forms of Christianity had been present for centuries in the Moluccas, North Sulawesi, the Sangir-Talaud islands and in Flores, Timor and Solor. Under the Portuguese and Dutch colonial governments, missionaries had previously viewed their main task as the spiritual care of the European colonialists. The christianization of the 'natives' was merely an afterthought for many of the early missionaries.[9] In the 1800s and to the early 1900s, a new breed of missionaries who had experienced the pietistic revivals of Europe came to Indonesia with the aim of preaching the 'Evangelical' gospel message to the 'natives'. This new breed of missionaries made inroads among ethnic religionists in North Sumatra (Bataks), Kalimantan (Dayaks), Sulawesi (Minahasa and Toraja), Eastern Indonesia and Central and East Java.[10] It is estimated that in 1900 there were as many as 100,000 Evangelical Christians in Indonesia and that by 1910 this number had increased to 300,000, said to be due to the teaching and preaching of these missionaries and 'native pastors', phenomenal 'revivals' and 'awakenings' and partly through 'folk movements'.[11] However strict Muslim areas and Hindu Bali were out of bounds

---

[8] C. Geertz, *The Religions of Java* (New York: The Free Press, 1969), 123.

[9] T. van den End, *Ragi Carita,* 256.

[10] Unknown Author, 'A History of the Pentecostal Movement in Indonesia', 133.

[11] J.E. Orr, *The Flaming Tongue* (Chicago: Moody Press, 1973), 114.

to the missionaries as the Dutch did not want religious disturbances in these regions.

Pentecostalism arrived in Indonesia somewhere between 1910 and 1921. While there are reports of Pentecostal/Charismatic phenomena occurring as early as 1910, the first classical Pentecostal missionaries from the West appear to have arrived in Indonesia in 1921. This was during the Dutch Colonial period and later stage of the Indonesian church history period of 'foreign missionary societies', which spanned from 1815 to 1930. [12] Pentecostal missionaries from America arrived in the 1920s with the 'full gospel' message of Jesus Christ as Saviour, Healer, Baptizer in the Spirit and Coming King. Two American missionary families of Dutch descent, the Groesbeeks and the van Klaverens, were sent in 1921 to Indonesia by their Pentecostal church, Bethel Temple in Seattle, USA. The Groesbeeks and van Klaverens are generally considered to be the founders of the Pentecostal movement in Indonesia. They started their work in Bali, East Indonesia. It is reported that when they prayed for the Balinese, supernatural healings of sick people occurred and a small church of Balinese Pentecostal converts began. [13] However, the Dutch colonial authorities expelled them because Bali was a Hindu region and in 1922 they moved to Surabaya, the largest city in East Java where they held church services and conducted healing meetings in public buildings. Encounters with the Holy Spirit, miraculous healings and conversions were reported and Pentecostal churches were started. Other Pentecostal missionaries such as Thiessen, Busby, Short and Devin and Dutch Protestant expatriates, such as van Alt and van Gessel, made a significant contribution to the early spread of the movement.

By the early 1930s the Pentecostal message had spread from Surabaya to other parts of Java. Among the Chinese people of East Java there were reports of people receiving their sight, the deaf hearing and lame people walking, with many converted to Christianity through the mass evangelistic meetings of the Chinese evangelist John Sung. The movement spread from Surabaya to Central and West Java, and to various outer islands. Most of the converts to Pentecostalism in Indonesia from 1921 to 1942 were non-Christians mainly of Chinese Buddhist-Confucian, Indo-European, Javanese and ethnic religious background, as well as some Dutch Protestants and Catholics.

The first generation Pentecostal converts by the 1930s had become leaders within the movement. The new Indonesian Pentecostal leaders partnered the missionaries in pastoring the churches and some went to other parts of Indonesia as missionaries themselves. It is significant that the first Pentecostal missionaries arrived at the beginning of the era of the indigenous church, because the events that mark this indigenous period of Indonesian church

---

[12] T. van den End, *Ragi Carita,* 256

[13] N.J. Sumual, *Pantekosta Indonesia: Suatu Sejarah* (Manado: Sario, 1981), 50.

history would influence the shape of the future Pentecostal church and its prospects for growth. The later formation of national church bodies free of foreign mission control would become significant in the indigenization process and development of the Pentecostal church.

In 1924, the Pentecostals were officially registered with the Dutch East Indies government under the name '*De Pinkster Gemeente in Nederlandsch Indie*'. This name was later 'Indonesianized' to *Gereja Pantekosta Di Indonesia* – the 'Pentecostal Church of Indonesia'. Most Pentecostals today trace their roots back to the original '*Pinkster Gemeente*'. During the Dutch Colonial period three groups developed from the original Pentecostal body: *Pinkster Zending* (1931), *Gereja Gerakan Pantekosta* (1932) and the United Pentecostal Church (1938). Some of these derivatives gave rise to further sub-groups: *Pinkster Zending* gave rise to *Gereja Sidang Jemaat Allah* (1931) – the Assemblies of God – and *Gereja Utusan Pantekosta;* and the United Pentecostal Church later gave rise to *Gereja Pantekosta Serikat* (1966).

Since its beginnings in 1921 the Pentecostal movement in the Dutch East Indies grew in numbers and expanded to many parts of the archipelago. This was largely because of the work of the pioneer missionaries. However, most significantly, a generation of indigenous Pentecostal leaders joined them in the work. These Indonesian leaders would provide the leadership during the next period.

Church Indigenisation in the Japanese Occupation and Struggle for Independence 1942-49

The arrival of the war and the Japanese occupation of much of the Dutch East Indies brought economic hardship and social upheaval to many Indonesians. The Pentecostal churches faced many challenges, not the least being the loss of the most experienced church leaders, the missionaries due to the outbreak of war. Some of the western missionaries fled the Japanese advance, some were captured and imprisoned and others were even killed. To add to the hardship, Indonesian Christians were viewed with suspicion by the Japanese, due to Christianity's identity at that time largely as the religion of the Allied powers. Many Indonesian Christian leaders were jailed and killed. Further to this, a heated debate broke out as the end of the war drew near about what should be the ideological base for the future of the new emerging nation. A sense of nationhood had been developing around Islam and an Islamic state, an outcome considered disastrous by Christians, was the objective of some Muslims.

The 'founding fathers' of Indonesia in 1945 debated whether the nation should have an Islamic or secular government. They were concerned about the unity of the diverse cultures, ethnic groups and religions that made up the Indonesian archipelago. On 17 August, 1945 the secular state of the Republic of Indonesia was proclaimed with Sukarno as the first president. Freedom of religion was enshrined in the '1945 constitution' in the form of the first principle of the *Pancasila* philosophy, that all Indonesians must have 'Belief in one God'. Some Muslims were bitterly disappointed when Islam was rejected as the basis of the state and vowed to continue the struggle.

With the adoption of the *Pancasila* as the governing philosophy of Indonesia, Protestant Christianity, including Pentecostalism as one of its forms, became officially recognized by the state. So the historical circumstances for Pentecostalism changed and Christians were able to continue practising their faith. While this change of events did not seem to immediately translate into dramatic growth, the new governing philosophy did provide opportunities for Indonesian Pentecostal missionaries to go to non-Christian regions that were previously restricted under the Dutch and Japanese.

After the war ceased in 1945 the Dutch returned to reclaim the 'Dutch East Indies' but the Indonesian nationalist forces resisted them. In 1949 after four years of bitter hostility and struggle the Dutch capitulated and Indonesia was indisputably recognized as a sovereign nation. When the missionaries returned to Indonesia they found that in their absence Indonesian Pentecostal leaders had stepped into the leadership positions of local churches and denominations that had been vacated. This was another significant turn around for the Pentecostal church as it speeded up the indigenization process.

Steady Success in Sukarno's Old Order 1949-68

After the war and throughout the 1950s, Pentecostals were part of a general 'Christ-ward movement'. [14] This 'Christ-ward' movement, however, was distributed unevenly among ethnic groups and geographical locations, not yet penetrating strong Muslim areas. Pentecostal churches grew steadily in the regions already evangelized and some attempts were made to penetrate the strict Muslim regions. After the Proclamation of Independence, many new Pentecostal denominations formed between 1949 and 1968, such as *Gereja Isa Almasih* (1946), *Gereja Bethel Injil Sepenuh* – Bethel Full Gospel Church (1952), *Gereja Pantekosta Pusat Surabaya* (1959) and *GPDI K.Sianturi Suhud* (1966). Some of these derivatives gave rise to further sub-groups that spread out across the nation creating a vast diversity of Pentecostal groups: *Gereja Bethel Injil Sepenuh* gave rise between 1953 and 1963 to *Gereja Bethel Tabernakel* (1957), *Gereja Tabernakel PDG Pasir* (1963) and *Gereja Bethel Indonesia* (1969); and *GPDI K.Sianturi Suhud* gave rise to *GPDI Sianipar* (1970). [15] As these diverse expressions of Pentecostalism continued to expand, the need for fellowship and cooperation between the different groups grew, resulting in the formation in 1961 of a national body, recognized by the

---

[14] A. Willis, *Indonesian Revival: Why Two Million Came to Christ* (Pasadena: William Carey Library, 1977), 2.

[15] N.J. Sumual, *Pantekosta Indonesia*, 74-75.

Indonesian government, called the *Persatuan Pendeta-Pendeta Aliran Pantekosta Seluruh Indonesia (PPAPSI)* or the Fellowship of Pentecostal Ministers in Indonesia.

Mass revival meetings were held during the 1950s and 1960s in Jakarta and Surabaya and other places that featured Pentecostal healing evangelists such as T.L. Osborne from the USA. Crowds of thousands attended the meetings where many miracles and conversions were reported. Healing evangelists, both foreigners and Indonesians, whether in the largest stadiums or big tents, raised the profile of the Pentecostal churches within the general community.

After the Japanese occupation, the major Pentecostal denominations started new Bible schools and expanded existing ones in several parts of Indonesia and trained Indonesians to plant and pastor churches.[16] The training of Indonesian Pentecostal leaders as pastors, evangelists and missionaries was significant in the development and expansion of the church during this period.

During the 1950s, continued failure by the government to produce political progress brought economic hardship and political instability. While the nation attempted to embrace democracy from 1950-57, the experiment failed.[17] Christians were concerned about the threats surrounding them, being caught between the two powers of Communism and Islam, both vying for political ascendancy. The outlook for the church was bleak, with the probability of either an Islamic or Communist state. Christians all over Indonesia prayed for divine intervention.

Accelerated Growth in Suharto's New Order 1968-98

The historical fortunes of Christianity changed with the failure of an 'attempted Communist coup' that occurred in September, 1965. President Sukarno was implicated in the attempted coup, which lead to his demise. On 11 March 1966, Major-General Suharto effectively took control of Indonesia. Assuming power formally on 27 March 1968, President Suharto inaugurated the 'New Order', promising better things ahead for the nation. The outlook for the church had suddenly changed. Protestant church attendance swelled in the 1960s. It is estimated that over 2 million Indonesians, particularly Javanese and Timorese, joined Evangelical and Pentecostal churches during the political and economic instability of the 1960s. The nation's upheaval caused Christians to pray more earnestly and many miracles, particularly in Pentecostal churches and 'spiritual awakenings' were reported. Due to the events surrounding the attempted coup, Christians would not have an antagonistic regime thrust upon them, either

---

[16] M. Devin, 'Information on Assemblies of God Work in Indonesia' (Unpublished paper, 1991), 3.

[17] M.C. Ricklefs, 'A History of Modern Indonesia since c.1300'.

Communist or Islamic, and Christianity, in its Catholic and Protestant forms, would continue to be state-sponsored.

Another major political development that had implications for the Pentecostal church and Christianity in general, began in 1965 when Suharto, by then operating as the head of the army, began to unleash recriminations upon the Communists, who were blamed for the attempted coup. It was decreed that every Indonesian must belong to one of the five major religions: Islam, Protestantism, Catholicism, Hinduism or Buddhism. The Pentecostal denominations were recognized by the government as an expression of Protestant Christianity. Anyone not joining one of these religions would be branded a Communist. State pressure to believe in one God and to have a 'proper' religion created some difficulties for the pre-existing indigenous religions, for example the Dayaks of Kalimantan, and the mystical groups in Bali and Java. This created new opportunities for the church as these people had to identify with Islam, Christianity, Hinduism or Buddhism. While some, particularly the Balinese, chose Hinduism, some chose Buddhism and still others Christianity. Many Indonesians began to regularly attend mosques and churches to avoid being labelled Communist. As such the government regulation compelled nominal affiliations with these mainstream religious traditions.[18]

Another implication for Christianity and Pentecostalism was that the army and Muslims, tracked down and killed at least 500,000 suspected Communists. Many Communists, particularly those who were ex-Muslims, fearing retribution from the army and Islamic groups, sought refuge in the churches. Churches, including Pentecostal ones, provided food and shelter to the poor and needy in the midst of the crisis. Pentecostal churches continued to grow into the early 1970s, in what has been referred to by one Indonesian church historian as 'growth by crisis'. During the 1970s, Pentecostalism and Evangelical Christianity had four outstanding church growth areas. They were East and Central Java, Karo-Batak land in North Sumatra, East and West Kalimantan and Timor.[19]

When President Suharto began his New Order government, political stability and economic development were the greatest needs. In the mid1960s Indonesia's economy was in shambles and many Indonesians lived in poverty. There was a great need for economic development and alleviation of poverty. The New Order's inauguration marked the beginning of a sustained period of economic growth, development and modernization, which changed the face of the country.[20]

---

[18] J.Z. Smith and W.S. Green (eds.), *The HarperCollins Dictionary of Religion*, 835.
[19] A. Willis, *Indonesian Revival*.
[20] R. Elson, 'Professorial lecture' (Griffith University, 1998).

The Charismatic movement, which began in the USA in the 1960s, appears to have come to Indonesia sometime in the 1970s.[21] This brought a more 'experiential' form of Christianity into some non-Pentecostal churches, renewing their more 'doctrinally-oriented' faith. While many Charismatic Christians stayed in their churches, others left, resulting in an influx of middle-class urban Protestant and Catholic Indonesians into Pentecostal churches. The Full Gospel Business Men's Fellowship also came to Indonesia in the 1970s and attracted Christian business people to Pentecostal churches. Another significant development for Pentecostals during the New Order period of accelerated growth was the establishment of a new national Pentecostal body. The Pentecostal Council of Indonesia (*Dewan Pentakosta Indonesia - DPI*) was formed in 1979[22] when the *Persatuan Pendeta-Pendeta Aliran Pantekosta Seluruh Indonesia (PPAPSI)*, which had formed in 1961, united with *Persekutuan Pentakosta Indonesia (PPI)*, formed in the early 1970s. This was important for the unity of the movement for better planning for future growth. Many Pentecostal denominations also stayed involved with other national Protestant bodies that they historically related to. By 1980 the Pentecostal denominations were said to be the fastest growing churches in Indonesia, with estimates of between 1.95 million[23] and 2.5 million[24] members in 5,000 Pentecostal churches. The largest denomination, *Gereja Pentakosta Di Indonesia*, was estimated in 1980 to have approximately 500,000 members.[25]

Against the backdrop of the rapid modernization, industrialization, economic development and Islamicization of Indonesia that characterized the 1980s and 1990s, the growth of the Pentecostal churches accelerated markedly, particularly among the Javanese people.[26] Indonesian society underwent rapid social and cultural change during the New Order period between 1968 and 1998, transforming it into a thriving, modern nation-state. Rapid modernization[27] became one of the most potent forces that shaped the development of Indonesian society. This economic growth delivered schools, medical facilities, roads, bridges and other facilities and created a kind of hybridized western metropolitan super-culture. In the 1980s and 1990s the development of a consumer culture transformed Indonesian society, particularly for those who lived in the cities.[28] The desire to modernize and the economic boom also brought about major demographic changes. The increase in

---

[21] T. van den End, *Ragi Carita*, 372.

[22] Ibid and Pentecostal Council 1998 official report to Ministry of Religion.

[23] D.B. Barrett, *World Christian Encyclopedia* (1982), 386-387.

[24] N.J. Sumual, *Pantekosta Indonesia*, 77.

[25] T. van den End, *Ragi Carita*, 259.

[26] P. Johnstone, *The Church Is Bigger than You Think*, 115.

[27] A. Hoogvelt, *Globalisation and the Postcolonial World*, 36.

[28] R. Elson, 'Professorial lecture' (Griffith University, 1998), 14

education and work opportunities brought about by economic growth and industrialization respectively caused large-scale rural to urban migration. A sizeable middle-class developed during this period, for the first time in the nation's history. While significant advances were made in alleviating poverty, many Indonesians, the urban poor, parts of rural Java and the outer islands peoples, still lived in poverty which has worsened dramatically since the 1997 economic crash. Rapid modernization and the ideological vacuum of the New Order are thought to have eroded the traditional cultural and social foundations in Indonesian society. This has produced new levels of openness, new values and lifestyles. This is thought to have created opportunities for new religious movements such as Pentecostalism.

Pentecostal growth during the 1980s and 1990s occurred in the cities, towns and villages of Indonesia, with the most rapid growth and the largest churches in the urban areas. A social shift began within Pentecostalism in the 1970s with the influx of middle class Indonesians, including professionals and business people, which later expanded to include the upper class. This provided an enhanced resource base to the Pentecostal churches for their objectives, in terms of finances and skilled personnel in important positions. Pentecostal Christians were able to resource the growth of the Pentecostal movement in Indonesia with minimal financial input from foreign groups. However, in this social shift they have maintained their social conscience, concern and compassion. This is evidenced by the development in this period of significant social welfare programmes, for example, schools, medical clinics, food banks and counselling services. While evangelism has been their main focus, alleviation of the poverty of their people is also an important mandate to Indonesian Pentecostals.

The growth of Pentecostal denominations from 1980-1990 continued to accelerate. The denomination, *Gereja Sidang Jemaat Allah*, the Assemblies of God, is said to have 'more than doubled in the ten years' from 1980-90. A new branch of *Gereja Bethel Indonesia (GBI)* church, referred to as *GBI Betani* (GBI Bethany), formed and grew rapidly to the point where it has large congregations, some with tens of thousands of people attending, in several Javanese cities. Pentecostal 'megachurches' sprang up in Jakarta and Surabaya in the 1990s. They emphasized 'signs and wonders', mass evangelism, 'high-tech' worship, modern marketing and church growth methods resulting in large numbers of conversions.

Pentecostal church growth continued in the 1990s, particularly in the previously evangelized regions among the Bataks, Chinese, Javanese, Timorese, Ambonese, Dayaks and in Sulawesi. However, most significantly, Pentecostalism made further inroads into strong Muslim and Hindu areas. Theological colleges in the 1970s had been training students for work among Muslims and many of the graduates had gone as missionaries to strong Muslim areas as part of the church planting 'plans' of their denominations. Due largely to the expressed concern of Muslims about the 'Christianization' of Indonesia,

President Suharto placed restrictions upon the churches regarding evangelism and missionary work. Suharto's pro-Islamic and anti-Christian policies fostered a climate of persecution of Christians by some Muslim groups. More Christian churches have been damaged, burned or destroyed since the mid-1990s than at any other time in Indonesian history. Tahalele blames the Suharto regime for transforming Indonesia from a society of religious tolerance to one of religious violence.[29]

By the mid-1990s there were increasing signs that the New Order was unable to contain social and economic currents with its earlier efficiency. The political instability of this time and the 1997 currency crisis brought about the collapse of the Suharto presidency in May 1998. During this upheaval the Pentecostal churches continued to grow significantly. Some denominations claim the growth of their churches in some regions has been exponential. By 1998 the Pentecostal movement in Indonesia had grown to an estimated membership of between seven and ten million people [30] with about 60 Pentecostal denominations and influence in most other Christian denominations in the form of Charismatic Christianity.

New Opportunities in the New Millennium 1998-Present

During the new democratic Indonesia that has been developing since 1998, Pentecostalism has continued to thrive amid the worst persecution the church in Indonesia has ever known. By 2000 the economy had made a slow recovery from the 1997 monetary crisis, but many Indonesians were living in poverty. Neither Presidents Habibie or Wahid were able adequately to resolve the country's ills.

In 2001, Patrick Johnstone, estimated that there were 10.878 million Pentecostal and Charismatic believers in Indonesia, representing 5.1% of the nation's population.[31] While this figure seems to be accurate, the number of Indonesian Pentecostal/Charismatic Christians in 2002 could be as high as 12 million people. Not only has this expansive movement grown to a most significant size, approximately 5-5.5% of the Indonesian population today and

---

[29] P. Tahalele and T. Santoso (eds.), *Beginikah Kemerdekaan Kita?* [Is This Our Freedom?] (Surabaya: Forum Komunikasi Kristiani Surabaya, 1997), 14.

[30] M. Robinson, 'Pentecostal Power among Pancasila People: reasons for the growth of a new religious movement in Indonesia' (Unpublished thesis, Griffith University, Australia, 2001), 50. Figures based on the 1998 Pentecostal Council report to the Indonesian government and personal communications with Indonesian Pentecostal Executive leaders.

[31] P. Johnstone and J. Mandryk, *Operation World: 21st Century Edition* (Paternoster, 2001), 339.

2% of the global Pentecostal population, but it continues to grow at an annual rate of 3.5%.[32]

The two largest Pentecostal denominations today are *Gereja Pantekosta di Indonesia (GPDI)* and *Gereja Bethel Indonesia (GBI),* estimated in 2001 to have 2.27 million and 1.08 million 'members and affiliates' respectively.[33] These two denominations both have local congregations with attendances in the tens of thousands. Two of the branches of the *Gereja Bethel Indonesia* church, *Betani* and *Tiberias,* appear to be the fastest growing Pentecostal churches in Indonesia today.

Pentecostal Experiences, Organisation and Activities as Reasons for Growth

The scope of this paper allows for only a brief overview of the reasons for the growth of Pentecostalism in Indonesia. Existing sociological explanations for the rapid growth of Pentecostalism in Indonesia include: political factors (government acceptance of Christianity, political instability), the 'this-worldly and transformative' nature of the Pentecostal message, the 'cultural fit' of Pentecostalism to Indonesian life and the 'modernity' argument that views Pentecostalism as having a modern appeal and as a movement that has responded well to modernization. While these arguments go part of the way to explaining the success of the movement, a truly in-depth understanding of the reasons for the growth is only possible by extending these existing explanations to give greater weight to the role of Pentecostal experience, organization and activities.[34]

Pentecostals largely attribute the growth of the Pentecostal movement in Indonesia to supernatural experiences and Pentecostal organization and activities. Experiences such as healings, deliverances, operations of the gifts of the Holy Spirit, 'dreams and visions' and other forms of the miraculous have regularly been reported in Pentecostal meetings throughout the twentieth century history of the movement. Many Indonesian Pentecostals have stated that the primary reason for their introduction to Pentecostalism was some kind of divine encounter with God that they experienced. The recurring nature of these experiences is also thought to contribute to the ongoing religious commitment of Pentecostal believers in Indonesia.

How Indonesian Pentecostals organize themselves and conduct their activities has also contributed to the movement's growth. Pentecostals in Indonesia emphasized a personal relationship with Jesus Christ largely through prayer, praise and worship and study of the Bible. Their message is about a

---

[32] Ibid., 339.

[33] Ibid., 339.

[34] M.Robinson, *Pentecostal Power among Pancasila People.* p. 108

'personal' and 'loving' God, assurance of personal salvation through Jesus Christ, personal devotion and commitment to God, personal integrity, the power of the Bible and the Holy Spirit to transform lives and the importance of loving and serving people. Pentecostals communicate their message using forms that are culturally appropriate and relevant to people of diverse ethnic, social and religious backgrounds. Pentecostal services and meetings typically follow simple formats that are less formal than those of traditional churches. They hold various types of meetings where the Holy Spirit can be encountered and new believers can grow in their faith. The main forms of meetings, which can occur seven days a week, include prayer meetings, church services with vibrant praise and worship followed by Bible preaching about matters that affect people's everyday lives, mass evangelistic or revival meetings, small 'cell' group meetings, specialized programmes that cater for interest groups (for example youth, children, women, men, business people, elderly people) and social programmes for the poor and needy. Pentecostal leaders are often committed to developing and training new ministers (including women and young people) and lay-leaders and encourage everyone in the life of the church to be active. Pentecostal churches commonly experience high levels of commitment from lay-leadership and laity in church life, community programmes, local evangelism and overseas mission. Pentecostals emphasize the Great Commission that Jesus gave his disciples to 'go and make disciples of all nations', and they do so with consuming evangelistic zeal.

Indonesian Pentecostalism is a modern movement, a fact that is reflected in the use of modern forms, particularly in urban environments, such as media, technology, marketing strategies, business management and transportation, to spread their message. They use high tech equipment in their services and programmes such as electronic musical instruments, computers and advanced lighting and sound systems. Pentecostal churches and denominations in Indonesia generally have simple organizational structures between and within congregations. The fastest growing movements are largely decentralized, with high levels of autonomy in the operation of local churches, in which apostolic senior pastors exert strong leadership. Indonesian Pentecostals are generally committed to establishing new church congregations and 'church planting movements' in places—regions, cities, suburbs, towns and villages— where no Pentecostal churches exist.

Conclusion

Indonesian Pentecostalism today is a multi-ethnic, multi-regional, multi-socio-economic and highly indigenized, expansive phenomenon. It has made an impact upon the poor, middle and upper classes. While foreign resources such as missionaries, visiting speakers and finances were significant in the expansion of the movement during the early and mid-1900s, since then Indonesian Pentecostalism has spread largely by its 'own autonomous power' and has developed its own cultural forms. The process of indigenization of Indonesian Pentecostalism, its separation from foreign input, seems to have contributed to its rapid expansion.

The resilience of Pentecostalism in Indonesia is attested to by the way that it has survived, grown and blossomed during some of the most turbulent times and antagonistic circumstances. Through economic hardship, political instability, internal strife, the Communist threat, Islamic opposition, modernization and consumerism, Pentecostalism has not only held its ground but has advanced, demonstrating an enormous capacity for adaptation and growth. Although the reasons for its success are many, in my view the supernatural experiences and Pentecostal organization and activities, are central to understanding the causes of the rapid growth of this movement.

In the new millennium, Pentecostal and Charismatic Christianity has entered the mainstream of socio-religious life in Indonesia and is gaining momentum. The movement shows every sign of continuing to grow, both in the areas it currently exists and into new regions. A new Asian tiger, Indonesian Pentecostalism, has emerged and is beginning to roar.

Pentecostalism in the Philippines

Joseph Suico

Introduction and Historical Background

This paper will discuss the history and development of Pentecostalism in the Philippines with a view to looking at the present situation in the country. Due to limitation of space and the nature of the paper, I will focus primarily on two major denominations: the Assemblies of God and the Jesus is Lord Church. The Assemblies of God in this case study will represent the classical Pentecostal churches because of its prominence in terms of growth and statistics. Of the three leading Pentecostal groups with strong ties in the USA (Assemblies of God, Foursquare Church in the Philippines and New Testament Church of God in the Philippines), the Assemblies of God has the largest number of foreign missionaries actively ministering in the country. To date their missionaries, although indirectly, still play an important role in the ministry of the member churches. They also constitute an organized Assemblies of God Missionary Fellowship (AGMF), the chair of which is usually a member of the executive presbytery of the Philippines General Council of the Assemblies of God (PGCAG). The Jesus Is Lord Church (hereafter cited JIL) headed by Bishop Eddie Villanueva will be taken as representative of other locally established Pentecostal churches with no link to the USA JIL is the most visible and the fastest growing Pentecostal group in the Philippines today because of its strong emphasis on evangelism.[1] JIL is to some extent indigenous, being founded locally and being in all respects autochthonous.[2]

This paper is to some extent a step towards the self-understanding of Pentecostalism in the Philippines. I also believe that to give just an account of the history and development of Pentecostalism without considering the larger framework of Philippine church history would be incomplete.

---

[1] Jesus is Lord Church is the only church in the Philippines included in C. Peter Wagner's *The New Apostolic Churches* (1998). These churches according to Wagner exhibit various components of the new wineskins that are shaping the church for the twenty-first century.

[2] That is. local and without foreign support.

The Republic of the Philippines is the only country in Asia with a Christian majority.[3] It has a unique heritage of Malay, Chinese, Spanish, and North American cultures. Today its cultural and religious characteristics are in some ways more akin to those of the nations of Latin America than those of South East Asia.[4] Despite Spain's long colonial rule, the Spanish language is now only spoken by less than 1% of the population, but the Spanish heritage is visible in other features of national life. One prominent example is that 83% of the population is Roman Catholic.

The Philippine Islands[5] were ruled by Spain for nearly 330 years until 1898 when they were ceded to the United States of America. According to historians, the islands were 'discovered' by Ferdinand Magellan (Fernão Magalhaes), a Portuguese commissioned by King Charles I of Spain.[6] Magellan was received by Rajah Humabon, the Sultan of Cebu, who after only a week was baptized along with several hundred other natives. However, when Magellan came to the neighbouring island of Mactan, he was met with fiery resistance from local warriors, which also cost him his own life. Out of the original five ships under Magellan's command, only three survived the Pacific crossing, but survivors of the Mactan skirmish sailed on in two remaining ships to the Moluccas, or Spice Islands.[7]

---

[3] Stephen Neill in his 'Foreword' to Gerald H. Anderson (ed.), *Studies in Philippine Church History* (1969), vii writes, 'More Christians live in the Philippines than in the whole of the rest of Asia put together'.

[4] The ten-nation geographic region to which it belongs. Paul Freston (1999) also notes 'Spanish colonial heritage, overwhelming Catholic majority, poverty, American influence in the twentieth century (although more directly in the Philippine case), the experience of dictatorship in the 1970s and 1980s, democracy consolidating reasonably well now and a Protestant community'.

[5] The Republic of the Philippines consists of 7,107 islands.

[6] Afterwards ruling as Emperor Charles V, the king made an agreement with Magellan which settled the different shares of ownership in the new discoveries and the rewards to be granted the discoverer and appointed him commander of the fleet. Otto Hartig, trans. by John Szpytman , *The Catholic Encyclopedia*, Volume IX, 1910 by Robert Appleton Company.

[7] Or substituted. e.g. dark wooden *anitos* (pagan gods) were exchanged for saints with Caucasian features. Maggay describes this as liturgical synthesis between Catholicism and the indigenous consciousness in *Filipino Religious Consciousness* (Quezon City: Institute for Studies in Asian Church and Culture, 1999), 14.

Roman Catholicism

It was during this period too that Roman Catholicism generally replaced[8] the traditional beliefs of most Filipinos. Eladio Neira in his book *Conversion Methodology in the Philippines,* claims that the conversion experience of the natives to Christianity was effective and real to the extent that sometimes they were willing to die for it.[9] Incorporated into this newly configured belief system were the colonisers' feudal aspects of their religion such as dogmatism, authoritarianism, and patriarchal oppression.[10] However, other writers like Melba Maggay believe what Filipinos call 'folk Christianity' can be traced back to a combination of pre-Hispanic religious imaginations and the Iberian variety of Catholicism.[11] This, she asserts is 'a branch of Christianity untouched by the upheavals of the Reformation and unscrutinized by the radical doubt of the Age of Reason'. Except in the Muslim south and in the remote interiors, Roman Catholicism became the dominant religion in the Philippines.

Magellan's expedition to the Philippines in 1521 brought the first priest to the islands. The first Augustinian missionary arrived in 1565 and the Dominicans established their university in 1611.[12] During the seventeenth and eighteenth centuries, the Philippines served as a mission base to Japan, China, and Cambodia.[13] It was only in 1905 that the first bishop was consecrated and in 1934, the first Filipino archbishop. The Filipinos saw their first cardinal in 1960. Today, the Philippines has the highest percentage of Catholics in Asia (83.6%) and the eighth highest percentage in the world.[14]

Catholicism as practised in the Philippines blended official doctrine with folk observance. In an intensely personal way, God the Father was worshipped as a father figure and Jesus as the loving son who died for the sins of each individual, and the Virgin was venerated as a compassionate mother. As in other Catholic countries, Filipinos attended official church services such as

---

[8] Eladio Neira, *Conversion Methodology in the Philippines* (Manila: University of Santo Tomas, 1966).

[9] José Rizal, martyr of struggle for independence from Spain wrote books (*Noli Me Tangere* and *El Filibusterismo*) attacking religious orders. He was executed in 1896.

[10] That is, the peninsula comprising Spain and Portugal. Jose M. de Mesa argues that the Spanish influence did not simply replace indigenous elements but the foreign elements were assimilated and modified into the native pattern (*And God Said, Bahala Na*, 1979). See also Delfo C. Canceran's *A Pagan Face of God* (1993) which provides a good background to Philippine history with a view to the process of early christianization in the Philippines from 1521–1665.

[11] C.R. Medina, *Towards Understanding the Religious Filipino* (Baguio City: St. Louis University, 1991), 12.

[12] C.R. Medina, *Towards*, 12.

[13] Felician AFoy, Rose M. Avato, *The Catholic Almanac* (Indiana: Our Sunday Visitor Publishing, 1998).

[14] Jaime C. Bulatao, 'Split-level Christianity', *Philippine Sociological Review* 13:2, 2.

Masses, novenas, baptisms, weddings, and funerals. They supplemented these official services with a number of folk-religious ceremonies basic to the community's social and religious calendar and involving just about everyone in the community. Catholic priest Jaime Bulatao, SJ contends that the Filipinos possess two inconsistent religious systems. In his article, *Split-level Christianity*, he points out that what Filipinos profess is not reflective of the way they actually lead their lives.[15] A Filipino can be very religious on Sunday but leads a lifestyle that is in contradiction to his faith during the week. The absence of a theology that addresses the everyday concerns of the Filipino such as farming, fishing, hunting or weather has led to this inconsistency. Strong belief in the power of the spirit-world continues until today. Leonardo Mercado, a Catholic theologian, argues, 'the Filipino is still an animist at heart, in spite of four centuries of Roman Catholicism'.[16]

Protestantism

Before the American civil government took control of the Philippines in 1901, Bibles found their way into the islands, largely through the efforts of the British and Foreign Bible Society.[17] Influenced by the reading of the Bible, the first Filipino evangelicals were produced, and according to historian Peter Gowing, 'even a few tiny underground congregations were started, well before the arrival of American Protestantism'.[18] However, it was not until Commodore Dewey's victory over the remaining Spanish forces in Manila that representatives of various mission boards in the United States met to plan for work in the Philippines.

---

[15] Leonardo N. Mercado, *Filipino Religious Psychology* (Tacloban City: Divine Word University Publications, 1977), 14.

[16] W. Canton, *A History of the British and Foreign Bible Society* (London: John Murray, 1910), 150. It was in 1873 that a translated Gospel of St Luke – the first portion in any of the Philippine dialects – was presented to the British & Foreign Bible Society. See also James Moulton Roe, *A History of The British and Foreign Bible Society: 1905-1954* (London: The British and Foreign Bible Society, 1965).

[17] Peter G. Gowing, *Islands Under the Cross: The Story of Church in the Philippines* (Manila: National Council of Churches in the Philippines, 1967), 125.

[18] Oscar Suarez, *Protestantism and Authoritarian Politics* (1999), 19. Suarez notes the works of Kenton J. Clymer, *Protestant Missionaries in the Philippines, 1898-1916* (Chicago: University of Illinois Press, 1986); Gerald Anderson, 'Providence and Politics Behind Protestant Missionary Beginnings in the Phlippines', in *Studies in Philippine Church History* (London: Cornell University Press, 1969); Peter G. Gowing, *Islands Under the Cross: The Story of the Church in the Philippines* (Manila: National Council of Churches in the Philippines, 1967); T. Valentino Sitoy, Jr., *Comity and Unity: Ardent Aspirations of Six Decades of Protestantism in the Philippines, 1901-1961* (Quezon City: National Council of Churches in the Philippines, 1989).

Oscar Suarez observes that most contemporary accounts of Protestant beginnings in the Philippines attribute to the American expansionist motive the urge for foreign Christian mission. Expansionism, according to such accounts, was a key factor that finally propelled evangelical mission in the Philippine islands. [19] A recent Evangelical interpretation of this is articulated in *Christianity Today*[20] during the centennial of Protestantism in the Philippines:

Evangelical leaders, however, assert that God's greater purpose for the Philippines transcended America's imperialistic design: Americans brought Bible-based Christianity; allowed religious freedom, which paved the way for vigorous evangelization and indigenous church planting; and taught English, which today is a major reason Filipinos are considered ideal ambassadors for Christ.

It is said that Protestantism arrived in the Philippines wearing an American soldier's uniform because the first Protestant minister by the name of Revd George C. Stull came as an army chaplain.[21] The first Protestant service of worship in the Philippines took place on 28 August, 1898 at the newly opened Young Men's Christian Association (YMCA). The succeeding years saw the coming of missionaries from various denominations: the Methodists in 1900, Episcopalians and Baptists the same year, United Brethren and Disciples of Christ in 1901, Congregationalists in 1902, Christian and Missionary Alliance and Seventh-Day Adventists in 1905. The first Pentecostal missionaries arrived in 1918 from the Church of God, then the Assemblies of God in 1926, and in 1937 the International Church of the Foursquare Gospel. Other denominations or religious groups also came during this period (1920 –40).

From the outset, Protestant churches in the Philippines were plagued with disunity and schisms. Kenton J. Clymer (1986) in *Protestant Missionaries in the Philippines, 1898–1916* writes that Protestant denominations during this period were much in competition with each other. Despite the founding of the Evangelical Union,[22] which sought to unite the Protestant churches thereby avoiding competition and duplication of work, division became inevitable.

---

[19] June 1998 issue.

[20] Gowing, *Islands*, 125.

[21] Founding members Methodist, Presbyterian, American Baptist and the newly arrived United Brethren missionaries met in April 1901 at the YMCA building in Manila. 'The Evangelical Union adopted two important measures: 1) a comity arrangement dividing the country among the various missions with a view to avoiding overlapping, competition, and duplication of work; and 2) the assumption of a common name for all the Protestant congregations – 'The Evangelical Church' – with the denominational name being added in parenthesis as appropriate to the geographical location of the local congregations' (Gowing, 1967:127). Catholic historian John H. Schumacher, S.J. (1979) notes the Episcopalians did not join the comity agreement which regulated proselytization of Roman Catholics.

[22] Gowing, *Islands*, 131.

Gowing cites the following reasons for this: 'principle of religious liberty, unavoidable personality differences and differences in understanding of the gospel, and the dynamics of Filipino nationalism—to say nothing of the misjudgements and mistakes of the American missionaries'.[23] The coming of other denominations in the 1920s and 1930s, which included Pentecostal churches, added to Protestant sectarian confusion because overall they were not ecumenical and did not have ties with the larger Protestant movement.

Although the goals of the Evangelical Union did not prevent schism within the Protestant body, it had significant accomplishments. For instance, the Evangelical Union's Committee on Order and Morals took a definite stand against opium traffic in the Philippines. It also supported public efforts to address the problems of prostitution, gambling and even imposed prohibition against alcoholic beverages. Gowing notes, 'Though these efforts very largely failed, the moral tone of the country was markedly improved by the unrelenting campaign against vice waged by the Evangelical Union'.[24] The member churches of the Evangelical Union early on made a strong statement that they wanted to minister to more than the spiritual needs of the people. Various institutions were then established to address such concerns as health, education, literacy and literature, agricultural improvement, and various types of social service.[25]

Protestantism resumed its earlier vision to evangelize the islands after World War II. The general picture was that of continued numerical growth, devolution to national leadership and expanding institutional and mission outreach. It was also during this time that the formation of the United Church of Christ in the Philippines (1948) and the National Council of Churches in the Philippines (1963) took place.

Pentecostalism

Pentecostalism, like Protestantism in general, has always been associated with the United States' influence in the Philippines. All major Pentecostal denominations in the USA and some minor ones sent missionaries to the Philippines initially to places not yet reached by Catholic priests or to remote areas where the Catholic Church did not have a strong presence. As a minority group, most Pentecostal churches to date are located outside of the city or town centres. Pentecostalism's strong emphasis on the miraculous and divine healing is a major factor in attracting people to its faith and practice. Another factor is the tendency to be 'member-oriented' and to effectively mobilize lay leaders in

---

[23] Gowing, *Islands*, 157.

[24] Gowing, *Islands*, 130.

[25] T.C. Esperanza, 'The Assemblies of God in the Philippines' (MRE dissertation, Fuller Theological Seminary, 1965), 17.

recruitment activities (evangelism). In contrast to established religions and churches, which tend to monopolize power in the hands of an elite clergy, Pentecostal churches empower their members through the gifts of the Spirit. This means that any member in the congregation has an equal opportunity to 'move in the Spirit' through such phenomena as prophesying, interpretation of tongues, healing, or discerning of spirits.

The Assemblies of God

The first Assemblies of God (USA) missionary to visit the country was Benjamin H. Caudle, who arrived in September 1926.[26] His ministry, though not very long, accomplished some measure of success in terms of conducting home Bible studies, university Bible classes, evangelistic meetings, and Christian literature distribution. Due to physical constraints, particularly with regard to Mrs Caudle, the first missionaries decided to leave the Philippines.

The influx of Filipino labourers to the USA paved the way for them to be exposed to the graces of the Pentecostal outpouring. Eventually they themselves became missionaries to their own people and pursued the earlier vision of developing Assemblies of God churches in the Philippines.[27] The first one involved in this endeavour was Cris Garsulao, who became a Christian while studying at university. His conversion led him to commit himself to the ministry. In 1928, after Bible school training in San Francisco, he went back to his hometown in the south west Philippines. The events that followed led to a beginning of something great in the development of Pentecostalism. Several other Filipinos with similar experience of that of Garsulao blazed the trail in other parts of the country, bringing the Pentecostal gospel to their own people.

In December 1939, Leland E. Johnson and his family arrived in Manila as an appointed missionary. The coming of the Johnsons was only the beginning of the influx of Assemblies of God missionaries to the Philippines.[28] Even during the invasion of the Japanese forces the work continued, though hindered by unfavourable circumstances wrought by the cruelty of war. Several American missionaries remained and were a source of strength and inspiration to the locals. During this time, a good number of both missionary and local outreaches were started all over the country. Later, these various outreaches as well as other Pentecostal groups went through the process of institutionalization. Because their mother churches in the USA supported most of the leaders, the process of institutionalization came naturally and without

---

[26] T.C. Esperanza, 'The Assemblies', 19.

[27] There are now 44 (31 couples and 13 singles) US Assemblies of God Department of Foreign Missions appointed missionaries in the country today (Mercy Balista, e-mail to author, 27 June, 2001).

[28] Esperanza, 'The Assemblies', 30.

much difficulty. Eventually, a group of Filipino Assemblies of God preachers in the USA joined their efforts in organizing the Philippine Assemblies of God. Their initial action was to request an appointed Assembly of God missionary to the Philippines to help them achieve this goal. Trinidad Esperanza explains the primary reason for this move:[29]

Their reason for this action was that the Philippines at that time was still under the United States protectorate with a Counsel General as the final seat of authority. A requirement for permitting any outside church denomination to operate in the Philippines was that it must seek registration with the United States Counsel General and have a duly appointed missionary or church leader from the home body in the United States.

When Leland Johnson arrived in 1939, he sought approval from the Counsel General to register an organization known as 'The Philippines District Council of the Assemblies of God Incorporated'.[30] It was only in 1953 that the localized Philippines General Council of the Assemblies of God was formed. With the new local congregations set up around the country came the need to train local workers. Bible schools were then established, initially with foreign missionaries as administrators.[31] Church programmes were adopted almost without question. In the early stages of the development of the Pentecostal movement in the Philippines, their theology 'created a sense of ideological separation that helped to solidify the group experience'. This was because the locals merely adopted the theology of their 'sponsors'. Despite strong persecution from the predominantly Roman Catholic country, the movement continued to grow rapidly. Arthur Tuggy in The Philippine Church: Growth in a Changing Society, writes:[32]

By 1949, 1822 members were reported. In 1952 there were 2,193. Then the Assemblies of God entered a new phase of rapid growth as the large Bethel Temple in Manila was begun under the ministry of Lester Sumrall. This church, which became the largest Protestant church in Manila, had its beginnings in 1952 and 1953.... By 1958 the Assemblies of God reported a membership of 12,022—an increase of almost 500% in five years!

Present membership statistical data is difficult to ascertain because of doubt as to which source is more accurate. The office of the Philippines General Council of the Assemblies of God does not have an up-to-date record.[33] Other source like the US Assemblies of God Division of Foreign Mission shows a more successful trend.

---

[29] Esperanza, *The Assemblies*, 30.

[30] Some Bible schools are still being administered by the missionaries.

[31] A.L. Tuggy, *The Philippine Church Growth In A Changing Society* (Grand Rapids: Eerdmans, 1971), 152.

[32] As of 28 June 2001.

[33] John W. Kennedy, 'Embracing the Challenge', *Pentecostal Evangel* (June 4, 2000), 5.

In the past 10 years, the Philippines Assemblies of God has grown from 1,230 churches with 198,000 members and adherents to 2,600 churches attended by 420,830 people, making it the largest evangelical body in the country. The fellowship exceeded its projected goal of new churches each year during the past decade. Last year alone 289 churches were established.[34]

In contrast, the World Churches Handbook edited by Brierley records a more conservative figure, which puts the Philippine Assemblies of God members only at 94,400 in year 2000. Kennedy's usage of 'members and adherents' and 'attendees' is ambiguous. It is not clear how many of the 420,830 attendees are actual members. Despite lack of proper record keeping, there is no question that the Assemblies of God in the Philippines through the years has experienced remarkable growth in both adherents and in the number of churches planted.

Jesus Is Lord Church

Bishop Eddie Villanueva, a former radical activist, Communist and atheist, founded the Jesus Is Lord Church (JIL) in 1978. Originally called Jesus is Lord (JIL) Fellowship, it had humble beginnings in small group Bible studies in various places in the Polytechnic University of the Philippines, where Eddie Villanueva was teaching. His exposure in leading people to protest against the evils of capitalism helped him to start a vibrant group of young people willing to sacrifice their time and efforts to advance the Kingdom of God by preaching the gospel of Jesus Christ. Today JIL has grown into a worldwide multi-ministry network, establishing churches from Asia to Australia, Europe, Africa, the Middle East, Canada and the USAAs of 1999,[35] JIL Church has 106 Sunday services in Metro Manila, 25 in Bulacan, 275 in other provinces all over the Philippines and 72 worldwide in 27 countries, with a total of 478 Sunday services, claiming altogether two million members. The church also owns a television station (ZOE TV-11) that broadcasts JIL's services on a regular basis. It is perhaps the only Pentecostal group in the country that owns and runs a school that provides education for nursery, kindergarten, complete elementary (first to sixth grade) and high school. There is also a plan to build a Christian university out of the existing structures.

Concerning socio-political involvement, JIL has been the most visible Pentecostal group in the last six years. Villanueva and his group publicly endorsed a presidential candidate in the 1998 presidential elections. 'Brother Eddie' runs and hosts a weekly television show which tackles current religious,

---

[34] Based on a faxed communiqué to Wonsuk Ma on 16 April 1999 but the figures may not be current.

[35] The Jesus Is Lord Church has also acquired a television station, the *Zoe TV-11*.

social and political issues.[36] Recently, with other Christian leaders, Villanueva campaigned for the revamping of the country's national film and television board due to the proliferation of pornography in the film industry. He also founded an organization called *Philippines for Jesus Movement,* composed of different Pentecostal and Evangelical churches. On a weekly basis, he writes a column for one of the major national newspapers. Through these vehicles he communicates his fellowship's stand on issues confronting both the Christian church and society. So far JIL has not only been involved in presidential elections and campaigns against pornography but has challenged some government policies and in 2000 asked the former president Joseph Estrada to step down from office. Because JIL is autochthonous it is not dependent on any kind of missionary leadership or even partnership.[37] Doctrinally, JIL's basic tenets of faith do not differ much from most Pentecostal denominations. Like most classical Pentecostals, the lack of contextual reflection in its theology is most noticeable. However, when it comes to socio-political issues—'Brother Eddie' is quite clear where his church should stand.

Other Pentecostal Groups

CLASSICAL PENTECOSTALS

Similar to the Assemblies of God structure is the Foursquare Church in the Philippines. In 1931 Vicente Defante, a US Navy cook became a convert and later worked with Aimee McPherson.[38]After attending LIFE Bible College in California, he went back to the Philippines as a missionary, returning to his home in Iloilo City and soon erecting the first Foursquare church building in 1937. By 1949, Foursquare churches had increased to thirteen in various parts of the country, eight in the Visayas region and four in Luzon. Later the work spread to Mindanao with missionaries from the USA helping to build a new Foursquare church there. In 1958, the denomination was organized into four districts: Northern Luzon, Luzon, Mindanao and Visayas. The church reported 56,700 members in 2000.

Another classical Pentecostal denomination worthy of mention is the Church of God (COG). With 540 churches, 65,354 members, 677 pastors and eight

---

[36] In contrast, the Assemblies of God has a school for evangelists, the founder and director of which, to date, is a missionary from the U.S.A.

[37] McPherson, a former Assemblies of God minister, founded the International Foursquare Church in the US

[38] Doreen Alcoran, e-mail to author, 29 July, 2001. The figures are from the souvenir programme of the Church of God Philippines Golden Anniversary in 1997. Present statistics are not available.

training schools,[39] the work of COG was begun in 1921 by Joseph Warnick. He, along with a local preacher Teodorico Lastimosa and a missionary from the United Free Gospel and Missionary Society, Frank Porada,[40] started a church in San Nicolas, Ilocos Norte (north of Manila). By 1947, the Philippine Church of God became an official extension of the mission work of the COG (Cleveland) in the USA. Other classical Pentecostal groups coming from the USA include the Pentecostal Holiness Church, which began work in 1954, Assemblies of the Firstborn, Christ to the Philippines, and Christ to the Orient, but statistics for these are not available.

INDEPENDENT PENTECOSTALS

I have chosen 'independent' because of the difficulty with the term 'indigenous'.[41] Various disciplines attribute different meanings to the term. It is widely accepted within missiological circles that self-government, self-support and self-propagation define what is an indigenous church. In the social sciences, however, as pointed out by Mullins, 'indigenization is understood as the process whereby foreign-born religions are transformed through contact with native religion and culture'.[42] Doctrinally, the basic tenets of faith of the independent Pentecostals are either similar to that of the classical groups or simply a derivative. In fact, many of them came to existence as splinter groups from the bigger, older Pentecostal denominations such as the Assemblies of God and Foursquare. While it can be argued that these congregations are 'self-propagating' and 'self-generating', and therefore indigenous, their basic theological perspective, in common with the classical Pentecostals, is one merely inherited from North America.

Some of them, like the Jesus is Lord Church (see above), do not receive outside support and are therefore autochthonous. However, a number of them maintain close relationships with outside bodies, mainly with American and/or Korean churches. The partnership usually consists of a missionary exchange programme or funding of local projects, particularly church planting. Some of the largest of these many independent Pentecostal groups include the following ten churches: 1) the Bread of Life, founded in 1982 by Butch Conde, who used

---

[39] He eventually affiliated with the Church of God Cleveland, TN, USA.

[40] Robert J. Schreiter, *Constructing Local Theologies* (New York: Orbis Books, 1985), 5 notes 'the difficulty with this term, at least in some places, is the history of the word "indigenous"'. In those parts of the world that once made up the British empire, "indigenous" connotes the old policy of replacing British personnel in colonial government with local leadership'.

[41] M.R. Mullins, 'The History, Spread and Internationalism of Pentecostal and Charismatic Christianity in South Korea and Japan' (A Paper presented at the Global Culture: Pentecostal and Charismatic Movements Worldwide, May, 1991).

[42] Robert M. Anderson's *Vision of the Disinherited* (New York: Oxford University Press, 1979).

to work with the Assemblies of God and now with over 12,000 members; 2) the Pentecostal Missionary Church of Christ, emerging as a secession from the Foursquare church in 1974; 3) the Keys of the Kingdom Ministries, founded in 1982 by an Episcopal (Anglican) priest; 4) Jesus Reigns Ministries which split from the Jesus is Lord Church in 1986; 5) the Christian Life Fellowship, whose founder was a US Assemblies of God missionary; 6) the Cathedral of Praise (formerly Manila Bethel Temple) and 7) Shekinah Christian Church, both of which seceded from the Assemblies of God; 8) Love of Christ Ministries, founded in 1981, whose leader was in the Filipino independent church Iglesia ni Cristo and which at one time had a close relationship with the Assemblies of God; 9) the Jesus Fellowship, formed by a Charismatic secession from the United Church of Christ in the Philippines, a mainline Protestant denomination; and finally, 10) Word for the World, founded in 1980 and seceding from the Church of God. All these independent churches subscribe to basic classical Pentecostal doctrine, which revolves around four cardinal truths: Christ the Saviour, Christ the Baptizer (baptism in the Holy Spirit), Christ the Healer, and Christ the Coming King.

Towards the Future: Limitations and Challenges

From the outset, Pentecostalism in the Philippines has been a globalized religion; its origin being North America via western-trained Filipinos. When the Pentecostal gospel came to the islands, it blended well with those at the grassroots level. The Filipinos' awareness of a 'spirit-world' was perfect for a religion that emphasizes the Spirit-gifts. The hundreds of thousands who usually attend the healing crusades of US-based evangelists is evidence of this. Through the years, the Pentecostal movement has witnessed and openly received the healing ministries of American evangelists like T.L. Osborn, Oral Roberts, Rex Humbard, Jimmy Swaggart, Morris Cerullo and, recently, Benny Hinn. The revival meetings of these evangelists undoubtedly has served as an impetus for Pentecostal church growth. In many instances, a congregation emerges after a series of healing crusades in a given area. Healing for the Pentecostal church is not an end in itself—it is often seen as a means of drawing people to the Lordship of Christ.

The influence of Pentecostalism in recent times has reached the upper strata of society and is gradually gaining more acceptance than ever before. In its incipient stage, it has flourished mainly among the poor, the uneducated, those from the margins of society and the oppressed. Today, Pentecostalism is increasingly reaching the middle and upper classes and is no longer restricted to the 'disinherited'.[43] Although the movement now represents all walks of life

---

[43] Although Pentecostal churches were accepted as early as the 1970s as members of PCEC, they did not have much influence in the organization.

and all educational levels, it is still in a minority. However, the Pentecostals' growing prominence within the Protestant and Evangelical movements is worth noting. It was not long ago that Pentecostals were on the margins and were not considered 'Evangelical',[44] but some Pentecostal leaders now play significant roles within the Evangelical movement. For instance, the 1998 presidential elections brought together some of the country's major Evangelical leaders to rally behind a candidate perceived to be a 'born-again' Christian and handpicked by the outgoing Protestant president. In April 1998, the JIL church held a *Jesus Declaration of Victory Grand Prayer Celebration*—a spiritual endorsement of a presidential candidate.[45] Despite the controversial nature of the meeting, Eddie Villanueva explained his view in his newspaper column:[46]

> I must admit that it is a high-risk decision to hold such prayer assembly for the nation at this crucial time. But the leaders of the Body of Christ squarely took that controversial position because we know that our collective prayers for enlightenment and direction are most needed right this very hour. Surely unless we are divinely guided, we are bent to make wrong decisions.

Other Pentecostal groups, including the top leaders of the Assemblies of God, also supported the well-attended meeting. What made it more controversial however, was the presence of the head of the Philippine Council of the Evangelical Churches. Because the 'Grand Prayer Celebration' turned out to be more of a campaign rally than a mere prayer meeting, many Evangelical leaders and members criticized the presence of PCEC's head in the meeting.[47] Bishop Villanueva became less visible following their candidate's defeat in the election. However, in October 2000 the new president, Joseph Estrada was rocked by a corruption scandal. His once close ally, a former provincial governor, accused him of pocketing roughly 12 million US dollars in bribes from gambling syndicates and tobacco taxes. The president's impeachment trial later evolved into the historic 'People Power 2' that eventually ousted him from office. As in the original 'People Power' of 1986 that brought down the dictatorial regime of Ferdinand Marcos, the Catholic

---

[44] Local newspaper columnist Max V. Soliven branded Eddie Villanueva's prayer rally 'an undisguised and unapologetic all-out campaign rally for Lakas-NUCD presidential candidate Jose de Venecia' (*Philippine STAR*, 28 April, 1998).

[45] Eddie Villanueva, 'Calling on God to intervene not putting his name in vain', *Philippine Star*, 30 April, 1998.

[46] Two months after the election, in June 1998, the General Secretary of PCEC circulated a letter of apology to all individual members and institutions. He regretted having publicly expressed his personal preference for a particular candidate.

[47] Richard Shaull and Waldo Cesar's *Pentecostalism and the Future of Christian Churches* (2000) provides a theologically informed sociological study of Pentecostalism in Brazil.

Church had a strong influence. But this time, more Evangelical churches participated—although the PCEC's involvement was more or less tentative. It is noteworthy that several months before the actual 'People Power 2' took place in January 2001, Eddie Villanueva had already called for Estrada to step down from office.

Currently, it seems that independent Pentecostal groups like the Jesus is Lord Church are moving towards emulating the example of Latin American Pentecostals in terms of socio-political involvement. Like its counterpart in Brazil, Pentecostalism in the Philippines has already penetrated the mass media.[48] Although the Pentecostals have for some time now aired their religious programmes on secular TV and radio stations, the JIL church was the first to own a TV station. The endorsement of a political candidate by a Pentecostal group in 1998 was the first time this had happened. Although we do not see a Pentecostal political party emerging yet, it may happen not long from now. Like in Latin America, Pentecostals converted by missionaries are more inclined to 'political withdrawal or passivity than of those who have an autochthonous or indigenous origin'.[49]

The socio-economic realities in the Philippines will to some extent influence the direction of a movement that was once limited to the margins of society. With the continuing slide of the country's economy, several classical Pentecostal groups who are still dependent on outside support will find it hard to be in real partnership with their foreign counterparts. Most of these groups have already celebrated their golden anniversaries, yet their ministry strategies have barely changed. Most social programmes are still organizationally dependent on foreign missionaries. The question some Pentecostals may need to ask themselves is whether Pentecostalism will be able to come out of its 'prolonged childhood'.[50]

The lack of theological reflection or contextual analysis in the movement is a perennial concern. Theological education in Pentecostal Bible schools still reflects educational approaches introduced by the missionaries in the 1960s. The study of local culture is almost non-existent in their curricula. Students, oftentimes through their theological training, are inadvertently detached from the values and needs of the local context. In the area of church ministries, church growth principles imported from Korea and California have not been analysed as to their relevance to the local setting. Overall, theological

---

[48] Jorge E. Maldonado, 'Building "Fundamentalism" from the Family in Latin America' in R. S. Appleby (ed.), *Fundamentalisms and Society* (Chicago: University of Chicago Press, 1993), II, 218.

[49] See Simon Chan, 'Asian Pentecostalism, Social Concern and the Ethics of Conformism', *Transformation* (January 1994), 29-32.

[50] See José Miguez Bonino, 'Pentecostal Missions is More Than What It Claims', *Pneuma:The Journal of the Society for Pentecostal Studies* 16 (Fall 1994), 28388.

formulations are still very much adopted from Anglo-Saxon Evangelical circles that were developed towards the end of the last century.[51]

The ability of the Pentecostals to create a Christian moral alternative that enables greater decision-making power is probably the greatest impact that Pentecostalism has had on Philippine society. There is an increasing recognition among sociologists and theologians who recognize the potential of a Pentecostal experience. However, it is likely that Pentecostalism will remain an imported movement unless the crucial issues above are carefully considered.

---

[51] The works of Shaull and Cesar (2000), Paul Freston (1994), David Martin (1993) and Chris Sugden (1999) are some of the examples.

Catholic Charismatics in the Philippines

Lode Wostyn

A description and evaluation of the Catholic Charismatic Renewal Movement (CCRM) in the Philippines[1] is a research matter which could lead to the publication of several studies. Based on my own pastoral experience, some interviews and a limited number of published materials, I attempt to give an initial sketch. After a short introduction about the origin of the CCRM, I look into three manifestations of the Charismatic Renewal in the Philippines: the CCRM that is guided by the episcopate, the El Shaddai movement of Brother Mike Velarde, and finally the meeting of the Charismatic Movement with Philippine Folk Catholicism. I conclude by presenting some principles for evaluating the significance of the CCRM for the renewal of Christian life in the Philippines.

I have never been a member of a Charismatic community. Hence this evaluation is written from the point of view of an outsider who has only a limited experience with Charismatic groups as pastor and as theologian, although I have taught for a short period at a Charismatic renewal centre.

The Origin of the Catholic Charismatic Renewal Movement (CCRM) in the Philippines

The Second Vatican Council (1962-65)

Yves Congar, one of the *periti* during the Second Vatican Council, believes that the Roman Catholic Church of the Middle Ages and Counter-Reformation caused an 'Eclipse of the Holy Spirit'.[2] Many theologians and church leaders

---

[1] The Philippine Islands, a group of islands in the Western Pacific, is divided into three areas: Luzon (North, where its capital Manila is located), Visayas and Mindanao (South). Its population: 81,159,644 (July 2000 estimate). Land Area: 300,000 square kilometres. Religions: Roman Catholic claims 83%, Protestant 9%, Muslim 5%, Buddhist and others 3%, of the ottal population.

[2] Caroline Joy R. Luz, 'Encountering the Spirit of Life: An Exposition and Conceptual Analysis of the Pneumatology of Jürgen Moltmann' (Unpublished study, Maryhill School of Theology, Quezon City, Philippines, 1999), 44-53. Luz refers to the work of Y. Congar and others.

have downplayed the role of the Spirit by a one-sided christomonism, by the conviction that the Spirit acts only through the intermediary of the church's institution and by the fear of a Spirit associated with freedom, risk and breaking away from structures. 'When I was young', writes the cardinal protector of the first generation of Catholic Charismatics, León Joseph Suenens, 'the church was presented to us as a hierarchical society: it was described as 'juridically perfect', having within itself all the powers necessary to promote its own existence'.[3] The Spirit was subordinated to the hierarchical church, 'making the Spirit appear as the Spirit of the Church, rather than the Church as the Church of the Spirit'.[4]

The Second Vatican Council corrected this situation by adopting a Trinitarian view of the economy of salvation in which the Holy Spirit is seen as the life-principle of the Church. Moreover, the Council also rediscovered the Pauline Charismatic view of the Church and reassessed the importance of the local churches. The Church should be seen as a communion of churches, with the Holy Spirit as principle of communion. This reaffirmation of the role of the Spirit was not free from ambiguity. In Chapter Three of *Lumen Gentium*, the Dogmatic Constitution on the Church, a legal-institutional view is set side by side with a salvation-historical approach. The Holy Spirit apparently remains the captive of the church's hierarchy.[5]

The Council is not the only event that made the appearance of the Charismatic movement possible in the Catholic Church. The liturgical movement, the scriptural renewal, Catholic action and other movements before the Council prepared the way for the renewal of ecclesiology. One of these movements, the *Cursillo de Cristiandad*, has greatly helped in the launching of the Charismatic renewal in the Philippines. The Cursillo (Spanish, meaning 'short course') originated in Spain in the 1940s, entered the Philippines via the United States and was a success in the 1960s and '70s. The pre-Vatican II Philippine Catholic Church was basically a sacramental service station for women that was run by a male clergy. The Cursillo had a great impact on the renewal of the church because it attracted the men. It was in fact a male movement during its early years. At a Cursillo weekend, participants went through a conversion experience and were encouraged to help other Cursillistas in fulfilling their baptismal vows. The group reunions or *Ultreya* (Spanish, meaning 'onward') renewed their conversion experience. Many of the Cursillistas became leaders of the parish renewal.

---

[3] Leon Joseph Cardinal Suenens, *A New Pentecost?* trans. Francis Martin (New York: Seabury Press, 1975), 1-2.

[4] Luz, 'Encountering the Spirit of Life', 50. Luz quotes Brian Gaybba, *The Spirit of Love* (London: Geoffrey Chapman, 1987), 111.

[5] Lode Wostyn, *Doing Ecclesiology* (Quezon City: Claretian, 1990), 43-60.

The Duquesne Experience[6]

The professors of Duquesne University who initiated the Charismatic movement in the Roman Catholic Church, were Cursillistas involved in prayer and social action groups. In their search to deepen their prayer experience they joined a Neo-Pentecostal group. This brought them in contact with the Azusa Street renewal, which is at the origin of the twentieth century's Pentecostal 'Fire from Heaven'.[7] Pentecost became a newly discovered reality for them. They received the baptism of the Spirit, which led to a transformation of their lives. The professors were advisers of a youth group and they shared their experience with them. The Spirit's response to the yearning of these young people was a similar renewal of life and commitment. The initial experience of this youth group took place in 1967. These young people shared their experience with the faculty and students of other universities. Prayer groups and communities sprang up, first in the United States and then in other countries. The CCRM was born.

Cardinal Suenens was instrumental in the acceptance of this new movement by the leadership of the Catholic Church. In 1974, the cardinal invited an international team of Charismatics and theologians to Belgium. They produced the Malines document,[8] which became a sort of reference point in the growth of the CCRM. In 1975, a convention of Charismatics was held in Rome; Pope Paul VI concelebrated with the cardinal and gave his official blessing to the movement.

Catholic Charismatics in the Philippines[9]

Several factors collaborated in the origin of the CCRM in the Philippines in the early 1970s. First, Protestant groups, influenced by the Neo-Pentecostal movement, organized prayer meetings in Manila that were also attended by Catholics. Second, Filipino members of religious orders experienced the CCRM in the United States and started Charismatic prayer groups in the Philippines. Prayer meetings even reached Mindanao through Maryknoll

---

[6] René Laurentin, *Catholic Pentecostalism* (London: Darton, Longman and Todd, 1977), 11-17; Mansfield, Patti G., *As By a New Pentecost* (Steubenville: Franciscan University Press, 1992), 3-28; Edward D. O'Connor, *The Pentecostal Movement in the Catholic Church* (Notre Dame: Ave Maria Press, 1971), 39-107.

[7] Harvey Cox, *Fire From Heaven* (London: Cassell, 1996), 45-78.

[8] 'Theological and Pastoral Orientations on the Catholic Charismatic Renewal' (Malines, 1974).

[9] Nazario E. Caparanga, 'The Spirit of Love Community: A Typological Description' (unpublished study, Maryhill School of Theology, Quezon City, 1998,), 11-15. Rev. Herbert Schneider, SJ, one of the pioneers of the CCRM in the Philippines, retold the story during an interview.

missionaries. Thirdly, Assumption sisters who came in contact with the Charismatic movement in Paris, founded a Charismatic prayer meeting. Some newcomers introduced the praying and singing in tongues. They spoke of the gifts of the Spirit. They asked for the baptism of the Spirit and the release of Charismatic gifts. From a small group in mid-1973, the Assumption prayer meeting grew to a number of more than one thousand in one year. Charismatic groups then spread all over Manila and the surrounding provinces.

The 'officially approved' CCRM that is sponsored by the Philippine episcopate has mainly been a middle-class movement. This is quite normal, because the majority of practising Catholics in the Philippines are middle-class people. The bishops set the boundaries of the movement at an early stage. Priests were assigned as spiritual directors and diocesan offices were organized. The institutionalization was partly motivated by the fear of 'losing' people to 'Protestant Pentecostalism', which was lumped together with the strongly proselytizing American fundamentalist groups. A dam had to be put up to stop the invasion of the 'sects'.[10]

In the promulgation of the 'Guidelines for the CCRM in the Archdiocese of Manila',[11] Cardinal Sin warns about the dangers of ecumenical or interdenominational Charismatic groups or activities. 'Indiscriminate or less prudent participation of Catholics in so-called ecumenical or Charismatic prayer groups has created considerable confusion in not a few of both faithful and pastors', writes the cardinal. His fear is somehow counteracted at the end of the Guidelines in which it is stated, 'that Catholics can worship together with other Christians without fear of intellectual and theological hostilities and debate is a welcome phenomenon...and a work of the Holy Spirit'.[12]

The Philippine Catholic Charismatic Renewal Movement

The Parish Groups[13]

Beautiful statements have been written in the Philippine Catholic Church about renewal and restructuring of the parishes, making them into a communion of Basic Christian Communities. This church has to become, not only a church

---

[10] *Catholic Guidelines on Fundamentalism* (Manila: Catholic Bishops' Conference of the Philippines, 1989).

[11] *Guidelines of the Catholic Charismatic Renewal Movement in the Archdiocese of Manila* (Archdiocesan Office for Research and Development, 1981), henceforth *Guidelines*.

[12] *Guidelines*, 26.

[13] Caparanga, 'The Spirit of Love Community', 16-30; *Guidelines*, 21-24, 33-34. I also relied on interviews with leaders of some parish groups.

for, but a church of the poor.[14] In the Archdiocese of Manila and many other dioceses the picture we get, however, is a very different one. The priest-centred parish with its 'mandated' organizations still follows very much the traditional pattern. Charismatic prayer groups have to fit in and become one of the mandated parish organizations, in which one or several groups of people have a prayer experience every week.

To become an official member of such a Charismatic prayer group, one has to attend a 'Life in the Spirit Seminar'. The seminars, mostly led by lay people of a covenant community and organized in the parish or in a Charismatic prayer centre, follow a fixed pattern. Seven topics are discussed: God's Love, Salvation, New Life, Receiving God's Gift, Manifestation of the Spirit, Growth, and Transformation. The speakers try to capture their audience by bringing in personal experiences and testimonies. Yet the basic truths have also to be presented. As a theologian, having attended some of the sessions of such a seminar, I admired the oratorial skills of the speakers but not the theological content of their talks.[15] Most of the CCRM groups have to catch up with the renewal in scripture study and in theology that has taken place in recent decades.

The culminating point of the Life in the Spirit Seminar is the baptism in the Spirit. This means for many of the participants a real conversion experience. They become new members of a prayer group, which has to sustain 'the life in the Spirit' that they received during the seminar. What happens during these prayer meetings depends very much on the leadership. In the beginning, many of these meetings were full of life and activity. People spoke in tongues. They were 'slain in the Spirit' and healers were called in. However, later, prayer meetings seem to have been tamed. They are very much limited simply to Bible study and the sharing of experiences. The Guidelines rightly lament that the charisms of the Spirit do not seem to go beyond the prayer group: 'Some groups appear to be reluctant to take active interest in the needs of those around them …and tend to become closed circles instead of springboards for service in the world'.[16]

In Metro-Manila, the 'Alliance of Parochial Charismatic Communities' is supplemented by the 'Community of Office-Based Prayer Groups'. People working in the offices of banking or business corporations meet during their break or after work in an office to have a prayer meeting or Bible study. Some

---

[14] *Acts and Decrees of the Second Plenary Council of the Philippines* (Manila: Catholic Bishops' Conference of the Philippines, 1991).

[15] *The Life in the Spirit Seminars* (Notre Dame: Charismatic Renewal Services Inc., 1973). The book of Herbert Mühlen, *A Charismatic Theology: Initiation in the Spirit*, trans. Edward Quin and Thomas Linton (London: Burns & Oates, 1978), would have been a better guide.

[16] *Guidelines*, 25.

of the office towers in the financial district of Makati have a chapel, sponsored by a business company. The Charismatic group meets in the chapel. Office groups attempt to reach out. Some succeed, for example, in creating new groups in government offices. They also take some initiative in helping poor people, the elderly, and the street children. Every month, office workers meet in the Greenbelt Church of Makati and celebrate a healing mass.

The Covenant Communities

The Life in the Spirit seminar, followed by prayer meetings and outreach programmes, have not been enough for some Catholics who have experienced a radical conversion. They looked for something more. The Senior Head Coordinator of *Ligaya ng Panginoon* (Joy of the Lord), the first covenant community in the Philippines, Brother Vic Gutierrez expressed this new call in the following words: 'We felt the challenge to explore how we can become practising Christians from Monday to Sunday'.

I briefly describe the history and organization of this first covenant community.[17] The original group of 41 were members of the Assumption prayer groups. In 1975, under the leadership of Rev Herbert Schneider, a Jesuit, they organized a weekend retreat at the East Asian Pastoral Institute. At the end of the retreat, the decision was taken to start a community. Yet how this could be done among married people was not very clear. Schneider brought them in contact with the Ann Arbor community in the United States. Some joined a workshop in Ann Arbor while leaders of the American community visited the Philippines and shared their expertise with the group. Among them were Stephen Clark and Ralph Martin. The group went into a long period of training. Finally, they made their covenant promise at the beginning of the 1980s. In their promise, which is repeated every year, each member pledges to live as a follower of Christ, to faithfully attend all the activities of the community, to relate with one another in love, and to give financial support to the community.

At present, Ligaya ng Panginoon is a cluster of covenant communities in the Philippines with about two thousand members. It created a network of movements for the evangelization of the different sectors of Philippine society: Brotherhood of Christian Businessmen and Professionals (BCBP), Christ's Youth in Action, Women for Christ, and so on. It also organized a partnership with covenant communities which it helped develop in India, Singapore, Pakistan, USA and Canada. Ligaya's main office reprints and distributes Catholic literature (Word of Joy Publications), runs a training centre (Institute for Pastoral Development), and is a member of two international organizations,

---

[17] See the Word of Joy publications. I rely mainly on an interview with Brother Vic Gutierrez.

the Christ the King Association (Catholic) and The Sword and The Spirit (Ecumenical).

In Manila, Ligaya ng Panginoon belongs to the Federation of Transparochial Communities. The federation has some thirty members. Among them are *Bukas Loob sa Diyos*, *Buklod ng Pagibig*, *Elim*, Spirit of Love Catholic Community, and so on. Some of these communities reach out beyond the boundaries of the Philippines. They have foundations, mainly among Filipino migrants, in Hong Kong, the USA and Canada. One organization, which has had a great impact in the Philippines and has spread to other countries, is the Couples for Christ (CFC). The CFC started from marriage encounters within the Ligaya ng Panginoon. It became a separate entity, which took as its mission the evangelization of families. At the same time, it refocused its thrust to include social responsibility to change the lives of the poor and the marginalized sectors of the country. The CFC participated in an active way in the recent campaign to oust President Joseph Estrada and in the election of a group of new senators.

Fringe Groups

Early Pentecostalism showed a pattern of division and proliferation. A similar pattern is present in the Philippine CCRM, notwithstanding the interventions of the Catholic hierarchy which tries to keep the movement within the diocesan and parochial boundaries. The leadership of many groups splits up and each leader starts his or her own group. Some of the priest leaders take part in movements towards division. The most famous among them is Archie Guiriba, a Franciscan priest, who founded *Shalom* and organizes his own TV masses and miracle crusades. In some dioceses bishops try to stop the spread of this group, yet people are very attracted by the healing sessions and keep flocking to the masses and prayer rallies of Guiriba.

One of the causes of the splitting up of the early Charismatic movement is its elitist character. Charismatics are middle class people who somehow realize that they have 'to put good order into their private life'.[18] This promise of generous, practising Catholics hardly addresses the chaotic world of the poor who have to survive in the slums of the cities. William Joseph Seymour, one of the initiators of Pentecostalism, believed 'that the breaking of the colour line was a much surer sign than tongue-speaking of God's blessing and the Spirit's healing presence'.[19] In the Philippines, the line to be broken is not colour but social classes. The boundary set by the official church to belong to a Charismatic group is formulated by the middle class clergy and laity. It is a

---

[18] See the 'The Promise of the Sacred Heart Community', a covenant community in Baguio City.
[19] Cox, *Fire from Heaven*, 64.

boundary of power and possession. Ordinary people are not able to cross this boundary to find a home within the Charismatic movement. They search for other Charismatic manifestations. This explains the El Shaddai phenomenon and the many popular expressions of charismata.

Brother Mike Velarde and El Shaddai

Described by *Asiaweek* in 1996 as a Filipino superstar and classified among the fifty most powerful people in Asia is the Catholic preacher Mario 'Mike' Z. Velarde. He is lovingly called 'Brother Mike' by the members of his El Shaddai congregation.[20] The story of Mike starts in 1978.[21] At the age of 37, he was waiting in hospital for heart surgery. He believes that he was miraculously healed after receiving a revelation. In the following years, as a movie producer and real estate developer, Mike gave his financial support to the CCRM in Manila. He founded the El Shaddai DWXI–PPFI (Prayer Partner Foundation, Inc.), and devoted himself to the radio apostolate. A new revelation in 1982 told him, 'Come, and build me a centre'. This led to the master plan of a huge basilica. He brought the plan of the basilica all the way to Rome to be blessed by the Pope. God had, however, other plans. Mike experienced three major setbacks that he attributed to the devil. In 1984, his business collapsed. This was followed by a crisis in his family and in his DWXI radio station. Within the experience of these crises, he understood the real meaning of God's call. God did not want him to build a basilica, but a holy temple of people.

In 1988, Mike Velarde's 'financial trouble was miraculously over'. Since then, 'the work of the Lord at DWXI-PPFI has spread unto the ends of the earth. Chapters in Hong Kong, Canada, USA, Singapore, the Middle East, Italy, United Kingdom and Japan have mushroomed'.[22] The El Shaddai organization has indeed experienced phenomenal growth and now has more than half a million card-bearing members in the Philippines and a hundred thousand abroad. Its real following by 'attendants' is much higher, estimated to reach as high as seven million.

During election campaigns, politicians attend El Shaddai rallies. Mike became President Joseph Estrada's spiritual adviser in 1998. He skilfully readjusted his position, however, after the fall of Estrada in 2001. Financially,

---

[20] *Asiaweek*, 22, 38 (September 20, 1996), 36-43. El Shaddai, the mountain (almighty) God, is an ancient name for Yahweh, found frequently in the P tradition (e.g. Gen 28.3, Ex 6.3).

[21] Brother Mariano 'Mike' Z. Velarde, *How to Win Your Battles All the Time* (Makati: El Shaddai Miracle Publ., 1992) and *El Shaddai. General Pastoral Guidelines for Service Volunteer Workers* (1994). See Esmeralda Fortunado-Sanchez, *Karanasan ng Ilang Kasapi sa El Shaddai – DWXI-PPFI* (Manila: University of Santo Tomas, 2001).

[22] Velarde, *How to Win*, 29.

the El Shaddai also became a success story. Its headquarters in the financial district of Makati is occupied by a group of enthusiastic people who run a huge organization. Many have questioned the non-transparency of the donations from Mike's followers. No doubt, money and Mike's political role have triggered a lot of controversy. Mike himself defends his position and is not afraid to mention his past as a gambler. Gambling becomes a metaphor for his leap of faith. 'So far', he says of the salvation business, 'this is my greatest risk'.[23]

The El Shaddai has its weekly celebration in a huge field near the Philippine International Convention Centre in Manila. The anniversary and Easter celebrations at Rizal Park draw crowds of a million and more. These celebrations are broadcast on television and radio and are often attended by the chaplain of the El Shaddai in the Archdiocese of Manila, Bishop Teodoro Bacani. On the local level, the El Shaddai have parish chapters supervised by parish priests who are spiritual directors. The chapters organize a monthly mass, weekly prayer meetings, monthly study of the Catholic Catechism, seminars and healing rallies. They not only fund their own activities and support the parish, but also contribute 20% to the national fund of the foundation. The El Shaddai tries to help its followers financially.

One who reads the booklet 'Pastoral Guidelines'[24] of the El Shaddai may feel rather uneasy when reading its conclusion in which is written: 'So we will always joyfully shout: Don't worry! Be happy!!! If you obey, your miracle is on the way!' The message of Mike Velarde is, indeed, not a complex theological treatise. It is straightforward language, which addresses the experience of people, especially of the poor. He tells them: 'God loves you. Do the will of God and the Lord will take care of you, even materially. Be generous and the Lord will be generous. God is present with his blessings, but we should also be willing to accept suffering in life'.

Mike's universe is the popular universe of indigenous religion, which is still very much present in the Philippines. Evil spirits control every disease; but by prayer, we will be able to expel these spirits. Brother Mike is a great speaker who puts all Catholic clerics to shame. He has a style of his own. He is relaxed and conversational. He gives sermons with humour and jokes, yet is authoritative. He feels one with the people, uses their symbols and give them homely reminders that touch their hearts. Theologians may suspect him of proclaiming the 'prosperity gospel' of the televangelists. But he is probably much more down to earth and his message is rooted in the very struggle of survival for the Filipino, in search of a job, food, health and a home.

---

[23] *Asiaweek*, 138.
[24] Velarde, 'El Shaddai: General Pastoral Guidelines'.

What explains the success of the El Shaddai? In an excellent study, Leonardo Mercado sums up eight factors.[25] I have mentioned some of them: the charisma of Mike, an attractive liturgy, effective communication, an inculturated message, and the empowerment of the laity. I would also like to quote the conclusion in the *Asiaweek* article.

> For all the priests and politicians that pay him homage, though, Velarde does not seem to fit the role of power broker. And for all the money El Shaddai draws, Brother Mike does not appear to be a cunning televangelist of the notorious American variety. If anything, he is most similar to a self-help guru, a preacher of positive thinking and mental healing. And like those spiritual cheerleaders, he offers a philosophy (I called it 'a theology') that seems sincere, if naïve. That his teachings have rekindled confidence and hope among many of the poor is perhaps, in itself, enough of a miracle.26

Folk Catholicism and the CCRM

Harvey Cox sees the widespread appeal of Pentecostalism in the light of what he calls the recovery of 'primal spirituality'.[27] People rediscovered within the Pentecostal experience the three dimensions of this elemental spirituality: primal speech, primal piety, and primal hope. In the popular El Shaddai movement, we see this spirituality at work. People experience a religiosity which is still very much alive in Filipino Folk Catholicism.[28] Filipinos are still at home in a universe in which the Great Creator, *Apo* (elder) *Dios* overlooks the world and brings life to it by being present through a wide variety of spirits and ancestors. Many communities still have their native priest/ess (*babaylan*, shaman) who functions as a kind of powerbroker. S/he helps people to be in harmony or to restore peace with this world of spirits. The priest/ess goes into a trance (*langkap, sinasapian*, means 'possessed by') and becomes the medium in prayer, prophecy and healing. Popular Catholicism adopted this primal worldview, but added its saints and the greatest mediators of all, Jesus and Mary. Mike Velarde's El Shaddai is a Charismatic movement that is inculturated within that universe of Popular Catholicism. Mike is the great mediator, prophet, and healer who brings people in contact with God and the spirits and mediates for them.

---

[25] Leonardo Mercado, 'El Shaddai and Inculturation', *Philippiniana Sacra* 35 (September-December 2000), 485-511.

[26] *Asiaweek*, 43.

[27] Cox, *Fire from Heaven*, 81.

[28] See the books of Leonardo Mercado, *Doing Filipino Theology* (Manila: Divine Word Publ., 1997) and *Filipino Popular Devotions* (Manila: Divine Word Publ., 2000).

Brother Mike has many companions. In the nineteenth century, religious millenarian movements in Mount Banahaw, south of Manila, attracted many followers. These communities are still alive today.[29] In 1914, Felix Manalo established the *Iglesia ni Kristo* (INK) among the uneducated labouring class. He was 'the angel from the east' (Is 43.5) and God's last messenger on earth. Manalo got his inspiration from messianic sectarian movements in the USA. Today, the *Iglesia* counts around three million followers.

Cities and towns in the Philippines still have an *Apo* (or *Ingkong*, elder) around, who functions as a mediator with the spirits. The *Apo* gets possessed by Santo Niño, Hesus Nazareno, Mary or one of the saints, and leads the community in communicating with the world of the Sacred. This manifestation of the Philippine age-old religion has been a fertile ground for some Charismatic leaders who founded their own communities. Only a few studies on recent religious movements are available. I briefly summarize one particular experience in which a group of Cursillistas and Catholic Charismatics founded 'Sacrifice Valley', a community led by *Ingkong Viring* (Virginia).

The community is situated in the countryside north of Manila. Virginia was a Cursillista who came in contact with Charismatic prayer groups in the beginning of the 1970s and had a new conversion experience. She believed that the Spirit took possession of her body and made her relive the experience of Jesus. She moved with her followers to a lonely place and set up a cluster of houses. Saturday is a day of worship. When her disciples pray together, Virginia gets into a trance and gives Jesus' messages, mostly about conversion because the end is coming. People approach her and ask for healing. In the healing sessions, Virginia uses holy water and herbal concoctions, often accompanied by a purification rite, in which people confess their wrongdoings. Some are 'slain by the spirit'.

During Lent and the Holy Week, devotees flock to the place of *Ingkong Viring* to witness her way of the cross, crucifixion, death and resurrection, while being possessed by Jesus' Spirit. This reenactment is followed, in the evening, by a healing session. On Saturday morning, at least during the first years of the community, one of the *apos* (elders) presided in the celebration of the Eucharist. How such a celebration led by a lay person could be a valid Eucharist was explained by pointing to the presence of *Ingkong* Virginia. Since Virginia was possessed by Jesus, the Holy Spirit was also present and took care of the consecration. In later years, the community tried to get the approval of the bishop of the place and desisted from celebrating the Eucharist without the presence of a Catholic priest.

Are 'Sacrifice Valley' and many other popular practices manifestations of the gifts of the Spirit? They certainly do not carry the official approval of the

---

[29] Robert C. Salazar (ed), *New Religious Movements in Asia and the Pacific Islands* (Manila: De La Salle University, 1994), 176-189.

Roman Catholic Church. And yet, the question has to be asked: Did the Catholic hierarchy not stifle the charisms of the Spirit within a legalistic and ritual structure which offered very little to the common people searching for some respite and wellbeing (*ginhawa*) in the midst of poverty, sickness and suffering? I will not enter into a full-blown discernment process about the validity of the different Charismatic experiences[30] I described. I end with some impressionist ideas about the significance of the CCRM for the Filipino Catholic Church and nation.

The Significance of the CCRM

Church Renewal

The renewal of the Catholic Church in the Philippines after the Second Vatican Council had a very slow start. Mike Velarde rightly claims that 'Filipino Catholics went over to the Born-Again groups because the Catholic Church has been sacramentalized; it did not evangelize'.[31] We are a priest-centred church and these priests are tied up with sacramental duties. The CCRM and the El Shaddai have contributed greatly to changing the face of the church by reconnecting with the biblical vision of the Church as a community of disciples, in service of one another and the world through a variety of Charismatic gifts.[32] Mary C. Grey[33] points out that Christianity has to confess to a disastrous neglect of the Holy Spirit. Charismatic Christianity has corrected this situation by putting a 'qualitative religious experience' at the centre of its renewal. The Spirit which started to breathe again in Pentecostalism, which has been manifesting itself in feminist spirituality, New Age groups[34] and liberation theology, has finally also breathed life into what has been called 'the frozen people of God', the Catholic Church.

I would like to sum up a few manifestations of this renewal. Dead rituals received life by making them into prayer experiences in which the whole community participated. The role of the laity was restored. Covenant communities became laboratories in which community life was rediscovered. The Bible regained its central place in Christian life. Lay people developed

---

[30] See David Middlemiss, *Interpreting Charismatic Experience* (London: SCM Press, 1996).

[31] Mercado, 'El Shaddai and Inculturation', 497, 500.

[32] 'Acts and Decrees of the Second Plenary Council of the Philippines', 35-54.

[33] Mary C. Grey, *The Outrageous Pursuit of Hope* (London: Darton, Longman and Todd, 2000), 62-78.

[34] See Lode L. Wostyn. *A New Church for a New Age* (Quezon City: Claretian Publ., 1997), 74-76.

their talents by serving the church and society through a variety of charisms.
Many groups got conscientized and developed programmes to rebuild Filipino
society, plagued by a greedy capitalism and a corrupt elite democracy. The
recent People Revolution and the revolt of the poor (Edsa II and Edsa III)[35]
confronted the church with its failure to reach the poor. The El Shaddai and
some covenant communities succeeded in addressing the poor. These
developments may finally give birth to the church of the poor that was
envisioned in the Second Plenary Council of the Philippine Catholic Church
and in the documents of the Federation of Asian Bishops' Conferences
(FABC).[36]

The Charismatic conversion of the Catholic Church has recently been
threatened by a conservative backlash. Pope John Paul II, surrounded by a
gerontocracy led by Cardinal Ratzinger, seems to rebuild the strongly
centralized fortress church of the Counter-Reformation. Reading the
'reflections on the CCR' by Archbishop Paul Josef Cordes, episcopal adviser of
the International CCR Office in Rome, I was rather astonished to find out that
'the charism of infallibility in matters of faith and morals' and 'the gift of
discernment of charisms', is endowed on the church's shepherds.[37] I thought
that the Second Vatican Council had affirmed that this charism belonged to the
whole church. Brother Vic Gutierrez of Ligaya ng Panginoon fears that the
CCRM will soon be a cleric-led movement instead of a lay movement.
Charismatic meetings are star-studded with priests and bishops. Priests get back
into the driver's seat, something that will be gladly given by the laity who feel
safer when a sacred man is around. How do we handle this conservative
backlash? I believe that the rediscovery of the Charismatic vision of the church
within the Catholic Church, with its long clerical past, has placed us in a
tension field. An awareness of these tensions may help us to keep the right
trajectory towards renewal.

---

[35] We witnessed in January 2001 a second people's revolution which overthrew
President Estrada. Edsa stands for the highway where the people's revolt took place.
Shortly after Edsa II, a crowd of poor people occupied the Marian Shrine on Edsa and
marched to the presidential palace where they were stopped by the police and army. This
was called the Edsa III revolt (end of April).

[36] In the theological vision of the FABC, we find a strong affirmation that the Spirit of
God is at work beyond the boundaries of the Christian churches, hence mission should
be conceived in terms of a threefold dialogue, with the poor, Asian cultures and
religions.

[37] Paul Joseph Cordes, *Call to Holiness. Reflections on the Catholic Charismatic
Renewal* (Collegeville: Liturgical Press, 1997), 44-47. Cordes refers to the *Catechism of
the Catholic Church*, articles 890 and 801.

Tensions

Harvey Cox sees a shift taking place in the struggle to be the ultimate source of meaning.[38] The two competitors of previous centuries, scientific modernity and traditional religion are two tired boxers. Two new competitors are entering the ring in the twenty-first century: fundamentalism versus experientialism. He places Pentecostalism in the experientialist camp. We can do the same with the CCRM and yet I share the doubt of Cox. The struggle between fundamentalism and experientialism cuts right through Pentecostalism, the CCRM, and the churches. Only a constant discernment in which we succeed in keeping a creative tension between these two competitors, will create the freedom to let the Church become a church of the Spirit a church of love, of order and peace (1 Cor. 12.31; 14.39-40). While listening to testimonies of members of the Filipino CCRM, I met several tensions and stumbling blocks which I summarize under five headings.[39]

I already mentioned the first one: the tension between charisms and the institution. In a strongly clericalized and centralized church, the temptation of the laity is to let the priests occupy the driver's seat, risking imprisoning the freedom of the spirit, manifested in a variety of charisms, within the cage of an institution. As a teacher of theology, I have been pondering for many years on the book of Ralph Martin, *A Crisis of Truth*.[40] He was one of the founders of the CCRM who suddenly turned conservative, if not fundamentalist and succeeded in condemning the best minds of present-day Catholic theology. I recently heard the same reaction from a group of Charismatic leaders who found it necessary to promise absolute obedience to the church's authorities and the teachings of the church. Not too much space will be left to the Spirit and his/her charisms, if they are hemmed in by the 'new' Roman Catechism, the papal moral code, and the Roman laws and rituals. A sound competition, an openness to pluralism, and a critical spirit of dialogue can be better alternatives.

A second tension creates an opposition between an often strongly emotional prayer experience and social involvement. In the course of my interviews, a leader of a covenant community expressed his frustration in trying to orient his group towards a stronger social commitment. We are good, he said, in handling prayer, in the study of and sharing about personal relationships, family life, sexuality issues and so on. We are a nice community in a warm nest of friendship, but we did not do enough to open our doors to the really poor people. We are trained to be Eucharistic ministers and counsellors but we do not know how to bring Christ to the slums. The vision is present among the laity. They know and they believe that evangelization and social action cannot

---

[38] Cox, *Fire from Heaven*, 299-321.

[39] Some of these tensions are discussed in Nigel Scotland, *Charismatics and the Next Millenium* (London: Hodder & Stoughton, 1995).

[40] Ralph Martin, *A Crisis of Truth* (Ann Arbor: Servant Books, 1982).

be separated. But in reality we all still have to learn to become more reflective of what the church wants to be: not only a church for, but a church *of* the poor.[41]

The struggle of ordinary daily life and the quest for the miraculous is a third tension field, which is difficult to handle in the Filipino setting. I keep remembering a healing session in which a Charismatic healer took away the crutches of a boy who was born cripple. The next thing that happened was a boy crawling over the floor until they lifted him and returned the crutches. Poor people flock to healing sessions and many are enthralled by the magic of Brother Mike who throws handkerchiefs containing three pieces of *calamansi* (small lemons) in the crowd, and blesses eggs, bottles of water and oil. They are symbols which fit within Filipino culture.[42] They may bring some joy and consolation, but the harshness of daily life still has to be faced. The health and wealth gospel stresses the joyful dimension in its meeting with the Spirit. Yet, poverty, suffering and pain are still there and will have to be overcome.[43]

A fourth tension field is created by a fundamentalist reading of the Bible which can hardly address present-day faith experience. The *Iglesia ni Kristo* and fundamentalist groups are keen to argue with Catholics by producing a chain of biblical quotations. Catholic apologists often get onto the fundamentalist platform, and they end up joining biblical shootouts. Catholics, especially Charismatics, have rediscovered the Bible. They also have made an attempt to bring the Word of God to their contemporary experience. Often, however, they have not fully succeeded in unearthing the riches of biblical texts because they are not familiar with the critical, historical tools of present-day exegesis. The Bible reports the faith experiences of a people. These experiences were interpreted and became a message about God and God's action in history. Some basic knowledge of the historical and cultural context in which Israel interpreted and expressed the presence of Yahweh can help us to reconstruct the underlying experiences of a people. Once we have uncovered these experiences, we can easily arrive at a dialogue with our own faith experiences. In such a dialogue, the message of the Bible is again a living Word addressing our own life situation. The meeting between Scripture and present-day experience often fails because the Bible is understood in a fundamentalist and literal way. Instead of a message rooted in the experience of a people, it becomes a chain of doctrinal and legal statements, imposing rules and regulations, apparently under the auspices of the Holy Spirit. Most Catholic Charismatics can hardly accept such a fundamentalist imposition. They find a way out of a literal reading by spiritualizing the biblical text. The meaning of the text is adjusted to fit into some very personal, spiritual experiences. For

---

[41] 'Acts and Decrees of the Second Plenary Council of the Philippines', 47-52

[42] Mercado, 'El Shaddai and Inculturation', 504-505.

[43] See Cox, *Fire From Heaven*, 315.

example, the master symbol of Jesus' preaching, the Kingdom of God is a political symbol which challenged the authorities of Jesus' time. The symbol gets spiritualized and now addresses nice people who are looking forward to the heavenly bliss in the kingdom of heaven. A spiritualized reading of the Bible is a poor alternative to fundamentalism.

A fifth tension field is created by the CCRM being challenged to enter into the political realities of the country. It is a known fact that political manipulation and powerplay have never been far away from the Philippine Catholic Church and its hierarchy. Politicians who attend the El Shaddai rallies do not fail to also visit the residence of Cardinal Sin, the Archbishop of Manila. Bishop Bacani, the chaplain of El Shaddai, has repeatedly stressed that the gospel failed to touch political life. Politics in the Philippines has never been evangelized. This task of evangelization belongs to the laity, but until now, the hierarchy has been in the lead. Some covenant communities and the leadership of El Shaddai have explored ways and means to be present in the political scene and to shake the foundations of a corrupt elite democracy. The task of the evangelization of politics is still ahead of us.

The Future

Prophetic movements, within a strongly institutionalized church, tend to be tamed and forced into the framework of the institution. This observation of the leader of a covenant community does not sound very hopeful. He feels that the CCRM is dying. The exercise of charisms has declined, prayer meetings have lost their freedom and creativity, the leaders are poorly trained. We are caught, he said, in patterns and prescriptions that sap the life from our prayer and community experiences.

Others, however, are more hopeful. The El Shaddai elders, for example, are full of enthusiasm. They express their hope in the following statements. 'We have to work hard and focus on evangelization. We can double our number. We have still a great harvest in front of us, especially among the poor and the migrant workers abroad'. These migrant workers themselves are missionaries in their host countries.

Pessimism or hope? I believe that by heeding the recommendations I received from some leaders, the CCRM can look forward in hope towards a promising future. What has to be done? First, leaders of the CCRM have to refocus on the baptism in the Spirit and the charisms. Second, they are to seek a better training programme for themselves. The gift of teaching is in the third place in Paul's list (1 Cor. 12.28). In our Catholic tradition, priests tend to claim all the charisms yet most of them are not exactly brilliant teachers. The CCRM leaders can express their support to the Spirit by creating possibilities for the laity to receive professional training as teachers and animators of the community. Thirdly, they are to develop real communities. The creation of Basic Ecclesial Communities has been the focus of pastoral planning in the

Philippine church. But pastoral action hardly got started because instead we have been busy writing position papers. Some Charismatic communities can show us the way. Finally, I got permission to quote Bishop Bacani and I hope I will be faithful. As Christians, we have to evangelize our society. It means, we have to address the social and political issues of the country. The laity needs to be encouraged to enter into the socio-political scene. The Roman Synod of 1971 on 'Justice in the World' (No 6) declared that social commitment is an integral part of evangelization. The task is ahead of us. I also share the prophetic dreams for the twenty-first century of Mary C. Grey, when she quotes Hyun Chung's sermon in Canberra (1991):

> Dear Sisters and Brothers, with the energy of the Spirit, let us tear apart all walls of division and the culture of death which separates us. And let us participate in the Holy Spirit's economy of life, fighting for our life on this earth, in solidarity with all living beings... Wild wind of the Holy Spirit blow to us. Let us welcome her, letting ourselves go in her wild rhythm of life. Come Holy Spirit, renew the whole of creation. Amen.[44]

---

[44] Grey, *The Outrageous Pursuit of Hope*, 78.

Filipino Independent Pentecostalism and Biblical Transformation

Jae Yong Jeong

Introduction

There are many denominational Protestant or Pentecostal groups and indigenous Protestant or Pentecostal groups that have been established since religious freedom was established in the Philippines.[1] I have selected three independent Pentecostal groups as examples of this phenomenon: Pentecostal Missionary Church of Christ (PMCC), Keys of the Kingdom Ministries Inc. (KKMI) and the Bread of Life (BL), and a religious movement that has syncretistically combined elements of Pentecostal practice and Filipino indigenous religion, *Santuala*. The study will also attempt to show the degree to which Filipino Pentecostalism has been indigenized or transformed according to the responses made by Filipino believers. Finally, the essay discusses how the Spirit is empowering Filipino people to respond to the Christian faith in such a way as to discover their own spirituality and to transform this into Christian spirituality. The implications of this for the relationship between the gospel and culture will be sketched in conclusion.[2]

---

[1] Douglas J. Elwood, *Churches and Sects in the Philippines* (Dumaguete City, Philippines: Sillinam University, 1968), 66. F.H. Chaffe (ed), *Area Handbook for the Philippines* (Washingon, D.C.: Government Printing Office, 1969), 168. Kenton J. Clymenr, *Protestant Missionaries in the Philippines: An Inquiry into the American Colonial Mentality* (Urban and Chicago: University of Illinois Press, 1986), 3. Stephen Neil, *A History of Christian Missions* (New York: Penguin Books, 1982), 292, 93. Jae Yong Jeong, 'Filipino Pentecostal Spirituality: An Investigation Into Filipino Indigenous Spirituality and Pentecostalism in the Philippines' (ThD Thesis, University of Birmingham 2001). Frances L. Starner, *The Rising Sun and Gangled Roots: A Philippine Profile* (Hong Kong: Christian Conference of Asia – International Affairs, 1986), 7.

[2] For more details on these topics, see Jeong, 'Filipino Pentecostal Spirituality', 51-55, 95-111, 182-236.

The Pentecostal Missionary Church of Christ (Fourth Watch)

The PMCC was founded in 1974; this indigenous Pentecostal church is one of the fastest growing independent churches in the Philippines. When the church first appeared, it was regarded as a 'cult', but it has since become one of the largest indigenous Pentecostal churches in the Philippines, with around 500 churches[3] and twelve missions in several Asian countries and further afield.[4] According to Eleazer Javier, the PMCC split from the Church of the Foursquare Gospel in the Philippines and was called the 'People's Missionary Church' before splitting again. After that it became known as the 'Pentecostal Missionary Church of Christ'.[5] Formerly it had strong links with the North American denominational Pentecostal church but separated in order to retain its identity and national independence.

Adherents of the PMCC believe that it is biblically founded on the Book of Acts and that Jesus Christ is its founder.[6] Just as the early Christian church had its own leaders, so the PMCC has its own apostle, Arisenio T. Ferriol, believed to be appointed by Jesus Christ, who continues to lead his churches and who has given Ferriol the authority to supervize this particular church.[7] The PMCC emphasizes the Pentecostal experiences of the early church in the Book of Acts and believes that the continuing presence of the Holy Spirit is the source of all spiritual gifts. The most important spiritual gift for them is the apostleship, for it still continues in the church through the leadership of Ferriol.[8]

The PMCC believes that 'in the church each one has a particular gift that is helping to serve, administer and strengthen one another'[9] and that these spiritual gifts are interrelated to edify the church.[10] The exercise of those spiritual gifts must be used according to the teachings of Ferriol because God placed the apostles first in the church.[11] Furthermore, 'since apostles are the ones laying the foundation as expert builders by the preaching of Jesus Christ,

---

[3] Jaime B. Rull, a pastor of the PMCC, interviewed on 14/04/1999 in Baguio City.

[4] Hong Kong, Macao, Singapore, Taiwan, Japan, New Zealand, Nigeria, Papua New Guinea, Saudi Arabia, Canada, Hawaii, the USA and other nations which are not listed, e.g., South Korea and China. According to 8th Convention: 17-23 November, 1997, Manila, Philippines, there are 206 churches in the Philippines. Rull, Interview.

[5] Eleazer Javier, interviewed at Taytay Methodist Community Church, Inc. in Taytay, Rizal in Greater Manila, 04/05/1999.

[6] Ibid.

[7] Ibid.

[8] Leticia S. Ferriol Maran, Maranatha Christian Academy (school Director), interviewed at Marikina Church in Manila 02/05/1999.

[9] Alex Dela Cruz, 'The Word: Evangelising the Lost', *Edifying the Saints*' 51 (June 1997), 3.

[10] Dela Cruz, 'The Word', 3.

[11] Ibid.

they are the authority to proclaim the good news (Romans 10.15)'.[12] In this belief the PMCC especially emphasizes the gift of apostleship, because it claims that other Pentecostals are practicing only limited spiritual gifts: 'speaking in other tongues, healing...but more we also believe to be Pentecostal'.[13] This belief leads to specific modifications in the function of the church through 'five-fold administrative gifts, apostles, prophets, evangelists, pastors and teachers'.[14] Therefore the existence of its apostleship is one of the most important beliefs of the PMCC, since it not only emphasizes the spiritual gifts, (which are also being practised by other groups), but it also continues to promote apostleship in the church in order to function more effectively, for 'every gift of operation we receive and apply has the same for the church'.[15] Regarding the PMCC's apostle, Art Ferriol has said, 'We have living apostles. In fact, the Word indicates this by the grace of God. God has confirmed, as Paul said in 2 Cor. 12.12 'the things that mark apostles, signs, wonders and miracles were done among you with great result''.[16] As a result, Arisenio Ferriol is now the PMCC's apostle appointed by Jesus Christ who thus demonstrates continuity of apostleship.[17]

The PMCC compares itself with other groups of Pentecostal churches in this context of leadership through an apostle. For example, if an apostle still exists today, there is no conflict of doctrinal problems or interpretation of the Bible on account of the presence of several Pentecostal denominations. Yet Pentecostal denominations other than the PMCC are concerned with promoting their particular doctrinal positions. The result is a lack of Christian unity among the Filipino Pentecostal church as a whole. To counteract this, the PMCC apostle, Arisenio Ferriol has appeared on Filipino television to explain his authoritative role with a view to attaining unity in the Pentecostal church.[18] Art Ferriol stated that the PMCC has only one authority invested in its apostle to lead its churches because his power is given by Jesus Christ himself. This kind of leadership demonstrates the restoration of the spiritual gifts just as Paul defined them and which were subsequently adopted in the doctrines of the early church. Arisenio Ferriol clearly defines the PMCC's own doctrines and teachings,[19] so his ministry is not limited to only one congregation but is extended to the other PMCC congregations in the Philippines and in other countries for the purpose of leading, serving and teaching members. Arisenio Ferriol not only has

---

[12] Ibid.

[13] Art Ferriol, Interview.

[14] Dela Cruz, 'The Word', 3.

[15] Ibid.

[16] Ibid.

[17] Rull, Interview.

[18] Art Ferriol, Interview.

[19] Ferriol Maran, Interview.

authority to interpret the Bible but also claims to be God's true representative for the PMCC.[20]

The meaning of the restoration of spiritual gifts, which has been already mentioned, needs to be explained. Firstly, the meaning of 'Pentecostal' in the PMCC differs from most other Pentecostal perspectives where the existence of an apostleship is generally denied. 'Pentecostal' for the PMCC means to revert to the early belief and practice of the first Christian church in the Book of Acts by having apostles in their churches today.

Secondly, Filipino Pentecostalism is an inadequate term to be used in the context of the PMCC because the PMCC prefers to be called 'Biblical Pentecostalism'; to name the church 'the Church of Christ, Pentecostal and missionary' is merely to indicate its general direction.[21] Thirdly, Pentecostalism not only refers to specific regions, nationals or even peoples in their own context in developing the idea of the work of the Holy Spirit, but according to the PMCC, Pentecostals must be biblical to achieve unity through an apostle's leadership.[22] Therefore using the words 'Biblical Pentecostal' for the PMCC restores the full meaning of Pentecostalism universally. Lastly, by being called 'Biblical Pentecostal' by its Filipino leaders, the PMCC increases its indigenization. The PMCC declares that it is wholly Filipino by maintaining its strong independence and it regards itself as an example for other Pentecostal denominations. It could be the means of uniting Pentecostals under Christ through the leadership of apostleship throughout the world.

The PMCC is identified with Filipino Pentecostal spiritualities which are trying to be 'Biblical Pentecostal' or manifesting the 'Restoration of the Spiritual Gifts' by the power of the Holy Spirit in the Philippine context. House to house visits, street evangelism, open-air preaching, 'little flock',[23] unity with holiness, strong leadership, the sacrificial service of workers and prayer are ways in which the spirituality of the PMCC is expressed in practice.[24]

The PMCC is developing an independent Filipino Pentecostal church, is strongly identified with the nationalistic identity and is accurately characterized as having native Filipino Pentecostal leaders rather than foreign Pentecostal ones. They have different views of Bible interpretation and the doctrinal conflicts between denominations. The PMCC is strongly independent of western Pentecostalism and concerned with constructing its own biblical belief system in the context of Filipino indigenous spirituality.

---

[20] Ibid.

[21] Ibid.

[22] Art Ferriol, Interview, and Ferriol Maran, Interview.

[23] Art Ferriol, Interview.

[24] Interviewed with one member of the PMCC, 18/04/1999.

Keys of the Kingdom Ministries

The KKMI started as Life in the Spirit Fellowship in about 1982. Michael Pangwi Sr priest for 23 years in the Episcopal Church, felt called by God for the KKMI and continues to be its leader.[25] Since its emergence in Baguio City, the membership of this fellowship has grown to approximately 5,000.[26] Fifty-eight daughter churches exist in nine local districts and, according to Pangwi, the KKMI has outreaches abroad in Hong Kong, Singapore, Macao and Taiwan. The KKMI is now challenging many Filipino churches in northern Luzon to establish indigenous forms of Pentecostalism while maintaining their independence. An interview with the leader of the group reveals its rapid growth as an independent Filipino Pentecostal church.

Michael J. Pangwi was uncertain of his future even as he was serving as an Anglican priest; he had been hospitalized many times and the struggle to find his true vocation during the 1970s led to a strong desire for spiritual renewal. He was invited to attend a seminar, 'Community Building and Development', at Ateneo de Manila in 1971 where he was taught a new concept called 'Liberation Theology'. This teaching promotes the concept of ministers who preach the gospel while at the same time emphasizing human rights,[27] which he thought was even more misleading! He reacted by saying 'instead, rebellion against authorities began to grip me'.[28] He continued to search for God's guidance and another opportunity arose to develop his gifts when he was invited to attend a seminar on 'Spiritual Renewal' on 20 March, 1973. This occasion allowed him to experience the power of the Holy Spirit; 'I was overflowing with the joy of the Lord, I received the baptism of the Holy Spirit!'[29] he exclaimed. Another spiritual experience occurred when he was invited to Singapore to attend a 'Spiritual Renewal Seminar', during the course of which he felt that his profound Christian living had started. When he returned to the Philippines, Pangwi received a 'New Direction', which brought him to a new revelation of the knowledge of God. This happened while he was praying in the mountains above Lubas (La Trinidad, Benguet, near Baguio City). He spent the whole day engrossed with God's word, communicating with him in such a way that he claimed he was directly entrusted with an inexpressibly beautiful experience which literally lifted him up to see 'the

---

[25] Michael J. Pangwi, pastor-director of KKMI, interviewed at Family Bldg., Km. 3 LA Trinidad Benguet 2061 Philippines, 15/04/1999.
[26] The Life in the Spirit Fellowship at Family Building Km. 3 La Trinidad, Benguet Philippines.
[27] Michael J. Pangwi. 'How Keys of the Kingdom Ministries was Conceived', in *Keys of the Kingdom Ministries, Inc.: 1991 Anniversary Magazine* (Life in the Spirit Fellowship, July 1991), 6.
[28] Pangwi, 'How Keys', 6.
[29] Ibid.

vision of the ministry and responsibility' being demanded of him. His understanding of this experience was clarified through being led to Jesus' reply to Peter's confession.[30] This personal experience totally changed his life, after which he began to proclaim the Good News and be led by the Holy Spirit.[31] This direct revelation from God gave him clear directions to build the KKMI, and many miracles followed.[32] A growing conviction of personal guidance through God's Word connects these ministries[33] and Pangwi continues to receive guidance[34] because he strongly believes that this ministry is carried on by the command of God and is based on Bible teaching.[35]

It is necessary to pose some questions relating both to Filipino indigenous spirituality as such and to its establishing a connection with Filipino Pentecostal spirituality: How is Pangwi's ministry related to the traditional belief system? Why did he separate from the Episcopal Church and how will the KKMI prove that Filipino Pentecostals promote the development of the individual? Actually, Pangwi had problems maintaining spiritual direction while serving in the ministry, for he was led by his appointment in the Episcopal Church to places where he had financial support from the denomination. Sometimes this caused him to disagree with the Bible while still depending on it. The church's doctrinal belief confused him and held him back, for if he really believed what the denominational teachings were that should be taught to members, he wondered whether they would have enough faith to be independent. There seemed to be many problems in his ministry at this point. However, Pangwi wanted to be spiritually renewed and this changed everything. The old traditional belief system of the Philippines was that the religious leaders had direct words from gods or ancestral spirits and a similar kind of Pentecostal practice convinced early Christian believers, since it related both to their daily physical and spiritual needs and to the belief in traditional spiritual leaders with authority to bestow on others anything from the supreme being or the ancestors. Being a leader of the KKMI, Pangwi has an absolute authority from Jesus Christ which is given to each local church's leaders, who thus become delegated ministers.[36] Many signs, wonders and miracles which show God's special appointment of the KKMI have increased the membership of the church.

---

[30] Matthew 16.17-19.

[31] Pangwi, 'How Keys', 7.

[32] Pangwi, Interview.

[33] Pangwi, 'How Keys', 8.

[34] Ibid.

[35] Ibid.

[36] Jeong, 'Filipino', appendix VII 'The Vision: Keys of the Kingdom Ministries, Inc. Life in the Spirit Fellowship.

One of the characteristics of the KKMI is its emphasis on reverting to the Bible. This is characterized by Pangwi's personal experience of the denominational belief system, which made him identify more clearly with the Word of God. He believes that the purpose of his ministry is as follows: 'The KKMI is to equip the saints with the living and revealed truth of God's Word, so that the Christian can truly be a powerful and effective witness in the Kingdom of God'.[37] As a priest, he was financially unstable; without support from the denominational organization he could not have had a ministry. This is true of most denominational ministers who depend not only on their groups but also on finding real identity with the Filipinos; the KKMI demonstrates that Filipinos are capable of creating indigenous Filipino Pentecostalism. Through Pangwi's personal involvement with the movement, the KKMI has established how the Filipino Pentecostal church can be independent by developing specific elements of indigenous Filipino Pentecostal spirituality. These relate to the following specific characteristics: his charismatic leadership, dependence on the Word of God, his ministry and sacrificial work accompanied by 'signs and wonders', independence of any foreign missions and being rather strongly identified with the nationalist identity and with development work. The KKMI is an example of an indigenous Pentecostal independent church in northern Luzon that has restored some elements of Filipino indigenous spirituality and it is a model of good practice both for Filipino Pentecostal churches and other denominational churches. It involves powerful elements of the work of the Holy Spirit in leading Filipinos according to God's providence and empowering them by biblical transformation to respond and discover their real identity within their existing context.

The Bread of Life

The BL church began in Manila on 12 August, 1982 when twelve people who believed they had experienced the life-changing power of Jesus Christ, including Butch Conde, the leader of this group, set out to establish the BL ministries in many different surrounding urban areas. Since the BL started, the membership of 'Crossroad 77', the mother or central church, has grown to over 12,500;[38] five Sunday services are held and there are five distinctive regional districts containing a total of 54 churches which are well established as rapidly growing local churches in urban areas.[39]

---

[37] Pangwi, Ibid.

[38] Miriam H. Carandang, Associate Resident Pastor of Touch of Glory Prayer Mountain of Bread of Life in the Philippines, interviewed at the office of the Bread of Life in Manila, 30/04/1999.

[39] Jeong, 'Filipino' appendix VIII 'The BL's Church Listing'.

According to *Crossroad 77: Bridging the Way to the twenty-first century*,[40] there were five stages of change in the growing membership when the Bread of Life Church moved from one place to another. On 14 November, 1982 there were 120 members at Maryknoll College (now Miriam College); by 15 January, 1984 the BL had temporary gatherings at the Heart Center in Quezon City in the Philippines. In the period from 22 January, 1984 to 29 March, 1987 the BL transferred to Celebrity Sports Plaza on Capitol Hills, Quezon City to accommodate another 1,200 members. On 5 April, 1987 the church moved again to the Circle Theater with around 1,800 to 2,000 members attending each of its five gatherings and lastly by 29 November, 1998, with the dedication of Crossroad 77, there were five gatherings averaging 2,500 members each. Here, it is necessary to consider only the origin of the BL.

While Butch Conde was studying at the Far East Advanced School of Theology[41] in Manila, he was deeply concerned about the economic situation of the Philippines and especially about the question of how Filipinos were to be spiritually renewed and their faith indigenized. His ministry was influenced by one particular Korean missionary, Won Suk Ma, who suggested a visit to Korea for him to see how churches there were growing.[42] There he observed the power of prayer in strengthening the church. He said 'Lord! Once I go to the Philippines, I will teach people how to pray'.[43] Actually he had a burning desire to minister to prostitutes in Olongapo where the American naval military base was located. Without telling anybody, led by God and keeping to his plan, he received a provision of 400,000 pesos that could be used for any spiritual purpose and he was also offered two hectares of land which in 1989 became a Prayer Mountain. At that time Conde was planning a halfway house for prostitutes, but the twelve members who started the BL discussed it and finally a more comprehensive plan was revealed during a church service.[44] Conde prayed for God's confirmation for the new work to open in Loyola Heights. The Catholic school, Maryknoll College, offered its auditorium for a Sunday gathering on 14 November, 1982; this was the start of the BL there as an independent church.

Several questions need to be considered to discover how the BL is related to Filipino spirituality and also how it contributed to the development of Filipino Pentecostal independent groups. Data supplied by the founder, Conde, reveals

---

[40] Benjie Cruz (ed.), *Crossroad 77: Bridging the Way to the 21st Century* (Manila, Philippines: Bread of Life Ministries, 1999), 6, 7.

[41] Far East Advanced School of Theology became Asia Pacific Theological Seminary which was with Bethel Bible College's campus in Manila and it was established for the purpose of Asian Pentecostal leaders of Assemblies of God.

[42] Carandang, Interview.

[43] Ibid.

[44] Cruz, *Crossroad*, 3.

that his personal calling from God is of primary importance in his ministry and in revealing Filipino identities in the changing social context. This is especially true of the urban areas, since his ministry is focussed in the metropolitan districts where the needs of the urban population are culturally different from those of rural Filipinos. Eleazer Javier says, 'The urbanized are more open, so more westernized, while those who grow up in rural areas are more strongly influenced by old Filipino values'.[45] In other words, 'It is very difficult for the Filipino Pentecostal to establish a Filipino or Filipinized biblical theology'.[46] Conde is strongly convinced that Filipinos can be independent through prayer and the power of the Holy Spirit, which is the way that indigenous values and practices can be embraced. For example, since the start of his ministry the importance of 'sacrifices' is emphasized: he receives no salary from the church, whereas many other denominational churches and some of their leaders depend on financial support from foreign sources. The BL, however, wants to show that God himself is providing for the Filipino churches.[47] Struggling with the colonial mentality, Conde wants to establish how the Filipino can be independent from foreign missionaries. This is one reaction to imperialism and post-colonialism. Following Conde's example, none of the BL ministers receives any salary from their churches but they do receive individual love offerings from church members. Carandang said, 'when a recognized minister is characterized and proves his work, he sacrifices his life to the Lord without receiving salary from the church'.[48]

Conde also finds that prayer is another source of recovering the Filipino identity. Prayer is emphasized at the Touch of Glory Prayer Mountain and many members and ministers are learning how to pray. Paul Yoo emphasizes the use of specific prayer methods: the early morning prayer, the prayer chain and fasting prayer.[49] The last is especially important to enable Filipino ministers to renew and deepen their spiritual experience. Once more than 300 pastors and ministers fasted up to forty days.[50] Prayer assures Filipinos that they are being revived, as are the churches, thus freeing them from the colonial mentality through the power of God.[51]

The BL emphasizes social development. For example, the BL established the SyCip Plantation Inc. (SPI), which is an extraordinarily integrated farming system involving the rotation of sugarcane, saltbeds, coconut trees, mango

---

[45] Javier, Interview.

[46] Ibid.

[47] Carandang, Interview.

[48] Ibid.

[49] According to Yoo and Carandang, the BL has these kinds of prayer meetings. Carandang, *Interview*.

[50] Yoo, Interview.

[51] Cruz, *Crossroad*, 27.

trees, milkfish ponds, prawn ponds, poultry raising, egg farming, cattle fattening and cattle breeding.[52] The purpose of the SPI is mainly to promote social responsibility by means of integrated farming based on ecological considerations, through personal empowerment seminars on improving work and living, team-building activities and through cooperatives and medical facilities working in the community.[53] Through the SPI, the BL wants to demonstrate how selfimprovement can be achieved in Manjuyod, Negros Orientals as many Filipinos are working abroad to resolve their financial problems. This produces a huge social problem of instability in which many women are sexually abused during long periods of separation from their husbands.[54]

Another area of social concern is the garbage removal from Metro Manila, a city choked with trash and full of foul-smelling streets and cockroach-infested public places. Here, through the programme of *Zero Kalat sa Kaunlaran*, every piece of trash and waste is being recycled by 25 volunteer families.[55] This is one example of how seriously the Pentecostal church is taking its social responsibilities.

Since the BL started, the House of Refuge (HR) has been a part of its ministries. In Metro Manila, many children are 'house refugees' and involved in prostitution, drug addiction, and gang warfare. The HR provides food, clothing and medical care and offers formal and informal educational programmes, including value formation classes. Furthermore, spiritual guidance and reconciliation either with original or alternative families are also part of its work.[56]

The founder of BL, Butch Conde, wants to build a strong national uniqueness by becoming independent of foreign sources. The previous concept of the Filipino identity did not distinguish between its own characteristics and new forms of foreign religious power. By rediscovering Filipino indigenous spirituality the BL is contextualized within the urban rather than the rural areas, where churches are already more strongly connected to the indigenous belief system than to any new religious movement. The BL emphasizes the independence of the indigenous Pentecostal church and is challenging other denominational churches to revive their identity through the Bible as well. From the beginning of Conde's ministry, his personal commitment demonstrates that his sacrificial offering to God is essentially as a model Filipino Pentecostal leader. The BL is characterized by prayer and sacrifice

---

[52] Ibid., 24.

[53] Ibid.

[54] See, appendix IV. 'What the Churches in Hong Kong are Doing to Help the Filipino Domestic Helpers'.

[55] Cruz, *Crossroad*, 25.

[56] Ibid.

based on the text from John 6.48; 'I am the bread of life, (NASB)'... 'Where we are only living on bread... we believe in five loaves and two fishes and we give thanks and offer them to God for him to multiply for us'.[57] This belief is founded on the distinction which the BL applies to the uniqueness of the Christian journey by emphasizing the centrality of Christ, the foundation of scriptures, prayer, the centrality of worship, operating by the power of God, the way of service through sacrifice and being people of faith.[58] These distinctive marks lead the members to responsible social involvement.

Santuala

Some church members, especially in Northern Luzon, are part of a religious movement called *Santuala,* which is at the same time misleading and attractive to some missionaries and church members who do not know much about it. This group is engaged in certain Pentecostal practices such as healing, dancing, trance experience, communicating with spirits and seeing visions. For the *Santuala*, the sacred days for worship are Friday and Sunday and during these days the members are strictly forbidden to work and even prohibited from taking a bath.[59] Furthermore, the *Santuala* includes syncretistic elements borrowed from Filipino indigenous religions.

According to information from a Methodist minister,[60] *Santuala* was founded by Maura Balagsa, an *Ibaloi*[61] woman, who was healed by the prayer of a Christian pastor when she was critically ill and her family and friends had given her up for dead. When the pastor prayed for her she had a vision that she would become an evangelist and preach about Jesus Christ and heal many sick people after she was healed. Maura Balagsa, who died aged 120, became a healer and founder of *Santuala* c. 1950. According to Julie Ma, from the 1950s to the 1970s *Santuala* enjoyed great success and hundreds came to join it.[62]

The practice of *Santuala* contains some interesting characteristics related to Filipino indigenous religions, as well as some characteristics that may have originated in the Pentecostal churches. The *Santuala* have no temples and meetings are usually held either in members' or leaders' houses—especially

---

[57] Carandang, Interview.

[58] Ibid.

[59] Mail interview with Patrick Aguiwas, pastor of Saddle Assembly of God Church in Benguet in the Philippines 30/05/1999.

[60] The interview was conducted in 1993. The Methodist pastor was an assistant pastor of the United Methodist Church in Baguio City. The pastor worked with *Santuala* because he believed in the work of the Holy Spirit and he tried to convert them to the Methodist church.

[61] One of the Igorot tribes.

[62] Julie Ma, 'Santuala: A Case of Pentecostal Syncretism' (Presented at World Pentecostal Conference at Full Gospel Church in Seoul in 1998).

where any important event such as a wedding, funeral, or thanksgiving is being celebrated. Occasionally a special service is held at a sick person's house, because the healing ministry is one of the most important functions for members. During the healing ministry, either in the middle or in the last part of their service, the members present the sick person. The leader asks if someone has a vision, which is called *buya*. The *buya* would be interpreted as meaning that the sick person needs to have a mission (*bonggoy*), which must be obeyed so that healing could take place. The members believe that the causes of sickness and disease are the sins of their forefathers so they need to ask forgiveness to restore their body and to have harmony with ancestral and spiritual beings.[63]

The *Santuala* uses the Bible and Christian hymns in the services; members usually sing *Baligi*, which means 'victory', a song which many Igorot Pentecostal churches now use in the course of their worship. The *Santuala* does not have a formal leader but an elder or elders who act as mediums between God and the members and give prophetic messages (*balakad*), which are interpreted by some of the members as either warnings or blessings in their services and other major activities.[64] The worship service of *Santuala* is clearly more related to Pentecostal practices than to those of other evangelical churches or Catholic services in the Mountain province. They also have a traditional dance, which the *Santuala* calls the 'holy dance', and there are other elements which Julie Ma and the writer observe in the *Santuala* which are similar to Pentecostal ways, while other elements have different forms and meanings. Those mentioned are ritual dancing, calling and appeasing spirits, praying for forgiveness of ancestral sins, concern for the ancestors, prolonged visions and looking for immediate answers to prayers.[65]

According to Julie Ma, the members of the *Santuala* do not have a specific time for hearing the word of God and studying the Bible, which they keep more as a symbolic object.[66] However, my interview with the Methodist pastor who had worked with the *Santuala* revealed that the members are eager to hear the word of God and study the Bible and are even attending the Bible study and worship services of Protestant and Pentecostal churches. The research showed that they have their own kindergartens or nurseries and that some members concealed their true allegiance to *Santuala* during Bible study and preaching and services on account of the secrecy which surrounds it. The reason they practise the beliefs of *Santuala* is that it connects them to their indigenous belief; they can experience spiritual power with the old elements of ritual practices found in their indigenous religions and they believe that visions,

---

[63] Aguiwas, Interview.

[64] Aguiwas, Interview.

[65] Julie Ma, 'Santuala'.

[66] Ibid.

trances, healing, and communication with the spirits are the work of the Holy Spirit. There are no theological foundations to this movement; it emphasizes experiencing the power of the spirits, supernatural elements and practising the culture and beliefs of Filipino indigenous religions rather than promulgating any theoretical ideas. Julie Ma sees the *Santuala* as a syncretistic group which has adopted Pentecostal forms to counterbalance inadequate Bible teaching. In contrast, some evangelical churches call it a 'cult' and not an authentic Christian movement. They even believe it to be pagan because the *Santuala* does not cooperate with any other Christian groups.

Understanding the *Santuala* movement theologically is difficult because the *Santuala* does not have any written form of doctrine, although it does contain elements of indigenous religions based on Pentecostal experience and the kind of adaptations which the Catholic and Protestant churches have also had to make in order to be relevant. In Julie Ma's view, the *Santuala* needs biblical guidance and real Christian experiences to be a potential means of challenging the established Pentecostal churches.

Transformation in Pentecostal Spirituality

Christianity was introduced to the Philippines through the colonial powers, first Spain and then the USA, but there have always been conflicts between nationalistic identity or indigenous spirituality and colonial belief systems, especially Spanish Catholicism and US American Protestantism, and this conflict led to the emergence of new adapted belief systems. Indigenous spirituality has been sustained and grounded in adapting Christian forms into syncretistic elements, but there is always tension between colonialism and nationalistic unity. Some Pentecostal liturgical elements have been introduced by foreign Pentecostal movements into the Filipino Pentecostal churches. These elements are similar to the practices of indigenous religions and some are found in the practices of new religious movements in the Philippines. These religious transformations have raised theological and missiological issues especially in regard to contextualization and inculturation.

There are several ways in which indigenous spirituality has linked with Pentecostal spirituality and been transformed as a result. Firstly, indigenous spirituality has syncretistic elements which have been evaluated negatively according to previous theological presuppositions. Beliefs and practices linked with indigenous religious practices are distinguished from these by their theological expression. This is one way of developing contextual theology[67] and this has also provided some theological understanding of Pentecostal practices. In this context, the PMCC is a good example of establishing a Filipino indigenous Pentecostal theological understanding of its own context.

---

[67] Tano, *Theology*, 149.

Secondly, following the example of African theology, traditional cultural values are the main source of a theology's own understanding and expression. This perspective can contribute to an understanding of distinctions between syncretistic elements and Pentecostal understanding. Early Filipino Pentecostal pioneers were influenced by classical Pentecostalism and adopted their doctrinal beliefs and denominational standards. In Pentecostal circles there is rejection of indigenous religious practices, but their indigenous spirituality is still continuing through the process of contextualization.

Thirdly, the theological criteria must be developed. Sepúlveda says,

> I would prefer to emphasize the spiritual freedom of Africans, as well as Asians, native and *mestizo* Latin Americans, ethnic minorities within the 'first world', and so on to express their religious experiences, church life and worship, in terms of their own cultural patterns. Chilean Pentecostalism is again a case in point: because of the absence of African elements in Chilean popular culture, the ways of expression of Chilean Pentecostals are rather different from the ways of black Pentecostals elsewhere...the Holy Spirit enables them to encounter God and worship him in terms of their own culture.[68]

This suggests that Pentecostal spirituality has its own forms of identity according to different cultural contexts. In other words, indigenous spirituality can be identified with different forms of Pentecostal practices and is flexible in accommodating and adapting Pentecostal forms. Korean, African, and Latin American Pentecostalism may differ from each other because they have different perceptions from classical Pentecostalism started in North America. In this context, indigenous spirituality has been linked with different Pentecostal expressions of theological understanding according to different contexts. Therefore according to their own cultural values and belief systems, theological understanding must be developed.

These suggestions can be related to the Philippine context, but need to be developed with the following further considerations. Firstly, theological educational institutions must be developed in the Philippine context. One of the legacies of colonialism is 'mis-education',[69] which has led to the loss of Filipino cultural uniqueness and to the ease of their adaptation to western culture without examining their own inheritance.[70] Bible School students learn western theology using the English Bible and textbooks—they even choose to speak English.[71] During a period of between three and four years, while they

---

[68] Sepúlveda, 'Indigenous', 133, 134.

[69] Miranda-Feliciano, *Filipino Values*, 34.

[70] Javier, Interview, 303, 304.

[71] Larry W. Caldwell, 'Towards the New Discipline of Ethnohermeneutics: Questioning the Relevancy of Western Hermeneutical Methods in the Asian Context', *Journal of Asian Mission*, 1:1 (March 1999), 25-29.

undergo Bible School training, they are becoming westerners rather than Filipino theologians.[72] More difficult situations have been encountered when they are in ministry because they are preaching in their own dialect while reading the Bible and commentaries in English, which creates crises between western and local cultures. These things make it very difficult to discern the real Filipino distinctiveness. Furthermore, their sources of training are mainly foreign e.g. course contents, materials and teachers, and this is a major concern in attempting to solve cultural and theological problems.[73] However, those in rural areas (especially those who never go to Bible School) are much more Filipinized than those in the urban areas. They use their own interpretation and preach in their own dialects, their Bible interpretation being dependent on their experiences. With some discipleship training they can give articulate biblical teaching. However in urban areas there are many regional or linguistic divisions, which are dependent on the migration patterns of different tribes from rural areas settling in the cities.

Secondly, theological expression must to be developed in the Philippine context. Two significant points of tension have arisen: one is the tendency to adopt western theology without experiencing any local cultural context in the understanding of religious experiences which make up their worldview. This is because western theological expression has depended on biblical interpretation and the rationalist approach in which 'the experience comes later'.[74] The other is that religious experiences occur first and are then subject to theological reflection to discover the relevance of Scripture: this leads to a more 'contextualized indigenous theological articulation and formulation'.[75] As Javier says, 'Filipinos are closer to the Bible than western theology'.[76] This foregrounding of experience is based on the belief system of the indigenous religion and worldview, which correlate with indigenous spirituality. But there is still a need for theological study to discover how Filipino indigenous spirituality can be expressed within the Filipino context of understanding supernatural power, which can lead to a real Filipino Pentecostal spirituality. Theologians in general need to develop their own experience of supernatural power and an understanding of the holistic worldview, which up to now western theologians have found difficult to express or theologize rationally.

---

[72] For example, the AG Bible schools have long been supervized by missionaries; this supervision includes financial support. Even in their curriculum, there is very scant or nonexistent emphasis on the local culture. Danny Esperanza, Interview, 287, 288, see also Joseph R. Suico, 'Pentecostalism: Towards a Movement of Social Transformation in the Philippines', *Journal of Asian Mission* 1:1 (March 1999), 18.

[73] Ferrez, Interview, 316.

[74] Go, Interview, 352.

[75] Ibid.

[76] Javier, Interview, 303, 304.

This worldview approach will help to produce a reshaped theology as well as develop a Filipino Pentecostal theology. Even though 'theology has yet to be translated into the local culture',[77] at present it is still in the process of becoming an indigenized theological reflection in the Third World.[78] At this point, Hollenweger suggests that western theologians have not been trained to deal with religious experiences of spontaneous healings, visions or dreams which are a daily experience for Asian people, so it is important for the Third World theologians themselves to develop theological vehicles that can accommodate such religious phenomena.[79]

Thirdly, Filipino Pentecostal spirituality needs to be developed within a global context. In the wider context of the comparison between indigenous spirituality and Pentecostal spirituality, it is necessary to develop the idea of transformation, especially concerning indigenous spirituality where it is evident in Pentecostal circles. Pentecostal spirituality's predominant spiritual element originates from Christian belief, but some elements of Filipino indigenous religious practices have been transformed into Pentecostal liturgy as spirituality. In the process of Pentecostalism expanding into a global phenomenon, Pentecostal spirituality must be rooted in God's Word found in Scripture and nurtured by the Holy Spirit, a necessity if Pentecostals are successfully going to deliver effective ministry in a post-modern world.[80] These can be developed through theological education, expression and global context according to the Philippine context. Therefore it is necessary to discuss how transformation can be traced through what I call 'empowered biblical transformation'.

Empowered Biblical Transformation

Empowerment is the work of the Holy Spirit which is the presence of God, but it must be followed by biblical understanding. Transformation can be promoted by interaction between all kinds of cultural and belief systems. Lesslie Newbigin says:

> The central responsibility of the Church is to proclaim this fact, to embody it in its own life, and to rely upon the Holy Spirit to transform the weak and foolish witness of the Church in the power and wisdom of God. It is to communicate this

---

[77] Suico, 'Pentecostalism', 18.

[78] Walter J. Hollenweger, 'Syncretism and Capitalism', *Asian Journal of Pentecostal Studies* 2:1 (January 1999), 52-61.

[79] Hollenweger, 'Syncretism', 52-62.

[80] Wonsuk Ma, 'Biblical Studies in the Pentecostal Tradition: Yesterday, Today, and Tomorrow', in Dempster et al (eds.), *The Globalization of Pentecostalism*, 64.

gospel to the world in a total activity, which encompasses word and deed, message and life, indissolubly held together.[81]

This idea indicates that God acts appropriately in the culture to proclaim the gospel more effectively. The colonial powers presented the gospel too but there were many failures because of misunderstanding of cultures and belief systems. The main problem encountered here is to discern how the gospel is relevant to people's lives and to adapt it meaningfully to their own cultural system. Newbigin argues that the Holy Spirit uses the people's culture and develops new understandings of the gospel because the empowerment of the work of the Holy Spirit makes possible the acceptance of failure of the ecumenical movement in its mission; despite this failure the gospel is proclaimed.[82]

Roli del la Cruz mentions that it is very hard to distinguish between folk Christianity and Pentecostal practices. Indigenous spirituality has so much parallelism with the Pentecostal practices such as indigenous religious beliefs of healing, trance, speaking in tongues, all of which have often been understood as syncretistic elements. However, among Pentecostals these things are usual phenomena of Filipino Pentecostal spirituality. Their theological understanding is not 'syncretistic' and is a common Filipino Pentecostal spirituality.[83] In this context, Pentecostal spirituality has the forms of indigenous spirituality. Developing their experiences into an understanding of the Bible and more recent denominational doctrines have given them a more concrete belief. For example the PMCC was strongly connected with denominational groups, but within their understanding of biblical truth it became an Apostolic Church which is based on the book of Acts.[84] Their biblical[85] understanding is based on the cultural, social and political situation in the Philippines. Denominational doctrines that had been incorporated confused theological understanding[86] but were transformed because of renewed theological interpretation through a new understanding of the Bible. This understanding is applied to their own context and well accepted by members.[87] Through the apostleship the interpretation of the Bible can be united just like the early leadership of the apostles. Furthermore, Michael Pangwi (the leader of the KKMI, a former Anglican

---

[81] Lesslie Newbigin, 'The Gospel in Today's Global City', *Occasional Paper* 16 (Selly Oak Colleges, 1997), 6.

[82] Newbigin, 'The Gospel', 3.

[83] Dela Cruz, Interview, unrecorded.

[84] Art Ferriol, Interview, 268, 273.

[85] Ibid., 269; Ferriol Maran, *Interview*, 350.

[86] Allan Delotavo, 'Toward a Christ-Centered Way of Doing Theology in Asia', *Asia Journal of Theology* 3:1 (April 1989), 330.

[87] Peter Tachau, 'Bible Study – Basis or Stumbling – Block? Observations in the Philippine Theological Seminaries', *The South East Asia Journal of Theology* 16:1 (1975), 19; Art Ferriol, Interview, 274.

priest) has had similar experiences. His theological training was more on denominational doctrines, which made him confused in his personal ministerial task and he was not able to meet the needs of the people. But through the empowering presence of God his ministry has been changed. Even then he came under accusation by people in denominational circles.[88] Pangwi's ministry has shown that the empowering presence of God has been revealed through his personal experiences. He applied them to his ministries which have been transformed through his members to demonstrate biblical truth.

The 'empowerment' is God's personal involvement in human life; through the work of the Holy Spirit believers can be 'empowered' for God's specific purpose. Through the empowering presence of God, people of different races or cultures or religious backgrounds can develop a theological framework according to their cultural contexts. In other words, 'biblical' exegesis and 'transformation' are informed by the cultural values, religious beliefs and practices mediated through experiencing the power of God. 'Biblical' understanding always takes place within the empowering presence of God who empowers believers to see the real context of their experiences in all situations, i.e. economic, racial and religious. 'Transformation' always plays the role between 'empowerment' and 'biblical' understanding because syncretistic elements of biblical understanding produce conflict between the gospel and culture. God's presence empowers this transformation into theological understanding according to experiences of the work of the Holy Spirit. Therefore 'empowered biblical transformation' in God's presence has empowered those who live in certain cultural belief systems making them understand biblical truth through their experiences. This transformation is an on-going process.

In the Philippines, the gospel was planted through Spanish Catholicism, Protestantism, and Pentecostalism, but there were strong reactions against the colonial mentality because of emerging nationalism. However religious syncretism has appeared as social, political and religious reactions.

Phenomenologically, religious transformation has been processed among indigenous religions and in Christian circles, but it is necessary to see that this indigenous spirituality has been transformed into Filipino Pentecostal spirituality within the understanding of the Bible, especially regarding the work of the Holy Spirit, i.e. speaking in tongues, visions and healing. Theological understanding of 'empowered biblical transformation' can be developed through a pneumatological hermeneutic. I have developed the concept of 'empowered biblical transformation' to clarify the relationship between a conceptual implication of inculturation, or contextualization and syncretism. Indigenous spirituality has been transformed through God's empowerment. That is, God has empowered Filipinos with indigenous religious and cultural

---

[88] Pangwi, Interview, 376.

backgrounds in order to understand biblical truth and transformation has been in process with God's empowering presence and biblical understanding.

PART FOUR

EAST ASIA

Pentecostal by Default?
Contemporary Christianity in China

Gotthard Oblau

Introduction

Protestant church reality in China is usually interpreted to the international visitor by the China Christian Council (CCC) as something close to evangelical mainline Christianity. However, such descriptions refer to only a part of the broad and multifaceted Christian reality in this vast country.

As international exposure is mostly limited to city churches and rural congregations closely affiliated with the institutionalized church, international observers tend to project on China an image of a church resembling their own experience of a structured, somewhat organized body with tensions or frictions along denominational, theological or political lines. Church leaders (as well as secular authorities) in China paint a less than favourable picture of a grassroots Christianity suffering from backwardness and a lack of education. Typical keywords used to describe China's village Christianity are: 'low quality faith'; 'superstition'; 'sects and heresies'; 'self-styled evangelists'; 'destabilization of the social order under the cloak of religion'; 'exploitation of the sentiments of religious people'.

Together with my wife, Claudia Währisch-Oblau, I worked for the Amity Foundation from 1985 to 1997. Countless trips through China, including many of her remoter parts, gave us the opportunity at least to catch some glimpses of a Christian reality which to us seemed to reflect not so much a religious deficiency but rather a spirituality of its own dignity, of biblical compatibility, contextual relevance and a liberating nature, though hardly reconcilable with mainline or evangelical faith life.

For the last three years I have been managing editor of *Unterwegs*, an independent German-language Christian magazine, which traces and reports on seeds of church renewal and innovative forms of Christian living. In this context, I have come across charismatic groups and individuals and entered into a dialogue with Pentecostals of German as well as African and Asian backgrounds. This new perspective has led me to re-evaluate much of what I have heard and seen in China, leading me to ask whether the majority of China's Christians feature a style of faith which elsewhere in the world is called Pentecostal.

My following deliberations are based on observations and interviews done by myself and my wife, on a limited range of literature portraying present-day Chinese Christianity and on some academic works on Pentecostalism providing a framework of interpretation. I am going to analyse China's Protestant church situation in terms of four different criteria: in terms of church structure (how common are charismatic over against bureaucratic structures?), in terms of salvation theology (how material/physical is the Chinese Christian concept of God's salvation?), in terms of communication (what is the role of oral tradition?) and in terms of human religiosity (what is the dominant kind of human piety and concept of God?).

I hope that my analysis will significantly substantiate the hypothesis that Christianity in China features a wide variety of Pentecostal characteristics. Though Christians in China do not call themselves Pentecostal, many of their groups and churches, particularly at the grassroots level, may be seen as Pentecostal in a broader theological sense.[1]

Finally, I will raise, though not answer, the question of where to find the origins of China's pervading Pentecostal spirit. According to my assumptions, a purely denominational perspective will hardly provide sufficient explanations. Institutional denominational structures, both western and indigenous, were forcibly disbanded and by the late 1950s no longer in existence, though today their undercurrents are still to be felt or, in the case of the indigenous movements, increasingly coming to the surface again. However, conditions that allowed indigenous Pentecostal denominations such as the True Jesus Church or movements like the Jesus Family to flourish in the first half of the twentieth century have in its second half nurtured countless other Christian communities too and led to an astounding growth of Christianity in most parts of the country.[2]

While an exclusively denominational approach to my question would therefore not suit the particular Chinese context, the assumption that Pentecostalism in its broader sense is confined to China's independent house church movement would be equally misleading. It would be a distortion of ecclesial realities in China if one tried to play off the house church movement

---

[1] In this I follow Walter J. Hollenweger, *Charismatisch-pfingstliches Christentum. Herkunft, Situation, ökumenische Chancen* (Göttingen: Vandenhoeck & Ruprecht, 1997). For Hollenweger, organizational fluidity, oral tradition, a holistic sense of salvation, an experience-oriented faith and an empowering and democratic church life are essential characteristics of Pentecostalism.

[2] According to statistics of the China Christian Council, the total number of China's Protestants in 1949 stood at 700,000. Since the early 1980s, the number has risen from 3 million to at least 15 million. Internal government reports are said to mention 25 and even over 30 million, whereas some independent, albeit less reliable, Christian claims are as high as 80 to 100 million.

against the institutional structure of the Chinese Protestant Three-Self Patriotic Movement (TSPM) or the established network of the CCC.[3] There is no need to distance oneself from these organizations to be Pentecostal and much of the Christian experience and witness within the realm of the CCC itself is fairly Pentecostal in nature.[4]

The reality of Christianity in China is more complex, or should I rather say much simpler than the usual stereotypes suggest - as the following narrative may show.

A Narrative

Xiyang, an extremely poor village with a population of 200 families, is located in the coastal mountains of northern Fujian province. In the 1990s, its Christian community of 42 families drew a lot of nation-wide attention, receiving praise from both the China Christian Council and the Communist Party for their contribution toward the village's social development and economic progress. *Tian Feng*, the CCC monthly magazine, featured Xiyang's case as a model for rural church work that manages to combine personal spiritual fervour with a strong sense of social commitment and a visible contribution to the country's modernization.[5] The Amity Foundation, a CCC-initiated development organization, gave funds for the setting-up of a fruit tree orchard which had been started as a Christian cooperative, and the Party honoured the village church leader You Muhua as an outstanding peasant woman on International Women's Day.[6]

---

[3] Today, TSPM and CCC are almost identical institutions, with most parallel positions in the two bodies held in personal union. Hence the Chinese usually speak of the *Liang Hui*, the 'Double Organisation'. In this paper, I use 'CCC' in the sense of the Chinese *Liang Hui*.

[4] In this I agree with Tony Lambert, *The Resurrection of the Chinese Church* (London/ Sydney/Auckland/Toronto: Hodder & Stoughton, 1991), 171, even though some groups of house churches may find TSPM representatives hostile toward healing prayer and charismatic leadership. See Tony Lambert, *China's Christian Millions. The Costly Revival* (London: Monarch Books, 1999), 66-67, and many evangelical or Pentecostal China watchers seem to project a simplistic dichotomy on a rather complex reality. See, for instance, *House Churches in China* by Paul Wong, a minister in the 'True Jesus Church', at www.biblesabbath.org/tss/486/house.html).

[5] *Tian Feng*, July 1992, the monthly magazine of Christianity in China published in Shanghai by the National Committee of the Three-Self Patriotic Movement of the Protestant Churches in China and the China Christian Council.

[6] *Amity News Service* (*ANS* henceforth, published by the Amity Foundation Overseas Coordination Office, Hong Kong), 93.1.13 (February 1993). *Amity Newsletter*, a Quarterly Bulletin of the Amity Foundation, 36 (1/1996), 1-3.

Things started with a young girl from Xiyang who was sold by her parents into marriage in another province. When she arrived at her in-laws, her husband-to-be had suddenly died. But instead of blaming her for bringing bad luck, which would have been expected, the grieving parents received her with generous hospitality. They turned out to be Christians and in their home the young lady from Xiyang learnt the basics about their faith, including singing, praying and reading the Bible. Soon after she decided to go home to bring the gospel to her native village.

In Xiyang she managed to win over not more than a few elderly ladies, until one day a nine-year-old boy fell into the village pond and almost drowned. He was pulled out of the water unconscious and carried home. Since the village had no real road connection and the next clinic was very far, any rescue efforts were out of the question. Yet while parents and neighbours resigned themselves to their fate, the Christian ladies came and sat at the boy's bedside, praying to God and pleading with him about the boy's life for over 24 hours, until finally the boy came to and recovered quickly and fully. This caused a Christian awakening; more and more young people and entire families joined the Christian group.

Later on, You Muhua married into Xiyang. She herself was a recent convert. Prayers in her aunt's house church had cured her of chronic fatigue and turned her into a fervent Christian. Her personal healing testimony plus her record of nine years of schooling gave her sufficient credentials to be put in charge of preaching and pastoring in the emerging house church in Xiyang.

At the same time, the social situation of the area was unhealthy and disheartening. Between 1978 and 1984, 28 young men were sentenced to death and executed for crimes including piracy. Poverty and destitution had led them to seek their fortune by robbing and sometimes murdering fish farmers and boat people down on the coastline. You's husband, too, had been involved in criminal activities. The young Christian lady, however, managed to win him over and told all who were willing to hear that the Lord Jesus wanted people to repent from their wrongdoings and in turn would provide for the believer's sustenance.

Xiyang's new converts developed an active social life. A visitation team regularly looked after all Christian families and cared for the sick, a production team organized assistance during times of sowing and harvesting for families with insufficient manpower, a know-how team of several young people was sent to the county town to attend courses in mushroom growing and the tending of orange trees. They shared their newly acquired knowledge with Christians and non-Christians alike and the entire village population benefited from the Christian presence in numerous ways.

After several years of volunteer pastoral work, You Muhua attended a lay training course of several weeks offered by the newly established Christian Council in the county town. This training helped her to refine her preaching and administrative skills, to improve her understanding of the Chinese catechism and to consolidate her biblical knowledge.

Charismatic and Bureaucratic Structures

Though very few local churches in China would establish production cooperatives, the case of Xiyang's Christian community is typical of the country's Christianity in a variety of aspects. First of all, it tells a lot about Protestant church structures.

For much of China's Protestant Christianity inside and outside the TSPM/CCC network I find true what Roswith Gerloff, with reference to social categories defined by Gerlach and Hine, writes about Black Pentecostalism in North America and world-wide: it features 'entirely different organizational and communication structures from those of the centralized, bureaucratic western denominations' and should be understood as 'movement organization'. [7] Its distinctive characteristics include 'a polycephalous organization', 'a mission that travels along preexisting daily social relationships', 'charismatic leadership which identifies with the needs of the people', 'a change-oriented and action-motivating message which is not abstract but can be easily communicated verbally' and a favour for 'the relevance and human power of each individual'. All of this applies to Ms You's church in Xiyang alongside countless other Christian communities in China. They are polycephalous, that is, the different local groups are led independently and are not linked together through a hierarchy. This is widely seen as the result of the dissolution of denominational church institutions in the 1950s and the persecution in the 1960s and '70s. However, the fact that Hong Kong also has a widely ramified polycephalous house church movement suggests that its roots reach deep into the soil of national culture and folk-religious history.[8] All in all, China's Christian world outside Roman Catholicism features what classical Protestant observers from the West would call an extreme congregationalist structure. Even within the CCC, each local church is completely independent in its local affairs including finances, personnel, pay scale and spiritual life. And although the CCC has formulated a minimalist church constitution to regulate and unify church life at the local level, it can do no more than recommend its application and completely lacks the power to impose sanctions in case of its

---

[7] Roswith Gerloff, 'Pentecostals in the African Diaspora', in A. Anderson and W. Hollenweger (eds.), *Pentecostals after a Century. Global Perspectives on a Movement in Transition* (Sheffield: Sheffield Academic Press 1999), 76.

[8] The classical 'locus' for the practice of Chinese folk religion was the village temple and the ancestral hall, both administered by the elders of the local clan. Hence grassroots religion has a particular earth-bound and family-oriented flavour.

violation (unless it 'borrows' government power through the Religious Affairs Bureau).

Christian mission within China is not the result of church planting schemes, evangelistic strategies, media presence or any other structured procedures from the side of professional church leadership but the spontaneous and accidental result of pre-existing daily social relationships. In the case of Xiyang village, the gospel arrived as a side effect of matrimonial arrangements and tragic coincidence. The classical fields of social contact, including the extended household, the neighbourhood, the workplace and the local market, have always been the typical transmission places for the gospel. Lately, long-distance connections such as domestic business trips, academic placement and labour migration can be added to the list.

Christian groups come freely into existence, divide and spread. I remember an encounter with Hou Xingde, a CCC-approved evangelist in a poor mountainous area, a peasant who in his spare time looked after the four dozen Christian meeting points of his county (there was no church and no theologically trained person far and wide). He told me how he once 'discovered' a group he had not known about before. People had somehow acquired a few Bibles and hymnbooks. Completely on their own and without any instruction, they had simply started to read the Bible and to recite the hymns in some form of self-invented chanting.

Just as You Muhua in Xiyang village, countless people, mostly women, serve as charismatic leaders of local Christian circles. Neither appointed nor elected, and without any training which would equip them for their task, they simply get involved. They see a need, feel an urge, believe in a calling and start things with personal fervour and rich emotional investment on the basis of trial and error, accompanied by much prayer, soul searching and spiritual pondering.

More than on any school education or social status, their credentials depend on their biographical encounters with the power of God and their personal charisma, which certainly includes a richness of social skills including human warmth, leadership qualities, rhetorical and organizational talents.

Finally, and typical for Pentecostal groups in many Third-World countries, the gospel in countless grassroots communities in China is rendered as a 'change-oriented and action-motivated message' which favours 'the relevance and human power of each individual'. In the case of Xiyang village, this is all too clear. Individual families start to coordinate their productive energies, former pirates become law-abiding citizens, drab and destitute lives gain dignity, hope and perspective. Such change results in an upward social mobility which has been widely observed in the case of Latin American Pentecostalism but can also be felt in China. A further parallel between China's grassroots Christianity and Pentecostalism elsewhere lies in the fact that very often it is the women who are attracted first and then in turn 'tame' the men, just as You Muhua did with her bridegroom. Though the women would not challenge patriarchal family structures in principle, they exert a religious and moral influence on their husbands which turns them into faithful and caring family heads who no longer waste their income with drinking and gambling.[9]

Where does, in view of this self-organizing religious grassroots movement, the China Christian Council (CCC) come into play? I have found it most helpful to differentiate, in very crude terms, between a charismatic structure from below and a bureaucratic structure from above, which partially overlap each other.[10]

The charismatic structure from below is mostly rural, dominated by volunteer workers of little formal education with many women in leadership roles. The bureaucratic structure from above, in contrast, is mostly urban, dominated by well-educated people with many theologians and mostly men in leading positions. While groups within the charismatic structure are mainly Pentecostal and often pre-modern in their orientation, preaching and teaching in the realm of the bureaucratic structure is dominated by the modern rationalism of evangelical or, at the very top, liberal theology.

The tension between these two structures can materialize between the CCC and independent house churches as well as within the CCC network itself. In the case of Xiyang, the tension has been a CCC-internal one and became visible, with a lot of power play and jealousy involved, between You Muhua as representative of the village church and the young men in charge of the county Christian Council.

The more the independent house church movement manages to organize itself (which recently seems to be the case with growing regional and national networks), the more the same structural and theological tensions will evolve within the house church movement itself.[11]

Physical Blessings

In Xiyang village, healing experiences in connection with prayer were essential for the start and growth of its Christian community. CCC representatives report that in rural areas generally at least half of all conversions are motivated by healing experiences that are either personal or witnessed in the family. In many

---

[9] Michael Bergunder, 'Pfingstbewegung in Lateinamerika: Soziologische Theorien und theologische Debatten', in Michael Bergunder (ed.), *Pfingstbewegung und Basisgemeinden in Lateinamerika: Die Rezeption befreiungs-theologischer Konzepte durch die pfingstliche Theologie* (Hamburg: Evangelisches Missionswerk), 14. Richard Shaull and Walso Cesar, *Pentecostalism and the Future of Christian Churches. Promises, Limitations, Challenges* (Grand Rapids/Cambridge: Eerdmans, 2000).

[10] I have developed this terminology together with Claudia Währisch-Oblau and used it in a number of unpublished papers.

[11] The Christian magazine *Dao* ('The Way'), anonymously published inside China, presents itself as a joint publication for a number of nation-wide house church networks and contains more or less evangelical views.

local places, church people claim a ratio as high as 90%. Though this is not much noticed internationally and has never been systematically researched, anecdotal evidence has been documented in a number of English language publications.[12]

In China, prayers for the sick are a common phenomenon in all local churches and by no means restricted to the countryside. They can be found among well-trained urban Christians too, and affiliation or non-affiliation with the CCC makes hardly any difference in this respect.[13] When in the summer of 2001 a student of Nanjing Union Theological Seminary, China's Protestant Seminary with the highest academic ranking, was hospitalized with a life threatening illness, a group of his classmates spent three days fasting and praying for his recovery.[14] Though the seminary leadership denounced this behaviour as superstition and took it as proof that the church suffers from a serious lack of theological thinking, the incident shows how close to the power centre of the bureaucratic church structure from above Pentecostal-style faith practice can be found.

Tony Lambert is correct in observing that both inside and outside the CCC network 'Chinese Christians adhere to a robust biblical supernaturalism which believes in a sovereign God who can answer the prayers of his people in remarkable ways. Eighteenth century rationalism [...] has had little influence in the Chinese church'.[15]

---

[12] *Bridge* (1984-1997), edited by the Christian Study Centre on Chinese Religion and Culture, Hong Kong; *Areopagus*, Magazine of the Tao Fong Shan Christian Centre, Hong Kong, Advent 1993; Claudia Währisch-Oblau, 'Healing Prayers and Healing Testimonies in Mainland Chinese Churches: An Attempt at Intercultural Understanding', *China Study Journal* 14:2 (August 1999), 5-21; Claudia Währisch-Oblau, 'God Can Make Us Healthy Through and Through: On Prayers for the Sick and the Interpretation of Healing Experiences in Christian Churches in China and African Immigrant Congregations in Germany', *International Review of Mission* XC, nos. 356/357 (January/April 2001), 87-102; Tony Lambert, *Resurrection*; Tony Lambert, *China's Christian Millions*; Alan Hunter and Kim-Kwong Chan, *Protestantism in Contemporary China* (Cambridge: Cambridge University Press, 1993); Ann Wire, 'Christian Miracle Stories and Modernization' (paper presented at a consultation on Christianity and Modernization, Beijing, October 1994).

[13] *Areopagus* (Advent 1993), 31 reports the story of evangelist Ye Zude, who is in charge of a local church affiliated with the CCC and once prayed for a little child already pronounced dead by a hospital doctor. The child came back to life shortly afterward and then gradually recovered in the hospital. Fearing that people might misinterpret the situation and start bringing the dead to the church, Mr Ye played down the experience but is quoted as saying: 'Did not Jesus heal the sick and cast out demons? How can we deny these miracles?'

[14] Oral report by Rev Bao Jiayuan in Hamburg, June 2001.

[15] Tony Lambert, *China's Christian Millions*, 110. Unlike Lambert, however, I would be careful with generalizing suspicions that 'believers may be left in a twilight world of

While in China, I have never come across, nor heard of, special healing services conducted by Christian communities. In many big churches, one can always see some believers staying behind after the regular worship service, praying in the pews or approaching the pastor or an elder with personal prayer requests. Most healing prayers, according to my impression, are conducted as part of home or hospital visits to the sick.

In contrast to many Pentecostal communities elsewhere, Chinese Christians tend to perform the prayer for the sick in a 'democratic' way; any believer can do it, no special healing charisma or any particular ecclesial status is required.[16] In other words, prayerful intercession in the field of physical well-being is part of the widely practised priesthood of all believers. In China, I have never heard of any healing crusades led by charismatic personalities basking in the limelight of star-cult, nor of any required ritual which would have to accompany the prayer - not even the anointing with oil. In the rather simple and unpretentious way in which the Chinese are accustomed to ask God for somebody's physical recovery, their prayers seem to be free of self-reflective bolstering, giving witness to the sole power of God. It is this attitude which makes people like Zhang Guangming, an almost illiterate peasant evangelist in Yunnan province, tell non-Christian clients requesting his healing prayer: 'I will gladly pray for you to my God. But if you don't recover, you must not blame me. If you recover, you should not thank me but give thanks to my God'.[17]

This democratic prayer practice does not necessarily focus on the miraculous; prayers are not spoken in vain if healing is neither quick nor thorough. More importantly, they are part and parcel of the communal love practised among the believers and of the care and comfort rendered to the sick in their midst. More often than not it is the commitment and human warmth with which church representatives keep visiting their members in the hospital rather than any spectacular recovery that makes Christianity attractive for doctors and other patients who observe this.

On the other hand, Chinese folk religion displays a remarkably pragmatic, even mercantile attitude toward the physical benefits of divine blessings. Truth is what works. Gods who can deliver are revered and deserve a place in the pantheon of the village temple. There is no doubt that the same religious flavour has permeated China's grassroots Christianity. The personal account of the fruit seller Li Shuying may stand for countless others:[18] Ms Li once suffered from serious anaemia which made her frequently faint, though she had to sell

---

folk-religion with a thin veneer of Christianity' and simply 'continue the practices of folk-religion using Christian terminology' (111). This is how Third-World Pentecostalism is commonly questioned by evangelical and liberal theologians alike.

[16] Claudia Währisch-Oblau, *IRM* 356/357, 89.

[17] Personal interview, Zhaotong, March 1994.

[18] *Areopagus*, Advent 1993, 28.

fruit in the streets every day. People kept gossiping that she was possessed by demons. Li was frightened and sought the help of a sorceress, spending a lot of money on her to no avail. One market day, she overheard people talking about the God Jesus who could heal the most stubborn illness. She learned that unlike other Gods Jesus did not take chickens or ducklings as offerings. Instead he wanted prayers and a moral conduct that included the refraining from cheating in the market place. In a local church Ms Li learnt to lead a Christian life. At first she lost money in her business, which antagonized even her mother. The long-term effects, however, turned out to be favourable. Her anaemia disappeared, harmony in her family was restored as all members converted and her business started to flourish.

This account is clearly shaped along the line of investment and return. Still, I would hesitate to denounce this kind of faith as religious syncretism or utilitarianism, as many of China's urban theologians would do.[19] Li's daily struggle for survival depends on the right balance of investment and return. In a way, her personal account constitutes a piece of authentic contextual theology. Also, in contrast to many evangelical theologians with their Greek-inspired emphasis on the immortal soul and non-material rewards of faith Ms Li may have instinctively grasped the biblical truth of the materiality of salvation, which according to Miroslaf Volf is an essential constituent not only of liberation theology but also of Pentecostalism.[20]

What Richard Shaull has observed among Pentecostals in Brazil is equally true for the great majority of China's believers: 'They not only understand the gospel stories of Jesus healing the sick and casting out demons, they also know them as part of their own experience'.[21] And 'In Pentecostalism, poor and broken people discover that what they read in the Gospels is happening NOW

---

[19] In *The Syllabus* 3/1989, its deputy editor and Nanjing Seminary theologian Kong Xiangjian castigates rural Christian faith motivated by healing experiences as folk religious syncretism: 'In their hearts they have replaced Jesus Christ with the boddhisattva Guanyin to protect them from harm, a Daoist god to exorcise evil spirits and the legendary healer Hua Tuo to restore health', quoted from the English translation in *Chinese Theological Review*, ed. Janice Wickeri, published by the Foundation for Theological Education in Southeast Asia, 1989, 121. In an officially published sermon, CCC-co-worker Xu Minghan of Shanghai subsumes Christian believers' hopes to gain material benefits through prayer under the Pauline term of 'knowing Christ after the flesh' and exhorts his audience that 'now our material knowledge of Christ has to become spiritual knowledge, our search for self-satisfaction, the pursuit of the words of eternal life', quoted from the English translation in *Chinese Theological Review* (1988), 155.

[20] Miroslav Volf, 'Materiality of Salvation: An Investigation in the Soteriologies of Liberation and Pentecostal Theologies', *Journal of Ecumenical Studies* 26:3 (Summer 1989), 447-67.

[21] Shaull, 131.

in their midst. The same Jesus is present with them, doing what he did in Galilee two thousand years ago. For them, the incredible witness of the Gospels to the resurrection is confirmed in their day-to-day experience. The impossible, the supreme miracle, has indeed happened'.[22]

Such experiences can develop in simple and often subdued people a feeling of an enormous empowerment and renewed self-respect. Just as You Muhua's aunt and her fellow worshippers claimed the right to approach God for You's health, so did the old ladies of Xiyang, prayerfully struggling for the life of the boy pulled from the pond. They dared to say: 'We refuse to accept this illness; we will not kowtow to this death'. Such audacity against evil, such determination for the betterment of life, first nurtured by the encounter with the unexpected, if not supernatural, has the tendency - as the story of Xiyang shows - to spill over into the realm of the natural and more common, into the fight against poverty and resignation, into the struggle for a better future, into everyday life with its dealings with querulous mothers-in-law, drinking husbands and stubborn party cadres. What Harvey Cox observed for African independent churches in North America is true also for Christian communities at China's grassroots: 'The concept of what was included in healing broadened. 'Healing' now came to include not just bodily recuperation but finding remedies for unemployment, family disputes, racism, marital discord, and controversies between factions in a tribe or village'.[23]

Oral Tradition

The Christian gospel found its way to Xiyang village through two young women who had learnt to know Jesus Christ as a mighty Lord through the experience of gracious hospitality and comfort, of prayerful encouragement and renewed physical energy. The good news they had in store was further shared and spread through oral testimonies, the retelling and reciting of biblical stories, the singing of Christian folk songs and hymns and certainly through the gentle but insistant pressures of moral exhortation and personal persuasion.

This kind of grassroots and person-to-person evangelism is the route the gospel in China today most commonly takes. During the early years of the Cultural Revolution, starting in 1966, countless homes of intellectuals and religious believers were ransacked by the Red Guards and libraries, both public and private, were burnt, which led to an irretrievable loss of literature in all of China's cities. Christianity and its way of tradition were deeply affected by this, leaving urban and well-educated Christians with no other way than to rely on

---

[22] Shaull, 185 (emphasis by Shaull).

[23] Harvey Cox, *Fire from Heaven: The Rise of Pentecostal Spirituality and the Reshaping of Religion in the Twenty-first Century* (New York: Addison-Wesley, 1994), 254.

memory and orality, something which had been the rule for rural Christianity all along. Though by today over 30 million Chinese Bibles have been printed and distributed, devotional literature and popular Bible explanations published in the PRC are still rather limited both in terms of titles and distribution.[24]

Between 1965 and 1981, practically no theological training had been possible in China. This fact, coupled with the fast spread and growth of Christian congregations since, has led to a severe shortage of trained pastors. Many counties with tens of thousands of believers and dozens of meeting points have no ordained pastor at all.[25] And even the ordained clergy can hardly be counted as academically trained, as most courses offered in provincial and regional seminaries last no longer than three years and are taken by people with often no more than nine years of schooling. In the remoter parts of the country, the situation is particularly strained. Zhaotong prefecture, for example, a backward mountain area in the northeast of Yunnan province with approximately 190,000 Christians, has only one ordained pastor.[26] She is a retired medical doctor who has received one year of seminary training in the provincial capital.

In such surroundings, itinerant evangelists with scant or no Christian training are a common sight, both inside and outside the CCC-network. A typical representative of her kind may be 'Sister Sun', as she was called by her fellow believers, of the Longquan county church in southern Zhejiang province.[27] She had never gone to school and started to be a Christian as a young mother, after she had become acquainted with Christians in the course of a long illness from which she was cured. At 72 years of age, after her husband's death, she started, with the consent of the lay leader of her local church, to regularly visit the 24 Christian groups in the villages of the surrounding hill area. When I met her in 1991, she had given up her home completely and was moving from place to place, staying in the homes of the Christian villagers and having hardly more possessions than what she carried with her in her little backpack. With a little regular pocket money from her daughter she could make ends meet and pay for board and lodging provided for her. While she could not even write her own

---

[24] Regular Christian publications for the laity with tens of thousands of copies printed and distributed nation-wide include *Tian Feng* ('Heavenly Wind', the monthly journal of the CCC), *Jiaocai* ('Teaching Materials', produced for Christian lay leaders by the Nanjing Theological Seminary on a quarterly basis) and *Jiang Dao Ji* ('Sermon Collection', published by the Zhejiang Provincial Christian Council with several issues per year).

[25] See, for example, the case of Guanyun County in Jiangsu province, as described in *ANS*, 99.1/2.5.

[26] Personal inquiry, 1996; see also *ANS*, 96.1.8.

[27] She is portrayed in Claudia Währisch-Oblau & Gotthard Oblau, *Kein Geheimnis Christ zu sein. Lebens-Bilder aus Chinas Gemeinden heute* (Neukirchen-Vluyn: Aussaat Verlag, 1992), 50ff.

name, she knew countless Bible stories and passages by heart and sang with the villagers the hymns and songs she had learnt in decades of regular church and home meeting attendance.

It was through the women and children that she found access to the population in the villages. Her message was clear and simple: Whoever wants to follow the way of Jesus must love one's family members and neighbours and forgo the usual gossiping and malevolence; this leads to harmonious relationships and good health in this life and to eternal salvation in the next.

An important part of China's non-academic and oral Christian tradition is constituted by a rich variety of grassroots spirituals. Everywhere in China, singing is an important part of Christian worship.[28] However, in rural churches most Christians feel the traditional western melodies and many of the Chinese hymns in the 'New Hymnal' published by the CCC difficult to follow.[29] In addition, many cannot read the texts and the music (which is in numerical notation).

In the rural churches in many Chinese provinces there are Christian 'bards' or 'minstrels'—most of them women. As Deng Zhaoming, the Hong Kong-based researcher and editor of *Bridge*, observes: 'Many rural women would never dare to speak up in the church. But as singers, they have a message to preach'.[30] Usually they adapt local popular folk song tunes to gospel texts or lyrics. Sometimes they compose or improvise simple melodies in their local ethnic style. Most of the lyrics are in colloquial language, easy to be picked up by the illiterate.[31]

In the countryside, many Christian congregations sing spirituals, for which no textbook exists, and which would be useless anyway as most of the singers are illiterate. Spirituals are passed down orally, memorized word by word through frequent singing. Their age and origins are usually unclear. Educated Christians here and there try to copy them by hand.

---

[28] Standard hymn books have been the *Hymns of Universal Praise*, ed. the United Hymnal Committee (Shanghai: Christian Literature Society, 1936), and the currently used *New Hymnal*, ed. the Hymn Committee (Shanghai: China Christian Council, 1983). The latter contains 300 Chinese translations of western hymns and 100 hymns of Chinese origin, half of which were written after 1949.

[29] Many Chinese find it difficult to sing the 4th and the 7th tone of the seven-tone scale correctly. This and the next paragraph is based on information from Nanjing Theological Seminary professor Chen Zemin given in a personal letter to Claudia Währisch-Oblau, May 1997.

[30] *ANS* 1997.5.6.

[31] In 1993, the churches in Harbin published a collection of 304 such 'short spirituals' with biblical texts, all composed and sung by singer-composer (Ms) Tian Huiyan and edited by Ma Cuilian, printed by the Amity Press in Nanjing.

Texts are diverse in form and drawn form a variety of sources. Many contain ethical exhortations with a strong emphasis on forgiveness and obedience,[32] including rules for proper behaviour in the family and during church service,[33] or general calls to follow the Lord. In a self-reflective way, they can even teach the benefits of the singing of spirituals:

> 1. The spirituals of Christ I must sing every day. I want to live a new life for my Lord, I also want to suffer for him. How good is this experience. The Lord gives me strength. Look to him alone!

> 2. The spirituals of Christ I must sing every day. I want to live a new life for the Lord, a new life, not worrying eating nor drinking. How good is this experience. The Lord gives me strength. Look to him alone!

> 3. The spirituals of Christ I must sing every day. We will overcome all our sufferings. The Lord gives me power. Look to him alone![34]

This text, already in existence when the Cultural Revolution started in 1966, was sung to the tune of 'The Three Main Rules of Discipline and the Eight Points for Attention' of the Liberation Army. This surely served as a convenient cover in a context of persecution, but it shows more: the method developed under Mao Zedong for the military training and behavioural education of illiterate peasants seems to have been copied and taken over by Christians for their basic catechetical education and spiritual formatting in a comparable social context.[35]

---

[32] 'When others hit us, we do not raise our hand; when they curse us, we do not open our mouths, we do not grow angry; when others curse us, we smile' (*Bridge* 25 [Sept./Oct. 1987], 15).

[33] The first stanza of an exhortational spiritual developed by Sister Lin Meng'en of Huang county, Shandong province, goes like this: 'Keep quiet when you come to worship. Do not talk, listen only. Make no hubbub, do not shout. Avoid gossiping and make less criticism' (*Bridge* 61 [Sept./Oct. 1993], 9).

[34] *Bridge* 61, 8 (English translation provided by *Bridge*)

[35] The following spiritual, recorded by *Bridge* 28 (April/May 1988), 11 from Wuyang prefecture in Henan province, follows the catechetical form of question and answer, sung in antiphony:

> I say, who will answer question number one?
> Who healed the sick and worked miracles?
> Who healed the sick and worked miracles?
> You ask who will answer question number one?
> I will answer it.
> Lord Jesus healed the sick and worked miracles.
> Lord Jesus healed the sick and worked miracles.

Affectionate Piety

Ecstatic worship does not seem to be the rule in China's churches. Personally, I have never encountered anything significant outside the sobriety of well-organized, orderly led gatherings, either in CCC-affiliated or in non-affiliated congregations, though there may be a world of worshipping spontaneity and spiritual impulsiveness in independent Christian circles I have never had access to.[36]

What can be encountered even by the international visitor, however, is a prayer practice in public worship which seems to be a common Pentecostal habit in other parts of the world and has been termed 'prayer concert' by Cheryl Bridges Johns.[37] In this form, worshippers pray out loud individually and simultaneously, thereby creating an acoustic sphere within which everybody plays an active but anonymous part in collective praise and lamentation, intercession and petition, and through which all worshippers are connected in a web of divine blessings mutually rendered and received. After a fixed period of time, the worship leader may ring a big hand bell to indicate the end of the prayer, after which the noise of human voices will gradually die down and the liturgy can go on.[38]

The subsequent stanzas follow the same pattern, all asking for important persons from the Bible:

> Who betrayed the Lord and deceived God? Judas.
> Who goes to heaven while he is living? Elijah.
> Who led the Israelites out of Egypt? Old Moses.
> Who went down to the lake of fire? The old rich man.
> Who was raised up after he died? Lazarus.
> Who was thrown into the fiery furnace? Three prophets.
> Who believed in the Lord and left his home? Elisha
> Who built the big ark? Noah.
> Who was carried away to heaven? Enoch.

This sung catechism betrays a faith agenda shaped by a context of persecution (betrayal of the Lord, liberation from Egypt, fiery furnace) and poverty (the perils of wealth: lake of fire) and dominated by clearly Pentecostal topics, including Jesus as healer and performer of miracles, itinerant evangelism (Elisha left his home) and a strong sense of immediate eschatology (Elijah, Lazarus, Noah and Enoch).

[36] The accounts given by a certain 'Brother Dennis', Danyun, *Lilies Amongst Thorns* (Tonbridge Kent: Sovereign World, 1991) which include a charismatic worship with literally earth-shaking effects (239-40 in the German translation: Danyun, *Aufbruch im Reich der Mitte* [Wiesbaden: Projektion J, 1997]), should be taken with caution; in addition, it is unclear how representative this book actually is.

[37] Cheryl Bridges Johns, 'Heilung und Befreiung aus pfingstkirchlicher Perspektive', *Concilium* 32 (1996), 241.

[38] Such practice has been witnessed by Claudia Währisch-Oblau in Wenzhou (1994) and Binhai (1995). It has also been tape-recorded and described to me by Deng Zhaoming in 1997.

Almost ubiquitous in Chinese Christian worship and easily to be observed are the mostly quiet but deep emotions flowing through a congregation, noticeable in the form of devoted concentration, in the tears and sobs and the passionate hymn singing of the mostly female believers in the pews. Chinese Christian religion, it seems, touches people much more deeply than an assumed utilitarian approach would suggest and it does so in much more gentle ways than eschatological threats and announcements of impending divine judgement would allow. What Harvey Cox has identified as Pentecostal faith in patriarchal Sicily[39] can also be found in China's hierarchical and male-dominated society under Confucianism-inspired rule: 'God is more lover than judge', 'more concerned with human affection than with commanding obedience', and is sympathetic with the 'murky emotions of the heart'.[40]

If this were taken as a yardstick for Pentecostal thinking, much of China's Christian preaching would qualify to be Pentecostal. Though at the surface, sermons in China display a lot of evangelical elements including human sin, God's wrath, Christ's death as a sacrifice to reconcile God, and human repentance as a precondition for escaping eternal damnation and gaining God's forgiveness, there is a discernible undercurrent expressing a much softer picture of God and of Jesus.[41]

Through his incarnation and life on earth, Jesus has become sympathetic with the poor and the downtrodden for whom it is difficult to live up to moral standards. Back in heaven after his resurrection and ascension, Jesus now pleads with his Father to have mercy on them and forgive their trespasses.[42] The temptation of Jesus in the wilderness is presented as a comfort for believers: He who was tempted like us can now understand our human troubles and tribulations; he who was able to gain victory over the devil is going to

---

[39] Harvey Cox, 201: 'The qualities that Pentecostals attribute to God, the Holy Spirit and Jesus Christ combine to produce a radical repainting of the traditional Sicilian portrait of the deity. [...] those qualities include distinctively feminine ones. The distant, jealous, and judgmental god of some traditional Catholic theology gives way to a Jesus who longs to embrace sinners, to enter into their hearts in what Cucchiari aptly calls a "soteriological romance"'.

[40] Harvey Cox, 201

[41] Based on research done on published sermons from China, the broadest source of which is 'Sermon Collection', *Jiang Dao Ji* (published by the Zhejiang Provincial Christian Council), I have analysed this phenomenon in greater detail in a paper on concepts of Jesus in contemporary Chinese Protestantism: Gotthard Oblau, 'Heiler, Tröster, Lehrer, Weltenherr: Jesusbilder im chinesischen Protestantismus', soon to be published in Roman Malek (ed.), *Jesus in China* (Nettetal: Steyler Verlag).

[42] Personally encountered sermon, Nanjing, Advent 1987; a similar portrait of Jesus is rendered by Xu Sixue, 'Reflections on the Gospel of Luke', *Chinese Theological Review* (1990), 163-176.

share this victory with all of us who are still under his dominion.[43] In other words, Jesus' ethical perfection does not distance him from his followers but instead binds him to them in sympathy, closeness and intimacy.

Jesus weeps for his people, showing mercy for them and acting as their great comforter. The most commonly used biblical image for Jesus is the Good Shepherd revealing the loving and caring nature of God. In this context, the second coming of Christ is anticipated as less a threatening judgement than the final triumph of his love, through which he will put right what is now wrong, make straight what is now crooked and heal what is now wounded.

Though the affirmation that Jesus died for our sins is a standard formula in countless Chinese sermons, this does not mean that the cross is interpreted within the theological paradigm of divine jurisdiction, the standard framework for western orthodoxy from Anselm of Canterbury up to contemporary evangelicalism. The Chinese instead have found their hermeneutic key in John 15.13: 'No one has greater love than this, to lay down one's life for one's friends'.[44] Jesus' arms, stretched and nailed to the wooden beam, are seen as the outstretched arms of love, his last cry as the shout of love.[45] It is certainly not accidental that of all elements of the crucifixion narrative the passage of John 19.25-27 finds particularly frequent recognition: From the cross, Jesus arranges for his favourite disciple to become the adoptive son of his mother. In this way Jesus proves his love for his mother and his most faithful disciple even at the hour of his death.

In the context of traditional Confucianism, which despite the Maoist onslaught of the last century is still alive in China as a cultural ferment shaping people's minds and much of their behaviour, it should come as no surprise that Jesus is pictured as parent and educator for his followers in many Chinese sermons and testimonies. However it is interesting to take note that it is not the commanding authority of a strict father or the rigid principles of austere upbringing that serve as the point of reference but, here again, the sympathetic, warning voice and the caring, self-sacrificing parental love.

Wang Weifan, a teacher of the older generation at Nanjing Theological Seminary who is both very familiar with China's classical cultural heritage and in close touch with ordinary people at the grassroots level of society, has personally experienced the hardships of political campaigns and persecution; he has also observed what these hardships mean for mothers who give their lives for the well-being of their children, asking neither payment nor a word of thanks. For Wang, this attitude becomes a parable of God: 'All human mother-love is embodied in the person of the Virgin Mary. And in the mother-love of Mary herself we find an image of the suffering Christ: a divine

---

[43] *Jiang Dao Ji* 21, 42.
[44] See, for example, *Chinese Theological Review* (1985), 158f. and (1990), 159ff.
[45] *Jiang Do Ji* 26, 72.

heart pierced by a sword and silently bleeding, yet returning this divine love to God and to all humankind! In this sacred mother-love, any isolated suffering heart can seek warmth; any reviled and wounded heart can be comforted. And through the warmth and comfort of divine love, every isolated, suffering, reviled and wounded heart can be transformed with the great love which can be returned to God and to all humanity!'[46]

God as mother, painted in distinctively female colours:; it would not be the first time in history that a foreign religion taking root in China has seen its male God turned into a loving and affectionate goddess. When the Buddhist Amitabha cult spread to China where it became popular as the sect of the 'pure land' or the 'western paradise', one of the Boddhisatvas associated with this cult went through a significant change of personality. The Indian (male) Boddhisatva Avalokitesvara gradually changed gender and became the goddess Guanyin, one of the major deities in Chinese folk religion.[47]

Pentecostal Origins

An important question, which I am in no position to answer, concerns the origins of Pentecostal realities in China. If it is true that Chinese Christianity, to a large extent and on a wide geographical scale, betrays Pentecostal characteristics, then what are the historical reasons to be identified and where are the sources to be found? So far, little research has been done on this.

To be sure, Pentecostals were active in China during the period of western mission presence before 1949. What, if any, has been the long-term impact of the 'Holiness Movement' which manifested itself in 1931 in Shandong province with its emphasis on visions, dreams, exorcisms, faith healing and tongues speaking?[48] To what extent can the legacy of John Sung (1901-44) be felt, who toured all of China and South-East Asia as a powerful and charismatic preacher before World War II and whose daughter Song Tianying played a formative role in the independent house church movement over the last two decades?[49]

When foreign missions were still building their own ecclesial institutions in China, indigenous denominations came into being in the early twentieth century. Among them was the *Zhen Yesu Hui* (True Jesus Church).[50] Though

---

[46] *Chinese Theological Review* (1988), 132f.; see also Wang's auto-biographical reflection in *Chinese Theological Review* 8 (1993), 92ff.

[47] Edward Conze, *Eine kurze Geschichte des Buddhismus* (Frankfurt/M:, suhrkamp taschenbuch, 1986), 106.

[48] Bob Whyte, *Unfinished Encounter: China and Christianity* (Glasgow: Collins, 1988), 176.

[49] Tony Lambert, *Resurrection*, 253-54.

[50] Its origins and founders are a matter of debate; see Bob Whyte, *Unfinished Encounter*,

independent denominational structures have long been dissolved in the PRC, there are still many local churches around which clearly identify themselves as adherents of the True Jesus Church tradition. Moreover, True Jesus churches exist in Chinese communities throughout South-East Asia and North America, presenting themselves as an explicitly Pentecostal denomination.[51]

An equally indigenous but less Pentecostal movement was the *Juhui Chu* (Christian Assembly, also known as Little Flock), founded by Ni Duosheng (Watchman Nee) in the 1920s. This group, too, maintains a discernible identity in the PRC while it has spread throughout the Chinese world around the Pacific.[52]

While both the True Jesus Church and the Local Assemblies are recognized by the CCC as legitimate expressions of Chinese Protestant Christianity and are partially integrated in the CCC network, other indigenous movements are branded by the government as sects or cults, having no chance of registration with the government. Among these are the *Mentu Hui* (Apostolic Church)[53] and

---

177, and *Bridge* 63 (Jan./Feb. 1994), 2.

[51] According to self-presentations on the internet (www.tjc.org.sg; www.tjc-ukga), the True Jesus Church sees itself as 'the revival of the true church in the apostolic time', with reference to Joel 2.23. It takes tongues speaking as an initial sign, observes the Sabbath and practises foot-washing. Baptism is only seen as valid if it is performed by complete immersion with the head facing downward in natural and living water (a stream or a river). In China, True Jesus Church congregations are integrated in or separated from the CCC, depending on the region. For instance, in Binhai (North Jiangsu) cooperation with the CCC seems to be very smooth. In Chongqing municipality, Zhongxian county, True Jesus Church adherents outnumbered believers in the local CCC-affiliated church and tried to lure away even more, which led to a severe conflict with the CCC pastor. When in the mid-1990s the county Religious Affairs Bureau went through the process of registering religious venues, it consulted the CCC pastor about the validity of the True Jesus group. He denounced them as sectarian, whereupon the local authorities turned down their application for registration under the pretext that their practice of baptizing people in the river even in winter endangered public health. As an unregistered religious group, the True Jesus Church in Zhongxian county became formally illegal.

[52] The Christian Assembly, originating from Shanghai, became part of a revival movement quickly spreading through Shandong, Jiangsu, Zhejiang and Fujian in the 1920s. It was fairly orthodox in nature. Ni Duosheng, for example, was critical of the Pentecostal practices of the 'Holiness Movement' in Shandong (Bob Whyte, 176). Today, congregations of the Christian Assembly are an integrated part of the CCC network in many parts of China. They have a very quietist influence on Chinese Protestantism and have so far blocked all attempts to develop the CCC into an institutionalized church through their refusal to recognize an ordained ministry.

[53] Like the Christian Assembly, the Apostolic Church favours a non-institutional model of the church, opposing the offices of pastor and bishop. Alan Hunter & Kim-Kwong Chan describe its adherents as mostly very poor peasants with a deep despair about this

the *Huhan Pai* (Yellers or Shouters),[54] both quite strong groups in certain areas. The *Yesu Jiating* (Jesus Family), originating from northern Shandong, used to be organized in Christian communes, which were forbidden by the socialist government soon after the Revolution. Some of their former adherents play a very constructive role in the CCC-affiliated churches of Shandong.[55]

Apart from traditional domestic Pentecostal groups, Pentecostal denominations from outside, too, may have their effects in China today. How should one assess the influence Pentecostals from Hong Kong exert on Christianity in the Pearl River Delta or international Christian broadcasting programmes have on the church in all of China? Are sectarian groups like the Yellers or the Spirit Church supported by Pentecostal forces abroad? And to what degree do these groups influence the broader Christian movement inside China?

For the time being, it is perhaps impossible to do serious research in this field, since most of such international connections are, according to China's standards, illegal and many of the above-mentioned religious groups inside China would not want their activities to be put under scrutiny.

---

world and inclinations to extreme forms of eschatology. They emphasize spirit baptism as well as exorcism, healing, vision and prophecy (199-210). A lot of the positive material and psychological effects of the Apostolic Church on its followers as described by Hunter & Chan I could observe among CCC-affiliated Christians in equally poor and remote areas. According to oral information, most CCC leaders regard the followers of the Apostolic Church not as sectarian but as partly misguided Christians.

[54] The group is dubbed 'Yellers' or 'Shouters' because of their style of praying. Little is known about them. They are branded a counter-revolutionary sect by the authorities and also the CCC distances itself sharply from the group. A wave of arrests in Henan in 1983 has attracted international attention (see Bob Whyte, 406f.; Tony Lambert, *Resurrection*, 90f.).

[55] The Jesus Family was started in the village of Mazhuang in 1921. According to Bob Whyte, 177, there were 140 communities in eight provinces by 1941. The movement's origins were clearly Pentecostal, with an emphasis on dreams and visions and commonly practised mass prayers and emotional worship. In 1994, attempts of re-establishing a Jesus Family community in north-western Shandong were stopped, its leaders arrested. During a visit in 1995, I learned that the TSPM chair-person of Weifang prefecture (northern Shandong), an elderly lady in her 80s, was a former Jesus Family member who now played a decisive role in promoting young seminary graduates and placing them in leadership positions. The founder of the first Christian hospital after the Cultural Revolution was a son of a leading Jesus Family adherent. When I featured this village hospital (*Amity Newsletter* 27 [Winter 1993/94], 1-3), I emphasized the communal, almost monastic style, in which doctors and nurses were organized. To mention the Jesus Family connection, however, would have violated the CCC policy of downplaying denominationalism and suppressing sectarianism.

Furthermore, it may be asked whether a denominational approach will be particularly fruitful after all.[56] Perhaps the answer to the question of why China's contemporary Christianity features so many and clear Pentecostal characteristics should not so much be sought in particular strands of Christianity and their individual historical or geographical impact today, but rather in China's cultural context in general. What elements in China's traditional religions, social organization, politics and common worldview help Pentecostal characteristics to emerge within its domestic Christianity? Is there a natural affinity between Chineseness and Pentecostalism?

However, even such a national or cultural approach could prove to be too narrow-minded. Perhaps scientific comparison with Pentecostal movements in other countries and continents may one day lead us to the conclusion that under certain social, economic and organizational conditions Pentecostalism can flourish anywhere in the world; that Pentecostalism is nothing other than Christianity in the form of 'primal religion' which comes to the surface wherever the subjects of religion are more or less left to themselves and to their fight for a decent life in a hostile and threatening environment, and where there are no forces strong enough to regulate, control, tame and refine the elemental human religious impulse. In other words, we may come to the conclusion that Pentecostalism is the universal form of Christianity's return 'to the raw inner core of human spirituality'.[57]

---

[56] Grace May, 'A Comparative Study of the Christian Assembly, the True Jesus Church, and the Jesus Family: Three Ecclesial Case Studies of Protestantism in China' (Unpublished paper presented at the Boston Theological Institute 1996); Orlando Costas, 'Modernization, the Church and the East Asia Experience' (Presented at Consultation on Global Mission). May summarizes the common features of the three more or less Pentecostal groups as: a) freedom to choose their own form of leadership, b) suffering during the Cultural Revolution and under the current administration, c) experiencing unprecedented growth, d) attributing this growth to the leading of the Holy Spirit, e) practising baptism by immersion, f) showing radical, if not fundamentalist, dependence on Scripture and g) putting great emphasis on Christian activity and little on theological reflection. According to my experience, however, all these features are by no means limited to the groups described in her paper. Rather they are common features of most Protestant groups and congregations in China, regardless of their denominational affiliation.

[57] Harvey Cox, 105.

Indigenous Chinese Pentecostal Denominations

Deng Zhaoming

In the rural and small towns in China, when asked about the rapid church growth most Christians would give you an immediate answer: the Spirit moves. If you urge them to further explain the phenomenon you might hear them say: 'It's God's mighty work, for without miracles, there would have been no Christianity'. What they mean here is faith healing, the most dominant factor in the spread of Protestant Christianity in China today. Indeed, in the so-called post-denominational Protestantism in China, the practice of faith healing is being seen everywhere. Thus faith evangelists who are equipped with the gifts of the Spirit, i.e. physical healing, speaking in tongues, prophecy, supernatural knowledge etc. are winning great popularity in the countryside.

The search for being filled with the Spirit and other gifts of the Spirit can be traced back to Pentecostal influences that resulted from the revivals of 1906-1907 in North America. The Pentecostal activists, fired by pre-millennial urgency, came across the Pacific to Hong Kong in August 1907, just short of a year after the great happenings at Azusa Street in June 1906 in Los Angeles. Other enthusiastic Pentecostals reached mainland China not later than 1908.[1]

As Prof Bays pointed out, the Pentecostals took the concept of the age of the 'latter rains' as a theological construct explaining why the Holy Spirit was especially active now and used the Book of Acts as a primitive normative model for church and mission. Their vision was to 'unite the Church and propel it backwards to the Apostolic age and forward to Christ's return'. Thus they often used the term 'Apostolic Faith' in their publications and for the name of Pentecostal groups, movements or congregations.[2]

But due to the strong suspicion of the traditional Protestant missions in China, their dreams of transcending denominational boundaries failed and in the end they could not but create their own mission structures. Nevertheless their ideas and practices had taken root in Chinese ground. Today Pentecostal foreign missions no longer exist in China, yet Christian groups of various

---

[1] See Daniel H. Bays, 'Pentecostalism in 20th Century China: Denominational Results of a Non-Denominational Movement' (A study delivered at the 2nd Symposium on the History of Christianity in Modern China, Deptment of History, Hong Kong Baptist University and Alliance Bible Seminary, Jan., 2001, Hong Kong).

[2] Ibid.

shades manifest themselves clearly in the Pentecostal mould, even though most of them now do not have the faintest idea about the origins of their traditions.

That Pentecostalism casts such a spell over many free-lance evangelists in China is because it fits well with traditional Chinese popular religion, which also stresses the miraculous and the supernatural. Its intense millenarianism and primitivism give its followers both a hope and an assurance in times of uncertainty caused by natural calamities and poverty, political tension and a sense of meaninglessness of life, as has often been the case in Chinese history. A hope, because in the imminent second coming of Christ people who are driven by stress think that they begin to see the light at the end of the tunnel. An assurance, because like Chinese scholars who care about the orthodoxy and purity of their teachings Chinese peasants too find much comfort in the belief that they are returning to the essential truths and behaviour of first-century Christianity. A further attractive point in Pentecostalism is its egalitarianism, which makes available God's revelation to all in dramatic fashion through the gifts of the Spirit. Any believer could have the same access to God and the same use of the gifts of the Spirit.[3]

This has facilitated the emergence and blossoming of home meeting points. As in pre-Liberation days, the overwhelming majority of their leaders do not go to seminaries and are seldom trained theologically. They study the Bible all by themselves and claim that they are guided by the prompting of the Spirit. No wonder old-time sects as well as newly arisen movements are ever more prominent despite intense political pressure for state control. For some time now, both the government sanctioned *lianghui*, meaning the China Christian Council (CCC) and the Three-Self Committee (TSPM), as well as the government Religious Affairs Bureau (RAB) find it necessary to focus on 'sects and heresies' and urge the Chinese church to stand up to the grim situation of 'fraudulent religion' in the same way that society must eliminate the fake goods that have flooded the market in recent years.

In the long list of 'evil sects' are found the *Lingling Jiao* which is a breakaway group from the True Jesus Church, the *Beili Wang* (Established King), the *Quan Fanwei* (All-Scope), the *Kuangye Hui* (Wilderness), the *Mentu Hui* (Disciples), the *Kupai* (Weepers), the *Chongsheng Dao* (Way of Rebirth), the Full Gospel of Blood, Water and Spirit (also known as the Apostolic Faith Church) and many others that are difficult to characterize.[4]

What I want to introduce to you are two old-time churches in China: the True Jesus Church and the Jesus Family. These two churches were founded and governed by Chinese Christians in the 1920s, which was a decade for new intellectual ideas in China. The famous May Fourth Movement took place in

---

[3] So Daniel Bays in his essay in Hong Kong.

[4] For a detailed report on the *Lingling* and *Beili Wang*, see my article 'Recent Millennial Movements in Mainland China: Three Cases', *Japanese Religion*, Jan, 1998.

1919 and set the stage for the anti-foreign mood of the 1920s. It was during this decade that the Communist Party was formed. National pride and a concomitant increase in national outrage toward foreign domination defined the era. Anti-western and anti-Christian movements became popular leaving the western-founded church in a difficult position. In this highly charged atmosphere of political and intellectual ferment, several indigenous churches were formed in response to the need for a truly Chinese church fit for a proud new country.

It might be argued that even these two churches had early formative connections with religious movements overseas. While this foreign connection seems to mitigate against the idea of a fully Chinese church, the paradox can be explained in this way. The patriotism and the antiwestern sentiments of the 1920s demanded a Chinese church that was not the running dog of the imperialists. American Pentecostalism and charismatic Christianity provided a form of Christian religious expression that was loose enough to allow for the emergence of such a church. What was especially significant about these two foreign religious movements was their stress on the leadership of the Holy Spirit and the resulting de-emphasis on educated (read western educated) ordained clergy. One need only experience the power of the Holy Spirit and then he or she was free to evangelize and start a movement. The result of this combination of Chinese patriotism with imported free-form Christianity was the first serious attempt at creating 'Three-Self' churches in China.

It is fair to say that of all the churches in China during the 1920s through the 1940s, these indigenous churches were self-supported to a greater degree than any of the others. In addition to their Three-Self aspirations, these churches shared several other characteristics. Their leadership espoused a rhetoric of egalitarianism and actively opposed the office of ordained clergy. At the same time, each of these churches was led, without exception, by autocrats and was structured in a very hierarchical fashion. The leaders demanded absolute obedience and were charismatic to the point where this obedience was freely pledged. The membership of them was overwhelmingly uneducated and many had experienced serious illnesses.

Healing and miracles often played the key role in attracting new members and the worship style was Pentecostal or Charismatic. Finally, these indigenous churches shared a particularly harsh and early demise at the hands of the Communist Party. Despite early efforts to adapt to the new political situation ushered in by the Communist revolution, each church failed to meet the political and religious demands of the TSPM. Whereas denominational churches founded by western missionaries were able to join together under the banner of the TSPM and continue functioning through 1966, the indigenous churches became the immediate targets of the Party. Their leaders were arrested and condemned; their churches were forcibly disbanded. All of this took place with the vehement support of the TSPM. The role of the TSPM as an accomplice in the demise of the indigenous churches has resulted in pronounced tensions between these churches and the patriotic movement that persist to this day.

The True Jesus Church

The True Jesus Church claimed to be the ark in the last days. 'It had the responsibility to preach the gospel of salvation, as well as the sacred mission of correcting the mistakes of all other churches'. Its goal was 'to revive the true Church like the one of the Apostolic Age' and to correct the many errors in the teachings of the various confessions, their own interpretation of the scripture, or their arbitrary additions and subtractions.[5]

Believing that there was only one body of Christ that was the Church, they asserted that there could only be one true Church. This being the case, all other churches were considered to have gone astray by changing the gospel through philosophy and empty deceit, according to human tradition, according to the elementary spirits of the universe, and not according to Christ (Col. 2.8-9; Gal. 1. 610).

The TJC believed that there were two phases of the promise of the Holy Spirit, the pouring out of the Spirit in the Apostolic Age called the autumn rain or the early rain and that before the second coming of the Lord in the last days called the spring rain or the latter rain (Deut. 11.14; Jer. 5.24; Joel 2. 23). It also believed that the early rain at Pentecost was the pioneering period of the Holy Spirit and the latter rain of the present day would be the perfecting period of the Spirit. The fact that the original True Jesus Church has been able to reappear today is believed to be the result of the outpouring of the latter rain spoken of by the prophet Hosea, 'Let us know, let us press on to know the Lord; his going forth is sure as dawn; he will come to us as the showers, as the spring rains that water the earth' (Hos. 6.3). Based on Ezek. 43.2,4 which states that the glory of God came from the East, the TJC asserted that the true church emerged in the East. The Apostolic Church was established by the Jews in the East, in the same way that the TJC was established by the Chinese in the East.

The word 'true' in the name TJC was always a source of contention in the larger Christian community. The TJC, however, claimed that their name was revealed through scripture. The proof text was 1 Cor. 11.3, 'I want you to understand that the head of every man is Christ' which unfolded in the following way: Christ was the head of every man, thus Christ had to be put above every man and the head of Christ is God, thus God is above Christ. God being true, Christ being Jesus, and every man being the church, thus revealed the name.

---

[5] The TJC in Taiwan has published a series of booklets to introduce itself. See *How Can I Join the 'True Church'?* and *A Brief Introduction to the TJC*.

| True | Jesus | Church |
| God | Christ | Every Man |

Pentecostal Origins and Belief

The founding of the TJC was influenced by both foreign and domestic causes. American Pentecostalism that sent its first missionary to Shanghai in 1907 constituted the foreign cause bringing with it tongues-speaking and faith healing. Domestically, the upsurge of nationalism at the turn of the century coupled with the concomitant anti-western and anti-Christian movements, caused many Christian groups to distance themselves from foreign missions.

The first TJC member to contact the Apostolic Faith Mission of the American Pentecostal church was Zhang Lingshen. He was a native of Weixian, Shandong and a Presbyterian deacon. In 1909 he heard of the charismatic movement and came to Shanghai to learn more about it. This first encounter with Pentecostalism had little effect, but on his second visit in December of the same year, he was 'filled with the Spirit'. The next year he took the baptism of immersion and was ordained as an elder by Elder Peterson of the Apostolic Faith Mission in Beijing. Shortly thereafter Zhang had a vision that the Sabbath was to be observed and convinced elder Peterson to change the day of worship to Saturday in July, 1916.

The second leader was a native of Rongyi, Hebei named Paul Wei. A member of the London Mission, he was cured of a serious illness through the laying on of hands of Elder Xin Shengmin of the Faith Mission in 1912. Shortly afterwards, while praying in his home in Beiping (now Beijing), he received the Spirit and baptized himself in living water.

The third of the triumvirate was Barnabas Zhang, with the original name of Dianju. He was also from Weixian and also a Presbyterian. In 1912, Zhang Lingsheng preached in his own county and Barnabas, after hearing him, received the baptism of the Spirit and began to speak in tongues on 16 March.

Moved by the Spirit, Paul Wei looked back over the preaching and the doctrines of the church and came to believe that many of the teachings ran contrary to Scripture. He was determined, therefore, to assume responsibility for correcting all the doctrinal errors that had crept into the other churches. In 1914, after selling his textile firm, he struck out in faith to preach under the banner of 'The Restored True Jesus Church of all Nations'. In 1918, Zhang Lingsheng came to Tianjin to receive the laying on of hands from Wei, and in the following spring Barnabas was also ordained by Wei as an elder in Weixian. In this way three lay businessmen, after giving up their trade, became founders of the TJC, which was to become one of the largest single churches in China.

Unfortunately, Paul Wei, the original founder, died in 1919, and the leadership fell to Zhang Lingsheng. The momentum of this new church, however, was never lost. By 1920, it had spread into Hubei and Hunan, by 1923 into Jiangsu, Zhejiang and Fujian. While preaching in Zhangzhou, Fujian, several Presbyterians from Taiwan were present. They accepted the new doctrine and invited Barnabas Zhang and Thomas Guo to go over to Taiwan to preach and set up churches in March, 1926.

In July 1926, the headquarters of the TJC was set up in Nanjing and at the same time the members began to publish the *Shengling Bao* (The Holy Spirit Monthly). In the following year, the headquarters was moved to Shanghai. In 1929 a split arose within the leadership over a difference of policy and Barnabas Zhang left the church and set up a new programme in Hong Kong. From Hong Kong he also branched out into Southeast Asia. Much confusion in the church resulted from this schism, and in April 1931 an emergency session was held in Shanghai to deal with the trouble. Barnabas was excommunicated and the churches in the north and south were invited again to be under one administration. Apparently, the evangelistic work had not been hindered. According to the investigation of the headquarters in Nanjing, by 1948 the TJC had spread to each province, with more than 700 churches.

The TJC exclusive attitude with regard to other churches and its self-understanding as the 'true church' whose mission was to correct the hypocrisy of others are evident in its credo. Attention to the correct way of performing rites is characteristic of their concern for being the Apostolic church. The considerable influence of American Pentecostalism can also clearly be detected. Of great importance to the TJC is the baptism of the Holy Spirit. It marks the difference between the weak, faltering pre-Pentecost Peter and the post-Pentecost Peter who was filled with a new power and wisdom from on high. Those who have received the Holy Spirit show bodily vibration and shaking of hands; even though a few of them might not have these physical signs, they all speak in tongues.

The TJC observes the Sabbath because it believes that changing the Sabbath to Sunday was accomplished by ecclesiastical decree at the Council of Laodicea in 336 and has no basis in the New Testament. The following is a translation of the Credo.

The Credo: the TJC Believes:

That Jesus Christ was the Word turned flesh; that he died on the cross for the redemption of sinners, resurrected on the third day and ascended into heaven; and that he is the only saviour of humankind, the Lord of heaven and earth and the only one true God.

That both the New and the Old Testaments are inspired by God, the only proof of the true Word and the criterion for Christian life.

That the TJC was founded by Jesus Christ through the latter rain Holy Spirit to restore the true church of the Apostolic Age.

That water baptism is a sacrament of remission of sin and regeneration. One must receive the baptisms of both the water and the Spirit, in the name of Jesus and be immersed in living water, with the head bowed in the likeness of Jesus' death.

That receiving the Holy Spirit is the guarantee of our inheritance of the Heavenly Kingdom. The speaking in tongues is the evidence of having received the Spirit.

That the sacrament of foot-washing is to have part in the Lord. It teaches us to love each other, to be holy, humble, to serve and to forgive. Every new convert must receive this rite once after baptism, in the name of Jesus. Mutual washing of feet is practiced when necessary.

That the Holy Communion is held as a memorial to the death of the Lord. It is the sacrament of eating the flesh and drinking the blood of the Lord together, to be united with the Lord for eternal life and resurrection in the last days. It needs to be administered frequently with unleavened bread and grape juice.

That the Sabbath (Saturday) is the day on which God gives his blessing. We observe it to remember his creation and redemption in grace and hope for an eternal rest in the age to come

That one is saved by grace through faith, but one must seek holiness, practise the teaching of the Bible, honour God and love one's neighbours through the prompting of the Spirit.

That the Lord will come at the end of the world to judge all people; the righteous will have eternal life, the sinners eternal punishment.

Among these, the following five are cardinal doctrines: Water baptism, Washing of feet, Holy Communion, Baptism of the Holy Spirit, and The Sabbath

The influence of Pentecostalism is also evident in the constitution of the TJC that emphasizes the democracy of the Spirit in its leadership style and its decision-making policies. At the same time, however, the constitution seeks to distance the TJC from the foreign church by insisting on its affinity with the Apostolic Church. By claiming that all churches since the Apostolic Church were heretical, the TJC was able to extract itself from centuries of western church history. This same move to connect itself with the pure Apostolic church and not with the foreign, tainted western church is evident in the above mentioned interpretation of Ezekiel where the TJC shares with the Apostolic Church its eastern origin. The desire to be separate is also shown through a pronounced concern for purity and a tendency to regard the rites and doctrines of other churches as 'contamination'.[6]

The Church Under Attack

Despite TJC's efforts to distance itself from the western church through association with the ancient and Eastern Apostolic church, it could not conceal its American Pentecostalist leanings. Before Liberation, it was possible for it to remain apolitical by exhorting such ideas as 'be spiritual in everything' or 'do not associate with atheists', 'loving the world and loving country show a lack of piety', and 'a true Christian should be above politics, above class, above nation, above the world and above everything'. With the advent of the Communist era in 1949, political neutrality ceased to be an option. In order to survive the church had to adopt a politicized Three-Self agenda in which self-government, self-propagation and self-support were put under the administration and censorship of the Communist Party.

Isaac Wei, the son of founder Paul Wei, for example, picked up the mirror of Mao Zedong thought and learned to 'carefully and honestly study the reflection of ourselves, our church, its clergy and laity'.[7] He was brought to see that his patriotic thinking' which he had valued previously was 'extremely muddled'. He realized that he had 'unconsciously become a tool of American imperialism'. The requisite pro-government stance of churches in the 'New Three-Self' movement established after the founding of New China became explicit in the Christian Manifesto in 1950 which described the goals of the movement as to 'give thorough-going support to the 'Common Political Platform', and under the leadership of the government oppose imperialism, feudalism and bureaucratic capitalism'. Christians were required to thoroughly remould their thinking and to take a firm 'people's standpoint' so as to better serve the broad masses of 'people'.

The establishment of the new Three-Self Reform Movement marked the beginning of a merciless attack on those indigenous churches which had sought to be three-self in an apolitical sense from the time of their founding. Isaac Wei's self-examination is a good example of the TJC's awakening to a new political environment. In it he admitted, 'I was detached from American imperialism only physically, but mentally I was still tightly bound by it. In fact, I was an accomplice of counter-revolution and a guide of the feudalistic landlord leisure class'.

---

[6] For the translation of the Constitution and a detailed report on the later development of the TJC, see my article in *Bridge* 62 (Nov-Dec, 1993).

[7] His self-examination was printed in *TF* 302 (1952).

At the end of Wei's examination, he tried to point the way for the TJC in the new era:

We should at once follow the call of Chairman Mao and by means of criticism and self-criticism reform our thinking as a basis for church reform.

If you know of any responsible person, preacher or spiritual brother who is anti-people, you should in the spirit of Jesus' teaching let your yea be yea and your nay be nay, frankly report it to the proper government authority, lest the holy church be corrupted.

We should all sign the Manifesto which Y.T. Wu and others have promulgated, and accept the leadership of the Preparatory Committee of the Chinese Christian Oppose-America/ Help-Korea Three-Self Reform Movement.

Every local church should earnestly study the *Tian Feng* weekly, for this is the organ of the Chinese Christian, Oppose-America Help-Korea, Three-Self Reform Movement Committee and it directs us how to promote the Three-Self Reform Movement (TSRM) and love both country and church.

We should encourage our members to join the Sino-Soviet Fellowship, and thus deepen the insoluble ties that bind these two great countries together.

We should become a Three-Self Reform Church, a religious institution of the Chinese people. In teaching we should warn against the poison of American imperialism, feudalism and capitalism. We should not lay so much stress on miracles, nor tell people that taking medicine and consulting a doctor are sins, but rather should train our preachers in the elements of public hygiene and midwifery, for greater service to the people.

Our preachers should at once take up some trade in which they can support themselves and adopt the standpoint of labour, for the Bible says, 'He that will not work, let him not eat'. Now under Chairman Mao's leadership we should obey this teaching, and thus obey his call for greater production and thrift, for economic advancement and the establishment of the New China.

Our church and other churches should come together in denominational union. Our own church should also show a greater spirit of unity, abolishing 'radical democracy', anarchic informality, subjectivism and individualism and thus accomplish real reform. In the spirit of persuasion we must introduce the practice of criticism and self-criticism, in order to reform our church, correct it, and make it a force for the creation of the New China.

The TJC, for the most part, followed what Wei proposed in his self-examination. *Tian Feng* played a vanguard role in the thought-reform programme. Apparently even the examination which Wei made leaned heavily on members of the Three-Self movement for direction and phraseology. His appeal to TJC followers to sign the Manifesto received a favourable response. He claimed that his church had more than a thousand churches, and those who signed the Manifesto numbered more than 13,000, ie, about one tenth of the total membership. Moreover in order to become a significant part of the reform movement, the General Assembly of the TJC held a special meeting from 1-10 April, 1953, in which a Preparatory Committee of the Three-Self Reform Movement (TSRM) of the TJC was created and a motion was passed to move the General Assembly from Beijing to Wuhan.

However all these efforts were not able to help the TJC keep its own identity, for the climate was for Christians to 'provide help to the government to crack down on counter-revolutionaries and scum who lay low in Christianity' on the one hand and to draw a line between the 'New Three-Self' and the 'Old Three-Self' on the other. The latter was attacked because 'the old Three-Self Movement realized its goals from a religious standpoint only, but neglected the issue of anti-imperialism and patriotism', so much so that it allowed 'its nature to be falsified by imperialism and itself to be a captive to the thinking of other people'.[8] 'So long as Old China, the whole country and the society had not been liberated from the rule of imperialism and Chinese reactionaries, it was only natural that Christianity could not [achieve] independence and liberation'.[9]

Bearing this climate in mind, it is not surprising to see that these independent churches were attacked and dissolved one after the other. In April, 1952, the founder of the Little Flock, Watchman Nee, was arrested during the 'Anti-Five' campaign. At almost the same time, a powerful team was sent by the 'Three-Self' Committee to Mazhuang, Shandong to investigate the Jesus Family. The thoroughgoing and painstaking investigation lasted more than four months. The result of it was an 'Exhibition Unmasking the Crimes Committed by the Leaders of the Jesus Family' which was first held in Beijing from the end of March to the beginning of April and also later in other cities. Then in June, 1953, 'the broad masses of Shanghai Catholics launched their struggle against the imperialists in the Catholic Church'. Shanghai newspapers began to report the great number of Chinese infants cruelly murdered by the imperialists in the past eighty some years in the nursery house of the Catholic Cathedral at Xujiahui. Given this environment of accusations and suspicions, the TJC could only anticipate its own downfall.

Isaac Wei's self-examination was not able to save him from an early arrest. More responsible leaders of the TJC fell in disgrace. It was forced to admit that faith hailing, exorcism and miracle performances were not only 'mistakes', but 'unlawful activities' that should be punished and cleared away. The situation was exacerbated; in 1960, the name of the TJC became bracketed signifying its non-existence. It had been cleansed and purged to the point of disappearance.

---

[8] *TF* 536 (17), 57/9/9, 23.
[9] *TF* 534 (15), 57/8/12, 13.

Resurrected with a Veangence

After the Cultural Revolution, the TJC resurfaced and reported rapid growth in North Jiangsu, Fujian, Hunan, Hubei, Sichuan, Shaanxi, Shanxi and Henan. A recent estimate claims that its membership is well over one million, ie, about 1/10 of Chinese Protestants. A visit to Xianyang district, Shaanxi might illustrate how they function at grassroots level.[10]

As elsewhere, the TJC here adopts a 'sheep leading another sheep in evangelism' from the very beginning. All their evangelists are volunteers and not one of them has had any regular theological training. Yet since 1989 the TJC has spread like wildfire. The reason for this rapid growth is quite simple, because it seems that all their believers are enthusiastic evangelists. Many of them come to church because they are discriminated against in their families. For example wives are maltreated by their husbands. As there is no other place for them to go, they come to Christ and pour out their grievances to him in prayer. What is surprising is the fact that once they are saved they keep an open door. Their healing power and their hospitality have moved many, including highly educated people, among them not a few Communist Party members.

TESTIMONY 1: ZHAO GUIFANG, FEMALE, AGE 53, PANGNAN VILLAGE, SHUANGZHAO XIANG, QINDU PREFECTURE

At the end of 1988, Zhao found herself with only skin and bone left. The hospital said she had hepatitis, appendicitis and womb cancer. Every night she had to put a big rock on her big stomach in order to get some sleep. Her case was diagnosed as incurable.

One day there was a kind of gathering in the village. A stranger came. She sang and prayed. Her strange behaviour drew the attention of quite a few people. Zhao heard the noise outside her home and wanted to know what was going on. But the big stomach made her walking difficult. For as soon as she walked, it ached and her head also pained. She could only inquire of her husband about it. Her husband, in order not to trouble her, said that there was nothing happening outside. Of course, Zhao did not believe him. She tried very hard to walk with her hands on the wall. The gathering was just around the corner from her home. When she arrived, the evangelist asked her to pray. She did not know what was praying, however. The evangelist then laid her hands on her head and prayed for her. After a while, she felt the pain in her head gone. In joy she told the crowd what had happened. In response they jeered at her, for they did not believe something like that could indeed take place. Zhao, however, knew that it was true. The fact that she could walk home without the pain she experienced when coming out was a proof.

---

[10] The following two testimonies are taken from my visit to the TJC in Jan. 1997.

Later, she found out that there were Christian meetings both Wednesdays and Fridays in the village. Having had the good experience the first time, she went out to join the meeting again. This time it took place in a home. As the few gathered in the house to pray, some one fell down to the ground from the kang (a heatable brick bed). She became unconscious and motionless. Then everybody knelt down and prayed for her. After about ten minutes, she woke up and gave praise to the Lord with the others. In February the following year, Zhao was baptized.

One month after her baptism, she saw a vision. She heard a voice at about 11 a.m. It told her to ask her husband to stand guard at the door, forbidding any one from coming into the house. She was lying on her kang, feeling faint. It seemed that angels were operating on her stomach. She could feel that it was opened. But she did not feel any pain. Finally the operation was over. One angel said: 'See how big is the tumour.Ah, the appendix is festering'.Another said: 'In the name of the Lord' and she touched all over her body.

Zhao rose again. It was 1 p.m. She was greatly relieved. Her stomach was no longer swollen and there was not one scar left on it. She was completely healed.

The whole village looked at her in great astonishment.

Before Zhao was healed, her husband was not happy about her going to the meetings. Afterwards however, he changed his attitude and agreed to be baptized in 1990. Since then, they have turned their home into a meeting point. The door is open from early morning to late evening. The sick are welcome. If needed, they are allowed to eat and stay there until recovery at no charge. On the average, about thirty people come to her daily.

Like Zhao, quite a number of TJC converts have the gift of an exceptional healing power. Out of gratitude, they reach out in their own villages and the neighbouring villages. In the past couple of years, Pangnan has developed into an important outpost of the TJC in the suburbs of Xianyang. It has now a membership of 500 people.

Testimony 2: Zhao Yu-e, female, age 40, Baihe village, Mazhuang xiang

Mazhuang lies in the northwest of Xianyang. There is a very good network of irrigation. The average annual income of peasants per capita can reach as high as two to three thousand RMB that is considered high in the comparatively poor Northwest region.

The introduction of the TJC to Mazhuang began in 1984. A sister came there in April and not until June was she able to convert a single person. In July there was a further convert. The pioneering work was therefore by no means easy. But at present there are more than 200 believers in Baihe that has a population of less than 900. And there are twenty-one villages in Mazhuang, with Christians in each village. The number of TJC members in Mazhuang is around 3,000 people. More surprising is the phenomenon that in some villages, like Baihe, every door and window is unlocked. Visitors can push open the doors and make themselves at home while the owners are working outside in the fields. This is because where Christians live together there is no fear of break-ins.

It all happened in 1992. Zhao Yu-e was an able-bodied peasant woman. She rode on a tricycle every day to market. One day, however, the tricycle dashed upon a concrete water pipe and threw her against the massive concrete. Her head was severely injured. When found, she was rushed to a hospital. Upon arrival she was certified dead.

The believers did not want to give up. They prayed at Yu-e's bed. A doctor said that it was useless and went away. The believers kept watch day and night. They took turns to pray for her. Yu-e was brought into the hospital at 10 am The next morning at 8 am, she suddenly regained consciousness. She opened her eyes as if nothing had happened. The whole hospital was taken by surprise. Both doctors and nurses could not believe their eyes. The superintendent was so moved that he inquired about how to believe in Jesus.

Recovering the 'True' Jesus Church?

The problem the TJC is facing at the moment is its attempt to rectify its name. All the time it claims that it is the 'True Jesus Church', not any 'Christian church'. The intention of the government is, however, also firm and clear not to let this happen. Knowing that it is impossible for them to have their own name, they prefer not having any. As a TJC in Liling, Hunan calmly remarked: 'We are now not allowed to have our sign engraved, we engrave it for the moment in our hearts. But when we build our churches, we always leave a blank space in the middle of the building. In due course, we will put our name back there'.

The Jesus Family

Founded in 1928 in Mazhuang, Shandong, the Jesus Family, a communitarian Protestant group and until today is little known to the outside world. The communitarian spirit of the Jesus Family was based on Acts, chapter 2 which reads, 'now the company of those who believed were of one heart and soul, and no one said that any of the things which he possessed was his own, but they had everything in common'. In the Jesus Family all things were communal, no one held private property. All members of the Family were required to live a simple and frugal life, to be hardworking and solid, ready to suffer for the Lord and each had to contribute his/her part to the Family, just like the disciples in the primitive church.

Jing Dianying, the undisputed family head, was raised in a Confucian environment. It was not until 1910 when he entered a middle school in Tai'an run by a Christian church that he came into contact with Christianity. Yet 'it seems that after his initial conversion to Christianity about 1913-14, he still flirted with becoming a Buddhist monk and in 1918 or 1919 may have joined the Shengxian Dao, a syncretiistic sect in the main White Lotus tradition that was prevalent in parts of Shandong even up to the 1960s'.[11] Then, in the mid-1920s, he was reconverted through contact with Pentecostal Christianity. 'Clearly it was contact with L. M. Anglin's Christian mission commune that gave Jing Dianying both the fervent religious Pentecostalism and the example of a self-sufficient egalitarian Christian community that fed directly into Jing's formation of the Jesus Family in 1927'. However, 'despite this joint sino-western origin, Jing never allowed any foreign influence on the later development of the group and foreign contact after 1927 was extremely limited'.

The perennial political unrest, economic hardship and finally the Japanese war provided the social context for the development of the Jesus Family. Indeed Jing's Christian movement had the initial goal of providing for the economic welfare of the needy. In 1921 Jing and others established in Mazhuang a Christian Savings Society on a cooperative store basis. It attempted to serve the needs of the economically and socially marginalized. By 1926, a silk reeling cooperative was formed which became the Jesus Family in 1927. As an economic co-op, the Jesus Family consisted of no more than ten people. They borrowed a house from a believer, rented a piece of land, bought three old looms and led a communal life. In order to subsist, each one had to toil unremittingly hard. As members increased, the Family moved to Beipo, about 1.5 km from Mazhuang, in 1930. Beipo was owned by the Jing family 'through providence' as legend would have it. There they built houses and gradually developed a whole range of economic activities that permitted the community to support and take care of itself. Besides basic agriculture, these activities included ironwork, shoe making, a medical department, construction, carpentry, needlework, a noodle factory and fruit orchards. The social structure of the Family was egalitarian. Those who joined had to renounce the world and all their goods, as well as their primary loyalties to Family members. Each member was required to commit him/herself totally to the community, unencumbered by other ties. To show that this Family was different from other families, Jing coined a new word. The Chinese character *jia*, which means house or home is composed of two radicals: *main*, a house and *shi*, pigs, meaning a house with livestock. Jing's new word was composed of 'people', instead of 'livestock', together with 'the Lord' who are now living in harmony in the house which is the Jesus Family.

After several years, the old home at Beipo, Mazhuang branched out. New homes were set up in the north, northwest and east of China. By the late 1940s there were over 100 Families with about 10,000 members. The largest community was still the old home in Mazhuang with about 500 members in the

---

[11] Daniel Bays in *Religion: Journal of the KSR* 26:1 (Oct., 1988).

late 1940s, over 100 houses and more than 10 working units.[12] Interestingly, over 95% of the Family members had not reached secondary education. The Jesus Family seemed to attract few intellectuals and people with money or property avoided it because of its communal and simple life.

Organization and Life

At the heart of the Jesus Family identity was the revelation and guidance of the Holy Spirit. To justify his understanding of ecclesiology, Jing initially did not devise any plan for church management. Everyone in the Family was trusted in the same way. Like other independent Christian groups, it also frowned upon the over-organization of conventional church structures. But as membership expanded, confusion arose and conflicts were unavoidable. Organization and management became a necessity as a small group evolved into a rigorous religious community. All members were taught the principle of 'from each according to his/her ability, to each according to his/her need' and 'no work, no food'. New members had to pass a stringent examination; visitors had to pay for their meals.

At first, admission into the Family was rigid. Everyone had not only to renounce their properties, but also to cut off their family ties with those relatives who refused to join the Family. This was described as 'joining the Family, losing the family'. Members were exhorted to love those in the Spirit more than those of the same blood; to love the Saviour more than one's life. The Family promised them 'wherever you are, there is your home, and your home is everywhere'. Not until 1948 did they adopt a more lenient approach, 'mutual seeking', i.e. believers were encouraged to try their best to bring their relatives and friends to the Family.

Within the Family, members were assigned to work in the different units mentioned above. Except for the youngest married couples, men and women lived in separate buildings. Engagements and weddings were arranged by Jing, the Family head. It happened that young teenagers were made to marry old men, the pretty were matched with the crippled and educated ones with the illiterate. Husbands and wives seldom had a chance to live together, for there were just a few rooms allotted to married couples which had to be shared by them in turn. Nurseries took care of the young children. Quite often, children of three to four years did not know who their parents were. But all received basic food, clothing, schooling and shelter at a subsistence level.

The day's regimen was scheduled around a cycle of religious activities. Pre-dawn prayer began after getting up at four in the morning. All knelt down to pray together until 5.30. Prayers were always interspersed with wailing and speaking in tongues. This was followed by singing spiritual songs and sharing

---

[12] *TF* 254 (Oct 3, 1951), 6-7.

testimonies, trances or dreams. Then came the exhortation of the Family head in the form of a sermon. Before it came to a close at 7.30, the whole congregation knelt down to pray aloud together and finally concluded with the Lord's Prayer. Only then were they allowed to retreat to their rooms to tidy up things and have their common breakfast.

After breakfast they worked in the different units until just before lunch when all people gathered together again in the chapel to sing and pray. There was a short recess after lunch, then they worked again. Post-dinner gatherings were filled with singing, praying, testimonies and exhortation.

Obedience is the principle of life. Every member is obliged to listen to the Family head. For example, Jing once said, 'if somebody received God's oracle in a dream to go to the east, the Family head can tell him to go to the west if he did not get the same oracle. The dreamer, for the sake of absolute obedience, must take the advice of the leader instead of God's command. Under such circumstances to obey man rather than God will not enrage God but will get His reward'.

Life is always simple in the Family. As one of their hymns describes, 'Eat a little bit slapdash, put on a little bit in rags, sleep a little bit off and on'. Even today, most Family members keep to a subsistence diet.

Theology in Hymns

The Family has yet to develop its theology. But it has a rich treasure house that is its hymnal. In addition to the contribution of Dong, Jing was also a gifted scholar. Hymns written by him numbered several dozen, all imbued with Christian Spirit and relevant to the Chinese situation and its cultural background. Whether his political ideal was revolutionary or counter-revolutionary can best be left to historians, but no one can deny that his hymns are very indigenous. The first hymn in their hymnal, for example, is the Jesus Family. It is a good example of inculturation. In it Jing tried to blend the ideal of the Confucian great harmony with the Bible stories, encouraging the believers to love each other in their sufferings so that they might see the coming of the Heavenly Kingdom on Earth through the life of the Jesus Family. It has twelve stanzas. The following are from the first through the fifth and the eighth:

1. The Jesus Family, full of love, in which the young are cared for; the old are in peace; widows, orphans, those left on their own and invalids are provided for; the sick are well taken care of and the dead buried properly; guests come and they feel as if they were a community of equality and mutual help. Soul brothers and sisters, we are all of one body.

3. The Jesus Family, full of joy, which has neither bitterness nor sadness. Real joy is flowing out from those who love each other. They praise [the Lord] morning and evening and they do not need musical instruments to accompany. All the

same there is sweet gratitude and love of the Lord. Are you not looking for fine art and recreation? When you are filled with the Spirit, your joy is untold.

4. The Jesus Family, full of hope, which does not love to eat or to dress up. High buildings and large mansions do not receive their admiration. Though our outer nature is wasting away, our inner nature is being renewed every day. The affliction of this world is slight and momentary. We deeply hope for the immediate return of Jesus, marching forward to welcome [him] in clothes of righteousness.

5. The Jesus Family, full of harmony, which has neither strife nor enmity. There is no boundary between races and nations. People from the east, west, south and north gather together; the yellow, the white, the red and the black form a single community of love, just as an undergarment is woven in one piece. The cross has wrought harmony. God's children, love your enemies.

8. The Jesus Family, full of Spirit, sees visions and speaks in tongues. They are all filled with the Spirit on the last day. Joyously they dance and sing spirituals; the power of God is made manifest through the healing of the sick and the casting out of demons. This is the witness of the Spirit himself. Are they filled with new wine? Or are they simply a public spectacle?

Hymn no. 63 is called 'Faithful Servants of the Family' which serves to explain the aim and fellowship of the Family. It has only two stanzas:

The Family is a fellowship of love, it is never a legal product. [In it they are all] fathers and sons, brothers and sisters. It is a meeting place for the weary and a place of comfort for the broken-hearted. On the last day when fierce winds and terrifying waves are raging and when laws both human and divine are defied, the Family of the Lord emerges at the right moment. It is like a hen just opening up her wings or a spiritual ark. You who labour and mourn, are you ready to return?

Peter left his net and followed the Lord; Noah gave up his family and built the ark. They were all chosen and became the leaders of soul saving. But now again, the water of the bitter sea is boundless and the waves of the flooding river reach far. How can we have shepherds like Noah who reform the church and build an ark to save the whole world? Can we expect that when the water rises the boat will go up and we will land in a green pasture to meet with the bridegroom forever?

In the Old Home in Mazhuang, the Family used to have a whole range of working units like ironwork, shoe making, poultry, needlework, etc. It is said that each unit was encouraged to write its own hymn to express their life and feelings. Without question the literary touch of Jing was everywhere. The following is a hymn of thanksgiving of the kitchen workers (no. 94):

In the big kitchen the sisters are numerous. We are weak; we dawdle and fret away the grace of the Lord. Because we are awkward in speech, we can only sing our thankfulness with one accord. Joy, joy, boundless joy, how joyful! Boundless joy, how joyful! We can only sing our thankfulness with one accord. Boundless joy, how joyful!

The big kitchen is most unusual, the more you work, the healthier you are. The Holy Spirit has shown us a vision. We see a long ladder standing on the top of the kitchen range and leading up to heaven. Only those who labour are allowed to climb it. The big kitchen leads up to heaven. The big kitchen leads up to heaven. We see a long ladder standing on the top of the kitchen range and leading up to heaven. Only those who labour are allowed to climb it. The big kitchen leads up to heaven.

Dissolution of the Jesus Family

In a time of radical political change, the Family with its communal pattern of organization, no foreign ties, no private property, ascetic life style, etc. made many outside observers believe that it would adjust smoothly to the new order. Indeed, it was even described as a 'proletarian church' and Jing himself took this interpretive stance in dealing with the new government. His group accounted for the largest number of initial signatures on the 'Christian Manifesto', the cornerstone of the Three-Self Movement and Jesus Family members actively supported the 'Resist-America/Aid-Korea Movement'. Even so, Jing was arrested in 1952 and the Family was disbanded. Charges were brought against Jing and other leaders. People who formerly praised the Family made an about-turn apologizing to the 'people' for their misleading articles.

In the wake of anti-imperialism in the church, only the Jesus Family was singled out for praise in *Tian Feng* in 1951: It is really touching to see their earnest and down-to-earth spirit of life, solid and hard-working; from childhood they are taught to bear hardships for the Lord. We believe that this single spark can burn in Wuhan, which will then attract many Christians to give up their private properties and march towards the communal life of 'from each according to his ability, to each according to his needs'.[13] For 'I have seen the most holy and beautiful faces in the world, these elders, brothers and sisters in the Family. The elderly ones of them are like Abraham, like Joseph; the younger ones like St John, like St Francis; the children like the child Jesus.... I love the young people in the Family, they love the Lord, love people, love poverty, love production, love labour'.[14]

Two years later, however, the tone changed completely. Led by the nephew of Jing, Zhendong, *Tian Feng* carried a series of diatribes against the Family

---

[13] Li Xing, 'My Impressions of the Jesus Family in Hankou', *TF* 249-250 (3 Feb., 1951).
[14] Jiang Yizhen, 'The Taste of the Jesus Family', *TF* 260 (21 April, 1951).

beginning from February, 1953. For example, 'In the past few decades, the Jesus Family has insulted the holy name of Jesus and endangered the Chinese people. From now on, this shameful name should not be heard again in New China'.[15] 'Jing Dianying colluded with Japanese invaders and the reactionary officers and officials of the puppet regime in the past thirty years; he also collaborated with the British and American imperialists, collecting information and engaging in anti-Soviet and anti-Communism propaganda'.[16]

The sudden turn of the event was, of course, the result of the 'painstaking and penetrating' efforts by the Preparatory Committee of the Resist-America and Aid-Korea Three-Self Reform Movement [predecessor of the TSPM]. In April, 1952 they sent a 'strong working team' to Mazhuang to help the Christians there reform themselves. After more than four months the task was successfully carried out. 'We have put an end to the control and exploitation of the Jesus Family in Mazhuang by the imperialist and reactionary, feudal influences'.[17]

To be sure, the dissolution of the Family was strongly politically motivated. Also not to be forgotten are the economic and realistic demands from inside. The isolation of the Family from all other churches could not but result in its radicalization and in its ability to keep people working and living in hardship while ignorant of the life outside. When the Family was dissolved, many of its young people came to see the real world for the first time and experienced a feeling of liberation.

A Church Incognito

Even after the Cultural Revolution, the Jesus Family were not allowed to organize themselves. They had to live incognito. The old home in Beipo was renamed Beixinzhuang (North New Village'). It was not until 1982 that the chapel there was renovated and re-opened. Without their own name, the believers insisted on their usual policy of 'no debt, no fundraising and no loan'. All expenditures were covered from the offering box. Though homes have now been normalized and there is no more communal meal, yet, symbolically, every year at Christmas, Easter, and Thanksgiving (after the autumn harvest in November), Christians still like to worship together and share a meal.

The following two cases show how difficult it is to live as a group for the Jesus Family believers.[18]

---

[15] Cheng Buyun, *TF* 357 (23 March, 1953).
[16] Zeng Guangxie, *TF* 357.
[17] See Note 18.
[18] The following two reports were written after my visit to Jinqu in April 1993 and to Duoyigou in February 1994.

CASE 1: JINQU, SHAANXI

The Jinqu village at Jiaofang, Mei Xian is a typical village in northwest China in which the inhabitants are hardworking, simple and honest. They have never dreamed to be rich, but they have also not complained of their poverty. As is the case in quite a few Shaanxi villages, the villagers of Jinqu are mainly from Shandong province and are still proud of their own dialect even though most of them were born in Shaanxi. In 1936, a year before the outbreak of the Sino-Japanese War, Jing Dianying, founder of the Jesus Family, decided to send his disciples out to various provinces to set up branch Families.

Most of those Christians who were sent, true to their tradition, were poor peasants. A few of them reached Jiaofang and began to build the Family there. They have been taught and trained in the spirit of sharing all possessions commonly patterned after the second chapter of Acts. They believed that the ark of Noah typified the church and all those who entered in it must sell their possessions and goods and distribute them to all, for the path of the Family is a path of renouncing and dying: Whoever strives to keep life loses it; whoever renounces it and denies himself enters life. They remembered the examples of the rich young man who had kept everything that he was expected to keep, yet because he was unwilling to sell what he possessed and give it to the poor, he was barred from entering the door of the family. They were also reminded of such leaders like Moses and Aaron who were finally not blessed with the entrance into the Promised Land. They know they were not better than the thousands who had died in the wilderness. But they were warned against going through the broad gate of worldly temptation, especially the temptation of going out for power and money.

Whether as a consequence of their belief or conditioned by the hard reality, the Christians at Jinqu have never tasted an affluent life. Not only their ancestors who pioneered in Shaanxi endured great hardships, even in the wake of a recent rush to get rich, the present generation is unmoved and happy with their simple but honest life. That means two meals every day, with a basketful of *mantou* (steamed buns) and a few pieces of home-made bean curd and self-cultivated vegetables. Meat is seldom served. Their economic straits do not, however, hinder their spiritual growth. Ten years ago when most churches in Shaanxi were still waiting to implement the government's religious policy, they turned aboveground and built their church with all their own resources, probably the first church built in the province after the devastating Cultural Revolution. After the dedication of the new church, Christians no longer needed to meet in crowded homes. Their number grew rapidly. Their old practice of having two big annual meetings, beginning from 15 January and 15 July respectively, was also reactivated. Each meeting usually lasted from five to seven days. Christians in other provinces gradually got wind of them and made their pilgrimages without invitation.

At the peak of the gatherings in 1988, Christians who made the pilgrimage came from as far as Xinjiang, Inner Mongolia, Hebei, Qinghai, Shandong and Anhui and certainly a lot more from the neighbouring provinces of Shanxi, Gansu and

Henan. At the 15 July meeting of 1989, the pastor of the Baoji TSPM was also invited. This man, suspicious of foul play in the Jinqu church, wrote a report to the national RAB around Christmas time accusing the church in Mei Xian of re-establishing the Jesus Family that had been dissolved by the government in 1952. Soon afterwards, both the Public Security Bureau and the Civil Administration Bureau of Mei Xian sent investigation teams to Jinqu. The day for the January [meeting] was approaching . To prevent Christians from coming from other provinces, the authorities instructed the Jinqu church to send telegrams to various provinces concerned, announcing that there would be no more 'spiritual mass meeting' in Jinqu.

However, many of them had arrived or had already been on their way. The Christians insisted, therefore, on meeting as usual. The magistrate of the county found it necessary to be present personally on the scene. He understood that the Jinqu Christians had no plan nor desire to recover their old name, though by and large they would follow the spirit of the Family. Yet he agreed that there should be no more mass meetings. The Christians could not understand why they were forbidden to hold their annual meeting. They never broke the law; they were always the first to pay government taxes and grain quotas. Furthermore, how could they ask their fellow brothers and sisters from afar to leave immediately? A concession was later made by the authorities that the January meeting be put off for another year. Still dissatisfied, the Christians kept their January meeting despite government warning. Then they met again ten days later for the latecomers. Consequences were taken. All leaders were summoned to undergo a study session, but the Christians had no fear. They knew the law of the government was meant for evil-doers; in addition, they themselves were strictly disciplined by the law of God. There was no question that they were good citizens. Indeed, during a period of more than forty days, the responsible cadres could not but put up their thumbs in praising them as 'really good Christians' or 'genuine believers in Jesus'. More gratifying to them is the fact that the name of Jesus Family has since spread near and far and this was done without intention.

However, the church was split. All Christians except for the elder who was appointed by the authorities and his family left the church. They met in private homes as they did more than ten years ago. For a long time to come, they will not be thinking of building another church.

CASE 2: DUOYIGOU, SHANDONG

Duoyigou is a village in Weishan, Shandong. It used to be a large meeting place for the Jesus Family. Its leader, Zheng Yunsu, was imprisoned for 20 years during the Cultural Revolution because he dared to preach Jesus. He was released shortly before church work was to keep their meeting going.

Zheng, in his 60s, is a talented person; he is also a specialist in shoe-making. The shoes made in the Family are a major source of revenue for the community. In addition, they also till the land and raise rabbits. As usual, the Family never borrows or raises money; its principle is self-reliance. But it is always hospitable.

In fact, many visitors got allowances for transportation from the Family. Yet the Family in Duoyigou is different from other Families in present-day China in that it has re-established the communal life that was practised in Mazhuang before being disbanded. Over sixty of them live, eat, and work together.

The community has seven thatched houses. The first Sunday in each month is the breaking of bread. On that day, believers flock to the church from everywhere. Thousands of them fill up the compound. Only those who are advanced in age are allowed to sit in the church. The rest must stand in the two big courtyards and in the streets.

On May 21, 1992, Zheng Yunsu went to Liuzhuang to celebrate the breaking of bread. Liuzhuang lies about nine kilometres from Duoyigou and has several hundred families, all belonging to the Jesus Family. When Zheng came, more than a thousand believers took part in the breaking of bread. But all of a sudden they were surrounded by a few dozen PSB officials. They wanted to arrest Zheng. The believers were angry and resisted. In the commotion one PSB official was pushed to the ground and stepped on.

When the PSB found that Zheng had escaped back to Duoyigou, they called in a helicopter that circled around Duoyigou for some time. Zheng knew he could not hide for long. Thinking that it would be better for him to be handed over to the provincial government than to the local PSB (he served out more than 10 years of his 20-year prison term during the Cultural Revolution), he hastened to travel to Jinan on the same evening. The next morning, however, he was arrested in Jinan, because he had been followed all the way. He was brought back to Zaozhuang for trial, and then to Weishan and he was finally sentenced in Hanzhuang (near Duoyigou).

After Zheng was taken away, his four sons were rather anxious. His eldest son Jiping and his third son Jike made their way to Beijing to inquire [about] the situation and to ask for leniency. They were not successful. Instead, the church in Duoyigou was levelled by a bulldozer of the PSB in July. All together 36 more people were arrested, among them the four sons and the third daughter-inlaw of Zheng. In September the court finally declared that they were guilty on two accounts: 1) 'swindle'(more then RMB 900 was found when the PSB searched their compound) and 2) 'disturbing of public order' (the church had nine loudspeakers mounted outside to ensure the large congregation of several thousands could hear the service). According to these accusations, Zheng was sentenced to twelve years' imprisonment, Jiping and Jike each to nine years and the two other sons received sentences of five to six years. All the rest got three -year sentences of 're-education through labour'.

The church at Duoyigou was built only two years earlier. At that time, the building of the church was opposed by the local PSB, because there was already a

Three-Self church opposite to it. The Three-Self church had very few attendants, while the Jesus Family had several thousand congregants. Zheng, in order to accommodate the large number of his followers, went to the provincial RAB in Jinan to inquire about the matter. The answer given was that he should sort things out with the local authorities. He then made up his mind to proceed with the building, knowing that it might one day be pulled down. Of the several thousand followers, about 30 of them (plus about 30 members of the Zheng family) lived a communal life. They took everything from home and brought it to the Family. They sewed clothes, made shoes, raised bean sprouts, sold bean curd and raised long-haired rabbits. There is no question they were able to save more than RMB 900 in a year. Now that more than 30 of them were arrested, it is feared that all the leaders who lived communally at Duoyigou would have been arrested.

Though the church at Duoyigou was levelled, believers kept coming back to worship. Further, Zheng's wife is suffering from liver cancer. Many believers want to visit her, but as soon as they come together, it is so natural for them to pray and sing. This, however, would be considered by the PSB as worshipping, and as such 'illegal'. Up to the time when we got this information, in June this year, Duoyigou had been strictly watched by the PSB. Any one coming from outside was searched. Their bikes, watches and money would be taken away. And sometimes a confiscated bike was sold immediately by the PSB at a bargain price of RMB 20!

On November 5, 1992, after the arrest of the many brothers and sisters, three of them wrote a letter to those who were outside the prisons.

Elders, brothers and sisters of the whole church, peace:

When you see this letter, you are seeing us who miss you very much. We are unworthy of your love and your tears that we can hardly repay. May God remember your tears.

Today, for the sake of loving God, we are imprisoned. We know that this is God's will for us. We are to present our bodies as a loving sacrifice, i.e. to present death on the altar. In this matter we have not our own wishes or choice, for this is the road of the cross on which God helps us to walk and of which we are unworthy to walk by ourselves. We have experienced the difficulties and hardships of walking on it, and we have also experienced the sweetness and comfort of it. By walking on this road, we are always filled up with the life of the Heavenly Kingdom. As it is written, though our outer nature is wasting away, our inner nature is being renewed every day.

Dear ones, wondrous is the grace of the Lord! We wish that you too exert yourselves on this road. The time is up, the Lord is coming soon. In this end time, the servant of God (meaning Zheng) keeps us company in the prison and see how he suffers. Brothers and sisters, what else can we not bear to part?

Time waits for no one. We also know that you have encountered difficulties on this road. But you must not be disheartened, nor be disappointed. Put down your heavy burdens of labour and walk! Our hope is in the Heavenly home.

Watch and pray all the time that you may not be left behind. If we do not see one another again in this world, we will meet again in the Heavenly home when the Lord comes. Dear ones, wait patiently, wait with patience!

Now, 18 sisters and 8 brothers are waiting for sentencing. We do not know how many years they will get for re-education. The servant of God and his four sons have already joined groups sentenced to reform through labour. Brothers and sisters, pray for your dear ones in prisons. We only hope to meet in the Spirit and pray for each other.

Though the road seems to end in a thread, it does not break in the presence of the Lord; the home is demolished, our mind in not changed; we die, we are faithful and march forwards; our clothes are stained with blood, we are going to see the Father.

We are writing this letter to you, dear ones, in the night when we are going to be transferred to another prison. We risk writing it without knowing whether you are going to get it. If you do receive it, show it to other brothers and sisters as well.

Because of the situation, we cannot write more.

Emmanuel!

Your members: Xiuling, Jingxiu, Fuqin

The Relationship between the Indigenous Churches and the Lianghui

The relationship between the indigenous churches and the *lianghui* (CCC and TSPM) remains tense and problematic. Even those churches that have joined the *lianghui* often show that their marriage is not a happy one. They are only seemingly in harmony, but actually at variance. For in addition to historical scores that are still to be resolved, the ecclesiastical and theological gaps between them are too wide to be bridged. Take for example, the indigenous churches which insist they are 'non-denominational'. In other words, each of them claims to be simply 'the church'. However, implied in this claim is that all others are not part of the church. On the other hand, the TSPM proclaims post-denominational unity, but the unity is defined and dictated by an understanding of church and ecumenism which grows out of the mainline Protestant denominations. Unity is not a goal which the churches are allowed to strive for through gentle negotiations and a gradual increase in mutual understanding. Instead, unity is a political requirement forced on all churches which wish to continue functioning above ground. Because of this continued tension, the joy that resulted from the reopening of the churches in the 1980s has gradually soured among many indigenous Christian groups. To be sure, a post-denominational church is an ideal for many. The question is, if the church in China really 'seeks common ground while reserving the differences', is excessive pressure and obvious high-handiness necessary in establishing the common ground, or are these methods not counter-productive?

'Yellers' and Healers – Pentecostalism and the Study of Grassroots Christianity in China

Edmond Tang

The origin of this paper is an attempt to move the present-day study of Chinese Christianity beyond its existing theological and methodological perspectives. For more than 50 years, religions in the People's Republic of China (hereafter abbreviated as PRC) have undergone dramatic changes in their fortunes—from near extinction to unprecedented growth – and yet so little knowledge is certain or verifiable regarding this extraordinary phenomenon. This is hardly surprising, given the draconian control over the religions in China as well as of any information about them. On the other hand it is not entirely true that no information, however indirect or fragmentary, is at all available. There are visitors' accounts, letters to fellow Christians, official reports in the press and underground publications that still filter through to journalists, churches and scholars outside China.

Among the many religions in China Christianity has received more attention than the others, partly due to the international interest in China's human rights situation and partly due to its missionary past. But because of these reasons, although there is more information on the Christian churches, this information is often 'packaged', either in the language of the human rights polemic serving to criticize the Chinese regime, or artificially in western theological categories of either the Protestant evangelical/liberal or Roman Catholic conservative/ progressive types. In these reports we often hear about the 'revivals' of presumed western forms of Christianity, without asking what are the impacts of the political campaigns, economic plans and social engineering of the last 50 years on the Chinese churches' belief systems, symbols, contents of worship, conversion patterns, organization and relation to society.

In admitting our general ignorance, we are at the same time pointing to our lack of satisfaction on two levels. Firstly, there is the difficulty in obtaining quality information about religions in China. Secondly, what we find often lacking are critical perspectives and appropriate analytical tools to render the information more useful. There is little the outside world can do to obtain more information short of infringing the sensitivity over security of the Chinese state. On the other hand, perhaps we can address the problem of interpretation by examining more closely our existing theoretical frameworks and try to bring in different perspectives to look at the existing information, particularly that of grassroots Christianity.

This perspective, which underlies the present enquiry, is inspired by the author's recent interest in Pentecostalism in Asia and the methodological questions raised by scholars in the subject. In other words, in order to focus our enquiry we deliberately pose the hypothetical question: Is Pentecostalism the dominant form of Protestant Christian expression at the grassroots in China? If so, why? Is this the result of missionary legacy, however remote, or a question of spontaneous emergence of indigenous forms? Is the phenomenon limited to Protestant Christianity? Are there Catholic equivalents? A number of recent studies seem to posit such a hypothesis, such as Anderson, Bays, Claudia and Gotthard Oblau.[1]

Such a hypothesis is tempting. In simply positing such a possibility, one is already struck by the similarities that can be drawn between what we observe in China and other movements of independent Pentecostal and charismatic churches in Africa and Asia. We are almost promised a readily available explanation of the outburst of activities on the ground – the prevalence of an emotional style of worship, emphasis on healing, opposition to the organized institutional churches and their liberal theology, resistance to any form of state control, as well as certain characteristics too often judged by others as 'sectarian' tendencies etc. On the other hand, we must be warned against the danger of imposing a ready-made explanation on an indigenous phenomenon. Or is it really indigenous? In fact, the comments above are already begging some important methodological questions before the data is adequately examined.

The study of Chinese Christianity after 1949

The study of religion in China had never been a well-established independent academic discipline even before the establishment of the PRC. There were hardly any Religious Studies departments in Chinese universities, except in Christian ones. The study of Buddhism and Taoism (or Daoism), the traditional religions of China, were carried out in the Departments of History and/or Departments of Chinese language and culture. The modern Chinese academia, even up to the present day, has been strongly influenced by a humanist and scientific-rationalist outlook that regarded religion as only the remnant of a pre-modern worldview. There were exceptions in the budding discipline of

---

[1] See, for example, recent studies by A.H. Anderson 'Pentecostalism in East Asia: Indigenous Oriental Christianity?', *Swedish Missiological Themes* 87:3 (1999); D. Bays, 'Christian Revival in China, 1900-1937', in Edith l. Blumhofer & Randall Balmer (eds.), *Modern Christian Revivals* (Chicago: University of Illinois Press, 1993); Gotthard Oblau, 'Pentecostalism by Default? Contemporary Christianity in China', in the present book; Claudia Waehrisch-Oblau, 'Healing Prayers and Healing Testimonies in Mainland Chinese Churches', *China Study Journal* 14:2 (August 1999), 5-21.

sociology in the tradition of Weber and Durkheim, but very little work of substance was produced before 1949. This tendency continued after the establishment of the PRC when the new Marxist view on religion became its natural heir.

Under the new state ideology, a combination of Stalinist and Maoist thought, every human endeavour, from economic production to scientific research, must be seen to serve the welfare of the people (read, 'to serve the purpose of politics') and must be brought under the direction of the State. Marxism has replaced, or subsumed under it, all the independent disciplines, including political science, economics, philosophy, psychology and sociology. In the study of religion, Marxism was the only legitimate theory. If there was any academic debate, it was only over the timing of the disappearance of religion – whether the 'opium of the people' would die slowly with the progress of economic and political forces that would eliminate all exploitation and ignorance, and whether it should be combated against vigorously to destroy its role in poisoning the consciousness of the masses.

Outside China, the study of Chinese religion was also influenced by the turn of political events. After the establishment of the PRC, access to the field was suddenly denied and information dried up. Scholars and church observers were also shocked by the violent means used to control religion. Scholarly attention turned firstly to the study of China's new religious policy and subsequently to how the churches responded to it. Without being conscious of it, the study of religion in China was cajoled into a tunnel vision.[2] The question of religious freedom, whether there is any or how much there is, has become an overriding concern from 1949 up to the present day.

For those who focussed their attention on the churches' response there was another trap. The United Front policy of the Chinese Communist Party led to the emergence of the Three-Self Patriotic Movement and the Catholic Patriotic Association. These organizations were given the task of reforming the churches and leading them into the orbit of government policies. It turned out to be a divisive issue. The denunciation campaigns and antagonistic methods of 'criticism' used by the government, and by church leaders against each other, certainly led to the split between the so-called Three-Self churches and the 'house churches', as well as the departure of a large part of the Catholic Church to the 'underground'. This history is well recorded in a number of classic studies.[3] The danger, however, is adopting the divisions as the only criteria to

---

[2] See the studies by L. Ladany, *The Catholic Church in China* (New York: Freedom House, 1987); R.C. Bush Jr., *Religion in Communist China* (Nashville, TN: Abingdon Press, 1970); J.T. Myers, *Enemies without Guns – The Catholic Church in China* (New Yprl: Paragon House, 1991), on the Catholic situation.

[3] Notable examples are the works by J. Chao (with Rosanna Chong), 'House Churches', in *A History of Christianity in Socialist China, 1949-1997* [in Chinese] (Taipei: CMI

identify various Christian groups - namely their acquiescence or opposition to state control. In time this developed into a stereotype that all serious studies could not escape. Some happily subscribe to this paradigm as a means to understand the development of Chinese Christianity, with little concern that this opposition was one-dimensional and could lead to the negligence of the multi-faceted developments at the grassroots.

These characteristic weaknesses continued even after the Cultural Revolution (1966-76) when all public expressions of religion were suppressed. Hope was revived in the Deng Xiaoping era, beginning with 1979 when the United Front was resurrected in order to rally the country in support of Deng's reform programme. Religious activities were again permitted and sometimes churches were even encouraged to take part in economic construction and social service. The study of religion was revived and it gained a new momentum, but again scholars returned to their old divisions. There were again those who paid attention only to the new 'post-denominational' official church led by the newly created China Christian Council (hereafter CCC), treating the 'house churches' as an insignificant aberration; while on the opposite spectrum, there were also those who still maintained that true Christianity could only come from the suffering church which stood fast against political persecution and that today's Christian revival can only come from the seeds of martyrs.

Interpreting Growth

There is no doubt from scanning both official and visitors' reports that the Christian churches are growing, particularly among Protestants and in the countryside. As early as 1987, in an internal document, the Chinese government identified this phenomenon in rural Henan and called it a 'religious fever'.[4] Do we know why? Since then many explanations have been given, but none of them convincing.

The government denied the growth in the beginning, but later acknowledged the existence of the phenomenon. Their explanation is reasonably common sense: there is still poverty and lack of access to health and education in the rural areas and these contribute to the spread of religion as an escape from the real problems. Another theory propounded by scholars from the state academies is based on the following argument: the growth of religion is a 'rebound effect' from the suppression of religion during the period of the Cultural Revolution.

Publishing, 1997), R. Paterson, *Heartcry for China* (Chichester: Sovereign World, 1989). Studies sympathetic to the official churches include: R.E. Whyte, *The Unfinished Encounter* (London: Collins 1984), and P. Wickeri, *Seeking the Common Ground* (Maryknoll, NY: Orbis, 1990).

[4] T. Lambert, *Resurrection of the Chinese Church*, 2nd ed. (Illinois: OMF IHQ, 1994), 139, n. 2, 309.

When it is allowed, everybody flocks to the formerly forbidden fruit, very much like the current explosion of interest in western goods as well as western habits and fashion, including western ideas. This theory, however, cannot explain the difference between the cities and the countryside, or the difference between religions and between Christian denominations.

The official Christian bodies, both Catholic and Protestant, try to explain this growth in their favour. According to them, it is thanks to the Three-Self Movement and the Patriotic Association that Christianity is now considered by the people to be truly Chinese; hence their willingness to become Christians. This explanation is justified to the extent that Christianity today is no longer considered by the ordinary Chinese to be a colonial religion and it is not shameful to become Christian. However, limited observation shows that, in the cities, the attraction to Christian belief is due less to the fact that it has become Chinese, whatever that means, than the fact that it is still western – therefore modern and fashionable. In the countryside, political ideas play an even smaller part in people's conversion to Christianity. It is the otherworldly and miraculous aspects of Christianity that appeal to them; in fact they abhor any politicization of the Christian faith, which they associate with urban, 'Three-Self' theology.

On the other hand it does not follow from the previous comments that the argument often put forth by Evangelicals is therefore correct. The grassroots resistance to political control is often exaggerated in their interpretation. In many instances, this resistance is not on theological grounds. If the government allows a certain space of movement and does not impose control through the 'patriotic' organizations, then most grassroots groups would happily accept registration and some form of government supervision.

It seems that the only certainty we have in the midst of divergent theories is that Christianity is growing very fast at the grassroots in China. It is not a uniform picture as it grows faster in some localities than others. In the case of Protestant Christianity, grassroots groups show clear affinity with so-called evangelical forms and some express clear charismatic tendencies. Apart from these general observations, do we really know what they believe, how they express their faith? How do they organize as church/community and what form of leadership do they accept? How do they worship and what are the prevalent forms? Where do these forms come from and what local creativity enters into the picture? How do they resolve doctrinal differences and relate to the official bodies?

The lack of reliable information that is not 'packaged' either by official bodies or by partisan scholarship, coupled with the difficulties in doing any field research, made it equally impossible to study religion objectively even in this relatively more open period. We are not any closer to a more objective understanding of the situation of Christianity on the ground. Hope was placed, however, on a group of new researchers inside China who made their mark in the mid-1980s by courageously challenging the conventional Marxist theory of religion by appealing to the young Marx. The theory of 'opium of the people' was re-interpreted not to mean the deliberate use of religion by the oppressive classes to dupe the people, but more as a means used by the people themselves in order to deal with the suffering and alienation as a result of their oppression. The tables were turned in the name of the 'people', and when the 'opium war' (of religion) was won, the new generation of researchers were free to taste the forbidden fruit for the first time. In the spirit of Deng's slogan: 'Seek truth from facts', many departments of religion at state academies as well as the universities have ventured to carry out the first empirical studies.[5] It is still too early to review the results of these studies, but generally they suffer from several weaknesses.

Firstly, they operate within the constraints imposed by the government's religious policy, or in some cases the lack of clarity on specific issues. If the state declares a certain group as a sect, then any objective research on that particular group becomes impossible. The Yellers (see later in the paper) and the Falun Gong sect are good examples. In the case of Rural Christianity, it was taboo for many years because the state refused open access to it – it seems the government does not want to know what is happening unless they are sure of the results! The lack of a clear distinction between religion and superstition also made scholars wary of exploring new theories regarding the rural phenomenon, where millennial cults and traditional folk religion intermingled with Christianity to create new churches/groups, some of which were later banned by the government.

Secondly, most research shows a rather simplistic approach to methodology. Questionnaires are often crudely constructed and are not published with collected data. The latter is correlated with simplistic criteria of social strata to produce generalized pictures of religious belonging. Anonymity of interviewees is often not protected. The status of the researcher is not declared and sometimes he/she is a government official, or accompanied by government department staff, which calls into question the reliability of the collected information. Published studies often organize their data along the lines of existing perceptions without challenging their validity.

Thirdly, most of the research suffers from a lack of historical perspective. Invariably the analysis starts with the statement: 'Since Liberation...', as if 1949 can be considered a clean slate to which all present developments can be traced. Missionary influence or denominational tradition is not allowed to be a

---

[5] The first empirical study was carried out by Luo Zhufeng and his colleagues of the Shanghai Academy of Social Sciences Luo Zhufeng (ed.), *Religion under Socialism in China*, trans. D.E. MacInnis and Zheng Xi'an (London: M.E. Sharpe, 1991). Their tradition is continued by SASS in their journal *Contemporary Studies of Religion*. Other studies can be found in a variety of academic journals. Many of these studies are published in *China Study Journal*, edited by the author.

factor in the analysis of the growth of Christian groups. This runs against simple common sense. For a proper understanding of the emergence and development of particular groups, it is important to compare both the continuity and discontinuity with previous forms of Christianity in the same locality. The official version says there are no Pentecostals in China, but can we be satisfied with this position when most grassroots groups show some charismatic characteristics, and some of them are so close to known forms of Pentecostalism that it would be wrong not to bring in some comparitive perspective, even if only as a hypothesis.

The 'Pentecostal' Temptation

Allan Anderson does not doubt that indigenous Christian groups outside of the China Christian Council are Pentecostals, especially the True Jesus Church, the Jesus Family and the Little Flock.[6] However, his study was based only on secondary sources and the Pentecostal identity of the groups he described was assumed rather than proven. It is also doubtful whether the Little Flock can be called Pentecostal at all if one takes a closer look at their beliefs and practices. Recent publications based on some field research, especially by Claudia and Gotthard Oblau,[7] have attempted to use a 'Pentecostal' paradigm to describe grassroots Christianity in China. In a recent paper on two grassroots Christian communities, Gotthard Oblau raises a rhetorical question: 'Are Chinese Christians Pentecostal by default?' Why 'by default'? The question summarizes the ambiguity of our existing knowledge and our lack of theoretical framework. How do we determine whether a group of Chinese Christians are Pentecostal or not? It seems to me there are three possible approaches to the question:

1. It is recognized by the group of Christians concerned, e.g. they are aware of their origins and links, and consciously subscribe to a set of beliefs and practices they can identify as Pentecostal.
2. They are recognized as such by other Pentecostals who are aware of the historical links and recognize parallels in their belief and practice.
3. Although the Christian groups concerned are not aware of their 'Pentecostal' beliefs and practices, and would object to being named as such, there are sufficient characteristics and parallels for the designation.

Gotthard Oblau has the taken the last approach. Following Hollenweger, he lists the following characteristics as typical of Pentecostal congregations: fluidity of organization, holistic view of salvation, non-literary communication

---

[6] Allan H. Anderson, 'Pentecostalism'.
[7] Gotthard Oblau, 'Pentecostal by Default?' in the current volume.

and transmission and an affective/ emotional experience. In applying these characteristics to the communities being studied, Oblau concludes that there is a 'wide variety of Pentecostal characteristics' (2), enough 'parallels' (6) to call them Pentecostal. But is that enough? Hollenweger has distilled these characteristics from communities clearly known as Pentecostal in order to describe their special character; the function of these characteristics is not necessarily meant to be used to identify new ones. If we attempt to do the latter, what was presupposed by Hollenweger cannot be assumed by us here. Besides the named characteristics there should be a clear defining characteristic such as an identifiable experience of the 'baptism of the Spirit', an 'empowerment by the Spirit' accompanied by some outward signs such as—but not necessarily limited to—speaking with tongues or some form of spiritual healing in the belief and practice of the groups.

There is no doubt many Christians in China feel empowered by an experience of God—experiences of deep conversion, feelings of inexplicable joy, repentance and forgiveness, etc. These experiences, however, are common to all Christian conversion to various degrees (even traditional Catholics! And the list of characteristics can be applied equally to basic ecclesial communities in Latin America and the Philippines). It seems therefore that some experience of the indwelling of the Spirit and recognizable forms of this, must be present to 'define' the Pentecostal. This is not to deny the usefulness of Gotthard Oblau's attempt, but further analysis seems necessary before the claims can be made. The dictum: 'the total is more than the sum of its parts' seems applicable here. The Pentecostal identity must be seen as an organic one, not just separate elements joined together, and these characteristics must centre round a core experience. In this case, it is the latter that is lacking in the analysis.

So, are there Pentecostals in China? In the following we shall look at a few cases, some with historical links, others with marginal claims and see if the Pentecostal paradigm can lead us any further.

The Case of the 'Yellers'

Are 'Yellers' Pentecostals? This is a borderline case that makes it a good illustration of the problem of classification mentioned above. Since both the leaders of the group and their followers claim to belong to a unique and indeed the only true form of Christianity, they are the first to deny any affiliation with existing denominations or movements. On the other hand, what if we look at their historical origins and doctrinal characteristics?

But first of all, who are the 'Yellers'? Sometimes also translated as 'Shouters' they are a group of Christians that gained widespread following in China in the 1980s, the first to be criticized by the China Christian Council and then condemned by the government as an 'evil cult' in 1983. They are a group under the leadership of a certain Li Changsou that broke away from another independent Christian group, the Little Flock, sometimes called the Assembly

Hall, founded by Watchman Nee in the 1920s. In 1949 Li took some of the Little Flock to Taiwan where he took charge of the Assembly Halls there and in Southeast Asia. In 1962 he carried out a successful mission in the USA and established the church there. In 1967 he started the movement of 'yelling'—a form of public, emotional repentance of sin by loud confession—and his followers took on that name. When China opened up in the late 1970s the group established itself along the south-eastern coast of China and spread to a number of provinces.[8]

Li believes that the time of the Word is past; it is now the time of the Spirit. All Christians must 'shout aloud the name of the Lord' in order to release the Spirit. Their services are characterized by collective emotional outbursts and noisy shouting. In many ways the Yellers have gone well beyond the orthodox teaching of Christianity, especially in placing the authority of the founder above that of Jesus Christ. Under the influence of Li, followers of the sect consider all other Christian churches heretical, and in China this exclusivist stand led to violent attacks on other Christian groups and attempts to take over churches and meeting points. They were also sent in teams of two or three to other churches where they denounced Three-Self churches as 'whores' and threatened to bring down 'Jericho' with their shouts. These extreme actions led to many divisions in Christian communities and violent clashes. In 1983 the Chinese government banned the group, with many of their local leaders sentenced to long periods in prison. However the ban by the Chinese government in 1983 did not stop them from spreading underground. By the time of the ban, the Yellers were already in most of the provinces of China, especially in Zhejiang, Henan, Fujian and Guangdong. Lushan, a small provincial city in Henan, became a stronghold of the Yellers and among a population of just over 100,000 there are tens of thousands of them.[9] In 2000 a Hong Kong businessman was arrested by the Chinese government for bringing in over 20,000 Bibles and other literature produced by the Yellers for distribution in China.[10]

It is not the purpose of this paper to discuss the orthodoxy of the Yellers; the followers of the sect who practise 'yelling' do not necessarily share the more extreme beliefs of the leader. The question that interests us is whether they can

---

[8] See *Tian Feng*, May 1983, 11-12 (official publication of the China Christian Council), and various issues in 1983 of the *Course Materials*, used by the correspondence course run by the Nanjing Theological Seminary. See also various issues of *Bridge*, a magazine published by the Christian Study Centre on Chinese Religion and Culture in Hong Kong and *China Study Journa*, published in London by the China Desk of Churches Together in Britain and Ireland.

[9] Deng Zhaoming, *The Torch of the Testimony in China* (Hong Kong: Christian Study Centre on Chinese Religion & Culture, 1998), 220.

[10] *China Study Journal*, April 2002, section K.

be associated with a Pentecostal interpretation: what are their historical origins? What is the context for their acceptance? Do groups influenced by them show similar charismatic characteristics?

The historical origins of the Yellers are well established. They can be traced to the Little Flock whose leader Watchman Nee was in turn influenced by the Brethren and their holiness stress on the Holy Spirit as well as other revivalist movements. One cannot help but speculate that it is this emphasis on the Holy Spirit that has become the source of Li Changshou's theory of the age of the Spirit. The emphasis on the Holy Spirit is not unrelated to the emotional character of the group's worship services, characterized by wailing and crying in order to release the Spirit. That seems to be a major factor in their appeal. In the areas where the Yellers are active there are also conventional groups of Christians, both government sanctioned as well as 'house churches', all of which are conservative and evangelical in nature. It seems that the Yellers are recruiting especially from existing congregations, leading us to believe that their appeal is precisely in their special form of affective expression and fierce independence from other denominations. Can it be their extreme emotionalism in worship and exclusivist stance fills a spiritual vacuum left by 20 years of harsh oppression and provides the necessary psychological outlet as well as identity through a strong social bond? It is worth noting that many of the sectarian movements also started in a similar period of time, when organized religions were only slowly responding to the religious needs of the population and there was no doctrinal authority to guide believers in their discernment.

Finally, it is interesting to note that at least two other groups are said to have issued from the Yellers, or at least been strongly influenced by them. One of these is the 'Established King' sect that was also banned by the Chinese government and their leader arrested and executed in 1994. The second, where the link is tenuous and not proven, is the Way of Rebirth that puts a strong emphasis on the Christian's rebirth in the Spirit. The group is active in Northern China and claims a large following. More research is necessary to study the links between these groups and the Yellers, between the Yellers and the Little Flock, and between the Little Flock and other revivalist movements in China and in the West. This would be a possible avenue to study the 'Pentecostal' influences within the 'lineage' of Chinese independent churches. Our suspicion is that it is not possible to determine the strict historical continuity between these groups, but it will help us to monitor the depth and breadth of charismatic traits in these churches.

To what extent can the Yellers be compared to 'Pentecostals'? The same question preoccupied scholars of earlier revival movements in China in the early part of the last century.

Clearly, emotional release was a major part of this experience. A sympathetic account, calling this 'the greatest spiritual movement in the history of missions in China', described how people would confess 'with sobs, shrieks, and groans', falling on their faces, until 'their separate cries were merged and lost in the swelling tide of general weeping'. The same account noted that 'strange thrills coursed up and down one's body', and that everywhere could be heard 'the agony of the penitent, his groans and cries and voice shaken with sobs'.[11]

This account, written 80 years before the Yellers, could very well be a present-day description of their yelling expressions. But Bays is reluctant to associate these revival activities of that time with Pentecostalism. He admits that it is easier to report the phenomenon than to analyse it, but he did relate it to the Welsh and Korean revivals and accepted that the phenomenon resembled early Pentecostal revivals.[12] Bays' prudence is that of an able historian and must be followed by students of present day Christianity in China. The 'Pentecostal' paradigm is tempting but further research must be done before we can come to any clear conclusions.

True Jesus Church, the 'Spirit-Spirit Sect' and Other Pentecostal groups

As opposed to the case of the Yellers, the Pentecostal nature of the True Jesus Church is not in doubt. It is a radically independent and sectarian Chinese church that began in north China in 1917. The history of this movement is well documented in a number of studies, and in great detail in Deng Zhaoming's recent paper.[13] Its main leader, Zhang Lingsheng, came from a Pentecostal mission background. According to Bays, the True Jesus Church is both revivalist and exclusivist in character. It is revivalist by both emphasizing spiritual renewal and by insisting that their members must renounce their old church affiliations in acknowledging their new faith to be the only true and unique dogma.[14] The emphasis on being filled with the Spirit, prayers in spirit language, baptism by immersion and keeping the Sabbath on Saturday etc. are also their characteristics. By 1949 they had established themselves in many parts of China, with over 700 churches and more than 100,000 members. Under the new regime they received harsh treatment. In parts of China they were banned and their leaders were put in prison, e.g. in Hubei, while in others they came under the banner of the Three-Self Movement but maintained a certain autonomy. After the Cultural Revolution they became active again and gained a strong influence among grassroots Christian groups in Jiangsu, Hubei, Hunan, Zhejiang, Fujian and Shanxi provinces. According to official figures they form

---

[11] Noted by Dr W. Phillips in *Chinese Recorder*, September 1908, 524. Quoted in D. Bays, 164.

[12] Ibid, 164.

[13] Deng Zhaoming, 'Indigenous Chinese Pentecostal Denominations: Two Examples', in present book.

[14] Bays, 170.

over 30% of the Christians in Jiangsu province and out of a total of 150,000 Christians in Hunan over 110,000 belong to their church.

The Pentecostal character of the True Jesus Church is evident both from its historical origins and from its patterns of belief and practice. It is also interesting to observe that a group, which may have branched off from the church, has further heightened these Pentecostal features. The Spirit-Spirit Sect (a poor translation of *Ling-ling Jiao*) was formed around 1985 in Jiangsu by Hua Xuehe and another True Jesus Church leader, Li Guiyao. The first 'spirit' in its name refers to the Holy Spirit, and the second 'spirit'—a play on Chinese tones—refers to the 'spiritual proof' of the work of the Spirit in the Christian. Members of the group perform 'spirit dances' and spontaneous 'spirit songs'. Like the True Jesus Church, it is also exclusivist in character, believing that all the older denominations are 'ineffective' and only by joining the sect can a Christian be saved. It became notorious in the mid-'90s when the official seminary in Yunan was closed after an open conflict between the teaching staff who became members of the sect and those who were against. It is now on the list of forbidden 'cults' of the Chinese government.

Besides the True Jesus Church there are a number of important Christian groups that can claim either some Pentecostal origins or can be described as Pentecostal from their actual belief and practice. These include the Jesus Family that was started in 1928 by Jing Dianying at Mazhuang, Shandong province. Jing was first converted to Christianity around 1913-14, but was reconverted in the mid-'20s after contacts with Pentecostalism, particularly L.M. Anglin's Christian mission commune which inspired the True Jesus Family's egalitarian communalism. The group emphasizes spiritual dreams and revelations. Other groups include the Disciple Faith Church (Shitou Xinxin Hui) in Shanghai that puts great emphasis on the external signs of being filled by the Spirit, such as speaking in tongues, leading a holy life. According to their belief, even a dead Christian must carry a smiling face as proof of salvation. Another group, the New Testament Church, is a recent import from Taiwan that follows the Pentecostal tradition. It believes the world is approaching the end-times and the church must return to the form of the early disciples and re-experience the power of the Spirit. Baptism of the Spirit and the speaking of tongues are obligatory for Christians.[15] Another group that can be included in the Pentecostal family is the Fangcheng Pai Church that has links with North American Pentecostalism.

Even a cursory treatment of independent groups in China reveals the extent of Pentecostal/charismatic influences among the grassroots Christian communities. Some can be identified as such while others are clearly on the borderline. In many cases, the parallels are so close that even if they cannot be

---

[15] Leung Ka-lung, *The Rural Churches of Mainland China since 1978* (Hong Kong: Alliance Bible Seminary, 1999), 180-81.

called 'Pentecostal' in the strict sense of the word – but how strict is the word? – the Pentecostal paradigm can provide an interesting perspective to understand and analyse the belief, practice, context of acceptance as well as influence of such independent church groups. This will change entirely the landscape of Protestant Christianity as we know it up to now; to which we shall now turn our attention. But before doing that, there must be a short note on the question of healing.

Healing and Conversion

There would be a big lacunae in the treatment of Pentecostalism in China if we did not touch on the phenomenon of healing, although it is not sure if this can be described as a defining characteristic.[16] All Christian churches in China practice some form of healing, including Three-Self churches. In fact, according to some surveys, 90% of new believers cite healing as a reason for their conversion. This is especially true in the countryside where medical facilities are often inadequate or non-existent. Normal Sunday worship is often interrupted by long periods of prayer for the sick and ends with Christians rushing forward to the altar to kneel in prayer for sick members of the family. In some churches there may be a weekday session devoted to healing. These sessions are not 'healing services' as commonly known outside China. They are simply prayer meetings with some emphasis on praying for the sick. If the leader is known to be blessed with special gifts of the Spirit, then the prayer meeting may emphasize the laying on of hands by the church leader or the sick may be brought to be touched by him or her. There are few structured services, and these 'democratic' prayers of healing are seen to be the duty of Christians – in fact, the main evangelistic witness. If healing is common to all Christian groups, nevertheless is is more prevalent in charismatic Christianity, and when the ritual of healing is incorporated into a Pentecostal type of religious service it also takes on a heightened intensity and meaning. However, the study in the field is only beginning.

The Changing Landscape of Protestant Christianity

Given the fragmentary nature of our information and the constraints discussed in the first part of the paper, it is not possible to provide an acceptable list of Pentecostal or quasi-Pentecostal groups in the People's Republic of China. On the other hand, with the limited information we have at hand, it is sufficient to call into question the existing models of interpretation and revise the landscape of Protestant Christianity in that country.

---

[16] See Claudia Oblau, 'Healing Prayers'.

That landscape, looked at from the grassroots level, is very different from the official picture promoted by the government and the officially sanctioned churches. While the official version emphasizes a sober, theologically liberal and politically motivated Christianity, what we can see on the ground are communities whose faith is experience-based, affective-emotional and materially efficacious. The social dimension is often absent. If the official version emphasizes some form of theological and political 'orthodoxy', then the grassroots communities stress more 'orthopraxis' (experience-based baptism of the Spirit, speaking in tongues, healing) and 'orthopathy' (deep sense of conversion and repentance that externalizes in yelling and weeping).

To approach the understanding of Chinese Protestant Christianity from the Pentecostal perspective serves several corrective functions. First of all, it shows the inadequacy of the simplistic division of Christians into so-called Three-Self churches and 'house churches'. The difference between them is often said to be political. There is some truth in that since most independent churches resist government interference and control. However, the differences go much deeper than that. If the differences are not strictly 'theological' in the sense that both camps subscribe to the same basic tenets of the Protestant creed, nevertheless, there is a huge divide in their religious sentiments and the way these are expressed.

Secondly, it is also clear from the above account that 'house churches' cannot be lumped together as a movement. There are as many common characteristics among all grassroots Christians as there are differences. Some are clearly Pentecostal, others are on the margin, while many are simply of the conservative evangelical type. Some are exclusivist to the extreme and reject the validity of any other group, while others are more conciliatory and willing to work together, including working with Three-Self churches.

Thirdly, in probing the Pentecostal/charismatic undercurrent of grassroots groups we are clearly reminded of the tradition of fierce independence of these groups which had its origin in the anti-missionary and anti-ecumenical period of the 1920s and '30s.[17] They have a tendency to distrust organized institutions and emphasize fluidity and democratic spontaneity. Any administrative measure to bring them into rigid structures will only end in antagonism and division. Since the 1980s, the official Protestant church has promoted the idea of a post-denominational church in China. It declared that the age of denominations was over. This is largely true concerning denominations of western origin such as Anglicans, Methodists or Presbyterians. It is also true that many new Christians are unaware of such divisions. On the other hand it is not entirely correct to say that denominations do not exist. Seventh Day Adventists are still functioning separately and from our description above it is clear that many independent churches still exist after the 1980s. These groups

---

[17] See D. Bays, 'Christian Revival'.

cannot be accused of foreign or missionary domination since they emerged in the earlier part of the last century as anti-foreign and anti-missionary groups. They are also 'independent' churches with closely-knit bonds and identities, a characteristic they also share with similar independent Pentecostal forms of Christianity in other parts of Asia and in Africa. It seems that any plans to create a super, national church or to establish one form of theology are almost doomed to failure from the start.

The theological task also looks very different once we accept Pentecostal characteristics as permanent features of Chinese Christianity. The rejection of existing paradigms will lead us to look afresh at some fundamental questions such as the growth of Christianity in the last 20 to 30 years, its function in society, possible forms of ecclesial life and ministry, relations with the state etc.

Further Questions

There is no doubt a sociological phenomenon is taking place which cannot be explained by superficial politico-theological theories. A proper study would discuss the sociological reasons for the spread of Pentecostal/ charismatic types of Christianity in China, e.g. the theory of functional substitution in a changing society.[18] Comparisons can be made with case studies in Korea, Singapore, Indonesia or South Africa to look at possible patterns of response to secular modernity.

The historical origins of Pentecostal groups merit further research. Although it is clear in some of them, such as the True Jesus Church, it is not clear if the historical link plays any important role in the other groups' self identity. In, others, such as the Little Flock, can the charismatic influence on the leader be confirmed also among his followers? Among recently established churches, are their Pentecostal characteristics a natural occurrence in a pre-denominational innocence? From a historical point of view, why were the independent Chinese revivalist groups in the early twentieth century fiercely nationalistic as well as exclusivist, a feature not shared by world Pentecostalism?

A final comment relates to the folk religions. A few Chinese scholars have already observed the parallels between grassroots Christian practices in China and the traditional folk religions.[19] The list of characteristics adopted by Gotthard Oblau can easily be applied to, for example, Daoist popular practices, which have strong 'animist' and shamanist undertones. Their organizations are fluid (forming when needed and disappearing when their function is fulfilled, without a professional full-time clergy), holistic (attention to both mind and body), employing predominantly non-verbal forms of expression (chants and

---

[18] David Martin, *Pentecostalism: The World their Parish* (Oxford: Blackwell, 2002).

[19] Gao Shining, 'Twenty-first Century Chinese Christianity and the Chinese Social Process', *China Study Journal*, 15:2/3 (December 2000), 14-18.

ritual dances), and affective/emotional experiences (trances). Of course the Christian symbolism is different, but we should not dismiss too quickly the possibility that there is cross-fertilization and even movement between the two. There are well-founded reports of folk religious practices seeping into Christian communities (talismans, exorcisms, worship of ancestral spirits, etc). Chinese scholars call this the 'folk-religionization' of Christianity.[20] Pentecostal groups that do not benefit from a clear denominational history are particularly vulnerable to various levels of syncretism. Oblau was rightly concerned that Christians can risk being 'left in a twilight world of folk-religion with a thin veneer of Christianity'.[21]

Our attempt to look at grassroots Christianity from a Pentecostal perspective has reaped some interesting results. It has put more mountains and rivers in our previously rather bland landscape of Chinese Christianity. It challenges our simplistic views and especially our lack of historical and analytical perspectives. The next step would be to set up comparative frameworks, initiate more fieldwork and individual case studies. The Pentecostal paradigm, from a methodological angle, is very tempting indeed.

---

[20] Ibid.

[21] G. Oblau, 'Pentecostals by Default?'

Pentecostals in Japan

Paul Tsuchido Shew

A New History of the Pentecostal Movement in Japan[1]

With news of the 'latter rain' flooding outward from the Azusa Street revival, missionaries began spreading the Pentecostal message around the world and it soon reached Japan. But when exactly has been a question of some dispute. The Japan Assemblies of God (JAG), the oldest and largest Pentecostal denomination here, has long dated its origins to the arrival of the Juergensen family in August 1913.[2] Most historical accounts of Protestant Christianity in Japan focus on mainline denominational history, ignoring Pentecostals altogether, while recent histories of Japanese Evangelicals take the official line of the JAG.[3] Scholars of the early history of Pentecostal missions should be familiar with M. L. Ryan and the adventures of his ill-prepared Apostolic Light missionary band in East Asia, but the history of the Pentecostal movement in Japan has remained largely obscured by the veil of time, untouched by scholarly examination until recently. This overview is an attempt to take a fresh

---

[1] This article is based on research conducted for my forthcoming doctoral dissertation from Fuller Theological Seminary, School of Theology. Japanese names are written in native order, surname first, then given name. Abbreviations employed in citations: FPHC (Flower Heritage Pentecostal Center) and AGWM (Assemblies of God World Mission).

[2] Japan Assemblies of God (ed.), *Mitama ni Michibikarete: Soritsu Sanju Nenshi* [Guided by the Spirit: The Thirty Year History] (Tokyo: Japan Assemblies of God, 1979). Japan Assemblies of God (ed.), *Mikotoba ni Tachi, Mitama ni Michibikarete: Nihon Assemburizu ob Goddo Kyodan Soritsu Goju Nenshi* [Standing on the Word, Guided by the Spirit: The Fifty Year History of the Japan Assemblies of God] (Tokyo: Japan Assemblies of God, 1999).

[3] Satoshi Nakamura, *Nihon ni okeru Fukuinha no Rekishi: Mo Hitotsu Nihon Kirisutokyoshi* [The History of Evangelicals in Japan: Another History of Christianity in Japan] (Tokyo: Word of Life Press, 2000). Nakamura's volume is a highly significant attempt to write an alternative history of Christianity in Japan that examines Evangelicals rather than simply focusing on the mainline denominations as church historians in Japan have done up to now.

look at the origins and developments of the Pentecostal movement in twentieth century Japan from primary sources.

The Pentecostal movement in Japan developed through a combination of influences, both from the international Pentecostal movement and from the larger Christian community in Japan which dates its history back to 1549. Although the original Jesuit missions to Japan in the sixteenth and seventeenth centuries touched a significant portion of the population, the following two and a half centuries of intense persecution and national seclusion succeeded in largely alienating Japanese people from Christianity. Missionaries returned to Japan in the late 1850s and the first Japanese Protestant church grew out of a 1872 revival. As a pro-western vogue swept the nation in the late 1870s and 80s, Christian churches exploded with growth, especially among the intellectual and social elites. Growth slowed in the 1890s accompanied by an anti-western backlash and for many Japanese Christian conversion was equated with forsaking one's family, heritage and nation, at least through the first half of the twentieth century. Despite the formidable social challenges Christianity continued growing through most of the twentieth century, slowing during the 1940s wartime crisis and from 1970 onward. When Pentecostals first entered Japan in the early 1900s the Protestant missionary community was well established, but the national church was still quite young.

Roots of Pentecostalism in Japan

Martin L. Ryan led a party of fourteen missionaries to Japan, arriving in Yokohama in late September 1907.[4] Some of the members continued on to China, but three families (the Ryans, the MacDonalds and the Colyars) and two single women (Cora Fritsch and Bertha Millligan) stayed in Japan and conducted mission work in Yokohama, Tokyo and Sendai. Ryan had published an article advocating xenololia for the purpose of world evangelization in the last issue of his circular, *Apostolic Light*, just before leaving for Japan, so his group may have had hopes of immediately evangelizing in the Japanese language.[5] But they soon settled in to the hard realities of adapting to a foreign country and language study. They were also joined by other early Pentecostal missionaries passing through Japan, including Mr and Mrs A.G. Garr and Lucy Leatherman.

Unfortunately, these early Pentecostal missionaries made very little impact upon Japan and the impressions that they left with many were negative. They were woefully unprepared for mission work in Japan and their work suffered from critical financial shortcomings and lack of knowledge about Japan or a

---

[4] There were an additional seven children in the group. Martin L. Ryan, 'Bound for the Orient', *The Apostolic Light* 183 (28 September 1907), 1.
[5] 'What Are the Gifts Needed?', *The Apostolic Light* 183 (28 September 1907), 1.

credible mission strategy. Before leaving Spokane, Ryan wrote that God would miraculously supply 'every means for the missionaries',[6] but when this clearly did not occur even Pentecostals began to question whether or not the call of all of the 'Apostolic Faith Missionaries was of the Spirit'. To Ryan's supporters the answer seemed obvious: 'The send-off on the Pacific coast to Bro. Ryan and his party was a wonderful time. People shouted 'Hallelujah', and spoke in tongues, and even got their baptism, but the 'Hooroar' soon died out of their Hallelujahs and they forgot to send on help'.[7] Indeed someone had missed the mark, and within a few years the Apostolic Light's members had all left Japan.

Perhaps their most lasting achievement was their influence on other Christians. The holiness movement in Japan picked up on their activities and denounced Ryan in their periodicals, while other missionaries gave them the same general unwelcome treatment. But they did have a number of converts and a few missionaries and other foreigners were open to this new outpouring of the Holy Spirit. By 1908, a student named Mr Ito, had received the baptism of the Holy Spirit, and Ryan claimed to have 100 converts in his fellowship, 60 of whom came from other churches.[8] Since none of the Apostolic Light missionaries spoke Japanese they tended towards English speakers and Ryan ended up pursuing ministry at a YMCA in Tokyo's student district. Ryan was the last of his group to leave, departing Japan in the fall of 1910, but a fresh wave of Pentecostal missionaries had begun to arrive.

Estella A. Bernauer and Tanimoto Yoshio met at Pentecostal fellowship in Indianapolis led by Zella Reynolds and J. Roswell Flower in the spring of 1909.[9] Tanimoto had come to the United States a few years earlier to study commerce with plans to return to Japan to succeed his father in business, but while at the Seventh Day Adventist College in Berrien Springs, Michigan, he became a Christian and soon felt called to return to Japan as a 'self-supporting

---

[6] Martin L. Ryan, 'Where the Means Come From', *The Apostolic Light* 183 (28 September 1907), 1.

[7] Sisson emphasized that despite the shortcomings of unmindful Pentecostal people, God had still 'brought them through'. Sisson, 'The Southerland Conference', *Confidence* (June 1908), 16.

[8] Martin L. Ryan, 'Victory in Japan', *The Pentecost* 1:4 (December 1908), 3. 'Statistics', *Japan Christian Yearbook 7* (1909), 490-93. Compared with other missions in Japan, this represented an extraordinarily high percentage of 'confirmations on confession of faith'.

[9] Reynolds and Flower's 1910 report on the Pentecostal work in Indianapolis, along with Tanimoto's and Bernauer's published testimonies are keys to understanding their relationship and early ministry. Zella H. Reynolds and J. Roswell Flower, 'The Power of Pentecost in Indianapolis', *The Latter Rain Evangel* (May 1910), 22-23. Yoshio Tanimoto, 'How a Japanese Missionary Received the Baptism of the Holy Ghost: His Own Testimony', *The Good Report* 7 (1 December 1913), 2. Estella A. Bernauer, 'A Call to Japan: Who will hold the ropes?', *The Latter Rain Evangel* (April 1913), 7-11.

missionary'. Estranged from his family by his new faith, he began working his way across America speaking in churches to raise support and discovered the new Pentecostal movement along the way. The Pentecostal fellowship in Indianapolis welcomed him and it was here that he received the baptism of the Holy Spirit. Estella Bernauer, widow of a Baptist preacher, happened to be a member of this church and she already felt a call to missions, but it was Tanimoto's passionate prayers for the people of Japan that convinced her that God was leading her to Japan.

Bernauer arrived in Yokohama in April 1910 accompanied by a younger woman, Ms Schoonover. Bernauer and Schoonover soon moved into the student district to a home about two blocks from Ryan and also began student ministry. They had hired a young man from Yokohama as their translator and guide but unfortunately he soon died of pneumonia and Bernauer herself became critically ill herself during the summer of 1911. She returned to the States in the fall of 1911 to recover, but was soon back to continue the mission in the student district by the fall of 1912. Meanwhile Tanimoto returned to Japan in September 1910 and began work in the Hiroshima area. He distributed tracts by bicycle through a large area of south-western Japan and gathered about 25 converts into a fellowship, but apparently his financial support was even more meagre than that of Ryan or Bernauer. After wearing himself out through full-time English teaching to support himself in addition to the mission work, Tanimoto appealed to Pentecostal circulars in 1914 to send him funds to be able to visit his supporters in the United States.[10] As far as we know he never received the funds, and this is the last we hear from him.

By 1914 at least an additional fourteen Pentecostal missionaries had arrived but many stayed only short-term and their impact was scarcely noticeable.[11] Like Ryan's group before them, the early Pentecostal missions in Japan were crippled by poor funding and planning, lack of language and cultural skills and habitual instability. It was not until the latter half of the 1910s that the Pentecostal community in Japan began to mature and produce significant results. An increase in funding, the development of organizational stability through mission boards such as the American Assemblies of God (General Council) and Japanese Pentecostal leaders were all key to this. During these early years of development the missionaries relied heavily on interpreters and

---

[10] Yoshio Tanimoto, 'Yoshio Tanimoto, Tanna, Akigun, Hiroshima, Japan', *Word and Witness* 10:7 (July 1914), 4. Yoshio Tanimoto, 'Tanna, Akigun, Hiroshima Japan', *The Pentecostal Evangel* (18 July 1914), 4.

[11] In chronological order, they include Robert and Bessie Atchison, Mr and Mrs Thomas Hindle, Edward Downing, Frank and May Gray and William and Mary Taylor, Carl and Frederick Juergensen, Margaret Piper and Mr and Mrs Barney Moore. Additionally other foreigners working in Japan assisted with these early Pentecostal missions, including I.G. Hitch, J.B. Ross and L.W. Coote.

Japanese pastors and leaders were rare. Only two of the 'native workers', Niki Makoto who worked with the Taylors and Takigawa Ichitaro who worked with Bernauer, had received the baptism of the Holy Spirit, and only Takigawa was ordained.[12] Without Japanese leaders baptized in the Holy Spirit it was very difficult for the missionaries adequately to teach such basic Pentecostal teachings, because interpreters who fundamentally disagreed with the content of the missionaries' sermons were naturally reluctant to faithfully translate the message.

Funds, stability and other mission factors improved throughout the 1910s, but the real change for Pentecostals in Japan came with the 1919 revival and outpouring of the Holy Spirit started under Leonard W. Coote in Yokohama.[13] By this time there were already numerous Pentecostal preaching stations and several churches, concentrated primarily in Japan's two largest urban centres: the Tokyo-Yokohama area and the Kobe-Osaka area. But few Japanese had received the classical Pentecostal experience of the baptism and speaking in tongues. Coote had arrived in Kobe in 1913 as a young businessman and, although already baptized at his father's request in a Methodist church before he left home, he experienced a born-again conversion under the influence of the holiness and Pentecostal missionaries in Kobe. He quickly became heavily involved in evangelistic activities and prayer meetings and received the baptism of the Holy Spirit at a dinner-turned-prayer-meeting hosted by Mary Taylor in 1917. After his five-year business contract expired he stayed on in Japan as a full-time missionary and moved north to Yokohama to help run the mission of Barney S. Moore, who was away on furlough. Starting in January 1919 Coote began holding 'An Every Night Campaign Until the Power Fell', but after about eight weeks of meetings the Christians in the congregation had almost entirely deserted him and even the Japanese workers and his interpreter considered him extreme.[14]

---

[12] Estella A. Bernauer, 'The Work in Tokyo, Japan', *The Bridegroom's Messenger* 8, no. 173 (1 July 1915), 3. Takigawa retained credentials through the General Council from 1917 through 1920, making him unique among his Japanese colleagues.

[13] Coote's autobiography is one of the earliest and most extensive narratives of the early Pentecostal community in Japan. Although it focuses on his personal experiences, the broad community of holiness and Pentecostal missions that interacted with one another are frequently mentioned. Leonard W. Coote, *Twenty Years in Japan* (Nara, Japan: Japan Apostolic Mission, 1933).

[14] Coote's autobiography contains a long narrative of the events and there were numerous contemporary letters about it published in Pentecostal circulars. The following are articles helpful in dating and substantiating the events. Frank H. Gray, Mr & Mrs, 'Yokohama, Japan', *The Pentecostal Evangel* (11 January 1919), 10. Frank H. Gray, 'Yokohama, Japan', *The Pentecostal Evangel* (8 March 1919), 11. Barney S. Moore, 'Good news from Japan', *The Pentecostal Evangel* (22 March 1919), 10. Leonard W.

Then one night, a young man kneeling at the altar was filled with the Holy Spirit and began to speak in tongues. As word of the miracle spread attendance at the meetings surged and suddenly others began receiving the same experience. Throughout 1919 Coote and his interpreter, Asakura, began holding revival meetings at each of the Pentecostal mission stations around the country, spreading the revival and outpouring as they went. Within a few months many of the Japanese workers of Pentecostal missionaries had received the baptism of the Holy Spirit, including Asakura, Tanimoto who worked with the Grays and Machida who worked with the Moores. This fundamentally altered their leadership role and perspective on basic Pentecostal doctrines.

Over the next few years the Pentecostal movement in Japan began to blossom. The number of missionaries swelled significantly by the early 1920s and increasing attention was paid to issues such as language acquisition for the missionaries and 'native' leadership training. By 1923 there were Pentecostal missionaries from England, Scotland, Canada, Greece, Norway and the United States, including at least 20 associated with the Assemblies of God, plus numerous independents. The Tokyo-Yokohama area remained the heaviest concentration and Yokohama had two of the most vibrant Pentecostal missions. Coote stayed in Yokohama to study Japanese after the Moores returned and soon founded another church which was experiencing a booming revival amid fierce persecution throughout 1923. A number of young Japanese men felt called to Christian ministry and Coote began holding morning Bible studies to train them. In August 1923 he rented a building for a Bible school, with classes scheduled to begin in the fall.[15] Meanwhile the Moores' church had been renovated and turned over to the leadership of a Japanese-Canadian Pentecostal pastor, Hasegawa. In the summer of 1923, Moore conducted his most successful tent revival ever and contracted with a carpenter to build another church. He had plans to start a curriculum in September for 'the training of native men and women for the care of these churches and for the evangelizing of their own people'.[16] Since Moore had recently completed an extensive fundraising tour of the United States and Canada seeking to raise $10,000 for the work in Japan, his mission was now positioned as one of the most experienced, well financed and aggressive in Japan.

All of this came crashing down on 1 September 1923 in one of the worse natural disasters of the twentieth century, the Great Tokyo-Yokohama Earthquake. Over 100,000 people perished in the quake and ensuing fires which

---

Coote, 'Testimony of an English Business Man in Japan', *The Pentecostal Evangel* (12 July 1919), 6.

[15] Leonard W. Coote, *Twenty Years in Japan* (Nara, Japan: Japan Apostolic Mission, 1933), 109-22, 54.

[16] Barney S. Moore, 'Greetings From Japan', *The Bridegroom's Messenger* 16, no. 246 (September 1923), 3.

destroyed all of Yokohama and most of Tokyo. The Yokohama churches were destroyed and the Moores barely escaped with their lives. Pastor Hasegawa was killed along with his wife and everything the Moores had built up was gone. They returned to the United States as refugees with nothing but the clothes they were wearing. Coote's church was also destroyed, but at the time he and his family were away. When Coote returned to Yokohama to help his flock, he had difficulty even locating the spot where the mission previously stood. He sent his family on a refugee ship to the United States and then relocated to Osaka, taking a number of the Christians with him as they too were now refugees. A great deal of mission funds were lost in the conflagration, and all the missions in the Tokyo-Yokohama area suffered damage. The greater Tokyo area was dedicated to recovery and rebuilding for the next few years.

Japanese Pentecostal Leadership and Denominations

Pentecostal missionaries in Japan were all essentially independent faith missionaries in the early years, but as denominational structures solidified in the West missionaries mirrored those alliances. By 1917 Pentecostal missionaries from throughout Japan were meeting to coordinate their work, and by 1923 the District Council of the Assemblies of God of Japan had been organized.[17] Such efforts were key to bringing the Pentecostal missionary community together, but divisive issues also arrived in Japan through mission conduits. The controversy of the 'New Issue' had reached Japan by 1916 and the missionaries were directly affected by a reduction in their financial support. But Oneness doctrines did not become a point of contention among the missionaries until 1919 after Moore returned from furlough. L.W. Coote and F.H. Gray were two of the early promoters of the doctrine of baptism in Jesus' name only, and as a result they were alienated from the dominant AG community.

Coote was in the vanguard of independent Pentecostal missionaries and during the later 1920s founded a number of churches in and around Osaka, pioneering efforts at Japanese leadership and self-support. He recruited about a dozen missionaries to join in his efforts and by the late 1920s was leading a substantially sized organization of missionaries and Japanese preachers.[18] To

---

[17] Barney S. Moore, Mr. & Mrs.; Piper, Margaret F.; Gray, Frank H.; Juergensen, Carl F., 'The Conditions of the Pentecostal Work in Japan', *The Pentecostal Evangel* (13 October 1917), 10. 'Council Meeting in Japan', *The Pentecostal Evangel* (5 January 1924), 11.

[18] According to the missionary directory of the 1928 *Japan Christian Yearbook*, 10 missionaries were associated with Coote's denomination. In English, he eventually settled on 'Japan Apostolic Mission' after briefly adopting the name of another group,

encourage independent, self-supporting churches, Coote instituted the establishment of 'barrack churches' which were very simple, partially finished structures that were built as follow-up for the converts at tent revivals. The new Christians then were responsible for finishing the buildings themselves, so that the churches were essentially self-supporting from their origin. To provide Japanese pastors, Coote founded Ikoma Bible School in 1929, located in Ikoma, Nara (near both Osaka and Kyoto). The first class of eight graduates in 1933 formed the core of the newly established Japanese denomination, *Nihon Pentekosute Kyokai* (Japan Pentecostal Church) and each graduate took charge of one of the churches that had been previously led by a missionary.

The Assemblies of God related missionaries also made considerable efforts to develop 'native' leadership for their churches, particularly under the influence of the Juergensen missionary family and Yumiyama Kiyoma. From the 1920s onwards, the Juergensen family, which included six career missionaries, became central to the Assemblies of God mission in Japan. Carl F. Juergensen came to Japan with this wife and two young daughters, Marie (age 12) and Agnes (8), in 1913, but had not yet established a stable church by the early 1920s.[19] Carl relied on interpreters until his daughter, Marie, learned Japanese and took over as his full time translator at age 14 in 1916. As a result the Juergensens did not partner with a full-time Japanese worker and after the 1919 revival theirs was the only established mission without a Japanese worker baptized in the Holy Spirit. This began to change, however, when their son, John, who had graduated from Bible school and been ordained in America, joined them as a missionary in late 1919, along with his wife Esther.[20] The rest of the family departed for furlough in 1922, leaving John in charge of the mission and he organized a Bible study for young men. Towards the end of that year Yumiyama Kiyoma, a young Christian evangelist seeking training, joined John's Bible class.[21] Yumiyama was baptized in the Spirit in 1923, and subsequently became a key leader in the burgeoning Assemblies of God mission.

Pentecostal Bands of the World. In Japanese, he originally used the name, *Pentekosute Kyokai* (Pentecostal Church) but latter prefixed *Nihon* (Japan) to it.

[19] Marie Juergensen, 'Heralding the Pentecostal Message in Japan', *The Pentecostal Evangel* (27 June 1931), 1, 6-7, 17. This feature article is one of the earliest attempts to narrate the history of the Juergensens' work in Japan including Yumiyama's story.

[20] *Kirisutokyo Nenkan 1927* [Christian Yearbook 1927] (Tokyo: Kirisuto Shimbunsha, 1926), 342. John's wife later died and he remarried, hence, seven Juergensen missionaries in total.

[21] Marie Juergensen, 'A Call from Japan: An Opportunity for Practical Missionary Work' (Springfield, MO: Assemblies of God, Foreign Missions Department, 1929), 4-9. This contains a biographical account of Yumiyama's testimony, and an account of how he began ministry with the Juergensens, some in his own words.

In January 1924, the missionaries of the AG District Council of Japan met to set a new course for the future which called for closer co-operation among the missionaries, the establishment of a Bible school and the building of a mission headquarters.[22] Informal training of 'native' leaders had occurred since early on, but the first systematic efforts were pioneered by John Juergensen from 1922-26.[23] Harriet Dithridge then opened the Berean Bible School for women in September 1926 in Tachikawa (25 km west of Tokyo) with 13 students.[24] These efforts began bearing fruit by 1926 when the Japanese workers organized themselves into an informal denomination, the *Nihon Pentekosute Kyokai* (Japan Pentecostal Church), which included six churches in the Tokyo area and two near Kobe.[25] Three of John Juergensen's students, Yumiyama, Tani Riki and Namiki Yoshimaro, were the first Japanese pastors. In 1929 they changed the name to *Nihon Seisho Kyokai* (Japan Bible Church, JBC) to avoid confusion with L.W. Coote's ministry.

The building project quickly evolved into Takinogawa Church, the 'first' AG church building in Japan, which would also serve as the mission headquarters and Bible school. None of the AG missions owned buildings or property at this point and it was a major financial step for the missionaries, requiring new levels of cooperation among themselves and with the American AG Foreign Mission Department. In 1925, they purchased land in Takinogawa, a Tokyo suburb, and dedicated the new church building in October 1927.[26] However, even before the building was up conflicts emerged regarding the use of resources, particularly concerning the women's Bible school.[27] In the 1929 meeting of the AG Japan District Council the missionaries voted to end support

---

[22] 'An Advanced Step in the Land of Opportunity', *The Pentecostal Evangel* (29 March 1924), 10.

[23] *Kirisutokyo Nenkan 1927* [Christian Yearbook 1927] (Tokyo: Kirisuto Shimbunsha, 1927), 33. John W. Juergensen, 'Missionary Victories', *The Pentecostal Evangel* (12 November 1927), 4. Coote and Moore also wrote about starting classes, but their plans were destroyed in the earthquake. John Juergensen's efforts were the first to produce results.

[24] Harriet E. Dithridge, 'Report of God's work in Tachikawa, Japan', *The Pentecostal Evangel* (12 March 1927), 11.

[25] This was not a legal body and was still under the authority of the missionaries (The Japan District Council). *Kirisutokyo Nenkan 1927* [Christian Yearbook 1927] (Tokyo: Kirisuto Shimbunsha, 1927), 33, 85-90.

[26] Juergensen, 'Juergensen Family Mission Report Circular', 2 March 1927 (Letter, FPHC Archive, 0781-029). 'The New Building in Japan', *The Pentecostal Evangel* (4 February 1928), 10. The church building is still in active use today. While Americans were dominant, AG missionaries also came from England, Australia and Canada.

[27] Juergensen, 'Juergensen Family Mission Report Circular', 2 March 1927 (Letter, FPHC Archive, 0781-029).

for Dithridge's school and instead would focus on a 'Men's Bible School'.[28]
The following year, Yumiyama took over as senior pastor of Takinogawa
Church and in 1931 became principal of the new school, *Seirei Shingakuin*
(Holy Spirit Seminary).

With Japanese Pentecostal leaders, trained under Yumiyama's tutelage, the
Japan Bible Church experienced steady growth through the 1930s. They
expanded geographically to cover a much wider area of Honshu, Japan's main
island and began partnering missionaries with Japanese pastors in all missions.
New churches were opened in many areas including Sendai, Yokohama,
Urawa, Nagoya, Kofu, Hamamatsu and Ibaraki; some without missionaries.
Each of the churches remained fundamentally independent and although there
was connection through denominational structures, allegiances were fluid
during this period. Some pastors, such as Tani Riki, transferred to holiness
churches, while pastors from other denominations and independents joined the
Japan Bible Church (JBC), such as Kawasaki Hajime of Nara. Some of the JBC
churches became independent, like Dithridge's fellowship in Tachikawa, while
some independents joined the JBC. Coote's Japan Pentecostal Church also
grew during this period and was an active part of this expanding Pentecostal
movement, but maintained a narrower geographic focus in the Kansai region.
The Pentecostal movement in Japan in the 1930s expanded beyond the borders
of the two 'Pentecostal' denominations and was increasingly a Japanese-led
movement. By 1937, not a single Pentecostal church reported a missionary as
its pastor to the *Kirisutokyo Nenkan* (Christian Yearbook) and by 1938 the JBC
had 19 churches and at least 22 Japanese pastors and evangelists (12 men and
10 women).[29]

The dynamic nature of this movement came with problems as well. The
Japan Bible Church, which was in fact more a federation of independent
churches than a unified denomination, made a new start in August 1937 headed
by Murai Jun, Norman Barth and John Juergensen. The Takinogawa mission,
calling itself *Takinogawa Seirei Kyokai* (Takinogawa Holy Spirit Church), then
seceded with its four churches, led by Yumiyama Kiyoma and Marie
Juergensen. Fifteen churches remained in the JBC. All of the missionaries were
united through the Assemblies of God and the two groups remained

---

[28] Carl F. Juergensen, 'Minutes of the Japan District Council and accompanying letter',
30 September 1929 (Council Minutes, FPHC Archive, 0295 403). Predictably, Dithridge
was not pleased with this and eventually left the AG. The AG Bible school accepted
women as well.

[29] The yearbooks report data for the year prior to the year of publication. Kirisutokyo
Nenkan 1938 [Christian Yearbook 1938] (Tokyo: Kirisuto Shimbunsha, 1938).
Kirisutokyo Nenkan 1939 [Christian Yearbook 1939] (Tokyo: Kirisuto Shimbunsha,
1939). The number of churches includes both JBC and Takinogawa Seirei Kyokai which
had just split that year. JBC alone submitted statistics for the number of workers.

theologically indistinguishable so they most likely split for political and financial reasons.[30] Despite the disagreements over organizational structure many of the pastors continued to have fellowship and co-operate with Yumiyama.

The War Years

The more serious problem in the late 1930s was the rise of fascism and militarism coupled with Japan's ongoing war with China. Christianity was associated with the West, and in the growing ultranationalistic, anti-western fervour Christians faced no small degree of persecution. Since almost all of the Pentecostal missionaries were from countries that were viewed as national enemies they began to suffer from surveillance and harassment as the wartime crisis unfolded. Naturally this accelerated the move to an entirely Japanese, self-supporting church. To mobilize the nation for war, the government enacted laws in 1938-39 to bring all activities under the control of the state, including Christian churches. Missionaries were legally excluded from official positions of leadership and then in 1939 the government began uniting all Protestants into a single denomination, *Nihon Kirisuto Kyodan* (NKK).[31] As independents, Pentecostals attempted to focus on maintaining normal church life as much as possible, but their work was increasingly restricted and missionaries described it as the most difficult time they had ever had in their ministry. Coote wrote of the almost daily disturbances at Ikoma Bible School by government officials and how police demanded to sit on the platform during his tent meetings and even review the entire text of messages before he was given permission to speak.[32] By 1940, the missionaries were becoming more of a liability than an asset and they began to return home. When all American assets in Japan were frozen by the government in July 1941 (in response to the US freezing Japanese assets), the remaining missionaries had no choice but to leave. When the Pacific war started with the United States in December 1941, only three

---

[30] *Kirisutokyo Nenkan 1939* [Christian Yearbook 1939] (Tokyo: Kirisuto Shimbunsha, 1939), 79-80, 123. *Kirisutokyo Nenkan 1940* [Christian Yearbook 1940] (Tokyo: Kirisuto Shimbunsha, 1940), 70, 75-76, 124-25. Number of churches compiled from the national directories of 'Churches and Pastors' in each volume. The four churches that seceded (Takinogawa, Jujo, Hamamatsu and Sendai) were all part of the 'Takinogawa Mission' and financially dependent on mission funds through Marie and Agnes Juergensen. Carl Juergensen was listed as the 'head', but he was by then retired and died in 1940 at age 77. Yumiyama's group also used the name *Seirei Kyokai* (Holy Spirit Church).
[31] Officially the name is translated 'United Church of Christ in Japan', but it literally means 'Japan Christ Association'.
[32] Leonard W. Coote, *Impossibilities Become Challenges*, 5th ed. (San Antonio, TX: Church Alive! Press, 1965; reprint, 1991), 178.

Pentecostal missionaries were left in Japan: Mr and Mrs. E Davies who were interned until being repatriated in 1942 and Jessie Wengler, who remained under house arrest for the duration of the war.

Japan Bible Church, Takinogawa Holy Spirit Church and Japan Pentecostal Church were all merged into the united Protestant denomination, which was officially incorporated in June 1941.[33] However, as loose associations of independent churches, these organizations had never been established as legal bodies, so each congregation made its own decision regarding its status with regard to the united church. Wengler wrote in May 1941 that she along with other AG related churches in her area had no plans to enter the united church but were going to try to continue registering each church independently, and missionary correspondence through the fall of 1941 shows no evidence that they had changed their position.[34] However after the Pacific War broke out in December 1941, the former denomination ceased to exist and many of the churches did join, at least as a formality.

Christian churches had difficulty amid the ethnocentric and jingoistic national spirit building up since Japan began full-scale war with China in 1937, but the social, political and economic situation accompanying the all-out war with the United States and the Allied powers ground church life to a standstill. Street meetings and public evangelistic activities were prohibited. Cut off from mission support, pastors and other church workers had to find outside employment. Families struggled for basic staples during the wartime shortages. Many of the men were drafted into the armed forces and military industries. Christians faced direct persecution from the government and holiness churches in particular were oppressed.

Over a hundred pastors of the former Holiness Church (having merged into the NKK) were arrested for claiming the supremacy of Christ over the Emperor. Seven died at the hands of their captors. Pentecostals, who would have given the same replies to inquisitors, were not singled out as the holiness groups were, only because they were too small a target and too decentralized. Travel for fellowship among pastors became impossible and a number of them died during the war, including Ito Chirukichi, pastor of the Yokohama church, who had been drafted into the army. During the fire-bombing of the cities some

---

[33] The NKK was divided into eleven groupings called 'blocks'. According to a June 1941 document by NKK, the Japan Pentecostal Church entered the seventh block which was for evangelistic associations such as the Japan Evangelistic Band, while the AG related groups entered the tenth block which was for independent churches. Nihon Kirisuto Kyodan Senkyo Kenkyujo, ed., *Nihon Kirisuto Kyodanshi Shiryoshu Dai Ippen (1930-1941)* [Compilation of Documents on the History of United Church of Christ in Japan, 1930-1941], 3 vols. (Tokyo: Nihon Kirisuto Kyodan, 1997), I, 315.

[34] Jessie Wengler, 'Exerpts of letter regarding response to 1941 church mergers', 6 May 1941 (letter, AGWM Archive).

of the church buildings were destroyed and Christians were scattered. By the time Japan was defeated the country was in ruins and Pentecostals, along with the rest of the nation, were struggling just to survive.

Despite the intense hardships of war there continued to be pockets of revival and important developments. By 1940 Murai Jun was head of the now entirely Japanese-led JBC and in 1941 he spent a month in Taiwan with several other JBC leaders, assisting evangelistic efforts of the True Jesus Church, an indigenous Pentecostal group (Taiwan was part of the Japanese Empire 1895-1945). Apparently he was influenced by the Oneness doctrines of the True Jesus Church and in November 1941 his wife received a divine vision to use the name *Iesu no Mitama Kyokai* (The Spirit of Jesus Church).[35] Murai went on to introduce other doctrines from the True Jesus Church, including an emphasis on foot-washing and baptism of the dead (in accordance with 1 Cor. 15.29). Because of the chaos of war and the unification of all churches within the NKK, Murai's influence was limited during the 1940s, but the Spirit of Jesus Church experienced phenomenal growth in the post-war period. Other indigenous Pentecostal groups trace their roots to outpourings of the Holy Spirit in this period including the *Kirisuto Kanan Kyodan* (Christian Canaan Church, 1940) and *Sambi Kyodan* (Praise Church, 1944).

New Beginnings

During the American occupation (1945-52) and the early post-war reconstruction, Pentecostal groups rapidly proliferated. With the restoration of religious freedom, missionaries returned and churches could exist outside of the NKK. Murai officially established the Spirit of Jesus Church under his charismatic leadership and by 1947 had gathered over 400 believers and soon thereafter opened Japan Bible Seminary.[36] Meanwhile, many of the former leaders of the JBC, including Yumiyama, began gathering for fellowship and held their first national revival meeting in April 1947, attended by seven pastors

---

[35] Japan Assemblies of God (ed.), *Mitama ni Michibikarete: Soritsu Sanju Nenshi* [Guided by the Spirit: The Thirty Year History] (Tokyo: Japan Assemblies of God, 1979), 22-23. This early history of JAG asserts that Murai left the JBC upon his return to establish the Spirit of Jesus Church but I can find no evidence that this actually occurred. According to the early post-war volumes of *Kirisutokyo Nenkan* (Christian Yearbook) he claimed that JBC developed into The Spirit of Jesus Church under his leadership. See also Mark Mullins, *Christianity Made in Japan* (Honolulu: University of Hawaii Press, 1998).

[36] Kirisuto Shimbunsha (ed.), *Kirisutokyo Nenkan 1969* [Christian Yearbook 1969] (Tokyo: Kirisuto Shimbunsha, 1969), 177, 407.

and 60 believers.[37] In March 1949 the Japan Assemblies of God (JAG) was established with thirteen churches, twelve Japanese workers and seven missionaries.[38] The Bible school was reopened in 1948 and was reorganized in 1950 as the Central Bible College on a new campus that also served as JAG headquarters.

Harriet Dithridge returned to Japan in 1949 and opened a church in Tachikawa in association with Bethel Pentecostal Temple from Seattle, Washington. Other missionaries soon followed her and Japan Bethel Mission was later established as a denomination. L.W. Coote also returned and Ikoma Bible School started classes again in 1950. During the war Coote had established a thriving church and the International Bible College in San Antonio, Texas which generously supported his return to Japan. Some of the first graduates of the Bible school became missionaries to Japan and by the early 1960s Coote had recruited about 25 missionaries to work in Japan. He also branched out to establish the Osaka Evangelistic Tabernacle which carried on nightly meetings for several years in the early 1950s, attended by thousands.

Coote was probably the single most significant Pentecostal missionary in the post-war period. In addition to his considerable skill as an evangelist and teacher, Coote was willing to step out in faith against all odds. He led people to salvation and preached the power of the Holy Spirit, but perhaps even more important for the rapid spread of the movement, he inspired leaders. Through the Ikoma Bible School, the Osaka Evangelistic Tabernacle and the numerous missionaries he brought to Japan, Coote influenced the formation and direction of a number of key Pentecostal denominations including Japan Pentecost Church (1950), Japan Evangelical Churches (1950), Next Towns Crusade (1956, Japan Next Towns Mission), Total Christian Church Group (1957) and the Flock of the Gospel of Jesus Christ (1961). Along with Ikoma Bible School, today these denominations are all self-supporting, self-governing, self-propagating, Japanese institutions.

Over two dozen new Pentecostal groups were established from the early post-war reconstruction period through the 1960s. The influx of missionaries peaked from 1950-55 during which 15 new Pentecostal groups were

---

[37] Japan Assemblies of God (ed.), *Mitama ni Michibikarete: Soritsu Sanju Nenshi* [Guided by the Spirit: The Thirty Year History] (Tokyo: Japan Assemblies of God, 1979), 39-41.

[38] Marie Juergensen, 'Inception of Assemblies of God Work in Japan' (unpublished manuscript, 1951, AGWM Archive). D.G. McLean, 'Precise History of the Japan Assembly of God' (unpublished Manuscript, 1978, AGWM Archive), 4. The name in Japanese, *Nihon Assemburizu obu Goddo*, is simply a transliteration of the English and sounds odd in Japanese. JBC was probably not chosen as a name, in part because they wanted to distance themselves from Murai who claimed that the 1937 reorganization of JBC was the start of the Spirit of Jesus Church. AG missionaries were also undoubtedly influential in the adoption of this Anglicized name.

established. Part of this rapid influx was due to China missionaries relocating to Japan after they were expelled by the Communists in 1950. Some of these missions were composed of just a few churches and disappeared with no permanent presence, but most thrived. Some of the significant arrivals include International Church of the Four Square Gospel (1950), Open Bible Standard Churches (1950), Church of God (Cleveland, TN, 1952) and Pentecostal Church of God (1954). Oneness groups also started mission work in Japan including the United Pentecostal Church International (1963). A number of Scandinavian organizations pioneered missions during this period including Fellowship of Christian Assemblies (1948), Swedish Free Missionaries (1950), Finland Free Foreign Mission (1950) and Free Christian Mission Group (1950, from Norway and Denmark). These Scandinavian groups later merged into the Independent Pentecostal Church Fellowship.

Growth and Challenges

The largest and fastest growing Pentecostal church was the indigenous Spirit of Jesus Church (SCJ). Starting from virtually nothing after the war, the church grew to be the second largest Protestant denomination in Japan by 1963 with 46,870 members and by the mid-1990s it claimed to have well over half a million members—approximately equal to all other Protestants combined. However from 1985 onward the *Kirisutokyo Nenkan*, the most authoritative source for statistics on Christianity in Japan, began excluding SCJ from its tallies. Not only was SCJ baptizing the dead, it was adding them to its rosters as well. These and other questionable doctrines alienated SCJ from other Christians in Japan and it is commonly considered heretical. In response SCJ sees itself as the only true church. In 1999, SCJ revised its figures down to approximately one tenth of their previous totals. But even so, the figures seem exaggerated since they only have 156 churches in Japan, only 94 of which have their own building. Based on the average size of Japanese congregations, I estimate that they have between 10,000 and 15,000 members living in Japan.[39]

Pentecostal denominations grew in numbers and in maturity over the next few decades. Unlike in the pre-war era, Japanese leaders quickly assumed top leadership positions and made the movement their own. There was also significant interaction among Pentecostals, particularly within geographic districts. But Pentecostals did not enjoy a positive relationship with either mainline Protestants or Evangelicals. The Charismatic Movement entered Japan

---

[39] The 2002 *Kirisutokyo Nenkan* statistical charts for SJC show 56,388 members and 236 churches (plus another 427 mission stations). But their church directory in the main volume (p. 20-27) lists 156 churches in Japan and 69 overseas, for 225 total. There were an average of 78 members per Protestant church in Japan for 2001. If SJC has average size congregations, then they would have a little over 12,000 members.

in the late 1960s and brought some conciliation with mainline Protestants and Catholics, but its influence was relatively minor. A number of individuals and churches welcomed this new movement of the Holy Spirit, but since charismatic expressions of faith were not generally accepted, some participants resorted to transferring to Pentecostal denominations which spread distrust of the movement.[40] The movement was perhaps better known and more significant for Pentecostals than for mainline churches. NKK leaders have tended to shun the Pentecostal and Charismatic movements as irrelevant and even today they are largely unknown among mainline Christians in Japan.[41]

International Pentecostal currents began flowing into Japan in the 1970s-'80s from Korea. But it was not the first time for Korean and Japanese Pentecostals to meet. In the pre-war period, both JBC and Japan Pentecostal Church included Korean congregations and JBC sponsored missions to Korea from 1928. Korean pastors had also trained at both Holy Spirit Seminary and Ikoma Bible School, and in 1939 Coote purchased land to build a Bible school in Korea. In the 1970s the tide turned and Korean Pentecostals began ministering in Japan. Yonggi Cho's Yoido Full Gospel Church started a branch in Japan in 1978. It is now one of the largest Pentecostal denominations with well over 7,000 members.[42] Their main church in Tokyo is today one of the largest in Japan with about 3,000 members, but there, as in most of their churches, Korean immigrants are dominant. Yonggi Cho has been deeply involved in mass meetings and church growth in Japan since the late 1970s.

International influences continued to be important, and from the mid1980s through the 1990s the Third Wave was introduced to Japan. Already well known in Japan among Evangelicals for his work on church growth, Peter Wagner held Charismatic seminars, as did Cindy Jacobs. A number of Japanese authors published on the theme and then Wagner's book *The Third Wave of the Holy Spirit* was translated into Japanese (1991) as was John Wimber's *Power Evangelism* (1994). Carlos Anacondia, Benny Hinn and other international

---

[40] Satoshi Nakamura, *Nihon ni okeru Fukuinha no Rekishi: Mo Hitotsu Nihon Kirisutokyoshi* [The History of Evangelicals in Japan: Another History of Christianity in Japan] (Tokyo: Word of Life Press, 2000), 242.

[41] The NKK has been preoccupied with internal struggles since about 1970 and its ignorance of the world-wide Pentecostal/Charismatic revival movement is due more to this than to a definitive theological position. However, when NKK publications mention charismatic expression of faith, they have been generally negative. In January 1998, the NKK Holy Spirit Regeneration Council was formed to break down prejudice and discrimination against Charismatic churches and Christians within the NKK.

[42] Kirisuto Shimbunsha (ed.), *Kirisutokyo Nenkan 2002* [Christian Yearbook 2002] (Tokyo: Kirisuto Shimbunsha, 2002). Statistical charts for the Full Gospel Church are not current. The above figure was obtained by totalling the members noted for each church in the directory. But as only half of the 34 churches reported such figures, total members must be much higher. As in Korea, each congregation tends to be large.

charismatic evangelists travelled to Japan for revival meetings in the 1990s. All of the major features of the Third Wave and various related worldwide outpourings of the Holy Spirit in the 1980s and 1990s were well publicized in Japan among both Evangelicals and Pentecostals.

The increasingly close relationship between Pentecostal and other Evangelicals around the world, and the prominent role that Pentecostals played in international Evangelical organizations began to have an effect on thawing relationships within Japan by the late 1980s. The first few interdenominational evangelical organizations in Japan excluded Pentecostals entirely. The Japan Evangelical Association (JEA) was formed in 1986 to replace previous organizations as a more inclusive body, but certain factions were still unsympathetic towards Pentecostals. At its founding the group approved a 'Provision on Charisma' denying Pentecostal doctrines and the application of the Japan Assemblies of God was rejected.[43] JAG leaders worked hard to clear up the 'misunderstandings' about Pentecostals and in 1988 they were inducted into the organization—a major turning point for Pentecostals in Japan. But some JEA members had increasing problems with developments in the Third Wave. In 1994 the Theological Committee of the JEA released a statement denouncing 'power evangelism' and the JEA was effectively split into pro and anti Third Wave factions, with the 'anti' faction in the majority.[44] This, along with the growing recognition of the limitations of the JEA, occasioned the formation of the Nippon Revival Association (NRA) in 1996. Welcoming Pentecostals, the NRA is a charismatic, evangelical organization dedicated primarily to revival in Japan. NRA began publishing The Revival Times in 1996 and has taken the bold step of maintaining a positive relationship with both JEA and its liberal counterpart, the National Christian Council in Japan.

Facing Forward

A perennial question for Christians in Japan is why the growth rate is so low. The same could be asked about Pentecostals. Pentecostals are growing exponentially around the world and neighbouring South Korea is leading the way. Why not in Japan? No one has satisfactorily answered this for Christians

---

[43] Yoshimasa Ikegami, 'Kindai Nihon ni okeru Kirisutokyo Seireiha no Keifu' [Lineage of the Christian Holy Spirit Tradition in Modern Japan], *Bulletin of Meiji Gakuin University Christian Research Center* 33 (20 January 2001), 83. Japan Assemblies of God (ed.), *Mikotoba ni Tachi, Mitama ni Michibikarete: Nihon Assemburizu ob Goddo Kyodan Soritsu Goju Nenshi* [Standing on the Word, Guided by the Spirit: The Fifty Year History of the Japan Assemblies of God] (Tokyo: Japan Assemblies of God, 1999), 168-69.

[44] Mamoru Ogata, 'Seirei no Daisan no Nami to Seirei Undo to Kongo to Tenkai' [Third Wave of the Holy Spirit and Further Developments of the Holy Spirit Movement], *Signs* 5 (September 2001), 195.

in Japan in general so I will not attempt to address the broader social, historical and theological reasons. There are, however, a few factors particular to Pentecostals. First, the major disruptions of the 1923 Great Tokyo-Yokohama Earthquake and World War II, devastated the churches, so after World War II the Pentecostal movement in Japan was practically starting over again from scratch. Second is the continuing friction with other Christians, both mainline and evangelical, which is much more pronounced than in many other parts of the world. After so many decades of enmity some Pentecostals in Japan suffer from a siege mentality, tending to be defensive of their orthodoxy and suspicious of other Christian groups. Third is the cultural clash between Pentecostals and Japanese society. The main currents of Pentecostalism in Japan are more focused on the West than on Japanese society for inspiration and guidance. While most Pentecostal groups in Japan today are truly Japanese-led, indigenous organizations, they tend to fall short of most definitions of contextualized ministry.

In spite of these problems, it is remarkable that Pentecostals are among the fastest growing of all Christian groups in Japan, and are significantly larger than the 'official' statistical charts in *Kirisutokyo Nenkan*. Like the pioneer Pentecostal missionaries of the pre-war era, submitting reports and statistics for posterity is not a priority—but evangelism is, and it shows. One example of a rapidly growing, indigenous, Charismatic denomination is The Lord's Cross Christian Centre which was founded in 1984. Today they have grown to 107 domestic churches and 22 overseas, with about 2,800 members in Japan.[45] While mainline Protestant churches in Japan have stagnated, Pentecostal denominations are almost all experiencing significant growth. Pentecostals are also cooperating at a national level more now than ever before. The Japan Pentecostal Council was established in May 1998 by ten Pentecostal denomination to 'promote the healthy growth and development of Pentecostal faith in Japan'. Pentecostals, in the broad sense of the term, show all signs of continuing these trends and are headed towards becoming a leading Christian movement in twenty-first century Japan.

---

[45] Figures obtained from their headquarters. For comparison, in the same 17 years, the NKK grew by a little less than 2%.

The Korean Holy Spirit Movement in Relation to Pentecostalism

Young-Hoon Lee

The Korean Protestant church has grown and developed rapidly enough to receive worldwide attention in its short history of one hundred and twenty years. The 'Holy Spirit movement' of the various Korean churches may be in good part responsible. The history of the Korean church can be divided into five periods of twenty years each. The Holy Spirit movement[1] in the Korean church generally shows unique features in each period which are related to the political, social and religious background of the period.

The First Period 1900-1920

During the first period, Korea was succumbing to Japanese occupation. It was a time of chaos both politically and socially and can be considered a period of religious vacuum. Since many Koreans had lost direction, they sought hope in Christianity.

The Great Revival of 1907

The Great Revival of 1907[2] that took place in PyongYang, currently the capital of North Korea, had a great influence on the lifestyle of Korean Christians. The revival started in a Bible study and prayer meeting that was primarily led by a Methodist missionary, R.A. Hardie, at Wonsan (North Korea) in 1903. It reached its peak at Pyong-Yang in 1907 and then spread throughout the country. The missionaries who had gathered when the revival broke out in Pyong-Yang went out to other places all over the country and led revival meetings in order to keep the fire of the Holy Spirit from dying out. The fire of

---

[1] I use the term 'the Holy Spirit movement' to embrace the conception of all spiritual/revival movements. I will specify which movement I refer to when necessary.

[2] This event was reported by William Blair. He called this event 'The Korean Pentecost'. He was living in Pyongyang (now the capital city of North Korea) as a missionary at that time. See in detail: William Blair and Bruce Hunt, *The Korean Pentecost and the Suffering Which Followed* (Carlisle: Banner of Truth, 1977), 71-74. See also Donald D. Owens, *Revival Fires in Korea* (Kansas, MO: Nazarene, 1977), 23-79.

the Spirit thus spread widely and brought about a great zeal for evangelism and a resulting explosive growth of the church.[3] According to the reports of missionaries, during the evening revival meetings people witnessed strong manifestations of the Holy Spirit.

> On Monday, January 14, 1907, about 1,500 gathered in the evening meeting. As it drew to a conclusion, Rev. William Blair reported, they received the power of the Holy Spirit. Rev. Graham Lee was leading the meeting that evening. After a short sermon, Rev. Graham Lee took charge of the meeting and called for prayers. So many began praying at the same time that Lee told the whole audience to pray together if they wished to pray aloud. The whole audience began to pray out loudly and in unison. People were feeling an urge to prayer.[4]

The prayer that sounded like a great waterfall captivated the whole congregation. One by one they began to repent of their sins publicly. It was reported that the experience of the Spirit at this meeting instantly solved the problem of individual sins and helped people release their grief over the fate of the nation. It was said that this was their first experience of feeling and tasting the dynamic power of the Holy Spirit. The Great Revival was never restricted to adult congregations but spread to children and high school students, especially to those who went to Christian schools. The movement of this period was open to all classes of people in all age groups.

Generally speaking the characteristics of Korean churches and their Christian lifestyle have been influenced by this movement. Bible study and ardent prayer, especially characterized by repentance, have become the most important religious traditions and integrally part of the Korean church.[5] The outstanding feature of this revival was repentance following the model of the early church as described in the New Testament. The repentance movement put its main stress on personal salvation and personal experience and for that reason was

---

[3] The following may be described as the background of the revival: 1) people wanted to find hope from Christianity while Korea was in trouble; 2) the revival came as a result of rapid westernization; 3) the old religions of Korea had failed the nation and thus Christianity was expected to bring new hope; 4) there was no great difficulty in the replacement of the old religions by Christianity. Like Confucianism, Christianity taught righteousness and revered learning. Like Buddhism, Christianity sought purity and promised a future life. Like shamanism, Christianity taught that God answered prayer and performed miracles. Donald D. Owens, *Revival Fires in Korea* (Kansas, MO: Nazarene, 1977), 25.

[4] William Blair and Bruce Hunt, op. cit., 73–74.

[5] Most church historians in Korea agree with this opinion. For example, see Kyung-Bae Min, *Church History of Korea* [in Korean], rev. ed. (Seoul: Christian Literature Society of Korea, 1982), 252–61; Allen D. Clark, *A History of the Church in Korea* (Seoul: Christian Literature Society of Korea, 1971), 165-66.

largely lacking in social concern. This tendency has passed into the mainstream of Korean church life.

The Second Period 1920-1940

The second period was a time when Korea was under Japanese occupation. The three Holy Spirit movements of the suffering church during this period can be described according to the different emphases of three outstanding and widely influential leaders. The first movement led by Rev. Sun-Joo Gil (1869-1935) emphasized eschatological faith and the imminent return of Jesus Christ. The second led by Rev. Ick-Doo Kim (1894-1950) emphasized the miraculous signs of the apostolic church and performed healing. The third movement led by Rev Yong-Do Lee (1901-33) stressed the suffering Christ and mystical union with Christ. Under the persecution of Japan, these three Holy Spirit movements with different emphases—eschatological faith, faith in divine healing and faith in mystical union with a suffering Christ—had a great influence on people. Since Christians had played a major role in the Declaration of Independence of 1 March, 1919, the Japanese began to persecute the churches severely. In the middle of this devastating situation Korean Christians were comforted by the Holy Spirit movements and as a result, became interested in having mystical experiences.

Sun-Joo Gil's Holy Spirit Movement

Sun-Joo Gil, a Presbyterian minister, led classes and revival meetings all over the country from 1907 to 1935. His emphasis on eschatology gave great hope for the future to people who despaired under the Japanese occupation. According to one estimate, during his 28-year ministry he preached more than 20,000 times to a total of 3.8 million people. He baptized more than three thousand and built more than sixty churches.[6] Numerous people became ministers, elders, and social workers under his influence. The main focus of Gil's theology was eschatology, as he emphasized the second coming of Christ and life after death. As a result of this emphasis, Korean Christians of the period tended to be concerned chiefly with the future life and personal salvation.

Ick-Doo Kim's Holy Spirit Movement

Ick-Doo Kim was a Presbyterian faith healer who provided vitality and new strength for the Korean people and church. Against the streams of new ideas and anti-Christian ideology that had begun to emerge in the 1920s, he was a

---

[6] Jin-Kyung Gil, *Sun-Joo Gil* [in Korean] (Seoul: Chongno, 1980), 326.

man of prophecy who maintained an orthodox faith and gave enormous hope to the lower class people, who had been neglected. Kim's revival ministry was a healing ministry through prayer. In October 1919, while leading a revival meeting in a church in Pyong-nam province, he was inspired by the Scripture verse in Mark 16.17, 'And these signs will accompany those who believe'. He believed that the same signs and wonders could take place as in the apostolic age when the Lord granted his grace and he ardently prayed for this manifestation of God's power. After a month he laid his hands on a paralytic man and prayed for his healing and it was reported that the paralytic was healed within a day. From this day forward he was convinced of the power of divine healing and many miracles were reported accompanying his ministry. According to the record of the minutes of the Ninth Annual Assembly of Presbyterian Churches, the blind regained their sight, the dumb spoke, paralysis and haemorrhaging were healed.

Kim's revival meetings had the following special features. First, they were public crusades. Second, his meetings had a unique schedule or time table. He led meetings four times a day: an early morning prayer meeting, a two to three hours long Bible class in the morning, a doctrinal study class in the afternoon and a revival meeting in the evening. Third, these meetings had a unique atmosphere, so that people said that his sermons stirred the hearts of those who gathered. Fourth, divine healing was the pre-eminent emphasis.[7] Kim's revival movement contributed greatly to the growth of the church. The most impressive feature of this movement was that Kim preached his message to lower class people who were neglected and suffering from poverty and disease. Furthermore his message was focused on the future life, proclaiming the eschatological millennium and criticizing sin and wealth.

---

[7] Divine healing is an important part of the modern holiness movement and the Pentecostal movement. A.B. Simpson, who had a great theological influence on the holiness movement, discussed the following four major doctrines found in the Bible: salvation, holiness, healing and the second coming of Jesus Christ. The Pentecostal movement took such doctrines from the holiness movement. Although the holiness churches do not emphasize divine healing as much as formerly, the Pentecostal movement still emphasizes and takes divine healing as an important doctrine. See Donald W. Dayton, *Theological Roots of Pentecostalism* (Grand Rapids, MI: Francis Asbury, 1987), 115–41; John Thomas Nichol, *Pentecostalism* (Plainfield, NJ: Logos International, 1966), 2–8, 15–17.

In the doctrine of the Presbyterian church, divine healing is not emphasized. Although Kim was a Presbyterian pastor and the former superintendent of the Presbyterian church council, his healing ministry was not very much emphasized. Only a brief comment has been made on his ministry in church history books written by Presbyterian scholars. See Yung-Hun Lee, *The History of the Korean Church* [in Korean] (Seoul: Concordia, 1992), 122–23.

Yong-Do Lee's Holy Spirit Movement

The Holy Spirit movement led by Yong-Do Lee in 1930, although brief, was strong; it stimulated and challenged the church and it stirred up a new enthusiasm for faith. Lee motivated a revival movement that emphasized 'Jesus-centred enthusiasm' and prayer, thus influencing the formation of patterns for the church, classified by many scholars as revivalism and mysticism. Yong Do Lee's movement had a great impact on the revitalization of a weak Korean church; it created an atmosphere favourable to its reform and as a consequence Lee became the target of severe criticism from existing churches. Yet he proclaimed the message of repentance wherever he went and is recorded as having said:

> Korea needs pioneers of the repentance movement more than any pioneers of doctrine or organization. A movement that does not bring regeneration by repentance does not have any significance at all. The pioneers of the church should be truly born-again Christians, dead to sin and born of righteousness, born-again by the Holy Spirit....[8] True repentance is long gone in the church. This is one of the major reasons why the church has not grown.[9]

He urged this repentance mainly upon the stiff-necked church, arrogant ministers and missionaries. The chief target of his criticism was the Christian congregation of Pyongyang, called the 'Jerusalem of Korea'.

Lee became a voice in the wilderness as he urged church reformation but was attacked for it. Although he lived for only thirty-three years, Lee influenced the Korean church quite crucially—both positively and negatively. His revival movement had a great impact on the church in many ways. First, he confronted a formalistic and lethargic faith and provided a chance to connect faith and life by an exercise of the emotions in their pure state.[10] Second, Lee stressed the prayerful life. He diagnosed that the church had become depressed due to a lack of prayer. Third, he started a new style of revival meeting that was mystical and indigenous to the Korean people, quite different from the Great Revival of 1907 that had been led by the missionaries. Fourth, Lee's revival meetings caused many young people to dedicate their lives to Christ.

---

[8] Jong-Ho Byun (ed.), *Diary of Yong-Do Lee* [in Korean] of (Seoul: Chang-Ahn, 1993), 59–60 (10 November, 1929). Jong-Ho Byun, as a follower of Yong-Do Lee, dedicated his life to research on Yong-Do Lee, defending him in regard to the charge of heresy on him and editing and publishing Lee's books. By Byun's effort, ten books of Yong-Do Lee were published, seven by Byun himself and the other three by Byun's wife after his death.

[9] *Diary* of 2 May, 1927, 33.

[10] Kyung-Bae Min, *History of Korean Christian Faith Movement under Japanese Occupation* [in Korean] (Seoul: Korean Christian Literature, 1991), 359.

Since these leaders, Gil, Kim and Lee, emphasized personal religious experiences, the church in this period was more concerned about individual faith.

The Third Period 1940-1960

The third period is considered, in retrospect, a period of confusion. During it Korea was liberated from Japanese occupation. A few years after liberation communist North Korea invaded South Korea and the war, which lasted three years, caused much suffering. The Korean churches, which up to then had been forcibly unified by the Japanese, began to divide by denomination. In almost all denominations today, after a series of divisions, two groups—conservative and liberal—coexist. Theological differences and conflicts between these two groups in each denomination also cause continuous tensions. As a result, the church lost the influence of its leadership in society, the various denominations became legalistic in orientation and they largely ignored the spiritual needs of people.

New Religious Sects

In parallel with continuous divisions in the churches, a number of 'heretical' Christian sects and *Sinhung Chonggyo* (syncretic religions) were born during this period. According to Myung-Hwan Tak, there were around two hundred new Korean syncretistic religions in the 1960s: 27 derived from Buddhism, 25 from Christianity, 14 from eastern learning, 5 from Japanese religion, 19 were Tangun sects, and 51 were Chungsan sects. These new syncretistic religions emerged from the opportunity presented by social chaos.[11] The best known of these were the Olive Tree Church and the Unification Church, which called itself the 'Holy Spirit Movement for the Unification of World Christianity'. These movements may be called 'pseudo-Holy Spirit' movements.[12] Against this background the preparation for the Pentecostal movement was in the making.

---

[11] Myung-Hwan Tak, *New Syncretic Religions in Korea* [in Korean], vol. 1, rev. ed. (Seoul: International Religious Research Institute), 1992, 35.

[12] Some scholars understand that both the Olive Tree Church and the Unification Church came into existence, being influenced by the mystical Holy Spirit movement of Yong-Do Lee. Young-Kwan Park, *Major Cults* [in Korean], vol. I (Seoul: Christian Literature Mission, 1976), 30–32, 129–31; Young-Kwan Park, *Major Cults* [in Korean], vol. II (Seoul: Christian Literature Mission, 1984), 35–38.

The Beginning of the Korean Pentecostal Movement

In this period the Assemblies of God, the largest Pentecostal body in the world, was organized in Korea where it is also known as the Full Gospel Church. This provided a direct connection between the Holy Spirit movement in Korea and the worldwide Pentecostal movement, since the former had developed quite independently.

The Pentecostal faith was first brought to Korea by Mary C. Rumsey in March 1928. Rumsey was the first missionary to Korea with a Pentecostal background. Originally she was a Methodist who participated in the Azusa Street revival meeting in 1906, received the baptism of the Holy Spirit, experienced tongues-speaking, received God's call to be a missionary to Korea and came to Korea twenty years later.[13] Upon arriving in Korea, Rumsey stopped off for some rest in the Chungdong hospital where Dr R.A. Hardie had been staying.[14] It is an important detail that the first Pentecostal missionary became connected with Hardie, who had initiated the Holy Spirit movement at Wonsan in 1903. Rumsey paid a visit to the headquarters of the Salvation Army in 1931 where she met Hong Huh who was working there and she asked him for help in her missionary work. Huh took Bible lessons from her and received the baptism of the Holy Spirit. Rumsey emphasized two characteristics of the Pentecostal faith—tongues-speaking and divine healing.[15] In March 1933 Rumsey and Huh together established 'Seobinggo church' in Seoul, the first Pentecostal church.

The Pentecostal church in Korea continued its ministry even in the face of Japanese opposition, growing rapidly until 1938, when it began to decrease as a result of continuous persecution by the Japanese. The Chosun Pentecostal churches were also persecuted for their opposition to Japanese Shinto-worship. The churches were shut down and the church members scattered.

When the country was liberated from Japanese occupation on 15 August, 1945, the Pentecostal church leaders came back to Korea after years of exile and the scattered Pentecostals gathered together and formed a Pentecostal denomination. The Pentecostal churches developed rapidly in the period of confusion after the Korean War. They gave people hope and a strong faith based on personal spiritual experiences, which most other churches were not paying attention to.

---

[13] Korea Assemblies of God, *The 30 Year History of Korea Assemblies of God* [in Korean] (Seoul: Jong Ryo, 1983), 28–29.

[14] This hospital was founded by William B. Scranton and Jack F. Heron. It was the first Methodist hospital. ITI, *The History of the Assemblies of God Churches in Korea* [in Korean] (Seoul: Seoul), 149–50.

[15] Jong-Ho Byun, *The History of the Pentecostal Faith in Korea* [in Korean] (Seoul: Sinsaengkwan, 1972), 90.

The Fourth Period 1960-1980

The fourth period was a time of explosive growth and revival for the church. Student demonstrations and military coups created an insecure atmosphere in Korean society and from it people began to find comfort in Christianity. The socio-political situation in this period called for two types of Holy Spirit movement. One was the *minjung* theology[16] movement advocated by people of a liberal group who recognised the 'third era of the Holy Spirit'.[17] The other was the Holy Spirit movement by a conservative group of people: the evangelical   movement   with   large-scale   crusades   and   the Pentecostal/Charismatic movement.

Evangelical Crusades

The Holy Spirit movement of Evangelicals and Pentecostals was carried out by large-scale crusades, thanks to the united efforts of many churches of different denominational backgrounds. This movement contributed at the same time to the growth of the individual churches. The growth of the Korean church in the 1970s is worth noting: the Christian population in 1974 was 3 million; in 1978, four years later, it had grown to 7 million. This indicates that Christians were added to the church at an average rate of 1 million per year.[18] According to statistics, six new churches were born every day in South Korea by 1978. Even in such a socio-political dark age, the Korean church grew remarkably, especially in the evangelical wings. The Pentecostal churches became prominent in this period.

---

[16] For an explanation of *minjung* theology, see: The Commission on Theological Concerns of the Christian Conference of Asia (ed). *Minjung Theology: People as the Subjects of History* (Maryknoll, NY: Orbis, 1983); Cyris H. S. Moon, *A Korean Minjung Theology—An Old Testament Perspective* (New York: Orbis, 1985); David Kwang-Sun Suh, *Theology, Ideology and Culture* (Hong Kong: World Christian Student Federation, 1983).

[17] This idea is similar to that of the monastic prophet of Southern Europe, Joachim of Fiore, in the Medieval age. He divided history into three ages. The Old Testament age has its time of beginning and bloom. So has that of the New Testament. But a third age is to follow. The first of the three ages was the age of the Father, the second the age of the Son, of the Gospel, and the sacraments, the third the age of the Holy Spirit, which was yet to come. David Schaff, *History of Christian Church*, vol. V, *The Middle Ages* (Grand Rapids, MI: Eerdmans), 373-78. cf. Paul Tillich, *A History of Christian Thought* (New York: Simon and Schuster, 1967), 175-80.

[18] Joon-Gon Kim, 'Six New Churches Everyday: Korean Church Growth' (Report for the Asian Leaders' Conference on Evangelism in Singapore, November, 1978), 5.

Minjung Theology

As the military government held power over a long period, groups of liberal church leaders raised protests against it. One outcome was *minjung* ('people's') theology, a unique indigenized Korean Christianity. This theology, which is a kind of re-casting of the liberation theology of Latin America, asserts the uniqueness of Korea. It stresses that the history of Korea is one of an oppressed, frustrated and neglected people. *Minjung* theology is deeply related to the Koreans' unique mind-set of *han*.[19] The *minjung* are *han*-ridden people. Andrew S. Park explains, '*Han* is an Asian, particularly Korean, term used to describe the depths of human sufferings'.[20] The *minjung* theology movement, which was advocated by the learned liberal Korean Christians, was well received by the world's Protestant churches. As *minjung* theology seems to place more stress on social concerns than theological concerns with their conventional religious traditions, it cannot escape being called a social rather than a theological movement.

The Fifth Period 1980-2000

In the fifth period, the Pentecostal/Charismatic movement spread throughout all the Christian denominations in Korea.

The Yoido Full Gospel Church and the Pentecostal Movement

As the Korean church grew explosively in the 1970s, one congregation attracted the attention of the churches of the world. That church was the Yoido Full Gospel Church (YFGC) pastored by Rev. Yonggi Cho. This church has the largest congregation in the world with a membership of 700,000 at the end of 1994. Yonggi Cho founded YFGC in 1958 and has pastored the church since then. Many view YFGC as the base of the Pentecostal movement in Korea.

---

[19] *Han* is a Korean word, which may be translated as 'grudge' or 'resentment'. *Han* is an underlying feeling of Korean people. Han is the anger and resentment of the *minjung* which has been turned inward and intensified as they become the objects of injustice upon injustice. It is the result of being repressed for an extended period of time by external forces: political oppression, economic exploitation, social alienation and restrictions against becoming educated in cultural and intellectual matters. Cyris H. S. Moon, op. cit., 1-2. See also Chimo Hong, 'Han is Minjung Theology',*Theological Studies* (Spring 1990), 136–51.

[20] Andrew S. Park, *The Wounded Heart of God: The Asian Concept of Han and the Christian Doctrine of Sin* (Nashville, TN: Abingdon, 1993), 15.

Yonggi Cho started a tent church in 1958. Its 44-year history may be divided into three periods: the pioneering period (1958-61)[21] in which YFGC was the instrument of the Pentecostal faith taking root in Korea by its strong 'full gospel' message and divine healing; the developing period (1961-73) when the church took the leadership role in the Pentecostal movement of Korea and spread the Pentecostal faith in the Korean church; and the period of expansion (1973 onwards) when the church has taken the lead in the Holy Spirit movement of the entire Korean church, has become mature enough to show its concern for Korean society and has greatly expanded the Holy Spirit movement.

Cho claims that the Holy Spirit movement can bear fruit when it is accompanied by the fullness of the Word, prayer and the Holy Spirit, for if one is neglected or overly emphasized the dynamic work of the Spirit will be impossible. The major factors in the growth of the church are: a powerful message, prayer, Spirit-baptism with speaking in tongues, divine healing and the cell group system.

Influenced mainly by the Yoido Full Gospel Church, the Pentecostal/ Charismatic movement has spread rapidly in all denominations. The churches involved in this charismatic movement have achieved remarkable growth which has brought them to the attention of the world churches. At present the leaders of the Holy Spirit movement are very involved with the ecumenical movement, and in working with it are trying to counter the negative influence of shamanism, and are also making preparations for the reunification of the country.

An Analysis of the Holy Spirit Movement

Unique Features

The Korean Holy Spirit movement is in some aspects unique. In the various periods demarcated above, it has been characterized by unique features, depending on the political and social situations of each period. It started as a repentance movement and developed into a movement of mystical union with Christ. It then became a recognizable evangelical movement with large-scale crusades, continuing on to a stress on *minjung* theology, then to Pentecostalism and finally to become a Charismatic movement pervading all churches. The various features of the Holy Spirit movement in the different periods coexist syncretistically in Korean churches today. It is particularly significant to this country that the Holy Spirit movement started at almost the same time as the

---

[21] ITI, *The Yoido Full Gospel Church: Its Faith and Theology* [in Korean], vol. II (Seoul: Seoul Logos, 1993), 96.

world Pentecostal movement, without any apparent connection or influence between the two. On the other hand, just as in the case of the first Pentecostal movement in the United States, the Holy Spirit movement in Korea was originated by a Methodist minister through Bible study classes and prayer meetings. In addition to these similarities, the Holy Spirit movement planted its roots in Korea as a repentance movement which was then formulated in an indigenous Korean Christian style. This kind of revival movement developed independently under the leadership of the three largest Protestant denominations in Korea—the Presbyterian, Methodist, and Holiness churches—until the Yoido Full Gospel Church, a Pentecostal church, took the lead in the 1970s.

Another feature of the Korean Holy Spirit movement is the house church movement that is called the 'cell group meeting movement'. The Yoido Full Gospel Church attained a 20-30% annual growth rate through its well-structured cell group ministries. Most Korean churches have adopted this system and employ the cell-group system as a fundamental source of church growth. This is a house-to-house ministry that recalls the early Jerusalem community described in the Acts of the Apostles.[22]

A unique feature of the Holy Spirit movement in Korea lies in its variety, with both conservative and liberal wings. The Confucian tradition of ancient Korean society and American Puritanism worked together to contribute conservative and evangelical characteristics to the Holy Spirit movement. But, just as significantly, the liberal tendencies of the Holy Spirit movement and its own uniqueness have come together to produce *minjung* theology, which may be described as a 'Koreanized' Holy Spirit movement. Such variety in the movement opens itself to the possibility of furthering the ecumenical movement. Since the Holy Spirit movement has spread through almost all the Protestant churches of Korea and among many Catholics as well, this breadth gives it an important position in the ecumenical movement in Korea.

Reasons for its Success

RICH RELIGIOUS SOIL

Koreans are known to be a religious people, which is to say that most of their lives have been based on some kind of religious belief. Shamanism, with five thousand years of Korean history, has taken its place in the mental structure of Korean consciousness. Buddhism, with 1,500 to 1,600 years of history, has also taken root in Korea because of the religious character of the people. This background of the Korean spirit is surely one of the reasons why there have

---

[22] Acts 2.42-47.

been so many converts, without any strong opposition, from the time the Holy Spirit movement was planted.

The influence of the shamanistic nature of old Korean religion should not be overlooked. The successes of the Holy Spirit movement would often be attributed to shamanism, since both appear on the surface to be quite emotional. Leaders of the Holy Spirit movement try to go beyond this criticism, however, by disciplining their members with intensive Bible studies and by also turning their interests to social concerns. Theologians and scholars must continue their explorations and research on this subject while the leaders of the churches need to work diligently to maintain sound doctrine.

CULTURAL BACKGROUND: IGNORANCE OF SPIRITUAL NEEDS

Confucianism is rooted in an ethos of the structure of consciousness of the Korean people. Influenced by Puritanism and Confucianism, the Presbyterian, Methodist, and Holiness churches all have the tendency to emphasise reverence and solemnity. This has given Korean Christianity something of a legalist and authoritarian cast. As an inevitable result, the major leading Protestant denominations have to some extent ignored people's spiritual needs. Spirit-oriented movements rose among the people in order to fulfil these needs. However these movements caused many problems in society and were soon judged 'heretical' by the major Christian denominations. It is against this background that the Pentecostal and Charismatic movements emerged.

UNSTABLE SOCIETY

Since the introduction of Protestant Christianity to Korea in the late nineteenth century the country has gone through the period of enlightenment, the colonial period, the nation's liberation, the Korean War, student revolts and a military take-over and dictatorship. As a result of such a series of events Korean society became unstable in many aspects. The people could not turn to and depend upon the traditional religions. In this matter, Christianity exerted a powerful influence on Korean society. The instability of Korean society has been a factor leading people to accept the Holy Spirit movement in their search for a stability and spiritual satisfaction they needed so desperately. Christianity is still developing rapidly in Korea, centred on the Holy Spirit movement.

Its Problems

The Holy Spirit movement in Korea is open to the following problems:[23]

---

[23] To solve these kinds of problems, Pentecostal churches try to participate in most ecumenical meetings and interdenominational crusades. They have begun to turn their interest to the needs of society. As an example, the Yoido Full Gospel Church has

SECTARIANISM

Until the early 1980s, the Korean Pentecostal churches had no close relations with other churches and for this reason were criticized for being anti-ecumenical. Since most of the churches involved in the Holy Spirit movement belong to the conservative wing, dialogue between the conservative and liberal groups is not actively carried out.

LACK OF SOCIAL CONCERN

Those oriented to Pentecostalism are criticized for their biased emphases on personal salvation and spiritual experiences. Since many churches that have participated in the Holy Spirit movement have not shown much interest in social justice and have ignored the problems of society, the influence of this movement on society has decreased.

LACK OF DOCTRINAL STANDARDS

The Holy Spirit movement may have achieved quantitative success in its rapid growth but this has not been accompanied by qualitative achievement. This calls for systematic theological education. A correct and sound doctrinal understanding of the action of the Holy Spirit in the life of the church is needed. Since each denomination of the Korean church has a different understanding of the Holy Spirit, it is urgently needed to establish a unified pneumatology through continuous theological research and dialogue.

AN EMOTIONAL TENDENCY IN CHRISTIAN FAITH

Since the Holy Spirit movement emphasized spiritual experience, it was inevitable that it had emotional tendencies. This tendency should be balanced to avoid an unstable and biased faith. Many people became over-emotional, emphasizing spiritual experiences only, while remaining ignorant of basic biblical doctrines. From this weakness of the Holy Spirit movement, many heretical tendencies have appeared. Therefore a sound doctrine of faith with balanced spiritual experience and biblical knowledge is urgently required. In addition to this a clear distinction must be made at all points between the negative dimensions of shamanism and the Holy Spirit movement.

Its Influences

SPIRITUAL AWAKENING

Passing through the five periods of Korean Protestant Church history, we have seen the Holy Spirit movement playing an important role in awakening

---

contributed over $11,000,000 for an apartment complex for poor factory workers project and has founded several institutions to educate its members.

spiritually powerless Korean churches in all periods. The Holy Spirit movement encourages people to realize the importance of spiritual experience which gives confidence to Christian life, helps Christians to dedicate themselves for the glory of God, and encourages them actively to spread the gospel.

ECUMENICAL MOVEMENT

Currently, the Holy Spirit movement has spread in almost all denominations. The big interdenominational crusades in the 1970s showed that the ecumenical movement is possible only by the Holy Spirit movement. This brought about remarkable church growth at that time.

CHURCH GROWTH

The Holy Spirit movement, with its prayer movement and house church movement (cell group movement) are becoming the most important factors of church growth. We find a good example of this in the Yoido Full Gospel Church.

Suggestions for the Future

A study of the Holy Spirit movement would be incomplete if it did not direct our attention to lessons and suggestions for the future. There should be no end to research in the Holy Spirit movement since there cannot be an end to the church growth or to the development of a theology of the Holy Spirit movement.

Concluding this paper, the following suggestions for the future are in order:

a) The Holy Spirit movement should be a way forward for ecumenism. Only the Holy Spirit movement can fulfil the ecumenical potential of Korea.

b) It should have solid social concerns. When the Holy Spirit movement loses its interest in social justice and the people who are oppressed and neglected, it will lose its influence on society.

c) It should be led by an intelligent group of people, theologically well-grounded, to prevent possible heresies. For this reason its theological standards should be derived from a theory of the Holy Spirit without neglecting the other great mysteries such as the Incarnation, the Divine Trinity, the Church, and the Life of Grace. At the same time, it should also be made firm through Bible study and prayer.

d) The Holy Spirit movement should guard itself from the negative influences of shamanism in Korean culture. It also should adapt the positive aspects of it and other religious traditions in Korea to the movement.

e) It should reflect the true picture of the Holy Spirit movement and its responsibilities as bearers of the gospel for society.

Full Gospel Theology and a Korean Pentecostal Identity

Hyeon Sung Bae

Introduction

The pace of change in Pentecostal theological circles during the twentieth century has been very rapid. How can we adapt ourselves to this change without losing our Pentecostal identity? At what point, and on what basis, should we withhold our consent to proposed changes? These are multifaceted questions which concern not only the Pentecostal world but the non-Pentecostal world also. The tremendous church growth in Korea has been, by and large, a result of Pentecostal influence. In an actual sense, it is Dr Yonggi Cho who extended Pentecostal influence not only in the Korean church, but also in the world church by his charismatic leadership and ministry in the Holy Spirit. We cannot underestimate his passion and devotion to Korean Pentecostalism. We might fail to discover or properly evaluate the real meaning of the Korean Pentecostal identity if we overlook his theological and pastoral contribution to world Christianity. 'Full Gospel'[1] theology enables us to grasp Dr Cho's theological view on Pentecostalism in Korea.

Bearing this in mind, it is timely and appropriate for us to make sure of our Pentecostal role and identity in Asia. Our main concern here is to explore the theological implications of a Korean Pentecostal identity by reflecting on the concept of Full Gospel theology as an indigenized form of Pentecostal theology in Korea. In an attempt to accomplish this goal, this paper analyses Full Gospel theology not only by exploring its Pentecostal concerns and uniqueness but also by criticizing its limits and bounds.

---

[1] Here, 'Full Gospel' is literally taking the gospel and accepting fully and totally all that is in the Bible in order to revitalize the faith and fullness of the Holy Spirit as was done at Pentecost. See, International Theological Institute (ITI), *The Church History of the Assemblies of God* [in Korean] (Seoul: Seoul Logos, 1998), 249.

Full Gospel Theology and the Analogy of Chopsticks

What is Full Gospel theology? How do we describe it? What are its theological implications for Pentecostalism? Why do we call it an indigenized Pentecostal theology? What unique contribution can it make to world Pentecostalism? The success of this paper depends on whether it gives proper answers to these questions. However, as a proper definition of Pentecostal theology remains elusive, so does Full Gospel theology, which identifies itself with the 'gospel of fullness' with its foundation in the unadulterated faith of the Word of God, standing on the basis of a God-centred theology.[2]

A proper definition of Full Gospel theology would be inappropriate at this stage as it has diverse theological implications. It is preferable to deliver images and symbolic meanings to Full Gospel theology rather than to give a more direct definition to it. Jesus Christ described the Kingdom of God without directly defining it, but rather, by using diverse metaphors and parables.[3] The same rule can be applied to introducing Full Gospel theology. I would like to offer 'chopsticks' as a crucial metaphor symbolizing the nature of Full Gospel theology, which illustrates the following distinctive features.

First of all, chopsticks imply the daily living culture of Korean people. Like cutlery, chopsticks are tools for having meals. So cutlery is to the western food culture what chopsticks are to the Korean one. For Korean people, chopsticks are indispensable tools for eating and maintaining their lives. In other words, chopsticks reflect the Korean people's living culture of *sitz im leben*.[4] Full Gospel theology regards the *sitz im leben* as an essential factor for completing one's 'holistic salvation' in one's life. Like chopsticks, Full Gospel theology reflects the Korean lifestyle and culture. That is the reason why Full Gospel theology can be called an indigenized form of Pentecostal theology.

Secondly, chopsticks illustrate the profound Korean philosophical principles of harmony. Here 'harmony' is 'the way in which the parts...are combined into a suitable and attractive arrangement'.[5] Chopsticks are always a pair—hence without interaction between the two sticks it is impossible for chopstick users to pick up or hold anything with them. This means that a principle of harmony is demanded when using them. Here, two sticks have the different functions of picking up and holding food by folding and unfolding them. Chopsticks need the principle of harmony between these two different functions, as there is a tension between them. In spite of this tension, the pneumatological mystery

---

[2] Yoido Full Gospel Church, *30-Years History of the Yoido Full Gospel Church* [in Korean] (Seoul: Yoido Full Gospel Church, 1989), 9.

[3] Matthew 13.34, 'he did not say anything to them without using a parable'.

[4] It is the German term indicating various circumstantial factors on which one's actual reality of life depends and is based. It is a barometer which evaluates whether one's life operates fairly or not in society.

[5] *Collins Cobuild English Language Dictionary*, 1994 ed., 664.

enables us to convert the tension to potential. This tension, therefore, is creative rather than destructive. Full Gospel theology is based on the Pentecostal orthodoxy of the early Christian church. Besides, it regards the missiological praxis of being witnesses to the ends of the earth as a theological motto. Because it achieves theological harmony by combining Pentecostal orthodoxy and praxis, Full Gospel theology is not partial but holistic. Harmony is an indispensable element in using chopsticks. Full Gospel theology has an holistic theological methodology which brings harmony between the opposites through a creative tension.

Chopsticks imply a communal relationship with God, the self, society and the cosmos. Likewise, the Chinese letter, 人 (*in*) which means 'human being', is composed of two persons and has symbolic meaning. From an eastern perspective, in order to become a human being a person needs a pair, becoming a couple who can help each other. In this connection, as this letter shows, the Chinese word, °N(human being) denotes that one props up the other, that is, human beings are beings who need their props. Thus we might say that chopsticks imply a communal culture from which one can get help from others. As in the early church, we could say that a communal relationship is what Pentecostals have sought. Full Gospel theology also entails a communal relationship between the self, others, the cosmos and God. Because of its positive nature, Korean churches have gradually recognised Full Gospel theology as a tool for introducing Pentecostalism in Korea.

Thirdly, chopsticks need users' experience and skill to handle them, so chopsticks users should spend time training themselves to use them well. If the chopsticks users use them impatiently, disregarding the rules, chopsticks are no longer chopsticks but sticks. Chopsticks are of no use for people who have never used them before. Therefore in order to use chopsticks well, people need experience in handling them. Full Gospel theology as an indigenized form of Pentecostal theology emphasizes the Pentecostal experience of baptism of the Holy Spirit, which is accompanied by speaking in tongues and a variety of manifestations of the Holy Spirit in public services. This experience has enabled the churches in Korea to be renewed and revived. This is the reason why Full Gospel theology is called a 'theology of experience'.

As we can see from the analogy, chopsticks give tremendous insights to those of us who attempt to identify the nature of Full Gospel theology. Summing up, Full Gospel theology is a theology for meeting the needs of the *sitz im leben*, whose theological concern lies in the Korean cultural context. In addition, the analogy implies that Full Gospel theology has a theological depth of harmony through which it can have a holistic theological methodology. Implicit in the analogy of chopsticks is that the basic foundation of Full Gospel theology lies in both the principle of harmony and the God-given dignity of the human person, viewed, naturally, in relation to the rest of God's creation. The analogy also plays a crucial role in evangelism by focusing on the communal mind and challenging people to have a mission-oriented mind.

Two Korean Theologies

There once was a time when Korean theologians simply used to introduce western popular theological issues and thoughts to Korea and translate them into Korean without full theological reflection on it.[6] Consequently, theology could not meet the needs of Koreans' *sitz im leben*. Theology loses its theological identity and relevance to the church and society if it is indifferent to people's actual reality. Considering this, the role of Korean theologians is something to do with developing a 'Korean theology'[7] by reflecting on the Korean *sitz im leben*. It is therefore necessary for Korean theologians to develop a way of expressing the truth, faith and life of Korean people by interpreting their *sitz im leben,* which is closely relevant to the Korean theological context.

If theology is healthy, it should help contribute to an alternative answer to the needs of grass-roots Koreans, suffering from their insecure *sitz im leben*. First century Christianity was not indifferent to dealing with the suffering of grass-roots people who were totally torn and broken socially and spiritually. In this connection, Pentecostal theology must be a holistic theology which can meet the social and spiritual needs of people. Considering this, we might say that there are two theologies in Korea which have shown those concerns for Koreans. They are *Minjung* theology and Full Gospel theology.

Minjung theology as a theology for social concern

Minjung theology is more familiar to western theologians as a Korean theology by its socio-political concerns for praxis. Here, the Korean term *minjung* can be generally defined as the grass-roots people who are oppressed politically, exploited economically, alienated socially and kept uneducated in cultural and intellectual matters. It was grass-roots so called *minjung* who participated in the original Pentecostal movement and built the early church in Jerusalem in the

---

[6] That atmosphere reached the peak in the early 1960s when some theologians returned home after finishing their study abroad and started to teach at theological schools. For a time, the churches in Korea had an adverse effect from them due to their consumptive, speculative attitude of doing theology. As a result, theology was becoming metaphysical and placed in an ivory tower without giving any theological relevance that could be applicable to people's actual life.

[7] What we mean by 'Korean theology' is a theology which seeks theological identity for Korea by interpreting and exploring the relationship between 'the gospel' and 'Korean culture'. Korean theology not only represents Christian spirituality in Korea but also conveys the cultural identity of Korea to the Korean churches. It necessarily asks for a new perspective on interpreting the text and the context. Korean theology is a theology which can be expressed by Koreans' intrinsic thought. See Chul Ha Han, 'The Concept of Korean Theology', *Church and Theology* (1971:5), 46.

first century. Without their passionate role and ministry, the Pentecostal movement would not have been handed down to us today. *Minjung* theology has originated from the unstable socio-political context of the 1970s in order to cope with social injustice and inequality in Korean society. It has drawn much attention to socio-political and economic issues in Korea. Regarding *Minjung* theology, Harvey Cox wrote that Korean Christians had 'invented their own form of 'liberation theology' called '*Minjung* theology', using the Korean term for the ordinary, non-elite people among whom Christianity first spread'.[8] He underlines *han* as the indispensable key to understanding not only *Minjung* theology but also the Korean soul itself.[9]

Boo Yoong Yoo tried to detect a convergence between Pentecostalism and *Minjung* theology. He calls it 'the meeting between socio-political *minjung* and Pentecostal *minjung*'.[10] He examined Korean Pentecostalism from a socio-political and cultural perspective by analysing the theological commonality between *Minjung* theology and Pentecostal theology.[11] One of the contextual theologies of Korea, *Minjung* theology has highlighted the issues of poverty, political violence, deprivation of rights, and discrimination against the grass-roots. It seeks to participate in and relive the agony of people by transforming unjust social structures and institutions. It is true to say that, due to its challenge, the churches in Korea awoke from their ignorance of social concerns during the 1970s and 1980s. But despite its merits, however, *Minjung* theology has its controversial points in underestimating the transcendental aspects of revelation and becoming a theory of sociology or political ideology. Like liberation theology, it no longer sees itself as an interpretation of the church's traditional doctrine of faith, but as a reflection on praxis and its critical accompaniment.[12]

Full Gospel Theology as a Theology for Holistic Concerns

The Korean Church also has Full Gospel theology, whose theological basis lies in Pentecostal theology. In contrast to *Minjung* theology, Full Gospel theology pertains to the theological harmony which satisfies both social and spiritual concerns. It aims at deepening and widening opportunities for the dignity of the grass-roots by practising Pentecostal dynamics. While *Minjung* theology is

---

[8] Harvey Cox, *Fire from Heaven: The Rise of Pentecostal spirituality and the Reshaping of Religion in the Twenty-first Century* (London: Cassell, 1996), 220.

[9] Ibid., 238.

[10] Quoted in Harvey Cox, ibid., 240.

[11] Boo Woong Yoo, *Korean Pentecostalism : Its History and Theology* (Frankfurt: Peter Lang, 1988).

[12] Walter Kasper, *Theology and Church*, trans. Margret Kohl (London: SCM, 1989), 133.

primarily a socio-political theology seeking to reform a distorted socio-political system and structure, Full Gospel theology is a holistic theology seeking harmony between Pentecostal orthodoxy and praxis, transcendence and reality.

Minjung theology and Full Gospel theology have played important roles in criticizing the rigidity, selfishness, schism and exclusive doctrinism in the existing society and churches in Korea. For this reason it will be superficial and even meaningless to understand Full Gospel theology without knowing the reality of its *sitz im leben*. Full Gospel theology seeks to guide the grass-roots to the holistic salvation of their spirit, soul and body by experiencing the works of the Holy Spirit. It is a theology of holistic salvation for the grass-roots. *Minjung* theology and Full Gospel theology have a common theological ground to share in that they are contextualized from *Minjung* theology and Pentecostal theology. What *Minjung* theology is to liberation theology, Full Gospel theology is to Pentecostal theology.

According to the use of the term, Full Gospel theology has two main dimensions. At first, it is related to the denominational dimension of the Assemblies of God in Korea, which represents Pentecostalism in this country.[13] Here, Full Gospel theology shares its theological nature with the classical Pentecostal movement started in the early twentieth century. In other words, it is a Pentecostal theology that is rooted in the Pentecostal events and movements described as 'the former rain and the latter rain'.[14] Secondly, Full Gospel theology has the specific personal dimension of Dr Yonggi Cho, the senior pastor of Yoido Full Gospel Church (YFGC), the largest church congregation in the world.

Full Gospel Theology and Dr. Yonggi Cho

In a certain sense, Full Gospel theology is Dr Cho's theology, in that his influence and contribution to it are fundamental. In dealing with the theological core of Full Gospel theology, Dr Yonggi Cho's theological concern for Pentecostalism through his passion and devotion to his Pentecostal ministry must be taken into account. The main reason for the rapid growth of YFGC was the great moving of the Holy Spirit, resulting in Dr. Cho's doctrine of the 'Fivefold Gospel'[15] and the 'Threefold Blessing'.[16] Here, the Fivefold Gospel is

---

[13] Korean Pentecostal denominations are mainly composed of the following denominations of Assemblies of God in Korea, Church of God in Korea, Church of the Foursquare Gospel in Korea, etc.

[14] See, Joel 2.23, 'He will cause to come down for you the rain, the former rain, and the latter rain in the first month'.

[15] This is a central theological issue of Full Gospel theology. It is composed of five essential messages of the Bible. These are gospel of Christ's redemption, gospel of fullness of the Holy Spirit, gospel of blessing, gospel of divine healing and gospel of

the theological theory and doctrine, whereas the Threefold Blessing is the practical application of it.[17] To put it another way, Dr Cho's theological creativity enabled him to construct the doctrinal essence of Full Gospel theology.

As Myung Soo Park points out, the crucial factors in shaping Dr Cho's Pentecostal theology are fourfold: 1) the world Pentecostal Movement; 2) Korean culture; 3) encounter with the Bible; and 4) experience-centred field theology.[18] These factors are integrated into his message. Dr Cho's message and Full Gospel theology have a deep relationship, like the relationship between John Wesley's message and Methodist theology. Dr Cho has been successful in delivering his theological emphases to people in Korea by proclaiming the message of the Fivefold Gospel and the Threefold Blessing. It is clear that Dr Cho's theological emphases have been developed by his messages, the nature of which is simple and practical but direct and effective. At this juncture, we might say that Full Gospel theology has resulted from the continual theological reflection on the biblical message. Considering his theological contribution to Full Gospel theology, it is not a coincidence to see the remarkable church growth of YFGC. Dr Cho's preaching reaches into the hearts of his congregation and blesses them by meeting their needs.

As one of the best-known leaders in the Protestant world, Dr Cho used to raise the question of how the Korean church could meet the needs of people who are broken economically, socially, physically and spiritually. His theology is a practical field-centred theology which concerns actual needs of people. The reason why Dr Cho has been sensitive to meeting the needs of the torn and the broken was due to his theological understanding of holistic salvation. He has tried to challenge people with his Pentecostal passion through focusing on baptism of the Holy Spirit, speaking in tongues and driving away evil spirits using the name of Jesus. In particular, facing up to the poor economic reality of Korea in the 1950s and 1960s, he prayed to God asking: 'God, where are you now? How can I give hope and new life to people who are in a desperate situation lacking a minimum level of clothing and meals?'[19] Being in agony

---

second coming of Jesus Christ. See, Yonggi Cho, *The Fivefold Gospel and the Threefold Blessings* (Seoul: Young San Publishing, 1983), 49-53.

[16] The Threefold Blessings is rooted in the Gospel of 3 John 1.2, 'Dear friend, I pray that you may enjoy good health and that all may go well with you, even as your soul is getting along well'.

[17] International Theological Institute, *Faith and Theology of Yoido Full Gospel Church* (Seoul, Seoul Logos. 1993), 35.

[18] Myung Soo Park, 'Pentecostal Movement and Rev Yonggi Cho's Theology', in International Theological Institute (eds.), *Studies on David Cho's Holy Spirit Movement* [in Korean] (Seoul: Seoul Logos, 2000), 43.

[19] Yonggi Cho, *The Threefold Salvation* (Seoul: Seoul Logos, 1989), 18.

with this question, he started to pray with eagerness. Thanks to his fervent prayer, Dr Cho could provide doctrinal principles to Full Gospel theology.

Summing up, Full Gospel theology has a concern to be relevant to the cultural context of Korea and to apply a Pentecostal theological basis to it. Due to Dr Cho's influence, not a few non-Pentecostal churches in Korea are gradually becoming aware of Pentecostalism and show a positive attitude in adopting Pentecostal concerns, faith, experience and dynamics.[20] In particular, we should not underestimate what Dr Cho has attempted to do towards inculturating the Gospel within Korean culture. However, the works of Dr Cho have been criticized more than once for appearing to be too accommodating to the cultural influences of the society around him.[21]

Full Gospel theology is not merely an imported theology from abroad but a Korean theology that has already become congenial to the Korean mind and spirit through its continual theological reflection and application to the churches in Korea. Therefore it is worth while reflecting on Full Gospel theology, through which we can envisage the portrait of a Korean Pentecostal identity. Full Gospel theology asks for the continual rediscovery of the Pentecostal value system.

The Theological Implications of a Korean Pentecostal Identity

We have noted above what Full Gospel theology means through exploring the analogy of chopsticks, by a comparison with *Minjung* theology and through sketching Dr Cho's theological perspectives. After all, what we perceived is that the nature of Full Gospel theology lies in developing Pentecostal potential and possibilities within the Korean church context. Thus Full Gospel theology reflects the particular context of the Korean church with the notion of *sitz im leben* of Koreans. In this section, the writer explores the theological implications of a Korean Pentecostal identity by analysing Full Gospel theology.

Full Gospel Theology and Meeting the Needs of Sitz im Leben

Through the ages Koreans have tried to achieve human wholeness[22] through a rich variety of moral and religious ways. A partial or narrow approach to

---

[20] Hyeon Sung Bae, 'Comments on *Minjung* and Pentecostal Movements in Korea', in Allan H. Anderson and Walter J. Hollenweger (eds.), op. cit., 161.

[21] Harvey Cox regards Dr Cho's Pentecostal ministry in YFGC as a massive importation of shamanistic practice into a Christian ritual. See, Harvey Cox, op. cit., 226.

[22] Human wholeness is what all human beings are commonly seeking for as God's creatures. Therefore, it entails not only an existential dimension but also a transcendental one. It is an ongoing journey requiring self-training and self-discipline.

human wholeness was certainly not qualified to solve the issue. Full Gospel theology has the theological premises of how to act in the world, acting out in the whole life of the whole world.[23] It is sensitive to meeting the people's contemporary needs. It does not neglect to respond to the way Koreans live. Regarding the role of Korean Pentecostalism, Harvey Cox wrote:

> Korean Pentecostalism must also help people cope with both the rampant urbanization and the wrenching demands of new economic and political realities, which have completely transformed the once isolated peninsula known as the Hermit Kingdom.[24]

Full Gospel theology is a theology of raising theological questions from people's *sitz im leben*. Besides, it has a responsibility to seek to heal the torn and the broken, not by simply making words but by performing works of the Holy Spirit. Full Gospel theology carries conviction to people, not by an abstract way but by a concrete way through God's presence within their *sitz im leben*. Full Gospel theology is concerned for practical directions about how to respond properly to the actual reality of people. Therefore, it seems clear that Full Gospel theology seeks the answers to the problems that people face in their everyday life situation, by discerning the will of God as well as practising the Pentecostal heritage. The main point I wish to make here is that the role of Full Gospel theology cannot be free from the issues of the actual living conditions of people struggling with their overall problems arising from their *sitz im leben*.

Full Gospel theology aims to look after the wounds of the people and to enable them to restore their human wholeness. It means that Full Gospel theology gives its theological motif to the recognition of people's *sitz im leben* through which people can experience God's presence. For this reason, *sitz im leben* is not only a place where people can experience God, but it is also a channel through which they can get the abundant blessings of God. It is Full Gospel theology that challenges people to pray to God for their daily bread.[25] Regarding meeting the needs of people, Dr Cho shows his theological direction like this:

> The problems of greatest concern to human beings are related to food, clothing and shelter. The ultimate goal of all ideologies is to solve these problems. What do you think God's idea is about these basic needs? God's idea is to give us our

---

See Hyeon Sung Bae, 'Towards a Theology of Harmony: A Study of Human Wholeness within the Korean Cultural Context' (Unpublished PhD Dissertation, Birmingham University, 1998), 8.

[23] Lesslie Newbigin, *The Open Secret: An Introduction to the Theology of Mission* (London: Gospel & Culture, 1995), 17.

[24] Harvey Cox, op. cit., 220.

[25] Yonggi Cho, *The Fivefold Gospel and the Threefold Blessing*, 13.

daily bread—a term that goes beyond food. It includes all things that are necessary to earn a living...Our Father God wants to fill all these needs.[26]

Supporting Dr Cho's theological position, Villa-Vicencio, a leading South African theologian, also raises a question on the practical role of a theology:

> A theology which fails to address the most urgent questions asked by ordinary people (and given the bias of the church in favour of the marginalized people, especially their questions) is not theology at all. It is little more than an academic exercise in uncovering archaic or dying religious beliefs and reified doctrines about God.[27]

Full Gospel theology is not only a theology for spiritual being but also a theology for actual being. It never neglects to meet the needs of Koreans' *sitz im leben,* where various theological motivations emerge. It needs to raise a theological question from the core of Korean contextual reality. Its theological nature is practical and dynamic rather than abstract and static. However, its theological aims are not limited to merely meeting the needs of people; its main concern lies in human wholeness. It means that the role of Full Gospel theology is to guide people to experience God's presence in their everyday life situation.

Full Gospel Theology and the Hermeneutical Dimension of Holistic Salvation

As Korean theologian Jung Young Lee argued, the task of theology is primarily to interpret 'ultimate reality to the people of its time'.[28] Lee's comment raises the issue of the hermeneutical dimension, which has arisen consistently throughout the last decade. Full Gospel theology is a hermeneutical tool for interpreting Pentecostal value systems through its doctrinal core of 'holistic salvation'. Here, holistic salvation denotes the doctrinal and practical essence of Full Gospel theology, whose theological ground is supported by 'the Fivefold Gospel' and 'the Threefold Blessing'. Full Gospel theology seeks the opening of a horizon by responding to the relationship between text and context. To put it another way, it asks for a new hermeneutical dimension which can interpret the gospel to Koreans. Moreover, it suggests to people the criteria that determine the interpretation and application of the gospel for

---

[26] Yonggi Cho, *Praying with Jesus* (Seoul: Seoul Logos, 1993), 140-142.

[27] Charles Villa-Vicencio, *A Theology of Reconstruction: Nation-Building and Human Rights* (Cambridge: Cambridge University Press, 1992), 40.

[28] Jung Young Lee, *The Theology of Change, A Christian Concept of God in an Eastern Perspective* (Maryknoll, NY: Orbis, 1979), 23.

holistic salvation.[29] Here, holistic salvation is what Full Gospel theology tries to seek through the hermeneutical dimension of 'the Fivefold Gospel' and 'the Threefold Blessing'. This is a state of perfection through which people cannot feel any want or suffering. God enables people to seek it wherever in the world they live and whatever their condition is. On the one hand, 'holistic' is derived from the Greek word *holos,* referring to an understanding of reality in terms of integrated whole. On the other hand, 'salvation' is derived from the Greek word *soteria,* implying health and wholeness.[30] Considering this, holistic salvation can be described as a concept of totality with physical, psychological, social, cultural and spiritual dimensions. After all, holistic salvation denotes a harmonious relationship between God, self and the world. We live in a society where people are still struggling to keep their dignity as human beings. With regard to this, Dr Cho suggests the following answer through the practical doctrine of 'the Threefold Blessing':

> Actually, today many people are crying out at the top of their voice due to the problems of purposelessness, a sense of futility, poverty, curse, sickness and fear of death. For them, it is 'the Threefold Blessing' that is necessary.[31]

Holistic salvation is life living under the reign of God, who is in perfect control. Regarding the ministry of Pentecostal churches in Korea, Harvey Cox pointed out three crucial factors of 'blessing, wholeness and healing' as its distinctive features. [32] In fact, his comments refer to the theological distinctiveness of Yoido Full Gospel Church as representative of Pentecostal churches in Korea. Here, blessing, wholeness and healing are central components of holistic salvation. The Kingdom of God is what Full Gospel theology eventually aims at through the concept of holistic salvation. As the Kingdom of God has two natures,[33] holistic salvation has two nature of both a

---

[29] Concerning salvation, an African theologian Manas Buthelezi regards it as 'wholeness' itself. See Manas Buthelezi, 'Salvation as Wholeness', in John Parratt (eds.), *A Reader in African Christian Theology* (London: SPCK,1997), 85-90.

[30] See, Charles Sherlock, *The Doctrine of Humanity* (Leicester, England: Inter-Varsity Press, 1996), 212-213.

[31] Yonggi Cho, *The Threefold Salvation*, 18-19.

[32] Harvey Cox, op. cit., 234.

[33] From the historical perspective, Tillich views the Kingdom of God as both an inner-historical and a trans-historical side. According to him, the former is manifested by the 'Spiritual Presence' while the latter is identical with 'Eternal life'. See Paul Tillich, *Systematic Theology*, vol. 3 (London: SCM, 1991), 357. According to Moltmann, the Kingdom of God is in the front line between the present and the promised future. See Jürgen Moltmann, *Theology of Hope*, trans. James W. Leitch (London: SCM, 1988), 225. Allison observes the two natures as both God's saving activity and the reality of his present-and-future reign. See J. B. Green, 'The Kingdom

present-oriented reality and a future-oriented one. While the former has a present dimension of 'here and now', the latter has an eschatological dimension of 'there and then'. These two natures of the Kingdom of God are indispensable elements for understanding holistic salvation. We are beings who live between the two realms of the present time and the time to come. The former asks for the power to fight against sin, sickness, darkness and curse, which prevent us from experiencing God's presence in the 'here and now' context. The latter asks for eternal life, through which Christians will be transformed into whole persons with no tears, suffering and death any more in the 'there and then' context.

Full Gospel Theology and Pneumatological Experience

As Donald Dayton once expressed it, Pentecostalism emerged in the midst of a unique form of doctrines and experiences.[34] The most important Pentecostal distinctive in the twentieth century is to acknowledge the works of the Holy Spirit in the life of ordinary individuals. This is true in that Pentecostals have sought to articulate Pentecostal value systems made possible through the experience of the Holy Spirit. The role of Pentecostals during the last century was to evoke the power of the Holy Spirit, manifested through signs, wonders, and charismata, to aid in personal transformation, to break down the destructive, sinful structures in individual lives and to bring relief from misery and death. In short, Pentecostals called the church's attention to the theological importance of the Holy Spirit and brought a heightened belief that God was as immanent as God was transcendent.

The theological foundation of Full Gospel theology also relies on the pneumatological experience, which is a crucial element for constructing Pentecostal identity. In spite of its theological importance, pneumatology seems to be a neglected dimension particularly in theological circles in that it eludes our grasp, our understanding and our academic probing and pursuit.[35] Full Gospel theology as a theology of the Holy Spirit has tried to get rid of that neglect in the Korean church. The issue of the Holy Spirit is dealt with as a

---

of God', in D. J. Atkinson and D.H. Field (eds.), *New Dictionary of Christian Ethics and Pastoral Theology* (Leicester: IVP, 1995), 530. An African theologian, Ukpong, describes the two natures of the Kingdom of God as a 'present reality' and a 'reality yet to be consummated'. See Justin S. Ukpong, 'Christology and Inculturation: A New Testament Perspective', in R. Gibellini (ed.), *Paths of African Theology* (London: SCM, 1994), 47.

[34] Donald W. Dayton, *Theological Roots of Pentecostalism* (Metuchen, NJ: Hendrickson, 1996), 16.

[35] See Allan Anderson, *Moya: The Holy Spirit in An African Context* (Pretoria: University of South Africa, 1991), vi.

central theme in 'the Fivefold Gospel' as the gospel of the fullness of the Holy Spirit. All who receive the fullness of the Holy Spirit receive power and are witnesses of Jesus Christ. To put it another way, we cannot keep our Christian identity if we are not filled with the Holy Spirit. The theological motif of Full Gospel theology relies on the twentieth century Pentecostal Movement, whose theological foundations are 'firmly planted in the nineteenth century Holiness Movement and American Revivalism'.[36] The Pentecostal Movement awoke people to experience the baptism of the Holy Spirit, through which Christians strengthen their convictions on Pentecostal faith. That is, when speaking of the nature of Pentecostal identity we cannot help emphasizing the works of the Holy Spirit. Theologians have attempted to understand the Holy Spirit according to their diverse theological perspectives.[37] With regard to the works of the Holy Spirit, Dr Cho says:

> The Holy Spirit is the Comforter who has been sent to help us. He is always with us. The Holy Spirit knows our infirmities and helps us. He knows even what we do not yet know and 'maketh intercession for us with groaning which cannot be uttered' (Rom. 8.26).[38]

The Holy Spirit not only draws our attention to Christ and enables us to open our spiritual eyes but also works through human beings by participating with them in human history. Furthermore, he gives us an eschatological hope by means of Christ's resurrection and allows us to be God's children and heirs of

---

[36] R.P. Menzies, 'Evidential Tongues: An Essay on Theological Method', *Asian Journal of Pentecostal Studies* 1 (1998), 111.

[37] Focusing on Christian faith and revelation, Martin Luther regards the Holy Spirit as a source for understanding God and as a goal for Christian life by experiencing him. According to him, 'no one can understand God or God's word unless he has it revealed immediately by the Holy Ghost; but nobody can receive anything from the Holy Ghost unless he experiences it'. Quoted in James D.G. Dunn, *Jesus and the Spirit: A Study of the Religious and Charismatic Experience of Jesus and the First Christians as Reflected in the New Testament* (London: SCM, 1978), 175. K. Barth interprets the Holy Spirit in relation to the 'Word' by saying 'The Holy Spirit is nothing else than a certain relation of the Word to man'. See Karl Barth, *Dogmatics in Outline*, trans. G.T. Thomson (London: SCM, 1949), 138. Arguing the term, Spirit, like all other statements about God as symbol, Tillich defines the Holy Spirit 'as the actualization of power and meaning in unity'. See Paul Tillich, *Systematic Theology*, vol. 3 (London: SCM, 1991), 111. Moltmann attempts to describe the Holy Spirit from the eschatological perspective by saying that 'Eschatologically, therefore, the Spirit can be termed 'the power of futurity' for it is 'the eschatological gift', the beginning (Rom. 8.23) and the earnest or guarantee (2 Cor. 1.22; 5.5) of the future'. See Jürgen Moltmann, *The Church in the Power of the Spirit: A Contribution to Messianic Ecclesiology*, trans. M. Kohl (London: SCM, 1977), 34.

[38] Yonggi Cho, *Praying with Jesus*, 93.

God.[39] The Holy Spirit eventually leads us to share God's glory. Considering these, pneumatological experience is an experience of Christ through the Holy Spirit for God's ministry. It is the force not only for breaking through the walls of human bondage but also for unity embodied in Christ.

What we wish to point out here is that pneumatological experience is a crucial factor which empowers believers to live under the presence of the Holy Spirit. The role of Full Gospel theology is to redirect our craving for the presence of the Holy Spirit. Here, what we mean by 'presence' is the experience of something that happens to somebody, namely the state of being touched by the Holy Spirit. In biblical sense, borrowing the Pauline term, 'new being' or 'new creation'[40] refers to the state of being grasped by the Holy Spirit. Therefore it needs to be considered that the experience of the Holy Spirit is vital to any understanding of Full Gospel theology.

Full Gospel theology depends on Dr Cho's perspectives for its theological direction. As Park analyses Dr Cho's pneumatology, its main theological concern is rooted in the baptism of the Holy Spirit, through which diverse theological issues come,[41] including issues of the fullness of the Holy Spirit, distinctions between being born again and the baptism of the Holy Spirit, speaking in tongues, the power of the Holy Spirit extended to mission and the fruits of the Holy Spirit. The early church was established on the foundation of pneumatological experience. Members of the early church were pneumatological in that they were those who were given charismatic gifts by the Holy Spirit. Even today, pneumatological experience is becoming popular for non-Pentecostals in Korea. The rapid growth of Pentecostal churches in Korea today is attributed to their strong pneumatological nature.[42]

Full Gospel Theology and Harmony as a Non-dualistic Methodology

As shown in the analogy of chopsticks, Full Gospel theology is underlined by the principle of harmony,[43] which has a non-dualistic methodology. Harmony has nothing to do with simply compromising and mixing factors in order to make one. There have been dualistic concepts of good and evil, sacred and

---

[39] See Hyeon Sung Bae, 'Paul's Christology from the Pneumatological Perspectives: Rom. 8.1-17' (Unpublished ThM Dissertation, Seoul Methodist Theological Seminary, 1991), 63.

[40] 2 Cor. 5.17.

[41] Myung Soo Park, 'Pentecostal Movement and Rev Yonggi Cho's Theology', op. cit., 33.

[42] Hyeon Sung Bae, 'Comments on *Minjung* and Pentecostal Movements in Korea', op. cit., 162.

[43] Here harmony is the term which involves an understanding of the East Asian cultural context. Harmony can be described as 'a state of equilibrium'. See Fung Yu-Lan, *The Spirit of Chinese Philosophy*, trans. E.R. Hughes (Boston: Beacon Press, 1953), 107.

secular, heaven and earth, life and death in the West. However, the ultimate truth does not lie in a dualistic approach but in a non-dualistic one. In his book, *A Coat of Many Colours*, Wilson strongly criticises the weakness of Western theology and suggests solutions like this:

> Western theology is one-eyed. It relies heavily on a tradition of academic debate. Its perception of Christianity is strongly left-brained and influenced by its development in a literary culture. Western theology is therefore a partial view of Christianity and is in need of healing itself. Inter-cultural dialogue can provide a necessary infusion of different points of view to make up a more whole theology.[44]

Full Gospel theology attempts to integrate extreme opposites in order to make its theological essence relevant to the living situations of Korea. We can find harmony and a non-dualistic methodology in Full Gospel theology. In the Threefold Blessing, we can find that the issues of the spiritual, material and physical needs of human being are well balanced. It is true to say that the mainline churches in Korea used to highlight the spiritual issue, neglecting the material and physical one. The apostle John says in 3 John 2.1, the biblical foundation of the Threefold Blessing, 'Dear friend, I pray that you may enjoy good health and that all may go well with you, even as your soul is getting along well'. Here, we can find harmony among one's spiritual, material and physical needs. God regards one's material and physical world as of great importance, as he does one's spiritual world. Regarding these, Dr Cho wrote:

> Today many people say that God does not concern Himself with material things. Some even assert that we should ask for spiritual things but not for our material needs to be met. But is God really indifferent to the physical world? The answer is definitely no. God prepared the physical world even before He created man and woman so that Adam and Eve did not have to worry about what they would eat, what they would put on, or what they would drink.[45]

Considering this, Dr Cho has a non-dualistic, harmonious methodology in forming Full Gospel theology. We can see the best example of this non-dualistic method in Christ's incarnation. That event symbolizes God's concern for harmony. In other words, that is the important event through which God showed the culmination of harmony between deity and humanity. When we look back over Christian history, we can find that dualism has been a serious problem. Full Gospel theology has a holistic methodology based on a holistic salvation. What is, then, the holistic theological methodology? Above

---

[44] M. Wilson, *A Coat of Many Colours: Pastoral Studies of the Christian Way of Life* (London: Epworth, 1988), 96.
[45] Yonggi Cho, *Praying with Jesus*, op. cit., 142.

all, it is a well-balanced perspective without having any prejudice and partiality. It guides us to see unity through diversity. Eventually it is a gateway to enter into the theological world of depth and meaning. Full Gospel theology integrates dual aspects of theology by its complementary and harmonious factors.

There have been some Western scholars who have attempted to overcome dualism by turning their faces to East Asian philosophical thought. For instance, Whitehead's theology seems to follow some aspects of East Asian thought more closely than other types of western thought.[46] Thus, even though western methodology has had a great influence on Korean theology, now it has become uncertain of itself and of its basis—at least in a Korean context. It means that Korean theology has begun to acquire a new self-confidence and a deep concern among Korean Christians for the last two decades. In this sense, Full Gospel theology cannot escape accomplishing its theological goal by developing its non-dualistic theological methodology. The non-dualistic theological methodology includes both 'theology of orthodoxy' and 'theology of praxis'. Reflecting on this, it seems clear that the non-dualistic theological methodology has not an 'either A or B' methodology, which forces people to select partial understanding of theology, but rather a 'both A and B' methodology, which focuses on theological wholeness. Full Gospel theology encompasses the complementarity of all opposites for the creative integration of the whole.

Full Gospel Theology and Pentecostal Healing

The journey towards human wholeness necessarily includes the issue of healing. Healing is an integral part of the Pentecostal message. The Fivefold Gospel includes the gospel of healing, which concerns a healing ministry manifesting signs, wonders and charismata to bring relief from misery and death in individual lives. With speaking in tongues, healing provides another distinctive identity for Pentecostalism. The issue of healing has been dealt with as of crucial importance in the Bible. Throughout the Bible, it was, and is, the very nature of God to effect healing. But churches in Korea in general were not concerned with it too much, just showing spiritual concern. In other words, they used to entrust medical doctors with the task. It was, however, Dr Cho who made the issue of healing the most essential Christian issue and put healing in theological and systematic order. In this connection, we cannot deny that his tremendous achievement in church growth resulted primarily from his Pentecostal healing ministry.

---

[46] Kim Sang-Il and Ro Young Chan (eds.), *Hanism As Korean Mind* (Los Angeles, California: Eastern Academy of Human Sciences, 1984), 2.

Jesus Christ never sent his patients back to their homes when they came to him for healing. Rather he healed everyone who came and asked for it. For Jesus, healing was crucial to his ministry of teaching and preaching. In particular, his methods of healing were not simply limited to the physical, but also to the holistic, in that he connected the cause of disease to the roots of a person's whole being. He showed the true way to reach human wholeness by healing people. It is therefore a quest for the divine that has been part of humanity, no matter what the cultural and ethnic distinctions, from the beginning of history.

In particular, the issue of healing is closely linked to the eschatological issue, which deals with the final history and the Kingdom of God.[47] Pentecostals perceive that the Kingdom of God becomes manifest and transformed into one's actual life, as the meaning of human wholeness. Therefore, a realised eschatology challenges us to pray for healing. Pentecostals relate physical sickness or material poverty to the spiritual dimension. Consequently, they view the spirit world as a present reality for which the divinely given charism, the discerning of spirits, is essential to any successful encounter with it.[48] Dr Cho regards the cause of disease as a spiritual problem.

> There are many people who become blind or dumb when they are possessed by the devil...Of course there are some who were born without eardrums or some whose eardrums have been ruptured. But there are some who cannot hear because of deaf spirits. And if these spirits are cast out in the name of Jesus, hearing can be restored miraculously and immediately. The Bible says that the devil causes all manner of diseases.[49]

Because the body is an evident, tangible aspect of a whole human being, a physical disorder not only affects our body but also our whole life. In the West, people used to understand the cause of disease from a biological perspectives. Contrary to the West, traditional Koreans linked it to both the biological and spiritual dimensions. That is the reason why traditional Koreans called for doctors as well as shamans when they become sick. In this connection, as Dong Sik Ryu points out, it is, to a certain extent, possible to consider that the

---

[47] As has been discussed about the Kingdom of God in the previous section, it has two natures. On the one hand, it has immediate dimension which is already established here and now. On the other hand, it has an eternal dimension which is not yet come, so we need to endure until the return of Christ.

[48] Opal L. Reddin, *Power Encounter: A Pentecostal Perspective* (Springfield, MO: Central Bible College Press, 1989), 291.

[49] Yonggi Cho, *Praying with Jesus*, op. cit., 246.

shamanistic nature of Korean culture has somewhat made Koreans equipped to understand biblical truths and value systems.[50]

What makes Dr Cho's understanding of healing distinguishable from other evangelicals is that he regards healing not as a selective matter but as a necessary matter. Dr Cho used to deliver healing messages proclaiming that 'Christ has diseases on his back'. This means that Christ not only redeemed our sin but also healed our sickness as well on the cross. In order to be healed, therefore, one has to repent of one's sin first and stand firm in the faith that he or she is already healed. Dr Cho has challenged the believers to rely on the cross of Jesus for it is not only the source of salvation but also the foundation of healing.

The physical body is 'a temple of the Holy Spirit',[51] a dwelling place of God. It is, therefore, obvious we should value the body and treat it with care and consideration. God intends the human body to be clean and beautiful and strong. Accordingly, without physical health we are hard-pressed to maintain human wholeness. Here, the word 'whole' denotes, 'healthy, free from wound or injury, healed'. What Full Gospel theology seeks is not merely limited to physical healing but is extended to holistic healing, embracing mental and spiritual wholeness as well. A life of wholeness is a life of health, because healing reconnects people with wholeness. In this connection, healing involves making human beings whole. It is a realization of potential.

Conclusion

Once P. van Dusen identified the Pentecostal Movement as 'the Third Force' in Christendom.[52] It has contributed to challenging the churches to open their eyes to see the unlimited potential of 'the Third Force'. It not only has reminded the churches in Korea of the works of the early church but also has envisioned believers to actualize Pentecostal power today. As a result, whichever denomination of the churches in Korea, whether Presbyterian, Methodist or Holiness, they have been, to a certain extent, Pentecostalized.[53] They began to be familiar with the Pentecostal atmosphere by adopting Pentecostal liturgy and prayer. It has been the role of Full Gospel theology to help the churches in Korea to adjust to the Pentecostal influence.

---

[50] Dong Sik Ryu, *Korean Religions and Christianity* (Seoul: Korean Christian Book Society, 1965)

[51] 1 Cor. 6.19.

[52] Henry P. Van Dusen, 'The Third Force in Christendom', *Life*, 44 (June 9, 1958), 113-24.

[53] H.J. Lee, '*Minjung* and Pentecostal Movements in Korea', in Allan H. Anderson and Walter J. Hollenweger (eds.), *Pentecostals after a Century: Global Perspectives on a Movement in Transition* (Sheffield, England: Sheffield Academic Press, 1999), 138.

As we have noted throughout, Full Gospel theology was not only a hermeneutical tool for interpreting the dynamic Pentecostal legacy but also a method of delivering a Pentecostal identity to Korean people. Full Gospel theology shares its theological identity with world Pentecostals. However we could never say that it is merely an imitation of western Pentecostal theology or an imported theology. Rather it is a Korean theology which is relevant and applicable to the Korean contextual reality, reflecting both Korean life and faith.

It has been our goal in this paper to examine the theological implications of a Korean Pentecostal identity by reflecting on the Full Gospel theology of Korea. Full Gospel theology has challenged the Korean church by suggesting a paradigm for theological renewal and revival. The essential point of Full Gospel theology is to recover a sense of a holistic mind in order to deal with the broken reality of society and church. In this connection, we call it a holistic theology and a theological methodology with concern for holistic salvation. In other words, Full Gospel theology has a non-dualistic methodology based on holistic salvation. It is far from the sort of theology whose boundary is limited to spiritual satisfaction or academic pride. As pointed out above, its theological implications vary from spiritual to cultural. Though it has various theological implications, its main concern is to recover God-given totality, 'the image of God' on the various levels.

Full Gospel theology is, in itself, an indigenized form of Pentecostal theology based on the Pentecostal and Charismatic experience. It seeks to discover its theological meanings from the Korean *sitz im leben,* where people can meet God and experience the presence of the Holy Spirit. It is sensitive to meeting the needs of people's *sitz im leben.* It is therefore a theology of the Holy Spirit as well as a theology of *sitz im leben.* Here, we cannot help mentioning the relationship between the Full Gospel theology and Dr Cho's role in it. The birthplace of 'the Fivefold Gospel' and 'the Threefold Blessing' was not a theological institution but a small room for prayer, where Dr Cho made supplication to God, weeping and kneeling down for the holistic salvation of the grass-roots people depressed by their insecure circumstances. It is also the place where he was busy due to his preaching, healing and teaching ministry.

It is necessary for Pentecostals to prepare a theological paradigm appropriate to the twenty first century by incorporating Full Gospel theology with an open mind. Therefore the future of Korean Pentecostalism depends on how well Full Gospel theology responds to Pentecostal issues with theological reflection. The core issue of this paper has been to construct the argument and setting for Full Gospel theology, which needs to be incepted in the context of Korean Christianity.

Given this point of view, it will be fruitful for Korean Pentecostals to develop Full Gospel theology, which is relevant and applicable to the spiritual and contextual reality of the Korean church. As far as Full Gospel theology is concerned, the twenty first century will be a turning point for the renewal and revival of the Korean church. In conclusion, Full Gospel theology has a long way to go for further development. It is not a ready-made theology but is still in its formative stage.

The Korean Charismatic Movement as Indigenous Pentecostalism

Chong Hee Jeong

Introduction

The formation and development of Korean Charismatic/Pentecostal Christianity during the past hundred years is one of the most remarkable stories in the church's history. It is difficult to classify or define the diversity and dynamism of Charismatic/Pentecostal Christianity historically, sociologically and theologically. Generally speaking, Charismatics in Korea differ from Pentecostals in several ways, including dates of origin and forms of institutionalization. In this paper, I will define 'Charismatics' as mainline Christians such as Presbyterians and Methodists who do not belong to Pentecostal denominations, even though Charismatics share with Pentecostals the affirmation of spiritual gifts, especially speaking in tongues, healing, and prophecy as a result of the work of the Holy Spirit. Western[1] Pentecostal scholars[2] who follow American paradigms see Classical Pentecostalism, those Pentecostal denominations formed since the Azusa Street revival (1906-1908), as the historical origin of the Pentecostal movement.[3] Vinson Synan, a well-known American Pentecostal church historian, classifies American Pentecostalism according to three historical stages: the development of Classical Pentecostals (1910s), mainline Protestant and Catholic Charismatic

---

[1] I will define western as Euro-American in my paper.

[2] Among Pentecostal scholars are Edith L. Blumhofer, Russell P. Spittler, Robert M. Anderson, Vinson Synan, Peter Hocken and Peter Wagner. Edith Blumhofer, 'Restoration as Revival: Early American Pentecostalism', in Edith Blumhofer and Randall Balmer (eds.), *Modern Christian Revivals* (Urbana: University of Illinois Press, 1993), 145-160; Russell P. Spittler, 'Are Pentecostals and Charismatics Fundamentalists? A Review of American Uses of These Categories', in Karla Poewe (ed.), *Charismatic Christianity as a Global Culture* (Columbia: University of South Carolina Press, 1994), 103-116; Robert M. Anderson, *Vision of the Disinherited* (New York: Oxford University, 1992); Peter Hocken, *The Strategy of the Spirit* (Guildford: Eagle, 1996).

[3] I use the term American here to speak of US American in my paper.

Movements (1960s), and the Third Wave renewal Pentecostals (1980s).[4] However, Allan Anderson points out the problem of Pentecostal historiography: 'The 1988 edition of the *Dictionary of Pentecostal and Charismatic Movements* is predominantly North American in focus, with some attention given to Europe, but the world of the great majority of Pentecostals is almost entirely absent'.[5] Because of a different process of Korean church history (quite unlike American Pentecostalism), Korean Charismatic Movements do not follow Classical Pentecostalism chronologically and Korean Pentecostalism does not have a three-fold development, as Synan has argued for the history of American Pentecostalism. The Korean field was already being prepared through the Charismatic Movement (1903-1907) before the first Classical Pentecostal missionary arrived in 1928. Historically speaking, there are two major streams in Korea, namely the Charismatic Movements (1910s-1940s) and the emergence of Pentecostal denominations (1950s-1980s).

However, the focus of this paper will be on reinterpreting the Korean Charismatic Movement from the perspective of indigenous Pentecostalism, because according to my reading of sources and secondary literature, Classical Pentecostalism and the western revival movements had a limited impact on Korean Pentecostalism.[6] The Welsh Revival and Korean Pentecostalism have been linked,[7] although Edwin Orr, the well-known English scholar explains that the Welsh Revival had only been known after the second wave of spiritual awakenings in Korea. In the opening of his chapter on 'The Korean Pentecost', Orr states, 'The awakenings of the 1900s in Korea were indigenous, of missionary derivation and part of a worldwide movement'.[8] He first stresses the indigenous character of the Korean Pentecost, then writes about the Canadian missionaries and hints to a link with the world-wide movement for 'the second

---

[4] See Vinson Synan, *The Holiness-Pentecostal Tradition: Charismatic Movements in the Twentieth Century* (Grand Rapids: Eerdmans, 1997); *The Spirit Said 'Grow': The Astounding Worldwide Expansion of Pentecostal & Charismatic Churches* (Monrovia, CA: MARC, 1992).

[5] Allan Anderson, 'Signs and Blunders: Pentecostal Mission Issues at "Home and Abroad" in the twentieth Century', in *Pentecostal Mission: Issues Home and Abroad at 2000 Conference Papers of the Society for Pentecostal Studies* (March, 2000), 1-16.

[6] I will use the word 'Korean Pentecostalism' as a collective term for a series of movements that emerged, of which some have grown while others remain small.

[7] See Edwin Orr, *Evangelical Awakenings in Eastern Asia* (Minneapolis: Bethany Fellowship, 1975); David Bundy, 'Keswick and the Experience of Evangelical Piety', in Edith Blumhofer and Randall Balmer (eds.), *Modern Christian Revivals* (Urbana: University of Illinois Press, 1993), 118-144; Blumhofer, 'Restoration as Revival: Early American Pentecostalism'; Daniel Bays, 'Christian Revival in China', in Edith Blumhofer and Randall Balmer (eds.), *Modern Christian Revivals* (Urbana: University of Illinois Press, 1993), 161-179.

[8] Orr, *Evangelical Awakenings in Eastern Asia*, 26.

wave of revival [that] swept Korea in 1905-1906'.[9] Nevertheless, he claims furthermore:

> The Welsh Revival was the farthest-reaching of the movements of the general Awakening, for it affected the whole of the Evangelical cause in India, Korea and China, renewed revival in Japan and South Africa, and sent a wave of awakening over Africa, Latin America, and the South Seas.[10]

Although these accounts were apparently very encouraging to missionaries, it is important to notice that the Korean Revival (1903-1907) had already started before the Welsh Revival (1904-1905) occurred.

The first American evangelical missionary came to Korea to evangelize in 1884.[11] William Blair who lived in Pyongyang as a missionary at that time experienced the 'Korean Pentecost', which progressed during 1903-1907.[12] According to the mission periodical, *The Korea Mission Field*, the fire of the Holy Spirit not only healed wounded hearts through Charismatic meetings and spread throughout Korea, but also brought about a powerful zeal for evangelism and an 'explosive' growth in the early Presbyterian and Methodist churches.[13] In other words, the Charismatic meetings (1903-1907) which were called the 'Korean Pentecost' created the historical formation of Korean Pentecostalism and gave a distinctive character to Presbyterian and Methodist

---

[9] Orr, *Evangelical Awakenings in Eastern Asia*, 27. Orr says, 'In 1906, Dr. Howard Agnew Johnston brought news of the awakenings in Wales and in India. Half the missionaries in Korea were…deeply moved by the accounts of revival among the Welsh Presbyterians and on their Asian mission fields'.

[10] Orr, *Evangelical Awakenings in Eastern Asia*, 14.

[11] A Korean Catholic church was built in Seoul for the purpose of forming a Catholic community in 1784. Protestant Christianity was then introduced in Korea when American missionary Dr Horace Allen came to Korea in 1884. Nevertheless, it is remarkable to remember that before any foreign missionaries actually engaged in evangelism on Korean culture, Protestant Christianity had been brought there by local evangelists (Su Jeong Yi ; Jin Gi Kim, Sang Ryun Seo and others). Pioneer missionaries H.G Underwood and Henry Appenzeller brought copies of the Korean translation of the Bible with them when they landed in 1885. Thus the origin and development of the Protestant Church in Korea from the first depended upon the efforts of the Koreans themselves. However, local evangelists did not make a great impact.

[12] See William Blair and Bruce F. Hunt, *The Korean Pentecost and the Suffering Which Followed* (Edinburgh: Banner of Truth Trust, 1977).

[13] W.G. Cram, 'A Genuine Change', *The Korea Mission Field* 3:5 (Seoul, Korea, May, 1907), 67-68; G. Lee, 'How The Spirit Came to Pyongyang', *The Korea Mission Field* 3:3 (March, 1907), 33-36; J.Z. Moore, 'The Great Revival Year', *The Korea Mission Field* 3:8 (August, 1907), 113-120; M.D. Myfrs, 'The Spirit's Quiet in Wonsan', *The Korea Mission Field* 3:4 (April, 1907), 54; W.C. Swearer, 'Gospel Progress', *The Korea Mission Field* 3:6 (June, 1907), 85-86.

churches[14] that will be described as the 'Korean Charismatic Movement'. Thus, the term 'Korean Charismatic Movement' may be used to describe an indigenous Charismatic event which has been integrated into mainline Korean Protestantism. Presbyterian pastors Sun-Joo Gil (1869-1935) and Ick-Doo Kim (1874-1950), and Methodist pastor Yong-Do Lee (190133), all played central roles in the Charismatic development of indigenous Pentecostalism thereafter. As a result, in 1931 *Sinhakjinam,* a well-known Korean journal, classified Pentecostalism as a distinct stream of Christianity which had three main paradigms: Roman Catholicism, which emphasized 'the structure of the church'; Protestantism, with 'its emphasis on biblical authority'; and Pentecostalism, which accented 'the empowerment of the Holy Spirit'.[15] *Sinhakjinam* also predicted, 'We shall see the great success of the Third Paradigm Shift in Korea through the Holy Spirit-orientated religion'.[16] Accordingly, the formation and development of indigenous Pentecostalism in Korea is different from that of Classical Pentecostalism, which more closely relates to the Azusa Street revival in Los Angeles (1906-1908) and the Welsh Revival (1904-1905). Hollenweger claims:

> A new generation of Pentecostal mission scholars will discover that the Holy Spirit was already present before the Pentecostal missionary or any other missionary arrived on the mission field, that the Holy Spirit also works through the Celestial Church in anglophone West Africa, the Kimbanguist Church in francophone Africa, and the Independent churches in Indonesia, Korea, Latin America, and the Caribbean.... They have produced their own theologies, liturgies, and ethics.[17]

So the term Pentecostalism in Korea must be defined in new ways for a better self-understanding as one of the expressions of world-wide Pentecostalism because 'Pentecostalism has had many beginnings and there are many Pentecostalisms'.[18]

---

[14] L.George Paik, *The History of Protestant Missions in Korea 1832-1910* (Seoul: Yonsei University Press, 1970), 361.

[15] Editorial, 'Gidokgyoeui Je3 Jeongi' [The Third Shift of Christianity], *Sinhakjinam* 13:1 (1931), 23.

[16] Editorial, 'Gidokgyoeui', 23.

[17] Walter Hollenweger, *Pentecostalism: Origins and Developments Worldwide* (Peabody, MA: Hendrickson, 1997), 301.

[18] Anderson, 'Signs and Blunders', 9; Walter Hollenweger, *The Pentecostals* (London: SCM, 1972), xxvii. Hollenweger says that 'we see now that these early tight clothes do not fit the worldwide Pentecostal revival. It is no longer sufficient to quote the truths of the past in order to be faithful to one's tradition and to the biblical message. Each age needs its own theological expression, and Pentecostalism is no exception to this'.

The Korean Charismatic Movement as the Contextual Healing of *Han*

The Korean Charismatic Movement has an indigenous formation in history, and did not develop in a vacuum. The Charismatic Movement, which was conditioned by the Korean *Sitz im Leben*,[19] did not emerge from a distinct religious and socio-political environment in Europe and America.[20] In Pentecostalism, which is fused with Korean culture, the division between gospel[21] and culture[22] cannot be sustained, because of the concept of *sintoburi* (身土不二).[23] In other words, the Korean Charismatic Movement can be understood in terms of *sintoburi*, the non-duality of gospel and culture, not in terms of dualism. I would say that the formation of Pentecostalism in Korea has already been deeply indigenized into Korean culture and history as *sintoburi*

---

[19] Korean Pentecostalism is relevant to Koreans' particularity (*Sitz im Leben*) as every historical event took place in a particular location as well as a particular time.

[20] For example, a Pentecostal scholar, Menzies insists on the limitation of western theology, and lists factors, such as 'theological bankruptcy' in the midst of humanistic intellectualism, and a tension between liberal Christianity with its social gospel and the opposite conservative camp characterized by fundamentalism.

[21] Theologically, by 'gospel', I mean both God's revelation of himself in history through his deeds and incarnation and the record of this revelation which is given in the Bible. For the useful discussion on the gospel and culture, see David Bosch, *Transforming Mission* (Maryknoll, NY: Orbis Books, 1996), 291-98, 420-32, 447-57; John Parratt, *A Guide to Doing Theology* (London: SPCK, 1996); Justin Ukpong, 'Towards a Holistic Approach to Inculturation Theology', *Mission Studies* XVI-2, 32 (1999), 100-124; Aylward Shorter, *Toward a Theology of Inculturation* (Maryknoll: Orbis Books, 1988), 17-30; B.J. Nicholls, 'Contextualization', in Sinclair B. Ferguson & David F. Wright (eds.), *New Dictionary of Theology* (Leicester: I.V.P., 1988), 164-67.

[22] Paul Hiebert, *Anthropological Insights for Missionaries* (Grand Rapids: Baker Book House, 1999). In this book, Hiebert shows that 'culture' is the 'integrated system of learned patterns of ideas, behaviour and products characteristic of a society'. Culture in this sense is both a bridge, which links different generations of people to one another; but as people cannot fully escape their own culture because it is within them, culture is also a barrier, when people defend themselves against other traditions or deliberately overcome that hindrance and enter a new culture. The relationship between gospel and culture is a much-debated topic.

[23] In Korea, *sintoburi* has been used in reference to the excellent efficacy of traditional Korean medicine for those who were born and live on the land. The term *sintoburi* originally meant the non-duality of body and earth. That is to say, the traditional term has been used to denote the close relationship between the human body and the earth on which it lives. The body cannot be isolated from the earth; neither can it be separated from the earth. Jesus was a historical person, and being historical, Jesus was chronologically, geographically, religiously, and culturally a first-century Jew. See Kim Kwang Shik, 'Non-duality of Body and Earth: Four Models of Indigenization', *Yonsei Journal of Theology* 3 (1998), 81-93; Kim Kwang Shik, 'Non-duality of God and Earth: The Problem of God's Name', *Korean Journal of Systematic Theology* 2 (1998), 45-55.

through the Korean Charismatic Movement (1903-1907). Accordingly, the Christian church in Korea grew not in the 'flowerpot of the West'[24] by missionary endeavours, but in the roots of Korean culture and history. In the Latin American context, David Martin argues for the significance of culture for Pentecostalism: 'The total autonomy of Pentecostalism is part and parcel of its immersion in Latin American culture'. [25] As culture is important for Pentecostalism, Newbigin contends that 'there is not and cannot be a gospel which is not culturally conditioned'.[26] Alan Neely concludes,

> Two conditions appear undeniable and inescapable. First, the gospel is not a-cultural, nor can it be a-historical. If it is to be understood and appropriated, it will have to be rooted in a particular historical context. But as the gospel is never a-historical, neither can it be a-cultural.[27]

A key question is therefore how the gospel has been communicated to the Korean people and their culture. What are the relationships between the Korean culture and the Christian gospel as introduced by missionaries? How has there been a genuine encounter or interaction between culture and the gospel, especially Pentecostalism in the Korean context? How has Korean Pentecostalism been meaningful and relevant to the Korean context and communicable to Korean people? One of the premier interpreters of Pentecostalism, Walter Hollenweger, also asks, 'What does it mean that our western form of Christianity and of Pentecostalism is by now a minority form, and that these other Christians, these other Pentecostals, are different—very different—from us?'[28] He remarks in his chapter entitled, 'Korea: The Oral Shamanist Culture in Pentecostal Transformation' that Korean Pentecostalism will, theologically, become more and more independent.

Shamanism has interacted with other religious traditions such as Buddhism, Confucianism and Christianity, permeating and influencing them.[29] Shamanism,

---

[24] D.T. Niles, 'Seongseoyeonguwa Tochakhamunje' [The Bible Study and Issue of Indigenization], *Christian Thought* (October, 1962), 67.

[25] David Martin, *Tongues of Fire: The Explosion of Protestantism in Latin America* (Oxford: Basil Blackwell, 1990), 282.

[26] Lesslie Newbigin, *The Gospel in a Pluralist Society* (Grand Rapids, MI: Eerdmans, 1989), 188.

[27] Alan Neely, *Christian Mission: A Case Study Approach* (Maryknoll, NY: Orbis Books, 1995), 3.

[28] Hollenweger, *Pentecostalism*, 289.

[29] Young-Hoon Lee, 'The Holy Spirit Movement in Korea: Its Historical and Doctrinal Development' (Ph D diss.: Temple University, 1996), 14-15. According to Lee, 'One distinctive characteristic of the history of Korean religions is that the dominating religions dramatically changed as ruling governments or dynasties changed. Shamanism was the dominating religion in prehistorical times; Buddhism in the Silra and Goryeo

as the 'primal spirituality'[30] or religion[31] of the Korean people, is called *mugyo* (shamanist teaching) or *musok* (shamanist practices). Shamanism is still rooted deeply in the minds of Korean people, in the depths of their religiosity, affecting their values and worldview. The negative characteristics that Koreans have that are influenced by Shamanism are an attitude of dependence, a short-sighted attitude, moral indifference, fatalism, escapism and self-centred interest. However, one important point here attracts our attention in the influence of Shamanism, which also has positive points in relation to Korean Pentecostalism: it was the unravelling of the *han* of people. Ko Eun, a renowned poet in contemporary Korea, writes, 'we Koreans were born from the womb of *han* and brought up on the womb of *han*'.[32] According to Katherine Wambold in 1908, Koreans expressed their *han* thus: 'I have no sense, my eyes are dim, my mind is dark, I cannot read, I have no money, I have no house, my husband is dead, I have no children, I have no son'.[33] Etymologically speaking, *han* (身) is composed of two Chinese characters. The first component of the word is *shim* (身), which means 'a heart', and the other is *geun* (身), which means the 'root'. In popular usage, *han* literally means the root of the heart. I

---

eras (from the seventh to the fourteenth century); Confucianism in the Joseon dynasty (from the fourteenth to the nineteenth century); and Christianity from the late Joseon era and following. Nevertheless, none of the religions became completely extinct in any period. All the religions took root in the Korean religious culture, influenced one another'. However, I would argue that Buddhism, Confucianism and Christianity were deeply influenced by Shamanism of primal spirituality or primal religion. So I can say shamanistic Buddhism, Confucianism and Christianity in Korean culture. Accordingly, I will focus on Korean Shamanism in my thesis.

[30] Harvey Cox, *Fire from Heaven: The Rise of Pentecostal Spirituality and the Reshaping of Religion in the Twenty-first Century* (Reading, MA: Addison-Wesley, 1994), 81-83. For Cox, primal spirituality has three dimensions that he calls 'primal speech' (ecstatic utterance), 'primal piety' (mystical experience, trance, and healing), and 'primal hope' (the unshakeable expectation of a better future). I will simply define primal spirituality as religiosity of human beings from the viewpoint of the Korean culture.

[31] Andrew Walls, *The Missionary Movement in Christian History: Studies in the Transmission of Faith* (T & T Clark: Edinburgh, 1996), 119, 136. I will use Walls' definition. He describes primal religion as underlying all the other faiths and often exists in symbiosis with them, continuing (sometimes more, sometimes less transformed) to have an active life within and around cultures and communities influenced by those faiths. Therefore nowadays Korean Shamanism is not only adjusting; some aspects have been revitalized in Korean Pentecostalism.

[32], Nam Dong Suh , 'Towards a Theology of *Han*', in Kim Yong Bock (ed.), *Minjung Theology: People as the Subject of History* (Singapore: Christian Conference of Asia, 1981), 54.

[33] Katherine Wambold, 'Thirty-Three Days of Country Classes', *The Korea Mission Field* 4:12 (December, 1908), 178.

will define *han* as the diseased hearts of people who are physically or psychologically associated with the suffering of survival created by wars, patriarchal suppression, poverty and sicknesses in Korean history.

The healing of *han* by Korean Pentecostalism is another characteristic of Korean culture, gospel and history. Ronald Kydd's book, *Healing through the Centuries: Models for Understanding*,[34] is an exploration of models of healing from a variety of eras, locales and doctrinal persuasions. He identifies the models as confrontational, intercessory, reliquarial, incubational, revelational and soteriological. Kydd states that 'comprehensiveness' has been a goal of the study to look at healing throughout the life of the Christian church. Kydd has given us a sweeping view of some of the variety and diversity that exist within western traditions. On this point, Cox finds that indigenous healings are part of the Charismatic message everywhere.[35] In particular, healings have been a major attraction for indigenous Pentecostalism in the Third World.[36] A vital element in this healing relationship is a growing mutual exchange between gospel and culture. Patrick Kalilombe describes the character of African religion as having a 'holistic and integrating nature' that 'pervades the whole of life, of individuals as well as of the community'.[37] On this point, Anderson claims,

> The central place given to healing is probably no longer a prominent feature of western Pentecostalism, but in the Third World the problems of disease and evil affect the whole community and are not simply a private domain relegated to individual pastoral care.[38]

Indigenous Pentecostalism generally regards the practice of contextual healing as good news for the poor, the sick and marginalized. In this context, every culture should be healed of its dehumanizing elements, and every culture needs the healing ministry of the gospel.[39] So Christians who live in the Third World understand that healing as the work of the Spirit comprises both eternal salvation for redeemed human beings and a concretely experienced wholeness and well being in this life for those who place themselves under his healing

---

[34] Ronald Kydd, *Healing through the Centuries: Models for Understanding* (Peabody, MA: Hendrickson, 1998).

[35] Cox, *Fire*, 222.

[36] Allan Anderson, 'Global Pentecostalism in the New Millennium', in Allan H. Anderson and Walter J. Hollenweger (eds.), *Pentecostals after a Century: Global Perspectives on a Movement in Transition* (Sheffield: Sheffield Academic Press, 1999), 219.

[37] Patrick Kalilombe, 'Spirituality in the African Perspective', in Rosino Gibellini (ed.), *Paths of African Theology* (London: SCM, 1994), 115.

[38] Anderson, 'Global Pentecostalism', 216.

[39] Cf. Isaiah 6.10; Hosea 6.1-2.

power. Similarly, contextual healing in Korea may be understood as the healing of *han*, as Korean 'lived soteriology', because the gospel of salvation has effected the healing of *han* among wounded people in the Korean churches. Interestingly enough, the historical process of Korean contextual healing can be seen as the extension of the healing of *han* under the Sino-Japanese War (1884-85), Russo-Japanese War (1904-1905) and the Japanese occupation (1910-45). So the main character of Korean ministry is nothing less than a movement of healing, as Korean people are caught up in a spirit of hopelessness and decline because Korean society, governed by wars and Japan, consisted largely of healing-oriented communities driven by Korean *han*.

The healing of *han* as the contextualization[40] of Korean Pentecostalism is one of the characteristics through 'the work of the Holy Spirit'. For Pentecostals, the Holy Spirit serves as the link between gospel and culture that has transformed Korean Protestant Christianity. He is seen as 'an active participant' who guides and energizes Korean Pentecostalism in a very significant way for contextualization.[41] Robert Schreiter claims, 'One cannot speak of a community developing a local theology without its being filled with the Spirit and working under the power of the gospel'.[42] Anderson argues that Pentecostalism in the Third World is more obviously a contextualization than a foreign imposition. He also thinks that the foundation of contextualization is the Holy Spirit.[43] The ability of Pentecostalism to indigenize Christianity takes place in its Charismatic emphasis on the transforming power of the Holy Spirit. Therefore, the Holy Spirit as a transformer is an enabler for the fulfilling of contextualization, so that all witnesses of the gospel have been part of a particular culture. Indigenous Pentecostalism can be seen as the direct result of people's experiences, which they have interpreted as an outpouring of the Holy Spirit who heals the diseased hearts of the Korean people.

The Korean Charismatic Movement (1903-1907)

The first outpouring of the Charismatic Movement in Korea began in the summer of 1903 at Wonsan, on the north-east coast, during a Bible study and prayer meeting among western missionaries. The climax of the Charismatic

---

[40] Originally the word 'contextualisation' is a derivative of the word 'context', with its roots in the Latin word 'contextus', which means 'weaving together'.

[41] Allan Anderson, 'The Forgotten Dimension: Education for Pentecostal-Charismatic Spirituality in Global Perspective', in *The 30th Annual Meeting of the Society for Pentecostal Studies*, Conference Paper (March, 2001), 18.

[42] Robert Schreiter, *Constructing Local Theologies* (Maryknoll: Orbis Books, 1985), 24-25.

[43] Allan Anderson, 'The Gospel and Culture in Pentecostal Mission in the Third World', *Missionalia* 27:2 (August, 1999), 220-30.

Movement was 'the Korean Pentecost' in Pyongyang in January 1907,[44] when people hungered for the Spirit to bring the healing of *han*, and more than 1,500 people gathered every night. Women were excluded due to lack of room. The main preacher during an evening meeting of the conference was Gil, but missionaries led the meeting.[45] After Gil's own confession, people began to confess their sins publicly. These spiritual experiences, namely *tongseonggido*,[46] with wailing, all night prayer, early morning prayer, fasting prayer and emotional conversion with Bible study, marked a great step in Korean church history during these special meetings. While the message was carried from place to place, a strong longing and desire for the same spiritual experiences were created in the minds of people all over the country. After the Charismatic Movement began in Pyongyang, wherever there were Christians, Charismatic experiences were repeated. An adequate description of the Korean Pentecost is almost an impossible task, nor is it necessary in the present investigation, but in order to aid our understanding of the nature of the Charismatic Movement, we shall give a contemporary account written in *The Korea Mission Field* of February and March 1907, which reported a manifestation of the presence of the Holy Spirit:

> The Spirit is coming with mighty power in this month of February to visit many of the cities and villages of every section. It was not 'will come' but 'is in the act of coming' and 'has come'. His visitation is mighty and wonderful.[47]

> 'And it shall come to pass in the last days, saith God, I will pour out of my Spirit upon all flesh'. This prophecy is being fulfilled in our midst today. During the past month the most marvellous working of the Holy Spirit in the hearts of the Christians of this city has been the subject of daily conversation.[48]

According to *The Religious Awakening of Korea: An account of the revival in the Korean Churches in 1907*, it was reported by the Board of Foreign Missions that 'The Holy Spirit performed his special work upon the church membership and the terrible manifestations of distress and agony were confined largely to

---

[44] Board of Foreign Missions, *The Religious Awakening of Korea: An account of the revival in the Korean churches in 1907* (New York: Methodist Episcopal Church, 1908), 7.

[45] Jin Kyung Kil , *Young Gyo Kil Seon Ju* (Seoul: Chongro Books, 1980), 191.

[46] *Tongseonggido* means simultaneous loud prayers with wailing

[47] Author unknown, 'The Holy Spirit in Korea', *The Korea Mission Field* 3:2 (February, 1907), 25.

[48] Author unknown, 'Recent Work of the Holy Spirit', *The Korea Mission Field* 3:3, Seoul, Korea: (March, 1907), 41.

the Christians themselves'.[49] American Methodist missionaries continuously acknowledged the Korean Charismatic Movement: 'The power of the Holy Spirit was present to heal' the Koreans' diseased hearts[50] and 'It was into hearts where were hid tragedies untold that God sent the power of his Holy Spirit to redeem and save'.[51] According to Brown, it was a reflection of the Korean Christians' character that they came to Christianity 'out of deeper sorrows than the self-confident Chinese and the masterful Japanese'.[52] This was an indication of the way that the moving of the Spirit especially encountered Korean diseased hearts and was perceived as an eschatological Spirit and a healing Spirit. In particular, the fire of the Spirit quickly spread through all parts of the land, and brought about a powerful zeal for the healing of *han*, and a resulting 'explosive' growth in the church. As Koreans said afterwards to the missionaries: 'Some of you go back to John Calvin, and some of you to John Wesley, but we can go back no further than 1907, when we first really knew the Lord Jesus Christ'.[53] Moffett explains that the Charismatic Movement was 'the spiritual seal on the founding charter of the Korean church'.[54] According to the Board of Foreign Missions, American Methodist missionaries reported that 'Out of it was born a new church and a new ministry in Korea'.[55]

Even today, Korean Christians have taken this experience as one of the main sources of their spiritual life. Korean mainline churches and denominations arrange at least two or three special Charismatic meetings a year, during which people gather for between a week and forty days. During these meetings, the community sings loudly with frequent hand clapping and prays aloud with many tears and emotional confessions. Most people at the meetings hope to be filled with the Holy Spirit, to gain assurance of forgiveness of sins as well as strength for the healing of wounded hearts, like the earlier Korean church. Therefore the contemporary Korean Charismatic churches,[56] which belong mainly to the Presbyterian and Methodist denominations, have also broadly

---

[49] Board of Foreign Missions, *The Religious Awakening*, 12.

[50] Board of Foreign Missions, *The Religious Awakening*, 24.

[51] Board of Foreign Missions, *The Religious Awakening*, 19.

[52] Arthur Brown, *The Mastery of the Far East* (New York: Charles Scribner's Sons, 1919), 539.

[53] Samuel Moffett, *The Christians of Korea* (New York: Friendship Press, 1962), 54.

[54] Moffett, *The Christians of Korea*, 54.

[55] Board of Foreign Missions, *The Religious Awakening*, 25.

[56] Today, there are many Charismatic Presbyterian mega-churches and Methodist mega-churches in South Korea, such as Onnuri (Presbyterian, Tonghap), Myeongseong (Presbyterian, Tonghap), Juan (Presbyterian, Tonghap), Sarangeui (Presbyterian, Hapdong), Sungeui (Methodist) and Geumran Church (Methodist).

become a 'Pentecostal type or distinctive'[57] through regular special meetings that have indigenized Christianity in Korea.

An Evaluation of the Charismatic Movement of the Contextual Healing

Many Korean scholars claimed for a long time that Charismatic meetings were designed as a search for pure religious experiences. The main features of the meetings were stirring sermons followed by public confession of sins, loud prayers and various forms of emotional expression. They thought that missionary reports of the Charismatic meetings revealed the positive impressions of the 'spirituality' of such a revival movement. The public confession of sin was ostensibly limited to immoral acts; but there was no mention of how people in 1907 felt about their national tragedy, the collective sin of the people as a nation and their social responsibility. Accordingly, Korean scholars insisted that the Charismatic Movement sets the tone for Korean Protestantism's main features: emotional, conservative, individualistic and characterized by faith in a heavenly world after death. These characteristics were inherited by the mainstreams of Korean Protestant Christianity.[58]

However, the Charismatic Movement created new social as well as individual transformations, within the contextual situation of oppression. Above all, the work of 'the Spirit' in these rituals, namely, *tongseonggido* with wailing, all night prayer, early morning prayer, fasting prayer and emotional conversion with agony, underpins the socially explosive nature of emotional pain, even if the eruptions took place in the hearts of individuals rather than in political upheavals. Each and every praying person sighed, pleaded and cried out before God in a deep sense of her or his *han*. This motive behind the people's conversion, which was closely related to their experience of oppression and poverty, however, was the collective experience of individuals. The weak and the small, the oppressed, and the poor received Pentecostalism as a uniting religion of new hope and power. The people were in dire need of sympathetic friends, hope and healing. As a result, the Charismatic meetings in 1907 solved a spiritual and a communal problem. What the missionaries or Korean scholars failed to notice, whether willingly or unwillingly, was this communal character of the experience of the healing of *han*. Today, looking back on the Charismatic Movement as the source of the spiritual renewal of Korean Christianity, even though the results were spiritual and cannot

---

[57] Jae Bum Lee , 'Pentecostal Type Distinctive and Korean Protestant Church Growth' (PhD dissertation, Fuller Theological Seminary, 1986), 7.

[58] Kwang Sun Suh , 'Hangukgidokgyoeui Jiseonggwa Banjiseong', in So Young Kim (ed.), *Hangukyeoksasokeui Gidokgyo* [Christianity in Korean History] (Seoul: KNCC, 1985), 287; Soon Kyung Park, *MinjokTongilgwa Gidokgyo* [The National Unification and Christianity] (Seoul: Hangilsa, 1987), 89-96.

adequately be assessed quantitatively, we find the collective healing experience of the 'Holy Spirit'. It transformed all dimensions of peoples' lives, including the personal, social and national strata. The Spirit of God seen as a liberator and healer was not limited to the subjective spirits of human beings. From the beginning, it was not meant to be a by-product of a social explosive or opium, but it brought about personal and social healings, which were unexpected.

In particular, social healing through the Charismatic Movement was very important within the cultural locus of Korean Pentecostalism. For example, the Charismatic Movement had an enormous religious impact on Korean people, who had been saturated by shamanistic and Confucian traditions for more than five hundred years. Many non-Christian Koreans, who were Confucianists and Buddhists, came to believe in Jesus Christ as a saviour and healer.

Furthermore, the great wave of the 'Korean Pentecost', spreading all over the nation gave rise to social movements and helped overcome structural evil under the Japanese regime.[59] The Christian contribution to Korean nationalism was extremely significant, especially through the mission schools. As an example, in 1911 the Japanese military police accused students at a Presbyterian school of plotting to assassinate the Japanese governor-general. The police arrested 123 Koreans for conspiracy, 82 of whom were Christian nationalists.[60] The history of Korean Christianity in relation to the nationalistic task reached its climax when Christians participated in the Independence Movement against Japanese colonial rule in 1919. Christians led the 1 March Independence Movement with the followers of Cheondogyo (a native messianic religion), Buddhism and Confucianism. It was a purely non-violent protest against Japanese colonialism, yet the Japanese killed almost 8,000 innocent Koreans, most of whom were Christians.[61] Fifteen signatories among thirty-three Koreans who signed the Korean Declaration of Independence were Christians, even though Christians represented only 1% of the total population at the time. Koreans from the Charismatic Movement were busy participating in the Independence Movement. It was obvious that from the Korean point of view, the church was no longer a Noah's Ark and that to be a Christian was to be a patriot. The Charismatic Movement in the healing of *han* led by 'the Spirit' continued to heal various lives in order to transform Korean *han* under

---

[59] Young Bok Kim, *Hangukminjungeui Sahoejeongi* [The Social Biography of Korean *Minjung*] (Seoul: Hangilsa, 1987), 121-24; Herbert Kane, *A Global View of Christian Missions: From Pentecost and the Present* (Grand Rapids, MI: Baker Book House, 1975), 268.

[60] The Institute of Korean Church History Studies, *Hangukgidokgyoeui Yeoksa I* [A History of Korean Church I] (Seoul, Korea: Christian Literature Press, 1989), 312-15.

[61] The Institute of Korean Church History Studies, *Hangukgidokgyoeui Yeoksa II* [A History of Korean Church II] (Seoul, Korea: Christian Literature Press, 1990), 35-41; Jong Chun Park, *Crawl with God, Dance in the Spirit: A Creative Formation of Korean Theology of the Spirit* (Nashville: Abingdon Press, 1998), 29-31.

Japanese occupation. Therefore Korean Pentecostalism was able to participate in political reform and went beyond individualistic healing, even though western missionaries seemed to ignore socio-political reform at that time.[62] As a result, indigenous Pentecostalism became the central force in the Independence Movement against Japan, and so influenced the social action of the Korean people. It also played an important part in sharing the suffering of people and in healing them, and the churches were widely identified with the Korean national cause.[63]

Conclusion

The Korean Charismatic Movement helped to relieve the *minjung's han*, stricken by despair and humiliation through wars and occupation. No part of Korea has been left untouched by indigenous Pentecostalism, thanks to the healing of *han* among the Charismatic *minjung*.[64] In 1908 Sung Man Yi, the future President of Korea, explained, 'She [Korea] has caught a vision. She has turned her eyes towards heaven and cried: O Lord, heal my wounded heart and lift me up in thine arms'.[65] The Charismatic Movement apparently placed Koreans 'in a position where the Holy Spirit can work on their hearts' for *han*.[66] Since the early Korean church was a contextual healing community, the development of Charismatic Pentecostalism as an extension of the healing of *han* among the *minjung* had been a major feature of mission throughout the last century.

---

[62] Klaus Fiedler, 'Evangelical Mission Theology I', in Karl Müller, Theo Sundermeier, Stephen B. Bevans, Richard H. Bliese (eds.), *Dictionary of Mission: Theology, History, Perspectives* (Maryknoll, NY: Orbis Books, 1998), 145.

[63] In Ung Son, 'Heundeulrineun Gyohoewisang Heundeulrilttae Seomgija' [The Church Crisis, The Diaconal Ministry], *Christian Thought* 475 (July, 1998), 39.

[64] *Minjung* theologians define *minjung* as the people who are politically oppressed, socially alienated, and economically exploited. Boo Woong Yoo views *minjung* as two kinds of *minjung*. The one is 'socio-political *minjung*' and the other is 'Pentecostal *minjung*'. However, I wonder whether socio-political *minjung* can be related to Korean Pentecostalism, because most *minjung* churches which were closely associated with *minjung* theology were short-lived in the 1980s. I will define Charismatic *minjung* as the mainline Christians who are associated with suffering of survival created by wars, patriarchal suppression, poverty and sicknesses in Korean history. See Boo Woong Yoo, *Korean Pentecostalism: Its History and Theology*, Studies in the Intercultural History of Christianity Series 52 (Frankfurt am Main, Germany: Verlag Peter Lang, 1988).

[65] Sung Man Yi, 'Appeals of Native Christians', *The Korea Mission Field* 4:6 (June, 1908), 96.

[66] Author unknown, 'The Korean Revival', *The Korea Mission Field* 4:4 (April, 1908), 62.

Moreover, it is important to point out that the Charismatic Movement was not led by Pentecostal denominations but by the mainline Korean churches, the Presbyterians and the Methodists.[67] In other words, the Charismatic Movement originated not primarily from a pre-determined impetus of American missionaries, their doctrine or from existing Pentecostal denominations, but rather from the same source as the Wesleyan revivals in England and Pentecostalism in America,[68] namely, a ritually perceived 'visitation of the Holy Spirit'. Therefore, Harold Hunter points out, 'paradigms designed for North American Pentecostals do not apply to Korea which has a totally different history'.[69]

In this context, one of the greatest mistakes made by western scholars is that they have not recognized the importance of the context for theology and religions, and hence have tried to force the transplantation of western form of worship onto other ethnic groups. In particular, Classical Pentecostal missionaries insisted that any variation from western norms was somehow 'un-Christian'. For example, Synan defines indigenous Pentecostalism like Korean Pentecostalism as 'quasi' Pentecostal movements because they were begun without 'western' Pentecostal mission board support.[70] Furthermore, Synan classifies the American Pentecostal movement and global Pentecostalism according to three historical stages with the development of Classical Pentecostals (1910s), mainline Protestant and Catholic Charismatic movements (1960s), and the Third Wave renewal Pentecostals (1980s).[71] They view Classical Pentecostalism as the historical origin and development of the Pentecostal Movement.[72] Moreover, Edwin Orr sees the Welsh Revival as the historical root of the modern Revival movements[73] even though he states that

---

[67] Hollenweger, *Pentecostalism*, 101.

[68] Martha Huntley, *Caring, Growing, Changing: A History of the Protestant Mission in Korea* (New York: Friendship Press, 1984), 131.

[69] Harold Hunter, 'Two Movements of the Holy Spirit in the 20th Century?- A Closer Look at Global Pentecostalism and Ecumenism', in Young Hoon Lee (ed.), *Asia Issues on Pentecostalism* (Seoul: International Theological Institute, 1998), 216.

[70] Vinson Synan, 'Perspectives on the Holy Spirit Movements of the Twentieth Century', in International Theological Institute (eds.), *The Works of Holy Spirit in Church History* (Seoul: International Theological Institute, 1995), 163.

[71] Synan, *The Spirit Said 'Grow'*.

[72] See Daniel Albrecht, *Rites in the Spirit: A Ritual Approach to Pentecostal/Charismatic Spirituality* (Sheffield: Sheffield Academic Press, 1999), 30-39.

[73] Orr, *Evangelical Awakenings in Eastern Asia*, X, 12, 14-15. Edwin Orr classifies the Evangelical revival according to five historical stages: 'The First Awakening ran its course in fifty years, and was followed by the Second Awakening in 1792, the Third in 1830, the Fourth in 1858-59, the Fifth in 1905 (X)'. He insists that 'It [the Welsh Revival as the Fifth General Awakening] was the most extensive Evangelical Awakening of all time, reviving Anglican, Baptist, Congregational, Disciple, Lutheran,

the Korean Pentecost was partly indigenous and of 'missionary derivation'.[74] He seems to understand Korean Pentecostalism as the historical extension of the Welsh Revival. However, the historical formation and development of Korean Pentecostalism was initially formed by the Korean Charismatic Movement (1903-1907), which had already started before the Welsh Revival (1904-1905).

Korean Pentecostalism differs from Classical Pentecostalism in three ways: 1) date and place of origin, 2) denominational background, and 3) contextual theology and praxis. An important distinction in the formation of indigenous Pentecostalism (1880s-1900s) in Korea is that the Korean Charismatic Movement (1903-1907) occurred before the coming of North American forms of Classical Pentecostalism, unlike in the USA. It also developed as a contextual healing movement, actualized by the Spirit, prior to the introduction of the 'divine healing' ministry of the Pentecostal denominations. It is significant to remember that healings of the Korean churches are contextual because of the cultural character of Korean Pentecostalism as the healing of *han*. Koreans responded to contextual healing from where they were, not from where the missionaries were. In other words, Koreans have contextually responded to ministry in Korean culture rather than to the American missionaries' experiences in their land. So many Protestants have been greatly affected by the Korean Charismatic development which related to the healing of *han* that existed in Korea. These factors explain why Korean Pentecostalism is so different from American Pentecostalism.

However, Peter Wagner explains that the Charismatic Movement began as a renewal movement within the mainline Protestant churches in North America in the 1960s. On this point, there will be a problem if scholars, consciously or unconsciously, view the local identity through their own lens of orientalism,[75] because Classical Pentecostal scholars who hold to mistaken views of

---

Methodist, Presbyterian and Reformed churches and other evangelical bodies throughout Europe and North America, Australia and South Africa, and their daughter churches and missionary causes throughout Asia, Africa, and Latin America, winning more than five million folk to each country' (12).

[74] Orr, *Evangelical Awakenings in Eastern Asia*, 26.

[75] According to Edward W. Said, he defines orientalism as more superior western identity in comparison with all of the Third World peoples and cultures. He points out, 'Orientalism is…a collective notion identifying "us" Europeans as against all "those" non-Europeans, and it can be argued that the major component in European culture is precisely what made that culture hegemonic both in and outside Europe. As a result, it could be regarded as 'the theatre of effective western knowledge about the Orient' while the period of orientalism coincides exactly with the period of European expansion. Edward W. Said, *Orientalism: Western Concepts of the Orient* (London, Penguin Books, 1995), 7, 41, 43; R.S. Sugirtharajah, *Asian Biblical Hermeneutics and Postcolonialism* (Maryknoll, NY: Orbis Books, 1998), 101-102.

orientalism, fail to explain the cultural identity of local Pentecostalisms, which may be different from western Classical Pentecostalism. Hollenweger predicts that an indigenous Pentecostal theology will emerge that will be 'different from western-based (Catholic, Protestant, evangelical and Pentecostal) theologies and missiologies'.[76] Global Pentecostalism must be delivered from 'its Babylonian bourgeois captivity'.[77] Therefore, we should interpret such localizing concepts as 'Pentecostal' only after researching carefully their contexts.[78] Each local Pentecostal movement must be studied from within its own internal culture and context, even if the universal nature of global Pentecostalism is recognizable in the construction of local identities. It should be acknowledged that what at first glance appears to be global Pentecostalism is in fact ultimately a series of different local Pentecostalisms.[79] It should also be accepted that as there was not a *kerygma* but the historical event in the beginning of the early church, in similar ways, as shown above, there was not a Pentecostal dogma, but Korean Charismatic existential experiences at the beginning of Pentecostalism in Korea. Korean Pentecostalism was not based on human-made doctrines or forms of institutionalization at the beginning of a mission stage, but on the reality of spiritual communities. What is true for Korea is one sign of the broad nature of Pentecostalism. Pentecostalism is not restricted to a narrow doctrinal and denominational level, but embraces many nations, including those in the West, Asia, Latin America and Africa.

---

[76] Hollenweger, *Pentecostalism*, 306.

[77] Hollenweger, *The Pentecostals,* xxvi. He acknowledges that 'they [global Pentecostals] also made it more difficult for me to accept only one valid interpretation of the Bible, namely the critical analytical western approach, which is so firmly rooted in the European Reformation with its emphasis on exact scholarly exegesis'; Hollenweger, *Pentecostalism*, 301, 303. Hollenweger seems to agree with Pomervile's assessment that 'Pomervile sees one of the great deficiencies of western theology as its tendency towards what he calls 'Protestant Scholasticism'.

[78] For the useful discussion on the local and global Pentecostalism, see Mike Featherstone (ed.), *Global Culture: Nationalism, Globalization and Modernity* (London, SAGE Publications, 1990); Sherron Kay George, 'Local-Global Mission: The Cutting Edge', *Missiology: An International Review* 28:2 (April, 2000), 187-97.

[79] Dana Robert, 'Shifting Southward: Global Christianity since 1945', *International Bulletin* 24:2 (April, 2000), 56.

PART FIVE

SUMMATION

Whither Pentecostalism?

Simon Chan

This conference on Asian Pentecostalism reflects in many ways common patterns and trends in Pentecostal studies in the wider world. This is to be expected as the Pentecostal movement is now perhaps the most globalized Christian movement (if David Barrett's statistics are any guide). What I would like to do in this summary reflection is to comment on a few conspicuous features and trends in current Pentecostal studies which reappeared at this conference. They involve methodological questions, but inevitably theological questions as well. They show at once both the exciting possibilities as well as potential dangers.

On the Term 'Pentecostal'

One of the issues that recurred throughout the conference is the question of definition. The problem is acute in view of the wide diversity of groups and movements described as Pentecostal or Charismatic. I suspect that the term has come to mean different things to different people, but most of us simply assume that everyone else knows what we are referring to when we use the term Pentecostal or Charismatic. It may be some time yet before scholars of Pentecostalism could come to a generally agreed definition. In the meantime, from now on, they will have to preface their study with some kind of working definition. On what basis do we consider a movement Pentecostal? Implied in this question is a crying need to refine our methodology. Current Pentecostal scholarship appears to favour a more phenomenological approach focusing on 'religious experience'. This is perhaps one of the most noticeable shifts in Pentecostal historiography in recent years.

Classical Pentecostal historians in the past had tended to view the origin of the Pentecostal movement as a single centre in North America, from where the movement fanned out into other parts of the world. This view has now been challenged by other historians. (See Hwa Yung and Allan Anderson's essays.) According to the newer view, not only are there many geographical centres of origin, Pentecostalism is from its beginning a multi-racial and multi-cultural phenomenon. That these facts were largely ignored previously is not only indicative of White bias but also of a certain hegemonic inclination prevalent among North American White Pentecostals. (One is immediately reminded of the way the White contemporaries of William Seymour consistently downplayed his significance in the development of Pentecostalism in North America).[1]

This newer Pentecostal historiography has no doubt contributed to a richer understanding of the nature of Pentecostalism. But I would like to raise a few caveats. I think it would be a mistake if one should think that the new explanation should replace the old, or that it is somehow 'better' than the old because of certain questionable assumptions commonly associated with the latter view. The fact that the older view has been associated with race bias and a colonialist mindset does not, for that reason, make it invalid. The fact of the matter is that both are conditioned by their respective historical contexts. Historical explanations are not value-free. If we grant that earlier histories have been coloured by the historian's social location, we must also grant the possibility of those favouring a multi-centre origin being similarly influenced. We live in what is being frequently described as a postmodern world. It is a world in which pluralism is as much taken for granted as 'universal reason' was the basic plausibility structure of the world of the Enlightenment. It is not difficult to see that a single-centre explanation fits well into a world where universal reason and the meta-narrative are taken as self-evident truths, whereas in a pluralistic culture a multi-centre explanation seems more plausible.

What this shift really entails is a redefinition of Pentecostalism itself and it is over the question of the definition of Pentecostalism that we must consider the relative strength and weakness of the two approaches. Is Pentecostalism to be defined in terms of actual historical links with a movement which calls itself Pentecostal? In this definition, history, tradition and key theological concepts are essential components in determining what it is that makes a movement Pentecostal. The advantage of this approach to the study of the history of Pentecostalism is that it sets clear parameters within which the term Pentecostal could be unambiguously applied. We could include under the term Pentecostal any movement that is historically connected with the original movement through persons with a set of similar beliefs and practices. (See Michael Berunger's essay.) The question that might be raised with this definition is whether it might be too limiting to be useful in assessing other Pentecostal-like movements that do not have any direct links with the 'original' movement, such as the indigenous Korean 'charismatic' movement. (See Chong Hee Jeong's essay.) Or is Pentecostalism to be defined in terms of a cluster of religious experiences understood phenomenologically? Here, what is crucial for understanding Pentecostalism are *practices* like healing, speaking in tongues, exorcism etc. rather than the *explanations* given by the practitioners themselves. Historical links are not crucial to the definition. The first definition is usually implied in the single-centre approach and the second definition is

---

[1] Douglas J. Nelson, 'For Such A Time as This: The Story of Bishop William J. Seymour and the Azusa Street Revival' (PhD. Dissertation, Birmingham, 1981).

implied in the multi-centre approach. Scholars of Pentecostalism will continue to struggle with the problem of definition for a long time yet. But this is not a new problem. Scholars of puritanism and pietism too encounter a similar problem.

Theological Criteria

For heuristic purposes I have stated their difference in rather stark terms. Modern Pentecostal scholarship appears to be clearly tilted towards a multi-centre approach. This is not necessarily a bad thing. For one thing, it opens up other ways of seeing how spiritual movements are connected besides the strictly historical connection. The possibility for such an approach exists, for example, in the case of the early Korean charismatic movement among Presbyterian and Methodist churches and the classical Pentecostal movement that came in later. What is problematic is that along with this approach, Pentecostalism is now largely understood in phenomenological and sociological terms.

But an adequate definition of Pentecostalism cannot be restricted to phenomenological description. It will have to include some historical and theological components. What we have noticed is that the theological component is decidedly muted. A spiritual movement is all too readily classified as Pentecostal largely on the basis of phenomenological similarities. This is the problem I have with Gotthard Oblau's essay. There are of course a number of explicitly theological papers at the conference, but the descriptive ones tend to leave out the significant theological symbols by which many Pentecostals define themselves. This has led one respondent to ask in the account of Pentecostalism in China why no reference was made to Spirit-baptism.

Classical Pentecostal beliefs like Spirit-baptism and initial evidence hardly feature in the definition of Pentecostalism. Critics may well have been right to point out that these doctrines were badly formulated to begin with. But any 'objective' investigation of Pentecostalism should at least ask questions like: Why are these doctrines so important to so many Pentecostals? Perhaps in their linking of baptism in the Holy Spirit with glossolalia they are trying to articulate something quite essential to their experience, even though they may have articulated it badly? What does that tell us about how Pentecostals understand themselves? If we ignore the theological criterion, we are eliminating what is perhaps the most essential dimension of a movement's self-understanding. A religious movement is what it is because it distinguishes itself from others by a set of beliefs, practices and ritual which reenacts the beliefs. By theological criterion I do not mean raising such questions as: Does (say) the Chinese Christians' practice of divine healing measure up to certain theological norms? Are their practices theologically sound or adequate? These are normative theological questions,[2] and a historian *qua* historian is not obliged to ask or answer such questions. Rather, what I mean by theological criterion is some such questions as: What are the central theological symbols in the various movements that we regard as Pentecostal that might help the historian have a better understanding of the way these movements understand themselves? How do they explain their own experience of the Spirit? Some of these movements may have more developed theologies than others. But even if their theology is of a rudimentary nature, it is still imperative to ask if it bears any affinity with the more developed forms. I would venture one step further; even if a movement has no explicit theology, one could still ask if there is an implicit theology that bears some similarities with those with an explicit theology. Without applying this theological criterion (the historical question aside), I do not think that it is legitimate to call a movement Pentecostal solely on the basis of common experiences. There is, after all, no such thing as a religious experience without any theological interpretation.

A phenomenological definition of Pentecostalism will tend to end up becoming too inclusive and overloaded. For instance, on the basis of a phenomenological definition, it would be difficult to see how the holiness movement and the Pentecostal movement could be distinguished from each other. Some holiness groups engaged in 'Pentecostal' practices like divine healing. Both use terms like baptism in the Spirit. Yet historically they became distinguished from each other as their traditions diverged and as their theological positions and practices became more finely nuanced. A phenomenological approach would not have been able to make the distinction. Yet in many instances, especially in studies of Pentecostalism in the non-western world, one often finds disparate movements lumped together (usually by western interpreters) as 'Pentecostal' when prior examination of their historical and theological traditions would have been required to determine if they are in fact related. (See Edmond Tang's essay.) Are they all Pentecostal only because they appear to have similar religious experiences? In what sense is folk Catholicism in the Philippines charismatic? (See R.G. dela Cruz' response to Lode Wostyn.) On what basis do we judge that their experiences are similar? If, as David Barrett affirms, there is such an 'incredible variety and diversity' of Pentecostalisms, so that one is forced to speak of 'prepentecostals', 'quasi-pentecostals', 'indigenous pentecostals', ethnic pentecostals', 'postpentecostals', 'indigenous charismatics', 'grassroots neocharismatics' and a host of other Pentecostals and Charismatics,[3] one

---

[2] For an example of raising normative theological questions, see David Middlemiss, *Interpreting Charismatic Experience* (London: SCM Press, 1996).

[3] David B. Barrett (ed.), *World Christian Encyclopedia*, 2nd ed. (Oxford: Oxford University Press, 2001), I, 19.

wonders if the term Pentecostal or Charismatic still serves as a useful term of predication. Is it not in danger of death by a thousand qualifications?

Responsible Syncretism?

The shift in understanding of Pentecostal origin is but one example of a number of significant changes that are taking place in current Pentecostal studies as Pentecostal scholarship gradually comes to terms with postmodernity. Another methodological issue is how Pentecostalism relates to the larger world. Hollenweger has thrown the challenge to Pentecostals to engage in 'responsible syncretism'.[4] Here again, basic methodological questions must be asked. I suspect that the call for Pentecostals to be engaged is usually based on a particular understanding of social engagement, namely, the Niebuhrian Christ-and-Culture model, where 'Christ' derives its meaning from the larger public discourse of 'culture'. But there are other models of engagement that may in fact be more appropriate for Pentecostals. Some stories of Pentecostal communities in Korea reveal another form of *Minjung* theology which influences society not by manipulating power structures but by being a 'community of character'. This type of engagement is closer to the model advocated by John Yoder and Stanley Hauerwas.[5] Many of the papers have demonstrated that Pentecostals are already engaging the world; the more important questions are, how are they engaging the world and how will they emerge from it? Before we can answer these questions, we need to ask a preliminary question of what syncretism is and how it compares with other forms of engagement, such as contextualization. Contextualization may be defined as the attempt to bring the gospel message to a context in a manner that is relevant to that context. The contextualizer is sensitive to the issues, concerns and thought forms of the context and seeks to present the gospel that addresses these issues and concerns and in a way that is consistent with the receiving culture's way of thinking. It may happen that in the process of contextualizing the gospel, terms and ideas are borrowed from the context but they are always reinterpreted in accordance with gospel norms. Syncretism, on the other hand, involves appropriating material contents from the context in order to bridge the gap between gospel and context.

The result of syncretism is that instead of the gospel challenging culture, it becomes a part of culture. Syncretism operates on two presuppositions:

1) that the gospel is too distant from the receiving culture because of excessive cultural accretions in the sending culture; and

---

[4] Hollenweger, *Pentecostalism: Origins and Development Worldwide* (Peabody, MA: Hendrickson Press, 1997), 132-41.

[5] John Yoder, *The Politics of Jesus* (Grand Rapids: Eerdmans, 1972); Stanley Hauerwas, *A Community of Character* (Notre Dame: University of Notre Dame Press, 1981).

2) that some of the material contents in the receiving culture are not only consistent with the gospel but actually a part of the gospel itself. The dissimilarities between cultures in the first presupposition are overcome by the substantial similarities in the second. The basis for the second affirmation is that God's Spirit is already at work in the receiving culture. This is the context in which the concept of *creator spiritus* is usually understood nowadays. Wonsuk Ma's analysis of Pentecostalism in Korea helps to clarify the difference between syncretism and contextualization. Ma argues that Pentecostalism in Korea as represented by Yonggi Cho is contextualization rather than syncretism. Cho's message addresses the problems and issues of the *minjung* and is presented in a thought form that the *minjung* are familiar with. At the same time, Pentecostal Christians, with their experience of radical conversion, have consistently distanced themselves from shamanism itself. If Ma is right, it shows that Pentecostalism at its best accentuates much more strongly the tension of being 'in the world' but not 'of the world'. It is because of this consistent distancing in the Pentecostal tradition that Pentecostals will not be comfortable with the call to engage in syncretism. Syncretism would simply dissolve the tension.

If we accept the above working definitions of contextualization and syncretism, many of the biblical examples of 'responsible syncretism' cited by Hollenweger are actually examples of contextualization rather than syncretism. The one remaining problematic is the concept of *creator spiritus*. Sometimes the way the problem is stated is as if it is between those who believe in the Spirit's working in the world and those who don't. But the issue is not whether the Spirit of God is at work in the world; the real issue is, *what* is the Spirit doing in the world? Increasingly *creator spiritus* has been invoked in connection with issues of ecology and the status of the world religions. Nobody would deny the importance of these issues. We live in a world where the ecological crisis has deeply affected all aspects of life everywhere; and in Asia, where Christianity exists side by side (sometimes uneasily) with the major world religions, no responsible Christian can afford to ignore the question of inter-religious relations. Hollenweger is therefore right to raise the issue with Pentecostals. Pentecostals (and all Christians, for that matter) need to find their proper place in a pluralistic world. But I have my doubts about whether the doctrine of the *creator spiritus* is the way to address the issues, especially the issue of non-Christian religions.[6] In both scriptures and the Christian tradition *creator spiritus* is a carefully nuanced doctrine and set squarely within the context of the history of redemption, in the history of the trinitarian life.[7] But in

---

[6] See my *Pentecostal Theology and the Christian Spiritual Tradition* (Sheffield: Sheffield Academic Press, 2000), 110-115.

[7] E.g. C.F.D. Moule, *The Holy Spirit* (London: Mowbrays, 1978); Tom Smail, *The Giving Gift: The Holy Spirit in Person* (London: Hodder and Stoughton, 1988).

our zeal for inter-religious dialogue, *creator spiritus* has been overwrought and made to do the work it is not meant to do. That this is largely an effect of our historical conditionedness can be seen in the way inter-religious dialogue has been understood by Christians over the years. In the 1960s and '70s the theological basis for dialogue was usually grounded in the cosmic Christ.[8] But with Pentecostalism now in ascendancy we appeal to *creator spiritus*. If we go further back into Christian history, the theological category for understanding God's relation to the world at large is neither the cosmic Christ nor the *creator spiritus* but the *vestigia Dei*. Within Christianity there has been a long history of positive relations with and assessment of other religions going all the way back to St Paul's preaching on Mars Hill and Justin Martyr among the church fathers. (Paul did not hesitate to identify the 'unknown god' of the Greeks with the Father of our Lord Jesus Christ.) But the link between Christianity and other religions was made mostly in terms of God the Father's creation of the world rather than in terms of Christology or pneumatology. This is very much in keeping with the first article of the creed. The God who created the world has left his footprints in creation—footprints that lead the truth seeker to God's revelation in Christ through the Spirit.[9] It is the *vestigia Dei* that sets the proper context for understanding the presence of truth in other religions. The *vestigia Dei* concept may provide a better account of the story of the Magi than the cosmic Christ and *creator spiritus* concepts alone could. What is *materially* present in the Magi, the substantial point of contact, are the footprints of God. The Magi followed the footprints of God and were led by the Star (something belonging to the order of creation) to worship the Son of God. All that is true in creation and in other religions is by virtue of the work of the Father, and is anticipatory of the gospel—a *praeparatio evangelii* and not the gospel itself. We know it to be true only when it leads to Christ. Perhaps some might find *vestigia Dei* too static a concept in a world accustomed to thinking in existential and dynamic terms, whereas *creator spiritus* implies a more dynamic and on-going relationship of God with the world. But isn't our preference for more dynamic categories itself largely a reflection of our historical conditionedness? In the world dominated by quantum dynamics in the physical sciences and process thought in philosophy and theology,[10] people are conditioned to react favourably towards dynamic images and negatively towards essentialist ones.

---

[8] As seen, e.g. in the East Asian Christian Conference (now the Christian Conference of Asia) 1970 statement on inter-religious dialogue. See Douglas J. Elwood (ed.), *What Asian Christians Are Thinking* (Manila: New Day Publishers, 1978), 335-38.

[9] Cf. the response of Korean Pentecostal Sang Hwan Lee to World Alliance of Reformed Churches-Pentecostal Dialogue. Lee noted that the role of the Father in his revelation in creation was neglected in the document. See *Pneuma* 23:1 (Spring 2001), 63-64.

[10] This may explain the attraction of some even among the more conservative Christians to 'open theism'.

The problem is that we are often not aware that our choices are shaped by our unconscious assumptions. This is evidenced by the fact that in our eagerness to find the *creator spiritus* in other religions, issues get blurred and distorted. For example, the call heard repeatedly to reassess the work of the Spirit vis-à-vis creation is often predicated on a rather romanticized vision of other religions. At the same time, we have been reminded not a few times at this conference of how Christians, especially western missionaries, in the past had simply dismissed other religions as 'of the devil'. In either case we are given at best a caricature. Such caricatures are not helpful if we are to develop a serious theology of religions. But the reason why such caricatures are often left unchallenged is because they have become part of our unconscious assumptions shaped by the prevailing plausibility structure.

The tendency to play fast and loose with *creator spiritus* extends also to the language of the demonic, another key area in Pentecostalism.[11] Traditionally, exorcism has been an important part of Pentecostal practice. This tradition goes back to ancient times, especially among the Desert Fathers. What is new is that martial language is spilling all over into other areas as well, especially in mission. To be sure, the warfare metaphor was used in the larger Christian tradition, e.g. among the Desert Fathers and the seventeenth century Puritans. But it was understood more broadly with reference to 'the three enemies of the soul': the world, the flesh and the devil. Nowadays, however, warfare language is applied rather narrowly to the demonic realm. At the same time the world and the flesh and a wide range of other concerns are subsumed under this narrowed understanding of spiritual warfare. This is due largely to the influence of the Third Wavers, especially Peter Wagner and Charles Kraft. Through the Fuller School of World Missions, a substantial number of missiologists from Asia[12] have been trained to engage in spiritual warfare, spiritual mapping, identifying territorial spirits etc. Mission is understood as power encounters; proclaiming the good news is translated into expanding the kingdom of God into enemy territory; prayer is the tool for tearing down spiritual strongholds etc. The language of warfare narrowly restricted to the demonic realm has become the dominant mode of expression in mission thinking and practice among many modern Pentecostals and Charismatics. Like *creator spiritus*, the language of the demonic has been overworked and made to do things it is probably not meant to do. Demonology has become a useful shorthand in modern parlance for dealing with things that one perceives as particularly hideous. Thus we hear of the demon of racism, sexism and patriarchy. But it is also the language that polarizes positions into sheer right and sheer wrong, pure

---

[11] See Amos Yong's essay. Yong's description of Pentecostal demonology is somewhat anachronistic, being based largely on Third Wavers' rhetoric.

[12] I understand that the Korean presence in the School of World Mission is especially strong.

light and pure darkness (cf. the late Ayatollah Khomeiny calling the United States of America 'the Great Satan'). Sometimes it is also used to transfer responsibility from human agents to some other extrahuman agent: 'The devil made me do it'; 'I'm a product of a deprived childhood, a victim of the demon of sexism'. Against this dangerous misuse of demonology language the Christian tradition offers a richer and more nuanced vocabulary when it distinguishes between the world, the flesh, and the devil.

If Pentecostal scholarship is to make real gains in the future it will need to exercise greater discernment of spirits. It must exorcise itself from obsession with the demonic (or, for that matter, with *creator spiritus*)! It cannot afford to simply flow with the modern Zeitgeist. Pentecostalism has a critical tradition of being 'not of this world'. Will it lose that tradition in the twenty-first century? It is ironical that in its obsession with the demonic, modern Pentecostalism has unwittingly accommodated itself to the other two enemies of the soul: the world and the flesh. It's easy to point out the worldliness among TV evangelists, but there is another kind of worldliness among Pentecostal scholars. Some perhaps in their eagerness to gain acceptability have simply jumped onto the latest theological bandwagon without much discernment. I cite one example: the use of inclusive language of a rather convoluted kind in a respectable journal like *Pneuma*. (Not all forms of inclusive language are wrong, but some are theologically doubtful).[13] It is these small adjustments which are a cause for concern. Pentecostals are in real danger of over-stretching their theological language to accommodate what they perceive to be the significant issues of the times. Ecology and religious pluralism are indeed vital issues that they must address. But in trying to discover a distinctively Pentecostal response, they run the risk of using their sources uncritically. As the Pentecostal movement gains wider recognition and respectability, it needs all the more to know who its real friends are. Like Rehoboam of old, we may find out too late that our real friends are not our contemporaries who would say nice things about us, but the trusted advisors of our forebears whose words may not be agreeable to our ears (1 Kgs 12. 6-11).

If Pentecostalism is to move forward over the next century as a vibrant, living tradition, it needs to reevaluate its present trajectory. Pentecostalism with its strongly eschatological focus is a forward-looking movement. Perhaps it is time to readjust its focus to include a backward look even as it seeks to grapple with current contextual issues. By looking back I do not mean merely back to Azusa Street or some other idealized 'Pentecostal-like' happenings. It needs to go much further back and relocate itself within the Great Tradition. The problem with most Pentecostals and Charismatics (other than those in the

---

[13] See David Wells' critique of the document on the dialogue between the World Alliance of Reformed Churches and the Pentecostals in *Pneuma* 23:1 (Spring 2001), 49-50.

Catholic and Orthodox traditions) is that any reference to tradition tends to trigger a negative reaction. Isn't Pentecostalism a protest movement against dead and stifling traditions? Isn't the scripture alone sufficient? Pentecostals (as well as most low church Protestants) need to learn that it is ultimately not Azusa Street but the Great Tradition that bequeaths to them and preserves their true identity as Pentecostals, enabling them to distinguish between essentials and peripherals, truth and falsehood. The Great Tradition is like a great river. At the edges we cannot quite tell where the river ends and the bank begins. This is the realm of the non-essentials, the place where we would do well not to dwell too long. But in the middle of the river we can say unambiguously: 'This *is* the River! This is where we reset our trajectory and negotiate safely into the future, to the End'. The fact that Pentecostalism is rooted in many Christian traditions, as Hollenweger has shown in *Pentecostalism: Origins and Development Worldwide*, is all the more reason why Pentecostals must not simply be content with telling their own hundred year old story. They must develop a catholic perspective, see their own story as part of the on-going story of the one holy, catholic and apostolic Church, if it is not to end up becoming 'more Pentecostal but less Christian' (Ma)—if it is not to end up becoming another ideology struggling to preserve its narrow, vested interest.

EPILOGUE

Allan Anderson

This has been an unusual book, not only because it is the first time this material has appeared in English, but because of the groundbreaking nature of its contents. We have sought to portray an important feature of Asian Christianity about which little has been written. These studies have raised many interesting methodological, historical and theological questions that the coming generation of scholarship will deal with. Although this book may have raised more questions than answers, we hope that it will be to some extent a benchmark for the future. One thing is for certain: these studies have demonstrated that the very nature of Christianity in Asia is changing rapidly, as it is doing in many other parts of the globe, and that the 'Charismatic face' of Christianity will continue to play a significant role in the religious world of the twenty-first century.

There are gaps in our knowledge. We have only scratched on the surface of the vastness of Chinese Christianity where western categories mean nothing at all. There are meaningful expressions of Christianity in Taiwan, Thailand, Vietnam, Nepal and the former Soviet countries of Central Asia, about which we know little. The questions surrounding the existence and role of a conservative and rather exclusivist form of Christianity in a religiously pluralistic society have hardly been touched on. Amos Yong's paper has sought to raise some of these issues in a Buddhist context. The diachronic and synchronic relationships between the earlier revival movements and the present-day Charismatic Christianity are still unclear, as is the question of origins.

It is my conviction that Pentecostals in different parts of the world have yet to come to grips with the particular role the 'freedom in the Spirit' has given them to formulate, often unconsciously, a theology that has meaning for people in different life situations. This is one of the most important features of Pentecostalism, and one that we often overlook. My own work among African Pentecostals has sought to demonstrate that theology is more than written, academic theology; it is also to be found in the preaching, rituals and practices of churches that have contextualized Christianity in such a way as to make it really meaningful to ordinary people. This is 'enacted theology' or 'theology in practice',[1] and it is found in Pentecostalism all over the world, and Asia is certainly no exception.

The extent of Pentecostal and Charismatic forms of Christianity in the religious diversity of Asia is seldom recognized. Indeed, many forms of Pentecostalism in much of the world are fundamentally different from the Pentecostal and Charismatic movements in the western world. This international movement is no importation of American Christianity. One of the main reasons for the phenomenal growth of Pentecostalism in the past century has been its remarkable ability to adapt itself to different cultural contexts and give authentically contextualized expressions to Christianity. Pentecostalism is inherently adaptable: the vibrancy, enthusiasm, spontaneity and spirituality for which Pentecostals are so well known and their willingness to address the problems of sickness, poverty, unemployment, loneliness, evil spirits and sorcery has directly contributed to this growth.

Evangelical scholars have spoken of 'indigenization' for a long time, and even Pentecostal missionary scholars like Melvin Hodges have written profoundly about an 'indigenous church'.[2] 'Indigenization' assumes that the gospel message and Christian theology is the same in all cultures and contexts, and tends to relate the Christian message to traditional cultures. Western Pentecostal missionaries have often supported the idea of a self-supporting, self-governing and self-propagating ('three self') church. But 'contextualization', on the other hand, assumes that every theology is influenced by its particular context, and must be if it is to be relevant. It relates the Christian message to all contexts and cultures, especially including those undergoing rapid social change. The ideas of 'contextual theology' were first formulated in the offices of the World Council of Churches in 1972.[3] Whereas In the West, particularly in North America where the evangelical/ ecumenical divide was most acute, this made the ideas more difficult for evangelical scholars to accept, although many of them had used different words to describe the same ideas, speaking of a 'deeper indigenization', or words to that effect. The rise of particular 'contextual theologies' like 'liberation theology' in Latin America, 'Black theology' among African Americans and South Africans, and 'Minjung theology' in Korea increased Evangelical concerns that this new trend in theology would lead to 'syncretism' and a placing of culture above God's revelation in the Bible. Gradually, evangelical scholars like Charles

---

[1] Allan Anderson, *Zion and Pentecost: The Spirituality and Experience of Pentecostal and Zionist/ Apostolic Churches in South Africa* (Pretoria: University of South Africa Press, 2000), 2; Allan Anderson, *African Reformation: African Initiated Christianity in the 20th Century* (Trenton, NJ & Asmara, Eritrea: Africa World Press, 2001), 217.

[2] Melvin L. Hodges, *The Indigenous Church* (Springfield, MO: Gospel Publishing House, 1953).

[3] Norman Thomas (ed.), *Readings in World Mission* (London: SPCK, 1995), 175.

Kraft and David. Hesselgrave began to give prominence to the importance of culture in the seventies and eighties.[4] Kraft spoke of 'the constant message in alternative forms', and of 'dynamic-equivalence theologizing',and that 'all theologizing is culture-bound interpretation and communication of God's revelation'.[5] South African missiologist David Bosch declares that all theologies were contextual theologies, but that we should not confuse the essential and universal aspects of the Christian message from the local, contextual ones.[6] Similarly, Lesslie Newbigin says that 'every communication of the gospel is already culturally conditioned', but reminds us that the gospel 'is not an empty form into which everyone is free to pour his or her own content', but that the content of the gospel is 'Jesus Christ in the fullness of his ministry, death, and resurrection'.[7]

The importance of contextualization is now more readily accepted by evangelicals, although they have their own interpretation of what this means. Dean Gilliland, a North American evangelical scholar, has recently defined the goal of contextualization as 'to enable, insofar as it is humanly possible, an understanding of what it means that Jesus Christ, the Word, is authentically experienced in each and every human situation'.[8] He says that the Christian message must be proclaimed in the framework of the worldview of the particular people to whom it is addressed, it must emphasize those parts of the message that answer the questions and needs of those people, and it must be expressed through the medium of the cultural gifts of those people. The Nigerian theologian Justin Ukpong says that 'in the process of evangelization each new culture with which Christianity comes into contact should be respected and given the chance to give its own expression to the Christian message'.[9] In assessing Pentecostalism in Asia, these considerations are very important. Culture and worldview, of necessity, include religious beliefs; and in a discussion of a 'contextual' theology we cannot avoid the questions of religious pluralism, especially in the contient of Asia.

Christianity in general and Pentecostalism in particular had taken on a distinctive form in Asia, very different from that found in the West. Observers

---

[4] Charles H. Kraft, *Christianity in Culture* (Maryknoll, NY: Orbis Books, 1979); David Hesselgrave, *Communicating Christ Cross-Culturally* (Grand Rapids: Zondervan, 1978).

[5] Kraft, 257, 291.

[6] David J. Bosch, *Transforming Mission: Paradigm Shifts in Theology of Mission* (Maryknoll, NY: Orbis, 1991), 423.

[7] Lesslie Newbigin, *The Gospel in a Pluralist Society* (London: SPCK, 1989), 142, 152-53.

[8] Dean Gilliland, 'Contextualization', in A. Scott Moreau, Harold Netland & Charles Van Engen (eds.), *Evangelical Dictionary of World Missions* (Grand Rapids, MI & Carlisle, UK: Baker Books & Paternoster, 2000), 225.

[9] Justin Ukpong, 'What is Contextualization', in Norman Thomas (ed.), *Readings in World Mission* (London: SPCK, 1995), 179.

who have tried to emphasize the 'North American' nature of Pentecostalism throughout the world or the 'Americanization' of Christianity in Korea and elsewhere often miss this important fact. Creative innovations and the selective transformation of 'foreign' symbols are constantly occurring, and naturally, a synthesising process takes place as new forms of Christianity interact with older religions. For example, the prayer mountain movement in Korea is well known. Mountains and hills as places of spiritual retreat and pilgrimage have been a characteristic of Korean religions for centuries. Beliefs in the mountain as the place to which God descends,[10] are not only part of Korean tradition but are also ideas fully at home in the Old Testament. Buddhist temples are usually built on mountainsides, and most Korean cemeteries are found on hills outside the residential areas. Traditionally, the many mountains of Korea were believed to be places where good spirits lived, and both shamans and ordinary pilgrims would receive power from the particular spirit on each mountain. At the risk of oversimplification, the prayer mountain movement may be said to be a culturally relevant form of Christian practice that reflects the ancient spirituality of Korean people. There are now many hundreds of Christian prayer mountains all over South Korea.

Pentecostals in Asia proclaim a pragmatic gospel and seek to address practical needs like sickness, poverty, unemployment, loneliness, evil spirits and sorcery. In varying degrees, Pentecostals in their many and varied forms, and precisely because of their inherent flexibility, attain a contextual character which enables them to offer answers to some of the fundamental questions asked by people. A sympathetic approach to national life, struggles and culture and the retention of certain ancient religious practices are undoubtedly major reasons for their attraction, especially for those overwhelmed by urbanization with its transition from a personal rural society to an impersonal urban one. At the same time, Asian Pentecostals confront old views by declaring what they are convinced is a more powerful protection against shamanism and a more effective healing from sickness than either the existing churches or the ancient rituals had offered. Healing, guidance, protection from evil, and success and prosperity are some of the practical benefits offered to faithful members of Pentecostal and Charismatic churches. All this does not say that Pentecostals and Charismatics provide all the right answers, a pattern to be emulated in all respects, nor to say that they have nothing to learn from other Christians. But the enormous and unparalleled contribution made by Pentecostals and Charismatics has altered the face of Asian Christianity irrevocably, and has enriched the universal church in its ongoing task of proclaiming the gospel of Christ by the proclamation of its message and the demonstration of its power.

---

[10] Sunghoon Myung, 'Spiritual Dimension of Church Growth as Applied in Yoido Full Gospel Church' (PhD dissertation, Fuller Theological Seminary, 1990), 156.

Select Bibliography

Albrecht, Daniel E. *Rites in the Spirit: A Ritual Approach to Pentecostal/ Charismatic Spirituality*. JPT Sup. 16. Sheffield: Sheffield Academic Press, 1999.

Anderson, Allan. 'The Gospel and Culture in Pentecostal Missions in the Third World'. Missionalia 27:2 (August 1999). 220-230.

_____. 'Pentecostalism in East Asia: Indigenous Oriental Christianity?'. *SMT: Swedish Missiological Themes/ Svensk Missions Tidskrift* 87:3 (1999), 319-40; and *Pneuma* 22:1 (2000), 115-132.

_____. 'Signs and Blunders: Pentecostal Mission Issues at "Home and Abroad" in the Twentieth Century'. *Journal of Asian Mission* 2:2 (September 2000), 193-210.

_____. 'The Significance of Pentecostalism in the Third World'. In Viggo Mortenson (ed.). *The Charismatic Movement and the Churches, Occasional Papers 2*. Center for Multireligious Studies: University of Aarhus, Denmark, 2001. 11-23.

_____. 'The "Fury and Wonder"? Pentecostal-Charismatic Spirituality in Theological Education'. *Pneuma* 23:2 (Fall 2001). 287-302.

_____. 'The Globalization of Pentecostalism and the Reshaping of Christianity in the 21st Century'. *Missionalia* 29:3 (November 2001). 423-43.

_____ and Walter J. Hollenweger (eds). *Pentecostals after a Century: Global Perspectives on a Movement in Transition*. JPT Sup. 15. Sheffield: Sheffield Academic Press, 1999.

Bae, Hyeon Sung. 'Towards a Theology of Harmony: A Study of Human Wholeness within the Korean Cultural Context'. PhD thesis, University of Birmingham, 1998.

Bays, Daniel. 'The Protestant Missionary Establishment and the Pentecostal Movement'. In E.L. Blumhofer, R.P. Spittler, and G.A. Wacker (eds.). *Pentecostal Currents in American Protestantism*. Urbana & Chicago: University of Illinois Press, 1999. 50-67.

Bergunder, Michael. 'Wenn die Geister bleiben...: Volksreligiosität und Weltbild'. In D. Becker, and A. Feldtkeller (eds.). *Es begann in Halle...* Erlangen: Verlag der Evangelisch-Lutherischen Mission, 1997. 153-166.

_____. *Die südindische Pfingstbewegung im 20. Jahrhundert. Eine historische und systematische Untersuchung*. Studien zur Interkulturellen Geschichte des Christentums, 113. Frankfurt am Main: Peter Lang, 1999.

_____. 'Ministry of Compassion: D.G.S. Dhinakaran—Christian Healer-Prophet from India'. In R.E. Hedlund (ed.). *Christianity Is Indian: The Emergence of an Indigenous Community*. New Delhi: ISPCK, 2000. 158-174.

_____. 'Miracle Healing and Exorcism: The South Indian Pentecostal Movement in the Context of Popular Hinduism'. *International Review of Mission* 90 (2001). 103-112.

Brouwer, S, P. Gifford, and S.D. Rose. *Exporting the American Gospel: Global Christian Fundamentalism*. New York & London: Routledge, 1996.

Burgess S.M., G.M. McGee and P.H. Alexander (eds.). *Dictionary of Pentecostal and Charismatic Movements*. Grand Rapids: Zondervan, 1988.

Chan, Simon. *Pentecostal Theology and the Christian Spiritual Tradition*. Sheffield: Sheffield Academic Press, 2000.

Cox, Harvey. *Fire from Heaven: The Rise of Pentecostal Spirituality and the Reshaping of Religion in the Twenty-first Century*. London: Cassell, 1996.

Csordas, Thomas J. *Language, Charisma and Creativity: The Ritual Life of a Religious Movement*. Berkeley: University of Caliofornia Press, 1997.

Dayton , Donald W. *Theological Roots of Pentecostalism*. Metuchen, NJ and London: Scarecrow Press, 1987.

Dempster, M.A., B.D. Klaus, and D. Petersen (eds.). *Called and Empowered: Global Mission in Pentecostal Perspective*. Peabody: Hendrickson, 1991.

_____. *The Globalization of Pentecostalism: A Religion Made to Travel*. Oxford: Regnum Books, 1999.

Faupel, D. William. *The Everlasting Gospel: The Significance of Eschatology in the Development of Pentecostal Thought*. Sheffield: Sheffield Academic Press, 1996.

Hedlund, Roger E. 'Indian Instituted Churches: Indigenous Christianity, Indian Style'. *Mission Studies* 16:1 (1999). 26-42.

_____. *Quest for Identity: India's Churches of Indigenous Origin, the 'Little Tradition' in Indian Christianity*. Delhi: ISPCK, 2000.

_____ (ed.). *Christianity Is Indian: The Emergence of an Indigenous Community*. Delhi: ISPCK, 2000.

_____. 'India's Quest for Indigenous Christianity: Some Examples from the Recent Past'. *Dharma Deepika: A South Asian Journal of Missiological Research* (January-June 2002). 19-29.

Hollenweger, Walter J. *The Pentecostals*. London: SCM, 1972.

_____. *Pentecost between Black and White*. Belfast: Christian Journals, 1974.

_____. *Pentecostalism: Origins and Developments Worldwide*. Peabody: Hendrickson, 1997.

Hwa Yung. *Mangoes or Bananas? The Quest for an Authentic Asian Christian Theology*. Oxford: Regnum Books, 1997.

Jeong Chong Hee. 'The Formation and Development of Korean Pentecostalism from the Perspective of a Dynamic Contextual Theology'. ThD thesis, University of Birmingham, 2001.

Jeong Jae Yong. 'Filipino Pentecostal Spirituality: An Investigation into Filipino Indigenous Spirituality and Pentecostalism in the Philippines'. ThD thesis, University of Birmingham, 2001.

Jongeneel, J.A.B. et al (eds.). *Pentecost, Mission and Ecumenism: Essays on Intercultural Theology*. Frankfurt: Peter Lang, 1992.

Kärkkäinen, Veli-Matti. *Spiritus Ubi Vult Spirat: Pneumatology in Roman Catholic-Pentecostal Dialogue (1972-1989)*. Helsinki: Luther-Agricola-Society, 1998.

_____. *Ad Ultimum Terrae: Evangelization, Proselytism and Common Witness in the Roman Catholic Pentecostal Dialogue (1990-1997)*. Frankfurt am Main: Peter Lang, 1999.

_____. *Pneumatology*. Grand Rapids: Baker Academic, 2002.

Kim Dongsoo. 'The Healing of Han in Korean Pentecostalism' (with response by Han Sang-Ehil). *JPT* 15 (1999). 123-43.

Kim Sung Kwang. 'Assessment on Dr Harvey Cox's Understanding of the Korean Pentecostalism' [in Korean]. *Korea Journal of Systematic Theology* 3 (1999). 167-194.

Lambert, Tony. *The Resurrection of the Chinese Church*. Wheaton: Harold Shaw Publishers, 1994.

Land, Steven J. *Pentecostal Spirituality: A Passion for the Kingdom*. Sheffield: Sheffield Academic Press, 1993.

Lee Hong Jung. 'Minjung and Pentecostal Movements in Korea'. In A.H. Anderson and W.J. Hollenweger (eds.). *Pentecostals After a Century: Global Perspectives on a Movement in Transition*. Sheffield: Sheffield Academic Press, 1999. 138-160.

Lee Jae Bum. 'Pentecostal Type Distinctives and Korean Protestant Church Growth'. PhD thesis, Fuller Theological Seminary, 1986.

Lee Young Hoon. 'The Holy Spirit Movement in Korea: Its Historical and Doctrinal Development'. PhD thesis, Temple University, 1996.

Liang Jialun. 'Rural Christianity and Chinese Folk Religion'. *China Study Journal* 14:2 (1999). 22-34.

Ma, Julie. 'A Comparison of Two Worldviews: Kankana-Ey and Pentecostal'. In W. Ma and R.P. Menzies (eds.). *Pentecostalism in Context: Essays in Honor of William W Menzies*. Sheffield: Sheffield Academic Press, 1997. 265-290.

Ma, Jungja. 'Pentecostal challenges in East and South-East Asia'. In M.W. Dempster, B.D. Klaus, & D. Petersen (eds.). *The Globalization of Pentecostalism: A Religion Made to Travel*. Oxford: Regnum Books, 1999. 183-202.

Ma, Wonsuk. 'Toward an Asian Pentecostal Theology'. *Asian Journal of Pentecostal Studies* 1:1 (1998). 15-41.

Ma, Wonsuk & Robert P. Menzies (eds.). *Pentecostalism in Context: Essays in Honor of William W Menzies*. Sheffield: Sheffield Academic Press, 1997.

McGee, Gary B. 'Pentecostal Phenomena and Revivals in India: Implications for indigenous Church Leadership'. *International Bulletin of Missionary Research* 12:3 (1996). 112-117.

_____. '"Latter Rain" Falling in the East: Early Twentieth Century Pentecostalism in India and the Debate over Speaking in Tongues'. *Church History: Studies in Christianity and Culture* 68:3 (1999). 648-665.

Moltmann, Jürgen & Karl-Josef Kuschel (eds.). *Pentecostal Movements as an Ecumenical Challenge*. Conciliom 1996/3. London & Maryknoll: SCM & Orbis, 1996.

Mullins, Mark R. 'The Empire Strikes Back: Korean Pentecostal Mission to Japan'. In Karla Poewe (ed.). *Charismatic Christianity as a Global Culture*. Columbia: University of South Carolina Press, 1994. 87-102.

Poewe, Karla (ed.). *Charismatic Christianity as a Global Culture*. Columbia: University of South Carolina Press, 1994.

Pomerville, Paul A. *The Third Force in Missions: A Pentecostal Contribution to Contemporary Mission Theology*. Peabody: Hendrickson, 1985.

Salazar, Robert C (ed.). *New Religious Movements in Asia and the Pacific Islands: Implications for Church and Society*. Manila: De La Salle University, 1994.

Satyavrata, Ivan M. 'Contextual Perspectives on Pentecostalism as a Global Culture: A South Asian View'. In M.W. Dempster, B.D. Klaus, & D. Petersen (eds.). *The Globalization of Pentecostalism: A Religion Made to Travel*. Oxford: Regnum Books, 1999. 203-21.

Shaull, Richard and Cesar Waldo. *Pentecostalism and the Future of the Christian Churches: Promises, Limitations, Challenges*. Grand Rapids & Cambridge: Eerdmans, 2000.

Synan, Vinson. *The Holiness-Pentecostal Tradition: Charismatic Movements in the Twentieth Century*. Grand Rapids & Cambridge: Eerdmans, 1997.

Währisch-Oblau, Claudia. 'Healing Prayers and Healing Testimonies in Mainland Chinese Churches: An Attempt at Intercultural Understanding'. *China Study Journal* 14:2 (1999). 5-21.

Yong, Amos. *Discerning the Spirit(s): A Pentecostal-Charismatic Contribution to Christian Theology of Religions*. JPT S 20, Sheffield: Sheffield Academic Press, 2000.

_____. *Beyond the Impasse: Toward a Pneumatological Theology of Religions*. Grand Rapids: Baker Academic, 2002.

_____. 'From the Arahant to the Desert Fathers: The Psychology and Technology of Liberation in Theravada Buddhism and Orthodox Christianity'. *Dharma Deepika: A South Asian Journal of Missiological Research* (forthcoming, 2002).

Yoo Boo Woong. *Korean Pentecostalism: Its History and Theology*. New York: Peter Lang, 1988.

_____. 'Pentecostalism in Korea'. In Jan A.B. Jongeneel (eds.). *Pentecost, Mission and Ecumenism Essays on Intercultural Theology*. Frankfurt am Main: Peter Lang, 1992. 169-176.

Name Index

Abeysekera, Fred, 115
Abraham, K.E., 160, 175, 176, 204
Abraham, Pastor S., 181
Abraham, Pastor T.S., 176
Abraham, Sara, 176
Abraham, T.P., 176
Abrams, Minnie F., 129, 154, 156, 174
Adhav, Shamsundar M., 6, 128
Adinata, Biworo G., 260
AFoy, Felician, 281
Agar, Miss, 136
Aguiwas, Patrick, 321, 322
Agur, C.M., 201
Ahmad, Aminah, 107
Ahn, Seen-Ok, 112, 113, 417
Ahone, Philip, 211
Albert, S.Vasantharaj, 188
Albrecht, Daniel E., 461, 481
Alcoran, Doreen, 288
Alexander, Patrick H., 46, 82, 481
Allen, Horace, 449
Aloysius Pieris, S.J., 99
Alvarez, Miguel, 46
Amarasingham, Lorna Rhodes, 89
Ames, Michael M., 89
Anacondia, Carlos, 410
Anand, N., 181
Anderson, Allan H., 3, 4, v, vi, vii, xi, xiii, 1, 3, 4, 8, 9, 33, 34, 35, 40, 118, 120, 124, 126, 129, 132, 133, 134, 137, 143, 159, 167, 168, 337, 380, 385, 434, 438, 444, 448, 450, 454, 455, 467, 477, 478, 481, 483
Anderson, Gerald H., 280, 282
Anderson, James, 257

Anderson, Robert Mapes, 119, 120, 289, 447
Anderson, Rufus, 168
Andersson, Karin, 156
Andreasson, B., 156
Andreasson, E., 156
Ang, Chui Lai, 242
Anglin, L.M., 367, 390
Appasamy, A. J., 38
Appenzeller, Henry, 449
Appleby, R. Scott, 187, 292
Aquinas, Thomas of, 19
Aristotle, 19
Aroolappen. John Christian, 36, 175
Arrolappen, John Christian, 36
Asakura, 400
Asamoah-Gyadu, Johnson, 123
Asanga, 85
Atchison, Robert and Bessie, 398
Atkinson, D. J., 438
Atyal, Saphir, 256
Avato, Rose M, 281
Ayatollah Khomeiny, 475
Azarcon-de la Cruz, Penny, 107, 108
Babalola, Joseph, 133
Babu, Y.S. John, 166
Bae, Hyeon Sung, vii, xi, 9, 427, 434, 435, 440, 481
Bailey, Brian, 240
Baird, Lula, 114
Balagsa, Maura, 321
Balista, Mercy, 285
Balmer, Randall, 380, 447, 448
Bao, Jiayuan, 340
Barney, Mr and Mrs, 398
Barratt, T.B., 152, 153, 155